Library and Book Trade Almanac™

formerly **The Bowker Annual**

2022 | 67th Edition

Library and Book Trade Almanac™

formerly **The Bowker Annual**

2022 | 67th Edition

Editor Kathleen Bayer

 **Information Today, Inc.**

Published by Information Today, Inc.
Copyright © 2022 Information Today, Inc.
All rights reserved

International Standard Book Number 978-1-57387-581-3
International Standard Serial Number 2150-5446
Library of Congress Catalog Card Number 55-12434

Information Today, Inc.
143 Old Marlton Pike
Medford, NJ 08055-8750
Phone: 800-300-9868 (customer service)
Fax: 609-654-4309
E-mail (orders): custserv@infotoday.com
Web Site: http://www.infotoday.com

Typesetting by Amnet Systems

Printed and bound in the United States of America

US $315.50
ISBN 978-1-57387-581-3

31550>

9 781573 875813

Contents

Part 1
Reports from the Field

Special Reports

Federal Agency and Federal Library Reports

National Association and Organization Reports

Part 5
Reference Information

Part 6
Directory of Organizations

Directory of Book Trade and Related Organizations

Preface and Acknowledgments

The staff of Information Today, Inc. presents the latest annual volume of *Library and Book Trade Almanac*.

A few highlights of the 2022 edition:

What do audiobooks, reflection rooms, augmented reality, fish tanks, and electronic braille keyboards have in common? A Special Report by Suzanne LaPierre answers that question and details how old and new ways of improving accessibility are shaping the future of libraries as well as the book publishing industry. She says, "All people exist on a spectrum of unique abilities and limitations. ... Our concept of disability should not be limited to people who are visibly disabled. ..." She explains how, at some point in our lives, each of us might need assistance—physically, mentally, or emotionally—and how libraries can play a role in helping us through the difficult times.

Our second Special Report, written by Michael Blackwell, director of St. Mary's County Library in Maryland, describes the forces at work that have created tension between libraries and book publishers over e-book pricing and circulation policies. He explains, "During the COVID-19 pandemic, ... the usage of e-books has exploded, and, accordingly, e-books have become even more contentious between libraries and publishers." Blackwell describes in detail how e-book lending policies have led to litigation and how the two sides—libraries and library organizations versus book publishers—have continued to seek common ground with only limited success.

Our third Special Report, by Barbie Keiser and Ruth Pagell, delves into the immensely important subject of the Sustainable Development Goals (SDGs) that were introduced by the United Nations and how academics, librarians, and publishers have been working together to achieve these goals. Everything, from reducing the environmental effects of shipping books and their packaging to making libraries greener and more eco-friendly, is being studied and, when appropriate, implemented.

There are many other features to recommend in this 2022/67th edition of *LBTA*—for instance, the extensive directory listings in Part 6. Another annual *LBTA* feature, "Career Resources and Job Listings for Library and Information Professionals," written by Susanne Markgren and starting on page 233, is a valuable resource for anyone interested in entering the field or migrating to a new position.

Keith Curry Lance and his colleague Debra E. Kachel contributed a report titled "School Librarian Employment in the United States." Their research is conducted for the SLIDE project. Learn more about this welcome initiative beginning on page 290, and be sure to visit its website.

To close, I want to acknowledge a number of talented individuals who have supported this production with skill and enthusiasm. Without repeating names seen above, special thanks go to contributors George Aulisio, Connie Harbison, Liz Page, Kathlin Smith, and Steve Zalusky.

A special thank you to all of those on the *LBTA* team: Terri Koenig; Owen O'Donnell, director of ITI's Reference Division; Jackie Crawford; Tiffany Chamenko; Tom Hogan, Sr., who edited the Special Reports; Vimali Joseph; and Nan Badgett. My personal thanks go to John Bryans, the previous editor of *LBTA*, who kindly passed on his knowledge and advice, which were essential to getting this year's edition completed.

To our readers, thank you for using *Library and Book Trade Almanac* in your work.

Part 1
Reports from the Field

Special Reports

Accessibility, Sci-Fi, and the Future of Books

Suzanne S. LaPierre

"We have the technology [to make him] better than he was before. Better, stronger, faster." That opening had kids of my generation slack-jawed in front of *The Six Million Dollar Man* television series based on Martin Caidin's 1972 bestselling novel *Cyborg*. The premise was mesmerizing: A NASA astronaut severely injured in an air crash is restored in an operation. One eye and multiple limbs are replaced with bionic substitutes, resulting in superhuman capabilities. The storyline plays into an enduring fascination. If we can mitigate disabilities with current technologies, can we also use those advances to make us all "better than before?"

While the Bionic Man's six-million-dollar upgrade ($42,419,072.16 today!) has faded into vintage sci-fi, it is true that advances developed for people with disabilities have revolutionized mainstream technologies and created more options for everyone. Within the library and publishing fields, a key example of this phenomenon is audiobooks. Originally developed for people with blindness, they are now a mainstay of the publishing industry, favored by millions who listen to books while exercising, commuting, or cooking.

According to data from 26 publishers in 2020, audiobook sales grew by 39 percent over the year and were the highest on record.[1] OverDrive, the leading digital platform for public libraries and schools, reported 138 million digital audiobook loans in 2020, a 20 percent increase over 2019.[2] These numbers are especially impressive considering the drastic reduction in commuting during the pandemic.

Evolution of Audiobooks

Audiobooks and long-playing (LP) records emerged together in the early 1930s when the American Foundation for the Blind began recording books on vinyl LPs. Shortly after, the National Library Service for the Blind and Print Disabled (NLS) began distributing them via the Talking Books program. Prior records had been inadequate for book-length content. In a stellar example of technology developed

Suzanne S. LaPierre is a Virginiana Specialist Librarian for Fairfax County Public Library in Virginia. Her writing has been published in national and international journals, including *Public Library Quarterly* and *Computers in Libraries*. She authors "The Wired Library" column for *Public Libraries Magazine*. LaPierre holds an M.L.I.S. from the University of South Carolina, an M.A. in museum studies from The George Washington University, and a B.F.A. from Rhode Island School of Design.

for people with disabilities transforming mainstream culture, LPs went on to rock the music industry, while audiobooks reshaped the publishing world.

Fast-forwarding through cassette tapes, compact discs, and thumb drives, NLS now offers audiobooks via the BARD app. These are customized to include descriptions of visual elements as well as content such as reader's guides often missing from commercially available audiobooks. Currently, NLS is field testing a voice-user interface program integrated into a handheld device to work with BARD audiobooks. This will enable people with visual or mobility challenges to browse the catalog using voice commands.

If searching the catalog by voice becomes more prevalent, this could influence some aspects of publishing and cataloging. Keyword search by voice is different than by text—voice-searchers tend to use longer strings of words and more natural language. Since search results by voice will vary from those by text, publishers may market titles accordingly, and catalogers may embed different keywords in bibliographic records for search optimization.

A more controversial issue in audiobooks currently is the use of artificial intelligence (AI) narration. Part of the appeal of audiobooks is favorite narrators, including authors, actors, and celebrities. However, some publishers are turning to AI narration to reduce costs and speed production. As of this writing, it is predicted that synthetic voices capable of the variety of tones and inflection necessary to be indistinguishable from human voices will be available in the next 12–24 months.[3]

As synthetic voices become more lifelike, they can be made to sound like particular individuals, potentially usurping human narrators and leaving some readers feeling less connected to the people behind the books. Many feel that hearing a book read by its author adds depth and meaning. The audio version of Michelle Obama's memoir *Becoming*, for example, had many print traditionalists migrating to audio to hear her delivery. Merely knowing that her voice had been used to create a convincing AI narration would not have appealed to those readers nearly as much.

Interestingly, however, many blind readers prefer synthetic voices because the lack of emotive interpretation is closer to the experience of reading text.[4] Blind readers may also be more accepting of automated voices because of their comfort level with text-to-speech technology. Feedback from these readers may indicate that robotic narration is an acquired taste.

The lower cost of AI can make audio versions of some reference materials more cost-effective to produce and thus more accessible. The ability to customize narrator voices—from an Aussie bloke to a Southern belle—might appeal to some users. Most likely, AI and human narration will exist on a spectrum: Reference material may be read synthetically while literary fiction read by well-known narrators and memoirs by their authors are offered as premium options.

Expanding Recognition of Disabilities

Just as options have expanded when it comes to reading technologies, so has recognition of a diverse range of disabilities, many of which are not easy to see. Greater awareness of neurodiversity has some libraries creating quiet rooms or calming kits to help customers overwhelmed by large, crowded, or noisy spaces, such as people with autism, anxiety, PTSD, or ADHD.

The University of Illinois undergraduate library calls theirs "reflection rooms." They may be used as "sensory safe spaces" for people who need relief

Modernist stairway and book stacks in Allen County Public Library, Fort Wayne, Indiana (Photo by Carol M. Highsmith)

from overstimulating environments. However, they are also used by anyone in need of a place to pray, meditate, or even stretch. One of the rooms includes a yoga mat and white noise machine. The other has a rocking chair and a "voice-activated light source that can be customized to provide light across the entire spectrum of colors depending on one's needs."[5]

Some libraries unable to devote an entire room for the purpose lend out "tranquility kits" instead. These may include stress balls, noise-canceling headphones, eye masks, fidget toys, liquid motion bubblers, and/or exercise bands. Fish tanks as environmental elements can relax anxiety and also give readers' eyes a break from printed text and computer screens. In the digital world, a variety of calming apps offer soothing audio or visual effects and/or breathing exercises.

Reading disabilities, typically invisible, are especially relevant to the book world. As of 2021 librarians and teachers are now among professionals authorized to certify people with reading disabilities for NLS services. Libraries are adjusting LibGuides and other web content to be easier to read. Some bookstores and libraries arrange nonfiction by subject, interfiling a variety of reading levels, as opposed to grouping all easier-to-read books in the children's section. In addition to people with dyslexia or learning disabilities, English-language learners frequently seek books with adult content but simpler text.

Advocates for people with disabilities caution that, while NLS services are essential, libraries relying exclusively on NLS to serve patrons with disabilities may be engaging in "separatist" or "segregationist" tendencies.[6] Similarly, while some libraries have a designated branch to serve those with disabilities, care should be taken to not refer customers to remote services when it is possible to integrate their needs.

St. Louis County Library staff deliver GrandPads to residents 75 and older during the pandemic.

Assistive Technology versus Universal Access

The very concept of disability is challenged by some advocates who contend barriers lie in the design of the environment rather than with individuals experiencing obstacles. Universal access and universal design promise spaces, products, and services that encompass a multitude of needs. This may be simpler to achieve online where factors such as font size and contrast are easily adjusted. Online text-to-speech and speech-to-text capabilities are being perfected, as is language translation.

In physical spaces, this means architecture and equipment that embrace diverse abilities and body sizes. As a general rule, universal design provides the same means of use for all people. Furniture is flexible for all body types. Equipment is simple and intuitive to use. Universal design encompasses everything from left-handedness to learning disabilities.

The typically abled also benefit from automatic doors that open when arms are full of books, elevators that accommodate strollers, and screen magnification for zooming in on details. In an ideal world, universal access would replace the need for assistive technology. In reality, ramps accommodate people operating wheelchairs but do not replace the wheelchair itself. Universal access and assistive technology work together but are not mutually exclusive.

Unfortunately, studies show a gap between how accessible librarians believe their services to be and how people with disabilities experience them.[7] In addition to obstacles that still exist in physical spaces, there are residents—such as those living in long-term care facilities and incarcerated people—who lack access to both technology and transportation. Thus, outreach is a vital form of access.

One example is the St. Louis County Library (SLCL) initiative to deliver GrandPads to residents ages 75 and older during the pandemic. The library used federal CARES Act funds to purchase and distribute 1,500 of the tablets designed for ease of use by people 75 and older. The GrandPad company, which provides 24/7 user support, documented robust usage of the devices. Many recipients confirmed the initiative helped them keep engaged during quarantine.

New and Old Book Formats

As bricks-and-mortar bookstores reopened post-vaccine, 2021 sales of physical books soared. In the 12 months ending June 2021, print book sales were eight times more than those of e-books, indicating that readers still love paper books.[8] Millennials, teens, and children tend to prefer traditional books, according to numerous surveys, demonstrating this is not simply a generational issue.

According to the results of the most recent Public Libraries Survey available from the Institute of Museum and Library Services (IMLS), U.S. public library users still prefer to borrow print books and physical reading materials over electronic options. Although electronic collection items available from U.S. public libraries now exceed the number of physical items, customers still utilize print items much more than alternatives. Libraries offered 3.1 e-books, downloadable audiobooks, and videos items per person, compared to 2.5 print materials and physical audio and video items per person. However, libraries circulated 5.8 physical items per person compared to 1.1 electronic items per person.[9]

This also holds true for braille material. Kristen Fernekes, head of communications and outreach for NLS, explained to me via phone that braille is "at the heart of literacy for many people who use it," and NLS remains committed to supporting braille in a variety of formats. Currently, it is partnering with libraries around the country to expand access to refreshable braille display, a technology that translates information from computers to tactile pins read as braille.

Maps, charts, and diagrams are a vital component of many nonfiction books, while pictorial illustration is integral to children's books and graphic novels for all ages. NLS is working to improve access to illustrative content for braille readers via tactile graphics—images with raised edges or multilevel emboss. Some libraries, such as New York Public Library, offer workshops for creating tactile graphics with equipment such as machines used to create raised and textured inkprints and tools that enable raised-line drawing on regular paper.

In the publishing world, accessibility developments include electronic files that allow content to be produced in various formats: audiobooks with synthesized or human narration, embossed braille, or electronic braille read via a refreshable braille keyboard. Universal design or "born accessible" publications enable the same content to be usable by everyone. Accessible Books Consortium offers accessibility guidelines for publishers.[10]

Bionic Eyes and Augmented Reality

Retinal implants are now commercially available as bionic eyes. While they lack the Six Million Dollar Man's ability to blast villains with eye lasers, most users have simpler goals, such as making everyday life easier and more enjoyable. The Argus II bionic eye implant, which debuted in 2009, has enabled some low-vision users to read large-print books. Another bionic eye converts images from a tiny video camera mounted on glasses into small electrical pulses delivered to the visual cortex, enabling some who are blind to regain visual perception.

Bionic eyes are for sighted readers as well. Telescopic contact lenses that allow users to switch between normal and ultra-magnified vision are being developed for military use. Soft contact lenses embedded with circuitry may soon allow imagery from computers to beam directly to the eye. Meanwhile, eye scrolling through smartphone content is already an option, while researchers fine-tune more precise eye-control functions.

Special glasses and apps are serving as augmented reality (AR) portals for books and libraries. AR advances combine physical books with digital enhancement, and they may open new avenues for accessible publishing. AR also enables book content to be appended without reprinting. Future AR developments may allow library or bookstore browsers to pick a book off the shelf and tap into a current message from its author or a booktalk from a librarian. AR apps for academic libraries are enabling students to explore facilities and access e-textbooks remotely. Miami University's ShelvAR app, designed to scan for misshelved books and tag them virtually, was exciting the library world years ago; however, it was discontinued due to an inventory tool previously patented by Amazon.

Will future readers be aided by AR librarians, similar to those in Neil Stephenson's *Snow Crash* and Matt Haig's *The Midnight Library*? These fictional librarians have no physical bodies—or minds, for that matter—yet they appear to the protagonists in reassuring human form. Gray-haired Mrs. Elm of *The Midnight Library* and the librarian sporting a tweed necktie in *Snow Crash* are no more than software or specters based on memory, but their familiar appearance makes it easier for the protagonists to accept and interact with them.

Like AI voices narrating audiobooks, AR librarians of fiction mimic humans in ways that are sometimes "good enough" for the purpose. It is likely to become a reality that AI takes over some librarian tasks, but it remains to be seen how well AI can replicate the personal interactions that many people seek from libraries. Probably, as with the array of audio narration varying from synthetic to human voices, AI will be accepted on a spectrum, depending on the task.

Conclusion

Current negotiations between our physical and virtual selves, further blended during the pandemic, have us questioning the concept of "presence" on multiple levels. Libraries are seeing increased use by people needing a physical space from which to launch their digital selves. Meanwhile, some librarians with disabilities are challenging the need to be physically present in library buildings to do their jobs.[11]

All people exist on a spectrum of unique abilities and limitations. As part of an aging population, each of us may eventually require mobility or vision assistance. Our concept of disability should not be limited to people who are visibly disabled, but neither should we overlook those most in need of assistance and outreach, regardless of how "universally accessible" we consider our buildings and websites. Often, personal contact is a necessary and irreplaceable link between people and information.

When it comes to the future of books, more choices enable more reading. While some technologies become obsolete with time, basics like paper books defy predictions of their demise. In all probability, we will have tangible tomes proudly displayed on our "credibility bookshelves" even when we have the choice to beam images directly to the eye or download content to the brain. The future is all about options.

Notes

1. Amy Watson, "Number of audiobook titles published in the United States from 2007 to 2020." Statistica. June 7, 2021. https://www.statista.com/statistics/261185/number-of-audiobooks-published-in-the-us.

2. Andrew Albanese, "OverDrive Reports Surge in Digital Library Lending in 2020." *Publisher's Weekly.* January 7, 2021. https://www.publishersweekly.com/pw/by-topic/industry-news/libraries/article/85253-overdrive-reports-record-surge-in-digital-library-lending-in-2020.html.

3. Thad McIlroy, "AI Comes to Audiobooks." *Publisher's Weekly.* Oct 29, 2021. https://www.publishersweekly.com/pw/by-topic/industry-news/publisher-news/article/87762-ai-comes-to-audiobooks.html.

4. Matthew Rubery, *The Untold Story of the Talking Book.* Harvard University Press, Cambridge, MA, 2016, p. 273–274.

5. Illinois University Library, "Reflection Rooms." 2020. https://www.library.illinois.edu/ugl/about/reflection-rooms.

6. Clayton Copeland, "Library and information center accessibility: The differently-able patron's perspective." *Technical Services Quarterly* (2011): 28(2), 223–241.

7. J.J. Pionke, "Toward holistic accessibility: Narratives from functionally diverse patrons." *Reference & User Services Quarterly* (2017): 57(1), 48–56.

8. NPD Group, "With More Bookstores Open, Soaring E-books Sales Fall Back to Earth, NPD Says." October 6, 2021. https://www.npd.com/news/press-releases/2021/2021-ebook-sales-data.

9. Institute of Museum and Library Services, Public Libraries Survey Fiscal Year 2019. Report date: August 2021. https://www.imls.gov/sites/default/files/2021-08/fy19-pls-results.pdf.

10. Accessible Books Consortium, "Accessible Publishing." Accessed November 14, 2021.

11. Fobazi M. Ettarh, "What does it mean to be present?" *WTF Is a Radical Librarian, Anyway? Librarianship, Education, Activism, and all the Intersections in Between.* November 8, 2021. https://fobaziettarh.com/2021/11/08/what-does-it-mean-to-be-present.

Of Progress and Plaintiffs:
E-Books in a Time of COVID

Michael Blackwell

For the past dozen years, e-books have been circulating ever more frequently while creating some discord between libraries and publishers. During the COVID-19 pandemic, however, the usage of e-books has exploded, and, accordingly, e-books have become even more contentious between libraries and publishers. The American Library Association's (ALA) Joint Digital Content Working Group released a 2021 statement on digital content in academic, public, and school libraries.[1] It provides a detailed context here, since this report will focus on public libraries. Andrew Albanese, who keeps a sharp eye on digital developments, said that the statement had "little new in terms of what the library community says it needs," while noting it shows "the pandemic has clearly changed the environment ... and upped the stakes for libraries."[2]

Libraries are still concerned, as they were a dozen years ago, about digital access (or lack thereof) to content as well as the terms under which that content is available. The clashing needs between the publishers and authors seeking revenue (rightly!) and the libraries providing access, especially in a time when print copies can be difficult or even impossible for library patrons to get, has led unfortunately but perhaps inevitably to litigation. The very gains we have made in the library digital ecosystem have exacerbated long-standing issues.

COVID-19 Effects

The pandemic has brought about a circulation jump in digital content that's unprecedented in the amount being circulated as well as the percentage increase. Industry leader OverDrive, for example, reported a 33 percent increase in digital circulation worldwide, with e-books up 40 percent from 2020 over 2019, to 289 million; digital audiobooks increased 20 percent to 138 million, a "lower growth rate due to less commuting."[3] In 2021 there was an increase of 16 percent overall for OverDrive, which the company attributed in part to "Simultaneous Use (SU), Lucky Day (also known as Skip-The-Line), and Cost Per Circ (CPC) access models [that] enable libraries to circulate higher-interest titles more quickly" and "U.S. librarians' usage of the American Rescue Plan Act (ARPA) funds to expand their digital collections."[4]

OverDrive can facilitate "Lucky Day" checkouts, but the other models it mentions are publisher dependent. Some of the Big 5 publishers have made beneficial changes in their licenses. The most noteworthy is Macmillan. The company dropped its "windowing" of titles, which had restricted libraries to only one copy of new releases in the first eight weeks of release.[5] It says this reprieve was intended to expand "libraries' collections in these difficult times."[6] ALA's #eBooksForAll campaign,[7] bringing in hundreds of thousands of signatures, and the library

Michael Blackwell is the director of St. Mary's County Library in Maryland, a member of the American Library Association's (ALA) Joint Digital Content Working Group, and the current chair of the ALA Ebooks Interest Group.

boycott of Macmillan[8] also likely played a role. Whatever the reason, the change was welcome. It may have partially eased the smart that many librarians felt in the years immediately before, when four of the Big 5 changed e-book licenses, eliminating perpetual access (it remains in two of the Big 5 for audiobooks) and relegating libraries to constant relicensing to keep series and other titles.[9]

Other Big 5 publishers made changes as well.[10] Macmillan, Penguin Random House (PRH), and HarperCollins lowered prices for a time. HarperCollins added some frontlist titles to its pay-per-use option. PRH added some license options. E-books could now be licensed for one or two years and audiobooks for perpetual one-user-per-copy or pay-per-use. The pay-per-use option, at 10 percent per cost of perpetual, was too pricy for most libraries: A $95 license (not uncommon for a new title) would be $9.50 per circ. The one-year e-book license proved helpful on high-demand titles: "normally we would buy eight or nine more copies under the 24-month license ... theoretically, we can [license] 16-18 copies for the same price with a 12-month license, and get folks through the holds queue twice as fast."[11] RBdigital offers a perpetual license but also a 100-circulation license on some older titles at an attractive price.[12]

The specific models noted here are less important than the fact that multiple models are offered. A ReadersFirst survey of librarians suggests that no single license model suits every library need.[13] Librarians want multiple models, from perpetual (even ownership) to short term, in order to allow the most efficient use of funds. We can hope that publishers will be willing try even more models, adjusting prices as is reasonable.

The Growth of Library Simplified

One recent welcome development is unrelated to the pandemic. LYRASIS and the Digital Public Library of America (DPLA) have partnered on a new version of Library Simplified (aka SimplyE) called Palace.[14] The partners will develop the app and a web version for personal computers and will rebrand the non-profit DPLA Exchange as the Palace Exchange. It will provide content from the Big 5 and many other publishers. New York Public Library (NYPL), which has been leading SimplyE, will continue development. NYPL is especially interested in enhancing accessibility features—a much-needed development since many commercial apps are sadly unresponsive to iOS and Android accessibility features. Amigos and Califa continue to deploy their own versions of SimplyE, while the Georgia Public Library Service has deployed a statewide version.[15] DPLA has been particularly active in seeking publishers to offer multiple license models. Currently, more than 25 offer four options: perpetual use, one-user-at-a-time; a 40-circulation bundle (ten may be simultaneous); bundles of five for titles libraries might wish to sample; and simultaneous unlimited multi-user.[16]

Such models offer the flexibility to meet nearly every library need. Unfortunately, no Big 5 publisher has yet partnered on them, but high-demand titles are available in these models from others. These developments would perhaps be less significant but for a major coup: Palace (and all SimplyE providers) will now be able to provide content never offered before to libraries from Amazon's imprints and from Audible.[17] Some 30,000 titles, many likely in high demand, will become available. A bonus: The titles will be in EPUB format, not Kindle, and Amazon will not have access to library patron reading, as it does (to the displeasure of many librarians) in Kindle format titles through OverDrive. Some have questioned Amazon's motives.[18] Is this dipping of the toe into the library market to be followed by working with other library vendors? Is it a ploy to comply with the Maryland e-book law (which we will explore soon), restricting offerings in a smaller vendor?

Palace/SimplyE does occupy a small part of the market now. It faces challenges in gaining substantial market share. The biggest obstacle, especially among libraries with only one library vendor platform, seems to be familiarity with existing systems. Libraries with only OverDrive, CloudLibrary, or Axis 360 (to name only the largest) may decide their platforms work well enough. They then do not have to teach staff and patrons something new. Libraries with multiple platforms (which Palace makes accessible in one place) or that want the new content may now wish to deploy. The Amazon/Audible deal is important for bringing libraries more content and for making a library-created, nonprofit platform more viable.

What Happens After the Pandemic?

Despite some progress, questions about digital content remain for librarians. Once the pandemic ends, will publishers retreat and even reconsider windowing? With ARPA funds no longer available, how might U.S. libraries meet demand for which this funding provided? While government agencies have worked to expand broadband, and libraries have worked with Wi-Fi hotspots and devices, Meredith Schwartz's concerns about the digital divide, expressed at the start of the pandemic, remain.[19] Will digital resources meet demand for the less affluent or in rural areas, and can libraries give up on those most in need? Is this at long last an inflection point—should libraries plan a large and more permanent shift to digital at the expense of print?

The answer, for many reasons, appears to be no. Most obviously, while digital occupies a higher percentage of circulation than ever before and is accessible during the pandemic, it has not displaced physical books, which still predominate in most libraries, if only via curbside delivery. Second, while preservation is not a concern for many, and perhaps not even for most public libraries, keeping access to titles, especially those that publishers deem to have lost commercial value, remains problematic in digital. Finally, at least among titles provided by the Big 5, libraries simply do not get the value from digital that they get from print.

Admittedly, this author is a digital advocate and can present arguments for why e-books are a great value, especially since print has "hidden" costs: processing; jobs that involve checking in, checking out, shelving, and (for multi-branch systems) transporting books; and buildings. I should also mention e-books' ability to change fonts for easier reading and how devices can suit people with limited hand mobility, in some cases, better than print books. But let's be honest. Processing is cheap, and those aren't just jobs. They are people, and they are one of the most important reasons patrons come to libraries. We're not going to give up the buildings because of all of their other uses. In digital, the "bang for the book" just isn't there. Here's a table of a week of recent *New York Times* bestsellers with a comparison, based on costs for my library at the time of this writing:

Title	Library E-Book Terms	Consumer E-Book Price (Amazon Kindle)	Library Actual Print Cost	Print Retail Cost
Fiction				
Go Tell the Bees That I Am Gone	12 months: $27.50 24 months: $55	$15.99	$20.45	$36
The Becoming	24 months: $60	$14.99	$16.38	$28.99
The Judge's List	12 months: $27.50 24 months: $55	$14.99	$16.92	$29.95
Fear No Evil	24 months: $65	$14.99	$16.39	$29
The Wish	24 months: $65	$14.99	$15.82	$28
Nonfiction	**Library E-Book Terms**	**Consumer E-Book Price (Amazon Kindle)**	**Library Actual Print Cost**	**Print Retail Cost**
The 1619 Project	12 months: $27.50 24 months: $55	$14.99	$21.47	$35
Will	12 months: $27.50 24 months: $55	$14.99	$16.95	$30
The Lyrics: 1956 to the Present	24 months or 52 checkouts: $200	$57	$56.50	$100
The Storyteller	26 checkouts: $34.49	$14.99	$16.94	$29.99
All American Christmas	26 checkouts: $34.49	$14.99	$16.94	$29.99
Taste	24 months: $59.99	$15.99	$15.82	$28
Total cost, fiction and nonfiction	$738.97	$208.90	$230.58	$404.92

E-book costs are 3.2 times what we pay for print. Print wears out, of course, but most libraries can typically keep hardcover books for 30 or even 70 or 100 circulations. Circulating for three weeks, the best one could hope for an e-book title in a two-year license is 34 circulations. At the end of two years, we can keep a print book or perhaps replace it inexpensively. Digital books are gone forever unless relicensed at a high cost.

Many medium and smaller publishers in fact offer better digital terms than previously cited. To those publishers, libraries are thankful. Yet this survey's small sample, suggesting e-books are often no bargain, would likely be replicated on any scale.[20] Inflated costs are the rub for librarians. Much controversy, many state bills or laws, the involvement of members of Congress, and two important lawsuits have emerged around the discrepancy between print and digital in libraries.

The Growth of Controlled Digital Lending

The lawsuit *Hachette Book Group, Inc.; HarperCollins Publishers, LLC; John Wiley & Sons, Inc.; and Penguin Random House, LLC v. the Internet Archive, et al.* arose after the Internet Archive opened the National Emergency Library during the pandemic. This move made some 1.4 million books, most of them from the 20th century and in mediocre quality scans, accessible for simultaneous access across the globe. It also extended the practice known as Controlled Digital Lending (CDL) beyond its usual scope, as noted in the "Position Statement on CDL by Libraries":

> [CDL] is an emerging method that allows libraries to loan print books to digital patrons in a "lend like print" fashion. Through CDL, libraries use technical controls to ensure a consistent "owned-to-loaned" ratio, meaning the library circulates the exact number of copies of a specific title it owns, regardless of format, putting controls in place to prevent users from redistributing or copying the digitized version.[21] [*Disclosure*—The author is among hundreds of institutional and individual signatories to the statement.]

The reaction by the Association of American Publishers (AAP) and four large publishers was swift. The Internet Archive's practices had long been attacked as being equivalent to those of "the world's most egregious pirate sites."[22] Now they were to be challenged in court. The Internet Archive responded by disabling the National Emergency Library and returning to the Open Library, which allows circulation of copies on a strictly "owned to loaned" ratio. It then asked the publishers to drop the suit.[23] The publishers were not willing, however, and continued with the suit, suggesting to libraries that the suit is not only about restricting CDL but also exercising total control over digital content, requiring compensation for every digital read.

The suit has been acrimonious and closely watched. Supporters of the Internet Archive claim that "the AAP desperately doesn't want the Internet Archive to know what it was talking about with the publishers" because "the only real 'harm' caused by its Open Library was that it made it more difficult for the large publishers to collude to jack up the prices on e-books sold (but not really sold) to libraries"[24] The plaintiffs have responded that the Internet Archive is "further attempting to litigate this case and their desired policy gains in the press based on a false narrative rather than in the courtroom based on the facts and the law."[25] Such discovery and legal disputes are to be expected in high-profile and important cases.

Meanwhile, a judge (and perhaps more than one judge, should the case be appealed) will need to decide if copyright is being violated by the Internet Archive's "continued efforts to lend books without compensating authors and publishers."[26] Does the fact that author and publisher were once compensated for the print work and a library legitimately owns that print work mean the library should be able to reproduce it digitally with adding "additional" copies and then circulating digital as if it were print? The case is much discussed as well as bitterly contested. Readers are encouraged to do further study, perhaps beginning with a somewhat neutral assessment.[27]

A New Nonprofit Group Begins to Influence the Conversation

The Internet Archive's position has been bolstered by the emergence of Library Futures, a nonprofit group bringing passion and legal expertise to the discourse. Its basic principles are as follows:

> For libraries to thrive, they must be able to purchase digital content, not "license" it within a twisted maze of terms. Libraries must be able to purchase, preserve, lend, and accept donations of digital materials. Library lending is enshrined in the copyright act, and libraries allow broad access to information by lending materials without restriction. We support digital lending that uses technology to mirror the library's right to loan legally acquired books under controlled conditions while respecting copyright.[28]

The group has released a detailed statement, "Controlled Digital Lending: Unlocking the Library's Full Potential," to support the legal basis of CDL.[29] [*Disclosure*—The author is not a member of Library Futures but has signed a statement advocating its principles.] As we shall see in the upcoming section on state laws, considerable further advocacy is likely from this group.

Many libraries, meanwhile, are proceeding as if the outcome of the Internet Archive suit does not affect CDL use in libraries. The International Federation of Library Associations and Institutions (IFLA), for example, has released a statement supporting CDL,[30] saying that "controlled lending has helped to fulfil the mission of libraries to support research, education and cultural participation within the limits of existing copyright laws." The Boston Library Consortium (BLC) announced, "The Davis Educational Foundation has awarded ... a two-year $215,000 grant to accelerate the implementation of controlled digital lending as a mechanism for interlibrary loan."[31] Meanwhile, "The National Information Standards Organization (NISO) announced that it has received a grant of $125,000 from The Andrew W. Mellon Foundation to support the development of a consensus framework for implementing controlled digital lending (CDL) of book content by libraries."[32] The NISO implementation group is proceeding on the assumption that CDL is legal, not that it might be. [*Disclosure*—The author is working in the group.] CDL looks to be an important future library tactic, even if not employed exactly as the Internet Archive has.

States Enter the Fray

Association of American Publishers v. Brian E. Frosh, Attorney General of Maryland is a lawsuit brought against the state of Maryland over Maryland Code, Education §§ 23-701, 23-702, the law that says any publisher offering to license "an electronic literary product" (defined as e-books and digital audiobooks) to consumers in the state is required to also offer to license the content to public libraries "on reasonable terms." As with the CDL lawsuit, this action has generated considerable controversy and opposing arguments. Many pages of pleading have emerged, and readers are encouraged to explore this further to gain a full understanding of the suit. The bill became law on June 1, 2021, but only came into force as of January 1, 2022. The reason for the delay: Amazon asked for an extension to comply with it and was happily granted one. The case is noteworthy for many reasons. First, the Maryland Library Association (MLA) has released a statement defining "reasonable"—certainly not binding on others but an attempt to summarize a tenable library position on digital content prices:

> Library eBooks and eAudiobooks with print-equivalent license terms (loaned sequentially for a limited lifespan) should have print-equivalent prices. Based upon a centuries old model, updated to the digital realm, print-equivalent terms could be fair to publishers, authors, libraries, and users, supporting the rich, healthy reading ecosystem on which we all depend.[33]

In short, whatever we pay for print, we should be paying for digital, adjusting for the many different license types possible, including perpetual, which might be priced at a high rate to reflect its not expiring. This definition of "reasonable" differs from the aims of Library Futures, which seeks ownership. For Maryland, and perhaps many libraries, licensing is not necessarily unfair, but it must be at lower costs than at least the Big 5 currently offer.

MLA was willing to suggest a compromise of print retail cost for a typical license of 30 or so circulations (based on a low average for circulation of print items). This offer has not, perhaps unsurprisingly, brought any individual members of the Big 5 to the bargaining table. (Note that publishers cannot collectively bargain or face U.S. Department of Justice scrutiny for price collusion.)

The Maryland legislative effort is also noteworthy for being one of many. It was, in fact, based on bills proposed in Rhode Island and New York but not acted upon due to COVID-19 closures of legislatures. It was merely passed first. AAP's challenge to the law came on December 9. Because AAP had since June to file, one might wonder why it waited. First, it wished to put time pressure on Maryland to prepare a response before January 1, when the bill became law. Maryland was, however, granted until January 14 for its response.[34] Second, AAP wished to put pressure on the governor of New York, where a similar bill was up for signature, to veto. In this, it succeeded. Much to the dismay of many librarians, the governor agreed that the New York bill might be unconstitutional, while saying it was "well intentioned" and perhaps leaving room to reframe it for an eventual signature.[35] Finally, AAP wished to chill action in other states, as noted by Samantha Handler, quoting a source opposed to the law: "The Maryland case is very, very significant because we're hoping and believe the court will say, 'You can't do this. This is unconstitutional,'" said Keith Kupferschmid, the president of the Copyright Alliance, a nonprofit that represents a broad group of creators. "And, presumably, other states would at least be a little more cautious. Hopefully they wouldn't introduce the bills at all."[36]

Kupferschmid's hopes have been dashed, however. Massachusetts continues consideration of its bill. A bill was introduced in Illinois on January 21, 2022, with modifications to what passed in Maryland, likely suggested in part by Library Futures. These bills clarify that "A contract or license shall contain no provision that restricts or limits a library's right to make non-public preservation copies of electronic books or digital audiobooks," which certainly opens a new front in library preservation, to the joy of academic librarians especially.[37] Rhode Island has reintroduced a bill,[38] emphasizing (as do all bills since Maryland's) that it applies to schools and higher education libraries. Those opposed to the bills suggest that state legislators do not understand copyright, or else they would not pass bills doomed to be invalidated. The legislators seem convinced that their states have an overriding interest in redressing an existing imbalance.

The state laws are notable, too, in that they occasioned the involvement of members of Congress. Sen. Thom Tillis (R-N.C.) asked the Copyright Office to opine on the Maryland law, asking for a review of its constitutionality.[39] Shira Perlmutter of the Copyright Office responded that the Maryland law "likely" would be preempted by federal law, while stating that "the state legislation at issue seeks to require licensing of works to libraries, which, while arguably a commercial transaction, ultimately serves a non-commercial goal of furthering the traditional mission of public libraries to provide free access to materials for their communities." She added, "It is unclear whether this would be a significant factor for a court considering the question of federal conflict preemption."[40] No exact legal precedent applies, hence Perlmutter's qualifying with the word "likely." ALA released a statement disputing Perlmutter's interpretation: "The American Library Association does not agree with [the] Copyright Office's conclusion that a court likely would find the state legislation at issue preempted under a conflict preemption analysis. To the contrary, the Copyright Office letter further bolsters our view that the legislation is not preempted. Of course, resolution of this question lies with the courts."[41]

Perhaps in response to Sen. Tillis and perhaps with the aid of Library Futures, Sen. Ron Wyden (D-Calif.) and Rep. Anna Eshoo (D-Ore.) sent letters first to the Big 5 publishers and subsequently to nine library e-book vendors, asking detailed questions about restrictions placed in licenses to libraries, revenues, the exact agreements, any changes made during COVID-19, and any legal actions taken toward libraries.[42] They noted, "E-books play a critical role in ensuring that libraries can fulfill their mission of providing broad and equitable access to information for all Americans, and it is imperative that libraries can continue their traditional lending functions as technology advances." They further stated, "Many libraries face financial and practical challenges in making e-books available to their patrons, which jeopardizes their ability to fulfill their mission. ... Under these arrangements, libraries are forced to rent books through very restrictive agreements that look like leases." Librarians can only be pleased that licensing arrangements are under intense scrutiny and will await the results of the investigation.

The Lawsuit in Maryland

Given these developments, a brief look at the AAP lawsuit against Maryland seems in order. It might foretell the outcome of other suits—assuming AAP can and will try to interdict any bill that becomes law. AAP, in its suit, public statements, and lobbying efforts, makes claims that, shall we say, stretch the truth. It will say that libraries are in league with "Big Tech" and "lobbying groups" to undermine copyright.[43] This is demonstrably untrue. Maryland and libraries have worked with their legislatures on their own, presenting evidence that they have been disadvantaged in the digital market for more than a decade.

In addition, AAP claims that Amazon's holdout of its imprints from libraries was the reason for Maryland's laws, and the law is unnecessary now that Amazon is participating. This claim is also untrue. The main impetus for the law was that Macmillan, one of the Big 5 publishers, was limiting content to libraries. AAP claims that the library e-books market has grown and is thriving. All that proves is that demand is high, especially as the pandemic limits access to physical materials. This claim ignores the costs libraries pay for access to e-books and digital audio, which greatly exceed the costs we pay for physical materials and that are based on licenses we must constantly renew to keep access, with costs for the same title escalating over the years. Libraries seek options that will allow us to use our resources more effectively. We could help readers discover even more authors, perhaps even helping sales for newer or less well-established authors, without increased digital spending. Ideally, better terms could even lead to a greater investment in digital as more library readers are able to benefit. In any case, the publishers would not see any less revenue from libraries. It is not illogical to think that their aim is to license more copies to consumers and limit the library market.

This brings us to the heart of the suit against Maryland. AAP says Maryland's law violates copyright, which is established by laws at the federal level. It states that copyright allows the owners to have complete control over their works, including control to license them through the publishers, and that the publishers have the right to license to whom they want at whatever rates they want. If they so choose, they should not have to license to libraries at all if they think libraries limit their sales. AAP says that federal law preempts any state law, and Maryland's law must therefore not be permitted to take effect.[44]

Maryland's attorney general, Brian Frosh, thinks otherwise. Frosh has mounted a spirited defense of the law.[45] "This case is not about copyright protection—it is about the unfair and discriminatory trade practices of publishers at the expense of public libraries," he says, adding that "the proliferation of digital media has outpaced the first sale doctrine, and publishers have capitalized on this loophole through both price discrimination against public libraries and withholding from public libraries access to e-books and audiobooks, to the detriment of library patrons." The statement further says that the "constitutional charge of copyright is not unlimited [but] is tempered by social and economic consequences"; that "preemption would not prevent the States from protecting 'rights not equivalent to any exclusive rights under copyright'"; that "publishers capitalize on the Digital Revolution at Libraries' Expense"; that AAP's request for injunction does not meet the "claim on which relief may be granted" for "irreparable harm"; that a thriving library market is no proof that inequities do not exist; that the law is clear on what Maryland libraries are; that "reasonable terms" are not too vague in terminology; and that self-published authors are not "publishers" and so not needlessly burdened.

Space limitations prevent a truly detailed consideration here, and the reader should investigate the situation in depth if seeking a full understanding. Each side has assembled a formidable list of precedents and a who's who of supporters, national and even international. The publishers'/AAP side has been joined by supporters from other media, such as television and film, eager to maintain control over content, especially streaming, through licenses. It is now up to the court (or courts, in case of a drawn-out and perhaps appealed process) to decide which side is correct. Readers might consult Andrew Albanese[46] for a more detailed consideration, but an objective lengthy and truly detailed analysis has yet to appear.

Conclusion

Predictions about the outcome of court cases and the future of libraries have one thing in common: They often turn out wrong. With that as a caveat, here a few thoughts on what is to come:

- More data is need for an assessment of how library use and publisher sales intersect, both in digital and print. Both sides could benefit and perhaps be able to craft reasonable deals. The question of who would manage the huge task of compiling detailed and anonymized data on which to make decisions remains an issue.

- In the digital area, libraries and publishers seem unfortunately likely to remain at loggerheads. Libraries need access to perform their mission, and publishers, or at least the largest ones, exist to turn a profit, which restricting library sales might bolster. Efforts to bridge the divide may be frustrated by extremist positions on both sides. Each side lacks single negotiating agencies that can speak for the whole. But, surely, more communication would be helpful. Perhaps, if they stand, Maryland's and other state laws will provide a framework for negotiations. Librarians and library associations should take a more direct role than they have in the past, speaking directly to publishers rather than relying on vendor intermediaries. Perhaps true negotiation can happen. It seems never to have happened before. Libraries and publishers have yet to meet as equals in good faith talks.
- Regardless of the outcomes of the Maryland lawsuit, state legislatures will, for now, lead in the fight over library access to e-books. The Maryland case may not set a precedent, no matter how it is decided.
- A win for Maryland, even with other states' laws being in place and upheld, will not guarantee change until the marketplace can agree on "reasonable" terms.
- Failing any agreement through the negotiation and the action of market forces—although the publishers may have incentive to negotiate if federal action seems necessary because of a patchwork of state laws—some sort of federal "digital right of first sale" may become necessary, as noted in a report on the Digital Millennium Copyright Act (DCMA).[47]

Caught among increased demand for digital resources in a pandemic that limits access to print, the ever-present need to fulfill our mission of providing resources while being good stewards of public funds, and recognizing the vital importance for our enterprise of creators and their agents, librarians have sought new means, including legislation, to achieve their ends. As an advocate and shaper of Maryland's law, this author can assert that it does not intend, even if upheld, action against publishers. It is, rather, an invitation to a dialogue. We cannot shrink from our responsibilities. We can, and should, embrace new and likely more sustainable and diverse content outlets, such as the Indie Author Project.[48] We should become local publishing leaders ourselves. Public demand and research trends are, however, unlikely to leave us free from the major publishers providing content in academic, school, and public markets. Is there a place where author, publisher, and library needs intersect fairly? A comparison of what we pay for digital versus print suggests we are not there now.

The precedent of more than a century provided by copyright and fair use is a useful "reasonable" guideline. So, librarians, let us listen to our best—and usual—selves. Let's hope for and work for true negotiations. If we cannot have them, then, alas, as we have shown ourselves willing since the pandemic and even before to take to figurative arms.

Notes

1. American Library Association Joint Digital Content Working Group. "The Need for Change: A Position Paper on E-Lending. (2021). https://www.ala.org/tools/sites/ala.org.tools/files/ content/The-Need-for-Change-A-Position-Paper-on-E-Lending-by-the-Joint-Digital-Content-Working-Group.pdf.

2. Andrew Albanese, "ALA Working Group Calls for Change in the Library E-book Market." *Publishers Weekly.* (2021). https://www.publishersweekly.com/pw/by-topic/industry-news/ libraries/article/86575-ala-working-group-calls-for-change-in-the-library-e-book-market.html.

3. 33% Growth for Digital Books from Public Libraries and Schools in 2020 Sets Records. OverDrive. Press Release. (Jan. 7, 2021).

4. Public Libraries and Schools Surpass Half a Billion Digital Book Loans in 2021. OverDrive. Press Release. (Jan. 5, 2022).

5. Chris Meadows, "Is Macmillan justified in windowing new-release library ebooks?" *Teleread.* (2020). https://teleread.org/2020/01/08/is-macmillan-justified-in-windowing-new-release-library-ebooks.

6. Porter Anderson, "Macmillan's Sargent: 'Differences Should Be Put Aside.'" *Publishing Perspectives.* (2020). https://publishingperspectives.com/2020/03/coronavirus-macmillan-penguin-random-house-ease-library-digital-book-programs.

7. American Library Association. #eBooksForAll. (2019). https://ebooksforall.org.

8. Carmi Parker and Dianne Coan, "Is the Macmillan Boycott Working?" ReadersFirst. (2020). http://www.readersfirst.org/news/2020/1/16/is-the-macmillan-boycott-working.

9. Sari Feldman, "Libraries Must Draw the Line on E-books." *Publishers Weekly.* (2019). https:// www.publishersweekly.com/pw/by-topic/industry-news/libraries/article/80689-libraries-must-draw-the-line-on-e-books.html.

10. Andrew Albanese, "Is the Covid-19 Crisis a Watershed Moment for Library E-books?" *Publishers Weekly.* (2020). https://www.publishersweekly.com/pw/by-topic/industry-news/ libraries/article/82834-is-the-covid-19-crisis-a-watershed-moment-for-library-e-books.html.

11. Andrew Albanese, "Is the Covid-19 Crisis a Watershed Moment for Library E-books?" *Publishers Weekly.* (2020). https://www.publishersweekly.com/pw/by-topic/industry-news/ libraries/article/82834-is-the-covid-19-crisis-a-watershed-moment-for-library-e-books.html.

12. Michael Blackwell, Dianne Coan, Cathy Mason, and Carmi Parker, "Digital Audiobooks in Public Libraries: A Current Assessment." *Computers in Libraries.* (April 2021). Information Today, Inc. https://www.infotoday.com/cilmag/apr21/Blackwell-Coan-Mason-Parker--Digital-Audiobooks-in-Public-Libraries-A-Current-Assessment.shtml.

13. ReadersFirst. The ReadersFirst Survey of E-Book Business Models. http://www.readersfirst. org/projects.

14. The Palace Project. Your Library is a Palace. https://thepalaceproject.org.

15. Georgia Public Library Service. What is SimplyE? (2021). https://georgialibraries.org/simplye.

16. ReadersFirst. DPLA Exchange Increases Number of Publishers Offering Flexible Terms. http://www.readersfirst.org/news/2021/4/13/dpla-exchange-increases-number-of-publishers-offering-flexible-terms.

17. Micah May, "Update on DPLA's ongoing talks with Audible." Digital Public Library of America. (2021). https://dp.la/news/update-on-dplas-ongoing-talks-with-audible.

18. Rebecca Klar, "Amazon takes big step in e-book deal with libraries, but activists want more." *The Hill.* (2021). https://thehill.com/policy/technology/556381-amazon-takes-big-step-in-ebook-deal-with-libraries-but-activists-seek-more.

19. Meredith Schwartz, "Lessons from COVID-19. Libraries Can't Be Our Only Safety Net." *Library Journal.* (2020). https://www.libraryjournal.com/story/Lessons-from-COVID-19-Editorial.

20. Michael Blackwell, Catherine Mason, and Micah May, "Ebook Availability, Pricing, and Licensing: A Study of Three Vendors in the U.S. and Canada." *Computers in Libraries.* (November 2019). Information Today, Inc. https://www.infotoday.com/cilmag/nov19/ Blackwell-Mason-May--Ebook%20Availability-Pricing-and-Licensing.shtml.

21. Controlled Digital Lending By Libraries. (2022). https://controlleddigitallending.org.

22. Publishers File Suit Against Internet Archive for Systematic Mass Scanning and Distribution of Literary Works: Ask Court to Enjoin and Deter Willful Infringement. Association of American Publishers. Press Release. https://publishers.org/news/publishers-file-suit-against-internet-archive-for-systematic-mass-scanning-and-distribution-of-literary-works.

23. Andrew Albanese, "Internet Archive to Publishers: Drop 'Needless' Copyright Lawsuit and Work with Us." *Publishers Weekly.* (2020). https://www.publishersweekly.com/pw/ by-topic/industry-news/libraries/article/83929-internet-archive-to-publishers-drop-needless-copyright-lawsuit-and-work-with-us.html.

24. Mike Masnick, "Internet Archive Would Like To Know What The Association Of American Publishers Is Hiding." TechDirt. (2021). https://www.techdirt.com/articles/ 20211031/23501047858/internet-archive-would-like-to-know-what-association-american-publishers-is-hiding.shtml.

25. Andrew Albanese, "Publishers, AAP Hit Back in Internet Archive Discovery Dispute." *Publishers Weekly.* (2021). https://www.publishersweekly.com/pw/by-topic/industry-news/ libraries/article/87810-publishers-aap-hit-back-in-internet-archive-discovery-dispute.html.

26. Copyright Alliance. "Internet Archive Continues To Harm Authors." (2021). https:// copyrightalliance.org/trending-topics/internet-archive-harms-authors.

27. Janko Roettgers, "With libraries shuttered, e-book lending booms, leading to new conflicts." Protocol. (2020). https://www.protocol.com/libraries-closed-ebook-lending-new-conflicts.

28. Library Futures. Our Principles. https://www.libraryfutures.net/our-principles.

29. Kyle Courtney, "Controlled Digital Lending: Unlocking the Library's Full Potential." Library Futures. (2021). https://www.libraryfutures.net/post/controlled-digital-lending-unlocking-the-librarys-full-potential.

30. International Federation of Library Associations and Institutions. IFLA Statement on Controlled Digital Lending. (2021). https://repository.ifla.org/handle/123456789/1835.

31. Boston Library Consortium. Davis Educational Foundation award accelerates Boston Library Consortium's controlled digital lending Implementation. (2022). https://blc.org/ news/148817.

32. NISO Awarded Mellon Funding for Controlled Digital Lending Project. NISO. Press Release. (2021). http://www.niso.org/press-releases/2021/09/niso-awarded-mellon-funding-controlled-digital-lending-project.

33. Maryland Library Association. A Maryland Library Association Statement on Maryland's Digital Content Law. (2021). https://www.mdlib.org/files/docs/press/statement.pdf.

34. CONSOLIDATED MEMORANDUM OF LAW IN SUPPORT OF DEFENDANT'S MOTION TO DISMISS ANDOPPOSITION TO PLAINTIFF'S MOTION FOR A PRELIMINARY INJUNCTION. (2022). https://storage.courtlistener.com/recap/gov.uscourts. mdd.504378/gov.uscourts.mdd.504378.10.1.pdf.

35. Andrew Albanese, "Hochul Vetoes New York's Library E-book Bill." *Publishers Weekly.* (2021). https://www.publishersweekly.com/pw/by-topic/digital/copyright/article/88205-hochul-vetoes-new-york-s-library-e-book-bill.html.

36. Samantha Handler, "Libraries, Publishers Battle Over Terms for E-Books' Use." Bloomberg Law. (2022). https://news.bloomberglaw.com/ip-law/libraries-publishers-battle-over-terms-for-e-books-public-use.

37. 102ND GENERAL ASSEMBLY State of Illinois 2021 and 2022 HB4470. (2022). https:// www.ilga.gov/legislation/102/HB/10200HB4470.htm.

38. AN ACT RELATING TO COMMERCIAL LAW—GENERAL REGULATORY PROVISIONS—ELECTRONIC BOOK LICENSES TO LIBRARIES AND SCHOOLS. STATE PF RHODE ISLAND IN GENERAL ASSEMBLY. (2022). http://webserver.rilin.state.ri.us/BillText/BillText22/HouseText22/H7113.pdf.

39. Andrew Albanese, "Senator Wants Copyright Office to Weigh in on Maryland Library E-book Law." *Publishers Weekly*. (2021). https://www.publishersweekly.com/pw/by-topic/industry-news/libraries/article/87194-senator-wants-copyright-office-to-weigh-in-on-maryland-library-e-book-law.html.

40. Shira Perlmutter, Letter to the Honorable Thom Tillis. (2021). https://www.publishersweekly.com/binary-data/ARTICLE_ATTACHMENT/file/000/004/4768-1.pdf.

41. "American Library Association Response to U.S. Copyright Office Analysis of Preemption Issues Relating to State Ebook Legislation." (2021). https://www.publishersweekly.com/binary-data/ARTICLE_ATTACHMENT/file/000/004/4769-1.pdf.

42. Wyden, Eshoo Press Big Five Publishers on Costly, Overly Restrictive E-Book Contracts with Libraries. United States Committee on Finance. Press Release. (2021). https://www.finance.senate.gov/chairmans-news/wyden-eshoo-press-big-five-publishers-on-costly-overly-restrictive-e-book-contracts-with-libraries.

43. Comment from Maria A. Pallante, President and CEO, Association of American Publishers on New York State Governor Kathy Hochul's Decision to Veto Unconstitutional eBooks Bill." Association of American Publishers. (2022). https://publishers.org/news/comment-from-maria-a-pallante-president-and-ceo-association-of-american-publishers-on-new-york-state-governor-kathy-hochuls-decision-to-veto-unconstitutional-ebooks-bill.

44. "Case 1:21-cv-03133-DLB Document 1: COMPLAINT FOR DECLARATORY AND INJUNCTIVE RELIEF." Association of American Publishers. (2021). https://publishers.org/wp-content/uploads/2021/12/AAP-v.-Maryland.pdf.

45. "Case 1:21-cv-03133-DLB Document 10-1: CONSOLIDATED MEMORANDUM OF LAW IN SUPPORT OF DEFENDANT'S MOTION TO DISMISS AND OPPOSITION TO PLAINTIFF'S MOTION FOR A PRELIMINARY INJUNCTION." Maryland Attorney General's Office. (2021). https://storage.courtlistener.com/recap/gov.uscourts.mdd.504378/gov.uscourts.mdd.504378.10.1.pdf.

46. Andrew Albanese, "Maryland Defends Its Library E-book Law, Seeks Dismissal of AAP Lawsuit." Publishers Weekly. (2022). https://www.publishersweekly.com/pw/by-topic/digital/copyright/article/88308-maryland-defends-its-library-e-book-law-seeks-dismissal-of-aap-lawsuit.html.

47. "Case 1:21-cv-03133-DLB Document 10-1: CONSOLIDATED MEMORANDUM OF LAW IN SUPPORT OF DEFENDANT'S MOTION TO DISMISS AND OPPOSITION TO PLAINTIFF'S MOTION FOR A PRELIMINARY INJUNCTION." Maryland Attorney General's Office. (2021). https://storage.courtlistener.com/recap/gov.uscourts.mdd.504378/gov.uscourts.mdd.504378.10.1.pdf.

48. The Indie Author Project. WHAT IS THE INDIE AUTHOR PROJECT? (2022). https://indieauthorproject.com/authors.

SDGs and the Scholarly Community

Barbie Keiser and Ruth Pagell

Whether you read scholarly articles or watch the daily news, you will probably be familiar with discussions on climate change, the green environment, and sustainability. The 2030 Agenda for Sustainable Development sets out 17 United Nations (UN) Sustainable Development Goals (SDGs). The 169 associated targets and 231 indicators underpinning the goals serve as a framework for countries, businesses and industries, and civil society organizations to address sustainable economic and social development (**Figure 1**). SDGs balance the three dimensions of sustainable development (the economic, social, and environmental), emphasizing human rights for all, gender equality, and the empowerment of women and girls (UN Department of Economic and Social Affairs, Sustainable Development, n.d.). This report highlights ways the scholarly community (publishers, educational institutions, and libraries) participates in sustainable development (SD) initiatives.

Researching SDGs: Finding Data, Analyzing Information, and Measuring Success

Progress made toward sustainable development is evaluated by words and actions. One approach is through scholarly output. The other approach uses metrics that evaluate country and university initiatives or highlight successful projects at an institutional level.

Members of the information supply chain—the LIS schools, individual librarians, and researchers—are responsible for disseminating unbiased information to

Figure 1 / Sustainable Development Goals

Barbie Keiser (https://orcid.org/0000-0003-0027-5795) is an information resources management (IRM) consultant who has created and reengineered corporate and academic libraries, government clearinghouses, and information centers. She is a former manager of information resources for the Penn Central Corporation and director of the Kathryn and Shelby Cullom Davis Library at the College of Insurance and is today a reference and instruction librarian at Northern Virginia Community College. A prolific author, Keiser writes a column for *ONLINE Searcher* magazine and is a contributor to Information Today, Inc.'s NewsBreaks (newsbreaks.infotoday.com).

Ruth Pagell (https://orcid.org/0000-0003-3238-9674), emeritus faculty librarian at Emory University, was founding university librarian for Li Ka Shing Library at Singapore Management University and an ALA-USIA fellow at the Asian Institute of Technology in Thailand. She has taught LIS courses for Drexel University, Clark Atlanta University, and the University of Hawaii and a knowledge management course at Nanyang Technological University in Singapore. She co-authored International Business Information: How to Find It, How to Use It.

their parent organizations, policymakers, and the public. Besides using research tools to find articles related to the goals, librarians need to be able to answer the question, "Is my country meeting its SD goals?"

Using Databases to Research the SDGs

The number of articles on SDGs grew almost 700 percent in the past six years. Three major information providers—subscription services from Elsevier and Clarivate and free and subscription services from Dimensions—apply different algorithms resulting in different outputs. The pre-generated searches use the indicators and target terms; the results presented may not refer specifically to sustainable development.

> **Elsevier.** In 2019 Elsevier created a search strategy for each SDG that serves as one indicator of the Times Higher Education Impact Rankings (Pagell, 2019). Elsevier uses AI and user input to modify the search strings; the search strategies are available for use by researchers (Jayabalasingham, 2019). Elsevier's SciVal analytics solution uses thousands of prepared search strategies to delve into subsets of SDGs organized into Topics and Topic Clusters. The top journals for Topic 564, "Information Literacy, Instruction, Libraries," for example, are library publications. RELX, Elsevier's parent, has a robust SDG Resource Centre (sdgresources.relx.com), replete with research and news about SDGs and trends in SDG research.
>
> **Clarivate.** In January 2022 Clarivate added SDGs as a Research Area for its research analytics tool, InCites, but not in Web of Science. InCites SDG search strategies are based on Eugene Garfield's original theory of using co-citations to create the Institute for Scientific Information's (ISI) citation indexes. "Navigating the Structure of Research on Sustainable Development Goals" (Nakamura et al., 2019) contains a detailed description of Clarivate's approach. Clarivate released its corporate Sustainability Report for 2020, outlining progress and its plans for the future.
>
> **Dimensions.** Digital Science's Dimensions classification scheme covers "areas of research associated with one or more SDGs (the majority of the SDGs are interrelated). The scheme uses automated allocation of the 17 SDGs and their associated targets and indicators to all fitting documents in Dimensions thereby addressing research areas aligned to the goals" (Dimensions, n.d.). Researchers can browse papers for each SDG through the Dimensions site (app.dimensions.ai/browse/categories/publication/sdg). "Contextualizing Sustainable Development Research" (Wastl et al., 2020) explains how Dimensions created its SDG search strategies. An updated release of the search strategies will be available in 2022. The Dimensions website (www.dimensions.ai/webinars/discover-and-analyse-research-in-context-of-the-united-nations-sustainable-development-goals) features an on-demand webinar, "Discover and Analyse Research in Context of the United Nations Sustainable Development Goals."

Table 1 compares articles across the sources and rankings; arrows indicate changes in rank from the pre-SDGs output (2000–2015) to 2016–2021.

Performing comparable free-text searches on "SDGs or Sustainable Development Goals" in Web of Science, Scopus, and Dimensions generates a list of top entities in all three databases (**Table 2**).

Measuring Success

Two comprehensive reports with accompanying datasets measure country progress toward meeting the goals. The first is the official UN report, "Sustainable Development Goals Report 2021." It includes in-depth information about each SDG, country reports with infographics, and an accompanying interactive database (unstats.un.org/sdgs/unsdg). The dataset covers all indicators for all countries

Table 1 / Research Output of SDGs, 2016–2021

SDG		Web Of Science InCites Rank		Elsevier Scopus Rank	Dimensions	
1	No Poverty	16		16	14	
2	Zero Hunger	9	↓	8	9	
3	Good Health & Well Being	1		1	2	
4	Quality Education	14	↓	15	3	
5	Gender Equality	2		14	15	
6	Clean Water & Sanitation	8	↓	12	11	
7	Affordable & Clean Energy	7	↑	2	1	
8	Decent Work & Economic Growth	12		9	7	
9	Industry, Innovation & Infrastructure	10	↑	13	16	
10	Reduced Inequalities	13	↓	11	8	
11	Sustainable Cities & Communities	3	↑	5	6	
12	Responsible Consumption & Production	11	↑	10	10	
13	Climate Action	4		3	5	
14	Life Below Water	6	↓	7	13	
15	Life on Land	5	↓	6	12	
16	Peace, Justice & Strong Institutions	15		4	4	
	Highest Output	889,011	SDG3	4,488,726 SDG3	886,390	SDG7
	Lowest Output	12,670	SDG1	16,447 SDG1	14,024	SDG9

Note: Databases update on different schedules; searches conducted in January 2022.

dating from 2000, but a good deal of the data is missing. According to the report, SDG 4 has been lagging its targets even before COVID; one year into the virus, reading proficiency for children from first to eighth grade as well as school funding have fallen on all continents (p. 34), as depicted in **Figure 2**.

The second source is "The Sustainable Development Report 2021: The Decade of Action for the Sustainable Development Goals." Cambridge University Press publishes the report and data under the auspices of the Sustainable Development Solutions Network (SDSN), a global initiative for the UN. Countries have an overall score and a rank; all the indicators are available. Japan is the only "top 20" country not in Europe.

Table 2 / Top institutions listed in all three databases: Web of Science, Scopus, and Dimensions

Institution	Country	Author	Publisher[4]	Publication
U College London[1]	US	Bhutta, A	MDPI	Sustainability
Oxford	UK[2]	Murray, CJL	Taylor & Francis	J Cleaner Production
Harvard	China[3]	Bartram, J	Elsevier	PLOS One
World Health Organization	Australia	Hay, SI	Taylor & Francis	Science of the Total Environment
London School of Hygiene and Tropical Medicine	Spain	Yaya, S	Oxford U Press	Int J of Env Res & Pub Health
	South Africa		Emerald	World Sustainably Series
	India		Wiley	

Clarivate:
1 - Also uses parent institution, University of London 2 - Includes UK and the individual countries
3 - Hong Kong and Macau are included in Clarivate's Chinese totals
Scopus: 4 – Does not have publishers

Search: "Sustainable Development Goals" OR SDGS in Title, Abstract Topic

Figure 2 / COVID-19 has wiped out 20 years of education gains

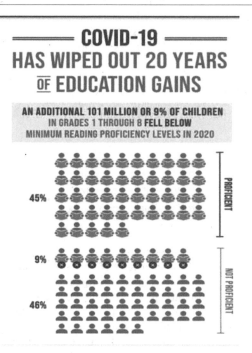

Source: *"Sustainable Development Goals Report 2021,"* p. 11

Users can explore and download "The Sustainable Development Report 2021" and country-level data via dashboards.sdgindex.org/downloads. The dataset includes color-coded composite data by SDG, indicating whether a country has met its goal (green), challenges remain (yellow), there are significant challenges (orange), and there are major challenges (red) for each SDG. Besides UN data, the report uses third-party data, such as the Times Higher Education Impact rankings and data from other international organizations. The download includes the codebook with URLs for each data source.

The report site features a dashboard of country profiles (dashboards.sdgindex.org/profiles). For the United States, there are also state-level profiles (us-states.sdgindex.org/profiles). Special reports include a 2019 ranking of 105 U.S. cities (sdsna.github.io/2019USCittiesIndex/2019USCitiesRankings.pdf).

The U.S. federal government has created an SDGs website (sdg.data.gov). A work in progress, the website provides data for the indicators at a national level. One positive aspect of this report is that it contains in-depth information about each metric (sdg.data.gov/reporting-status), including the source, a definition, and comparable information for the UN's data on the indicator. Despite lags in the data, there is adequate, accessible data to report progress for countries and individual U.S. states.

Publishers' and Information Vendors' Take on the SDGs

Almost every industry is tackling the 17 SDGs, and the publishing industry is no exception. Asfrid Hegdal of the Norwegian Publishers Association notes in "Publishers and the United Nations Sustainable Development Goals" that some publishers seek to drive progress by becoming agents of change, "giving a voice and platform to those who can shape society and our culture for the better." Others examine their business practices to ensure they operate sustainably and equitably (Hegdal, 2020, p. 1).

Some publishers concentrate on internal projects, such as creating awareness among staff of the firm's SDG commitments; others distribute research about sustainable development, including expanding the number of titles available via open access (OA) or creating resources to support instruction. Exchanges of ideas can be limited to academic scholars or address a broader audience, including policymakers and the public.

Academics, librarians, and publishers have been working together on SDGs since the run-up to the United Nations Conference on Sustainable Development (Rio+20) in 2012. As the final goal (17) is Partnerships for the SDGs, professional and trade associations assist their members in identifying potential approaches to meeting the world SDGs.

How Publishing Associations Encourage Their Members to Act

Together, the International Publishers Association (IPA) and the UN have identified ten challenges for action, known as the SDG Publishers Compact. The compact is a voluntary commitment to publish books and journals that accelerate progress toward achieving the SDGs. Signatories to the compact agree to actively acquire and promote content that advocates for SDG themes, reporting on progress toward achieving these goals by raising awareness about them; advocating, promoting, and collaborating across boundaries; dedicating resources toward accelerating progress; and acting on at least one SDG goal (SDG Publishers Compact, n.d.).

The Higher Education Sustainability Initiative's (HESI) SDG Publisher Compact Fellows consists of publishers, librarians, and academics working in "groups to create useful tools and important outcomes for the academic international community":

- The Academic Societies and Textbooks group develops "ways for publishers to recognize and address the lack of SDG-related content in their education materials."
- The Connecting Academic Researchers and Practitioners group develops best practices to "foster and build strong relationships between research and those who use research," including businesses.
- The Impact and Reach group is "changing the traditional ways research impact is viewed, specifically looking at academic rankings and incentives."
- A Changing Culture subgroup "is taking steps to affect [sic] culture change throughout the academic and publishing ecosystem" (Martin, 2021).

National publishing associations and allied organizations, such as the Copyright Clearance Center (CCC), work to achieve sustainable development goals through initiatives at the association level and among their member companies:

- The Association of American Publishers' (AAP) commitments to diversity and inclusion consist of recruiting women and persons of diverse backgrounds to the industry and members to publish "works that represent the widest range of voices and perspectives" (Association of American Publishers, n.d.).
- In its "Responsible Sourcing of Printed Material," "the Norwegian Publishers Association (NPA) recommends that its members refrain from contributing to deforestation and practice zero tolerance for tropical deforestation" (Den Norske Forleggerforening, 2019, p.4).
- Established in 2020, the Green Book Alliance (GBA) is a joint effort of BISG (formerly known as the Book Industry Study Group), BookNet Canada, and Book Industry Communication to develop supply chain standards in the United States, Canada, and Great Britain. GBA promotes "information sharing, joint planning and research, events and other sustainability initiatives," including creating a central source for environmental information, hosting global green book supply chain events, and developing a green global supply chain award (Reid, 2021).

Efforts by Individual Publishers

Most publishers have a webpage announcing their commitment to the SDGs, mention the SDGs in their annual reports, or are otherwise transparent and accountable for their firm's progress. Relatively few provide sufficient data about the actions taken, implementation strategies, or how they measure progress.

Exemplary practice highlighting internally focused and outward-facing initiatives: Since 2018, Penguin Random House UK's Creative Responsibility Reports illustrate the progress made in reading, community, inclusion, and sustainability through book donations to school libraries, food banks, prisons, and homeless shelters (Penguin Random House, n.d.). The company's 2020–2021 report provides greater detail about its direct and indirect carbon footprint, presenting a detailed methodology for the calculated impact on raw material use, the value chain, distribution, and logistics (Penguin Random House, 2021).

Many publishers address SDGs as an extension of traditional publishing roles, such as issuing new OA journals dealing with SDGs, for example, three new academic journals for environmental research launched by the Institute of Physics Publishing. Other publishing companies curate collections covering the SDGs for classroom use. Taylor & Francis, for example, has mapped its digital content to the SDGs, creating a Sustainable Development Goals Online collection featuring book chapters, articles, essays, presentations, videos, case studies, teaching guides, and lesson plans for each SDG.

How Publishers Deal with Diversity, Equity, and Inclusion (DEI)

Aspects of diversity include a mix of race, ethnicity, religion, nationality, gender identity and expression, socioeconomic background, sexual orientation, disability status, marital or familial status, and geography. Publishers strive to balance perspectives by expanding the representation of previously unrepresented groups among authors, editors, and corporate executives. Organizations such as PublisHer encourage more specific groups, in this case, women, to participate in all aspects of publishing and help publishers address imbalances and inequities in the publishing world (PublisHer, 2019). The Elsevier Foundation supports women researchers from developing countries through New Scholars grants and capacity-building projects in developing countries (Elsevier Foundation, 2021). Publishers are also making their materials more accessible to other groups, such as the visually impaired, by committing to EPUB3 standards and using alt text descriptions, and to girls with depictions of females in nontraditional professions.

Examples of DEI collections offered from database vendors are:

- EBSCO's Diversity, Equity and Inclusion Resources (www.ebsco.com/products/diversity-equity-and-inclusion-resources)
- ProQuest's Diversity Collection (about.proquest.com/en/products-services/diversity-collection) includes Ethnic NewsWatch, GenderWatch, and Alt-Press Watch.
- Gale OneFile: Diversity Studies (www.gale.com/c/onefile-diversity-studies) is global in scope.
- Harvard Business Publishing has assembled cases and course materials to address diversity, inclusion, and belonging (hbsp.harvard.edu/diversity-resources-for-educators).

Publishers increasingly assist researchers from the Global South, helping them find funding for research projects or paying article processing charges (APCs). SAGE MILES (Manuscript Improvement and Language Editing Services, sagemiles.com) "includes copyediting, proofreading, formatting assistance, and expert advice in terms of context and logical flow within manuscripts submitted to SAGE Publications India" (Keiser, 2020, p. 18).

The target of publishers' SDG 3 initiatives (Good health and well-being) might be their employees, the researchers whose works they publish, or the public. One of many efforts by Taylor & Francis to support researchers is Knowledge Retreat (knowledgeretreat.taylorandfrancis.com). The site presents self-care tips and expert advice for exercising the mind and overcoming periods of brain fog, fatigue, or writer's block (Taylor & Francis, 2021).

Rethinking Raw Materials, Water Usage, Energy, Climate Change, and the Environment

Increasingly, publishers are actively reducing their use of materials that will harm the environment in products and production; using less electricity, water, and even plastic in their offices; and avoiding damage to the environment by redesigning waste disposal. Most have set targets to reduce their carbon footprints, some committing to net-zero emissions by a specific year. Publishers are also concerned about the environmental effects of shipping physical books and their packaging (Publiship, n.d.). Their commitments extend to reducing the amount of waste sent to landfills and the amount of water used in the pulping of books. Bertelsmann's ambitious targets to achieve climate neutrality by 2030 include changes to materials used, energy, water discharge, emissions, and waste disposal (Bertelsmann, 2022).

Many publishers have committed to the environment and climate change for a decade. Examples include Macmillan's pledge to lower its overall carbon emissions. The company's sustainability website (sustainability.macmillan.com) explains how it reduces carbon emissions, presenting data it has collected. The transparency of Macmillan's data is lacking in other publishers' reporting of progress.

Print on demand, which is closer to end users, is another way that publishers reduce transportation impact and costs, and greater reliance on recycled paper is making the supply chain greener (Publishers Weekly, 2021). Some booksellers and libraries commit to using recycled paper. RecycLivre (recyclivre.com) sells secondhand books over the internet, donating 10 percent of the profits to educational charities. Little Free Libraries (littlefreelibrary.org) make reading accessible to communities by establishing pop-up bookcases in convenient locations. Readers can take a book from the shelves and leave one in its place.

Industry, Infrastructure, and Innovation

Digital infrastructure allows progress toward SD goals, but energy consumption continues to rise as industry and academia rely on high-powered servers to store and deliver data to researchers. Several publishing companies, such as Otava in Finland, take a more holistic approach, converting the entire group to green energy.

Others purchase credits to offset their carbon footprint. The Penguin Group USA, for example, buys credits to offset 100 percent of the electricity used by its distribution center in Westminster, Maryland.

"Smart cities" and 5G mobile networks reduce the need to commute to the office or campus to access research from libraries that are able to deliver digital magazines, journal databases, and e-books cost-effectively. However, bandwidth continues to be a challenge for remote access in developed nations; unreliable electricity in the Global South remains an issue for access to academic resources and data analysis.

Institutions of Higher Learning

In addition to teaching and researching, many universities now have offices of sustainability with roles for building awareness about the SDGs and changing operations to support the goal of becoming net carbon-neutral campuses. Several offices fund projects led by student and faculty groups, such as Emory University's Office of Sustainability Initiatives (OSI). This year's OSI grant recipient projects "support biodiversity, save energy, reduce waste and increase engagement with climate action and racial justice at Emory" (McCormack, 2021).

The Association for the Advancement of Sustainability in Higher Education (AASHE) is home to the Sustainability Tracking, Assessment, & Rating System (STARS; reports.aashe.org/institutions/participants-and-reports/?sort=country). University libraries are featured in two indicators: Support for Sustainability Research and Waste Minimization and Diversion. Unfortunately, most of the 350 universities filing sustainability reports are in North America, which limits STARS's claim of global scope. Universities choose to participate by sharing initiatives with the Times Higher Education Impact Rankings or the UI GreenMetric World University Ranking. (greenmetric.ui.ac.id). UI GreenMetric evaluates universities according to 39 indicators in six groupings: setting and infrastructure, energy and climate change, waste, water, transportation, and education and research (Fourtane, 2022; Pagell, 2021).

Infrastructure, Energy, and Waste

Energy-inefficient buildings contribute to greenhouse gas emissions. Institutions constructing buildings or retrofitting existing structures are increasingly turning to renewable energy, decarbonizing heating systems, adding gardens on roofs, and making other changes to help them achieve carbon neutrality (Cities Today, 2022). Some have turned to architectural firms utilizing the Leadership in Energy and Environmental Design (LEED) certification, "a framework for healthy, highly efficient, and cost-saving green buildings" (USGBC, n.d.). Washington University in St. Louis, Missouri, "holds the most Platinum-level certifications among U.S. universities" (Grauerholz, 2021).

Alternative means of transportation on campus lower carbon emissions and pollution. Universities can encourage the use of electric vehicles by installing electric charging stations, rewarding carpooling, providing campus buses, and making the campus bicycle-friendly and pedestrian-friendly.

Exemplary Practice: The University of Sao Paulo takes measures "to increase and enhance diversity in the student population by increasing under-represented minority groups and those students from lower socio-economic backgrounds. ... The University has successfully implemented environmental sustainability policies and programmes to reduce energy use across campuses," fostering "carbon free transport through free bikes for students," establishing bike lanes, and working "with local communities on initiatives to protect biodiverse areas and native forests" (The RELX SDG Customer Awards 2021, n.d.).

Academic librarians and campus facilities engineers collaborate to make their libraries greener and eco-friendly. LEED architecture for new building design, and retrofits for existing structures, are becoming more commonplace as librarians provide input on library construction projects. According to the Green Libraries website (greenlibraries.org), there are 42 green libraries listed in the United States and Canada, with more under construction. A resource list is available on the site for librarians wishing to explore ways to make their library green (greenlibraries. org/resources). For those considering turning their library greener, the Association of College and Research Libraries (ACRL) LibGuide offers an extensive collection of resources for sustainable academic library building design (acrl.libguides. com/buildingresources).

Educating for Sustainability

SDGs expire in 2030, but the need for sustainable development does not. The Organisation for Economic Co-operation and Development (OECD) introduced a broader vision of "global competence" as "a multi-dimensional construct that requires a combination of knowledge, skills, attitudes and values successfully applied to global issues or intercultural situations." The only way to accomplish this is through education. Schleicher (2020) believes that education can reconcile the needs and interests of individuals, communities, and nations within an equitable framework based on open borders and a sustainable future. Only then will the underlying principles of the SDGs become a real social contract with citizens.

OECD, UNESCO, and the Sustainable Development Solutions Network (SDSN) contribute to promoting education for sustainability by providing tools for educators and learners through conferences, surveys, webinars, and learning academies. SDSN offers free, self-paced classes open to learners at any educational level (unsdsn.org). In addition to SDSN's Global Schools Program, the SDG Academy (sdgacademy.org) creates and curates free massive open online courses (MOOCs) and educational materials on sustainable development and the SDGs (usdsn.org/sdg-academy or edx.org/school/sdgacademyx). In 2015 SDSN launched an all-volunteer network of youth hubs (sdsnyouth.org).

In response to COVID, UNESCO formed the Global Education Coalition (globaleducationcoalition.unesco.org), a group of 275 organizations from the public, private, and nonprofit sectors to protect the right to education during unprecedented disruption, from response to recovery. The coalition has 233 projects in 112 countries. An important initiative is its Global Skills Academy (globaleducation coalition.unesco.org/global-skills-academy), which offers free, online technical and vocational training by its select members, such as IBM and Dior.

The Australia, New Zealand & Pacific SDSN site (ap-unsdsn.org/regional-initiatives/universities-sdgs) offers links to events concerning actions on SDGs in various educational settings as well as guides such as Getting Started with the SDGs in Universities (ap-unsdsn.org/regional-initiatives/universities-sdgs/university-sdg-guide) and Accelerating Education for the SDGs in Universities (ap-unsdsn.org/regional-initiatives/universities-sdgs/university-sdg-guide). The guides are available in multiple languages; the most recent addition is a guide supplement with new case studies.

The Global MDP Master's in Development Practice program (mdpglobal.org) is a consortium of 35 institutions from 24 countries on all continents. The program consists of a core curriculum tailored to individual and institutional needs; a Global Classroom, including students communicating remotely; and a field training overview. At Emory University (https://web.gs.emory.edu/mdp/about/index.html), the librarian for sociology, African studies, and development studies teaches the Research Methods class.

TeachSDGs (teachsdgs.org) is a volunteer organization providing official UN resources for teachers and students, supported by the United Nations Foundation.

Many education conferences emphasize the need for integrating sustainable development into curricula. Examples include:

- The 10th International Conference on Sustainable Development (ICSD) 2022, Creating a Unified Foundation for the Sustainable Development Research, Practice, and Education (ecsdev.org/conference/10th-icsd-2022)
- The 3rd World Higher Education Conference (WHEC2022), Reinventing Higher Education for a Sustainable Future (en.unesco.org/news/unesco-world-higher-education-conference-2022), sponsored by UNESCO, in partnership with OECD

Sustainability Courses for LIS and iSchools

According to the International Association of Universities' (IAU) "2nd Global Survey Report on Higher Education and Research for Sustainable Development," 65 percent of 352 universities responded that they have specific courses on sustainable development or integrate SDGs into other courses. An example of a standalone course's approach is the "University of Auckland's three SUSTAIN courses, which teach what sustainability means, its underpinning values, and the role individuals and organisations play in creating solutions at the local and international level. The courses are available to arts and science students, with the first-year course available to all students as a General Education option" (India Education Diary, 2022). The University of Technology Sydney (sustainability.edu.au) embeds sustainability into the curriculum for all courses. It also maintains the national Teaching and Learning Sustainability website for Australia, including lists of educators, courses, and teaching materials.

The IAU report includes an extensive bibliography and sample university strategic plans (Mallow, Toman, and van't Land, 2020). Noticeably absent are courses or programs in schools of library and information science (LIS) or iSchools. The American Library Association (ALA) lists areas of concentration/career pathways within ALA-accredited programs (www.ala.org/CFApps/lisdir/index.cfm); none include sustainability.

> **Exemplary Practice:** The University of Florida (UF) created a resource for developing greater global awareness and sustainability literacy: Sustainable Development Goals in the Classroom: a UF Faculty Guide for Using the United Nations SDGs (https://dcp.ufl.edu/sbe/wp-content/uploads/sites/32/2021/02/UN-SDGs_InTheClassroomAtUF_2021-01-00.pdf).

Chowdhury and Koya (2017) argue that one essential element to achieving SDGs is access to information. Their article, "Information Practices for Sustainability: Role of iSchools in Achieving the UN Sustainable Development Goals (SDGs)," includes a recommended framework for teaching and research in iSchools for promoting SDGs:

1. Sustainable information systems and infrastructure
2. Sustainable information practices
3. Sustainable information policies and governance
4. Essential user education, training, and literacy

The article does not mention libraries. There is agreement on the importance of education in achieving the SDGs; however, LIS and iSchool programs have been slow to integrate sustainability into their curriculums.

Pre-Tertiary Education

The long-term future of the planet depends on Generation Z and those who come after. The OECD survey of 15-year-olds' accomplishments in reading, math, and science, known as PISA (Programme for International Student Assessment), asks questions about student awareness of the global environment. According to the 2018 results, 78 percent of the students across OECD countries agreed or strongly agreed that looking after the global environment is important to them and that they know about climate change and global warming. However, they are not being proactive in their actions (OECD, 2020). Ninety percent of school principals reported that their curriculum covers climate change and global environment.

The "Think Green Education and Climate Change: Trends Shaping Education #24" report summarizes the PISA report, recommends steps for universities to take through changing pedagogy and working with other organizations, and incorporates supporting data (OECD, 2021). The OECD 2008 Workshop for Sustainable Development included a curriculum guide for education for sustainable development for primary, secondary, and tertiary levels (www.oecd.org/green-growth/41078703.pdf) that remains relevant today.

The Sustainable Development Goals and Libraries

Libraries partner with other libraries and library associations to learn about and participate in sustainable development efforts and activities. Academic libraries collaborate with other departments to promote SD across their campuses, participating in SD events and initiatives.

Library and Information-Related Associations

International, regional, and national library and information-related organizations conduct surveys, issue reports, and hold events related to sustainable development. For example, the global membership organization OCLC, known to many librarians as the provider of WorldCat, has a productive research team. In 2020 it conducted a survey of library staff to determine how aware they are about SGDs and how libraries are using SDGs "to inform their strategic directions" (OCLC, 2021). The survey found that awareness concerning SDGs was lowest in the Americas. Also, explicitly incorporating SDGs into library strategic planning was below 15 percent in all regions. Links to the survey findings and a series of on-demand webinars are available at https://www.oclc.org/research/publications/2021/sustainable-development-goals-study-2021.html.

The International Federation of Library Associations and Institutions (IFLA) has been among the most active organizations at the global level. As part of the 2020 United Nations SDG Action Week, IFLA listed eight ways to promote SDGs:

1. Use IFLA's posters on websites and social media.
2. Contribute a story to the Library Map of the World.
3. Organize and present your own advocacy resources.
4. Take the message to decision-makers and influencers.
5. Access your capacity to advocate around SDGs by using IFLA's SDG capacity grid.
6. Build relations with decision-makers.
7. Build advocacy partnerships.
8. Evaluate advocacy (IFLA advocacy capacities grid, 2020).

IFLA's Environment, Sustainability and Libraries (ENSUBLIB) section is now in charge of the association's Green Library Award, presented since 2006. There is an award for the best library building and the best library project. In 2021 the Edmonton Public Library's revitalization project was the 2021 building winner, and Finland's Oulu City Library received the project award (https://www.ifla.org/news/ifla-green-library-award-2021-winners-announced). Past winners and runners-up are listed at https://www.ifla.org/g/environment-sustainability-and-libraries/ifla-green-library-award.

As of February 2022 31 countries have submitted stories to IFLA's Library Map of the World Sustainable Development Goals and Stories (https://librarymap.ifla.org/stories), highlighting ways in which their libraries reach out to their communities about sustainable development. Noticeably absent from the map are the United States and the U.K. One story represented on the map is the Charles Darwin Research Center's (darwinfoundation.org) traveling library, which is designed to increase conservation literacy and awareness across the four Galapagos Islands (SDGs 4, 11, 13, 14, and 15). The center's library staffers support primary teachers and students through email and social media.

Regional Library Associations

Giuseppe Vitiello, director of the European Bureau of Library, Information and Documentation Associations (EBLIDA) clarified the European Union's (EU) approach to Agenda 2030 and the role of EBLIDA (personal communication January 20, 2022). The EU takes a holistic approach to the SDGs (https://ec.europa.eu/info/strategy/international-strategies/sustainable-development-goals/eu-holistic-approach-sustainable-development_en), creating a set of 100 indicators bundled into six priorities: European Green Deal, economy that works for people, Europe fit for the digital age, European way of life, stronger Europe in the world, and European democracy.

EBLIDA supports library associations and libraries in the 47 countries of the Council of Europe (www.coe.int/en/web/portal/home), encouraging libraries to see beyond education, culture, and the environment. The association partners with European organizations, sharing resources and ideas for integrating the SD goals into libraries' core mission, such as:

- EBLIDA Matrix (www.eblida.org/Documents/ELSA-WG-implementation-SDG-Indicators-in-EU-Libraries.pdf), which presents in-depth information on each SDG and how libraries can relate to them
- The SDG-KIC-Knowledge Information Centre (www.eblida.org/activities/sdg-kic), a resource for politicians, library policymakers, and staff implementing SDGs in libraries
- The European Libraries and Sustainable Development Implementation and Assessment (ELSIA) Expert Group (www.eblida.org/about-eblida/expert-groups/eu-libraries-sustainable-development-implementation-assessment.html), which deals with the implementation of the 2030 Agenda in European libraries
- The December 2021 EBLIDA Newsletter (mailchi.mp/316f692cdbdd/eblida-newsletter-4870162?e=[UNIQID]), which provides summary data from the "Second European Report on Sustainable Development and Libraries"

Australia, its universities, and library associations have been active in SDG initiatives. The Australian Library and Information Association (ALIA), the Australian Libraries and Archives Copyright Coalition, Blue Shield Australia, the Council of Australia University Librarians (CAUL), and the National and State Libraries of Australia have worked together to identify 10 targets covering the six different goals listed, referred to as "Stretch Targets." The 10 targets and the SDGs they support are:

1. Libraries contribute to literacy, including media literacy, and are embedded in national strategies (SDG 4.6).
2. Adopt open access practices and principles (SDG 16.10).

3. Achieve copyright reform (SDG 16.10).
4. All Australians have access to public library services online, and 90 percent have access to a public library service point (SDG 16.10).
5. In collaboration with indigenous people, adopt practices to collections and services that are culturally informed and respectful (SDG 4.7).
6. ALIA has an open and transparent position on climate change (SDG 13).
7. Public libraries are acknowledged as centers for personal development and well-being (SDG 3).
8. Library collections and services reflect the diversity of Australia's population, including asylum seekers and refugees (SDG 4.7).
9. We commit to lifelong learning for our own workforce and provide opportunities for all Australians to pursue lifelong learning (SDG 4).
10. Australian library and information sector professionals are actively engaged with libraries and library associations in the region and internationally (SDG 17) (Sustainable Development Goals: Stretch Targets for Australian libraries 2020–2030, n.d.).

ALA established its International Relations Round Table (IRRT) in 1949. In 2002 IRRT launched the International Sustainable Library Development (ISLD) interest group. ISLD acts as a clearinghouse of sustainable library-based projects in developing areas of the world. In 2020 ALA created the ALA Task Force on United Nations 2030 Sustainable Development Goals (www.ala.org/aboutala/ala-task-force-united-nations-2030-sustainable-development-goals), which is still in the formation stage. The site provides links to archived webinars from a variety of sources.

Exemplary Practice: A university library, library association, and publisher supporting SDG 17, Partnerships for the Goals (www.las.org.sg/wp/blog/announcements/why-should-i-care-libraries-advocacy-and-the-un-sdgs)

In September 2021 Singapore Management University Libraries hosted the webinar, "Why Should I Care: Libraries, Advocacy, and UN SDGs," co-hosted by the Library Association of Singapore and Taylor & Francis. The speakers included Loida Garcia-Febo, chair of the ALA Task Force on United Nations 2030 Sustainable Development Goals, and Don Low, journals sales director at Taylor & Francis.

These are examples of professional organizations supporting libraries' involvement in sustainable development. As Vitiello tells us, "Professional organizations and librarians' associations have a great role to play in raising librarians' awareness about SDGs."

Libraries Large and Small

Libraries address sustainable development through traditional activities and innovative SD initiatives. As librarians consider the inclusive nature of their collections, they turn to independent booksellers and small presses to find more diverse titles. Academic libraries are examining catalog records for the use of outdated and inappropriate terminology in subject headings (e.g., replacing "Aliens" with "Noncitizens"). Some libraries are examining their archival holdings for collections to share about historical injustice, such as the Syracuse University Libraries Special Collections Research Center's new digital exhibition, A Courageous Stand: The Story of the Syracuse 8, about "a group of Black student-athletes who boycotted the University football program until it addressed their allegations of racism in 1970" (Hatem, 2021).

> **Exemplary Practice:** Academic libraries are creating research guides dealing with the SDGs, such as the University of Michigan's effort to document resources for conducting SDG research (guides.lib.umich.edu/sdg). Other libraries develop research guides for individual SDGs, such as the University of South Florida LibGuide on DEI (guides.lib.usf.edu/diversity) and the Resisting Racism Research Guide from the University of Washington (guides.lib.uw.edu/resistingracism).

Library-led SDG awareness campaigns include hosting in-person events and online webinars that feature expert speakers from their faculty and using the library blog to post articles about the SDGs. Using SDGs as examples during library instruction classes is another way librarians integrate sustainable development into the curriculum.

> **Exemplary Practice:** Hong Kong University of Science and Technology (HKUST) works closely with university researchers through its blog, "Research Bridge" (library.ust.hk.sc/adg). Gabi Wong described a library-led project to put HKUST research output in context and raise researchers' awareness of SDGs (personal communication, January 18, 2022). HKUST's publishing profile was compared to the Scopus dataset.

Library Services beyond the Traditional

Libraries are known as social agents for promoting the good health and well-being of their communities (Schofield, n.d.). During the pandemic, libraries assumed information-adjacent roles, including distributing food and masks and acting as COVID testing and inoculation sites.

The public turns to libraries for accurate information, often beyond the training of library staff. Social workers can help patrons access resources and services beyond what is available in the library ("Davenport Library Becomes Iowa's First to Hire Social Worker," 2022). Libraries benefit when there is a social worker to address the psychosocial needs of library patrons, including the homeless and mentally ill (Wahler et al., 2020).

Exemplary Practice: The Sustainable Libraries Initiative (sustainablelibrar iesinitiative.org) creates awareness of the library ecosystem and libraries' role as sustainability leaders in their communities. The project offers professional development opportunities for library staff to become certified Sustainability Coordinators. The website features libraries that have found ways to reduce energy, redirect waste, and increase collaborations with other groups in their communities.

Programming at the public library might feature cooking demonstrations and nutrition classes. Libraries participating in the USDA's Summer Food Service Program (SFSP) provide meals and nutritious snacks to children and teens in low-income areas during the summer. "Offering meals and snacks through the federal meal programs not only allows libraries to become key allies in eliminating childhood hunger and promoting healthy foods, but it helps attract children to the libraries' resources and activities" (Food Research & Action Center, p. 1).

According to a survey conducted in 2020 by the Hope Center for College, Community, and Justice, 39 percent of student respondents at two-year institutions and 29 percent at four-year institutions were food insecure (Hope Center for College, Community, and Justice, 2021). Each campus and library customizes a response to meet the nutritional needs of its students and the institution. Some colleges locate their food pantries in the library "because of the library's expansive hours and student traffic" (Wood, 2020). The College & University Food Bank Alliance (CUFBA) has a toolkit and other resources to help libraries when considering opening a food pantry (cufba.org/resources).

Libraries help students with childcare while they attend class or study. At Monroe Community College in Rochester, New York, the libraries have family-friendly study rooms replete with educational toys and books to keep children occupied (Ithaka S+R).

"More than 90 percent of academic institutions have affordable learning initiatives" (*Library Journal*, p. 9). At the institutional level, these initiatives include reduced tuition and greater flexibility in the time allotted to complete courses required for graduating with a degree. Libraries participate by assuring fair access to resources and eliminating fees for access to research and fines for the return of overdue material. "The coronavirus pandemic has taken a financial toll on college students and sped up the process of going fines free" (Chung, 2021).

During the pandemic, academic libraries were the logical choice to spearhead efforts by colleges to lend laptops, iPads, Chromebooks, and hotspots to students whose classes had shifted online. Since libraries already lend books, it was simply a matter of sourcing the technology from information technology departments.

Academic libraries recognize a need to place greater emphasis on DEI initiatives. Responding to a *Library Journal* survey, libraries indicated they would use unexpected increases in budgets to purchase more electronic resources (65 percent of respondents), increase staff (44 percent), fund digitization (42 percent), and fund DEI initiatives (37 percent). Funding DEI initiatives placed higher on the list of priorities than building/facilities improvement (36 percent), OER initiatives (32 percent), or pay increases (31 percent) (*Library Journal*, p. 29). While there were some regional differences, both Europe and North America included DEI among their top priorities (*Library Journal*, p. 30).

Whether taking a comprehensive approach to sustainable development or targeting their efforts, libraries strive to make their communities more sustainable. Some libraries are leading the way; others are just beginning. There is no end to the opportunities to participate.

A Prescription for Progress

The UN SDGs provide a framework for addressing the many complex and systemic challenges facing the world today. A sustainable future requires innovation, with all segments of the scholarly community working together: teachers and scholars, publishers and database providers, libraries and professional organizations. There is no one right path for achieving sustainability. Each member of the scholarly community can follow internal best practices to support individual SDGs and communicate the importance of SDGs to their stakeholders. They may have already been doing many of these activities but have neither connected nor integrated them into sustainable development initiatives. The following recommended practices supporting sustainable development provide entities with practical ideas for beginning their SD efforts.

Recommendation #1: Make others aware of your organization's commitment to sustainable development.
- Enumerate the actions your organization is taking toward SDGs.
- Use multiple channels to inform, describe, and convince others to participate in your SDG-related initiatives or events.
- Encourage and amplify the SD initiatives of your organization (and those of others).
- Help researchers promote their work to scholarly and non-academic markets.
- Create mechanisms to assure effective transfer of knowledge ("lessons learned") from one program to another, one institution to another.

Recommendation #2: Encourage and support research that creates new knowledge about SD.
- Work with your university to incorporate the SDGs in its research framework.
- Support efforts to integrate SD across the curriculum.
- Create targeted workshops, drop-in sessions, meetups, webinars, seminars, and conferences for researchers; expand the subjects covered in these sessions; and increase the number of participants from your community and beyond.

- Assist researchers to deal with intellectual property rights.
- Embrace the future of open access, including the underlying data for research output, by adopting the FAIR (Findable, Accessible, Interoperable, and Reusable) data principles and making informed decisions about where to publish.
- Coordinate with relevant departments in your institution to create a repository for research and data to maximize discovery.

Recommendation #3: Educate your staff, students, instructors, and community about SD.
- Use a mix of SDG learning opportunities (e.g., lectures by experts, webinars, and podcasts) to extend your reach about SD to those in and beyond your community.
- Develop research guides, conduct literature reviews and arrange for subject experts to create systematic and/or scoping reviews, create annotated bibliographies related to the SDGs, and make alerts on each topic available to interested parties.
- Examine your collections for SD-related materials, highlight SD in exhibitions, and acquire SD-related materials to be included in classroom instruction to excite the next generation of researchers.

Recommendation #4: Be deliberate about sustainable development by including SD in your strategic plans. Commit resources to each effort, including financial and human resources.
- Identify SDG opportunities as part of your organization's planning session.
  - Include your staff in the planning to increase chances for success.
  - Identify potential partners within and outside your organization whose resources could help you reach the goals.
  - Set priorities by selecting high-impact and highly visible projects.
- Holding a staff member accountable for SD activities will help the department achieve its targets.
- View SDGs through the lens of organizational activities, connecting existing activities to the SDGs.

Recommendation #5: Use the scholarly supply chain to collaborate and communicate with other libraries, library organizations, and publishers.
- Inform publishers, database vendors, and platforms of SD gaps in their offerings.
- Encourage interdisciplinary collaboration on SD-related projects, with multiple institutions and countries.

Recommendation #6: Identify key performance indicators (KPIs) for specific goals.
- Track and disclose historical data to be used as a benchmark for assessing progress.

- Work with departments in your institution to align targets and coordinate assessments.
- Provide transparent progress reports.
- Report for impact by making reports meaningful and accessible to others as models.
- Take responsibility for following and understanding the national and international third-party rating of SD research and activities to inform the organization and its researchers on how to improve their visibility and positions.

References

Association of American Publishers. AAP Programs. (n.d.). https://publishers.org/aap-programs.

Benson, Darian. "Why your local library might be hiring a social worker." NPR. (January 3, 2022). https://www.npr.org/sections/health-shots/2022/01/03/1063985757/why-your-local-library-might-be-hiring-a-social-worker.

Bertelsmann. Corporate Responsibility: GRI 300 Environmental. (2022). https://www.bertelsmann.com/corporate-responsibility/reporting/gri-300-environmental.

Blankstein, M. and Wolff-Eisenberg, C. Planning, Partnering and Piloting: A Community College Library Service Innovation Playbook. Ithaka S+R. (May 18, 2020). https://sr.ithaka.org/publications/planning-partnering-and-piloting.

Cardoso, Nathalice Bezerra. How to contribute to the Sustainable Development Goals (SDGs): checklist for libraries. (April 2021). https://libraryscience.de/wp-content/uploads/2021/05/CheckList-ENG.pdf.

Chowdhury, G. and Koya, K. "Information practices for sustainability: role of iSchools in achieving the UN Sustainable Development Goals (SDGS)." *Journal of the Association for Information Science and Technology.* 68(9): 2128-2138 (2017). https://nrl.northumbria.ac.uk/id/eprint/28569/3/SDG%20and%20iSchools%20JASIST%20Paper%20Revied%20Version%20Clean.pdf.

Chung, F. "Reconsidering overdue fines in the midst of a pandemic." *Public Services Quarterly* 17:2, (2021). 136-140, DOI: 10.1080/15228959.2021.1899101.

Clarivate. (2021). Clarivate Releases Annual Sustainability Report Outlining 2020 Progress and Plans for the Future. Press release. https://clarivate.com/news/clarivate-releases-annual-sustainability-report-outlining-2020-progress-and-plans-for-the-future.

Claudio, A. "Librarians Now Frontline Workers in Combating Covid-19." *Route Fifty.* https://www.route-fifty.com/health-human-services/2022/01/librarians-now-frontline-workers-combating-covid-19/361230.

Cyr, C. and Connaway, L.S. "Libraries and Sustainable Development Goals: The Past, Present, and Future." (2020). Submitted to ASIS&T Annual Meeting 2020. https://www.oclc.org/content/dam/research/publications/2020/Cyr_C%20AM20%20Short%20Paper.pdf.

Dankowski, D. "Public libraries are using licensed professionals to address homelessness and mental health issues." *American Libraries.* (March 21, 2018).

https://americanlibrariesmagazine.org/blogs/the-scoop/pla-social-worker-walks-library.

"Davenport library becomes Iowa's first to hire social worker." *Quad-City Times.* (January 17, 2022). https://www.victoriaadvocate.com/ap/state/davenport-library-becomes-iowas-first-to-hire-social-worker/article_64a15642-95f8-5c80-a797-e815621fd9b4.html.

Dimensions Webinars. "Discover and analyse research in the context of the United Nations sustainable development goals." (n.d.). (register for access) www.dimensions.ai/webinars/discover-and-analyse-research-in-context-of-the-united-nations-sustainable-development-goals.

"An Eco-Friendly Approach to Publishing: Close-up on HP Publishing Solutions." *Publishers Weekly.* (April 19, 2021). https://www.publishersweekly.com/pw/by-topic/industry-news/publisher-news/article/86119-an-eco-friendly-approach-to-publishing-close-up-on-hp-publishing-solutions.html.

Egmont. "CSR Report: Communication on Progress 2018." (June 2019). https://www.egmont.com/sites/default/files/2019-06/CSR_Report_2018.pdf.

The Elsevier Foundation. Past Programs. (2021). https://elsevierfoundation.org/past-programs.

Food Research & Action Center. FRAC Facts for Libraries: Participating in Summer and Afterschool Meals. (n.d.). https://frac.org/wp-content/uploads/frac-facts-libraries-summer-afterschool-meals.pdf.

Fourtane, S. "Key Elements of a Sustainable University." *Fierce Education.* (January 21, 2022). https://www.fierceeducation.com/leadership/key-elements-sustainable-university.

Grauerholz, M. "Washington University leads in LEED Platinum certifications." U.S. Building Consulting Group. (October 20, 2021). https://www.usgbc.org/articles/washington-university-leads-leed-platinum-certifications.

Guaglione, S. "What goals publishers have set for becoming carbon-neutral." *Digiday.* (January 4, 2022). https://digiday.com/media/what-goals-publishers-have-set-for-becoming-carbon-neutral.

Halligan, N. "What are the UN's sustainable development goals and why do they matter?" *The National.* (January 18, 2022). https://www.thenationalnews.com/uae/environment/2022/01/18/what-are-the-uns-sustainable-development-goals-and-why-do-they-matter.

Hatem, C. "New Digital Exhibition Features Story of The Syracuse 8." Syracuse University Campus & Community. (August 28, 2021). https://news.syr.edu/blog/2021/08/28/new-digital-exhibition-features-story-of-the-syracuse-8.

Hegdal, A. "Publishers and the United Nations Sustainable Development Goals." International Publishers Association and Norwegian Publishers Association. (2020). https://www.internationalpublishers.org/images/aa-content/ipa-reports/State_of_Publishing_Reports_2020/Publishers-and-The-United-Nations-Sustainable-Development-Goals.pdf.

Hope Center for College, Community, and Justice. "#RealCollege2 2021: Basic Needs Insecurity During the Ongoing Pandemic." (March 31, 2021). https://hope4college.com/wp-content/uploads/2021/03/RCReport2021.pdf.

IFLA Advocacy Capacities Grid. International Federation of Library Associations and Institutions. (September 3, 2000). https://repository.ifla.

org/bitstream/123456789/1284/1/ifla_advocacy_capacities_grid_3_sep_2020.pdf.

Jackson, P. "From Stockholm to Kyoto: A Brief History of Climate Change." *UN Chronicle*, 2: XLIV (2007). https://www.un.org/en/chronicle/article/stockholm-kyoto-brief-history-climate-change.

Jayabalasingham, B. et al. "Identifying research supporting the United Nations Sustainable Development Goals." (October 22, 2019). DOI 10.17632/87txk-w7khs.1.

Keiser, B. "Supporting libraries, scholarship, and publishing in the global south." *ONLINE Searcher.* (January/February 2020). 44: 14-21.

"Laying the foundations for a green building revolution." Cities Today. (January 20, 2022). https://cities-today.com/industry/laying-the-foundations-for-a-green-building-revolution.

Mallow, S., Toman, I., and van't Land, H. "Higher Education and the 2030 Agenda: Moving into the 'Decade of Action and Delivery for the SDGs.'" International Association of Universities. (2020). https://www.iau-aiu.net/IMG/pdf/iau_hesd_survey_report_final_jan2020.pdf.

Martin, R. "Partnerships to achieve the Sustainable Development Goals." International Publishers Organization. (December 10, 2021). https://www.internationalpublishers.org/blog/entry/partnerships-to-achieve-the-sustainable-development-goals.

McCormack, C. "Sustainability grants fund innovative projects across campus." Emory News Center, Emory University. (December 8, 2021). https://news.emory.edu/stories/2021/12/er_sustainability_incentives_fund_08-12-2021/campus.html.

Melvern, L. "The world's forgotten first environmental conference." *The Day.* (December 20, 2009). https://www.theday.com/article/20091220/OP03/312209788.

Nakamura, M. et al. "Navigating the Structure of Research on Sustainable Development Goals." Clarivate. (April 2019). https://clarivate.com/webofsciencegroup/campaigns/sustainable-development-goals.

Den Norske Forleggerforening. "Responsible sourcing of printed material: A guide for members of the Norwegian Publishers Association." (2019). https://forleggerforeningen.no/wp-content/uploads/2019/10/DnF_veileder_EN_Interaktiv.pdf.

OCLC, Inc. "United Nations Sustainable Development Goals Study 2021: Findings from the 2020 OCLC Global Council Survey." (September 2021). https://doi.org/10.25333/6jr4-cc46.

OECD. "PISA 2018 Results (Volume VI): Are Students Ready to thrive in an Interconnected World?" (2020). https://doi.org/10.1787/d5f68679-en.

OECD. "Think green: education and climate change. Trends Shaping Education Spotlights, No. 24." (2021). https://doi.org/10.1787/2a9a1cdd-en.

Pagell, R. "Ruth's Rankings 38: Coming Attractions, UN Sustainable Development Goals and Times Higher Education Innovations and Impact Rankings Demystified." Access. (2019). https://librarylearningspace.com/ruths-rankings-38-coming-attractions-un-sustainable-development-goals-times-higher-education-innovation-impact-rankings-demystified.

Pagell, R. "Ruth's Rankings 48 Part 1: How Green is My University? Ranking Green Universities–New Metric, New Leaders." Access. (2021). https://librarylearningspace.com/ruths-rankings-48-part-1-how-green-is-my-university-ranking-green-universities-new-metrics-and-new-leaders.

Pagell R. "Ruth's Rankings 41: THE's University Impact Rankings and Sustainable Development Goals." Access. (2019). https://librarylearningspace.com/ruths-rankings-41-thes-university-impact-rankings-sustainable-development-goals-impactful-universities-world.

Penguin Random House. (n.d.). Creative Responsibility. https://www.penguin.co.uk/company/creative-responsibility.html.

Penguin Random House. "Creative Responsibility Report 2019." (October 20, 2021). https://penguinrandomhouseuk.shorthandstories.com/CR-Report-2019/index.html.

PublisHer. About PublisHer. (2019). https://womeninpublishing.org/about.

RELX SDG Customer Awards 2021. University of Sao Paulo. (n.d.). https://stories.relx.com/sdg-awards-2021/index.html#group-section-University-of-Sao-Paulo-OsiGg2oy3N.

Rea, A. "LJ's State of Academic Libraries Survey Reveals Challenges, Priorities." *Library Journal*. (October 21, 2021). https://www.libraryjournal.com/story/news/LJs-State-of-Academic-Libraries-Survey-Reveals-Challenges-Priorities.

Reid, C. "BISG Annual Meeting Examines Sustainability on a Number of Levels." *Publishers Weekly*. (April 27, 2021). https://www.publishersweekly.com/pw/by-topic/industry-news/publisher-news/article/86187-bisg-annual-meeting-green-book-publishing.html.

Roberts, A. "NOPL Cicero Library Farm grows a new record." *Eagle News Online*. (January 12, 2022). https://eaglenewsonline.com/opinion/point-of-view/2022/01/12/nopl-cicero-library-farm-grows-a-new-record.

Sachs, J., Kroll, C., Lafortune, G., Fuller, G., and Woelm, F. "Sustainable Development Report 2021." Cambridge: Cambridge University Press. (2021). doi:10.1017/9781009106559.

Schleicher, A. "Are students ready to thrive in an interconnected world? The first PISA assessment of global competence provides some answers." OECD Education and Skills Today. (2020). https://oecdedutoday.com/students-ready-thrive-interconnected-world-first-pisa-assessment-global-competence.

Schleicher, A. "Green at 15—what schools can do to support the climate." Australian Council for Educational Research. (2021). https://www.teacher-magazine.com/au_en/articles/green-at-15-what-schools-can-do-to-support-the-climate.

Schofield, A. "Social Workers and Librarians—A Case for Why We Are BFFs." "Intersections." (n.d.). https://www.ala.org/advocacy/diversity/odlos-blog/social-workers.

Selin, H. and Linner, B.O. "The Quest for Global Sustainability: International Efforts on Linking Environment and Development". CID Graduate Student and Postdoctoral Fellow Working Paper No. 5. Cambridge, MA: Science, Environment and Development Group, Center for International Development, Harvard University. (January 2005). https://dash.harvard.edu/handle/1/37366427.

Springer Nature. Springer Nature signs England's Time to Change mental health pledge and commits to supporting staff wellbeing. Press release. (January 17, 2019). https://group.springernature.com/gp/group/media/press-releases/springer-nature-signs-englands-time-to-change-pledge/16402358.

"State of Academic Libraries Benchmark Survey 2021." *Library Journal*. (Summer 2021). https://www.libraryjournal.com/story/research.

"Sustainable Development Goals: Stretch Targets for Australian Libraries 2020-2030." Australian Library and Information Association. (n.d.). https://read.alia.org.au/sustainable-development-goals-stretch-targets-australian-libraries-2020-2030.

Taylor & Francis. The Knowledge Retreat. Taylor & Francis. (2021). https://knowledgeretreat.taylorandfrancis.com.

Taylor & Francis. (n.d.). SDG Online. https://www.taylorfrancis.com/sdgo/?context=sdgo.

Tisley, A. "Dispensing Computers" *Inside Higher Ed*. (February 8, 2013). https://www.insidehighered.com/news/2013/02/08/libraries-turn-laptop-vending-machines-fulfill-students-late-night-studying-needs.

Udell, E. "Food for thought: Academic libraries are fighting campus food insecurity with onsite pantries." *American Libraries*. (May 1, 2019). https://americanlibrariesmagazine.org/2019/05/01/library-campus-food-insecurity-food-for-thought.

United Nations. SDG Publishers Compact. Sustainable Development Goals. (2020). https://www.un.org/sustainabledevelopment/sdg-publishers-compact.

United Nations Department of Economic and Social Affairs, Sustainable Development. Transforming our world: the 2030 Agenda for Sustainable Development. (n.d.). https://sdgs.un.org/2030agenda.

United Nations Sustainable Development Goals (SDGs). Dimensions. (n.d.). https://app.dimensions.ai/browse/categories/publication/sdg.

United Nations. "The Sustainable Development Goals Report 2021." (2021). https://unstats.un.org/sdgs/report/2021/The-Sustainable-Development-Goals-Report-2021.pdf.

"University of Auckland: Students' Sustainability Projects Shared at United Nations Workshop." India Education Diary. (January 29, 2022). https://india-educationdiary.in/university-of-auckland-students-sustainability-projects-shared-at-united-nations-workshop.

Wahler, E.A., Provence, M.A., Helling, J., and Williams, M.A. "The Changing Role of Libraries: How Social Workers Can Help." *Families in Society: The Journal of Contemporary Social Services*, 101(1), (January-March 2020). 34-43. https://doi.org/10.1177/1044389419850707.

"What Effect Does the Shipping of Books Have on the Environment?" Publiship. (n.d.). https://publiship.com/a-look-at-the-environmental-impact-of-book-shipping.

What is LEED? U.S. Green Building Council. (n.d.). https://www.usgbc.org/help/what-leed.

Wood, L.M. "Empty shelves: How your academic library can address food insecurity." *College & Research Libraries News*, 81:7. (2020). https://crln.acrl.org/index.php/crlnews/article/view/24532/32372.

Wastl, J. et al. "Contextualizing Sustainable Development Research." Digital Science report. (May 2020). https://digitalscience.figshare.com/articles/report/Contextualizing_Sustainable_Development_Research/12200081.

Zillman, J. "A History of Climate Activities." *Bulletin*, World Meteorological Organization, 58(3), (2009). https://public.wmo.int/en/bulletin/history-climate-activities.

Federal Agency and Federal Library Reports

Library of Congress

10 First St., S.E., Washington, DC 20540
202-707-5000
https://loc.gov

Carla Hayden
Librarian of Congress

The Library of Congress is the largest library in the world, with more than 173 million items in various languages, disciplines, and formats. As the world's largest repository of knowledge and creativity, the Library has as its mission to engage, inspire, and inform the United States Congress and the American people with a universal and enduring source of knowledge and creativity.

The Library's collections are housed in its three buildings on Capitol Hill and in climate-controlled facilities in Fort Meade, Maryland. Its audiovisual materials are held at the Packard Campus of the National Audio-Visual Conservation Center in Culpeper, Virginia. The Library also provides global access to its resources through its website, https://loc.gov.

Highlights of 2021

In fiscal year (FY) 2021 the Library of Congress:

- Responded to 730,682 reference requests from Congress, the public, and other federal agencies[1]
- Recorded a total of 173,731,463 physical items in its collections
- Recorded 86 petabytes of digital storage in use. The material on the Library's websites alone totals 5 petabytes.
- Recorded more than 178.1 million visits and 617.7 million page views on its web properties
- Welcomed 29,939 visitors to its Capitol Hill campus
- Circulated more than 21.5 million copies of braille, audio, and large print items to patrons, via the National Library Service for the Blind and Print Disabled and its network of state and local libraries

[1]Direct use of Congressional Research Service reports is included in this calculation.

- Issued 403,771 copyright registrations and recorded 8,252 documents containing 961,291 titles
- Employed 3,194 permanent staff members
- Circulated 154,505 items for use inside and outside the Library
- Performed approximately 2.2 million preservation actions on items in the Library's physical collections, with a further 3.4 million pages of materials prepared and shipped to vendors for preservation reformatting services
- Placed more than 7.5 million items under inventory control in its preservation facility at Fort Meade
- Operated with a total budget authority of $802.128 million, including $757.346 million in appropriations and the additional authority to spend $44.782 million in offsetting receipts.

The Library recorded a total of 173,731,463 physical items in collections, including:

- 25,252,360 cataloged books in the Library of Congress classification system
- 15,752,924 items in the nonclassified print collections
- 132,726,179 items in the nonclassified (special) collections, including:
  - 4,178,059 audio materials
  - 75,737,064 manuscripts
  - 5,648,316 maps
  - 17,516,607 microforms
  - 1,879,626 moving images
  - 8,231,662 items of sheet music
  - 2,034,666 other (including machine-readable items)
  - 17,500,179 visual materials

The Library and the COVID-19 Pandemic

In an effort to reduce the spread of COVID-19, the Library of Congress closed to the public in March 2020 and adopted new approaches that allowed the institution to safely carry out its mission of serving Congress and the public.

As conditions improved in late spring 2021, the Library implemented a plan to incrementally reopen reading rooms to a limited number of registered readers, restore limited access to Library buildings for the general public, and begin transitioning staffers who were working remotely back into the office environment.

On June 1 the Law Library, Manuscript Division, Geography and Map Division, and Newspaper and Current Periodical reading rooms reopened to registered readers, with reduced hours of operation—more than 14 months after the Library first closed its facilities to the public. Readers were required to make appointments to use the reading rooms and to follow Library health and safety procedures, including health screening, social distancing, and mask wearing.

Other reading rooms followed suit in stages. The Performing Arts, Recorded Sound, Prints and Photographs, and Moving Image reading rooms reopened on

June 14. The Main Reading Room and the American Folklife Center, Microform and Electronic Resources Center, and Rare Book and Special Collections reading rooms reopened on June 28. The African & Middle Eastern, Asian, European, and Hispanic reading rooms reopened on July 12.

Around that time, the Library reopened its doors to visitors. Beginning July 8 the public was allowed to visit the Jefferson Building on a limited basis on Thursdays, Fridays, and Saturdays from 10 A.M. to 4 P.M. To facilitate social distancing, visitors were required to reserve free, timed-entry tickets in advance. The following week, on July 15, the Library's major exhibits reopened to the public.

Researcher Access

The General and International Collections Directorate, and particularly the staff of the Researcher and Reference Services Division (RRS), played a key early role in adjusting operations to facilitate researcher access in light of pandemic restrictions. RRS staff members established the temporary Electronic Resources Center, from September 2020 through May 2021, to provide limited, appointment-based access to researchers throughout Phase 3.1 of the Library's restoration of services plan. In addition, the staff of the Newspaper and Current Periodical reading room provided limited on-site support for researchers, scanning documents from print materials and delivering them. RRS staff members then led a team to implement a researcher appointment-scheduling system, supporting documentation and operational procedures in preparation for the reopening of the reading rooms.

When the Law Library, Manuscript, Geography and Map, and Serial and Government Publications divisions reopened their reading rooms, special service routines ensured physical distancing and safety for staff and researchers alike. Staff members employed new researcher-appointment software and retrieved collection materials in advance so that visitors could be as productive as possible during each four-hour appointment.

To enhance Library outreach and support collection use while the reading rooms were closed, Library Services personnel created more than 1,000 online resources for researchers and users. These resources included Encoded Archival Description finding aids, digitized collections, research guides, blog posts, story maps, podcasts, videos, and webcasts.

The Acquisitions and Bibliographic Access Directorate resumed Surplus Books Program operations in March 2021, with services limited to congressional staff by appointment only. In six months, the program distributed 12,258 books, selected by congressional staff, to congressional offices, schools, libraries, and nonprofit organizations.

Public Events and Outreach

Despite the pandemic, the Library's Center for Learning, Literacy and Engagement (CLLE), in partnership with divisions across the Library, produced a year full of nearly all virtual programs.

The Library presented 375 virtual events with a viewership of 370,570 guests in the first 30 days the programs were posted online. Those events included concerts, author talks, lectures, orientations, workshops, and many others. In addition, the virtual National Book Festival programs, featuring 100 authors, rolled out over ten days and generated more than 3.9 million content views. The Library Events

Office played a leadership role in transitioning major events to a virtual format, including the Madison Council and National Film Board and Recording Preservation Board meetings and the Library of Congress Lavine/Ken Burns Prize for Film Award Ceremony.

To promote further understanding of the pandemic and encourage a dialogue with scientists, the Science, Technology and Business Division (ST&B) collaborated with the Library's Health Services office to provide a series of online COVID-19 panel discussions with invited experts. Throughout the year, ST&B and Health Services engaged with 1,678 attendees during the series of six virtual events.

The Digital Services Directorate's continued expansion of the By the People crowdsourced transcription program allowed the Library to engage with users in new ways while providing metadata for improved digitized collections searching. At the start of the pandemic, the By the People team met the challenges of sudden remote work by creating a space on the platform for projects specifically for Library staff. Although these staff-only projects decreased over time with the gradual return to on-site work, By the People transcription campaigns remained popular with both volunteers and Library employees. By the close of FY 2021 By the People transcribers saved more than 700,000 transcriptions, and more than 150,000 of those were ingested back into the Library's collections.

Collections Care in the Pandemic

In FY 2021 the Preservation Directorate continued its support of the RE-opening Archives, Libraries, and Museums (REALM) project and conducted research on hand sanitizers to understand the impact of COVID-19 safety measures on collection items. The directorate also played an important role in enabling the Library to continue productive telework by managing the inventory control and collections safety measures that allowed more than 80 staffers to bring more than 32,000 items home for cataloging or use in research and then safely return them to the Library.

The Library also reached an important milestone during the pandemic, with more than 7.5 million items under inventory control in its preservation facility at Fort Meade and a new collection storage module completed. Large-scale services for reformatting and after-market library binding returned to regular operating capacity during FY 2021, and conservation and scientific staff found a mix of practical and innovative solutions to continue working under restricted operating conditions, ultimately completing about 2.2 million preservation actions.

The National Audio-Visual Conservation Center implemented a new telework-based workflow that enabled audio preservation laboratory staff members to preserve nearly 3,000 endangered sound recordings on the fragile CD-R format as a telework assignment using newly acquired portable digital-audio workstations. The center acquired the workstations after the midpoint of the year, yet the technology allowed laboratory staff to achieve pre-pandemic preservation goals in just six months, despite on-site facility access restrictions. The workstations also support file quality-control activities and will be utilized in a variety of future preservation projects.

Digitization and COVID-19

Despite the challenges presented by the pandemic, digitization work continued at the Library. Digitization Services Directorate (DSD) management returned to on-site operations in October 2020 to shut down, move, and rebuild the Digital Scan Center. In June 2021 imaging specialists and technicians returned as a part of the Library's Phase 3.1 restoration of on-site operations to restart digitization operations within curatorial divisions.

With the opening of the new Digital Scan Center in July, digitization support successfully resumed on the continuing stream of scan-on-demand requests and other digitization projects. The DSD resumed additional projects with increases in on-site staffing as Phase 3.2 commenced. In addition, a collaborative effort between the DSD and the Office of the Chief Information Officer enabled digitization contractors to streamline their workflow by ingesting digital images directly into the Library's Content Transfer System rather than download to hard drives first.

Serving Congress

The Library of Congress was established in 1800 to provide resources to members of Congress for use in their work. The Joint Committee on the Library—the oldest continuing joint committee of Congress—was created through legislation in 1802, providing for congressional oversight. The unique collaboration between Congress and the Library has allowed them to serve the nation together for more than 220 years.

In FY 2021 the Library supported members of Congress, their staffs, and constituents in a variety of ways, such as providing reference, research, and analysis on key issues and supplying surplus books to congressional districts. The Library also continued to implement new technologies to make the legislative process more accessible and transparent to the public.

Legislative Support

The Congressional Research Service (CRS) in the Library serves Congress with the highest-quality research, analysis, information, and confidential consultation to support the exercise of its legislative, representational, and oversight duties in its role as a coequal branch of government. The work of CRS is authoritative, confidential, objective, nonpartisan, and timely. CRS examines pressing legislative issues facing Congress; identifies and assesses policy options; and provides analysis, consultation, and briefings to support Congress throughout the legislative process across the full range of public policy issues.

In FY 2021 CRS responded to more than 71,000 congressional requests. The CRS website for Congress, crs.gov, drew more than 900,000 views, including more than 321,000 views of the service's reports and general distribution products.

Congress established the Law Library of Congress in 1832 with the mission of making its resources available to Congress and the U.S. Supreme Court—a mission that expanded to include other branches of government and the global legal community. Librarians and foreign law specialists respond to congressional inquiries about U.S., foreign, comparative, and international legal and legislative research, drawing upon the world's largest collection of legal resources. The collection comprises more than 5 million items, including 2.9 million bound volumes and global legal materials in various formats.

In FY 2021 the Law Library's Public Services Division and two Foreign, Comparative, and International Law divisions responded to 383 research requests from Congress and provided assistance to congressional offices on 444 reference questions. In total, the Law Library provided 827 responses to congressional offices. The Law Library's reference librarians assist congressional staff any time either chamber of Congress is in session, no matter the hour.

Copyright Law and Policy

The U.S. Copyright Office, headed by the register of copyrights, administers the nation's copyright laws for the advancement of the public good and the benefit of authors and users of creative works. The register's duties under the Copyright Act include registering works of authorship, recording information about copyright ownership, and administering certain statutory licenses. The Copyright Office also provides expert impartial assistance to Congress, the courts, and executive branch agencies on questions of domestic and international copyright law and policy and develops educational resources and events for the public.

The Copyright Office worked throughout FY 2021 to set up the new Copyright Claims Board (CCB), as required by the Copyright Alternative in Small-Claims Enforcement (CASE) Act of 2020. The CCB will serve as a voluntary, streamlined adjudication process in the Copyright Office to resolve copyright disputes regarding small claims with a monetary value not exceeding $30,000. The CASE Act was the culmination of years of work by the Copyright Office at the request of Congress to address the need for a more efficient and economical option for resolving such claims. The law required the CCB to be operational by December 27, 2021, or up to 180 days thereafter.

Congressional Preservation Efforts

The Library leads several major preservation initiatives at the behest of Congress to capture and preserve American history and culture for generations to come. Congress passed the National Film Preservation Act of 1988 and the National Recording Preservation Act of 2000 to ensure preservation of the nation's audiovisual heritage. This legislation directs the Librarian of Congress to select "culturally, historically or aesthetically" significant films and sound recordings, respectively, for the National Film Registry and National Recording Registry. To date, the Librarian has selected 800 films and 575 sound recordings for preservation.

In FY 2021 the Library reconstituted the 44-person rosters of the National Film Preservation Board and National Recording Preservation Board. As mandated by the legislation, the 17 statutory organizations on each board received requests to nominate three individuals, from whom the Librarian selected a board member and alternate. The Librarian separately appointed 10 at-large representatives for each board and worked with organizations such as the Congressional Hispanic Caucus to identify potential candidates for these prestigious positions.

Established by Congress in 2000, the Veterans History Project (VHP) in the Library's American Folklife Center preserves the memories of those in our nation's armed services who served from World War I through recent conflicts. During FY 2021 the VHP received 1,464 collections and reformatted 7,100 items for preservation. VHP now holds more than 112,000 collections from veterans across the nation, including 207 collected under the Gold Star Family Voice Act. In addition, VHP worked with more than 50 congressional offices to promote the project in members' home states and create special video messages featuring the Librarian of Congress.

Supporting the Library

The president signed the Consolidated Appropriations Act, 2021 (P.L. 116-260) on December 27, 2020, providing the Library with a total budget authority of $802.128 million for FY 2021, including $757.346 million in appropriations and $44.782 million in offsetting receipts authority. Before enactment, the Library operated under five continuing resolutions at FY 2020 funding levels. Continuing resolutions funding was provided from October 1, 2020, to December 11, 2020; December 18, 2020; December 21, 2020; December 22, 2020; and December 28, 2020.

Total Library budget authority increased approximately 2.7 percent over FY 2020. The funding supported the Visitor Experience Master Plan initiative, cyber-security enhancements, and compact shelving replacement for the Law Library. The funding continued to support the VHP and CLLE's Teaching with Primary Sources (TPS) program.

The 2021 enacted budget continues a multiyear strategic modernization in all areas—information technology standardization, optimization, and moderniza-tion; infrastructure; business processes; and targeted workforce skills to increase accessibility and to engage "user centered" customer service to Congress and the American people.

Librarian of Congress Carla Hayden testified about the Library's FY 2022 budget request before the House Appropriations Subcommittee on March 3, 2021, and before the Senate Appropriations Subcommittee on April 28, 2021. The Library's FY 2022 request focused on resources to sustain the mission to Con-gress, provide access to the creative record of the United States, and provide stew-ardship of the cultural heritage of the American people. The request also continued ongoing efforts to make the Library more user-centered and data-driven. Subcom-mittee members inquired about Library programs, including CRS productivity and diversity, the Library's safety and security measures, impacts of the pandemic, and the Visitor Experience Master Plan initiative. The House subcommittee also heard separate testimony from the director of CRS and the register of copyrights.

The Library of Congress Trust Fund Board, created in 1925 by an act of Congress, acted as trustee of private funds invested for the benefit of the Library. Its work supports Library literacy programs, exhibitions, acquisitions, scholarly programs and fellowships, concerts, and initiatives.

Collections

The Library of Congress is both the nation's library and the largest library in the world. The institution's vast collections encompass virtually all formats, languages, and subjects. It is perhaps the most comprehensive accumulation of human knowledge ever assembled.

In FY 2021 the Library's collections grew to more than 173.7 million items. The Library added 1,096,408 physical items to its collections during the year through purchase, gift, exchange, or transfer from other government agencies. The U.S. Copyright Office transferred 534,493 works with an estimated value of nearly

$45 million to the Library's collections during FY 2021. The Library received more than 510,000 of these transfers from publishers via mandatory deposit. A total of 112,675 tangible items acquired through transfer—including 53,871 print books, 50,769 print serial issues, 1,629 films, and 6,406 sound recordings—were selected for the permanent Library collections. The Library also received 128,396 e-serial issues via eDeposits and 33,682 e-books through the Cataloging in Publication Program.

The Acquisitions and Bibliographic Access Directorate (ABA) acquired 1,096,408 items for the Library's collection through cost-effective methods, including purchase and exchange, and facilitated the acquisition of 331,698 collection items through solicited gifts to the Special Collections and General and International Collections directorates. Factoring in additional acquisitions, such as additions through arrearage-reduction projects, the Library's collection increased by more than 2.1 million items in FY 2021.

The Library maintains six overseas offices, located in Cairo, Islamabad, Jakarta, Nairobi, New Delhi, and Rio de Janeiro. These offices acquire, catalog, preserve, and distribute library and research materials from parts of the world where such materials are largely unavailable through conventional acquisitions methods. In FY 2021 the overseas offices acquired approximately 180,000 collection items, on a cost-recovery basis, for the more than 100 U.S. libraries participating in the Cooperative Acquisitions Program.

Collection Development

The Collection Development Office (CDO) supports the Library's strategic goal of acquiring and maintaining a universal collection of knowledge and the record of America's creativity to meet the needs of Congress, researchers, and the American public. It ensures that the Library's physical and digital collections reflect the breadth and depth of knowledge published in all media, languages, and regions of the world.

CDO continued its program to review and update, on a cyclical basis, all of the Library's collections policy statements and associated supplementary guidelines. Eight documents were reviewed and updated, while two new documents were created and approved. The office also launched a general collections assessment, completing a pilot that covered the fine and decorative arts segment of the classification and beginning the U.S. history segment assessment.

In FY 2021 the Library developed a new digital collections strategy for 2022–2026, which was approved by Librarian of Congress Carla Hayden in September. This new strategy, led by CDO in partnership with the Digital Services Directorate, succeeds the Library's former digital collecting plan, implemented in 2017, which had provided a blueprint for acquisition by the Library of born-digital content as part of a coordinated strategy. The new plan incorporates the full life cycle of born-digital materials, from acquisition to preservation and user access, and aligns with the goals prioritized within the Library's strategic plan.

FY 2021 began with a pause in new collecting under the web-archiving program due to anticipated web-crawling capacity limitations. However, CDO worked during the year with the Digital Collections Management and Services Division to balance resources to allow a resumption of new web archive nominations and collecting activities. CDO also conducted a web archives assessment, which documented the collection's exponential growth from 2018 through 2020. Based on the results of that assessment, the office worked with the Collections Policy Committee to set priorities for web collecting in underrepresented subjects and geographic regions.

Preservation

The Library's mission to provide a "universal and enduring" record of knowledge and creativity guides the work of the Preservation Directorate, which ensures that the Library's historical artifacts and collections remain available in the evolving array of formats needed by users today and in the future. The directorate uses established technologies, practices, and procedures to address risks to these materials, and it engages in fundamental research to explore new approaches to preserve and enhance our knowledge of Library collections.

To that end, the directorate is responsible for the execution of millions of preservation actions each year in stewardship of the national collection. Expert staff members perform preventative and corrective treatments and transfer information from obsolete or at-risk media into new formats. They manage secure, environmentally optimized storage facilities and maintain inventory control, enabling the fulfillment of thousands of loans each year to support Congress and serve researchers around the world. The directorate is a center for fundamental research and education, and its insights and innovations set standards and enhance preservation and conservation practices worldwide.

In FY 2021 the directorate performed 2.2 million preservation actions on books, serials, prints, photographs, manuscripts, and other items, with a further 3.4 million pages of materials prepared and shipped to vendors for preservation reformatting services. During FY 2021 110,955 items received new library bindings; 19,172 were treated or repaired in conservation labs; protective containers or housings were provided for 21,284 items; and 118,471 book equivalents and 426,600 sheets were deacidified. Staff members surveyed the preservation needs of 652,938 items from the general and special collections, monitored more than 230 environmental data loggers, and continued to play a key role in the Library's security and emergency-response programs.

Reformatting is a critical process that ensures the long-term availability of informational content on original media at risk of deterioration, and reformatting via digital transformation was an important focus during FY 2021. The directorate reformatted more than 1.5 million pages, including 869,718 digitized from custodial divisions and 644,295 microfilmed from overseas offices.

Newspapers

The National Digital Newspaper Program, jointly sponsored by the Library of Congress and the National Endowment for the Humanities, supports the enhancement of access to American newspapers. Through various partnerships and collaborations, cultural heritage institutions select and digitize representative newspapers from their states or territories for contribution to the Chronicling America website.

During FY 2021 the Chronicling America website recorded 44.1 million visits and 4.1 million page views. The collection now includes 2,558,924 issues of 3,515 titles from 48 states, two territories, and the District of Columbia. In addition to the Chronicling America historic newspaper collection, other publicly available digitized newspaper collection items received 1.4 million page views and 715,575 visits.

Audiovisual Collections

The Packard Campus of the National Audio-Visual Conservation Center, located in Culpeper, Virginia, houses the Library's recorded sound and moving image collections—the world's largest and most comprehensive.

In FY 2021 the Moving Image Section acquired 6,215 analog items. The largest gift was 3,557 reels of 35 mm and 16 mm films, consisting primarily of American features acquired from the BBC. In addition, the section acquired 27,232 born-digital items, including 23 files from the copyright collection, 1,387 files via direct transfer from the Senate, and 20,277 files from the Vanderbilt Television News Archive, which features newscasts from 2019–2020.

On December 14, 2020 the Librarian of Congress named 25 films to the National Film Registry, bringing the total to 800.

Sound Recordings

The Recorded Sound Section is committed to building and enhancing a collection of commercial and noncommercial recordings in all formats from all periods. In FY 2021 the section acquired 26,426 physical audio recordings, 27,788 manuscript items, and 3,869 born-digital recordings.

On March 24, 2021 the Librarian of Congress announced the addition of 25 sound recordings to the National Recording Registry, bringing the total to 575.

Access

The Library makes its multiformat collections publicly available in its multiple reading rooms and research centers on Capitol Hill and at the Packard Campus of the National Audio-Visual Conservation Center and through its website. By cataloging its holdings in English and other languages, the Library provides expanded bibliographic access to its vast and growing collections. Through shared and cooperative cataloging, the Library helps the nation's libraries provide better access to their collections.

Visitors to the Jefferson Building from July through September 2021, when the Library reopened on-site operations, totaled nearly 30,000. In normal years, the Library's public spaces and exhibitions remain open to the public Monday through Saturday year-round, with the exception of Thanksgiving, Christmas, and New Year's Day. Typically, the Main Reading Room serves as a venue for many special Library events, including open houses. As a necessary precaution against the spread of COVID-19, the Jefferson Building was open on limited days, at 25 percent capacity, beginning July 8, 2021.

Reference Services

In June 2021 the Library began the incremental process of reopening reading rooms to a limited number of visitors by appointment, and it resumed issuance of new reader-identification cards. A total of 2,718 new cards were issued from June through September, and Library staff responded to a total of 75,373 reference requests during FY 2021, including 65,541 requests received online, via email, and through services such as Ask a Librarian. In addition, the Library circulated 113,029 physical items on-site in FY 2021. More than 41,476 items were circulated off-site to authorized borrowers; other items were circulated to on-site researchers and staff.

In order to ensure congressional access to collections stored off-site, Collections Management Division (CMD) staff remained available to retrieve material from the Library's Fort Meade and Cabin Branch facilities. CMD Capitol Hill staff provided on-site support throughout the pandemic to ensure materials were properly charged and delivered to congressional offices. Members of Congress and congressional staff members received 2,609 items during FY 2021.

Cataloging

The Library managed 53,911,967 MARC records in its integrated library system during the year. It cataloged 242,481 new works in addition to 1,131,614 manuscript items on 176 bibliographic records. The Cataloging-in-Publication program cataloged 50,165 titles, and the Electronic Cataloging-in-Publication E-book Program prepared cataloging in advance of publication for 26,289 e-books. The Library established 252,191 name and series authorities, 11,551 subject headings, and 8,499 new Library of Congress Classification numbers. The Dewey Program, which supports libraries worldwide that classify their titles in Dewey Decimal Classification (DDC), assigned DDC to 102,564 titles.

During the year, the Library's curatorial divisions created 194 new Encoded Archival Description finding aids, bringing the total number of researcher-accessible archival items in the Library's collections to more than 77 million.

Bibliographic Framework Initiative

The BIBFRAME initiative began in FY 2011 as a replacement for the cataloging metadata standard known as MARC 21. The Library's BIBFRAME progress accelerated in FY 2021, as more than 100 cataloging staff continued to produce BIBFRAME descriptions in a simulated cataloging environment, adding 10,943 descriptions to the publicly shared BIBFRAME database.

The Library's Network Development and MARC Standards Office continued to refine the BIBFRAME-to-MARC conversion tool and supporting tools. These refinements ultimately will permit distribution of BIBFRAME descriptions to OCLC and other Cataloging Distribution Service customers in the MARC formats. The advances made in FY 2021 improved productivity and helped BIBFRAME progress toward becoming the Library's primary production environment for bibliographic metadata.

Access for the Blind and Print Disabled

In FY 2021 the National Library Service for the Blind and Print Disabled (NLS) added 5,796 talking books and 835 braille books to its catalog.

In February 2021 NLS implemented a long-awaited change that made it easier for people with reading disabilities to enroll for services. The change required congressional amendment of the eligibility language in NLS's authorizing legislation. The final regulatory step was publication of the new language in the Federal Register, which was done in the winter of FY 2021. The new language allows reading specialists, educators, librarians, and school psychologists, among others, to certify the eligibility of applicants with reading disabilities. NLS always has made its services available to people with reading disabilities; however, a doctor of medicine or osteopathy was required to certify that an applicant's reading disability was "the result of organic dysfunction." This requirement was a high bar for potential patrons, and network libraries had urged NLS to relax it. The change resulted in a 21 percent increase in reading-disabled individuals served.

Throughout FY 2021 NLS continued its rollout of Duplication on Demand (DoD) to libraries in its nationwide network. The DoD system allows libraries to create their own talking-book cartridges on-site from NLS-produced digital files, making it easy to fill patron requests quickly and reducing costs associated with maintaining large physical collections. In addition to its other advantages, DoD allows libraries to distribute multiple books on a single cartridge. As of September 2021 53 network libraries were using some form of DoD. The remaining network libraries expect to complete conversion to DoD operations in FY 2022.

The Library's Website, Digital Collections and Social Media

The Library's website, loc.gov, provides users with access to the institution's unparalleled resources, such as online catalogs; selected collections in various formats; copyright, legal, and legislative information; exhibitions; and videos and podcasts of events. In FY 2021 the loc.gov website recorded more than 178.1 million visits and 617.7 million page views.

The Library launched several sites that were new, redesigned, or enhanced to support divisions and programs, including Poetry & Literature, the Lavine/Ken Burns Prize for Film, the Congressional Relations Office, the Asian Division reading room, Library of Congress Pathways, the National Book Festival, the Law Library, and the Library of Congress Literacy Awards Program.

In FY 2021 the Library added 36 new digital collections to loc.gov and significantly upgraded 53 digital collections. New digital collections included the John and Alan Lomax papers; the initial release of the United States Congressional Serial Set (a collaborative project with the Government Publications Office); Living Nations, Living Words; Early Motion Picture Copyright Descriptions; Sheet Music of the Musical Theater; and 11 new web archives collections. Key collections that were upgraded or migrated include the Hannah Arendt Papers, Native American Constitutions and Legal Materials, and Selections of Arabic, Persian and Ottoman Calligraphy.

In collaboration with WGBH in Boston, the National Audio-Visual Conservation Center launched 10 new online collections as part of the American Archive of Public Broadcasting (AAPB). Among the new collections are 9/11 Special Coverage, Línea Abierta from Radio Bilingüe, Pacifica Radio Archives, Prospects of Mankind with Eleanor Roosevelt, and Wall $treet Week with Louis Rukeyser. The National Audio-Visual Conservation Center also debuted three online AAPB exhibits in collaboration with WGBH: Exploring Public Media in the Peabody Awards Collection; Freedom Song: Interviews from Eyes on the Prize: America's

Civil Rights Years, 1954–1965; and Native Narratives: The Representation of Native Americans in Public Broadcasting.

The By the People (BtP) crowdsourced transcription program continued to expand. New collections and campaigns were launched, including the papers of Rosa Parks, George S. Patton, Theodore Roosevelt, and others. By the close of FY 2021 BtP transcribers saved more than 700,000 transcriptions, and more than 150,000 of those were ingested into Library collections. Moreover, BtP campaigns in 2021 incorporated new formats, such as sheet music, and more than 5,000 transcriptions were completed for BtP's first non-English transcription campaign, Herencia: Centuries of Spanish Legal Documents.

Each month, the Library streams videos of concerts, lectures, panel discussions, and other events on YouTube and Facebook. Once public events were limited due to the pandemic, the Library premiered prerecorded videos. During FY 2021 105 premiere videos were published. The premiere videos and livestreams included the National Book Festival; a VHP anniversary series; National Book Festival Presents events, including discussions by Jon Meacham, Danielle Allen, and Walter Isaacson; the 2020 Library of Congress Lavine/Ken Burns Prize for Film ceremony; and numerous concerts.

The Library maintains 20 blogs that serve as vehicles for sharing collection discoveries and engaging with users. Two of those blogs—"Of the People: Widening the Path" and "Guardians of Memory"—were added during FY 2021. The Library's blogs published 1,478 posts during the year, drawing more than 5.6 million page views for a lifetime total of more than 26.7 million. The Library's blogs collectively drew 48 percent more visits than in FY 2020.

In FY 2021 the Library maintained 14 public-facing Twitter accounts and one CRS-protected Twitter account for members of Congress and congressional staff. The public-facing accounts issued 6,008 tweets during the year, gaining 91,623 retweets and 6,861 replies. The public accounts also gained 25,158 followers (for a total of more than 1.65 million) and received more than 71.2 million impressions.

In addition to its main Facebook page, the Library offers Facebook pages for the Law Library, the American Folklife Center, Performing Arts, VHP, NLS, and the Library's international collections. During FY 2021 the Library posted 3,659 times on those pages, gained 11,474 followers, and received 295,115 likes on posts and more than 51.3 million impressions. Library Facebook accounts have a combined 575,255 followers, and posts on them have received 489.9 million lifetime impressions.

During FY 2021 the Library made 535 new videos available on its main YouTube channel, which were liked 133,316 times and viewed more than 14.4 million times—an increase of 118 percent over FY 2020. The channel gained 68,397 subscribers during the year. The Copyright Office also made 29 new videos available, which were viewed 147,708 times.

The Library's podcast account features selected podcasts, historical films from Library collections, and video and audio recordings from collections and of events at the Library. During FY 2021 the Library added 21 files to Apple podcasts. The account gained 951 new subscriptions and drew 43,401 visitors and 62,971 consumptions. Since launching the account in 2009, the Library has added 4,041 files and attracted 231,774 subscriptions and more than 1 million visitors, with a total consumption of over 4.5 million.

Using the photo-sharing project on Flickr, photography enthusiasts continued to help identify the subjects appearing in Library photos from the early 1900s. During FY 2021 the Library added 2,182 photos to the main Library account, bringing the total to 39,412. Over the account's lifetime, the Library has accumulated 74,865 followers and nearly 420 million image views. A second account, Library of Congress Life, features photos and videos of Library buildings and events. During the year, the Library added 55 photos to the account, bringing the total to 1,024. The account has accumulated 200 followers and 803,663 image views in its lifetime. The account COVID-19: American Experiences added 1,770 photos for a lifetime total of 2,863. It also added 909 members for a total of 1,384.

The Library's Instagram account continued to share images from events and exhibitions. It added 16,623 new followers for a total of 95,567 at the end of FY 2021. It received 244,762 likes for a lifetime total of 765,435.

The Library offers 68 email alerts, including all Library and copyright-related topics for subscription. Loc.gov sent 4,209 bulletins in FY 2021 and recorded 262,156 new subscriptions. Copyright.gov sent 143 bulletins and recorded 90,475 new subscriptions.

Promoting Creativity, Scholarship, and Lifelong Learning

The Library of Congress collections chronicle centuries of human creativity—a rich, diverse and enduring source of knowledge for the American people and scholars around the world. Through its many public programs, the Library also promotes creativity and cultural literacy. The Library is a catalyst for promoting scholarship through the John W. Kluge Center and the American Folklife Center, which offer fellowship and internship opportunities in various disciplines and publications that showcase the Library's unparalleled collections.

In addition to its fellowships, research services, and collections access, the Library promotes lifelong learning and literacy through CLLE and K–12 educational outreach efforts, which assist the nation's teachers in engaging students through the use of primary sources in the classroom.

Educational Outreach

Reaching educators and providing them with useful opportunities and materials was more important than ever during this year, when the pandemic forced many schools to online learning. Through CLLE's TPS program, the Library provides educators across the grade spectrum, the curriculum, and the country with easily accessible, high-quality professional-development programs and classroom materials. These opportunities and tools help educators use digitized primary sources, event recordings, and other materials from the Library's online collections in their teaching.

In FY 2021 TPS—through the efforts of both Library staff and TPS consortium members—continued to serve tens of thousands of teachers, helping them achieve curricular standards while engaging students in authentic inquiry experiences and encouraging student research. The TPS team responded to the needs of teachers and librarians and the students they serve by developing innovative programs that leveraged distance-learning capabilities and harnessed new and existing partnerships. In doing so, the program's reach and scope expanded. Despite the limitations on in-person programming, consortium members and the Library staff delivered 889 presentations and professional development events for nearly 38,000 educators.

Consortium members reported that TPS-related curricular materials or online interactives and apps were downloaded from their websites 2,233,518 times. In addition, the TPS Teachers Network website, a professional networking site for educators who use the Library's primary sources in the classroom, continued to grow in use. At the end of FY 2021 11,825 educators were enrolled on the site.

The Library's website for teachers, loc.gov/programs/teachers, continued to grow as a hub for the educator audience. The site, which provides teacher resources on a wide range of topics as well as free professional development, was visited more than 7.5 million times in FY 2021.

The "Teaching with the Library of Congress" blog marked its tenth anniversary and continued to build its audience. In FY 2021 it published 121 posts and was visited more than 295,325 times, a 21 percent increase over FY 2020, with more than 33,000 subscribers.

Celebrating Achievement

Throughout the year, the Library of Congress celebrates the achievements of the nation's creative and scholarly communities. The Library also recognizes the accomplishments of its staff members. In addition, it sponsors privately endowed programs that honor achievement in the humanities. Through these awards and prizes, the Library honors those who have advanced and embodied the ideals of individuality, conviction, dedication, scholarship, and lifelong learning.

Kluge Prize

The rollout of the 2020 Kluge Prize winner was reimagined by Librarian of Congress Carla Hayden. In FY 2021 the Library held a series of events with 2020 winner Danielle Allen titled Our Common Purpose: A Campaign for Civic Strength at the Library of Congress. Three public discussions moderated by Allen were held on political institutions, a shared historical narrative, and civic media. In addition, Allen led four workshops on civic education in conjunction with outside partners and the office of educational outreach at the Library. These workshops gathered 30 middle school and high school teachers from around the country, giving them a chance to discuss and engage with key Library collections.

Library of Congress Prize for American Fiction

The prize honors an American literary writer whose body of work is distinguished not only for its mastery of the art but also for its originality of thought and imagination. On June 30 the Library announced Joy Williams as the recipient of the 2021 prize. Williams is the acclaimed author of four short story collections, two works of nonfiction, and five novels, including the recent *Harrow*.

Literacy Awards

Created and sponsored by philanthropist and Madison Council chairman David M. Rubenstein, the Library of Congress Literacy Awards seek to reward organizations that have done exemplary, innovative, and easily replicable work over a sustained period to promote literacy in the United States and abroad.

David M. Rubenstein Prize ($150,000)

The 2021 winner was Dolly Parton's Imagination Library of Pigeon Forge, Tennessee. The Imagination Library is an initiative of the Dollywood Foundation, a nonprofit organization founded by Dolly Parton in 1988. Dedicated to improving the lives of children by inspiring a love of reading, it provides books free of charge to families through local community partnerships.

American Prize ($50,000)

The 2021 winner was Parents as Teachers National Center of St. Louis. The center builds strong communities and thriving families and children by matching parents and caregivers with trained professionals who make regular personal home visits during a child's earliest years in life, from the prenatal period through kindergarten.

International Prize ($50,000)

The 2021 winner was the Luminos Fund of Boston. It provides transformative education programs to thousands of out-of-school children, helping them catch up to grade level, reintegrate into local schools, and prepare for lifelong learning.

Federal Library and Information Network

Laurie Neider
Executive Director

The Federal Library and Information Network (FEDLINK) is an organization of federal agencies working together to achieve optimum use of the resources and facilities of federal libraries and information centers by promoting common services, coordinating and sharing available resources, and providing continuing professional education for federal library and information staff.

FEDLINK serves as a forum for discussion of the policies, programs, procedures, and technologies that affect federal libraries and the information services they provide to their agencies, Congress, the federal courts, and the American people.

In spite of challenges created by the ongoing COVID-19 pandemic, during fiscal year (FY) 2021 FEDLINK continued its mission to achieve better utilization of federal library and information resources by providing the most cost-effective and efficient administrative mechanism for delivering necessary services and materials to federal libraries and information centers.

FEDLINK Executive Report

FEDLINK's Advisory Board (FAB) focused its bimonthly meetings on a variety of broad federal information issues, including administrative issues related to market sustainability and system updates for the FEDLINK-assisted acquisition model. At several sessions, members discussed customer satisfaction surveys, directional planning, online training, and FEDLINK program fees.

FEDLINK held two expositions in FY 2020. The 2021 Spring Expo, "Reaching for New Information Horizons," featured a keynote address by Tiffany L. Smith, acting chief knowledge officer for NASA, and plenary sessions on trends in library systems technology, information accessibility, reimagining professional development opportunities, and e-discovery tools. The Fall Expo, "Federal Librarians: The Vanguard of the Hybrid Infospace," opened with a keynote address from Shakima Tozay, chief of clinical services at Naval Station Everett's Fleet and Family Support Center, and featured an afternoon keynote presentation from Dr. Ursula Gorham, director of the library and information science program at the University of Maryland, on current trends in library school curriculum. The expo also offered sessions on federal library technicians responding to COVID-19 and the stewardship of digital assets.

FEDLINK Working Group Highlights

FEDLINK Awards Committee

To honor the many innovative ways federal libraries, librarians, and library technicians fulfill the information demands of government, business, research, scholarly communities, and the American public, the Awards Committee administered a series of national awards for federal librarianship.

Winners of the FY 2020 awards, announced In May 2021, were:

2020 Federal Library/Information Center of the Year

Large library/information center (staff of 11 or more federal and/or contract employees): The Joint Base Lewis-McChord Library System in Washington was recognized for its commitment to providing high-quality, in-demand programs and services to the entire base community of military service members, their families, retirees, civilian employees, contractors, and students. The system ensured service members had the materials needed to access necessary educational programming while providing opportunities for families during times of transition. From a focus on early literacy for children to online training for adults, the library system provided services to 200,000 patrons who borrowed 109,000-plus items, more than any other Army Morale, Welfare and Recreation Library in the world. Despite limitations caused by the COVID-19 pandemic, the library system still offered 439 programs, including bilingual story hours, prerecorded story times, interactive online programming, and summer reading programs.

Small library/information center (staff of 10 or fewer federal and/or contract employees): Barr Memorial Library at Fort Knox in Kentucky was recognized for its quick and responsive innovation in adapting existing services to the virtual world. The library developed and implemented a popular contactless carryout service, a model adopted by several other Army libraries. Its outreach efforts increased adult reading program participation by more than 50 percent, and the library's 356 programs, which included author events, story hours for preschool children, and craft programs for all ages, attracted nearly 20,000 in-person and virtual participants. The library developed and led 20 Army Morale, Welfare and Recreation Libraries in the creation and support of Fantober, a comic-themed event at 20 different installations that reached 8,400 participants with 155 unique programs. Beyond attracting new or lapsed users to libraries, the event created partnerships with 35 on-post agencies, attracted eight sponsors, and created collaborations with 32 private, commercial, and individual partners.

2020 Federal Librarian of the Year

Mariana Long, from the U.S. Department of Justice (DOJ) in Washington, D.C., was recognized for her outstanding service at DOJ libraries. Long and her staff of 12 provided research support to four of the seven litigating divisions at DOJ, including civil, civil rights, criminal and environment, and natural resources. Long and her staff handled nearly 40 percent of the library's 36,651 research and reference queries. Additionally, she taught docket research to more than 100 attorneys and support staff and coordinated a continuing legal education class series assisting more than 300 attorneys with their legal education requirements. She also provided orientations to more than 100 attorneys and staff from across the department. As co-chair of the library's marketing committee, Long anticipated the needs of customers and widely promoted services, resources, and collections. She took the lead in improving instruction and training for staff on expert witness vetting and, with her staff, vetted more than 300 experts in FY 2020.

2020 Federal Library Technician of the Year

Sharon D. Pemberton, from the Cyber Research Center at the Cyber Center of Excellence in Fort Gordon, Georgia, was recognized for her dedication to the library's mission and its community. In the midst of the pandemic, the Cyber Research Center migrated to a new library services platform. Pemberton navigated this change between two cataloging systems, cataloging more than 100 books in each system; set migration priorities; and offered insightful ideas for improvements. Dedicated to supporting the research, customer service, and the cataloging needs of the center, she implemented a new concierge system for book lending and created interactive forms and spreadsheets to track the library's budget, expenditures, and yearly metrics. Offering excellent support for military education students' research projects and assignments, Pemberton's work was essential to executing the training and education missions of the center.

FEDLINK Working Groups

The eResources Working Group hosted presentations on approaches and best practices involving subscription license agreements and vendor negotiations, open access in the federal environment, bibliometrics, and general data management, with speakers from the National Science Foundation, the National Oceanic and Atmospheric Administration (NOAA), and the Smithsonian Libraries and Archives. The Preservation Working Group featured a session on the Federal Depository Library Program Web Archive, with speakers from the Government Publishing Office. The Information Technology Working Group held discussions on IT lessons learned during the pandemic and current IT infrastructure available across the federal workspace.

FEDLINK Publications and Education Office

FEDLINK continued to develop targeted resources to support the FEDLINK program, including governing body and educational programming support; directional, business, and customer service plans; promotional materials; and supporting materials for both exposition programs and working group projects and events. FEDLINK offered a two-day introductory preservation training program, virtual updates on FEDLINK books and serials assisted acquisitions programs, and a meeting of current vendors. New resources for federal librarians include "Top 10 Reasons Federal Agencies Need Libraries," research on data metric tools, purchasing trends, and open access; and a series of newsletters for members and vendors. FEDLINK continued its publication program as a digital communication provider and used its website and community listservs for outreach on critical advocacy and program information to more than 2,000 electronic subscribers.

FEDLINK Contracts and Network Operations

FEDLINK provided assisted acquisition services to the federal information community by procuring publications in a wide variety of formats (print and electronic journals; print and electronic books; sound recordings; audiovisual materials items via document delivery and interlibrary loan; and access to databases of full text, indexes, abstracts, and a variety of other data) and library support services (cataloging and related technical processing services, staffing support, information management, resource sharing, integrated library systems, digitization, digital archiving, and preservation services).

Through interagency agreements (IAAs), FEDLINK's contracts and network staff members worked on behalf of federal agencies with more than 100 vendors to conduct competitions, issue orders, and resolve issues with vendors. FEDLINK continued to provide assisted acquisition services to its members, with $62.5 million in transfer pay services and $165.5 million in the direct express services.

National Agricultural Library

U.S. Department of Agriculture, Agricultural Research Service
Abraham Lincoln Bldg., 10301 Baltimore Ave., Beltsville, MD 20705-2351
E-mail agref@nal.usda.gov; https://www.nal.usda.gov

Paul Wester

Director

The U.S. Department of Agriculture's National Agricultural Library (NAL) is one of the world's largest and most accessible agricultural research libraries, offering service directly to the public either on-site in Beltsville, Maryland, or via its website, https://www.nal.usda.gov.

The library was established in 1862 at the same time as the U.S. Department of Agriculture (USDA). It became a national library in 1962, when Congress established it as the primary agricultural information resource of the United States (7 USCS § 3125a). Congress assigned to the library the responsibilities to:

- Acquire, preserve, and manage information resources relating to agriculture and allied sciences
- Organize agricultural information products and services and provide them within the United States and internationally
- Plan, coordinate, and evaluate information and library needs relating to agricultural research and education
- Cooperate with and coordinate efforts toward development of a comprehensive agricultural library and information network
- Coordinate the development of specialized subject information services among the agricultural and library information communities

NAL is located in Beltsville, Maryland, near Washington, D.C., on the grounds of USDA's Henry A. Wallace Beltsville Agricultural Research Center. Its 14-story Abraham Lincoln Building is named in honor of the president who created the Department of Agriculture and signed several of the major U.S. laws affecting agriculture.

The library employs about 100 librarians, information specialists, computer specialists, administrators, and clerical personnel, supplemented by about 50 contract staff and cooperators from NAL partnering organizations.

NAL's reputation as one of the world's foremost agricultural libraries is supported and burnished by its expert staff, ongoing leadership in delivering information services, expanding collaborations with other U.S. and international agricultural research and information organizations, and extensive collection of agricultural information, searchable through AGRICOLA, the library's bibliographic database.

In 2012 NAL reorganized to better align its functions with its overall strategic plan, which includes simplified access to all NAL content, expansion of digital content, and the integration of scientific datasets and discovery tools.

The Collection

The NAL collection dates to the congressionally approved 1839 purchase of books for the Agricultural Division of the Patent Office, predating the 1862 establishment of USDA itself. Today NAL provides access to billions of pages of agricultural information—an immense collection of scientific books, journals, audiovisuals, reports, theses, artifacts, and images—and to a widening array of digital media, as well as databases and other information resources germane to the broad reach of agriculture-related sciences.

The library's collection contains more than 8 million items, dating from the 15th century to the present, including the most complete repository of USDA publications and the world's most extensive set of materials on the history of U.S. agriculture. Publications are selected for the collection based on the National Agricultural Library Collection Development Policy.

Building the Collection

NAL is the only U.S. national library with a legislated mandate to collect in the following disciplines: plant and animal health, welfare, and production; agricultural economics, products, and education; aquaculture; forestry; rural sociology and rural life; family and consumer science; and food science, safety, and nutrition. In addition to collecting as comprehensively as possible in these core subject areas, NAL collects extensively in many related subjects, such as biology, bioinformatics, biochemistry, chemistry, entomology, environmental science, genetics, invasive species, meteorology, natural resources, physics, soil science, sustainability, water quality, and zoology. The library has primary responsibility for collecting and retaining publications issued by USDA and its agencies. As well, NAL collects publications from around the world.

Special Collections

The NAL Special Collections program emphasizes access to and preservation of rare and unique materials documenting the history of agriculture and related sciences. Items in the library's special collections include rare books, manuscripts, nursery and seed trade catalogs, posters, objects, photographs, and other rare materials documenting agricultural subjects. Materials date from the 1500s to the present and include many international sources. Detailed information about these special collections is available on the NAL website at https://specialcollections. nal.usda.gov.

Special Collections of note include the following:

- The U.S. Department of Agriculture History Collection (https:// special collections.nal.usda.gov/usda-history-collection-introduction-index), assembled over 80 years by USDA historians, includes letters, memoranda, reports, and papers of USDA officials, as well as photographs, oral histories, and clippings covering the activities of the department from its founding through the early 1990s.
- The U.S. Department of Agriculture Pomological Watercolor Collection (https://naldc.nal.usda.gov/usda_pomological_watercolor) includes more

than 7,000 detailed, botanically accurate watercolor illustrations of fruit and nut varieties developed by growers or introduced by USDA plant explorers. Created between 1886 and the 1940s, the watercolors served as official documentation of the work of the Office of the Pomologist and were used to create chromolithographs in publications distributed widely by the department. Although created for scientific accuracy, the works are artistic treasures in their own right.

- The Henry G. Gilbert Nursery and Seed Trade Catalog Collection (https://specialcollections.nal.usda.gov/guide-collections/henry-g-gilbert-nursery-and-seed-trade-catalog-collection), begun in 1904 by USDA economic botanist Percy L. Ricker, has grown to comprise more than 200,000 U.S. and foreign catalogs. The earliest items date from the late 1700s, but the collection is strongest from the 1890s to the present. Researchers commonly use the collection to document the introduction of plants to the United States, study economic trends, and illustrate early developments in American landscape design.
- The Rare Book Collection (https://specialcollections.nal.usda.gov/guide-collections/rare-book-collection) highlights agriculture's printed historical record. It covers a wide variety of subjects but is particularly strong in botany, natural history, zoology, and entomology. International in scope, the collection documents early agricultural practices in Britain and Europe, as well as the Americas. Manuscript collections (https://specialcollections.nal.usda.gov/guide-collections/index-manuscript-collections), now numbering more than 400, document the story of American agriculture and its influence on the world.

NAL continues to digitize these and other unique materials to share them broadly via its website and has published detailed indexes to the content of many manuscript collections to improve discovery. AGRICOLA, NAL's catalog, includes bibliographic entries for special collection items, manuscripts, and rare books. The library provides in-house research and reference services for its special collections and offers fee-based duplication services.

Preservation/Digitization

NAL is committed to the preservation of its print and nonprint collections. It continues to monitor and improve the environmental quality of its stacks to extend the longevity of all materials in the collection. The library has instituted a long-term strategy to ensure the growing body of agricultural information is systematically identified, preserved, and archived.

NAL's digital conversion program has resulted in a growing digital collection of USDA publications and many non-USDA historical materials not restricted by copyright. NAL is in the midst of a large-scale project to digitize agricultural literature and provide online access to the general public. Important and distinctive items were selected from the NAL collection, with an initial focus on USDA-issued publications and nursery and seed trade catalogs. Publications are accessible at NAL's Internet Archive collection (https://archive.org/details/usda-nationalagriculturallibrary) and in the National Agricultural Library Digital Collections (https://naldc.nal.usda.gov).

Library Services

Reference Services

NAL serves the agricultural information needs of customers through a combination of web-based and traditional library services, including reference, document delivery, and information centers. The NAL website offers access to a wide variety of full-text resources, as well as online access to reference and document delivery services.

The main reading room in the library's Beltsville facility features a walk-up service desk, access to an array of digital information resources (including full-text scientific journals), current periodicals, and an on-site request service for materials from NAL's collection. Services are available 8:30 A.M. to 4:30 P.M. Monday through Friday, except federal holidays.

NAL's reference services are accessible online using the Ask a Question form on the NAL webpages; by use of e-mail addressed to agref@usda.gov; by telephone at 301-504-5755; or by mail to Research Services, National Agricultural Library ARS/USDA, 10301 Baltimore Avenue, Beltsville, MD 20705. Requesters receive assistance from research services staff in all areas and aspects of agriculture, but staff particularly answer questions, provide research guidance, and make presentations on topics not addressed by the seven subject-focused information centers of the library.

Information Centers and Partnerships

NAL's information centers and partnerships provide comprehensive, science-based information on key aspects of U.S. agriculture, providing timely, accurate, and in-depth coverage of their specialized subject areas. Their expert staff offers extensive web-based information resources and advanced reference services:

- The Alternative Farming Systems Information Center (AFSIC) (https://www.nal.usda.gov/afsic) specializes in identifying and accessing information relating to farming methods that maintain the health and productivity of the entire farming enterprise, including natural resources. This focus includes sustainable and alternative agricultural systems, crops, and livestock.
- The Animal Welfare Information Center (AWIC) (https://www.nal.usda.gov/awic) provides scientific information and referrals to help ensure the proper care and treatment of animals used in biomedical research, testing, teaching, and exhibitions, and by animal dealers. Among its varied outreach activities, the center conducts workshops for researchers on meeting the information requirements of the Animal Welfare Act.
- The Food and Nutrition Information Center (FNIC) (https://www.nal.usda.gov/fnic) provides credible, accurate, and practical resources for nutrition and health professionals, educators, government personnel, and consumers. FNIC maintains a staff of registered dietitians and nutrition experts who can answer questions on food and human nutrition.
- The Food Safety Research Information Office (FSRIO) (https://www.nal.usda.gov/fsrio) delivers information on publicly funded—and, to the extent

possible, privately funded—food safety research initiatives. The Research Projects Database provides more than 17,000 active food safety research projects in a searchable database of U.S. and international agencies. The Research Publications Feed offers access to real-time updates of peer-reviewed publications in food safety.

- The National Invasive Species Information Center (NISIC) (https://www.invasivespeciesinfo.gov) delivers accessible, accurate, referenced, up-to-date, and comprehensive information on invasive species drawn from federal, state, local, and international sources.
- The Rural Information Center (RIC) (https://www.nal.usda.gov/ric) assists local officials, organizations, businesses, and rural residents working to maintain the vitality of rural areas. It collects and disseminates information on such diverse topics as community economic development, small business development, healthcare, finance, housing, environment, quality of life, community leadership, and education.
- The Water and Agriculture Information Center (WAIC) (https://www.nal.usda.gov/waic) collects, organizes, and communicates scientific findings, educational methodologies, and public policy issues related to water and agriculture.

In addition to these information centers, NAL manages the popular Nutrition.gov website (http://www.nutrition.gov) in collaboration with other USDA agencies and the Department of Health and Human Services. This site provides evidence-based nutrition information for the general consumer and highlights the latest in nutrition news and tools from across federal government agencies. A team of registered dietitians and nutrition experts at NAL's Food and Nutrition Information Center maintains Nutrition.gov and answers questions on food and nutrition issues.

The Agricultural Law Information Partnership is a collaboration among the National Agricultural Library, National Agricultural Law Center (NALC), and Center for Agriculture and Food Systems (CAFS) at Vermont Law School. The partnership supports the dissemination of agricultural and food law information to key audiences, including attorneys, agricultural professionals, and the general public involved in agricultural industries in the United States. Agricultural law is defined broadly to include land-based agriculture, food and fiber production and systems, aquaculture, and energy issues. Explore the partnership at https://www.nal.usda.gov/aglaw/agricultural-law-information-partnership.

Document Delivery Services

NAL's document delivery operation responds to thousands of requests each year from USDA employees and from libraries and organizations around the world. NAL uses the Relais Enterprise document request and delivery system to support document delivery. With Relais fully integrated with the Voyager library system, with DigiTop, and with other Open-URL and ISO ILL-compliant systems, NAL customers can request materials or check on the status of their requests via the web, and the needed materials can easily be delivered electronically. Document requests can also be submitted via OCLC (NAL's symbol is AGL) and DOCLINE

(NAL's libid is MDUNAL). Visit https://www.nal.usda.gov/services/request.shtml for details.

Scientific Research Data Services

In 2012 NAL began including digital scientific research data as part of its mission in support of federal open data and public access requirements. NAL data services help USDA-funded research communities make their data "Findable, Accessible, Interoperable, and Reusable (FAIR)." NAL does this by providing research communities with expert metadata and informatics expertise to help create rich, well-structured, machine-readable metadata, offering a channel to publish data and metadata, and delivering the infrastructure for data preservation. NAL's role is to help the agricultural research community prepare data to be accessed and reused for analytical applications.

NAL services currently support a number of domains, including arthropod genomics, life cycle assessment, geospatial modeling, food and nutrition, and animal welfare to name a few. Products that underpin these services include:

- USDA Food Composition Database (https://ndb.nal.usda.gov)
- I5K Workspace@NAL (https://i5k.nal.usda.gov)
- Life Cycle Assessment Commons (LCA Commons; https://www.lca commons.gov)
- Dr. Duke's Phytochemical and Ethnobotanical Databases (https://phyto-chem.nal.usda.gov)
- Geospatial Data Catalog (GeoData; https://geodata.nal.usda.gov)

Digital Products

NAL's website (https://www.nal.usda.gov) is the primary entry point to all of the following online resources.

AGRICOLA

AGRICOLA is an online catalog of NAL collections, and the article citation database delivers worldwide access to agricultural information through its searchable web interface (http://agricola.nal.usda.gov). Alternatively, users can access AGRICOLA on a fee basis through several commercial vendors, or they can subscribe to the complete AGRICOLA file, also on a fee basis, directly from the library by e-mailing AgricolaPublishers@usda.gov.

The AGRICOLA database covers materials in all formats, including printed works from the 15th century onward. Its records describe publications and resources encompassing all aspects of agriculture and allied disciplines. AGRICOLA, updated daily, includes the following two components:

- NAL Public Access Catalog, containing more than 1 million citations to books, audiovisual materials, serial titles, and other materials in the NAL collection. (The catalog also contains some bibliographic records for items cataloged by other libraries but not held in the NAL collection.)

- NAL Article Citation Database, consisting of more than 6 million citations to journal articles, book chapters, reports, and reprints. NAL has implemented automated indexing/text analytics software to produce its Article Citation Database. This application combines semantic analysis, machine learning, and human rules to automatically assign subject terms to journal articles.

DigiTop

DigiTop, USDA's Digital Desktop Library, delivers the full text of 7,000-plus journals and more than 5,000 newspapers worldwide and provides 27 agriculturally significant citation databases, including AGRICOLA, BIOSIS Previews, Business Source Premier, CAB Abstracts, GEOBASE, GeoRef, Scopus, and Web of Science. DigiTop also supplies a range of digital reference resources and offers focused, personalized services. Navigator is a component of DigiTop that allows cross-searching of multiple bibliographic databases. This discovery service includes citations from academic journals, newspapers, magazines, and nonprint sources. DigiTop is available to on-site visitors and to the entire USDA workforce worldwide—more than 100,000 people—around the clock. NAL staff provides help desk and reference services, continuous user education, and training for DigiTop users.

Ag Data Commons

Ag Data Commons (https://data.nal.usda.gov), a scientific research data catalog and repository, supports USDA's objectives to make USDA-funded research data FAIR. Through Ag Data Commons, NAL provides scientific research data description, publishing, and preservation services for agricultural research communities. Ag Data Commons serves as USDA's central point of access to open agricultural research data. Its catalog, with more than 4,000 records, is a gateway to data from USDA-funded research. Its repository also publishes and preserves data files from intramural and extramural grant programs. Standardized metadata records describe datasets in detail and link them with information, related data, publications, and people, using persistent identifiers. The goal of Ag Data Commons is to enable data reuse to compound the value of USDA science and engender science-based decision-making.

Ag Data Commons uses a customized version of the open source DKAN software, which is compliant with U.S. Project Open Data standards for federal agencies. The system includes both a catalog function describing the data and pointing to its online location and a repository holding and publishing data that's not otherwise available.

National Agricultural Library Digital Collections

National Agricultural Library Digital Collections (NALDC) (https://naldc.nal.usda.govl) offers easy access to collection materials available in digital format. NALDC provides rich searching, browsing, and retrieval of digital materials and collections and delivers reliable, long-term online access to selected publications. NALDC includes historical publications, USDA research, and more.

PubAg

PubAg (https://pubag.nal.usda.gov) provides discovery of and access to full-text articles authored by USDA employees and citations to the peer-reviewed journal literature of agriculture. These citations have been enriched through subject analysis and application of terms from the National Agricultural Library Thesaurus (NALT).

National Agricultural Library Thesaurus (NALT)

Redesigned as part of NAL's NALT for the Machine Age initiative, NALT 2022, 20th edition, is a state-of-the-art multischeme concept space with added structural features for enhanced scalability and machine readability.

2022 Inaugural Schemes

- NALT Core, a trim NALT subscheme with just 13,791 frequently used agricultural concepts, including 4,396 agriculturally important organisms (taxa) and structural updates for a lean and efficient machine-readable agricultural knowledge base
- NALT Full, all NALT concepts and NALT Core plus more than 48,000 additional agricultural related organisms (taxa) and several thousand less-frequently used concepts for a total of 76,933 concepts. NALT Full is a more granular knowledge base.

New NALT 2022 Structural Features

- Streamlined top concepts reflect USDA programs and services to support data linkages and transparency and to enhance agriculture research and information discoverability:
  - Animals, Livestock, One Health
  - Economics, Trade, Law, Business, Industry
  - Farms, Agricultural Production Systems
  - Fields of Study
  - Forestry, Wildland Management
  - Geographical Locations
  - Human Nutrition, Food Safety and Quality
  - Natural Resources, Conservation, Environment
  - Plant Production, Gardening
  - Research, Technology, Methods
  - Rural Development, Communities, Education, Extension
  - Taxonomic Hierarchy
- Maintained natively as a linked data graph, also known as a knowledge graph (SKOS concept scheme)
- The knowledge graph enables linked open data mappings across the Internet, harnessing the power of the semantic web.
- Mapping to other resources: Library of Congress Subject Headings, CAB Thesaurus, AGROVOC, Global Agricultural Concept Space (GACS), and

Wikidata. NALT 2022 mappings have increased since last year by 70 percent to 50,275.

- NALT persistent uniform resource identifiers (URIs) are upgraded to HTTPS (Hypertext Transfer Protocol Secure), ensuring secure access to NALT concept descriptions. Legacy HTTP NALT URIs are currently supported by redirects.
- NALT concept types (Organism, Chemical, Product, Geographical, Topic) express the most salient features of the concept space.
- Product-to-organism relationships are added to capture deeper knowledge of agricultural production from farm to fork.
- The NAL project NALT for the Machine Age, along with interested agricultural subject matter expert communities, is working to create additional subschemes within the NALT concept space.

Networks of Cooperation

The NAL collection and information resources are supplemented by networks of cooperation with other institutions, including arrangements with agricultural libraries at U.S. land-grant universities, other U.S. national libraries, agricultural libraries in other countries, and libraries of the United Nations and other international organizations.

AgNIC

The Agriculture Network Information Collaborative (AgNIC) is a voluntary alliance of member institutions, mostly U.S. land-grant university libraries, dedicated to enhancing collective information and services among the members and their partners for all those seeking agricultural information over the Internet. More information about AgNIC and its activities can be found at https://www.agnic.org.

USAIN

The United States Agricultural Information Network (USAIN) is a professional membership organization that provides a forum for members to discuss food and agricultural issues and seeks to take a leadership role in the formation of a national information policy as related to food and agriculture. Central to its mission is cooperation with and support of the NAL. Learn more about USAIN at https://usain.org.

AGLINET

Through the Agricultural Libraries Network (AGLINET), NAL serves as the U.S. node of an international agricultural information system that brings together agricultural libraries with strong regional or country coverage and other specialized collections. NAL functions as a gateway to U.S. agricultural libraries and resources, fulfilling requests for information via reciprocal agreements with several other libraries, information centers, and consortia. As an AGLINET member, NAL agrees to provide low-cost interlibrary loan and photocopy service to other

AGLINET libraries. Most materials requested through AGLINET are delivered digitally, although reproductions via fiche or photocopy are used when appropriate. AGLINET is administered by the Food and Agriculture Organization of the United Nations.

Information Management and Information Technology

Over the past quarter century, NAL has applied increasingly sophisticated information technology to support the ever-more complex and demanding information needs of researchers, practitioners, policymakers, and the general public. Technological developments spearheaded by the library date back to the 1940s and 1950s, when NAL director Ralph Shaw invented "electronic machines" such as the photo charger, rapid selector, and photo clerk. Over the years, NAL has made numerous technological improvements, such as automating collections information and delivering full-text and image collections digitally on the Internet.

NAL has fully implemented the Voyager integrated library system from Ex Libris. The system supports ordering, receiving, and invoice processing for purchases; creating and maintaining indexing and cataloging records for AGRICOLA; circulating print holdings; and providing a web-based online catalog for public searching and browsing of the collection. In addition, the system is fully integrated with an automated interlibrary loan and document delivery system by Relais International that streamlines services and provides desktop delivery of needed materials.

NAL is in the process of migrating its Voyager and Islandora data to Alma, Ex Libris's library services platform. Alma will allow NAL to integrate AGRICOLA platforms and services and modernize NAL infrastructure. NAL's go-live date for Alma is September 2022.

National Library of Medicine

8600 Rockville Pike, Bethesda, MD 20894
301-496-6308, 888-346-3656, fax 301-496-4450
E-mail nlmcommunications@nlm.nih.gov
http://www.nlm.nih.gov

Jody Nurik

Director, Office of Communications and Public Liaison

The National Library of Medicine (NLM) is the world's largest biomedical library and a leader in biomedical and health data science research. NLM's research and information services support scientific discovery, healthcare delivery, and public health decision-making. NLM pioneers new ways to make biomedical data and information more accessible, builds tools for improved data management and personal health, and helps create a more diverse and data-driven workforce. NLM's work enables researchers, clinicians, and the public to both access and utilize a wealth of biomedical data to improve health. There is not a biomedical discovery, public health advance, or clinical care action in the past 30 years that has not benefited from NLM resources.

Leveraging its 185-year history, NLM develops and applies innovative approaches to acquire, organize, curate, and deliver current biomedical information across the United States and around the globe. NLM's advanced biomedical information services are among the most visited webpages in the federal government digital landscape, providing researchers, healthcare professionals, and the public unfettered access to high-quality biomedical information and data, including biomedical literature, genomic data, clinical trial data, and chemical data.

NLM's innovative research and training programs—focusing on artificial intelligence (AI), machine learning, computational biology, biomedical informatics, and health data standards—help catalyze basic biomedical science, data-driven discovery, and healthcare delivery.

NLM continues to strive to achieve key objectives of its strategic plan—to accelerate discovery and advance health through data-driven research, reach more people in more ways, and build a workforce for data-driven research and health. NLM also supports National Institutes of Health (NIH)-wide efforts to answer the call to respond to national priorities, including the COVID-19 pandemic, and close the gap in health disparities. NLM achieves this through effective preservation of valued scientific and data resources, judicious investments in extramural and intramural research, informed stewardship of federal resources, and innovative partnerships to align priorities and leverage investments across the U.S. Department of Health and Human Services, the federal government, and the biomedical research community.

NLM's Response to COVID-19: Highlights

At the onset of the COVID-19 pandemic, NLM responded swiftly and provided both public and professional audiences with the resources and information needed to combat this global public health threat. NLM facilitated scientific discovery of SARS-CoV-2 (the virus that causes COVID-19) by connecting data and information resources. Used by scientists across the globe, NLM resources accelerated the development of new approaches for COVID-19 testing, evaluation of vaccine candidates, and validation of effective and innovative treatments.

In 2021 to support coronavirus research and response efforts, NLM rapidly increased access to full-text coronavirus-related scientific journal articles through PubMed Central (PMC), NLM's digital archive of free, full-text biomedical literature. NLM worked with the global publishing community to make tens of thousands of research publications related to coronaviruses freely and immediately available to the public in ways that supported automated text mining, allowing for seamless search and retrieval of information. NLM released a vast collection of coronavirus-related information accessible to AI and machine learning researchers to accelerate discoveries about COVID-19. This effort involved collaborating with publishers, scholarly societies, and leading IT companies. More information on NLM's continued response to the COVID-19 pandemic can be found throughout this narrative.

NLM worked across multiple fronts to improve researchers', clinicians', and public health professionals' understanding of SARS-CoV-2 and COVID-19. In 2021 activities included:

- Adding 3.7 million genetic sequences and 800,000 complete SARS-CoV-2 genome records to GenBank, a database of all publicly available DNA sequences
- Creating a dedicated website, the SARS-CoV-2 Data Resources page, to help researchers search, retrieve, and analyze data for the more than 6 million digital genomic sequences of the virus available from GenBank and the Sequence Read Archive (SRA). This resource continues to provide free access to SARS-CoV-2 viral genome sequence data and ensures rapid dissemination and maximum impact of these data.
- Facilitating access to COVID-19 data through SRA, the world's largest publicly available repository of unprocessed sequence data. COVID-19-focused datasets made available through this cloud-based platform allowed researchers to access, download, and/or compute on datasets directly within the cloud, giving researchers the ability to compute across the full SRA dataset for metagenomic research on the new coronavirus in ways not previously possible.
- Collaborating with other NIH institutes and centers, as well as other federal agencies, such as the Centers for Disease Control and Prevention (CDC), on surveillance data for tracking of COVID-19 community spread. As part of these collaborative efforts, NLM calculated the viral mutations and variants present in the GenBank and SRA SARS-CoV-2 samples and has made this analysis available for more than 6 million datasets through cloud-based platforms.
- Updating LitCovid, a special subset of articles pertinent to post-acute sequelae of COVID-19 (also known as long COVID). NLM continued to work with publishers, both domestic and international, to get as much coronavirus research into PMC, in support of LitCovid, for free and immediate

access in machine-readable formats. The original set of free full-text articles related to coronavirus grew with the addition of more than 340,000 articles in the past year. The PMC Open Access Subset currently includes more than 3.4 million journal articles and preprints on all biomedical topics that are made available under license terms that allow reuse and data mining.

- Continuing the NIH Preprint Pilot to test the viability of making preprints searchable in PMC and discoverable in PubMed, starting with COVID-19 preprints reporting NIH-supported research. More than 2,700 preprint records were available in these databases, while 45 percent were unavailable in published journals.

- Adding nearly 125,000 COVID-19-related citations to PubMed. NLM helped users retrieve comprehensive results when accessing this rapidly growing corpus by automatically expanding searches for COVID-19 to include additional key terms and PubMed Clinical Queries to include special COVID-19 filter categories.

- Posting more than 7,000 clinical studies related to COVID-19 and SARS-COV-2 on ClinicalTrials.gov, NLM's database of privately and publicly funded clinical studies conducted around the world, to reach a milestone of approximately 400,000 total registered studies. Trials were summarized by location, funding, and whether the drug or vaccine being studied was available on the ClinicalTrials.gov COVID-19 webpage. ClinicalTrials.gov also listed nearly 6,000 international COVID-19-related studies registered with the World Health Organization, providing users with a more comprehensive registry.

- Identifying, selecting, and archiving more than three terabytes of web and social media content documenting the COVID-19 pandemic as part of NLM's Global Health Events web archive. This collection encompasses federal, state, and local government COVID-19 webpages, websites of aid organizations and nongovernmental organizations, and content documenting health disparities, life in quarantine, prevention measures, vaccines, the experiences of healthcare workers, patients, and more.

Accelerating Data-Driven Discovery and Health

NLM works to accelerate discovery and advance health through data-driven research, to reach more people in more ways through enhanced dissemination and engagement, and to build a workforce for data-driven research and health. NLM continued its work across many projects to improve data standards and tools for precise representation of social determinants of health and other concepts that are essential to advancing health equity around the COVID-19 pandemic. In addition to activities driven by the COVID-19 pandemic, NLM continued to advance support for professionals within and outside the field of information science. Every day, millions of scientists, health professionals, and members of the public from around the world use NLM's online information resources to translate research results into new treatments, develop new products, inform clinical decision-making, and improve public health.

Outreach and Engagement

NLM's Office of Engagement and Training (OET) serves as a strategic connector between NLM and its many stakeholders throughout the United States and internationally. OET develops community partnerships with an emphasis on reaching and engaging underserved populations, and it coordinates the Network of the National Library of Medicine (NNLM). NNLM leverages more than 8,000 academic health science libraries, hospital and public libraries, and community organizations across the United States to improve access to health information for all. In 2021 NNLM funded more than 150 outreach projects across the country to enhance awareness and access to health information and to address health literacy issues.

In its response to the COVID-19 pandemic, NLM supported NIH through the following activities:

* Joining and serving on the executive committee of the Reopening of Archives, Libraries and Museums, a partnership with the Institute of Museum and Library Services, OCLC, and others
* Supporting the NIH Researching COVID to Enhance Recovery (RECOVER) initiative to enable and rapidly advance understanding of the recovery process, the epidemiology, and the natural history of post-acute sequelae of SARS-CoV-2
* Contributing to the NIH Community Engagement Alliance (CEAL) Against COVID-19 Disparities initiative by creating and sharing educational videos (available in English and Spanish) on various relevant topics, including vaccinations, clinical trials, and COVID-19 treatments

NLM also leveraged NNLM to provide additional support to NIH by:

* Investigating the need to develop and strengthen the infrastructure, mechanisms, and tools to support U.S. public and academic libraries and underserved communities
* Hosting symposia in support of library workers, including "Responding to the COVID-19 Infodemic" and "BLOSSOM: Building Life-Long Opportunities for Strength, Self-Care, Outlook, Morale and Mindfulness"
* Offering hundreds of other activities, events, and trainings to address issues related to COVID-19
* Partnering with the NIH All of Us Research Program to provide virtual health programming to support public libraries and their patrons through virtual events spanning topics in citizen science, genetics, and maternal health

Enhancing Information Delivery

NLM strives to reach more people in more ways through the innovative delivery of information across digital platforms. In 2021 activities included:

* Indexing approximately 1.6 million new journal articles for PubMed, NLM's most heavily used database, which contains records for more than 33 million citations for biomedical literature

- Growing PMC with 900,000 full-text additions for a total of more than 7 million available articles
- Expanding ClinicalTrials.gov and continuing a multiyear effort to modernize ClinicalTrials.gov to deliver an improved user experience on an updated platform, accommodate growth, and enhance efficiency
- Increasing entries in NLM's database of Genotypes and Phenotypes (dbGaP), which connects individual-level genomic data with individual-level clinical information. The dbGaP resource now contains data from more than nearly 1,811 studies, comprising de-identified data from more than 3 million study participants. This database allows unrestricted access to summary-level genomic results, primarily from NIH-supported genomic studies. More than 2,500 research papers have been published based on new analyses of these data.
- Adding nearly 40 million sequence records (an increase of 15 percent) to NLM's Reference Sequence (RefSeq) collection, which provides a comprehensive collection of reference sequences and genes against which individual variations can be compared
- Expanding NLM's historical collections, including 35 now fully digitized manuscript collections housed in NLM Digital Collections, a freely accessible digital repository. This collection includes more than 73,000 prints and photographs, 1,000 audiovisual titles, and 34,000 rare or unique books.
- Curating and archiving a series of virtual free history talks by a diverse group of researchers who have completed research using NLM's vast collections, along with interviews featured on the NLM History of Medicine Division's popular blog, "Circulating Now." Notable among these programs was the timely talk "Peril in the Air: Pollution Activism on Film" and the related NLM exhibition Fifty Years Ago: The Darkening Day.
- Continuing to enhance clinical terminologies and terminology services to support changing research, clinical practice, and public health needs due to COVID-19. Such changes included adding 23 new COVID-19-related terms to the Medical Subject Headings thesaurus (MeSH); creating a new resource, COVID-19 Vaccines and Medications in RxNorm, for rapid dissemination of new RxNorm terms as they are published; supporting creation and dissemination of new COVID-19-relevant codes and mappings involving the vocabularies for SNOMED, LOINC, and ICD-10; and inclusion of new and provisional codes in value sets in the NLM Value Set Authority Center.

Promoting Public Awareness and Access to Information

NLM offers plain-language, direct-to-consumer information through its flagship consumer health website, MedlinePlus.gov. This resource includes information about a broad variety of health topics, human genetics, medical tests, medications, and dietary supplements, as well as healthy recipes. MedlinePlus now offers more than 1,000 health topics in English, Spanish, and many other languages.

In response to the COVID-19 pandemic, MedlinePlus added several new health topics in English and Spanish. These pages help the public find accurate, up-to-date information about COVID-19 symptoms, prevention, testing, and vaccines from the federal government and other trusted sources.

Consumer health information from MedlinePlus and several other NIH institutes and centers is also accessible through MedlinePlus Connect. This service received more than 150 million requests for targeted health information from health information technology and electronic health record systems.

In collaboration with other NIH institutes and centers, NLM also produces the NIH MedlinePlus digital magazine (available in both English and Spanish). A digital publishing model ensures that the magazine content remains robust, timely, and topical. A special spring 2021 issue, featuring NIH leaders Dr. Francis Collins and Dr. Anthony Fauci, included extensive coverage of the NIH response to the COVID-19 pandemic. Overall engagement on the digital platform continued to increase in page views, users, new users, and sessions.

Research and Development for Advanced Information Systems, Standards, and Research Tools

Intramural Research Programs

Under the leadership of NLM's scientific director of Intramural Research Programs (IRP), the Computational Biology Branch and the Computational Health Research Branch develop and apply computational approaches to a broad range of problems in biomedicine, molecular biology, and health.

The IRP's website was recently redesigned to reflect its evolving research priorities. In computational health research, the focus includes natural language processing, clinical image processing, biomedical ontologies and information models, and clinical analytics. In computational biology research, topics include transcription, chromatin, and networks; structure and function; sequence statistics; and evolutionary genomics.

The NLM IRP also provides training and research opportunities for future computational health and bioinformatics leaders. This includes postdoctoral fellowships, internships, and volunteer programs.

Standards and Terminology

NLM has been a major force in the field of health data standards for more than 30 years. NLM supports the development, maintenance, and dissemination of health data standards and associated tools used widely in health care and research, including LOINC (Logical Observation Identifiers Names and Codes) and SNOMED CT (Systematized Nomenclature of Medicine, Clinical Terms). Importantly, NLM support allows key health data standards to be used free of charge in the United States and widely implemented in health care, public health, biomedical research, and product development.

The Unified Medical Language System (UMLS) integrates and distributes key terminology, classification and coding standards, and associated resources to promote the creation of more effective and interoperable biomedical information systems and services. UMLS resources help computer programs to interpret biomedical text and health data correctly in NIH-funded research, in commercial product development, and in many electronic information services.

RxNorm is a widely used drug terminology system developed by NLM and is used for electronic prescription and exchange of drug information. NLM has developed a graphical user interface and application programming interface to facilitate access by researchers, industry, and the public.

NLM has been an active proponent of the Health Level Seven Fast Healthcare Interoperability Resources (FHIR) standard that is supported at the NIH level to support data science. Both the Office of the National Coordinator for Health IT and the Centers for Medicare & Medicaid Services include requirements for use of FHIR in recent rulemaking related to the 21st Century Cures Act. NLM has also developed several software tools to facilitate use of FHIR.

In response to the COVID-19 pandemic, NLM, CDC, the Food and Drug Administration, Regenstrief Institute, the Association of Public Health Laboratories, and the In-Vitro Device (IVD) Industry Connectivity Consortium (IICC) developed a catalog that provides guidance for reporting SARS-CoV-2 test results using LOINC, SNOMED CT, and device identifiers. The use of this mapping tool (the LOINC In-Vitro Device specification, or LIVD) is intended to reduce inaccuracies and time spent on the import of laboratory test results sent through laboratory information systems.

The Value Set Authority Center, in response to the COVID-19 pandemic, adapted to stakeholders' needs for timely updates of provisional codes that several standard terminologies currently produce and frequently update. NLM stewards the NIH Common Data Elements (CDE) Repository, a free, collaborative platform for sharing and discovering structured, human, and machine-readable definitions of data elements, variables, and measures recommended for use in NIH-funded clinical research.

Extramural Programs

NLM funds extramural research, resources, and workforce development grants that build important foundations in biomedical informatics and data science, bringing the methods and concepts of computational, informational, quantitative, social/behavioral, and engineering sciences to bear on problems related to basic biomedical/behavioral research, health care, public health, and consumer use of health-related information. NLM offers several types of grants within the following three general categories: research, resource, and workforce. Research grants include research projects grants, grants for small businesses, and small exploratory/developmental research projects. Resource grants include those for scholarly works in the history of science and medicine and information resources to reduce health disparities, and workforce grants include university-based training, fellowships, and career transition grants. NLM funded 186 awards, including 22 that were co-funded with other NIH institutes and centers.

Biomedical Informatics and Data Science Research

NLM's Extramural Program research project grants support pioneering research and development to advance knowledge in biomedical informatics and data science. Complementing initiatives at other NIH institutes and centers, these grants support investigator-initiated innovation in basic and applied research, ranging from small proof-of-concept projects to larger, sustained collaborations, creating and testing approaches and tools that will be valuable to more than one domain of interest.

The Extramural Program issued 36 new research project grants, including one exploratory/developmental award that reflects current and expanding investments in data science, as well as investments in data science applications for patients. Several of these awards address data analytics topics, including collaborative filtering for improved information retrieval, 360-degree automated characterization of the built environment, and evidence-based communication of numbers in health. New awards in translational bioinformatics focus on reconstruction and modeling of dynamical molecular networks, inference of molecular mechanisms of complex disease, and panomic analytics for microbiome data. In support of the NIH Next Generation Researchers Initiative, NLM awarded new research project support to ten early-stage investigators.

NLM sets aside funds to support small business innovation and research and technology transfer (SBIR/STTR). NLM met its required set-aside by funding four new and three continuing SBIR/STTR awards; NLM's allocation of funds for SBIR/STTR was more than $2 million. The new projects center on decision support for real-time trauma resuscitation, a blockchain enabled healthcare network for population health data, and a home-based monitoring system for children with cerebral palsy.

Resource Grant Programs to Reach More People in More Ways

Nine awards were made to grantees under NLM's unique Information Resources to Reduce Health Disparities program. This program aims to bring useful, usable health information to populations experiencing health disparities. Topics supported include information resources for deaf and hard-of-hearing populations, support for communities at risk for Chagas disease, and environmental health literacy resources for Appalachian Kentucky. NLM continued to support the Scholarly Works resource grant program; seven new and three continuing grants were awarded that were targeted to the interests of biomedical terminology specialists, public health officials, and clinical informaticians.

Research Management and Support

Research Management and Support activities provide administrative, budgetary, communications, and logistical support for NLM programs to ensure strategic planning, messaging, and evaluation; regulatory compliance; policy development; international coordination; and partnerships with other federal agencies, Congress, the private sector, and the public. NLM is streamlining its organizational and administrative structure to enhance collaborative leadership, innovation, and customer service.

Administration

The director of NLM, Patricia Flatley Brennan, R.N., Ph.D., is guided in matters of policy by a board of regents consisting of ten appointed and nine ex-officio members.

United States Government Publishing Office

732 North Capitol St. N.W., Washington, DC 20401
http://www.gpo.gov

Gary Somerset
Chief Public Relations Officer
202-512-1957, e-mail gsomerset@gpo.gov

The U.S. Government Printing Office (GPO) was created when President James Buchanan signed Joint Resolution 25 on June 23, 1860. GPO opened its doors for business nine months later, on March 4, 1861, the same day Abraham Lincoln took the oath of office to become the 16th president of the United States. On that day, GPO began operation in buildings purchased by Congress, at the same address it occupies today.

A historic moment occurred for GPO in December 2014, when President Barack Obama signed into law a bill changing the agency's name to the U.S. Government Publishing Office. The new name reflects the increasingly prominent role that GPO plays in providing access to government information in digital formats through GPO's govinfo (govinfo.gov), apps, e-books, and related technologies. The information needs of Congress, federal agencies, and the public have evolved beyond only print, and GPO has transformed itself to meet its customers' needs.

Under Title 44 of the United States Code, GPO is responsible for the production and distribution of information products for all three branches of the federal government. These include the official publications of Congress, federal agencies, and the courts. Today GPO provides products in print and a variety of digital forms, all of which are born digitally. In addition, GPO produces passports for the Department of State and secure credentials for many government agencies.

As the federal government's official resource for gathering, producing, cataloging, providing access to, and preserving published information in all forms, GPO has disseminated millions of publications to the public. GPO's Superintendent of Documents and its Library Services and Content Management (LSCM) organizations administer and manage the four programs required by Title 44:

- The Federal Depository Library Program (FDLP)
- Cataloging and indexing
- Distributing government publications to the International Exchange Service
- The By-Law Program, under which certain government publications are distributed to members of Congress and to other government agencies as mandated by law

FDLP dates back to 1813, when Congress first authorized legislation to ensure the provision of certain congressional documents to selected universities, historical societies, and state libraries. At that time, the secretary of state was responsible for distributing publications. In 1857 the secretary of the interior assumed oversight of printing and the designation of depositories. In the Printing Act of 1895, the governance of the depository program was transferred to the Office of the Superintendent of Documents at GPO. Duties remained largely unchanged until 1993, when Public Law 103-40, the Government Printing Office Electronic Information Access Enhancement Act, amended GPO's duties to not only provide public access to printed publications but to Internet-accessible publications as well.

Two centuries after the start of FDLP, the program continues to serve a vital need of the public through the partnership with federal depository libraries located in nearly every congressional district. GPO is obviously a much different agency in the digital age than it was years ago. While its name has changed, its mission—Keeping America Informed—is as important and relevant as ever. GPO's public information programs are examples of the agency's long-standing commitment to free, permanent public access to U.S. government information.

The Superintendent of Documents and LSCM organizations support GPO's continued digital transformation through initiatives to enhance historic and current content on govinfo.gov and the Catalog of U.S. Government Publications (CGP), as well as through the development of free online tools and resources to help FDLP libraries manage their depository library more effectively and efficiently. Additionally, beginning in fiscal year (FY) 2020, LSCM has been working closely with libraries to help preserve tangible government documents in FDLP library collections.

In an effort to further openness and transparency, the Superintendent of Documents seeks comments from the depository library community, interested stakeholders, and the general public on various documents, including draft policies. In FY 2021 the Superintendent of Documents established a more formal process to obtain, report, and retain comments received. Two new webpages were added to FDLP.gov: Open Requests for Comments (https://www.fdlp.gov/about-fdlp/18-supdocs/4956-open-requests-for-comments) and Closed Requests for Comments (https://www.fdlp.gov/about-fdlp/18-supdocs/4957-closed-requests-for-comments). When comments are sought, there will be an entry on the Open Requests page for the duration of the comment period. The Closed Requests page serves as a record of the comment process, providing an entry for any document for which a call for comments was made.

COVID Support Services for FDLP Libraries

As a result of the COVID-19 pandemic, GPO has strived to provide needed services to FDLP libraries. Available through the COVID-19 Tool Kit: Federal Depository Library Program (https://www.fdlp.gov/promotion/covid-19-fdlp-toolkit) is the following:

- Information for federal depository library staff on FDLP operations during the pandemic
- Information for libraries in general
- Reliable U.S. government information resources for FDLP patrons
- Downloadable images for library websites to link patrons to COVID-19 information pages or research guides
- Infographics to share with patrons
- Recorded webinars for library staff and patrons

Since information on the pandemic is constantly changing, GPO is continuing to update this resource with new information as it becomes available.

Nationwide, FDLP libraries have accumulated many lessons learned and best practices related to COVID-19, such as for working remotely and the process of reopening. Librarians and staff have been sharing information with GPO about what initiatives have been incorporated into their "new normal" environment to enhance and strengthen the overall public service experience. A webpage under the COVID-19 Toolkit serves as a collection of related information to share among the FDLP community (https://www.fdlp.gov/covid-19-best-practices-lessons-learned-for-fdlp-libraries). It includes best practices, success stories, and articles of interest.

Key Stakeholders: The Libraries in FDLP

GPO Partnerships

Since 1997 GPO has developed strategic partnerships with federal depository libraries, federal agencies, and other institutions to increase public access to electronic and tangible U.S. government information.

GPO's partner categories are:

- Preservation Steward (for historic tangible content)
- Digital Preservation Steward
- Digital Content Contributor
- Digital Access Partner
- Cataloging and Metadata Contributor
- Other/Specialized

Partnering is an integral part of how GPO is "Keeping America Informed," and over the past two decades, these partnerships have grown and evolved. At the close of FY 2021 there were 71 official GPO partnerships: 43 Preservation Stewards, 1 Digital Preservation Steward, 7 Digital Content Contributors, 17 Digital Access Partners, and 3 Cataloging and Metadata Contributors.

GPO Collaborations

In FY 2021 LSCM staff contributed to and collaborated with groups in support of the FDLP and Cataloging & Indexing Programs, including:

- GPO is collaborating with the Law Library of Congress to digitize and make accessible volumes of the U.S. Congressional Serial Set dating back to 1817. The initial public release of content in the govinfo Serial Set collection was on September 28, 2021. This release contains selected volumes from the 69th Congress (1925–1927), the 82nd Congress (1951–1953), and several 19th-century Congresses. The public can access these volumes of the Serial Set on govinfo (https://www.govinfo.gov/app/collection/serialset). Additional volumes will be added to the collection as they become ready.

- In a collaboration with the Law Library of Congress in a multiyear project, LSCM is cataloging thousands of digitized and born-digital historic legal reports to increase public access. GPO has now cataloged more than 1,000 of these reports, which are accessible through CGP.
- Through its partnership in the Civics Renewal Network (CRN), a consortium of organizations committed to strengthening civic life in the United States by increasing the quality of civics education in our nation's schools, LSCM makes available, through the CRN website, K–12 resources that support civics education.
- LSCM continued its partnership in the Technical Report Archive & Image Library (TRAIL). LSCM and TRAIL members work together to ensure that federal technical reports are openly accessible, and participating LSCM staff members offer expertise in cataloging and other areas and participate in the exchange of information about U.S. government scientific and technical information.
- The Digital Public Library of America (DPLA) and LSCM continued their collaboration to broaden public access to the information made available via CGP. Through the partnership, more than 234,700 records from CGP are available to the public via the DPLA website. Examples of records include the federal budget; laws; federal regulations; and congressional hearings, reports, and documents. LSCM and DPLA also partner to provide e-books to the DPLA Exchange, making this government content even more widely accessible.
- LSCM continues to be heavily involved in cooperative cataloging and metadata activities with members of the library community. LSCM is an active participant in all components of the Program for Cooperative Cataloging (PCC), which is managed by the Library of Congress, including the Bibliographic Record Cooperative (BIBCO), Cooperative Online Serials (CONSER), the Name Authority Cooperative (NACO), and the Subject Authority Cooperative (SACO).
- GPO has been a member of OCLC since 1976 and contributes bibliographic records for U.S. government information to the international database daily.
- LSCM is part of the Electronic Cataloging in Publication Program (ECIP). ECIP provides cataloging records for books in advance of publication. The publisher then includes the record on the verso of the publication's title page. Through ECIP, LSCM is creating prepublication bibliographic records for publications from federal agency publishers. LSCM has been a part of ECIP since 2015, and its staffers have created ECIP records for GPO, the Combat Studies Institute, the Air Force Research Institute, the Smithsonian Institution Scholarly Press, USGS, and the National Gallery of Art, to name a few.
- Through another collaboration with the Library of Congress, LSCM is cataloging Congressional Research Service (CRS) reports for CGP and OCLC. At the close of FY 2021 LSCM's Library Technical Services staff had cataloged more than 7,550 separate, unique CRS report titles, approximately 80 percent of all reports available on the site.

LSCM Pilot Projects

LSCM Pilot Projects are an opportunity for collaboration between LSCM and federal depository libraries. These jointly conducted projects are envisioned to benefit the larger FDLP community and ultimately to enhance access to the National Collection of U.S. Government Public Information.

With a framework developed in FY 2021, Pilot Project Opportunity 1 was announced to federal depository libraries in August 2021. It focused on cataloging, inventory, condition assessment, and digitization of certain publications from the U.S. Department of War. Another pilot opportunity will be announced in early 2022.

FDLP Academy

The FDLP Academy (https://www.fdlp.gov/about-the-fdlp/fdlp-academy) was launched to support the FDLP community's education and training needs and to advance U.S. government information literacy.

The FDLP Academy enhances U.S. government information knowledge through events, conferences, webinars, and webcasts coordinated by GPO that cover a variety of government information topics. Many sessions are presented by GPO staff, while others are presented by staff from other federal agencies and from members of the FDLP community, as recruited and hosted by GPO.

Since its inception in 2012, the FDLP Academy has hosted almost 600 webinars, with more than 75,000 combined registrants and almost 150 recorded webcasts. Training topics cover all aspects of government information resources and librarianship.

Enhancing Content in Govinfo

LSCM has worked closely with GPO's Office of Programs, Strategy, & Technology (PST) throughout the development and ongoing enhancement of govinfo.gov. Continuing to add to the collections currently available on govinfo is of the highest priority, with a goal of offering complete and historic holdings to its collections.

Notable additions in FY 2021 include:

- Monthly Catalog of U.S. Government Publications and Government Document Indexes
- New publications from Digital Content Contributors:
  - University of Florida
  - Boise State University
- Release of ten additional years of Bill Status XML Bulk Data, from the 108th Congress to the 112th Congress (2003–2012)
- Addition of linked HTML in the Congressional Record Index for 1983–2011
- Statute Compilations in USLM XML
- Completion of the Federal Register Index collection
- Final Report of the Committee on the Modernization of Congress

- *Women in Congress, 1917–2020* e-book
- 2020 United States Policy and Supporting Positions, or the "Plum Book"
- Senate Manual for the 116th Congress
- Congressional Directory for the 116th Congress
- 2021 Economic Report of the President
- Constitution of the United States of America: Analysis and Interpretation (CONAN), 2020 Supplement
- Thirteen new courts opted into publishing to the U.S. Courts Opinions collection, bringing the total number of courts participating in the program to 148.

Govinfo Certification as a Trustworthy Digital Repository

Since 2015 GPO has worked to be named as a Trustworthy Digital Repository (TDR) for government information through certification of govinfo under ISO 16363:2012. Certification under ISO 16363 provides GPO stakeholders, including the FDLP community, with assurance that govinfo is a standards-compliant digital archive in which government information shall be preserved, accessible, and usable well into the future. Certification of govinfo validates GPO's commitment to standards-based digital preservation practices and activities across 109 criteria in the areas of:

- Organizational Governance
- Digital Object Management
- Infrastructure and Security Management

Trusted Digital Repository certification has been a key GPO strategic initiative and a joint effort between GPO's LSCM and PST business units.

On December 28, 2018, GPO made history by becoming the first organization in the United States and second organization in the world to achieve ISO 16363:2012 Certification. The Primary Trustworthy Digital Repository (TDR) Authorization Body Ltd. awarded GPO ISO 16363:2012 for govinfo and publicly announced the certificate on its website. In summer 2021 GPO initiated the first phase of its recertification audit of govinfo to maintain ISO 16363:2012 compliance.

FDLP LibGuides

FDLP LibGuides (https://libguides.fdlp.gov) is a service provided by GPO for depository libraries and the public. Guides are created by LSCM staff on a variety of topics, including those requested by the FDLP community. All guides are available for free use. Libraries and agencies can also submit their own guides for inclusion on the FDLP LibGuides Community page. In an effort to provide resources that are useful to all FDLP libraries, LSCM staff members continue to review the site and make enhancements to its look and content. FDLP LibGuides has had more than 76,000 views to the 160 guides offered.

Catalog of U.S. Government Publications

CGP (catalog.gpo.gov) is the finding tool for locating publications produced by the federal government, both current and historic. Students, researchers, community leaders, and anyone who needs to find information published by the U.S. government can get help from this online resource. Users can access library catalog records on a wide range of topics, including defense, citizenship, U.S. laws, health, science, and more. There are also direct links to the documents—unless the publication exists only in print. CGP even has a feature called MetaLib, which lets users research and retrieve reports, articles, and citations by searching across multiple U.S. government databases at once. What's more, there's a collection of U.S. government e-books from a variety of federal agencies, all free to access.

There were more than 25 million successful searches of CGP in FY 2021.

A service was launched in October 2017 to provide sets of bibliographic records from CGP free of charge on a monthly basis via GPO's CGP on the GitHub repository site. The CGP on GitHub datasets contain records produced by GPO staff according to national standards such as Resource Description and Access (RDA) and Anglo-American Cataloging Rules (AACR2) and include GPO Historic Shelflist project brief bibliographic records and other retrospective records.

Web Archiving and the End of Term Harvest

The FDLP Web Archive (https://www.archive-it.org/home/FDLPwebarchive) provides point-in-time captures of U.S. federal agency websites while preserving the functionality of the sites to the greatest extent possible. The aim is to provide permanent public access to federal agency web content. GPO harvests and archives the websites with Archive-It, a subscription-based web harvesting and archiving service offered by the Internet Archive.

LSCM continues to harvest digital publications and websites in order to advance FDLP collection development efforts. Throughout FY 2021 LSCM has:

- Increased the size of the FDLP Web Archive collection to 35.2TB, with more than 341,000,000 URLs
- Made available 211 website collections in the FDLP Web Archive on Archive-It and 266 records available through CGP

LSCM is currently monitoring collections in the web archive that are releasing information about COVID-19 to ensure timely capture of these collections.

GPO was again a partner in the End of Term Web Archive, which captures U.S. government websites at the end of a presidential administration. The 2020 End of Term Web Archive crawl is complete, and the collection is publicly available at the Internet Archive (https://archive.org/details/EndOfTerm2020WebCrawls?tab=collection).

FDLP Distribution Facilities

At GPO's Distribution Facility in Laurel, Maryland, the GPO staff continues to distribute publications, fulfill claims, and send special mailings of tangible items to federal depository libraries and international libraries participating in the International Exchange Service. In FY 2021 the staff distributed 2,708 titles, totaling 474,139 copies of materials, to FDLP libraries.

At GPO's Distribution Facility in Pueblo, Colorado, the staff distributes FDLP promotional items to FDLP libraries nationwide. As of the end of FY 2021 the Pueblo staff managed the inventory and dissemination of 28 different types of FDLP handouts and promotional items.

askGPO

askGPO is a GPO website used to facilitate questions from federal depository libraries, federal agencies, and the public. LSCM's askGPO Salesforce platform went live in 2020, retiring the more than 17-year-old RightNow system. The askGPO platform provides a 360-degree customer relationship management tool. It is a robust multi-task platform for delivering customer support and strengthening GPO's partnerships within FDLP. Benefits include:

- Improved customer interaction with a consolidated communication channel that places all library information in one location, providing anyone in LSCM with a clear picture of library activities and interactions
- Comprehensive information for each library, including historic information (all digitized) for those libraries that have been in FDLP since the mid-1800s
- Offering consistent response and information to libraries, providing help with training and instruction, and strengthening partnerships with library groups, while addressing the individual needs of libraries
- Accounts for all federal agency publishers that GPO staff work with on a regular basis or have a partnership agreement with

The Federal Depository Library Directory

A newly redesigned Federal Depository Library Directory (FDLD; https://ask.gpo.gov/s/FDLD) was released in July 2021 as a component of askGPO. FDLD enables the public to find local federal depository libraries in their area. The directory includes features such as:

- Library names and parent institutions
- Websites
- Street addresses and phone numbers
- An FDLP Network map
- Exterior library building photos
- Location maps on individual FDLP library pages

National Technical Information Service

U.S. Department of Commerce, Alexandria, VA 22312

Wayne Strickland

Associate Director, Office of Program Management

The National Technical Information Service (NTIS) has long been in the forefront of information collection and retrieval. Established in 1945 as the Publication Board to collect and disseminate government-sponsored research, NTIS became the first major computerized database of scientific and technical information in 1964. In the 1990s NTIS began digitizing the full texts of the reports in its collection and in 2009 began an online subscription service to make those full-text digital copies immediately downloadable.

NTIS manages the largest publicly available U.S. government-sponsored collection of technical and scientific reports, which totals more than 3 million publications. This collection is called the National Technical Reports Library (NTRL), a data dissemination program that involves a multistep process, including document acquisition, indexing, summarizing, and archiving. Through NTRL's online portal, this collection is also made available for comprehensive online bibliographies, commercial database vendors, and document delivery services.

Today, almost one-third of NTRL's 3 million federal research documents (approximately 998,000 documents comprising 3.2 terabytes of data) are available as fully digitized text to download at no charge. The database covers a wide variety of topics, including aeronautics, artificial intelligence, chemistry, energy, environment, health care, library and information sciences, mathematics, medicine and biology, pandemics, physics, and transportation, to name a few. In all, there are 39 major subject categories and 375 subcategories. The database is updated weekly, and, historically, more than 10,000 federally funded scientific reports are added every year.

To ensure perpetual access to authentic federally funded scientific research data in a "raw" format for academia, industry, and promoting innovation, Chapter 23 of Title 15 of the United States Code (15 U.S.C. 1151-1157) codified NTIS's basic authority to operate a permanent clearinghouse of scientific and technical information. With this chapter, NTIS was also given authority to charge fees for its products and services and to recover all costs through such fees "to the extent feasible."

This authority was restated in the National Technical Information Act of 1988, codified as 15 U.S.C. 3704b. That act gave NTIS the authority to enter joint ventures and declared the clearinghouse to be a permanent federal function that could not be eliminated or privatized without congressional approval.

The American Technology Preeminence Act of 1992 (Public Law 102-245) (1) required all costs associated with bibliographic control to be recovered by fees; (2) required agencies to make copies of their scientific and technical reports available to NTIS; and (3) directed NTIS to focus on developing new electronic methods and media for disseminating information.

In 2016 NTRL was transitioned to be publicly accessible for free while serving active consumers who include technical professionals and librarians. Through its stewardship, NTIS recognizes the value of this digital asset and strives to provide a web-friendly NTRL customer experience, which enables straightforward access to such a unique, original, and authenticated collection of scientific, technical, and engineering information. NTIS removed its cost-recovery subscription service and began providing free public access to the entire NTRL clearinghouse. This open access for NTRL publicly expanded the advanced search capabilities for title words, source agency, authors, publication year, and full-text availability. NTIS's Office of the Chief Information Officer (OCIO) team created the infrastructure for a metadata bibliographic database management system (MBS).

The future of NTRL will include exploring open-source publishing technologies and the development of application architecture for automated cataloging and indexing. Such technology modernization will ensure efficiencies for even greater compliance with §3704b, which mandates the transfer of federal scientific and technical information through the encouragement of the head of each federal executive department or agency in a timely manner to NTIS. Ongoing efforts to upgrade the NTRL content management system have become a NTIS priority. A primary focus is to make sure that the public and the research community benefit from the eventual digitization of all tangible formatted legacy documents.

Unfortunately, due to the COVID-19 pandemic and the need to safeguard the workforce, NTIS is in maximum telework status, and all handling of legacy content has been suspended. During this period, telework status does afford opportunities to collaborate with federal agency modernization strategies for the submission of future content digitally. Additionally, NTIS has begun investigating and implementing innovative options for automated cataloging and indexing of new scientific content. As science dictates, NTIS will also ensure updates to researched information categories in NTRL.

The 21st-century goal for NTRL is to continue being at the forefront of promoting economic growth by ensuring perpetual availability of federally funded scientific research in all data formats. NTRL will comprise important information that will be readily reproducible, discoverable, and openly accessible. Establishing trusted relationships with federal labs, federal agencies, the library community, researchers, industry, and the public will provide an economic growth pipeline for showcasing federal research, authorship, and achievement to better serve the public.

More than 300 U.S. government agencies and federal laboratories contribute to the NTIS collection, including the National Aeronautics and Space Administration; the Environmental Protection Agency; the departments of Agriculture, Commerce, Defense, Energy, Health and Human Services, Homeland Security, Interior, Labor, Treasury, Veterans Affairs, Housing and Urban Development, Education, and Transportation; and numerous other agencies.

National Technical Reports Library (NTRL) on the Web

NTIS offers web-based access to federal information and data on scientific, business, and technical research products at https://ntrl.ntis.gov/NTRL/.

Since NTIS discontinued its operating cost-recovery efforts in 2016 for NTRL (which historically utilized a fee-based subscription model), NTIS has been providing the public with NTRL service for free while continuously exploring alternative funding models and partnerships to minimize operating loss and modernize maintenance of this valued U.S. government-sponsored collection through automation technologies. In recent years NTIS succeeded in cost-saving efforts that helped dramatically lower operating losses. In fiscal year 2022 NTIS will develop a three-to-five-year Project Charter for upgrading the transition of NTRL into a cloud infrastructure for content management and open access to further reduce costs.

Key NTIS/NTRL Contacts

Email

ntrlhelpdesk@ntis.gov

Mail

National Technical Information Service
5301 Shawnee Rd.
Alexandria, VA 22312

National Archives and Records Administration

700 Pennsylvania Ave. NW, Washington, DC 20408
1-86-NARA-NARA or 1-866-272-6272
https://www.archives.gov

The National Archives and Records Administration (NARA), an independent federal agency, is the nation's record keeper. NARA safeguards and preserves the important records of all three branches of the federal government so that the people can discover, use, and learn from this documentary heritage. NARA ensures public access to government records, which strengthens democracy by allowing Americans to claim their rights of citizenship, hold their government accountable, and understand their history so they can participate more effectively in their government.

NARA carries out its mission through a national network of archives and archival field offices and records centers, stretching from Boston to San Francisco and Atlanta to Seattle, in addition to 15 presidential libraries that document administrations back to that of Herbert Hoover—a total of 44 facilities nationwide.

The agency includes the National Historical Publications and Records Commission (NHPRC), the grant-making arm of NARA; the Office of the Federal Register, which publishes the official records of the actions of the government; the Information Security Oversight Office (ISOO), which oversees the government's classification programs; the National Declassification Center (NDC), which is streamlining the declassification process; and the Office of Government Information Services (OGIS), which reviews agencies' Freedom of Information Act (FOIA) administration and practices.

NARA also assists federal agencies, the courts, and Congress in documenting their activities by providing records storage, offering reference service, administering records management programs, scheduling records, and retiring noncurrent records to federal records centers. NARA also provides training, advice, and guidance on many issues relating to records management.

NARA's constituents and stakeholders include educators and their students at all levels, a history-minded public, family historians, the media, the archival community, and a broad spectrum of professional associations and researchers in such fields as history, political science, law, library and information services, and genealogy.

The size and breadth of NARA's holdings are staggering. NARA's electronic records holdings amount to 1,265.7 terabytes of data. This consists of records that were "born digital" and managed in a digital form throughout their life cycle.

In addition, NARA maintains traditional holdings that will be converted to digital form for preservation purposes and to ensure access to them far into the future. This, along with the ever-growing quantity of born-digital records, creates a big data challenge for NARA and the federal government. NARA's current traditional holdings include more than 15 billion pages and 44 million photographs.

NARA is about to issue a new Strategic Plan for fiscal years (FY) 2022 through 2026, setting its long-term objectives. It has four strategic goals: Make Access Happen, Connect with Customers, Maximize NARA's Value to the Nation, and Build Our Future through Our People. Specific initiatives are underway at NARA to reach each goal.

Records and Access

Information Security Oversight Office (ISOO)

ISOO is responsible to the president for policy and oversight of the government-wide security classification system, the National Industrial Security Program, and the emerging federal policy on "controlled unclassified information" (CUI). ISOO receives policy and program guidance from the assistant to the president for national security affairs and National Security Council staff in the Executive Office of the President.

ISOO oversees the security classification programs (classification, safeguarding, and declassification) in both government and industry. It is also responsible for exercising NARA's authorities and responsibilities as the executive agent for controlled unclassified information. ISOO contributes materially to the effective implementation of the government-wide security classification program and has a direct impact on the performance of thousands of government employees and contract personnel who work with classified national security information. For more information on ISOO, visit archives.gov/isoo.

National Declassification Center (NDC)

In December 2009 Executive Order 13526 established NDC within the National Archives to address declassification of classified federal government records. The focus of this effort was to promote transparency and accountability of records created by the Executive Branch of the U.S. government.

NDC led a process that streamlined the declassification review processes for classified historical records and eliminated a 350-million-page backlog at the National Archives. NDC is committed to completing QA on all accessioned classified records no later than one year after they have been transferred to our custody. To facilitate public access to these records, NDC established an "Indexing on Demand" process that allows a researcher to request priority indexing and release for eligible record series.

NDC also processes requests for classified records under the Freedom of Information Act (FOIA) and Mandatory Review Provisions of Executive Order 13526 (MDR). To respond to these requests, NDC works closely with other agencies to ensure exempted records are reviewed by the appropriate equity agency, then processes declassified and redacted records for release. For more information about NDC, go to archives.gov/declassification.

Office of Government Information Services (OGIS)

As the FOIA Ombudsman, OGIS educates stakeholders about the FOIA process, resolves disputes, and assesses agency compliance.

The Open Government Act of 2007 created OGIS within the National Archives. The statute requires that OGIS offer mediation services to help resolve FOIA disputes and review agency FOIA policies and procedures. FOIA also charges OGIS with identifying methods to improve compliance with the statute.

The OGIS director chairs the FOIA Federal Advisory Committee. The committee brings together FOIA experts from inside and outside of government to identify major issues with the implementation of FOIA and develop consensus solutions. The OGIS director also serves as the co-chair of the Chief FOIA Officers Council.

For more information about OGIS, visit archives.gov/ogis or follow OGIS on Twitter @FOIA_Ombuds.

Electronic Records Archives (ERA)

NARA uses the Electronic Records Archives (ERA) system to take in and store electronic records from the White House, Congress, and agencies across the federal government. In addition, since 2012 NARA has required all federal agencies to use ERA to submit records schedules to NARA for approval by the Archivist of the United States, as well as to manage the transfer of all permanent records, electronic and non-electronic, to NARA. The adoption of ERA by federal agencies and the use of ERA to support the transfer of electronic presidential records have led to the transfer of increasing volumes of electronic records to NARA for preservation and eventual access through its public access portal, the National Archives Catalog (NAC).

In late 2018 NARA launched a new system, ERA 2.0, to update and enhance the agency's capabilities to meet the ever-expanding challenges in preserving born-electronic records and digitized material. ERA 2.0 uses cloud services for greater scalability in terms of storage and computer processing to increase NARA's ability to preserve and provide access to greater amounts of digital material over time.

The ERA 2.0 system consists of three major components: a digital processing environment, a digital object repository, and a business object management component. The processing component provides the capability to upload digital material of all types, gives staff a variety of software tools for verification and processing, supports the creation and editing of metadata, and allows users to submit packages of processed digital material to the repository component for preservation. The repository supports the capability to ingest processed digital material to provide for safe archival storage, delivers advanced staff search and discovery capabilities, provides digital material for further processing for preservation, and makes copies of records available for public access through NAC. The business object management component, slated for deployment to federal agencies by early 2023, will provide a redesign of the online forms and approval workflows used by NARA and federal agencies to schedule and transfer records to NARA. For more information about ERA, see archives.gov/era.

Applied Research Division

NARA's Applied Research Division serves as the agency's center for advanced and applied research capabilities in the fields of computer science, engineering, and archival science. The division's staff conducts research on new technologies, both for awareness of new types of electronic record formats that will need to be preserved and to evaluate new technologies that might be incorporated into electronic records management and preservation systems at NARA to increase their effectiveness. The staff also helps NARA managers and employees acquire the knowledge and skills they need to function effectively in e-government through presentations on new technologies. For more information, visit archives. gov/applied-research.

NARA's Website

The online entrance to the National Archives is archives.gov, which provides the most widely available means of electronic access to information about and services available from NARA. Links to various sections provide help to the particular needs of researchers, including veterans and their families, educators and students, and the general public—as well as records managers, journalists, historians, and members of Congress.

The NARA website provides the following:

- Directions on how to contact NARA and conduct research at its facilities around the country
- Direct access to certain archived electronic records at archives.gov/aad
- Digital copies of selected archived documents
- A contact form, at archives.gov/contact, for customer questions, reference requests, comments, and complaints
- Electronic versions of *Federal Register* publications
- Online exhibits
- Classroom resources for students and teachers at archives.gov/education
- Online tools such as eVetRecs (archives.gov/veterans/military-service-records), which allows veterans and their next-of-kin to complete and print, for mail-in submission, requests for their military service records

Public Access Projects

NARA's Office of Innovation is responsible for oversight of the digitization of NARA's holdings and for ensuring public access through NAC (catalog.archives.gov). The Office of Innovation is constantly developing improved tools, techniques, and workflows to accelerate access. In the coming years the Office of Innovation will continue to find new ways to improve digitization and access as we work toward our strategic goal of 500 million pages available in the catalog by the end of FY 2024. For more information, see https://www.archives.gov/about/plans-reports/strategic-plan.

Engagement with "citizen archivists" also represents a critical component to improving access. The tagging, transcribing, and commenting performed by public volunteers help to make NARA's holdings more discoverable to researchers through the addition of critical metadata and searchable text.

The History Hub (History.gov) is another tool that helps expand access to the nation's history and to NARA's holdings. After registering on the History Hub, individuals can submit questions about U.S. history; the platform allows responses from NARA staff, staff at other participating cultural heritage organizations such as the Library of Congress, and the public. This crowdsourced platform helps eliminate the silos that exist between information residing at different organizations and allows researchers, citizen historians, and archival professionals to more easily find answers to their questions.

Social Media

NARA uses multiple social media platforms to increase access to the records in its holdings, which is at the heart of its mission. The main goals of social media at NARA are to increase awareness about archival holdings and programs and to enrich the agency's relationship with the public through conversations about its mission, services, and holdings. In addition to expanding access, use of social media creates a more collaborative work environment and increases communication and knowledge sharing both within NARA and externally with other federal agencies.

The National Archives has 18 blogs, including one by the Archivist of the United States. NARA also offers historical videos from its holdings and videos of recent public events on the agency's 12 YouTube channels. The agency shares photographs and documents from its collections through Flickr Commons. Across the country, more than 200 NARA staff contribute actively to the agency's 120-plus social media accounts, including Facebook, Twitter, Tumblr, Instagram, LinkedIn, and others.

Social media also allows NARA's researchers and friends, as well as the public, to become citizen archivists by tagging, sharing, and transcribing documents. For more information, go to archives.gov/citizen-archivist.

Additional information about NARA's social media projects is available at archives.gov/social-media.

National Archives Museum

The National Archives Museum, a set of interconnected resources made possible by a public–private partnership between NARA and the National Archives Foundation, provides a variety of ways to explore the power and importance of the nation's records.

The Rotunda for the Charters of Freedom at the National Archives Building in Washington, D.C., is the centerpiece of the National Archives Museum. On display are the Declaration of Independence, the Constitution, and the Bill of Rights—known collectively as the Charters of Freedom. The Public Vaults is a 9,000-square-foot permanent exhibition that conveys the feeling of going beyond the walls of the Rotunda and into the stacks and vaults of the working archives. Dozens of individual exhibits, many of them interactive, reveal the breadth and variety of NARA's holdings.

Complementing the Public Vaults, the Lawrence F. O'Brien Gallery hosts a changing array of topical exhibits based on National Archives records. The 290-seat William G. McGowan Theater is a showplace for NARA's extensive audiovisual holdings and serves as a forum for lectures and discussions.

The David M. Rubenstein Gallery houses a permanent interactive exhibit, Records of Rights, which documents the struggles and debates over civil rights and liberties throughout American history. The Rubenstein Gallery is also home to a 1297 copy of the Magna Carta, owned by Rubenstein.

The Boeing Learning Center is an open and engaging educational space for teachers, parents, and families to explore documents found in the exhibits and in the NARA catalog. The center's education Learning Lab offers an immersive field trip adventure for middle and high school students that links NARA holdings to the curriculum in the classroom. Weekly programs are offered in the Boeing Learning Center for elementary school children as well as families. The center also offers educators professional development opportunities throughout the year as well as weeklong summer workshops.

DocsTeach (docsteach.org) is an education website designed to provide instructional resources to teachers in order to support best practices of teaching with primary sources. Using documents in NARA's holdings as teachable resources, DocsTeach provides teachers with the tools and resources they need to foster civic literacy and civic engagement. This site gives all teachers access to primary sources, instruction in best practices, and opportunities to interact with their counterparts across the nation.

When developing the DocsTeach site, the agency established an online community that serves as a virtual meeting place for NARA's education team and colleagues from schools, institutions, and organizations nationwide to collaborate and share innovative ideas and best practices for this online resource.

The National Archives' New York City field office is located in the Alexander Hamilton U.S. Custom House at the southern tip of Manhattan. There, NARA has a large research center as well as diverse educational and program activities offered for free in the Learning Center. The Learning Center incorporates many of the resources and activities found in the Washington, D.C., building but also includes New York-specific offerings.

At its Kansas City, Missouri, field office at 400 West Pershing Road, NARA also has a welcome center, changing exhibitions, workshops, and other public programs.

A set of webpages now makes the National Archives Museum available anywhere. An illustrated history of the Charters of Freedom can be found there, as well as information on educational programs, special events, and current exhibits at the National Archives.

Those traveling to Washington can bypass the public line during peak tourist season by making online reservations at recreation.gov. For more information, see the National Archives Museum at museum.archives.gov. An online version of the Records of Rights exhibition is available at recordsofrights.org.

National Archives Research Centers

At the Robert M. Warner Research Center in the National Archives Building in Washington, D.C., and the Steny H. Hoyer Research Center at the National Archives at College Park, Maryland, researchers can consult with staff experts on federal records held in each building and submit requests to examine original documents.

The Warner Research Center holds approximately 275,000 rolls of microfilmed records documenting military service prior to World War I, immigration into the United States, the federal census, the U.S. Congress, federal courts in the District of Columbia, the Bureau of Indian Affairs, and the Freedmen's Bureau. The center also contains an extensive, ever-expanding system of reference reports, helping researchers conduct research in federal documents.

Executive branch records housed in the National Archives Building include those of the Bureau of Indian Affairs and of civilian agencies responsible for maritime affairs. Military records in this building include those of the Army before World War I and the Navy and Marine Corps before World War II. In addition, the National Archives Building holds many records relating to the federal government's interaction with individuals; these are often consulted for genealogical research.

The Steny H. Hoyer Research Center holds textual records of civilian agencies from 1789; investigative records and military holdings that include those from the Army and Army Air Forces dating from World War I; and Navy, Marine Corps, intelligence, defense-related, and seized enemy records dating from World War II. In addition to textual records, special media records include motion pictures, still photographs and posters, sound recordings, maps, architectural drawings, aerial photographs, and electronic records. A research room for accessioned microfilm holds records of the Department of State's Berlin Document Center and other World War II-era captured documents.

Field Archives

NARA has 12 field archives where the public can do research. They are located in or near Boston, New York, Philadelphia, Atlanta, Chicago, St. Louis, Kansas City, Fort Worth, Denver, Riverside (California), San Francisco, and Seattle. Archived records of significance, as well as, in some locations, immigration records, are available for use by the public in these field archives.

Presidential Libraries

NARA operates presidential libraries for the 15 most recent U.S. presidents, from Herbert Hoover through Donald J. Trump. Presidential libraries bring together the documents and artifacts of a president and his administration and make them available to the public for study and discussion without regard for political considerations or affiliations. In addition to archiving and preserving presidential papers and objects, presidential libraries bring history to millions of visitors from around the world through public and educational programs, exhibits, and other outreach activities. At archives.gov/presidential-libraries, visitors can learn about the presidential library system as a whole and link to individual library websites to learn about the lives of the presidents and the times in which they served.

Federal Records Centers Program

NARA also serves federal agencies, the courts, and Congress by providing records storage, reference service, life-cycle management, and guidance on many issues relating to records management. A network of 18 Federal Records Centers (FRCs) stores 27 million cubic feet (about 52 billion pages) of noncurrent records for 200 agencies.

The Federal Records Centers program is nationwide. NARA has records centers in or near Atlanta; Boston; Chicago; Dayton; Denver; Fort Worth; Kansas City; Miamisburg, Ohio; Lee's Summit, Missouri; Lenexa, Kansas; Philadelphia; Pittsfield, Massachusetts; Riverside, California; St. Louis; San Francisco; Seattle; Suitland, Maryland; and Valmeyer, Illinois.

Genealogy Research

Genealogy research brings thousands of people to NARA facilities every year. In its holdings, NARA has census records dating back to 1790, records dealing with immigration, land and pension records, and passenger lists from ships arriving from all over the world.

NARA is often considered the first stop in searching for one's ancestry, either at its facilities in the Washington, D.C., area or one of its 12 field archives around the country. At these locations, NARA staff offer genealogy workshops to show the public how to look through documents dating back to the Revolutionary period.

NARA also offers an annual Genealogy Fair that is now a virtual event at which NARA staffers provide tips and techniques for researching genealogy records at the National Archives. Lectures are designed for experienced genealogy professionals and novices alike. Watch past fairs online at archives.gov/calendar/genealogy-fair.

NARA maintains close relationships with genealogical associations as well as organizations such as Ancestry.com and Fold3, whose online resources can be accessed without charge at any NARA location.

The National Archives has the census schedules from 1790 to 1940 available on microfilm. (Most of the 1890 census was destroyed in a Department of Commerce fire, although partial records are available for some states.)

Archives Library Information Center (ALIC)

The Archives Library Information Center (ALIC) provides access to information on American history and government, archival administration, information management, and government documents. ALIC is located in the National Archives at College Park, Maryland. Customers also can visit ALIC on the Internet at archives.gov/research/alic, where they will find "Reference at Your Desk" Internet links, staff-compiled bibliographies and publications, and an online library catalog. ALIC can be reached by telephone at 301-837-3415.

Government Documents

Government publications are generally available to researchers at many of the 1,250 congressionally designated federal depository libraries throughout the nation. A record set of these publications also is part of NARA's archival holdings. Publications of the U.S. Government (Record Group 287) is a collection of selected publications of government agencies, arranged by the SuDoc classification system devised by the Office of the Superintendent of Documents at the U.S. Government Publishing Office (GPO).

The core of the collection is a library established in 1895 by GPO's Public Documents Division. By 1972, when NARA acquired the library, it included official publications dating from the early years of the federal government and selected publications produced for and by federal government agencies. Since 1972, the 25,000-cubic-foot collection has been augmented periodically with accessions of government publications selected by the Office of the Superintendent of Documents as a by-product of its cataloging activity. As with the federal depository library collections, the holdings in NARA's Record Group 287 comprise only a portion of all U.S. government publications.

NARA Publications

Historically, NARA has published guides and indexes to various portions of its archival holdings. Many of these are still in print, although the most up-to-date information about NARA holdings is now available almost exclusively through online searches at archives.gov. The agency also publishes informational leaflets and brochures.

Some publications appear on NARA's website (archives.gov/publications/online), and many are available from NARA's Customer Service Center in College Park, Maryland, by calling 866-272-6272. The NARA website's publications homepage (archives.gov/publications) provides more detailed information about available publications and ordering.

General-interest books about NARA and its holdings that will appeal to anyone with an interest in U.S. history as well as facsimiles of certain documents are published by the National Archives Foundation. They are for sale at the foundation's National Archives Store in NARA's downtown Washington, D.C., building and through the store's website at nationalarchivesstore.org.

Federal Register

The *Federal Register* is the daily gazette of the U.S. government, containing presidential documents, proposed and final federal regulations, and public notices of federal agencies. It is published by the Office of the Federal Register and printed and distributed by GPO. The two agencies collaborate in the same way to produce the annual revisions of the *Code of Federal Regulations* (*CFR*). Free access to the full text of the electronic version of the *Federal Register* and *CFR*, and to an unofficial, daily-updated electronic *CFR* (the e-CFR), is available via fdsys. gov. *Federal Register* documents scheduled for future publication are available for public inspection at the Office of the Federal Register (7 G Street, N.W., Suite A-734, Washington, DC 20401) or online at the electronic Public Inspection Desk (federal register.gov/public-inspection). Federalregister.gov provides access to proposed rules, and rules published in the *Federal Register* are open for public comment. (The website federalregister.gov and the multiagency website regulations.gov also provide the means to comment on these documents.)

The full catalog of other Office of the Federal Register publications is posted at ofr.gov and includes the *Compilation of Presidential Documents*, *Public Papers of the Presidents*, slip laws, *United States Statutes at Large*, and the *United States Government Manual*. Printed or microfiche editions of Office of the Federal Register publications also are maintained at federal depository libraries (gpo.gov/libraries).

The Public Law Electronic Notification Service (PENS) is a free subscription email service for notification of recently enacted public laws. Varied subscriptions to the daily *Federal Register* are available from federalregister.gov. Additional information about Office of the Federal Register programs appears on Facebook (facebook.com/federalregister) and Twitter (@FedRegister).

The Office of the Federal Register also publishes information about its ministerial responsibilities associated with the operation of the Electoral College and ratification of constitutional amendments and provides access to related records. Publication information concerning laws, regulations, and presidential documents and services is available from the Office of the Federal Register (telephone 202-741-6070). Information on Federal Register finding aids, the Electoral College, and constitutional amendments is available through archives.gov/federal-register.

Publications can be ordered by contacting GPO at bookstore.gpo.gov or by toll-free telephone at 866-512-1800. To submit orders by fax or by mail, see bookstore.gpo.gov/help-and-contact.

Grants

The National Historical Publications and Records Commission (NHPRC) is the national grants program of the National Archives. The Archivist of the United States chairs the commission and makes grants on its recommendation. NHPRC's 14 other members represent the president (two appointees), the Supreme Court, the Senate and House of Representatives, the departments of State and Defense, the Librarian of Congress, the American Association for State and Local History, the American Historical Association, the Association for Documentary Editing, the National Association of Government Archives and Records Administrators, the Organization of American Historians, and the Society of American Archivists.

NHPRC's mission is to provide opportunities for the American people to discover and use records that increase understanding of the nation's democracy, history, and culture. Through leadership initiatives, grants, and fostering the creation of new tools and methods, the commission connects the work of the National Archives to the work of the nation's archives. NHPRC grants help archives, universities, historical societies, professional organizations, and other nonprofit organizations to establish or strengthen archival programs, improve training and techniques, preserve and process records collections, and provide access to them through finding aids, digitization of collections, and documentary editions of the papers of significant historical figures and movements in American history. The commission works in partnership with a national network of state archives and state historical records advisory boards to develop a national archival infrastructure. For more information about the commission, visit archives.gov/nhprc. For more information about the projects it supports, go to faccbook.com/nhprc.

Administration

The head of NARA is David S. Ferriero, who was appointed Archivist of the United States in 2009 by President Barack Obama and is set to retire in April 2022. As of January 2022 the agency employed 2,551 people working at NARA locations around the country.

National Center for Education Statistics

U.S. Department of Education, Institute of Education Sciences
Potomac Center Plaza, 550 12th St. S.W., 4th fl., Washington, DC 20202

Christopher A. Cody and Tara Lawley
Academic Libraries, Integrated Postsecondary Education Data System

Maura Spiegelman
School Library Media Centers, Schools and Staffing Survey/
National Teacher and Principal Survey

In an effort to collect and disseminate more complete statistical information about libraries, the National Center for Education Statistics (NCES) initiated a formal library statistics program in 1989 that included surveys on academic libraries, school library media centers, public libraries, and state libraries. At the end of December 2006, the Public Libraries Survey and the State Library Agencies Survey were officially transferred to the Institute of Museum and Library Services (IMLS). The Academic Libraries Survey and the School Library Media Centers Survey continued to be administered and funded by NCES. However, the School Library Media Centers Survey was incorporated into the School and Staffing Survey (SASS), and the Academic Libraries Survey was incorporated into the Integrated Postsecondary Education Data System (IPEDS).

The library surveys conducted by NCES are designed to provide comprehensive nationwide data on the status of libraries. Federal, state, and local officials, professional associations, and local practitioners use these surveys for planning, evaluating, and making policy. These data are also available to researchers and educators.

Past information about elementary and secondary public school library media centers is available on the School and Staffing Survey website, http://nces.ed.gov/surveys/sass/. The Library Statistics Program's website, http://nces.ed.gov/surveys/libraries, provides links to data search tools, data files, survey definitions, and survey designs for the complete Academic Libraries Survey files from 1996 to 2012. The IPEDS Academic Libraries Information Center, http://nces.ed.gov/ipeds/Section/Alscenter, contains current survey definitions and designs, and the IPEDS Use the Data Website at https://nces.ed.gov/ipeds/Home/UseTheData contains complete data files for the Academic Libraries component beginning in 2014. The two library surveys conducted by NCES are described below.

Academic Libraries

The IPEDS Academic Libraries (AL) component provides descriptive statistics from academic libraries in the 50 states, the District of Columbia, and, if applicable, other U.S. jurisdictions (Guam, the Commonwealth of the Northern Mariana Islands, Puerto Rico, and the U.S. Virgin Islands).

NCES surveyed academic libraries on a three-year cycle between 1966 and 1988. From 1988 to 1998, AL was a component of IPEDS collected on a two-year cycle. From 2000 to 2012, the Academic Libraries Survey (ALS) separated from IPEDS but remained on a two-year cycle as part of the Library Statistics Program.

During this time period, IPEDS and ALS data were still linked by the identification codes of the postsecondary education institutions. In aggregate, these data provide an overview of the status of academic libraries nationally and by state. Beginning with the 2014–2015 collection cycle, AL was reintegrated back into IPEDS, and the AL component became a mandatory, annual survey for all degree-granting Title IV institutions. It was at this time that many questions from the 2012 ALS collections and services sections were removed or revised. Since 2014, the AL component has undergone many changes.

Currently, the 2021–2022 AL survey collects data on libraries in the entire universe of degree-granting Title IV postsecondary institutions using a web-based data collection system. The survey component collects the counts and the circulation/usage of books, serials, media, and databases, both in physical and electronic formats. Additionally, academic libraries report on interlibrary loan services. Also, starting 2020–2021, the AL survey began collecting again information on library staff.

Institutions with reported total library expenditures over zero or institutions that have access to a library collection are required to report collections data, while those with expenditures equal to or greater than $100,000 are required to report collections and detailed expenditures data. Academic libraries report expenditures for salaries, wages, and fringe benefits, if paid from the library budget; materials and services expenditures; operations and maintenance expenditures; and total expenditures.

For the 2020–2021 Al survey, institutions were asked to report data to accurately reflect the time period corresponding with the IPEDS survey component, even if such reporting is seemingly inconsistent with prior-year reporting. NCES expected that some data reported during the 2020–2021 data collection year would vary from established prior trends due to the impacts of coronavirus pandemic. Additionally, for the AL survey, institutions were asked to include any library-related expenses that are covered by the Higher Education Emergency Relief Fund (HEERF) grants funded under the Coronavirus Aid, Relief, and Economic Security (CARES) Act, Coronavirus Response and Relief Supplemental Appropriations Act (CRRSAA), and American Rescue Plan (ARP) Act in the appropriate expense sections. These same reporting requirements were required for the AL Survey for the 2021-22 collection cycle.

For the final 2012 ALS data collection, a First Look report, "Academic Libraries: 2012" (NCES 2014-038), was released on the NCES website in February 2014, as were the final data file and documentation for the 2012 ALS (NCES 2014-039). NCES also has a web-based peer analysis tool for AL called "Compare Academic Libraries" (https://nces.ed.gov/surveys/libraries/compare/) using AL 2012 data. Beginning with the 2014–2015 IPEDS collection cycle and ending with the 2017–2018 IPEDS collection cycle, the following First Look reports were released for Academic Libraries:

- "Enrollment and Employees in Postsecondary Institutions, Fall 2014; and Financial Statistics and Academic Libraries, Fiscal Year 2014" (NCES 2016-005)
- "Enrollment and Employees in Postsecondary Institutions, Fall 2015; and Financial Statistics and Academic Libraries, Fiscal Year 2015" (NCES 2017-024)

- "Enrollment and Employees in Postsecondary Institutions, Fall 2016; and Financial Statistics and Academic Libraries, Fiscal Year 2016" (NCES 2018-002)
- "Enrollment and Employees in Postsecondary Institutions, Fall 2017; and Financial Statistics and Academic Libraries, Fiscal Year 2017" (NCES 2019-021)

Beginning with the 2018–2019 IPEDS collection cycle, IPEDS no longer produces First Look reports; however, AL data, web reports, and tables from 2014 and on are available via the IPEDS Use the Data website (https://nces.ed.gov/ipeds/Home/UseTheData). Academic library statistics information can be obtained from Christopher A. Cody, Integrated Postsecondary Education Data System, e-mail IPEDS@ed.gov.

School Library Media Centers

National surveys of school library media centers in elementary and secondary schools in the United States were conducted in 1958, 1962, 1974, 1978, and 1986, 1993–1994, 1999–2000, 2003–2004, 2007–2008, and 2011–2012.

NCES, with the assistance of the U.S. Bureau of the Census, conducted the School Library Media Center Survey as part of the Schools and Staffing Survey (SASS). SASS is the nation's largest sample survey of teachers, schools, and principals in K–12 public and private schools. Data from the school library media center questionnaire provide a national picture of public school library staffing, collections, expenditures, technology, and services. Results from the 2011–2012 survey can be found in "Characteristics of Public Elementary and Secondary School Library Media Centers in the United States: Results from the 2011–2012 Schools and Staffing Survey" (NCES 2013-315).

NCES also published a historical report about school libraries titled *Fifty Years of Supporting Children's Learning: A History of Public School Libraries and Federal Legislation from 1953–2000* (NCES 2005-311). Drawn from more than 50 sources, this report gives descriptive data about public school libraries since 1953. Along with key characteristics of school libraries, the report also presents national and regional standards, and federal legislation affecting school library media centers. Data from sample surveys are provided at the national, regional, and school levels, and by state.

NCES recently redesigned the Schools and Staffing Survey as the National Teacher and Principal Survey (NTPS). NTPS focuses on teachers, principals, and the schools in which they work. The 2017–2018 survey counted the number of school library media centers; data on library media center staff were not collected but will be part of the next NTPS. For more information about the NTPS or to review data collected in the 2015–2016 and 2017–2018 school years, visit https://nces.ed.gov/surveys/ntps/.

Additional information on school library media center statistics can be obtained from Maura Spiegelman, e-mail maura.spiegelman@ed.gov.

NCES has included some library-oriented questions relevant to the library usage and skills of the parent and the teacher instruments of the new Early Childhood Longitudinal Study (ECLS). For additional information, visit http://nces.ed.gov/ecls. Library items also appear in National Household Education Survey

(NHES) instruments. For more information about that survey, visit http://nces.ed.gov/nhes.

NCES included a questionnaire about high school library media centers in the Education Longitudinal Study of 2002 (ELS: 2002). This survey collected data from tenth graders about their schools, their school library media centers, their communities, and their home life. The report, "School Library Media Centers: Selected Results from the Education Longitudinal Study of 2002" (ELS: 2002) (NCES 2005-302), is available on the NCES website. For more information about this survey, visit http://nces.ed.gov/surveys/els2002.

How to Obtain Printed and Electronic Products

Reports are currently published in the First Look format. First Look reports consist of a short collection of tables presenting state and national totals, a survey description, and data highlights. NCES also publishes separate, more in-depth studies analyzing these data.

Internet Access

Many NCES publications (including out-of-print publications) and edited raw data files from the library surveys are available for viewing or downloading at no charge through the Electronic Catalog on the NCES website at http://nces.ed.gov/pubsearch.

Ordering Printed Products

Many NCES publications are also available in printed format. To order one free copy of recent NCES reports, contact the Education Publications Center (ED Pubs) at https://www.usa.gov/federal-agencies/education-publications-center-edpubs, by e-mail at edpubs@edpubs.ed.gov, by toll-free telephone at 877-4-ED-PUBS (1-877-433-7827) or TTY/TDD 877-576-7734, by fax at 703-605-6794, or by mail at ED Pubs, P.O. Box 22207, Alexandria, VA 22304.

Many publications are available through the Education Resources Information Clearinghouse (ERIC) system. For more information on services and products, visit https://eric.ed.gov.

Out-of-print publications and data files may be available through the NCES Electronic Catalog on the NCES website at http://nces.ed.gov/pubsearch or through one of the 1,250 federal depository libraries throughout the United States (see http://catalog.gpo.gov/fdlpdir/FDLPdir.jsp). Use the NCES publication number included in the citations for publications and data files to quickly locate items in the NCES Electronic Catalog. Use the GPO number to locate items in a federal depository library.

Defense Technical Information Center

Fort Belvoir, VA 22060
https://discover.dtic.mil

The Defense Technical Information Center (DTIC) is a Department of Defense (DoD) field activity, under the leadership of the Office of the Under Secretary of Defense for Research and Engineering. DTIC aims to be the premier knowledge resource for defense research, providing a robust science and technology (S&T) knowledge base to enable research and engineering and connect scientific communities.

With more than 4.7 million documents, DTIC is DoD's central resource for scientific and technical information, enabling the entire DoD research community to build on the accumulated knowledge base produced from the department's multibillion-dollar annual investment in S&T. DTIC provides digital applications and services that facilitate search, analysis, and collaboration, making information widely available to decision makers, researchers, engineers, and scientists across DoD.

In this capacity, DTIC has three main focus areas. Collection entails the gathering, preservation, and management of defense technical information. Dissemination involves the distribution of content across DoD to facilitate collaboration and discovery. Finally, the DoD Information Analysis Centers (DoD IACs) help solve DoD's technology challenges through rapid, flexible, and low-cost research services to acquisition program managers, DoD laboratories, Program Executive Offices (PEOs), and Combatant Commands.

Ultimately, DTIC aims to maximize the availability and use of DoD-funded technical information, while balancing information-sharing with information protection.

Reaching across the Federal Government

DTIC offers its capabilities to a broad user base within the federal government. Although some applications are publicly available on https://discover.dtic.mil, many are restricted to registered federal government and contracted personnel. Federal employees and contractors with a public key infrastructure card can access these sites with their credentials. More information about the benefits of and eligibility for restricted access can be found at https://discover.dtic.mil/dtic-registration-benefits.

Who uses DTIC applications and services? Among its registered users are:

- Acquisition personnel
- Active duty military personnel
- Congressional staff
- DoD contractors
- Engineers
- Faculty and students at military schools and universities
- Historians

- Information professionals/librarians
- Program analysts
- Program executive offices
- Researchers
- S&T advisors
- Scientists
- Security managers
- Small-business owners
- Software engineers and developers

Collection

DTIC's holdings include both public and access-controlled documents. Its information collection activities include working with DoD organizations and contractors; other U.S. government organizations and their contractors; and nonprofit organizations on gathering, managing, and preserving the results of DoD-funded scientific, research, and engineering activities. DTIC primarily accepts information electronically and, when necessary, in physical print and digital formats such as CD and DVD. More information about submission and selection is available at https://discover.dtic.mil/submit-documents.

DTIC's holdings include more than 4.7 million documents, such as technical reports on completed research, research summaries of planned and ongoing work, independent research and development summaries, defense technology transfer agreements, DoD planning documents, DoD-funded journal articles, DoD international agreements, conference proceedings, security classification guides, command histories, and special collections dating back to World War II.

Dissemination

The Research and Engineering (R&E) Gateway—accessible only to authorized users via https://www.dtic.mil—is the entry point to DTIC's full suite of applications, some of which are also available on the public website, https://discover.dtic .mil. In an access-controlled environment, the R&E Gateway offers access to DoD research, other scientific and technical information, and collaboration with other subject matter experts.

By providing the highest awareness of relevant information, the R&E Gateway helps the defense research community build on past work and collaborate on current projects. The broad availability of DTIC documents helps avoid duplication of effort and maximize the efficient use of DoD project funds.

DTIC's applications and products include:

- R&E Gateway Search—Available to registered users, Search is DTIC's principal application for discovering scientific and technical information from DTIC's repository of 4.7 million documents. With Search, users can access DoD's body of S&T knowledge to quickly find the most relevant information for their research needs.

- *Journal of DoD Research and Engineering (JDR&E)*—*JDR&E* is published quarterly for registered users. An access-controlled forum, *JDR&E* advances the development of DoD priority technologies through rigorous peer review of scientific research. The journal provides visibility into controlled defense research and promotes the scientific collaboration that results in new warfighter capabilities.
- PubDefense—In 2013 the White House Office of Science and Technology Policy mandated that federally funded, scholarly journal articles must be made available and free to the public following a 12-month embargo. PubDefense is DTIC's publicly accessible tool to access journal articles, conference papers, and related materials resulting from research funded by DoD and the Office of the Director of National Intelligence/Intelligence Advanced Research Projects Agency. Public datasets associated with these scholarly publications are also available through PubDefense. The application is available at https://publicaccess.dtic.mil/padf_public/#/home.
- Horizons—Horizons is an aggregate tool that enables users to track DoD research across its life cycle. Horizons has recently expanded to show growing technology areas, as well as research and funding sources, including DoD Grant Awards, research clustering, project maturity, and performance tracking. Horizons intends to deliver the information needed to deduplicate similar efforts and provide focus on DoD modernization priorities. The tool will also continue to provide additional datasets, linkages, and functionality over time.
- DTIC Thesaurus—Available to the public at https://discover.dtic.mil/thesaurus, the DTIC Thesaurus provides a broad, multidisciplinary subject-term vocabulary that aids in information search and retrieval. Subject terms, called Descriptors, are organized into hierarchies, where series of narrower terms are linked to broader terms.

DoD Information Analysis Centers

DoD IACs provide research and analysis services to, and develop scientific and technical information products for, the DoD S&T community in the broad domains of cybersecurity and information systems, defense systems, and homeland defense and security. DoD IACs draw on the expertise of scientists, engineers, and information specialists who provide research and analysis to customers with diverse, complex, and challenging requirements.

DoD IACs develop and provide a broad variety of research and analysis products and services, including customer-driven research and analysis; prototyping; answers to scientific and technical inquiries; access to the S&T community's subject matter experts; technical training; and wide-ranging scientific and technical reports, articles, factsheets, State-of-the-Art Reports (SOARs), and other technical information products.

DoD IACs deliver requirements-driven research, development, analysis, prototyping, testing, and concept-design services to DoD and other government agency research challenges requiring up to five years of effort and costing hundreds of millions of dollars. DoD IACs provide access to low-cost research and development contract vehicles with highly qualified, pre-vetted industry leaders across a broad swath of 22 technical areas of interest to DoD: Software and Data Analysis, Cybersecurity, Modeling and Simulation, Knowledge Management and Information Sharing, Advanced Materials, Autonomous Weapon Systems, C4ISR, Directed Energy, Energetics, Military Sensing, Non-Lethal Weapons and Information Operations, RMQSI, Survivability and Vulnerability, Weapons Systems, Homeland Defense and Security, Critical Infrastructure Protection, Weapons of Mass Destruction, CBRN Defense, Biometrics, Medical, Cultural Studies, and Alternative Energy.

Education Resources

National Library of Education

Knowledge Use Division
National Center for Education Evaluation and Regional Assistance
Institute of Education Sciences, U.S. Department of Education
400 Maryland Ave. S.W., Washington, DC 20202
https://ies.ed.gov/ncee/projects/nle

Karen Tate
Director

The U.S. Department of Education's National Library of Education (NLE), created in 1994, is the primary resource center for education information in the federal government, serving the research needs of the Department of Education, the education community, and the public. NLE resides in the Institute of Education Sciences' National Center for Education Evaluation and Regional Assistance.

NLE was created by Public Law 103-227, the Educational Research, Development, Dissemination, and Improvement Act of 1994, and reauthorized under Public Law 107-279, the Education Sciences Reform Act of 2002. The act outlines four primary functions of NLE:

- Collect and archive information, including products and publications developed through, or supported by, the Institute of Education Sciences, and other relevant and useful education-related research, statistics, and evaluation materials, as well as other information, projects, and publications, that are consistent with scientifically valid research or the priorities and mission of the institute and that are developed by the department, other federal agencies, or entities
- Provide a central location within the federal government for information about education
- Provide comprehensive reference services on matters relating to education to employees of the Department of Education and its contractors and grantees, other federal employees, and the public
- Promote greater cooperation and resource-sharing among providers and repositories of education information in the United States

NLE works closely with the Education Resources Information Center (ERIC). ERIC collects and archives information and provides a central location within the federal government for information about education.

The primary responsibility of NLE is to provide information services to agency staff and contractors, other government agencies, and the general public. Located in the agency's headquarters building in Washington, D.C., the library houses current and historical collections and archives of information on education issues, research, statistics, and policy; there is a special emphasis on agency publications and contractor reports, as well as current and historical federal education legislation.

NLE's primary customer base includes about 4,000 department staff nationwide, department contractors performing research, education organizations, education researchers, and the general public.

Collections

The focus of NLE's collection is on education issues, with an emphasis on research and policy, with some materials on related topics, including law, public policy, economics, urban affairs, sociology, history, philosophy, psychology, and cognitive development. In addition to current materials, the collection has books dating from the early 19th century, including approximately 800 books on education research in the United States and more than 25,000 historical textbooks. Some of these books were donated to the library by Henry Barnard, the first U.S. commissioner of education.

NLE maintains collections of historical documents associated with its parent agency, the U.S. Department of Education, having a complete collection of ERIC microfiche; research reports reviewed by the What Works Clearinghouse and special panels; and publications of or relating to the department's predecessor agencies, including the National Institute of Education and the U.S. Office of Education in the Department of Health, Education, and Welfare. These collections include reports, studies, manuals, statistical publications, speeches, and policy papers. NLE also serves as a selective federal depository library under the U.S. Government Publishing Office program.

Services

NLE provides reference and other information services, including legislative reference and statistical information services, to department staff, the education community at large, and the general public, as well as offering document delivery services to department staff and interlibrary loan services to other libraries and government agencies.

Contact Information

The National Library of Education's reference desk is available by e-mail at askalibrarian@ed.gov and by telephone from 9 A.M. to 5 P.M. weekdays, except federal holidays, at 800-424-1616 (toll free) or 202-205-5015. For the hearing-impaired, the toll-free number for the Federal Relay Service is 800-877-8339. The library is open to researchers by appointment from 9 A.M. to 5 P.M. weekdays, except federal holidays.

National Association and Organization Reports

American Library Association

225 N. Michigan Ave., Suite 1300, Chicago, IL 60601,
800-545-2433; http://www.ala.org

Patricia "Patty" Wong.
President

The American Library Association (ALA) was founded in 1876 in Philadelphia and later chartered in the commonwealth of Massachusetts. ALA has 49,851 members, including librarians, library trustees, and other interested people from every state and many nations. The association serves public, state, school, and academic libraries, as well as special libraries for people working in government, prisons, and other institutions.

ALA is home to eight membership divisions, each focused on a type of library or library function. They are the American Association of School Librarians (AASL); the Association for Library Service to Children (ALSC); the Association of College and Research Libraries (ACRL); Core: Leadership, Infrastructure, Futures; the Public Library Association (PLA); the Reference and User Services Association (RUSA); United for Libraries; and the Young Adult Library Services Association (YALSA).

ALA hosts 20 roundtables for members who share interests that are outside the scope of any of the divisions. A network of affiliates, chapters, and other organizations enables ALA to reach a broad audience.

ALA offices address the broad interests and issues of concern to ALA members. They track issues and provide information, services, and products for members and the public. Current ALA offices are the Chapter Relations Office (CRO); the Communications and Marketing Office (CMO); the Development Office; the Executive/ALA Governance Office; the Human Resources Office; the International Relations Office (IRO); the Library and Research Center (LARC); the Office for Accreditation; the Office for Diversity, Literacy and Outreach Services (ODLOS); the Office for Human Resource Development and Recruitment (HRDR); the Office for Intellectual Freedom (OIF); the Public Policy and Advocacy Office (PPAO); the Public Programs Office (PPO); and Publishing and Media.

With headquarters in Chicago, ALA's PPAO is based in Washington, D.C., and United for Libraries is in Exton, Pennsylvania. ALA also has an editorial office for *Choice*, a review journal for academic libraries, in Middletown, Connecticut.

Leadership and Strategic Planning

Patricia "Patty" M. Wong, city librarian for the city of Santa Clara, California, was inaugurated as 2021–2022 ALA president at the association's 2021 Annual Conference, held virtually. Lessa Kanani'opua Pelayo-Lozada, adult services assistant manager at Palos Verdes Library District in California, was chosen as 2021–2022 ALA president-elect. Other officers are Julius C. Jefferson, Jr., immediate past-president; Maggie Farrell, University of Nevada–Las Vegas, treasurer; and Tracie D. Hall, ALA executive director. Wong is the first president of Asian American heritage. Her major initiative was "Libraries Connect." Part of her commitment is to generate attention toward Asian American voices and communities, including an event at LibLearnX, ALA's new midwinter event, inaugurated in 2022, featuring interviews with Asian American leaders.

Amplifying Asian American and EDI Support of ALA Efforts

Wong worked with her team to bring additional attention and recognition of ALA and its core values to the greater Asian American community and to establish relationships with organizations serving underserved Asian Americans.

ALA Connect Live

In November 2021 Wong hosted an ALA Connect Live online program looking at equity, diversity, and inclusion (EDI) through the lens of programs, initiatives, and scholarships. Nicole Cooke, the Augusta Baker Endowed Chair and an associate professor at the University of South Carolina's School of Library and Information Science, facilitated a discussion that included Ray Pun, president of the Asian Pacific American Librarians Association (APALA), and Pambanisha Whaley, head of user services at Vassar College Libraries.

Connectivity Corner

This new Instagram Live bimonthly series (@americanlibraryassociation) focused on local library practitioners who are keeping their communities connected. The first Connectivity Corner event took place on September 17, 2021, on ALA's Instagram account (@americanlibraryassociation). Wong spoke with Chris Martinez, division director of information technology at Harris County Public Library (HCPL) in Texas, about his library's innovative efforts to connect the 13.6 percent of households in the county without internet access. Their conversation covered HCPL's recent application for thousands of hotspots and Chromebooks through the Emergency Connectivity Fund, a new Federal Communications Commission program to help schools and libraries provide tools and services for remote learning during the COVID-19 emergency period.

American Libraries columns

Wong's columns in *American Libraries* focused on universal broadband and digital access and the intersection of EDI and social justice in ALA's work. Hall wrote a series of columns that brought attention to such crucial issues as equitable information access as a matter of social justice and dismantling the school-to-prison pipeline.

ALA Statements

ALA issued a statement opposing widespread efforts to censor books in U.S. schools and libraries, particularly those focusing on LGBTQIA+ issues and books by Black authors or that document the Black experience or the experiences of other BIPOC individuals.

The ALA executive board released a statement opposing initiatives to censor information resources, curricula, and programs addressing racial injustice, Black American history, and diversity education.

The ALA executive board issued a statement in support of APALA in condemning ongoing anti-Asian hate crimes.

ALA praised the Library of Congress's decision to update the cataloging subject headings "Aliens" and "Illegal aliens." The Library of Congress's Policy and Standards Division, which maintains Library of Congress Subject Headings, announced the decision to replace the terms with new subject headings "Noncitizens" and "Illegal immigration" at its regularly scheduled meeting on November 12, 2021.

The ALA executive board joined the American Historical Association's (AHA) condemnation of the 1776 Commission report, which, according to AHA, is "an apparent attempt to reject recent efforts to understand the multiple ways the institution of slavery shaped our nation's history."

Contributed Revenue and COVID-19 Relief Grant Making

Hall stressed the goal of positioning ALA to earn enough contributed revenue to allow it to significantly expand its capacity to disseminate grants to the libraries experiencing funding and service reductions. Funds received from two funders, the Acton Family and the Andrew W. Mellon Foundation in fiscal year 2021, allowed ALA to distribute grants that made a significant difference in their communities

eLearning Website

ALA launched ALA eLearning, a new centralized web portal that brings together the most comprehensive digital collection of professional development for library and information professionals anywhere. Hall said, "ALA eLearning brings together the association's unrivaled capacity for education, enrichment, and advancement across all library types and services."

Sustainability Committee

In 2021 the ALA Council created the Sustainability Committee. The committee is charged with overseeing ALA strategic initiatives that promote the core value of sustainability within the policies, procedures, practices, and professional activities of the association. The committee works in collaboration with the ALA board and president, ALA Council, ALA divisions, ALA offices and units, ALA round tables, ALA committees, ALA affiliates, and ALA staff. In particular, the committee maintains a working relationship with several ALA offices and groups to affect meaningful sustainability-related outcomes and model best practices across the association.

ALA Honors

Martin Garnar Receives IFRT Immroth Memorial Award

ALA's Intellectual Freedom Round Table (IFRT) Immroth Award Committee named Martin Garnar the recipient of the 2021 John Phillip Immroth Memorial Award, which honors significant contributions defending intellectual freedom. The director of Amherst College Library, Garnar has served as a trustee and president of the Freedom to Read Foundation, chair of the ALA Intellectual Freedom Committee, chair of the ALA Committee on Professional Ethics, chair of the IFC Privacy Subcommittee, trustee of the Leroy C. Merritt Humanitarian Fund, editor of the tenth edition and co-editor of the ninth edition of the *Intellectual Freedom Manual*, and councilor of IFRT.

Robert Randolph Newlen Wins Lippincott Award

Robert Randolph Newlen was the recipient of the 2021 Joseph W. Lippincott Award. This award is sponsored by Joseph W. Lippincott III and presented by ALA for distinguished service in the profession of librarianship. The jury for the 2021 award honored Newlen for his many accomplishments during a long, varied, and distinguished career at the Library of Congress. He retired from his position as Deputy Librarian of Congress after 43 years of service. He currently serves as the executive director of the Dwight D. Opperman Foundation.

ALA Names Robert Wedgeworth Honorary Member

The ALA Council elected former ALA executive director Robert Wedgeworth to honorary membership in the association on January 26, 2021, during the Virtual Midwinter Meeting & Exhibits. Honorary membership, ALA's highest honor, is conferred in recognition of outstanding contributions of lasting importance to libraries and librarianship. Wedgeworth was nominated in recognition of significant contributions to the profession at large and the extraordinarily important work he did while leading ALA as its chief executive officer.

Milestones

Effective September 1, 2021, ALA Publishing, which includes ALA Graphics, ALA Editions/ALA Neal Schuman, *American Libraries*, Booklist, eLearning Solutions, Digital Reference-RDA, and Production Services, was renamed ALA Publishing & Media, reflecting general trends and areas of work as well as ALA strategic imperatives.

PLA welcomed Mary Davis Fournier as its new executive director. Fournier is a 20-year veteran of ALA, having served in various roles, including, most recently, as deputy director of PPO. At ALA, she spearheaded dozens of groundbreaking projects that have paved the way for innovation in the library field, including Libraries Transforming Communities; the National Impact of Library Public Programs Assessment (NILPPA); Building Common Ground: Discussions of Community, Civility and Compassion; and the first "One Book" resource, Planning Your Community-Wide Read.

Mary Mackay, ALA's publishing and media department head, was named interim senior associate executive director. In addition to her experience leading one of ALA's largest revenue streams, Mackay brings into her new role her considerable knowledge of publishing and conference services operations and insight gained overseeing the precursor to ALA's new Continuing Education revenue stream.

Robert Jay Malone became the new executive director of ACRL in early September 2021. Malone comes to ALA from the History of Science Society (HSS), where he served for 23 years. As HSS's first executive director, Malone furthered the organization's advocacy agenda, promoted EDI, oversaw and implemented strategic planning, created a fundraising infrastructure, served on a 22-member board, and worked with hundreds of volunteers.

Deb Robertson retired in October 2021 after nearly 40 years at ALA. Robertson founded PPO in 1992 to empower libraries to create vibrant hubs of learning, conversation, and connection through library programming. Under her leadership, the office has supported thousands of libraries with grants, program models, materials, and professional development. Among the most familiar are Let's Talk About It reading and discussion programs, Live at Your Library writer and artist programming, and a traveling exhibition program in collaboration with major museums and national libraries. Over the years, she raised more than $30 million to fund library programming initiatives while supporting ALA's strategic goals and forged countless internal and external partnerships, including with foundations such as the Bill & Melinda Gates Foundation, W.K. Kellogg Foundation, and John and James L. Knight Foundation and with institutions such as the Smithsonian, the U.S. Holocaust Memorial Museum, the Louisiana Endowment for the Humanities, and Tribeca Films. Melanie Welch now serves as interim director of PPO.

Aimee Strittmatter, ALSC's executive director, resigned from ALA effective August 31, 2021. Strittmatter joined ALSC as deputy executive director in April 2005, bringing to the division extensive experience as a children's librarian and children's services supervisor. In 2009 she was named executive director. In her 16 years, Strittmatter has provided leadership, strategic direction, and management oversight across a wide spectrum of ALSC's programs, initiatives, and operations and effectively managed and grew ALSC's resources and capacity by increasing its operational fund balance fourfold. Alena Rivers, ALSC's deputy director, is serving as interim executive director.

Kevin D. Strowder was brought on in June 2021 as the director of ODLOS. Strowder comes to ALA from Embarc Chicago, an organization that serves low-income high school students and prepares them for college and career success, where he was senior program manager for climate and culture. His previous positions include work with Chicago Cares, the Center on Halsted, and Mercy Home for Boys and Girls.

Lorelle R. Swader was named associate executive director for human resources after serving as interim in that capacity since March 2020. She was hired in 1992 as program officer/deputy executive director for the American Library Trustee Association (ALTA), which is now United for Libraries. In 1997 she became the director of HRDR. In this role, she was chiefly responsible for the ALA JobLIST Placement & Career Development Service. In 2011, while remaining director of HRDR, Swader became the director of the ALA-Allied Professional Association.

ALA welcomed Dina Tsourdinas as its new chief financial officer. Tsourdinas has worked in leadership roles in finance at several nonprofit and educational institutions, including the University of Illinois–Chicago; SOS Children's Villages Illinois, where she was chief financial officer; Childserv, where she was chief financial officer and vice-president of finance; and Adler University, where she served as associate vice-president of finance.

Melissa Walling was named the new associate executive director for ALA Offices and Member Relations (AOMR). She joined ALA in June 2019 as director of member relations and services.

Events and Celebrations

AASL National Conference

In the first face-to-face ALA meeting in almost two years, more than 1,500 school librarians, administrators, authors, and exhibitors convened in Salt Lake City, Utah, for the 2021 AASL National Conference. During the event, held October 21–23, 2021, attendees shared ideas, held conversations, engaged in sessions and programs, and reaffirmed their commitment to the school library profession.

Speakers included Omékongo Dibinga, author of *The UPstander's Guide to an Outstanding Life*, and Kekla Magoon, the 2021 Margaret A. Edwards award-winning author of more than a dozen novels and nonfiction books for young readers.

The General Session featured an intimate conversation among four school superintendents and principals who spoke about how administrators can empower a school librarian's leadership role to impact all learners as well as what administrators need and expect from their school librarians and school libraries.

There was also an advance screening of the award-winning documentary *TRUST ME*, a collaboration between AASL and the Getting Better Foundation (GBF) that shows how an avalanche of biased news and misinformation is undermining trust in society.

ACRL 2021 Virtual Conference

The ACRL 2021 Virtual Conference was held April 13–16, 2021. The event attracted 3,660 registrants and exhibitors who explored the complex issues impacting the future of library service. Themed Ascending into an Open Future, the conference included more than 300 programs addressing issues affecting higher education and libraries.

The session The Library Never Closes: Assessing Resources and Services after a Crisis showed how COVID-19 disrupted academic libraries, with librarians from three universities sharing data on their users.

Invited presenters included Kaetrena Davis Kendrick, dean of the Ida Jane Dacus Library and the Louise Pettus Archives & Special Collections at Winthrop University in Rock Hill, S.C., whose presentation was Creating an Open Vision for 21st-Century Libraries and Archives. Jennifer Brown, Jennifer Ferretti, and Charlotte Roh, administrators of We Here, an online community for BIPOC in LIS professions and educational programs, presented the session Systemic Oppression Requires Systemic Change: Recasting the Roles of Academic Libraries in Contemporary Contexts.

ALA Midwinter Meeting & Exhibits

ALA hosted the 107th and final Midwinter Meeting & Exhibits online Jan. 22–26, 2021. The event attracted more than 7,100 participants.

The second ALA conference to be presented virtually due to the COVID-19 pandemic, Midwinter connected librarians and library workers and offered inspiring educational sessions, featuring tools and best practices to navigate new paths in this time of uncertainty. The conference offered more than 30 educational sessions in the Symposium on the Future of Libraries and News You Can Use programs; more than 25 ALA division-hosted discussion groups; peer-to-peer live chat opportunities; and more than 50 committee meetings, most of which were open to observers.

ALA president Julius C. Jefferson, Jr. opened the event by welcoming attendees and noting that librarians have faced the need to pivot during the pandemic with innovation and resilience. Opening session speakers Ibram X. Kendi and Keisha N. Blain discussed their co-edited book, *Four Hundred Souls: A Community History of African America, 1619–2019*, a "choral history" of African Americans covering 400 years of history in the voices of 80 writers.

The ALA President's Program featured Joy Harjo, a member of the Muskogee (Creek) Nation and the first Indigenous U.S. Poet Laureate, who read several poems, including *My Man's Feet*, and from her latest collection, *An American Sunrise*.

Other featured speakers included actor, author, and member of the New York Public Library board of trustees Ethan Hawke, who lauded libraries; actor and author Cicely Tyson, who shared stories from her memoir, *Just as I Am*; Grammy-winning musician and children's book author (*Music Is in Everything* and *My Dog Romeo*) Ziggy Marley; author Natalie Baszile, who offered a heartrending discussion about her new nonfiction book, *We Are Each Other's Harvest: A Celebration of African American Farmers, Land & Legacy*; and author Emmanuel Acho, who explained why he chose to write his first book, *Uncomfortable Conversations with a Black Man*.

Special featured guests included National Youth Poet Laureate and Inaugural Poet Amanda Gorman, who read from her lyrical picture book debut *Change Sings*, and U.S. Sen. Jack Reed, who, in his special interview with Jefferson, spoke of his advocacy for public libraries and how it stems from a desire to help library staff on the front lines tackle such issues as information literacy and the digital divide.

Attendees visited with more than 220 participating exhibitors and enjoyed programs on 11 presentation stages in the Library Marketplace: Exhibits, Stages & Resources. They could browse Library Champion Spotlight sessions featuring new book titles; Book Buzz Bites; Live from the 25, a podcast listening booth; the Festival of Shorts, featuring short films and trailers; the Diversity in Publishing Showcase, an exhibit of diverse books and authors; and Swag-a-Palooza, with hundreds of free items for attendees. The Library Marketplace was open to all attendees January 22–25.

The Library Marketplace also featured keynote presenters, including comics authors Stan Sakai, Max Brooks, and Christian Cooper; children's book authors Matt de la Peña and Christian Robinson; HGTV host and new author

Mina Starsiak-Hawk; organizational psychologist and author Adam Grant; and activist Ruby Bridges in conversation with Carla Hayden, Librarian of Congress.

A highlight for many members of the library community and beyond, the celebration of the annual ALA Youth Media Awards honored the top books, digital media, video, and audiobooks for children and young adults—including the Caldecott, Coretta Scott King, Newbery, and Printz awards. The John Newbery Medal for the most outstanding contribution to children's literature was awarded to *When You Trap a Tiger*, written by Tae Keller, and the Randolph Caldecott Medal for the most distinguished American picture book for children went to *We Are Water Protectors*, illustrated by Michaela Goade.

The I Love My Librarian Awards were presented to ten outstanding winners whose exemplary service positively impacted their communities. The winners came from academic, public, and school libraries and were nominated by patrons nationwide for their expertise and dedication to their work. ALA received 1,865 nominations for this year's award, and the ten winners demonstrated the incredible achievements of librarians across the country. Their swift and effective response to the COVID-19 pandemic included hosting virtual programs, distributing books and technology safely to those in need, and ensuring uninterrupted access to books and resources.

Before the closing session, Jefferson announced the long-awaited new meeting concept from ALA. Scheduled to kick off in January 2022, LibLearnX (LLX), the library learning experience, is a dynamic, member-focused education experience designed to motivate, inspire, and engage attendees in discussions that will shape the future of libraries and their communities. LLX will emphasize active and applied learning, networking opportunities for library professionals, and a celebration of the positive impact libraries have on society.

First Lady Jill Biden, in a memorable closing session conversation with Jefferson, shared her commitment to education and literacy—and her love for libraries. Biden addressed the audience of librarians saying, "Never forget that what you're doing matters. Right now, someone out there is a better thinker because of you. Someone is standing a little taller because you helped them find the confidence they need."

Event sponsors included EBSCO, Gale, OverDrive, OCLC, Innovative, and Mango Languages. ALA student members and library professionals who had been furloughed, laid off, or experiencing a reduction of paid work hours attended the event at no cost.

ALA Annual Conference & Exhibition—Virtual

ALA hosted the ALA Annual Conference & Exhibition—Virtual, June 23–29, 2021. It attracted 9,142 attendees and 306 exhibitors. Designed to educate, entertain, and inspire librarians and library workers, the conference featured more than 200 educational live and on-demand sessions, live chat opportunities with authors and speakers, 28 featured speaker sessions, more than 175 publisher and exhibitor sessions on new book titles, 140-plus author sessions, a virtual exhibit floor with more than 300 participating exhibitors, Swag-a-Palooza with hundreds of free items for attendees, and more.

Day 1 of the conference focused on The Library Marketplace: Exhibits, Stages & Resources, with more than 300 exhibitors, Meet the Authors sessions, Book Buzz sessions, Book Buzz Bites, Library Champion Spotlight sessions, Swag-a-Palooza, and eight presentation stages. The Library Marketplace program kicked off with Youth Poet Laureate Amanda Gorman and her *Change Sings* book illustrator, Loren Long, in conversation with Librarian of Congress Carla Hayden.

Keynote speakers included President Barack Obama in conversation with secretary of the Smithsonian Institute, Lonnie Bunch, III, who discussed Obama's book, *A Promised Land* and Obama's appreciation for libraries. Pulitzer Prize-winning journalist and creator of The 1619 Project, Nikole Hannah-Jones, offered a look inside the project and discussed her two new books, *The 1619 Project: A New Origin Story* and *Born on the Water*.

The President's Program featured speaker, journalist, and author Isabel Wilkerson, the first African American woman to win a Pulitzer Prize. She is the author of *Caste: The Origins of Our Discontents*, which explores the structure of an unspoken system of human ranking and reveals how our lives are still restricted by what divided us centuries ago.

Other featured speakers included Stanley Tucci, author of *Taste: My Life Through Food*; Billie Jean King, author of *All In: An Autobiography*; Trisha Yearwood, author of *Trisha's Kitchen: Easy Comfort Food for Friends and Family*; David Copperfield, author of *David Copperfield's History of Magic*; Melissa de la Cruz, author of *Never After: The Thirteenth Fairy*; Eve L. Ewing, author of *Maya and the Robot*; Areli Morales, author of *Areli Is a Dreamer*; Savala Nolan, author of *Don't Let It Get You Down: Essays on Race, Gender, and the Body*; Charles Person, author of *Buses Are a Comin': Memoir of a Freedom Rider*; Leana Wen, author of *Lifelines: A Doctor's Journey in Public Health*; and Judy Tyrus and Paul Novosel, authors of *Dance Theatre of Harlem: A History, A Celebration, A Movement*.

Other highlights included a conversation with 2020–2021 ALA president Julius C. Jefferson, Jr. and IMLS director Crosby Kemper, III and a conversation with 2021–2022 ALA president Patty Wong and Chicago Public Library commissioner Chris Brown.

Favorite educational sessions, as indicated by attendee preferences, included Intellectual Freedom Is Meaningless Without Social Justice; Take Up the Challenge: An Actionable and Accountable Racial Justice Program; What's In a Name?: LGBTQ+ and Latinx Perspectives on Access Terminology—Challenges and Solutions; Why Psychological Safety Matters More Now Than Ever; and Libraries Are for Everyone: In-Person and Virtual Programming for Adults with Disabilities.

Event sponsors included EBSCO, Infobase, bibliotheca, China National Publications Import & Export (Group) Co., Gale, Modern Language Association, OCLC, OverDrive, Iowa School of Library and Information Science, Be Internet Awesome-Google, Iron Mountain, LibLime, MK Solutions, Mango Languages, OECDiLibrary, Reading Plus, SAGE, Springer Nature, Tutor.com, Virco, and VizMedia.

Banned Books Week

At a time when LGBTQIA+ books and books that focus on racism and racial justice are challenged for removal from library and school bookshelves, Banned Books

Week (September 26–October 2, 2021) was a reminder of the unifying power of stories and the divisiveness of censorship. This year's theme—Books Unite Us, Censorship Divides Us—underscored how books reach across boundaries and build connections between readers. Typically held during the last week of September, Banned Books Week spotlights current and historical attempts to censor books in libraries and schools. It brings together the entire book community—librarians, booksellers, publishers, journalists, teachers, and readers of all types—in shared support of the freedom to seek and to express ideas, even those some consider unorthodox or unpopular.

Giving Tuesday

The Development Office supported executive director Tracie D. Hall in ALA's Giving Tuesday (November 20, 2021) campaign. Donors were encouraged to help ALA in its fight against censorship. The 2021 campaign raised $31,045 on Giving Tuesday alone.

Library Card Sign-up Month

Each September, ALA and libraries around the nation celebrate Library Card Sign-up Month. In 2021 libraries participated by using such free tools from ALA as promotional artwork featuring the 2021 Library Card Sign-up honorary chair, Marley Dias, the 16-year-old author, executive producer of Netflix's *Bookmarks: Celebrating Black Voices*, and founder of #1000BlackGirlBooks; audio public service announcements featuring Phil Morehart, host of *American Libraries* magazine's Call Number podcast; and social media graphics in both English and Spanish. Libraries and library lovers were encouraged to share their stories on Facebook, Twitter, and Instagram using the hashtag #LibraryCardSignUpMonth. ALA's digital graphics are free for all to use on their websites and social media accounts. Since 1987 Library Card Sign-up Month has been held each September to mark the beginning of the school year. During the month, ALA and libraries unite together in a national effort to ensure every child signs up for their own library card.

National Friends of Libraries Week

United for Libraries coordinated the 16th annual National Friends of Libraries Week, held October 17–23, 2021. National Friends of Libraries Week offers a threefold opportunity to celebrate Friends—promoting the group in the community, raising awareness and increasing membership, and giving libraries and boards of trustees the opportunity to recognize the Friends for their help and support of the library. In conjunction with National Friends of Libraries Week, two awards of $250 are given to Friends of the Library groups for activities held during the celebration.

National Library Week

National Library Week was celebrated April 4–10, 2021, with the theme Welcome to Your Library. Key events included the launch of School Library Month on April 4, the release of the "State of America's Libraries Report 2021" on April

5, National Library Workers Day on April 6, National Library Outreach Day on April 7, and Take Action for Libraries Day on April 8. On Friday, April 9, ALA announced a new grant initiative to support libraries whose communities are experiencing information access and digital connectivity disparity. Additionally, in partnership with the Association of Bookmobile and Outreach Services and the Association for Rural and Small Libraries, ALA celebrated the first ever National Library Outreach Day.

Actor and author Natalie Portman served as 2021 National Library Week honorary chair. Journalist Dan Rather was interviewed over Zoom by *Booklist*'s Donna Seaman on Take Action for Libraries Day during an event hosted by United for Libraries.

AASL advocated for well-equipped and well-staffed libraries during School Library Month, which celebrates the essential role of strong school libraries in transforming learning. Various resources were available for download, emphasizing the message that school libraries are welcoming places that empower students and transform learning. Videos from past School Library Month spokespeople—including Dav Pilkey, Jason Reynolds, and Julianne Moore—provided powerful testimony about the value of school libraries. Other resources included an Open Education Resources toolkit and the AASL Developing Inclusive Learners and Citizens activity guide.

Preservation Week

Preservation Week, April 25–May 1, 2021, promoted the role of libraries and other institutions in preserving personal and public collections and treasures. Through a variety of resources, Preservation Week provides ideas for public events that can be held at libraries, institutions, and other community spaces and tips and tools for preservation and disaster planning. It is supported by Core: Leadership, Infrastructure, Futures, a division of ALA.

The 2021 theme for Preservation Week was Preserving Community Archives. Community archives are organized by members of physical or self-identified communities—specifically those marginalized by traditional collecting institutions—and are focused on documenting and interpreting their own histories. Institutions around the world use the hashtag #preswk to talk about their preservation programs and services.

Pulitzer Prize-winning investigative reporter and *New York Times Magazine* journalist Nikole Hannah-Jones was the honorary chair of Preservation Week 2021. As a journalist and founder of The 1619 Project, Hannah-Jones understands the significance of local and community archives collecting and preserving stories that counter dominant historical narratives. By exploring the history of civil rights and racial injustice in the United States, Hannah-Jones helps us examine and gain a better understanding of how these issues impact American society.

Sharjah International Conference and National Libraries Summit

The 8th Sharjah International Conference was held November 9–11, 2021, with 223 registrants from 17 countries. Live streaming of the keynotes reached close to another 400 virtually.

In addition to the Sharjah Conference, ALA's IRO and the Sharjah Book Authority created the National Libraries Summit, which was held November 8–9, 2021. Despite the inability of some national library leaders to attend due to the pandemic, representatives from 19 national libraries participated: six each from Africa, Europe, and the MENA Region, as well as Librarian of Congress Carla Hayden. The four topics of the summit were Visibility, Engagement, Impact, and Collaboration. The event allowed ALA to increase its contacts with national libraries.

Highlights of the Year—Offices

Chapter Relations Office

In 2021 ALA provided $1.25 million in emergency relief grants to 34 libraries that experienced substantial economic hardship due to the coronavirus pandemic. Through the ALA COVID Library Relief Fund, grantees representing academic, public, school, and tribal libraries received grants between $30,000 and $50,000 to support library services and operations. The ALA COVID Library Relief Fund was supported by Acton Family Giving as part of its response to the pandemic. The Andrew W. Mellon Foundation provided initial seed funding as part of its efforts to bolster educational and cultural organizations devastated by the economic fallout from COVID-19.

Communications and Marketing Office (CMO)

Media Relations

During 2021 32,470 articles mentioned ALA, with a total circulation of 35.7 billion. (Circulation rate is calculated using the number of articles/mentions multiplied by the monthly unique visitors for each media outlet's website.)

I Love Libraries

I Love Libraries is an initiative of ALA created to spread the word about the value of today's libraries. The site promotes the value of libraries and librarians, explains key issues affecting libraries, and urges readers to support and take action for their libraries.

I Love My Librarian Award

ALA received more than 1,300 nominations from library users for the 2021 I Love My Librarian Award, which demonstrates the breadth of impact of librarians across the country. Hundreds of nominations focused on librarians' swift and effective response to the COVID-19 pandemic, such as hosting virtual programs and distributing books and technology safely to those in need. The 2021 award recipients include four academic librarians, four public librarians, and three school librarians. Honorees each received a $5,000 cash prize, a $750 donation to their library, and complimentary registration to ALA's LibLearnX.

Public Service Announcements

CMO partnered with two celebrities to promote the value of libraries. YouTube sensation Blippi has entertained millions of preschoolers for years with his viral videos and catchy songs and has racked up more than a billion views a month on YouTube. Actress and author Isla Fisher voices the character Maddie, a poisonous (and adorable) Taipan snake, in Netflix's latest animated adventure, *Back to the Outback*.

Libraries Transform

Libraries Transform closed out the year with more than 18,600 libraries and library advocates using the free program in all 50 states, more than 100 countries, and all 6 inhabited continents.

International Relations Office (IRO)

ALA's Disaster Relief Fund sent $12,000 to the Bibliothèque Nationale d'Haïti to reestablish two of its public libraries whose locations were damaged and made uninhabitable due to the earthquake that struck Haiti in August 2021.

Development Office

The Development Office supported president Patty Wong, executive director Tracie D. Hall, and ALA's Philanthropic Advisory Group in hosting a celebration of ALA's donors and stakeholders, which attracted over 50 attendees.

Office for Diversity, Literacy and Outreach Services (ODLOS)

DEI Scorecard

The ALA Committee on Diversity created the Diversity, Equity, and Inclusion (DEI) Scorecard for Library and Information Organizations. The DEI Scorecard promotes accountability and transparency in gauging institutional performance on five measures of DEI presented in rubric format along with supplemental reflection questions: Embeddedness of DEI into the Culture and Climate of the Organization; Training and Education; Recruitment, Hiring, Retention, and Promotion; Budget Priorities for DEI; and Data Practices.

Rural Libraries Summit

From May 25–26, 2021, ALA's Rural, Native and Tribal Libraries of All Kinds Committee (RNTLOAK) hosted the inaugural Rural Libraries Summit in partnership with the Association of Bookmobile and Outreach Services, the American Indian Library Association, and the Association for Rural and Small Libraries. The two-day summit was attended by more than 100 and included sessions on supporting staff and the community during the pandemic and opportunities to increase library revenue through unique funding.

National Library Outreach Day

In collaboration with the Association for Rural and Small Libraries and the Association of Bookmobile and Outreach Services, ODLOS rebranded the former National Bookmobile Day as National Library Outreach Day, celebrated on April 7, 2021. In light of the invaluable role libraries have played in response to the COVID-19 pandemic, ODLOS and its affiliate partners were compelled to recognize all outreach efforts, including and beyond outreach vehicles.

Spectrum Scholarships

ODLOS awarded Spectrum Scholarships to 60 exceptional students pursuing graduate degrees in library and information studies for the 2021–2022 academic year. In addition, ODLOS received funding from IMLS for the four-year project, Spectrum Doctoral Fellowship Program: Catalysts for Change. With co-project director Nicole A. Cooke, ODLOS will recruit a cohort of 8–10 racially and ethnically diverse doctoral students focused on advancing racial equity and social justice in LIS curricula. The project will also build capacity and cooperation among partnering LIS degree programs to expand social justice curricula and increase support for BIPOC doctoral students and faculty in LIS.

In May ACRL, ARL, ODLOS, and PLA announced the formation of the Building Cultural Proficiencies for Racial Equity Framework Task Force. The group is charged to create a framework for cultural proficiencies in racial equity that can be used in public and academic libraries through conducting an environmental scan, drafting the framework, and seeking comments from stakeholders and the broader library community.

Human Resource Development and Recruitment (HRDR)

The Emerging Leaders Working Group has selected 49 people to participate in the 2022 class of Emerging Leaders. This includes 13 people who work in academic libraries, 28 who work in public libraries, seven who work in schools, and one who works in a special library. All but two, who work in Canada, work in the United States, and 65 percent of the participants are sponsored. The participants will work on 11 different projects.

Office for Intellectual Freedom (OIF)

OIF received an unprecedented number of challenge reports throughout fall 2021. From September 1 through December 1, 2021, 330 unique cases were reported to OIF, with December's reports still to be tallied. This can be compared to the 156 unique cases reported to OIF in 2020, a year marked by school and library closures, and the 377 unique cases reported to OIF in 2019 for the entire 12 months of that year. OIF staff provided confidential counsel in 275 of those cases, consulting on policy and procedure, providing legal information related to case law and legislation, and sharing information about challenged titles.

OIF worked with ALA's executive board, PPAO, and CMO to draft and publish a public position statement addressing the coordinated campaign to censor diverse materials in school and public libraries. The ALA executive board approved the Statement on Book Censorship on November 29, 2021, supporting those libraries and library staffers working to defend students' and library users' freedom to read across the United States.

In October 2021, with the support of ALA's executive board, OIF and PPAO convened a state legislative summit to examine adverse trends in state legislation that threaten libraries, library workers, or the ability of patrons to freely access information and to determine a course of action that leverages the full strength of the library ecosystem in responding to those trends. In early January OIF and PPAO released the State Legislative Toolkit, a public-facing resource with member access to sensitive or proprietary information. The toolkit will continue to evolve based on member feedback and legislative activity.

Public Programs Office (PPO)

ALA Editions and PPO published *Going Virtual: Programs and Insights from a Time of Crisis*, written by Sarah Ostman (2021).

PPO held a meeting for the Public and Cultural Programs Advisory Committee (PCPAC) at Midwinter 2021. For the ALA Annual Conference in 2021, the committee met again, and PPO, alongside PCPAC's Small and Rural Subcommittee, hosted three "coffee chat"-style events during the morning sessions of the conference. Each session was attended by at least 200 library workers to network and chat about programming during the pandemic.

With funding from the National Endowment for the Humanities (NEH) through the American Rescue Plan Act (ARPA) of 2021, the American Rescue Plan: Humanities Grants for Libraries opened applications to distribute up to 200 ARPA grants of $10,000 each to libraries, with an emphasis on reaching libraries in historically underserved and/or rural communities.

ALA and the FINRA Investor Education Foundation collaborated with a team of librarian advisors to develop a book list that eschews stereotypes and embraces diversity in telling stories and sharing skills related to personal finance and financial capability for children. The final guide will be free and available for download in March 2022.

Library workers were invited to apply for Let's Talk About It: Women's Suffrage, a reading and discussion project that will spark conversations across the United States about the women's suffrage movement.

The 2021 Libraries Transform Communities Engagement grant went to Albany Public Library in New York for Branching Out, a community program that aims to uplift local Black voices in music and art. The library received the second annual $2,000 grant, part of ALA's Libraries Transforming Communities (LTC) community engagement initiative. The Libraries Transforming Communities: Focus on Small and Rural Libraries initiative announced a total of 567 libraries to receive $3,000 to tackle issues such as media literacy, COVID-19 safety, and unemployment.

The inaugural Peggy Barber Tribute Grant, a programming grant named after the transformative ALA leader, went to Harrison Public Library in New York, the Montana Department of Corrections's Library, and West Liberty Library in Ohio. With funding from the Library of Congress's Teaching with Primary Sources program, the Teaching with Primary Sources: Women's Suffrage & Libraries initiative selected four advisors to take part in an effort to create and widely disseminate a programming guide, based on Library of Congress digital collections, that will help library workers nationwide lead informal education programs about the U.S. women's suffrage movement.

Highlights of the Year—Divisions

American Association of School Librarians (AASL)

AASL posted a letter to President-elect Joe Biden and incoming U.S. Secretary of Education Miguel Cardona stressing how school librarians are an equity-oriented solution to some of the most pressing concerns facing education. The letter was cosigned by ALA, 48 state-level school library associations, and the leadership of the AASL Chapters Assembly.

AASL concluded a year of snapshot surveys capturing national data on how school librarians are integral in uncertain times. Whether in virtual, hybrid, or in-person settings, school librarians were essential in helping and often leading the efforts of their educator colleagues to transition to remote teaching and learning. Results are a powerful advocacy tool to use in discussions with administrators to demonstrate the critical contributions of school librarians.

Association of College and Research Libraries (ACRL)

The ACRL board of directors approved funds to support up to 50 memberships for ALA and ACRL (a value of more than $200 per membership) for Black, Indigenous, and BIPOC library workers, especially those who serve underrepresented populations.

In 2021 25 outstanding individuals and institutions received ACRL awards recognizing their accomplishments. ACRL's top honor, the Academic/Research Librarian of the Year Award, was presented to Julia M. Gelfand, applied sciences and engineering librarian at the University of California (UC)–Irvine. ACRL continues to present the Excellence in Academic Libraries Award to recognize the staff of a community college, a college, and a university library for exemplary programs that deliver outstanding services and resources to further the educational mission of their institution. This year's recipients were the Davidson College E.H. Little Library (Davidson, North Carolina), the Tulsa Community College Library (Tulsa, Oklahoma), and the Loyola Marymount University William H. Hannon Library (Los Angeles, California).

ACRL's book publishing program was very active during 2020–2021, releasing 14 new books, including titles on information literacy, library outreach, open educational resources, student wellness, practitioner research, and more. In addition, the 2019 edition of *Academic Library Trends & Statistics* was issued in October 2020.

C&RL News, the official newsmagazine and publication of record of ACRL, adopted an online-only publication model beginning in January 2022. The December 2021 issue was the final print issue of the magazine. The ACRL board of directors and the *C&RL News* editor-in-chief sought input from the Budget & Finance Committee, *C&RL News* editorial board, ACRL Publications Coordinating Committee, ACRL Membership Committee, and ACRL Section Membership Committee on a variety of potential publication models for the magazine. The shift to an online-only publication model brings *C&RL News* in line with the *College & Research Libraries* (*C&RL*) journal, which moved to an online-only model at the beginning of 2014.

The ACRL Rare Books and Manuscripts Section's RBMS 2021 Conference was held virtually June 8–10, 2021. The conference critically examined the existing power structures that have shaped and continue to impact special collections and archives by exploring the power dynamics within our profession and the ways in which we experience, exert, and/or defy power. Conference programs provided participants with tools and strategies to inspire and lead to transformative change.

In October 2021 ACRL and PLA launched Benchmark: Library Metrics and Trends to power library data analysis and visualization. This new digital resource can help libraries plan, make informed decisions, and tell the story of their impact. Through Benchmark, library professionals have access to a centralized collection of their library data and the ability to compare with peer libraries using a robust set of visualization and reporting tools. Academic libraries also have access to ACRL's Academic Library Trends and Statistics Survey data. Subscribers will find an intuitive interface that supports analysis and reporting efforts. Virtual data dashboards and customized comparison tools are interactive and user-friendly.

Kristen Totleben was appointed the next editor of *C&RL* by the ACRL board of directors. Totleben, the librarian for modern languages and cultures at the University of Rochester's River Campus Libraries, will serve as editor designate from July 1, 2021–June 30, 2022, when she will assume full editorial responsibility for the journal. In the position of editor, Totleben will also serve as chair of the *C&RL* editorial board. She succeeds Wendi Arant Kaspar, professor of library practice at Texas A&M University.

In 2021 *Choice* launched Toward Inclusive Excellence (TIE), a multimedia platform devoted to social and racial justice. Under the general editorship of Alexia Hudson-Ward, associate director of research and learning at MIT Libraries, the service explores issues of EDI, particularly, though not exclusively, as they affect the academic library community. TIE incorporates weekly blog posts, as well as occasional podcasts and webinars, in which contributors explore the intricacies of racial identity as they relate to implicit bias, systemic racism, and ableism, among other pertinent topics.

Association for Library Service to Children (ALSC)

The Newbery Medal, established in 1921 and first awarded in 1922, is celebrating its 100th anniversary. The 100th medal and honored books were announced in January 2021. A yearlong anniversary celebration that kicked off in summer 2021 includes a host of special Newbery-related activities and resources to encourage widespread involvement and will culminate with the ALA 2022 Annual Conference. Commemorative merchandise featuring a 100th anniversary logo and limited-edition designs from Newbery-winning illustrators Cece Bell, Jerry Craft, Kevin Henkes, Victoria Jamieson, and Grace Lin is available for purchase in the ALA Graphics Gift Shop.

Día

Last year marked the 25th anniversary of the celebration of Día (Children's Day/Book Day). Messaging and graphics were produced in English and Spanish with Día champions and similarly focused organizations. Día booklists provide engaging stories representing a variety of cultures and backgrounds to share with children from birth through eighth grade. Illustrator Reggie Brown created a special image that is featured on commemorative Día merchandise available for purchase from the ALA Graphics Gift Shop.

The 2021 ALSC Children's Literature Lecture Celebration

The 2021 celebration was held virtually on December 2, 2021, and honored the work of Rudine Sims Bishop, who was given the Children's Literature Lecture Award for 2021. Due to unforeseen circumstances, Bishop did not deliver the lecture. In lieu of a lecture, the event celebrated Bishop's work and her impact on the field of children's literature. A live, moderated discussion featured thought leaders in children's literature: Violet J. Harris (University of Illinois–Urbana-Champaign), Dianne Johnson-Feelings (University of South Carolina), Alexandra Kennedy (Eric Carle Museum of Picture Book Art), and moderator Jonda C. McNair (Ohio State University). The celebration also presented prerecorded remarks from numerous children's literature authors, illustrators, and leaders in the field, including Bishop.

A Celebration of Illustration!

This one-day virtual conference focused on art and illustration in children's literature was held on May 14, 2021, prior to the ALA Annual Conference. The event reached more than 100 people and included two general sessions and six education programs.

Charlemae Rollins President's Program

The 2021 Charlemae Rollins President's Program, The POW(!)er of Graphic Novels to Support Youth Literacy: Creators Speak, was held virtually on July 20, 2021, and featured a panel including Nidhi Chanani, Jerry Craft, Varian Johnson, and Nadia Shammas. The event reached more than 300 people. The POW(!)er of Graphic Novels to Support Youth Literacy: Successes in Libraries, ancillary programming to the President's Program, was held virtually on June 1, 2021. This panel of library practitioners discussed how to advocate for and incorporate graphic novels in home library collections and programming. The event was recorded and later presented on demand as part of the Comic-Con@Home Education Programming, in partnership with Comic-Con International.

Book & Media Awards Shelf

In March 2021 the Book & Media Awards Shelf was launched. This database-driven resource is a one-stop destination for approximately 2,000 ALSC award-winning titles, representing 100 years of awards history. The Book & Media Awards Shelf was designed to help library staff, educators, and families find books and media that support their needs and appeal to their interests.

Core: Leadership, Infrastructure, Futures

ALA and Core welcomed the removal of offensive "Illegal aliens" subject headings by the Library of Congress. Core president Lindsay Cronk said, "With the leadership and expertise of Core groups including the Subject Analysis Committee (SAC), Core is committed to pursuing approaches to address systemic equity issues in description [that] are sustainable, actionable, and appropriate."

The Core board of directors endorsed the Cataloguing Code of Ethics for use by the cataloging community. It was developed by the Cataloging Ethics Steering Committee in consultation with six working groups and members of the international cataloging community of practice.

Core e-Forum topics included Instructional Technologies and the Effects of COVID-19 on Library Instruction.

Eight libraries were chosen for the 2021 John Cotton Dana (JCD) Award, which recognizes recipients for their strategic communications efforts and provides grants for libraries that demonstrate outstanding library public relations. The award is managed by Core and consists of $10,000 grants from the H.W. Wilson Foundation.

Trevor Owens has been selected as the recipient of the 2021 Frederick G. Kilgour Award for Research in Library and Information Technology, sponsored by OCLC and Core.

Public Library Association (PLA)

PLA publishing had an active year in 2021, releasing *Pivoting during the Pandemic: Ideas for Serving Your Community Anytime, Anywhere*; *Strategic Planning for Public Libraries*; *Guidance for Social Work Positions at the Library*; the PLA 2022 Early Literacy Calendar (in English and Spanish); "2020 Public Library Technology Survey"; and "Benchmark Briefings."

PLA launched several online training series, including the PLA Leadership Lab: Embedding EDI in Library Leaders; Public Libraries: Partners in Workforce Development; Advancing Family Engagement in Libraries: A PLA Professional Development Series; and Census Data Literacy.

Benchmark: Library Metrics and Trends

PLA partnered with ACRL to launch Benchmark: Library Metrics and Trends to power library data analysis and visualization. This new digital resource can help libraries plan, make informed decisions, and tell the story of their impact. Through Benchmark, library professionals have access to a centralized collection of their library data and the ability to compare with peer libraries using a robust set of visualization and reporting tools. Public libraries have access to PLA survey data, Public Libraries Survey data (reported to IMLS), and census data. The new Benchmark tool provides the most comprehensive data available, aligning with ALA's commitment to serving as a clearinghouse for library data and trends. It fills gaps in U.S. libraries' ability to understand their performance in context with peers. Peer comparisons, or benchmarking, can help libraries support everyday decision making, establish baselines, and identify opportunities to improve service. PLA also teamed up with AT&T to improve digital literacy and promote broadband adoption among families and communities, particularly those who are newly connected to the internet and navigating homeschooling, employment, and other activities made challenging due to the COVID-19 pandemic. PLA and AT&T will offer a specially curated collection of digital literacy courses based on PLA's DigitalLearn.org training.

Inclusive Internship Initiative

After a one-year pandemic pause, PLA completed the fourth year of its IMLS-funded Inclusive Internship Initiative. Since its inception, 194 high school students at 141 libraries in 44 states have learned about careers in librarianship. Through community-based projects developed by the interns, many libraries have been able to reach new audiences and create partnerships that had not been possible before. Project highlights from the 2021 cohort included feminist book clubs, new partnerships to help immigrants navigate community college, and English-language learner programs for middle-school students. In the 2021 evaluation, 91 percent of mentors reported that the program allowed their library to increase their capacity to provide programming for diverse audiences and support diverse professionals. PLA will launch a toolkit in 2022 to support local and independent adoption of the Inclusive Internship Initiative model by libraries.

Reference and User Services Association (RUSA)

BRASS Fall Thing

The first ever BRASS Fall Thing, a new virtual event open to all, was held October 19–21, 2021. The theme was business information literacy. The event included a combination of live programming and access to vaulted programming. The seven hours of live programming included workshops and lightning talks focused on business information literacy; the Framework; and teaching students how to find, use, and evaluate business resources and information.

Carnegie Awards

Deacon King Kong, by James McBride, published by RiverheadBooks, an imprint of Penguin Random House, was chosen as the winner of the 2021 Andrew Carnegie Medal for Excellence in Fiction, while *Fathoms: The World in the Whale*, by Rebecca Giggs Higginbotham, published by Simon & Schuster, won the 2021 Andrew Carnegie Medal for Excellence in Nonfiction. The selections were announced at RUSA's Book and Media Awards ceremony, sponsored by NoveList.

EDI Speakers Series and Definition of Reference Update

RUSA held three programs as part of its Equity, Diversity and Inclusion Speaker Series. The series was free and addressed EDI issues in RUSA affecting whether to volunteer, the impact on recruitment, continued membership and possible burn-out, and any barriers or policies that may hinder participation.

RUSA updated the "definition of reference" in 2021. It had last been updated in 2008. RUSA examined the current definition of reference, how it compares to the current practice of reference, and what would be needed for a reaffirmation or redefinition of reference.

ASGCLA Group Onboarding

RUSA brought into its membership three former Association of Specialized, Government, and Cooperative Library Agencies (ASGCLA) groups: the Federal and Armed Forces Libraries Interest Group (FAFLIG), the Physical Delivery Interest Group, and the Accessibility Assembly. Since coming to RUSA, FAFLIG has updated its administrative structure and approved a new operating manual. The Physical Delivery Interest Group was added to RUSA's Sharing and Transforming Access to Resources Section (STARS) section. Upon coming into RUSA, the Physical Delivery Interest Group held a popular open discussion where the members were able to both introduce themselves and share examples of their current work with all of RUSA. The Accessibility Assembly continues its commitment to diversity and to accessibility of library and information services for all, including people with physical, sensory, or mental disabilities, as reflected in the ALA policy on library services to people with disabilities.

'Decolonizing the Catalog' Webinar

In RUSA's "Decolonizing the Catalog" webinar, a panel of experts explored recent efforts to draw attention to and amend harmful language in library records related to the African American experience in the United States.

United for Libraries

United for Libraries launched a monthly online program for members, United for Libraries Learning Live, which was held on the fourth Wednesday of each month through 2021.

Young Adult Library Services Association (YALSA)

YALSA and IBM are collaborating to offer a series of skills-based trainings and webinars to their librarian network across the United States aimed at helping diverse teens gain access to key technical and professional skills.

Teen's Top Ten

YALSA officially announced the 2021 Teen's Top Ten winners. The Teen's Top Ten is a "teen choice" list, for which teens nominate and choose their favorite books of the previous year. Nominators are members of teen book groups from 16 school and public libraries around the country selected by YALSA to participate.

Young Adult Services Symposium

The 2021 Young Adult Services Symposium, with the theme Biggest Little Safe Spaces: Serving Teens during Times of Adversity, was held with a hybrid virtual/in-person format November 5–7, 2021, in Reno, Nevada.

Publishing and Media

ALA Editions | ALA Neal-Schuman

Professional development books published by ALA in 2021 included:

- *Pivoting during the Pandemic: Ideas for Serving Your Community Anytime, Anywhere*, edited by Kathleen M. Hughes and Jamie Santoro
- *Intellectual Freedom Manual, Tenth Edition*, Martin Garnar, editor, Trina Magi, assistant editor, for the ALA Office for Intellectual Freedom (OIF)
- *RDA Glossary*, by the RDA Steering Committee (RSC)
- *The Six-Step Guide to Library Worker Engagement*, by Elaina Norlin
- *Cataloging Correctly for Kids: An Introduction to the Tools and Practices, Sixth Edition*, edited by Michele Zwierski, Joanna F. Fountain, and Marilyn McCroskey
- *32 Virtual, Augmented, and Mixed Reality Programs for Libraries*, edited by Ellyssa Kroski
- *Advancing a Culture of Creativity in Libraries: Programming and Engagement*, by Megan Lotts

- *Telling the Technical Services Story: Communicating Value*, edited by Kimberley A. Edwards and Tricia Mackenzie in collaboration with Core Publishing
- *Library Programming for Autistic Children and Teens, Second Edition*, by Amelia Anderson
- *Books under Fire: A Hit List of Banned and Challenged Children's Books, Second Edition*, by Pat R. Scales
- *Launching Large-Scale Library Initiatives: Innovation and Collaboration*, by Valerie Horton
- *Rightsizing the Academic Library Collection, Second Edition*, by Mary E. Miller and Suzanne M. Ward
- *Transfer Student Success: Academic Library Outreach and Engagement*, edited by Nancy Fawley, Ann Marshall, and Mark Robison
- *Learning Centers for School Libraries*, by Maura Madigan for the American Association of School Librarians (AASL)
- *The One-Shot Library Instruction Survival Guide, Third Edition*, by Heidi E. Buchanan and Beth A. McDonough
- *Introducing RDA: A Guide to the Basics after 3R, Second Edition*, by Chris Oliver
- *Going Virtual: Programs and Insights from a Time of Crisis*, by Sarah Ostman for the ALA Public Programs Office (PPO)
- *Let's Talk about Race in Storytimes*, by Jessica Anne Bratt
- *Fundamentals for the Instruction Coordinator*, by Caitlin A. Bagley
- *Foundations of Information Literacy*, by Natalie Greene Taylor and Paul T. Jaeger
- *Library Services and Incarceration: Recognizing Barriers, Strengthening Access*, by Jeanie Austin
- *Transforming Print: Collection Development and Management for Our Connected Future*, edited by Lorrie McAllister and Shari Laster in collaboration with Core Publishing
- *Libraries and Sustainability: Programs and Practices for Community Impact*, edited by René Tanner, Adrian K. Ho, Monika Antonelli, and Rebekkah Smith Aldrich
- *The Disaster Planning Handbook for Libraries*, by Mary Grace Flaherty
- *Introducing Scholarly Research: Ready-to-Use Lesson Plans and Activities for Undergraduates*, by Toni Carter
- *Compact Copyright: Quick Answers to Common Questions*, by Sara R. Benson
- *Profiles in Resilience: Books for Children and Teens That Center the Lived Experience of Generational Poverty*, by Christina H. Dorr
- *The Readers' Advisory Guide to Horror, Third Edition*, by Becky Siegel Spratford
- *Fundamentals of Planning and Assessment for Libraries*, by Rachel A. Fleming-May and Regina Mays

- *A Basic Music Library: Essential Scores and Sound Recordings, Fourth Edition, Volume 3: Classical Music*, compiled by the Music Library Association (MLA)
- *Creating Fundable Grant Proposals: Profiles of Innovative Partnerships*, by Bess G. de Farber
- *Library Programming for Adults with Developmental Disabilities*, by Barbara Klipper and Carrie Scott Banks

The publications board of the Society of American Archivists (SAA) selected for its 2020–2021 One Book, One Profession reading initiative the ALA Neal-Schuman title *A Matter of Facts: The Value of Evidence in an Information Age*, by Laura A. Millar.

ALA Graphics

ALA Graphics, home of the iconic Celebrity READ campaign and exclusive art from award-winning children's book illustrators, is also the official source of materials for National Library Week, Library Card Sign-up Month, and Banned Books Week, among other events. In 2020 American ice-dancing duo and Olympic bronze medalists Maia Shibutani and Alex Shibutani joined the Celebrity READ campaign, as did Marley Dias, the 15-year-old founder of #1000BlackGirlBooks. And from a galaxy far, far away, The Child (aka Baby Yoda, or Grogu) from the Disney+ live action television series *Star Wars: The Mandalorian* appeared on a READ poster and bookmark.

With a focus on diversity, new posters and bookmarks celebrated Black history, women's history, and Asian/Pacific American heritage, illustrated by Ekua Holmes, Laura Freeman, and Dan Santat, respectively. Sophie Blackall created a new poster and bookmark inspired by her 2019 Caldecott Medal-winning picture book, *Hello Lighthouse*.

American Libraries

American Libraries magazine is the flagship publication of ALA and its members, covering news, trends, professional development, commentary, and product information. It is published six times per year, plus one digital-only issue and occasional supplements.

In 2021 stories included a look at how the COVID-19 pandemic was affecting accessibility (March/April); Marshall Breeding's Library Systems Report (May); "The Reader's Road Trip," a feature celebrating 35 years of literary landmarks (June); the annual Library Design Showcase (September/October), recognizing the architectural innovation of new and renovated buildings; and a look at how libraries are adapting services to help small businesses during the pandemic (November/December).

Other highlights included previews and coverage for ALA's Midwinter Meeting and virtual annual conference and interviews with musician Ziggy Marley, TV personality Padma Lakshmi, and authors Isabel Allende, Kazuo Ishiguro, and Colson Whitehead.

American Libraries Online

Nearly 150 online-only features and "Scoop" blog posts were published at American Libraries Online (americanlibraries.org) in 2021. Much of the year's coverage centered on how COVID-19 continued to affect the library world, virtual and in-person library conferences, and library updates from Capitol Hill.

AL Direct

AL Direct is *American Libraries*'s award-winning weekly e-newsletter, covering library news, activities, technology, events, state and federal legislation, and more. It is delivered to nearly 31,000 library professionals every Wednesday.

Call Number Podcast

Call Number continues to release monthly, half-hour episodes (with occasional bonus installments) featuring conversations with librarians, authors, celebrities, and scholars on topics affecting the library world. Popular episodes in 2021 included Libraries and Hip-Hop, Serving Our Veterans, and the podcast's Halloween episode, Zombies!

Booklist Publications

Booklist's internationally recognized, award-winning publications include *Booklist*, the premier prepublication book review collection development resource for libraries; *Book Links*, publishing the very best literature-based resources for educators and school librarians; and, new in 2021, *Booklist Reader*, a monthly readers' advisory magazine for libraries and library patrons. The Booklist publications remain the most trusted collection development and readers' advisory resources in the field, publishing more than 8,000 original reviews annually. With counsel from its diverse advisory board members, and in addition to reviews, Booklist publications offer columns, essays, author interviews, lists, read-alikes, core collections, trend alerts, trade secrets, and other related content. Booklist also hosts informative and well-known webinars and the popular Shelf Care podcast. Booklist is the sponsor or cosponsor of various ALA media awards, including the Andrew Carnegie Medals for Excellence in Fiction and Nonfiction, the Michael L. Printz Award, the William C. Morris Award, and the Odyssey Award.

American Booksellers Association

333 Westchester Ave., Suite 202, White Plains, NY 10604
914-406-7500
www.bookweb.org

Founded in 1900, the American Booksellers Association (ABA) is a national not-for-profit trade organization that celebrates and supports independent bookstores. ABA provides information, education, business tools and services, author programming, advocacy, and an e-commerce platform for 2,400 members throughout the country. These stores prove that independent booksellers are more than transactional retailers—they are literary institutions, community centers, and third places that promote books and reading, support diverse authors, create a forum for an open exchange of ideas, offer cultural enrichment, add character to their neighborhoods, and contribute to the economic vitality of their towns and cities by keeping tax dollars and jobs local.

2021

In 2021 independent bookstores continued to rise to the challenge of the COVID-19 pandemic with the spirit, creativity, resilience, and passion that has historically defined this industry. In 2021 ABA prioritized six key initiatives to support its members: Antitrust Advocacy, Advocacy, Education, E-Commerce, Freedom of Expression, and Publisher Advocacy.

Antitrust Advocacy

ABA actively investigated and reported on how Amazon has impacted book sales with the end goal of bringing about the regulation of Amazon and its breakup into four separate businesses. To that end, ABA advocated in support of the Twenty-First Century Antitrust Act in New York state and the Ending Platforms Monopoly Act in the U.S. House of Representatives; came together with other organizations and businesses to form Small Business Rising and Rein in Big Tech, two coalitions protesting Amazon's antitrust violations and lobbying for legislation to protect small business; and promoted an ABA-published white paper, shared with all U.S. attorneys general, stating that Amazon has used anticompetitive behavior to monopolize the retail and technology industries.

Advocacy

In 2021 ABA lobbied for the interests of our members—pushing for a federal e-commerce assistance program to help independent retailers improve their e-commerce presence; lobbying to increase competition and control rates related to debit card interchange fees; and ensuring that the availability and conditions for Paycheck Protection Program (PPP) money took into account the needs of small businesses.

Education

ABA continued its primary mission of providing members with education, and as COVID continued, programming continued to be virtual. Virtual programming provided the benefit of accessibility as well as the flexibility for the association to offer continuous education throughout the year. In addition, ABA's two regular in-person conferences, Winter Institute and Children's Institute, both occurred online in 2021, with 1,600 and 650 attendees, respectively. ABA also provided networking opportunities for members to come together to crowdsource best practices through ShopTalks, meetups, an online forum, a Discord group, affinity groups, and other idea exchanges. During 2021 ABA produced more than 100 education sessions for members as well as dozens of educational resources.

E-Commerce

For many years ABA has provided an e-commerce solution for almost 600 of its member stores. Historically, e-commerce sales have been less than 1 percent of most stores' sales, but in 2020, as COVID shut down stores and consumer buying habits shifted, stores' e-commerce sales spiked to 80–100 percent, depending on the store's circumstances and COVID shutdown status. In 2021, as sales leveled off but remained significantly higher than they were pre-COVID, ABA began a two-year, $3 million upgrade to its platform to meet the needs of stores as they prepare for a post-COVID future of hybrid shoppers who shop equally in-store and online.

Freedom of Expression

As a wave of book bans started across the country in 2021, ABA provided resources and assistance to member stores that were faced with local school and library book-banning challenges. ABA partnered to produce and promote Banned Books Week to educate people about the dangers of book banning, and it partnered with other coalitions to speak out against the violations of the First and Fourteenth Amendments that the current bans represent.

Publisher Advocacy

In 2021 ABA continued to meet regularly with publishers to convey the value of the independent bookstore channel and advocate for better terms and support on behalf of its members. ABA produced a member store video to share bookstore stories as case studies to help educate publishers about members' businesses and their needs. ABA also conducted its first survey of members about publishers' performance in categories such as damages, diversity initiatives, and business-to-business terms. Results were analyzed for best practices to then share with publishers to improve their support for bookstores. These conversations and initiatives resulted in several programs and changes that helped bookstores.

Antiracism, Equity, Access, and Representation

In 2021 ABA continued the commitment to antiracism, equity, access, and representation that the association institutionalized in 2020 as an ends policy, with several new initiatives: an Advance Access program for underrepresented voices to introduce booksellers to diverse authors; a new diversity, equity, inclusion, and access membership manager position to better support diverse members; advocacy in support of more representation among publisher sales forces; a monthly affinity group for LGBTQIA2S+ members; a monthly affinity group for neurodiverse members; a quarterly LGBTQIA2S+ forum for community members to meet with ABA staff to share their needs and concerns; an expanded ABA Diversity, Equity & Inclusion Council to ensure more representation and support of historically marginalized members; an updated ABA code of conduct to address microaggressions at ABA events; the addition of closed-captioning for virtual events; institutional changes in programming to ensure significant representation among authors; an institutionalized land acknowledgment for virtual conferences that included a regular donation to the American Indian College Fund; waived fees for new BIPOC members; and a member dashboard to increase access to ABA's offerings and collect optional demographic information to better inform programming and support all members.

In addition to these 2021 priorities, ABA continued to support members through events (Independent Bookstore Day, Indies First, a national indie bookstore event for Lin-Manuel Miranda, and Indies Present for *Universe of Wishes*), collaborations with Oprah's Book Club and *Good Morning America*, indie-branded book promotions (Indies Next List, Kids' Next List, Indies Introduce debut author program), marketing (holiday shopping and seasonal assets), financial benchmarking, and its investment in BookShop as a minority partner of this e-commerce platform that shares 80 percent of its profits with local, independent bookstores.

Statistics

In 2021 215 independent bookstores opened, 41 bookstores closed, and 38 bookstores changed ownership.

Members

The pandemic hit members hard. In June 2020 a membership survey revealed that 20 percent of stores were in danger of closing by the end of the year. Bookstores saw a rally in Q4 2020, though, as stores started receiving PPP money, ABA launched a viral marketing campaign—#BoxedOut—reminding people of the costs and consequences in their communities of shopping at Amazon, and neighborhoods faced with more and more empty storefronts due to the pandemic rallied to keep their local stores and restaurants in business. The momentum continued in 2021. A February 2022 ABA membership survey revealed that 89 percent of reporting members reported higher sales in 2021 compared to 2020, and 70 percent reported higher sales in 2021 compared to 2019. However, those statistics only reflect gross sales. Throughout 2021 independent bookstores continued to experience an increase in costs, labor shortages, supply chain issues, and uncertainty in an industry notorious for its already thin margins.

Board and Staff

ABA has 40 full-time employees. ABA's chief executive officer, Allison K. Hill, began her tenure on March 2, 2020, just as the COVID-19 pandemic began. Hill is the first woman to serve as chief executive officer of the association. As of January 2022 ABA's executive team consists of chief operating officer Joy Dallanegra-Sanger, chief communications officer Ray Daniels, and chief financial officer PK Sindwani. ABA also has a volunteer board of 13 booksellers and bookstore owner members. ABA's 2021 board of directors included ABA president Brad Graham of Politics & Prose Bookstore in Washington, D.C.; co-vice-president/secretary Kelly Estep of Carmichael's Bookstore in Louisville, Kentucky; co-vice-president Christine Onarati of WORD Bookstores in Brooklyn, New York, and Jersey City, New Jersey; Kenny Brechner of DDG Booksellers in Farmington, Maine; Danny Caine of The Raven Book Store in Lawrence, Kansas; Jenny Cohen of Waucoma Bookstore in Hood River, Oregon; Cynthia Compton of 4 Kids Books & Toys in Zionsville, Indiana; Jake Cumsky-Whitlock of Solid State Books in Washington, D.C.; Kris Kleindienst of Left Bank Books in St. Louis, Missouri; Melanie Knight of Books, Inc. in San Francisco, California; Michelle Malonzo of Changing Hands in Tempe and Phoenix, Arizona; Angela María Spring of Duende District Books in Washington, D.C., and Albuquerque, New Mexico; and Tegan Tigani of Queen Anne Book Company in Seattle, Washington.

The Future

Like so many industries, independent bookstores experienced significant disruption to their businesses during the COVID-19 pandemic in 2020 and 2021. This meant significant challenges, but it also meant innovation in operations, experimentation with store models, and creative approaches to serving customers—all of which will continue to serve the industry into 2022 and beyond.

Association of Research Libraries

21 Dupont Circle NW, Washington, DC 20036
202-296-2296, email webmgr@arl.org
http://www.arl.org

Kaylyn Groves
Senior Writer and Editor

The Association of Research Libraries (ARL) is a nonprofit organization of 126 research libraries in Canada and the United States whose mission is to advance research, learning, and scholarly communication. The association fosters the open exchange of ideas and expertise; advances diversity, equity, and inclusion (DEI); and pursues advocacy and public policy efforts that reflect the values of the library, scholarly, and higher education communities. ARL forges partnerships and catalyzes the collective efforts of research libraries to enable knowledge creation and to achieve enduring and barrier-free access to information.

Following are highlights of ARL's achievements in 2021, many of which were undertaken in partnership with member libraries or other organizations. For more details, visit https://doi.org/10.29242/annualreport2021.

2021 Highlights

On reflection, 2021 represents a year in which ARL member institutions, like so many other organizations, faced daunting operational and strategic challenges resulting from COVID-19 and its reverberations, political polarization, ongoing mis/disinformation, and persistent violence against BIPOC people. In the evolving context, ARL came together virtually and strengthened through informal conversations, association meetings, and the largest number of attendees ever at the Fall Forum. We welcomed two new member institutions and engaged even more research library and archives employees in our Action Plan priorities and work.

This report outlines the association's progress in advocating for policies and practices that support expanding equitable access to information. Together with our partners, we advanced our commitment to accessibility, digital rights, and university-based publishing and advanced research policies related to funding, international students, research data, open scholarship, and the future of scholarly communications. This report describes the association's work to create diverse, equitable, inclusive, and accessible work environments, services, and collections, including revising ARL's governance structure to address structural inequities, relaunching the ARL Leadership Fellows program, and joining the U.S. Truth, Racial Healing, and Transformation Movement to establish a U.S. Commission on Truth, Racial Healing, and Transformation and an Archive of Racial and Cultural Healing. This report provides an overview of ARL's 2021 assessment activities, data collection, and analysis and showcases the association's efforts to shape and inform leadership practice throughout research libraries. It highlights how, during a year of continued turmoil, the association engaged with key stakeholders, partners, and the media to raise their awareness of the impact of member library and archives' contributions to the broader ecosystem.

2021 by the Numbers

Convene

- 125 member institutions
- 1 new member institution: Texas State University
- 17 member and interim member representatives new to the association
- 2,502 attendees at ARL events

Inform

- 254,000 active users and 359,000 sessions on the flagship website ARL.org
- 6,332 subscribers to daily and weekly ARL newsletters (Day in Review and ARL News)
- 24 briefings (10 member briefings, 14 public policy briefings)
- 13 member events (in addition to association meetings) on presidential records, publisher negotiations, digitization, research security, anti-racism, leadership and diversity strategies, talent management, career paths, organizational development, COVID-19 operations, and budgeting
- 10 presentations to external organizations about ARL's strategic priorities (AAU/APLU Summit on Accelerating Public Access to Research Data, Confederation of Open Access Repositories, Council on Governmental Relations, Digital Public Library of America, Federal Demonstration Partnership, Federation of American Societies for Experimental Biology, Jisc, National Information Standards Organization, North Carolina Summit on Accelerating Public Access to Research Data, and Society for Scholarly Publishing)

Shape

- 35 participants in the Digital Scholarship Institute Summer Virtual Series
- 20 Leadership Fellows representing the broadest range of research institutions and communities in the program's history and 80 participants in ARL diversity programs
- $474,020 invested in fellows and scholars programs (including sponsorships)
- A $300,000 new grant awarded to ARL to conduct research, develop models, and collect costing information for public access to research data across five disciplinary areas
- 8 board/steering committee memberships (AGU Publications Committee, Coalition for Networked Information, Dryad, Global Sustainability Coalition for Open Science Services, Research Organization Registry, SPARC, U.S. National Academies's Board on Research Data and Information, and U.S. National Committee for CODATA)

Influence

Representing institutions collectively serving millions of professionals, students, faculty, researchers, innovators, and the public from around the world:

- 174 media mentions (digital and print media)
- 46 public policy positions, including 26 sign-on letters, 14 public statements submitted to the U.S. government, and 6 public statements

Advocate for Public Policies in Support of Our Mission and Shared Objective

Our objective is to advocate and advance law and policy for balanced copyright that safeguards the interests of researchers and learners by ensuring that libraries can acquire, share, lend, reformat, and preserve content with maximum digital affordances.

Scholarship and Policy Team

In 2021 ARL's Scholarship and Policy Team collaborated on cross-cutting issues, such as research security, producing an issue brief and member session; scientific integrity, through submitting comments in response to a U.S. federal request for information; and science funding legislation, issuing a public statement welcoming increased investment in research and data-sharing. ARL kept the membership and the community informed through a monthly Public Policy Briefing, more than 15 "ARL Views" blog posts, and social media engagement.

Advocacy and Public Policy Committee (APPC)

The Advocacy and Public Policy Committee's (APPC) contributions to the 2021–2022 Action Plan were centered around safeguarding libraries' digital rights. With a new visiting program officer from Louisiana State University, we researched and identified the special exemptions and limitations within the Copyright Act that enable libraries and educational institutions to fulfill their missions—with a particular focus on the digital environment and digital lending in particular. We held discussions with members of APPC and the University Information Policy Officers (UIPO) to understand the legal and policy barriers embedded in licensing digital scholarly materials in research libraries. We held meetings with congressional offices informing them of challenges for libraries in these areas. Finally, while copyright is a cornerstone of ARL's advocacy work, the association remains firmly committed to open and public access policies that would resolve many of the conflicts of copyright of scholarly works for libraries and the research community. Our work in this area in 2021 laid the foundation for our forthcoming launch of a refreshed KnowYourCopyrights.org website with public position papers on research libraries and digital rights.

ARL/CARL Joint Task Force on Marrakesh Treaty Implementation

The ARL/CARL (Canadian Association of Research Libraries) Joint Task Force on Marrakesh Treaty Implementation expanded its structure and capacity. We added a visiting program officer to the task force and created new technical and beneficiary working groups. With accessibility as a core area of focus for APPC, we are able to connect the Marrakesh work to our broader digital-rights strategy, including our work on the triennial rulemaking for Section 1201 of the Digital Millennium Copyright Act on circumventing technological protection measures.

Section 230 of the Communications Decency Act

ARL led the library voice in policy discussions around reform of Section 230 of the Communications Decency Act. In collaboration with our colleagues in the Library Copyright Alliance, the Internet Infrastructure Alliance, and EDU-CAUSE, we developed an issue brief on Section 230 and libraries that was member-informed and recognized as extremely helpful by congressional offices and member libraries. Based on the brief and accompanying webinar, a key member of Congress contacted us to understand our position on specific bills that would reform Section 230. APPC is tracking congressional proposals to reform Section 230, as well as broader conversations about online transparency and privacy that also have implications for Section 230 and the open Internet.

U.S. Commission on Truth, Racial Healing, and Transformation

We developed a research library advocacy strategy to advance legislation on Truth, Racial Healing, and Transformation. In 2021 ARL joined a broad-based coalition of academic, artistic, civic, and faith organizations calling for the establishment of a U.S. Commission on Truth, Racial Healing, and Transformation (H. Con. Res. 19). Libraries and archives are in this movement to advance a more just and equitable society by bringing our expertise, collections, and relationships to advance truth for teaching and scholarship, remembrance, community-building, and healing. Leaders of the movement worked with committee members on a panel discussion with ARL members in October 2021. ARL partnered with the American Library Association (ALA) and the Society of American Archivists to develop a statement for the National Day of Racial Healing in January 2022, signaling the commitment of libraries and archives to collaborate and to document the diverse history of the U.S.

Catalyze Collective Efforts to Achieve Enduring and Barrier-Free Access to Information

Our objective is to enhance partnerships within the greater research ecosystem in order to strengthen research libraries within the "open science by design" framework and related open scholarship initiatives.

Partnerships

A key outcome of 2021 is increased visibility of research libraries among stakeholders and partners in higher education and national agencies. Our work has resulted in renewed opportunities and relationships, particularly in the area of research data, with the U.S. National Committee for CODATA, Council on Governmental Relations, U.S. National Academies's Board on Research Data and Information, U.S. National Institute of Standards and Technology, and U.S. National Science Foundation.

ARL/CARL Joint Task Force on Research Data Services Report

ARL and CARL published the final report of the ARL/CARL Joint Task Force on Research Data Services, with recommendations for the roles of research libraries with regard to research data principles, policy, and strategy for managing research data. The report also offers guidance on discipline-specific research data approaches, priorities for automation of processes, economic models to scale and sustain shared resources, prioritization of research data to steward, and decision-making rubrics. The task force engaged 24 deans, directors, and data librarians from the ARL membership across Canada and the United States to complete this work.

Grant Project

The Scholars and Scholarship Team kicked off a two-year, $300,000 National Science Foundation grant project to study the realities of academic data-sharing. This project builds upon the U.S. National Library of Medicine's prior work on the costs of public access to research data and continues the outcomes recommended by the Association of American Universities (AAU) and the Association of Public and Land-Grant Universities (APLU) in their Accelerating Public Access to Research Data initiative. Specifically, this project will work with six ARL member organizations to answer the following questions:

1. Where are funded researchers across these institutions making their data publicly accessible, and what is the quality of the metadata?
2. How are researchers making decisions about why and how to share research data?
3. What is the cost to the institution to implement the federally mandated public access to research data policy?

NIST Research Data Framework (RDaF)

In collaboration with AAU and APLU, ARL co-convened a cross-sectional group of institutional administrators and service providers to pilot the NIST Research Data Framework (RDaF). RDaF is meant to be a map of the institutionally based research data landscape and a guide for various stakeholders in research data to understand best practices for research data management and dissemination. The first of the pilot meetings was held in November 2021, with additional meetings expected to be scheduled throughout 2022.

Toward an Open Monograph Ecosystem (TOME)

The Toward an Open Monograph Ecosystem (TOME) initiative marked its fourth year in 2021. This initiative, which is a collaboration among AAU, ARL, and the Association of University Presses, provides a subvention award of up to $15,000 per monograph to create a digital open access version of the title. To date, more than 100 books have been published under TOME, which represents an investment of more than $1.5 million dollars in supporting open humanities and social sciences scholarship. At the 2021 meeting of TOME stakeholders, featuring presentations and discussions of several open access monograph initiatives, participants affirmed the ongoing need for a collective approach (like TOME) to funding open monographs.

Create Diverse, Equitable, Inclusive, and Accessible Work Environments, Services, and Collections

Our objective is to advance sustainable and systemic change particularly as it relates to racism by helping ARL members recruit, retain, and advance people of color and other underrepresented populations, as well as through programs, frameworks, and partnerships to build structural equity and inclusion.

Building Structural Equity and Inclusion

In 2021 ARL engaged in numerous efforts aligned with its goal of advancing sustainable and systemic change to build structural equity and inclusion. ARL continues its work as a member of the joint task force to develop a framework for proficiencies in racial equity for libraries and archives. This group is led by the Association of College & Research Libraries (ACRL), ARL, ALA, and the Public Library Association (PLA). The framework working group, which convened in spring 2021, shared the draft framework with the full task force over the summer and initiated an open comment process in January 2022. Additionally, the Diversity, Equity, and Inclusion Committee partnered with the ARL Academy Advisory Committee to draft the ARL Learning & Development Framework. This framework, which was presented to the ARL board in February 2022, establishes an intentional structure to provide guidance, organization, and consistency to learning and development opportunities for ARL community members, while remaining adaptable in order to encourage innovation and to respond to unpredictable circumstances.

Leadership and Career Development Program (LCDP)

ARL continues to deepen its long-term commitment to diverse populations throughout their careers through enhancements made to the Leadership and Career Development Program (LCDP) and Kaleidoscope Program. The 2020–2021 LCDP cohort—"The Pandemons"—comprised 24 fellows who successfully navigated the unprecedented circumstances of COVID-19. After their in-person orientation in March 2020, the fellows adapted to a virtual structure that included extending their fellowship for six months. The cohort presented their experiences during the fall 2021 association meeting and called on member representatives to identify active ways to cede or share power and make actionable changes in order to create more space and opportunities for rising BIPOC leaders. Twenty-four leaders from ARL and non-ARL institutions served as career coaches and hosted virtual visits for their matched fellows. Preparations for the 2022–2023 LCDP cohort began at the end of 2021, which included soliciting applications for fellows as well as launching the LCDP Task Force and LCDP Selection Working Group.

Kaleidoscope Program

Seventeen diversity scholars from the 2019–2021 cohort completed the Kaleidoscope Program. Another 18 diversity scholars from the 2020–2022 cohort completed the first year of the program, which included attending the virtual 2021 Leadership Symposium and the Research Library Site Visit at Arizona State University. These diversity scholars will continue to receive financial, mentoring, and job-search support through their second year in the program. Additionally, 18 diversity scholars were selected for the 2021–2023 cohort, which began meeting in September 2021. We selected a mentoring consultant who successfully matched all 18 scholars with their mentors. The mentoring consultant, who also serves as an ARL visiting program officer from the University of California–San Diego, is developing materials and resources to strengthen and enhance the mentoring components of the Kaleidoscope Program for the scholars and mentors.

Framework for Change

ARL's intentional focus on structural inequity includes centering anti-racism and developing a framework to scaffold systemic change. After a delay in 2020, ARL began work in fall 2021 on Diversity, Equity, and Inclusion Institute planning, which is supported by an Institute of Museum and Library Services Fiscal Year 2020 Laura Bush 21st Century Librarian Program award (RE-246354-OLS-20). The DEI Institute Task Force, supported by a research scholar from the University of Illinois–Chicago, launched in December 2021. Additionally, in lieu of hosting the IDEAL: Advancing Inclusion, Diversity, Equity, and Accessibility in Libraries & Archives Conference in 2021, ARL was a Diamond/Diamante Sponsor for the REFORMA National Conference VII. This opportunity, which celebrated the 50th anniversary of REFORMA, included conference registration for three Kaleidoscope Diversity Scholars, the sponsorship of four conference sessions—all of which involved colleagues from ARL member institutions—and a virtual exhibit space. Toward the end of 2021 the ARL Diversity, Equity, and Inclusion Committee began initial planning for the next IDEAL Conference with the hope of hosting it in 2023.

Provide Data and Analytics on Research Library Practices, Effectiveness, and Impact

Our objective is to implement a research agenda for the association that enables research libraries to address impact and outcomes.

Research and Analytics Program

In 2021 the Research and Analytics program focused on implementing initiatives to improve the Salary Survey and the ARL analytics experience, as well as strategizing for the future. Putting past recommendations generated from direct engagement with the membership into practice and initiating conversations about the future of research and analytics at ARL moved our agenda forward substantially.

Resource Updates

Two major accomplishments of note were launching a revised ARL Statistics website and implementing improvements to the ARL Annual Salary Survey put forth by the ARL Salary Survey Task Force and approved by the board of directors. Collectively, these efforts make ARL data easier to gather and access and make the data more relevant to today's library environment. The revised ARL Statistics website provides a cleaner interface, more efficient workflow for members, and several new tools and functionality to make it easier to use. Implementing recommendations from the Salary Survey Task Force provides critical updates to this valuable dataset that will allow member libraries to obtain insights that are more applicable to their institutions.

ARL Statistics Survey

Strategically, the Research and Analytics Committee began the important work of rethinking the data collected through the ARL Statistics survey. Through consultation with the board of directors, executive committee, and ARL staff, the committee crafted an approach centered on member engagement to refresh this flagship survey.

ACRL/ALA/ARL Joint Advisory Task Force on IPEDS Academic Libraries Component Definitions

The ACRL/ALA/ARL Joint Advisory Task Force on IPEDS Academic Libraries Component Definitions submitted its recommendation to the U.S. National Center for Education Statistics (NCES) on adding a question to the Academic Libraries Survey (ALS) about shared collections. Further, the IPEDS Task Force also contributed comments to a report about the implications of moving the ALS from NCES to the Institute of Museum and Library Services.

LibQUAL Survey

ARL continued its work to revise the LibQUAL survey and plans to launch a pilot with a partner institution in 2022 to complete additional testing. In 2021 46 institutions ran a LibQUAL survey.

Shape and Inform Leadership Practice throughout Research Libraries

Our objective is to implement a strategy for leadership and organizational development through programming and events that develop library deans, directors, and employees to meet the challenges and opportunities presented by the significant changes underway in research, teaching, and learning. ARL advanced this objective in 2021 by laying the foundation for deepening and delivering on critical work for library leaders at all stages of their leadership development. The following are major achievements from the year.

Redesigned Leadership Fellows Program

We launched the revamped Leadership Fellows program with the most diverse class (institutions, individuals, perspectives) ever. The program and curriculum have been completely redesigned and re-implemented. The program has now established an ARL approach to leadership and mentorship that provides fellows with insight into the day-to-day leadership challenges and opportunities they can expect to encounter regularly as senior leaders. Fellows are offered advice and counsel for learning about topics covered by monthly sessions, applied best practices related to those topics, and stakeholder connections in institutional settings that shape those topics in practice.

ARL Academy's Name Change

The ARL Academy prepared recommendations for a name change in order to better convey that learning facilitated by ARL is continuous and ongoing, that it happens at all levels of the organization, that it fosters a community of practice and inquiry, and that, through learning, ARL shapes libraries of the future. ARL members have been polled to determine the best name for the Academy Advisory Committee to present to the board of directors.

ARL Learning & Development Framework

In partnership with the senior director of Diversity, Equity, and Inclusion, we completed the ARL Learning & Development Framework, which was presented to the board in February 2022. The framework establishes an intentional structure to provide guidance, organization, and consistency to learning and development opportunities for ARL community members, while remaining adaptable in order to encourage innovation and to respond to unpredictable circumstances.

Leadership Research Task Force

The Leadership Research Task Force completed its work to examine the changing roles of library leaders, identify gaps between current and future needs, determine any necessary skill sets that would enable research library leaders to better engage with their campuses, and inform ARL programming and strategic priorities. Moving forward, the Academy Advisory Committee plans to mine the data that has been collected to find opportunities for publication and further analysis of those findings.

AUL/Senior Leadership Institute

The ARL Academy established a new working group to update, design, and implement content for mid-career and senior leaders via the AUL/Senior Leadership Institute. The ARL Academy AUL/Senior Leadership Institute is a professional development opportunity for senior leaders of research libraries to strengthen strategic thinking and decision-making skills to ensure effective leadership of research libraries in a time of rapid, continuous change. The institute will teach participants ways to strengthen their individual leadership qualities, including integrity, empathy, and collegiality, as they develop their strategic leadership skills. The institute will be open to current associate and assistant deans and directors of research libraries and other senior managers who report directly to the university librarian/dean/director.

Deepen and Expand Understanding of Research Library Impact in the Research Enterprise and More Broadly

Our objective is to deepen and expand the understanding of the research library's value and brand identity, particularly in terms of its impact in the research enterprise and more broadly. During a year of continued turmoil in our countries, institutions, and individual lives, the association engaged with key stakeholders, partners, and the media to raise their awareness of the impact of member library and archives' contributions to the broader ecosystem.

Research Libraries Report

In partnership with CARL, ARL engaged Ithaka S+R to interview key stakeholders in higher education to identify their strategic priorities and the role of research libraries and archives in achieving them. The report is forthcoming in early 2022, along with case studies and key indicators to assist member institutions in identifying opportunities for increased alignment. More than 60 stakeholders enthusiastically participated, and our partners in higher education expressed their interest in working with the association going forward to develop a deeper understanding of what research libraries contribute.

Social Media and Marketing

ARL expanded its reach in sharing news about member institutions and our collective initiatives through social media and email marketing, which are up since 2020. Between December 2020 and December 2021 ARL's Twitter following increased 8 percent from 11,490 to 12,460. Followers also increased on both Facebook and Instagram. The Day in Review newsletter, launched in June 2020, increased its number of subscribers in 2021 by 129 percent from 1,014 to 2,321. The weekly ARL News email grew its subscriber base in 2021 by 47 percent from 2,719 to 4,011. Additionally, we launched the "ARL Views" blog's first podcast in a series, covering topics such as copyright, the Marrakesh Treaty, and the social impact of research libraries.

Media Coverage

ARL press releases and public comments reached various media outlets and publications with readership from the low thousands to the millions. Media outlets that cited ARL in 2021 included *Library Journal*, *Inside Higher Ed*, and *Chronicle of Higher Education*. Media coverage focused on ARL's advocacy and public policy initiatives, along with our work on DEI. In 2021 we began highlighting member library events and resources covering holidays, commemorations, and other important events. ARL Communications will continue its focus on showcasing the work of member libraries and demonstrating brand value.

The Scholarly Publishing and Academic Resources Coalition

Heather Joseph

Executive Director

1201 Connecticut Ave. NW, #608, Washington, DC 20036
202-630-5090, sparc@sparcopen.org
https://www.sparcopen.org

Background and Mission

The Scholarly Publishing and Academic Resources Coalition (SPARC) is a global advocacy organization working to make research and education open and equitable by design. Representing 200-plus academic and research library members, SPARC's work is built on the premise that sharing knowledge is a fundamental human right. As a catalyst for action, SPARC works at the local, national, and international level to change policies, educate and activate stakeholders, and incubate projects that advance a world where everyone can fully participate in research and education systems.

Supported by members in the United States and Canada, as well as a strong network of active international affiliates in Africa, Europe, and Japan, SPARC promotes collective action based on shared values with key stakeholders, from faculty and administrators to research funders and the public. To create an open and equitable ecosystem for this and future generations, SPARC places a premium on empowering students and early career professionals.

Responding to COVID-19

As the global pandemic enters its third year, SPARC continues agile programming priorities and supporting resources for its members and the broader community. SPARC is structured to function largely as a virtual organization, having moved away from large in-person meetings to more targeted regional and virtual events. Additionally, SPARC's key focus areas—providing open access to research articles and data, as well as promoting open educational resources—continue to be central to enabling higher education's continuity of operations throughout the pandemic. SPARC also established COVID-19 resources to equip members with the tools to help them pivot to address the "new normal" circumstances on their campuses.

Strategy

To promote the changes in both scholarly infrastructure and culture, SPARC's strategy centers on:

- Advocating for policies that enable open practices throughout research and education

- Educating stakeholders on opportunities to change the scholarly communication system
- Incubating projects that promote new models for sharing research outputs and developing educational materials that support the needs of scholars and society

SPARC works to identify shared values and opportunities for action between its library members and stakeholders in the global research and education environment, including faculty and administration, public and private research funders, and the public. SPARC places a premium on empowering students and early career professionals and actively incorporates collaboration with them across all program areas.

Priorities

SPARC's work promotes barrier-free sharing of research and educational materials to enable an open and equitable global ecosystem for scholarship—democratizing knowledge sharing, accelerating discovery, and increasing societal and economic returns.

As a catalyst for action, SPARC's pragmatic agenda focuses on encouraging new norms, practices, and policies that promote open and equitable access to and participation in research and education. SPARC is committed to designing equity and inclusion into the foundation of the initiatives it leads and the communities it cultivates and to advocating for these core values in all of the spaces where SPARC is active.

The following were key priorities in 2021:

Driving Policy Change

SPARC will continue its leadership role in advancing policies that enable an open and equitable global ecosystem for scholarship. SPARC's work will include:

- Educating key policymakers (including the U.S. Congress, the U.S. Executive Branch, the Canadian administration, state and provincial governments, and global public and private funders) on SPARC's policy priorities
- Deploying proactive campaigns to expand policy progress in the United States, as well as defending against threats to existing policies
- Advocating for the U.S. Executive Branch update of the 2013 Office of Science and Technology Policy's (OSTP) Memorandum on Increasing Access to the Results of Federally Funded Scientific Research to reflect emerging global norms: zero embargoes; full reuse rights; adoption of FAIR data principles; harmonization of article and data-sharing requirements; inclusion of code, software, and algorithms, etc.
- Clearly communicating the potential social equity impacts of proposed policies, particularly APC-based models
- Advocating for state and federal policies that incentivize the adoption of open educational resources, including continued funds for the federal Open Textbook Pilot

- Promoting full implementation of the OPEN Government Data Act through the Federal Data Strategy
- Leveraging leadership of and participation in coalitions and communities (the Open Access Working Group, the Data Coalition, OpenCon, etc.) to speed policy progress
- Working with the media to promote public awareness of the benefits of open policies

Enabling Community-Controlled Infrastructure

SPARC will promote initiatives that enable the academic community to retain and regain control of crucial infrastructure—and attendant data—underpinning the open scholarly ecosystem. SPARC's work will include:

- Deploying a comprehensive campaign to "lock the market open for competition," including dissemination of comprehensive, expert market analysis of the current status of infrastructure across the higher education sector and the implications for libraries/academic institutions and proposed strategic responses
- Strengthening the community's ability to secure long-term control of infrastructure by developing values-based contracting terms for collective use
- Retaining expert financial and legal counsel to ensure that strategic responses are viable, sustainable, and designed to scale effectively
- Leading research/development efforts on economic and organizational models for the collective provisioning of community-controlled infrastructure, including support for targeted new investment instruments
- Actively collaborating with existing community efforts to accelerate progress toward an open/community-owned ecosystem
- Advocating for policies that empower institutions to retain control over their research and education infrastructure, including content and data

Catalyzing the Realignment of Research Incentives

SPARC will promote the realignment of existing reward and incentive structures to advance an open scholarly ecosystem. SPARC's work will include:

- Continuing to organize the joint Open Research Funders Group (ORFG)/ National Academies of Sciences, Engineering, and Medicine's Roundtable on Aligning Incentives for Open Science, equipping funders and higher education leaders to actively promote practices and policies to reward the open, equitable sharing of research outputs and educational resources
- Preparing and supporting the ORFG member funders to serve as champions and peer influencers to promote incentive realignment
- Supporting the National Academies' Roundtable, working on encouraging department-level development of proposed rewards/recognition for open practices to be included in evaluation and promotion guidelines

- Supporting research into current evaluation, reward, and incentive structures and promoting exemplars that have made demonstrable progress toward realigning research incentives and rewards
- Increasing opportunities for early career professionals to participate in shaping rewards and incentive systems through deeper integration of the OpenCon community with the SPARC community

Supporting Direct Library Actions

SPARC will support and enhance our members' ability to take timely and informed actions. SPARC's work will include:

- Expanding our Negotiation Community of Practice to provide comprehensive data, resources, and support for libraries that are considering "Big Deal" cancellations to improve their negotiating position with vendors
- Retaining high-level financial and legal expertise to better inform library negotiations and decision-making processes
- Identifying and promoting specific opportunities for libraries to move out of "Big Deal" subscription packages and reinvest in support of an open, equitable ecosystem for scholarship
- Providing professional development opportunities to empower people as catalysts for advancing open, including the SPARC Open Education Leadership Program
- Partnering with funders and scholarly societies to explore shifts in business models
- Providing up-to-the-moment updates and analyses of key policy and scholarly communications-related trends and developments
- Issuing action alerts and other opportunities for timely member library participation in advocacy, education, and partnership initiatives
- Delivering tools and resources to support campus advocacy and education activities

Global Collaboration

SPARC continues to reflect and support the global nature of scholarly communications by:

- Advocating for better global representation in the leadership of open and scholarly communications-related initiatives
- Drawing attention to the need for more globally inclusive business models for the communication of research results
- Coordinating and promoting International Open Access Week as a catalyst for action across the community
- Identifying new opportunities and establishing partnerships with key stakeholders in other global regions

Supporting Students and Early Career Researchers

SPARC promotes the inclusion of students and early career academic professionals in all areas of open access by:

- Supporting the OpenCon community for students and early career academic professionals
- Continuing joint advocacy efforts to leverage community presence on open access, open data, open education, and related issues
- Maintaining relationships with key national and international organizations representing students and early career academic professionals

Program Activities and Outcomes 2021

Policy and Advocacy

- Spearheaded advocacy for national policies to make federally funded research articles, data, and code more openly and equitably available
- Secured language supporting faster access to taxpayer-funded research in the Senate's U.S. Innovation and Competition Act (S. 1260)
- Coordinated community response to the OSTP's Request for Information to Improve Federal Scientific Integrity Policies, as well as for the U.S. Department of Education's evidence-building plan, the Learning Agenda
- Secured $7 million in federal funding for the U.S. Open Textbook Pilot grant program in fiscal year (FY) 2021, with an additional $14 million proposed in the Senate's FY 2022 appropriations bill
- Successfully advocated for $115 million in funding for open education resources in California
- Coordinated the open agenda for private funders via ORFG

Equipping Members for Successful Publisher Negotiations

- Provided SPARC members with resources (including contract libraries, pricing information, guidance on data analysis for negotiation, and more) to better prepare for journal negotiations
- Convened regular vendor-specific negotiation discussions for SPARC members to share strategies and learn from one another's experiences
- Hosted regular discussions on topics related to negotiations, including a Negotiations 101 and 201 series co-hosted with the Association of College and Research Libraries (ACRL) to better support libraries and library workers in building their skills for negotiation with vendors

Centering Anti-Racism, Diversity, Equity, and Inclusivity

- Thoroughly examined and revised SPARC's recruitment processes for both staff and governance positions
- Partnered with the Knowledge Equity Lab to launch the *Unsettling Knowledge Inequities* podcast series and produce its second season

Realigning Research Incentives

- Partnered with the National Academies of Sciences, Engineering, and Medicine to convene the ongoing Roundtable on Aligning Incentives for Open Science to reform research incentives to support open science
- Led the development and launch of a new Open Science Toolkit for use by institutions and funders

Empowering Librarians through Online Resources and Development

- Launched a new informational resource, InclusiveAccess.org, for members to get the facts about automatic textbook billing
- Provided intensive online professional development through the fifth year of the popular SPARC Open Education Leadership Program
- Served as lead organizer of the international 2021 Open Education Conference
- Collaborated with the United Nations' Dag Hammarskjöld Library to organize the 2nd Open Science Conference
- Released the COVID Impact Survey, which was undertaken to better understand libraries' pandemic-related budgetary challenges, with a focus on understanding how they affected attitudes toward content, collections, and open initiatives

Raising Competition Concerns with Regulators

- Worked with antitrust and legal experts to file a challenge urging the Federal Trade Commission to block the proposed merger of Clarivate and ProQuest
- Proactively worked with regulators and legislators to educate them on issues in the scholarly publishing market and to initiate interventions where necessary

Supporting Community-Controlled and Open Infrastructure

- Provided competitive analyses and recommendations for actions that institutions can take to retain control of critical infrastructure and data, including the 2021 Update to the SPARC Landscape Analysis and Roadmap for Action
- Monitored and educated members on the growing risk of data privacy and surveillance issues in critical library infrastructure
- Catalyzed the creation of a repository network in the United States with the addition of a SPARC/Confederation of Open Access Repositories (COAR) Visiting Program Officer

Communication and Media

SPARC is regularly consulted and quoted as an expert source on topics relating to scholarly communications. Its programs have been featured in both the national and trade press by such outlets as *Forbes, Nature, BBC, Business Wire, The Chronicle of Higher Education*, and *Scientific American*.

SPARC–ACRL Forums

In May and June 2021 SPARC and ACRL co-hosted Negotiations 101 workshops that focused on providing a better foundation for librarians tasked with negotiating on behalf of their library. This training provided an introduction to negotiating theory followed by a real-world exercise in which the participants worked in small groups to prepare, execute, and reflect on a negotiation.

Building on the Negotiations 101 sessions, ACRL and SPARC also co-hosted a series of Negotiations 201 workshops to provide deeper dives into specific aspects of negotiating strategy and how they can be put to use.

Governance

SPARC is guided by a steering committee. The committee members are Jennifer Beamer (The Claremont Colleges), Gwen Bird (Simon Fraser University), Chris Bourg (Massachusetts Institute of Technology), Talia Chung (University of Ottawa), Vicki Coleman (North Carolina A&T State University), Christopher Cox (Clemson University), Karen Estlund (Colorado State University), Antoinette Foster (Oregon Health & Science University), Scarlet Galvan (Grand Valley State University), Carrie Gits (Austin Community College), Harriett Green (Washington University in St. Louis), Lorraine Haricombe (University of Texas–Austin), April Hathcock (New York University), Mary Lee Kennedy (Association of Research Libraries), Beth McNeil (Purdue University), Carmelita Pickett (University of Virginia), Ariana Santiago (University of Houston), Virginia Steel (University of California–Los Angeles), and Elaine Thornton (University of Arkansas).

Council on Library and Information Resources

211 North Union Street, Suite 100-PMB1027, Alexandria, VA 22314
https://www.clir.org
Twitter @CLIRNews

Kathlin Smith
Director of Communications

The Council on Library and Information Resources (CLIR) is an independent, nonprofit organization that forges strategies to enhance research, teaching, and learning environments in collaboration with academic and cultural institutions, scholars, specialists, and practitioners. CLIR president Charles Henry leads the 22-member staff and works in close liaison with seven CLIR Distinguished Presidential Fellows.

CLIR is supported by fees from sponsoring institutions, grants from public and private foundations, contracts with federal agencies, and donations from individuals. A list of current sponsors, members, and funders is available at https://www.clir.org/about/current-sponsors-and-funders.

CLIR's board establishes policy, oversees the investment of funds, sets goals, and approves strategies for their achievement. A full listing of CLIR board members is available at https://www.clir.org/about/governance.

Ongoing Response to the COVID-19 Pandemic

The pandemic continued to affect all aspects of CLIR's work. With few exceptions, conferences, meetings, and workshops were held virtually throughout 2021. Timelines for grantees, fellows, and projects were extended, as staffing, services, and travel continued to be profoundly disrupted. More detail is provided in the following overview of CLIR's activity.

Fellowships and Grants
Digitizing Hidden Special Collections and Archives

Digitizing Hidden Special Collections and Archives is a national grant competition administered by CLIR for digitizing rare and unique content in collecting institutions. Supported by the Andrew W. Mellon Foundation, the program is built on the model of CLIR's Cataloging Hidden Special Collections and Archives program, which ran from 2008 to 2014.

Since 2015 Digitizing Hidden Special Collections and Archives has awarded $24.2 million to institutions holding collections of high value for research, teaching, and learning. A review panel, comprising experts from a range of scholarly and technical disciplines, evaluates proposals and recommends award recipients. Awards range from $50,000 to $250,000 for single-institution projects and $50,000 to $500,000 for collaborative projects.

In March 2021 CLIR announced the award of just more than $4 million to 16 projects proposed during the 2020 award cycle. (Announcement of the awards, typically made in early January, was delayed until spring because of the pandemic's impact on application and review activities.) The funded projects cover subjects ranging from hip-hop, fashion, and public media to plant specimens and whale reproduction.

Also in March 2021 CLIR launched a new iteration of the grant program, called Digitizing Hidden Special Collections and Archives: Amplifying Unheard Voices (DHC-AUV). The program focuses on projects to digitize materials that deepen public understanding of the histories of people of color and other communities and populations whose work, experiences, and perspectives have been insufficiently recognized. The new program expands eligibility to include Canadian nonprofit institutions, which were previously allowed to participate only as supporting partners to U.S.-based institutions. Recipients from the 2021 award cycle will be announced in April 2022.

Following the new program's launch, CLIR commissioned two researchers to conduct an external assessment of the DHC-AUV initiative. With expertise in digital archives, community-based research, and grantmaking, the team will help CLIR create more inclusive, equitable, and broadly accessible regranting initiatives that serve a diverse range of organizations. The study is running concurrently with the application and review cycle as researchers gather data from applicants, reviewers, and staff.

More information about the Digitizing Hidden Special Collections and Archives program, including a list of funded projects, is available at https://www.clir.org/hiddencollections.

Recordings at Risk

Launched in 2017 with funding from the Andrew W. Mellon Foundation, Recordings at Risk is a national regranting program to support the digital preservation of rare and unique audio, audiovisual, and other time-based media of high scholarly value. It is intended to encourage professionals who may be constrained by limited resources or technical expertise to act against the threats of media degradation and obsolescence. The program also helps institutions identify priorities and develop practical strategies for digital reformatting, build relationships with partners, and raise awareness of best practices.

In April 2021 CLIR awarded $552,905 to 17 projects that preserve materials ranging from radio and television broadcasts to oral histories, music recordings, films, and performance videos.

The ninth call for proposals opened in September 2021, with applications due in December 2021. In response to work slowdowns caused by COVID-19, CLIR also extended the grant terms of recently funded projects from 12 to 18 months and gave reporting extensions to other active grants as necessary.

Grants range from $10,000 to $50,000. To date, the program has awarded $3.95 million. More information about the program, including a list of funded projects, is available at https://www.clir.org/recordings-at-risk.

Postdoctoral Fellowship Program

CLIR's Postdoctoral Fellowship Program offers Ph.D. graduates an opportunity to work on projects that strengthen connections among library collections and services, promote the effective use of collections and technologies, and curate and preserve the products of current research. Launched in 2004, the program has supported 215 fellows at 93 partner institutions across the United States, Canada, and overseas. Fellowships are typically for two or three years.

In the academic year 2020–2021 fellows worked in one of three areas: (1) data curation for African American and African Studies funded by the Andrew W. Mellon Foundation, (2) data curation for the energy social sciences supported by the Alfred P. Sloan Foundation, and (3) digital humanities and digital scholarship funded by individual host institutions. In January 2021 the Andrew W. Mellon Foundation awarded CLIR $2.01 million to extend Fellowships in Data Curation for African American and African Studies. The funds enable current fellows whose work was negatively affected by the global pandemic to extend their time at host institutions by up to two years.

Throughout 2021 fellows collaborated on a writing project called Curated Futures, focusing on the possibility of a third library—a space within or outside institutions that challenges conceptions of libraries of the past. The project, which encompasses podcasts, essays, and a visualization, was published in early 2022.

In February 2021 CLIR published "Capacity Assessment of Latin American and Caribbean Partners: A Symposium about Open Access, Technological Needs, and Institutional Sustainability." The report, available in five languages, presents recommendations from a virtual symposium organized by four postdoctoral fellows in April 2020.

Additional information about the Postdoctoral Fellowship Program, including a list of current and former fellows, is available at https://www.postdoc.clir.org.

Mellon Dissertation Fellowships

CLIR awarded the final round of CLIR-Mellon Fellowships for Dissertation Research in Original Sources in spring 2019. Funded by the Andrew W. Mellon Foundation since 2002, the program has supported 258 fellows, who together represent 59 U.S. universities. These fellows have conducted research at more than 1,700 sites in 86 countries worldwide. They have worked with original materials of every sort, from handwritten and illuminated manuscripts, ancient pottery, and medieval paintings to early films and vinyl LPs; from medical, corporate, and prison records to political pamphlets from flea market bins. In pursuit of their research, these scholars have traveled the globe, becoming experts in scholarly research both in the United States and across national borders, often working in settings with very different approaches to cultural heritage and information management.

To celebrate and reflect on the program's two decades, CLIR will host a symposium for alumni in 2022 to share lessons learned through the fellowships. The symposium will focus on the evolution of original source research since the program's inception and consider what the future may hold for archives and researchers. Fellows will discuss how broad global changes have affected original source research and the risks facing researchers and collections today. They will also consider the role that archives and archival research will play in addressing the social, political, and environmental challenges of the coming decades.

More information on the fellowship program, including a list of fellowship recipients, is available at https://www.clir.org/fellowships/mellon/fellowshiprecipients.

Programs and Partnerships

Digital Library Federation

A program of CLIR, the Digital Library Federation (DLF) is a community of practitioners who advance research, learning, social justice, and the public good through the creative design and wise application of digital library technologies. DLF connects CLIR's vision and research agenda to a network of practitioners working in digital libraries, archives, labs, museums, and elsewhere.

In June 2021 Jennifer Ferretti joined CLIR as DLF senior program officer, filling a leadership position that had been vacant since the departure of Bethany Nowviskie in 2019. Formerly a digital initiatives librarian at the Maryland Institute College of Art on Piscataway land in Baltimore, Ferretti is also founder and principal of We Here, a community dedicated to supporting Black and Indigenous people and people of color in library and information science professions.

DLF Forum

DLF's annual signature event, the Forum, is open to digital library practitioners from member institutions and the broader community. The Forum provides an opportunity for DLF's advisory committee, working groups, and community members to conduct business and present their work. It also enables community members to share experiences and practices with one another and support a broader level of information-sharing among professional staff. The Forum allows DLF to continually review and assess its progress with input from the community at large.

The 2021 DLF Forum and affiliated events took place virtually for the second year, from November 1 to 10, 2021. The Forum, the National Digital Stewardship Alliance's Digital Preservation 2021: Embracing Digitality, and Learn@DLF encompassed presentations, panels, lightning talks, and workshops that drew more than 1,400 attendees.

The 2022 Fall Forum will take place October 9–13 in Baltimore, Maryland.

Working Groups

DLF's 12 working groups represent a community of practitioners who collaborate year-round to solve problems in a variety of digital library subfields, from project management and assessment to labor and accessibility. Working groups are organized across institutional and geographical boundaries, and participation is open to anyone, regardless of institutional affiliation.

Highlights of 2021 included the following:

- In October 2021 the DLF Digital Library Pedagogy group shared instructional resources in its #DLFteach Toolkit 2.0, which focuses on lesson plans to facilitate disciplinary and interdisciplinary work engaged with 3D technology.
- The Digital Accessibility Working Group began work on a how-to manual for accessible information technology policies and workflows.

Working groups are open to all interested professionals. A full list of DLF groups is available at https://www.diglib.org/groups.

National Digital Stewardship Alliance

DLF serves as the host institution for the National Digital Stewardship Alliance (NDSA), a consortium of organizations, including universities, professional associations, businesses, government agencies, and nonprofit organizations, committed to the long-term preservation of digital information. NDSA activities are organized by three interest groups (Content, Infrastructure, and Standards and Practices), out of which smaller working groups often emerge. NDSA hosts the annual Digital Preservation Conference, which, since 2016, has followed the DLF Forum and—like the Forum—was held virtually in November 2021. More information about NDSA is available at https://ndsa.org.

Digital Library of the Middle East

In June 2021 CLIR, Stanford University Libraries, and Qatar National Library announced several major improvements to the Digital Library of the Middle East (DLME). DLME is a public, open platform that aggregates digital records of published materials, documents, maps, artifacts, audiovisual recordings, and more from the Middle East and North Africa (MENA) region. The site, at https://dlmenetwork.org/library, is fully navigable in Arabic and English.

The improvements offer new capabilities for browsing, searching, and organizing content. Site curators are now able to organize material into categories and subcategories with which users can interact. The multilingual interface has also been improved, and searchers are now easily able to toggle between the Hijri and Gregorian calendars as they browse DLME collections.

Since its launch in July 2020, DLME has grown to more than 150,000 objects in more than 100 collections from 35 institutions from around the world. It also provides an array of applications, tools, and descriptions that enrich the content and facilitate browsing, searching, and interpretation.

Iraqi-Jewish Archives Exhibitions

In 2003 a U.S. Army team found a collection of more than 2,700 books and tens of thousands of documents recording centuries of Jewish life in Iraq in a flooded basement of the Iraqi intelligence headquarters. To ensure the survival and accessibility of the materials, the U.S. National Archives and Records Administration and its partners preserved, cataloged, and digitized the books and documents. An online exhibit at https://ijarchive.org/exhibit-pages/discovery-recovery.html describes the collection and its discovery. Traveling exhibits were also initiated, although they have been paused until additional resources and support are secured.

In October 2020 CLIR signed a memorandum of understanding with the U.S. Department of State's Bureau of Near Eastern Affairs to collaborate in seeking support for exhibits of the material, as well as for potential meetings, conferences, and symposia. Although COVID-19 paused much of the momentum for planning a traveling exhibit and website redesign, a meeting was held in March 2021 to discuss the future of the physical collection.

HBCU Library Alliance Partnership

In July 2019 CLIR and the HBCU Library Alliance announced a long-term partnership to foster awareness of and access to collections held by Historically Black Colleges and Universities (HBCUs). In late 2020 the two organizations received a grant from the Andrew W. Mellon Foundation for a project to identify common values, priorities, and needs for describing and managing special and archival collections for HBCU Library Alliance members. In spring 2021 three researchers began conducting interviews and focus groups to help the HBCU Library Alliance envision how its member institutions can work together to preserve, describe, and digitize their unique collections. A public report of their findings is expected in early 2022. More information about the HBCU Library Alliance and CLIR partnership is available at https://www.clir.org/initiatives-partnerships/hbcu-library-alliance.

CLIR also began work on season three of its podcast, *Material Memory*, in close collaboration with the HBCU Library Alliance. Seven episodes, to be released in spring 2022, will spotlight people and collections in libraries at six HBCUs and offer insights on these cornerstones of culture and historical knowledge.

Leading Change Institute

The Leading Change Institute (LCI), cosponsored with EDUCAUSE, brings together information sector leaders, including deans, librarians, and information technologists, who seek to advocate for and advance change in today's rapidly evolving higher education environment. Each summer, a weeklong residential institute is held for a new cohort of participants who learn from and discuss current developments with colleagues from academia, associations, grant-making agencies, industry, and government. After attending the institute, participants join other alumni in monthly chats.

The COVID-19 pandemic forced postponement of what would have been the 2020 LCI. In response, deans Joanne Kossuth and Elliott Shore increased the frequency of the monthly alumni Zoom meetings to once per week and invited members of the 2020 class to participate. This helped to engage the new class and served as a way for alumni from all years to support one another and exchange strategies for leading their departments during a challenging time. With the rise in vaccinations and the loosening of restrictions in Washington, D.C., CLIR was able to hold an in-person institute July 12–16, 2021.

Since the institute's inception as the Frye Leadership Institute, more than 800 people have participated, representing a broad range of both domestic and international institutions of higher learning. A list of participants is available at https://leadingchangeinstitute.org/alumni.

Chief Information Officers Group

Since 2002 CLIR has facilitated a semiannual forum of directors of organizations that have merged their library and information technology units on the campuses of liberal arts colleges and small universities. The group held virtual monthly meetings in fall 2021 and an in-person meeting in December.

At their meetings and through a listserv, members discuss library and computing issues as an integrated whole. They have explored such topics as organizational models for optimizing success; governance structures; fostering diversity, equity, and inclusion in merged organizations; data security and privacy; and digital scholarship. A list of current members is available at https://www.clir.org/initiatives-partnerships/cios.

Affiliates

CLIR establishes collaborative relationships and cross-institutional initiatives with organizations that have similar missions in the pursuit of common goals. The affiliates program allows CLIR to serve as a fiscal or administrative home for mission-aligned organizations that may not need to be independent legal entities. Affiliates have their own governance and mission, while CLIR provides integrated services and access to tools, platforms, research, and expertise to reduce costs, create greater efficiencies, and enable affiliates to better serve their constituencies.

CLIR's affiliates are code4lib, the Institute for Liberal Arts Digital Scholarship, the International Image Interoperability Framework, the International Internet Preservation Consortium, NDSA, Open Repositories, the Scholastic Commentaries and Texts Archive, and Weave.

Publications

Pocket Burgundy series. In June 2021 CLIR invited proposals for a new publication series modeled on its "burgundy reports," so named for their cover color. The series departs from CLIR's traditional reports in that they will be shorter, the ideas will be generated by the community, and submissions will be reviewed by an editorial committee. Five proposals were selected and announced in December 2021 at https://www.clir.org/2021/12/clir-announces-awards-for-new-publication-series. The reports will be publicly available in 2023.

Material Memory **podcast.** Season two of CLIR's podcast, which concluded in April 2021, explores the impact of the climate crisis on communities and their cultural heritage. In eight episodes, host Nicole Kang Ferraiolo, director of global strategic initiatives at CLIR, talks with guests about the roles of information and cultural heritage professionals in responding to the crisis and how different approaches to preservation can help or harm affected communities. Season three, planned for release in spring 2022, will spotlight people and collections in libraries at six HBCUs and offer insights on these cornerstones of culture and historical knowledge. Episodes are available through major podcast apps, as well as at https://material-memory.clir.org.

"Capacity Assessment of Latin American and Caribbean Partners: Report of Symposium and Recommendations," by Hadassah St. Hubert, Jennifer Isasi, Nicté Fuller Medina, and Margie Montañez. Drawing from discussions at a virtual symposium held in April 2020, this report offers recommendations for equitable practices to enhance cultural engagement through collection development that fully acknowledges Latin American and Caribbean organizations as equal partners with a voice in decision making for projects and grant funding. The report is available in English, French, Haitian Creole, Portuguese, and Spanish at https://www.clir.org/pubs/reports/pub178.

Year of CLIR. From January 2020 to April 2021 CLIR published a weekly blog series, Year of CLIR, highlighting a key activity from each year since its founding in 1956. It is available at https://www.clir.org/pubs/resources/a-year-of-clir.

CLIR Issues 139–144. CLIR's bimonthly newsletter is available at https://www.clir.org/pubs/issues.

Association for Library and Information Science Education

ALISE Headquarters, 4 Lan Drive, Suite 310 Westford, MA 01886
978-674-6190, e-mail office@alise.org
http://www.alise.org

Lisa O'Connor
President 2021–2022

The Association for Library and Information Science Education (ALISE) is an independent, nonprofit professional association founded in 1915 as the Association of American Library Schools (AALS). It changed to its current name in 1983 to reflect more accurately the mission, goals, and membership of the association. Its mission is to promote innovative, high-quality education for the information professions internationally through engagement, advocacy, and research.

Membership

Membership is open to individuals and institutions. Personal members can include anyone interested in the objectives of the association, with categories including full-time (faculty member, administrator, librarian, researcher, or other interested individual), emerging professional (doctoral students as they transition to faculty member status, maximum of three years), part-time/retired (part-time or adjunct faculty or retired professionals), and student (doctoral or other students, maximum of six years). Institutional members include schools with programs that offer a graduate degree in library and information science or a cognate field. International affiliate institutional membership is open to any school outside the United States or Canada that offers an educational program in library and information science at the professional level as defined or accepted by the country in which the school is located. Associate institutional membership status is accorded to libraries and organizations other than schools of library and information science.

Structure and Governance

ALISE is constituted of operational groups, including the board of directors; committees; the Council of Deans, Directors, and Program Chairs; school representatives; and special interest groups (SIGs). The association has been managed since October 2018 by McKenna Management, Inc. in Westford, Massachusetts, with Cambria Happ as executive director. The board of directors is composed of seven elected officers serving three-year terms. Officers for 2021–2022 were Lisa O'Connor (University of North Carolina–Greensboro), president; Rong Tang (Simmons University), president-elect; Sandra Hirsh (San José State University), past president; Shimelis Assefa (University of Denver), secretary/treasurer; Denice Adkins (University of Missouri), director for membership; Monica Colon-Aguirre (University of South Carolina), director for community building; and Mega Subramaniam (University of Maryland), director for programming. At the end of the annual conference in October 2022, Hirsh and Adkins will conclude their terms of service, and two newly elected officers will join the board: a new vice-president/ president-elect and a new director for membership.

The board establishes policy, sets goals and strategic directions, and provides oversight for the management of the association. Face-to-face meetings are held in conjunction with the annual conference to focus on policy, planning, programming, and other matters. For the remainder of the year, business is conducted through teleconferences, an online collaborative work platform, and e-mail.

Committees play a vital role in carrying out the work of the association. Since fall 2008 an open call for volunteers to serve on committees has been used to ensure broader participation in committee service, with members for the coming year appointed by the president-elect for most committees. Principal areas of activity include awards, conference program planning, governance, nominations, research competitions, advancement, programming, community building, and membership. (See https://www.alise.org/alise-committees for a full list.) Each committee is given an ongoing term of reference to guide its work as well as the specific charges for the year. Task forces can be charged to carry out tasks outside the scope of the existing standing committees.

The ALISE Council of Deans, Directors, and Program Chairs consists of the chief executive officers of each ALISE institutional member school. The group convenes at the annual conference and discusses issues via e-mail in the interim. Anthony Chow (San Jose State University), Raj Dewan (Syracuse University), and Sanda Erdelez (Simmons University) serve as the 2021–2022 co-chairs.

Within each institutional member school, a school representative is named to serve as a direct link between the membership and the ALISE board. These individuals communicate to the faculty of their school about ALISE and the association's events and initiatives and provide input on membership issues to the ALISE board.

SIGs enable members with shared interests to communicate and collaborate, with a particular emphasis on programs at the annual conference. New SIGs are established as areas of interest emerge. Ongoing SIGs, grouped by thematic clusters, are:

- Roles and Responsibilities: Doctoral Students, Part-Time and Adjunct Faculty
- Teaching and Learning: Curriculum, Innovative Pedagogies
- Topics and Courses: Archival/Preservation Education, Disabilities in LIS, Equity and Social Justice, Gender Issues, Health, Historical Perspectives, Information Ethics, Information Policy, International Library Education, School Library Media, Technical Services Education, Youth Services

Communication

Announcements, notifications, and membership updates are posted to the ALISE membership listserv. News and events are published on ALISE's official website (http://www.alise.org). The organization has been actively using its social media accounts, including Twitter (@alisehq) and Facebook (https://www.facebook .com/ALISEHQ) to connect with its members and communities, as well as to post announcements and ALISE-related events in a timely manner.

Publications

The ALISE publications program has four components:

- The *Journal of Education for Library and Information Science* (*JELIS*) is a peer-reviewed quarterly journal edited by John Budd and Denice Adkins. It is a scholarly forum for discussion and presentation of research and issues within the field of library and information science (LIS) education. The University of Toronto Press began to serve as the publisher of *JELIS* in 2018. The journal is open access at a green level. It is indexed in Elsevier's Scopus, among other indexing sources.
- The *ALISE Library and Information Science Education Statistical Report* publishes data collected annually from its institutional members on their curriculum, faculty, students, and income and expenditures. Members can gain free access to existing reports by logging in to the members-only area of the ALISE website.
- The ALISE Book Series, published by Rowman & Littlefield, addresses issues critical to LIS education and research through the publication of epistemologically grounded scholarly texts that are inclusive of regional and national contexts around the world. The series editors are Jaya Raju (University of Cape Town) and Dietmar Wolfram (University of Wisconsin–Milwaukee). The first two books in this series were published in 2020: *The Information Literacy Framework: Case Studies of Successful Implementation* and *E.J. Josey: Transformational Leader of the Modern Library Profession.*
- The ALISE website is the public face of the association and provides information about the association and news of activities and opportunities of interest to members. It provides login access to the MemberClicks system, where members can access members-only benefits (reports, a member directory, etc.), renew membership, register for the conference and webinars, and access other services.

Annual Conference

The 2022 annual conference will be held in Pittsburgh, Pennsylvania, on October 24–26, 2022. The conference theme is Go Back and Get It: From One Narrative to Many. Program co-chairs Jenny Bossaller (University of Missouri) and LaTesha Velez (University of North Carolina–Greensboro), with president O'Connor, are planning the conference. The event will offer presentations, poster sessions, and networking and placement opportunities, along with the unCommons—a gathering place to share, debate, brainstorm, and network. The ALISE Academy will immediately precede the conference. Conference proceedings are housed by the IDEALS repository (https://www.ideals.illinois.edu/handle/2142/98928).

Professional Development

ALISE offers regular, free webinars to members to facilitate virtual engagement with research and other membership interests during the year between conferences.

Recent webinar offerings have included "Student Use of Mobile Devices for LIS Coursework: Implications for Educators," "The Rising Phoenix: Perspectives on Resilience for Education, Research, and Practice," and "Accessibility in Online Learning Environments: Practical Steps for Making Your Course Accessible." Those who are interested in offering a webinar may submit a proposal through the webinar submission webpage (http://www.alise.org/webinar-proposals).

ALISE redesigned its Leadership Academy (https://www.alise.org/lead ership-academy) in 2022 through the work of its programming committee. The redesigned event features a series of five webinars throughout 2022 that are free to members. The academy will culminate with an in-person workshop immediately following ALISE's 2022 annual conference in Pittsburgh, Pennsylvania. In 2019 ALISE initiated the Leadership Academy to create communities within library and information science for the exploration of leadership roles as chairs, directors, and deans. It aims to build interest in leadership and to build the confidence of prospective leaders. The academy also provides prior attendees with a forum to reconvene, to reflect on their learnings from the past year, and to gain new insights to deploy in the future.

Grants and Awards

ALISE supports research and recognizes accomplishments through its grants and awards programs. Research competitions include the ALISE Research Grant Competition, the ALISE/Bohdan S. Wynar Research Paper Competition, the ALISE/ProQuest Methodology Paper Competition, the ALISE/Eugene Garfield Doctoral Dissertation Competition, and the ALISE Community conn@CT Mini-Grants. Support for conference participation is provided by the University of Washington Information School Youth Services Graduate Student Travel Award, the Doctoral Student to ALISE Award, the ALISE/Jean Tague Sutcliffe Doctoral Student Research Poster Competition, and the ALISE Diversity Travel Award to the ALISE Annual Conference. This last award was created in collaboration with the ALA Office for Diversity Spectrum Scholarship Program, which created a parallel award, the ALA/ALISE Spectrum Travel Award, partially funded by ALISE.

Awards recognizing outstanding accomplishments include the ALISE/Norman Horrocks Leadership Award (for early-career leadership), the ALISE/Pratt-Severn Faculty Innovation Award, the ALISE Service Award, the ALISE Award for Professional Contribution, the ALISE/Connie Van Fleet Award for Research Excellence in Public Library Services to Adults, and the ALISE Excellence in Teaching Award. Winners are recognized at an awards luncheon at the annual conference. For a list of award winners, see http://www.alise.org/awards-grants.

Collaboration with Other Organizations

ALISE seeks to collaborate with other organizations on activities of mutual interest. ALISE members also serve on committees for various national organizations, including American Library Association (ALA) committees.

ALISE continues to build its international connections, with members serving on International Federation of Library Associations and Institutions (IFLA)

Standing Committees that address education and research. ALISE has been expanding its collaborations with peer organizations, including the Association for Information Science and Technology (ASIS&T) and the iSchools Organization; the partnership of these three organizations is called the iFederation.

Impact of COVID-19

Throughout the pandemic, ALISE continued to organize webinars to help its members cope and shift to teaching in our new online-centric environment.

Due to the pandemic, ALISE held its 2021 annual conference virtually rather than as planned in Milwaukee, Wisconsin. The virtual conference was well-attended, and more people from outside the United States and Canada were able to participate. Many presentations, posters, and discussions focused on the pandemic and social justice, for example, "Still Struggling to Breathe: Another Conversation on Libraries and Communities in Crisis," Beyond Resilience: Moving from Self-Care to Collective Care," Examining the Impacts of the COVID-19 Pandemic on Library Makerspaces and LIS Makerspace Curricula," and "Engaging with Global at the Local: Developing Equity, Diversity and Inclusion through International Education Experiences." The 2022 annual conference is planned for an in-person experience with precautions in place to follow all guidance from public health authorities. Going forward, ALISE will continue to explore ways to offer ALISE members more enriching content virtually and to provide ALISE members with opportunities to engage with each other in virtual formats.

Conclusion

ALISE is guided by its strategic plan. In 2020 the 2017–2020 strategic plan was closed out, and the association underwent a significant strategic process that resulted in a completely updated strategic plan for 2021–2025 (https://www.alise .org/history-strategic-direction). ALISE looks forward to continuing its leading role in LIS education and research.

International Reports

International Federation of Library Associations and Institutions

Postal Address: P.O. Box 95312, 2509 CH Den Haag, Netherlands
Visiting Address: Prins Willem-Alexanderhof 5, 2595 BE The Hague (Den Haag), Netherlands
Tel. +31 70 3140884, fax +31 70 3834827, e-mail ifla@ifla.org
http://www.ifla.org

Beacher Wiggins
Director for Acquisitions and Bibliographic Access, Library of Congress
Secretary, IFLA Standing Committee on Acquisition and Collection Development, 2019–2023

Susan R. Morris
Special Assistant to the Director for Acquisitions and Bibliographic Access, Library of Congress
Member, IFLA Standing Committee on Cataloguing, 2019–2023

The International Federation of Library Associations and Institutions (IFLA) is the preeminent international organization representing librarians, other information professionals, and library users. The federation's major work in 2021 fell into three areas: presenting the annual conference virtually, implementing a new governance structure to support the IFLA Vision and Strategy, and optimizing the IFLA website, http://www.ifla.org, as a resource for planning, assessment, and advocacy. Carrying out these major projects during the global COVID-19 pandemic, IFLA proved itself both idealistic and realistic in promoting its four core values: freedom of access to information and expression, as stated in Article 19 of the Universal Declaration of Human Rights; the belief that such access must be universal and equitable to support human well-being; delivery of high-quality library and information services in support of that access; and the commitment to enabling all members of IFLA to participate without regard to citizenship, disability, ethnic origin, gender, geographical location, political philosophy, race, or religion.

86th World Library and Information Congress (WLIC): First Virtual IFLA Congress

In the face of the continuing global COVID-19 pandemic, the IFLA governing board announced in September 2020 that the 2021 World Library and Information Congress (WLIC) would be held virtually, following the outright cancellation of the 2020 Congress. The 2021 WLIC had originally been planned for Rotterdam, Netherlands, and the city of Rotterdam and the Dutch National

Committee for the Congress were instrumental in organizing more than 160 virtual events for the conference from August 17–19, 2021, followed by the virtual IFLA General Assembly of all members on August 25. Congress and assembly participation was enthusiastic, with more than 2,750 registered attendees from 125 countries and more than 11,461 comments submitted over chat in online sessions. The online sessions were organized in four tracks, each with a keynote speaker:

- Libraries Inspire—Keynote speaker Karima Bennoune, United Nations Special Rapporteur for cultural rights
- Libraries Include—Keynote speaker Emilia Saiz, secretary general of the international umbrella organization United Cities and Local Government
- Libraries Engage—Keynote speaker Teddy Woodhouse, research manager for access and affordability at the Alliance for Affordable Internet
- Libraries Innovate—Keynote speaker Darren Tang, director general of the World Intellectual Property Organization

Also in September 2020 IFLA announced plans to design a new, hybrid virtual-physical format for future congresses, with a view to facilitating participation in all countries, for all who wish to attend. The conference exhibitor fees and registration fees are higher than for most conferences in the library community, but revenue from WLIC historically has not loomed large in IFLA's funding model; in fact, the most recent in-person WLIC in Athens, Greece, in 2019 ran a deficit of €46,152 (more than $50,000 U.S.). The custom of convening all registered participants in opening and closing ceremonies limits the number of potential host cities to those with conference halls seating at least 3,000 people. In response to members' concerns about expense and inconvenience, IFLA livestreamed 11 key sessions at WLIC 2019 for audiences around the world and made them available free of charge on the WLIC website and YouTube. After WLIC 2021, IFLA made the online sessions available in its conference eLibrary. The governing board agreed in late 2020 to undertake further work and investigations into sustainable ways to hold WLIC. Any plan for an all-virtual WLIC would begin in 2024 at the earliest, because IFLA has contractual obligations to hold WLIC in person in Dublin, Ireland, in July 2022 and in Rotterdam in 2023.

IFLA Global Vision and IFLA Strategy 2019–2024

To provide direction and inspiration for all of its activities, IFLA in 2018 adopted a global vision of "A strong and united global library field powering literate, informed and participatory societies." The IFLA Strategy 2019–2024 was developed from the IFLA Global Vision. Glòria Pérez-Salmerón, president of IFLA from 2017–2019, and Gerald Leitner, secretary general from June 2016– March 2022, unveiled the IFLA Strategy 2019–2024 at WLIC 2019. The IFLA Strategy presents four strategic directions: strengthen the global voice of libraries, inspire and enhance professional practice, connect and empower the field, and optimize the organization. Each strategic direction is supported by four key initiatives, forming a call to action for all libraries to inspire, engage, enable, and connect with their societies.

After working intensively since December 2019 to reexamine IFLA's organization and governance, IFLA now operates with a streamlined and more participatory governance structure. Pledging "no decisions about you without you," the governing board and IFLA headquarters staff issued an initial draft in June 2020, followed by a member survey and virtual workshops seeking feedback from individuals. A final proposal for a new governance structure and revised IFLA Statutes was accepted by the General Assembly in November 2020, and the governing board approved it in February 2021. The new governance structure and IFLA Statutes took effect on August 26, 2021.

The highest governance level of IFLA is its General Assembly of all members, meeting annually during WLIC and voting in person or electronically. The General Assembly determines the purposes and values of IFLA, approves amendments to the IFLA Statutes, determines the conditions of membership, and receives and approves the annual financial statements.

The new, streamlined governing board has only 11 members, eliminating the need for the former executive committee. The governing board members are the president, president-elect, and treasurer of IFLA; the chairs of the Professional and Regional councils; the chair of the Management of Library Associations Section, currently Halo Locher of Switzerland; and five elected members-at-large. Currently, the members-at-large are Ayub Khan, U.K.; Jonathan Hernández Pérez, Mexico; Kirsten Boelt, Denmark; Mandla Ntombela, South Africa; and Yasuo Inoue, Japan. The IFLA secretary general is the nonvoting secretary of the governing board.

A new Regional Council guides, supports, and sets priorities for IFLA's advocacy work in each of six regions of the world. Six new regional divisions report to the Regional Council: Asia and Oceania, including Australia and New Zealand; Middle East and North Africa; Latin America and the Caribbean; Sub-Saharan Africa; Europe, including Turkey; and North America. Because the six regional divisions follow the United Nations pattern of political divisions, the North America regional division includes only Canada and the United States (50 states and the District of Columbia), with Mexico and Puerto Rico assigned to Latin America and the Caribbean. The establishment of regional divisions, which prior to 2021 were a single division, will provide greater visibility to IFLA's regional advocacy work and foster greater participation in countries with developing economies. The first chair of the Regional Council is Nthabiseng Kotsokoane of South Africa.

Forty-two sections continue as professional units, organized in eight divisions, reporting to the Professional Council. The chair of the Professional Council is currently Adjoa Boateng of Germany. The chair of each professional unit's standing committee is authorized to appoint five additional members to ensure that each region of the world is represented on the standing committee. The four IFLA strategic programs have been replaced by four advisory committees reporting to the governing board: Standards, Cultural Heritage, Copyright and Other Legal Matters, and Freedom of Access to Information and Free Expression. In contrast to the previous structure, the advisory committees report to the governing board but do not automatically have seats on the Professional Council. The new structure allows sections or divisions to sponsor special interest groups that may exist for two four-year terms before either disbanding or becoming full-fledged sections.

Standards

Guided by the Advisory Committee on Standards (ACOS), IFLA's professional units—sections and review groups—develop conceptual models, rules for library resource description, digital format codes, guidelines, and statements of best practice for the full range of library work. IFLA Standards include the Statement of International Cataloguing Principles (ICP) and IFLA Guidelines for Library Services to People Experiencing Homelessness. The ICP and Library Reference Model (LRM) are the foundation of many national and international cataloging codes, such as RDA: Resource Description & Access. ACOS has centralized procedures for development and approval of new standards in the IFLA Standards Procedures Manual. During 2021 ACOS reviewed an update to the 2011 edition of the International Standard Bibliographic Description (ISBD) and forwarded it to the Professional Council for endorsement. It also undertook a final review of Common Practices for National Bibliographies in the Digital Age, submitted by the IFLA Section on Bibliography.

Copyright and Libraries

IFLA advocates vigorously for open access to digital content and for the right of libraries to benefit from fair use and exemptions from copyright restrictions. IFLA's Advisory Committee on Copyright and Other Legal Matters (CLM) represents the organization on the World Intellectual Property Organization's (WIPO) Standing Committee on Copyright and Related Rights (SCCR). IFLA monitors participation in the Marrakesh Treaty, which reduces barriers to libraries' provision of copyrighted resources to people with disabilities in formats they can use. The update prepared in 2021 and issued in January 2022 shows that a large majority of signatories are choosing not to impede libraries in these efforts. At the annual WIPO Assemblies in October 2021, IFLA attended virtually and stressed the role of WIPO, as a United Nations agency, in ensuring that intellectual property laws support sustainable development.

Cultural Heritage

IFLA's strategic direction recognizes culture as a basic human need and calls for sustained effort to preserve cultural heritage. In 1996 IFLA was a founding member of the International Committee of the Blue Shield and its successor, Blue Shield International, to protect cultural property in the event of natural and human disasters. Its current Blue Shield partners are the International Council on Archives, the International Council on Monuments and Sites, and the International Council of Museums.

Since 2016 IFLA has maintained a Risk Register for Documentary Cultural Heritage, a confidential repository of information about unique documentary heritage assets, including indigenous languages and digital cultural heritage resources, deemed to be at risk from natural or human-caused disasters. In 2021 the IFLA Preservation and Conservation Centre in Qatar contributed to rescuing collections of the National Library of Lebanon, which was heavily damaged in an explosion in August 2020. In August 2021 outgoing IFLA president Christine Mackenzie and Gerald Leitner issued a call for the human rights of the people of Afghanistan to be respected and for the country's libraries to be safeguarded.

Freedom of Access to Information and Freedom of Expression

The Advisory Committee for Freedom of Access to Information and Freedom of Expression (FAIFE) works with partner organizations, including UNESCO, the World Summit on the Information Society, Internet Governance, and the Office of the United Nations High Commissioner for Human Rights, to raise libraries' profile in the areas of intellectual freedom and other core library values. In 2021 FAIFE participated in the Dynamic Coalition on Public Access in Libraries (DC-PAL), which engaged partners to recognize libraries' value to a digitally empowered society. At the annual Internet Governance Forum in December 2021, FAIFE and DC-PAL held a session on access to the Internet in libraries as it supports community development and connection. The session highlighted projects in African countries, Indonesia, Peru, and Poland. FAIFE stresses relevant legal matters but also publicizes technological options for expanding public access, for instance by publicizing low-Earth orbit satellite connectivity in remote areas. In December 2021 FAIFE and the nonprofit organization Electronic Information for Libraries issued a working draft on the uses and benefits of public Internet access in libraries. FAIFE also provided IFLA's input to the World Summit on the Information Society's annual reporting, stressing the importance of expanded access in libraries.

Grants and Awards

IFLA continues to work with corporate partners and national libraries to maintain programs and opportunities for librarians and libraries in developing countries. Numerous awards and travel grants are expected to continue when in-person congresses resume. Such awards include the Standing Committee for the IFLA Academic and Research Libraries Section travel grants, cosponsored by SAGE and awarded to four candidates from Argentina, Brazil, Philippines, and Uganda in 2021; registration awards for 40 first-time conference attendees through IFLA WLIC Participation Grants, including the Bersekowski Awards; the IFLA New Professionals WLIC Attendance Grants; and the Dr. Shawky Salem Conference Grant.

The IFLA PressReader International Marketing Award was presented in 2021 to the libraries of Monash University in Australia and Pennsylvania State University in the United States for their Monash and Penn State Great Rare Books Bake Off. The finalists were the City Libraries of Jinan, China, for its Delivery Buddies Post, and LGMA (Local Government Management Agency)/Libraries Ireland for the campaign "Your Library—Take a Closer Look." The award recognizes creative, results-oriented marketing campaigns in the library field and usually includes a cash stipend and support for travel to WLIC.

More IFLA awards recognize exemplary libraries or librarians. The IFLA Green Library Award, established in 2015, recognizes a green or sustainable library project. Sponsored by De Gruyter, it was designed by the IFLA Environment,

Sustainability, and Libraries Special Interest Group (ENSULIB). In 2021 the recipients were the Edmonton Public Library in Canada for Best Green Library and the Oulu City Library in Finland for Best Green Library Project.

The IFLA/Systematic Public Library of the Year Award recognizes a library that best combines innovative architecture with information technology solutions, accounting for digital developments and local culture. The winning library must operate in a building that is newly built or repurposed as a library. With a prize of $5,000 from Systematic, this is one of IFLA's most generous awards. Library buildings that were completed in both 2019 and 2020 were considered for the 2021 award, which went to the Deichman Bjørvika Oslo Public Library in Norway.

The IFLA Dynamic Unit and Impact Award for 2020 was presented to the Document Delivery and Resource Sharing Section at the 2021 WLIC and General Assembly. The 2021 award was presented to the Academic and Research Libraries Section, also at the 2021 conference.

The IFLA Honorary Fellowships, IFLA Medal, and IFLA Scroll of Appreciation recognize service to IFLA by individuals. At the August 2021 General Assembly meeting, five individuals received the IFLA Scroll of Appreciation, including Ann Okerson of the Center for Research Libraries, who is a longtime leader in digital librarianship. Past president Glòria Pérez-Salmerón was named an Honorary Fellow, IFLA's highest honor, recognizing her immense impact on the international library field.

Membership and Finances

IFLA has more than 1,500 members in 135 countries, including 300 American members. As of November 2020, members included 136 national and international library associations. Initially established at a conference in Edinburgh, Scotland, in 1927, IFLA has been registered in Netherlands since 1971 and has headquarters facilities at the Koninklijke Bibliotheek (Royal Library) in The Hague. Although IFLA did not hold a General Conference outside Europe and North America until 1980, there has since been steadily increasing participation from Asia, Africa, South America, and Australia. IFLA maintains regional offices in Pretoria, South Africa; Singapore; and Buenos Aires, Argentina. The organization has seven official working languages—Arabic, Chinese, English, French, German, Russian, and Spanish. It maintains four language centers: for Arabic, in Alexandria, Egypt; for Chinese, in Beijing, China; for the French-speaking communities of Africa, in Dakar, Senegal; and for Russian, in Moscow, Russia. The language centers provide translations of IFLA publications and serve in local or regional professional events.

IFLA offers a range of membership categories: international library associations, national library associations, other associations (generally regional or special library associations), institutions, institutional subunits, one-person libraries, school libraries, national association affiliates (limited to three consecutive years and open only to national associations with operating budgets of €10,000 or less to encourage membership in countries with developing economies), personal affiliates, student affiliates, new graduate members, and nonsalaried personal members. Association and institution members have voting rights in the IFLA General

Assembly and IFLA elections and may nominate candidates for IFLA offices. Institutional subunits, one-person libraries, and school libraries have limited voting rights for section elections, association affiliates and personal members do not have voting rights but may submit nominations for any IFLA office, and individuals may run for office themselves. Except for affiliates, membership fees are keyed to the UNESCO Scale of Assessment and the United Nations List of Least Developed Countries to encourage participation regardless of economic circumstances. Membership dues are quite low, ranging from €52 per year for individual students, recent graduates, and retirees to more than €26,000 per year for the largest national library associations.

UNESCO has given IFLA formal associate relations status, the highest level of relationship accorded to nongovernmental organizations. In addition, IFLA has observer status with the United Nations, WIPO, the International Organization for Standardization (ISO), and the World Trade Organization, and it has associate status with the International Council of Scientific Unions. IFLA participates in the Internet Governance Forum, under United Nations auspices.

Leading corporations in the information industry have formed working relationships with IFLA as Corporate Partners. The Corporate Partners provide financial and in-kind support and in turn gain the opportunity to convey information about their products and services to IFLA members and others who pay attention to IFLA's publications and activities. Several levels of corporate partnership are available. Most prominently, OCLC has been IFLA's first and sole Platinum Partner since 2014, providing extraordinary support, and served as Presenting Partner for WLIC 2021. Delegate Connect was WLIC's Technology Partner, ProQuest was the Accessibility Sponsor, IEEE Xplore Digital Library was Subtheme Sponsor, and LexisNexis was the Gamification Sponsor. The national Dutch libraries with NBD Biblion also contributed major support.

The IFLA Foundation (Stichting IFLA or SIF) was established in 2007. The foundation accepts private donations and bequests and is also funded by other IFLA income. It gives funding priority to proposals and projects that promise to have a long-term impact in developing and strengthening IFLA, are clearly related to at least one of IFLA's strategic priorities, and are not likely to be funded by other bodies. The foundation also occasionally makes grants for attendance at WLIC; the grants are administered by the IFLA headquarters and governance structure rather than directly by the foundation. The foundation's board of trustees does not respond directly to requests for foundation grants, which are considered by IFLA headquarters and other appropriate IFLA units.

Stichting IFLA Global Libraries (SIGL) was established in November 2016 as a legacy partner of the Bill and Melinda Gates Foundation's Global Libraries initiative. The secretary general of Stichting IFLA Global Libraries is Gerald Leitner, and its chair is Glòria Pérez-Salmerón. Its two additional appointed trustees are currently Deborah Jacobs and Inga Lundén. Stichting IFLA Global Libraries focuses on strengthening the library field and empowering public libraries.

Personnel, Structure, and Governance

The secretary general from 2016–March 2022 was Gerald Leitner of Austria. In April 2022 he left the federation, and Halo Locher of Switzerland, chair of the

IFLA Management of Library Associations Section, was appointed interim secretary general. His e-mail address is iflasg@ifla.org. Helen Mandl is the deputy secretary general and the manager for member services. Her e-mail address is helen.mandl@ifla.org. In addition, IFLA headquarters has 22 staff members.

The editor of the peer-reviewed quarterly *IFLA Journal* is Steven W. Witt of the University of Illinois–Urbana-Champaign. The journal has a 12-member editorial committee, chaired by Anne Goulding from Victoria University of Wellington in New Zealand and reporting to the IFLA Professional Council. The journal is published by SAGE.

Barbara Lison, director of the Stadtbibliothek Bremen in Germany, is president of IFLA for 2021–2023. Her email address is barbara.lison@stadtbibliothek.bremen.de. She has adopted the presidential theme Libraries Building a Sustainable Future in recognition that during her term, libraries must help to rebuild societies after the COVID-19 pandemic, help drive sustainable development worldwide, and ensure the institutional sustainability of the library space. Christine Mackenzie of Melbourne, Australia, is IFLA's past president. Antonia Arahova, director of the Presidential Library of Greece, was selected as president-elect for 2021–2023, but she stepped down in April 2022 because of urgent, long-term family responsibilities. Nthabiseng Kotsokoane of South Africa, chair of the IFLA Regional Council, is the temporary president-elect. The elected treasurer, Perry Moree, chief executive officer of the Library of Zeeland in the Netherlands, also stepped down in April 2022. Kirsten Boelt of Denmark accepted the duties of IFLA treasurer on a temporary basis. In April 2022 IFLA began the process of elections for permanent replacements.

The IFLA Voucher Scheme enables libraries to pay for international interlibrary loan requests using vouchers purchased from IFLA rather than actual currency or credit accounts. Since 2019 IFLA has charged a handling fee in addition to the voucher cost, but by eliminating bank charges and invoices for each transaction, the voucher scheme continues to reduce the administrative costs of international interlibrary loans and allows libraries to plan budgets with less regard to short-term currency fluctuations. The voucher scheme has also encouraged participating libraries to voluntarily standardize their charges for loans.

The IFLA Data Protection Policy complies with the General Data Protection Regulation (GDPR) of the European Union. Under the revised policy, IFLA can publish contact details of its officers, staff, standing committee members, and special interest group conveners on its website and in section newsletters and the *IFLA Journal*. Consent from individuals is gathered on a data protection registration form. IFLA does not sell contact information for other individuals. IFLA is registered with the Chamber of Commerce in The Hague, no. 40407191. Its primary bank is the ABN-AMRO Bank in Amsterdam, Netherlands.

Library and Archives Canada

Leslie Weir
Librarian and Archivist of Canada

In 2020 the global pandemic took Library and Archives Canada (LAC) into uncharted territory. Placing a strong emphasis on collaboration and its role in Canada's documentary heritage community, in 2021 LAC continued providing as much access as possible to our users, with the health and safety of our staff remaining a top priority.

Service Points

Due to changing health restrictions in response to the fluctuation in COVID-19 case numbers across Canada, the reopening of LAC service locations (Vancouver, Winnipeg, Ottawa, and Halifax) has been in flux since September 2020, when our research rooms and service points across the country started reopening in accordance with directions from provincial health bodies. Some of the protocols we introduced over the months included quarantining archives and books for three days (72 hours) after being handled (which was later reduced). We also limited the number of staff and visitors authorized to be on-site to ensure physical distance. All visits, in all locations, continued to require a booking in advance.

In order to inform LAC's regular clients and future visitors about our most up-to-date service offerings, the communications team developed a webpage that pulled together all relevant information. Before reopening our facilities to the public, we wanted to ensure that our clients were aware of all of the health and safety measures we were taking. To inform them, we produced a short video that was promoted on social media. We also created a user-friendly, online, step-by-step process for our clients to book appointments with staff and in our consultation rooms.

To strengthen communications with LAC users and all Canadians, the social media team worked with the government of Canada to create its priority messaging around COVID-19 and public health messages. LAC also helped to produce social media content that used material from our collection to reference historical situations in which Canadians had to pull together for a common cause. This content was used to promote the government of Canada's COVID-19 Alert app and, later, to communicate information about the vaccine.

Currently, most of LAC's on-site services have resumed. Our four service points are open, and all collections are accessible, including textual, photo, art, maps and plans, and publications. LAC continues its gradual return to regular operations, paired with an increase in capacity. The health and safety of employees and clients remains our priority, and several health measures are being maintained until further notice.

Digital Services

Despite the pandemic's impact on LAC's services, we have a strong online service component to our work and, although business could not continue as usual,

LAC staff stayed connected to our users as much as possible. Since the beginning of the pandemic, LAC never stopped providing research support and orientation services. We continued to help users find online content or analog documents that could be digitized on demand via our Copy Services and oriented them to the services or programs specific to users' needs. Reference archivists and librarians, genealogy consultants, and archival and orientation technicians also came on-site, whenever possible, to access the collection on behalf of our users in order to provide enhanced reference services when our consultation and reference rooms were still closed.

A number of services were able to continue, almost as normal, despite the closures. These services continued because they had always been conducted online (or remotely) or because they are considered critical to Canadians, such as online client registration, remote research support (by phone, e-mail, correspondence, or videoconference), responses to urgent Access to Information and Privacy (ATIP) requests that required on-site consultation of records (for example, for clients in failing health), responses to ATIP requests that could be completed in a remote working environment, and review of the historical document collections related to class action lawsuits.

LAC has been able to continue the development of its podcasts, blogs, Flickr, and Co-lab "challenges." Co-lab is an online tool that the public can use to transcribe, tag, translate, and describe digitized images in LAC's collection. The more material that people transcribe, tag, translate, or describe in Co-lab, the more accessible and usable our digital collection becomes for all Canadians. Contributors have added tags, transcriptions, and descriptions to more than 4,000 images in LAC's collection so far this fiscal year, more than four times as many as last year.

Work also continued, with minimal interruption, on developing and enhancing LAC's digital services. We continued to invest in improvements to Collection Search (our online catalog), including developing a new template to target a search to a particular collection (*The Canada Gazette*); launched a new user interface for Co-lab based on user feedback and testing; and launched the new My Account feature in February 2022 that allows users to log in, create, save, and share research lists. Over time, new features will be added to allow for more self-service and personalization options for LAC services.

Throughout the pandemic, we continued to make regular improvements to Collection Search to address feedback from clients and to fix bugs. In addition to working on Collection Search, enhancements were made to the online legal deposit submission process, an improved deposit system to make depositing digital publications easier for Canadian publishers and self-publishers. The system features new and easy-to-use web forms to deposit monographs (books) published in digital format, as well as a bulk submission option to deposit multiple publications in a single submission. The system will allow LAC to more efficiently receive, preserve, and make available digital publications. LAC plans to incorporate the deposit of other types of publications and productions in the future.

Additionally, the request for funding applications process as well as other online applications, such as the Canadian Library Directory, were improved over the course of the year.

The COVID-19 pandemic demonstrated that web archiving is one of the few immediate actions information professionals, digital librarians, and archivists can take to preserve primary resources related to an extended crisis. From the beginning of the COVID-19 pandemic, LAC was fully engaged in documenting its evolution and its effects on Canadian society. The team curated a diverse collection that includes websites from government and nongovernment sources, as well as social media relating to the pandemic's impact on life in Canada. To date, we have collected approximately 15 terabytes of website data and captured almost 3.5 million tweets related to COVID-19. The digital information harvested will be used for future research and will help tomorrow's Canadians understand what it was like for those living through the crisis. Having this information preserved will provide future leaders with important background, data, and experiences to help guide their decisions.

Online Public Programming

LAC also reached audiences through public programming activities that were adapted to be offered online. LAC hosted online roundtables, information sessions about collections and how to do research at LAC, subject-oriented lectures, webinars, and virtual tours of 395 Wellington, LAC Winnipeg, and LAC Vancouver. This online programming was paired with virtual tools such as videos, quizzes, and games.

One of our most popular events was a workshop and webinar via LAC's Facebook page called "In the Trenches: Digitized Records of the First World War." LAC also collaborated with the Vancouver Public Library to pilot a virtual version of its weekly "Connection to Kith and Kin" (Indigenous genealogy cafe) via Zoom. LAC is building on this experience and continues to develop and offer workshops to help users discover and explore its rich collection. A recent example would be the webinar "No. 2 Construction Battalion: Explore Library and Archives Canada's First World War Records," presented in collaboration with the Canadian Museum of Immigration at Pier 21 on February 26, 2022. During the First World War, more than 800 Black men served in No. 2 Construction Battalion. Mobilized at Truro, Nova Scotia, in 1916, the battalion was the only segregated unit in the Canadian Expeditionary Force.

As part of our Signatures Interview Series, we hosted a number of online conversations with well-known Canadians featured in our collection. These interviews are a unique opportunity to see behind-the-scenes photographs and documents with personal commentary from the public figures themselves. One of our interviewees was Gabor Szilasi. LAC recently announced the acquisition of an important collection of Szilasi's works covering nearly seven decades of the photographer's life and career. The event dove into his work, which contains more than 80,000 negatives and 42 photographic prints. These include negatives of early photographs taken in Hungary during the uprising against the Soviet invasion, as well as photographic prints from Montréal and rural Quebec.

Our online programming also included collaborative events with other institutions, both local and international. For example, the German National Library and LAC collaborated to present a four-part series of conversations between October 2020 and October 2021 to explore the effects of digitization on our respective institutions and priorities.

Our virtual programming has been a massive success and has kept us connected to our users and a diversity of communities.

Acquisition and Description

LAC's Published Heritage Branch continues to refine and improve the modified and digitally focused workflows established during the COVID-19 pandemic. Most staff tasked with supporting analog collections have returned to physical workspaces, and teams continually adjust to maintain new digital competencies acquired over the past year while ensuring analog collections are maintained. The Digital Asset Management System (DAMS) initiative is advancing on schedule, and published acquisition staff have successfully introduced new tools that support the smooth ingest of electronic books and publisher-supplied metadata via Legal Deposit; this greatly improves services to digital publishers and adds to the comprehensiveness of the National Collection. More than 650 digital publishers have registered to participate in the program, and LAC is receiving new digital content and associated metadata from Canadian publishers daily. Published Acquisitions continues to run pilot initiatives to continue to expand and optimize digital approaches.

LAC's Description Division has significantly advanced work on needed improvements to the Canadian Subject Headings (CSH). Because the language describing Indigenous materials in CSH is often not reflective of the terminology preferred by First Nation, Inuit, and Métis Nation communities in Canada, in 2019 LAC started a review and revision of CSH headings. This work continued in 2021–2022. LAC consults broadly on its revisions and looks to examples set by others doing similar work to ensure that a culturally appropriate and respectful approach is taken. We publish the full list of CSH, as well as the list of CSH related to Indigenous Peoples, on our marc21.ca website, so Indigenous-related terminology can be seen in context and our progress can be tracked by users.

Given the ever-increasing volume of digital content generated by Canadian publishers, donors, institutions, and the government of Canada, LAC is undertaking the multiyear DAMS implementation to streamline all stages of the digital asset management process. In 2021–2022, the Published Heritage Branch implemented a new workflow to harvest electronic books and Government of Canada Publications using DAMS and has begun the analysis to create workflows for ingesting publications with their associated ONIX metadata. The Cataloguing in Publication (CIP) Program, which produces standardized bibliographic descriptions for forthcoming Canadian publications, has seen continuous growth in demand in the past few years and is on track to break its record for highest number of descriptions produced in a year. This increase in requests has continued despite the challenges faced (by both publishers and LAC staff) of working during the pandemic. In 2021–2022, for example, we have seen an increase of 12 percent in requests.

Looking Ahead

Over the course of the pandemic, virtual events, such as the Ministerial Round-table on Libraries and Archives, cohosted by LAC and Canadian Heritage, have allowed us to discuss the impacts of COVID-19 on our sector and reflect together on sustainable solutions to a variety of issues faced by culture and heritage institutions in Canada. In order to continue this crucial dialogue within our community, LAC hosted a Galleries, Libraries, Archives, and Museums (GLAM) Think Tank during winter 2021 to further explore the ways in which COVID-19 has challenged how we deliver our services, our employees' ability to carry out their work, and the finite institutional resources and capacities we possess. The think tank brought together key players from the Canadian GLAM community in order to discuss the themes of enhancing the digital presence of GLAMs, promoting GLAMs' social value in a post-COVID-19 landscape, demonstrating GLAMs' relevance in a crisis context, building capacity at the local level, and ways in which GLAMs can reinvent themselves.

LAC is also revisiting the plans for Ādisōke, its future joint facility with the Ottawa Public Library, in light of the lessons learned from the pandemic. The design is being reexamined, and LAC services are being transformed with a goal of better aligning on-site and online experiences.

The year 2022 continues to be challenging due to the pandemic, although with a recent improvement and easing of restrictions. Despite the uncertainty, LAC continues to focus on its staff and on doing our best to provide Canadians with access to our collection and services. Going through the health crisis as a community and as an institution has led us to adapt and learn with a hopeful eye to the future.

International Board on Books for Young People

Nonnenweg 12, 4055 Basel, Switzerland
E-mail ibby@ibby.org
http://www.ibby.org

Mingzhou Zhang
President, 2018–2022

Liz Page
Executive Director

The founding of the International Board on Books for Young People (IBBY) was the result of the visionary commitment of Jella Lepman (1891–1970). Born in Stuttgart, Germany, she became a politically active journalist. In 1936 she emigrated with her son and daughter from Nazi Germany to London and became a British citizen, working for the British Foreign Office and the BBC during World War II and, beginning in 1941, for the American Broadcasting Station in Europe.

When the war ended, Lepman was engaged at the American headquarters in Germany as an adviser for questions relating to children and young people. Despite a lack of funds, she organized an exhibition of children's illustrations and children's books from 20 countries in Munich in 1946. Three years later, with initial funding from the Rockefeller Foundation, she established the International Youth Library in Munich and was its director until 1957.

In the postwar years, individuals actively engaged in the field of children's literature in many countries became aware of the importance of children's books as a means for promoting international understanding and peace. They realized that children everywhere should have access to books with high literary and artistic standards and thus become enthusiastic and informed readers.

With this vision in mind, in November 1951 Lepman organized a meeting in Munich under the title International Understanding through Children's Books. The goal of the meeting was the foundation of an international organization to promote children's books. The speeches and discussions at the event were covered by news media worldwide. The meeting resulted in the establishment of a committee to form the International Board on Books for Young People (IBBY).

The committee met in Munich in 1952 and made a formal declaration of intent. The meeting was chaired by Swiss publisher Hans Sauerländer, and the effort was international in character from the beginning, as the meeting included representatives from Austria, Germany, the Netherlands, Norway, Sweden, and Switzerland.

The success of this preparatory work resulted in the establishment of IBBY, which was registered as a nonprofit organization in Switzerland when the new organization's first General Assembly and Congress were held at the Swiss Federal Institute for Technology (ETHZ) in Zurich in October 1953. The congress brought together the organization's founding members, including authors Erich Kästner, Lisa Tetzner, Astrid Lindgren, Jo Tenfjord, Fritz Brunner, and Pamela Travers; Swiss illustrators Alois Carigiet and Hans Fischer; publishers Sauerländer and Bettina Hürlimann; and specialists in reading research, such as Richard Bamberger.

The initial capital for the founding of IBBY was donated by the Swiss foundation Pro Juventute, and its secretary general, Otto Binder, was elected as

IBBY's first president. In the early years IBBY also received support from the International Youth Library. However, the dues from the ten national sections that had joined IBBY by 1956 were not sufficient to establish a permanent office, and IBBY's activities were mainly carried out through donations and voluntary work. The organization of the administration was the task of the acting presidents who served for two-year terms during the first decade. Succeeding Otto Binder were Swedish publisher Hans Rabén (1956–1958), Italian professor of education Enzo Petrini (1958–1960), and Lepman (1960–1962).

A notable professionalization of IBBY and an extension of membership were achieved during the presidency of Bamberger (1962–1966). In addition, the publication of IBBY's quarterly journal, *Bookbird*, edited by Lepman, Bamberger, and Lucia Binder, became a permanent activity at this time. During the presidencies of Slovenian publisher Zorka Persic (1966–1970) and Finnish school principal Niilo Visapää (1970–1974), IBBY grew so large that it was no longer possible to rely entirely on voluntary work. In 1974 a permanent office, the IBBY Secretariat, was established in Basel. Leena Maissen was appointed its director and remained in that post until her retirement in 2003. The post is currently held by Liz Page.

IBBY is a nonprofit organization that represents an international network of people who are committed to bringing books and children together. The annual dues from the national sections are IBBY's only source of regular income; projects are supported by sponsors. IBBY cooperates with many international organizations and children's book institutions around the world and exhibits at the International Children's Book Fair in Bologna and other international book fairs.

The biennial IBBY Congresses, which have taken place in 27 countries, have become increasingly important meeting points for the worldwide membership, now comprising 79 national sections, to share information and experiences.

Mission and Programs

IBBY's mission is:

- To promote international understanding through children's books
- To give children everywhere the opportunity to have access to books with high literary and artistic standards
- To encourage the publication and distribution of quality children's books, especially in developing countries
- To provide support and training for those involved with children and children's literature
- To stimulate research and scholarly works in the field of children's literature
- To protect and uphold children's rights as outlined in the United Nations Convention on the Rights of the Child

As part of its mission, IBBY administers three major international awards: the Hans Christian Andersen Award, which is presented to an author and illustrator whose body of work has made lasting contributions to children's literature; the IBBY-Asahi Reading Promotion Award, which is given to a group or an institution whose activities are judged to be making a lasting contribution to reading promotion programs for children and young people; and the IBBY-iRead Outstanding Reading Promoter Award, which recognizes outstanding individuals who are working to promote the expansion and development of children's reading. All three awards are given biennially and presented at the IBBY Congresses; the next awards will be presented at the 38th IBBY Congress in Putrajaya, Malaysia, in 2022.

The IBBY Honour List is a biennial selection of outstanding recently published books, honoring writers, illustrators, and translators from IBBY member countries. An annotated catalog is published for each Honour List selection.

The IBBY Collection for Young People with Disabilities offers information and documentation services for organizations, research workers, teachers, students, librarians, publishers, authors, illustrators, policymakers, and the media who work with young people with special needs. The IBBY Selection of Outstanding Books for Young People with Disabilities is prepared biennially and presented in an annotated catalog. The collection is based at the North York Central Library Branch of the Toronto Public Library in Canada.

Traveling exhibitions of the IBBY Honour List and the Outstanding Books for Young People with Disabilities selections can be booked from IBBY. Detailed information can be found on the IBBY website (http://www.ibby.org).

IBBY established International Children's Book Day in 1967 to inspire a love of reading and to call attention to children's books. Each year the day is sponsored by an IBBY national section and is celebrated on or around Hans Christian Andersen's birthday, April 2.

The IBBY Yamada workshop and project program relies on its international network to help produce and develop book cultures for children within regions that have special needs and lack support.

IBBY established its Children in Crisis program to provide support for children whose lives have been disrupted by war, civil disorder, or natural disaster. The two main activities supported are the therapeutic use of books and storytelling in the form of bibliotherapy and the creation or replacement of collections of selected books that are appropriate to the situation. The Sharjah/IBBY Fund for Children in Crisis was active from 2012 to 2016. The fund supported projects in Afghanistan, Iran, Lebanon, Palestine, Pakistan, and Tunisia.

In response to the waves of refugees from Africa and the Middle East arriving on the Italian island Lampedusa, IBBY launched the project Silent Books, from the World to Lampedusa and Back in 2012. The project involved creating the first library on Lampedusa to be used by local and immigrant children. It also developed a collection of silent books (wordless picture books) that could be understood and enjoyed by children regardless of language. These books were collected from IBBY National Sections. The books are deposited at the documentation and research archive in Rome (Palazzo della Esposizioni), while a second set is deposited at the library in Lampedusa, and a third makes a traveling exhibition for the IBBY network.

Congresses

IBBY's biennial World Congresses, hosted by different national sections, bring together IBBY members and other people involved in children's books and reading development from all over the world. In addition to lectures, panel discussions, seminars, and book exhibitions, the IBBY Membership Assembly takes place. The presentation of the Hans Christian Andersen Awards, the IBBY-Asahi Reading Promotion Award, the IBBY-iRead Outstanding Reading Promoter Award, and the IBBY Honour List are highlights of the biennial congresses. The 38th IBBY Congress will be in Putrajaya, Malaysia, in 2022.

IBBY national sections also organize regional conferences to improve communication, networking, and professional exchange and to strengthen ties of friendship and cooperation among the sections in the region.

Bookbird: A Journal of International Children's Literature is a refereed quarterly journal published by IBBY and is open to any topic in the field of international children's literature. *Bookbird* also has occasional themed issues. Calls for manuscripts are posted on the IBBY website. Regular features include coverage of children's literature studies, IBBY activities, and children's literature awards around the world. *Bookbird* also pays special attention to reading promotion projects worldwide. Its editor works in cooperation with an international editorial review board, guest reviewers, and correspondents who are nominated by IBBY national sections.

IBBY cooperates with several international organizations, including the International Federation of Library Associations and Institutions (IFLA), the International Publishers Association (IPA), and the International Literacy Association (ILA).

IBBY's U.S. National Section

The United States Board on Books for Young People (USBBY) is the U.S. national section of IBBY. It is a nonprofit organization devoted to building bridges of international understanding through children's and young adult books. The Friends of IBBY in the United States was founded in 1976 and became a national section of IBBY in 1984. Membership in USBBY is open to individuals and organizations interested in its mission.

A volunteer board includes USBBY's president, president-elect, past president, recording secretary, treasurer, and 12 directors, four elected and eight appointed, representing the membership as well as the patron organizations that support USBBY, such as ILA, the Children's Book Council (CBC), the American Library Association (ALA), and the National Council of Teachers of English (NCTE).

USBBY offers a forum for those interested in national and international activities relating to children's literature. It publishes a semiannual newsletter for its members, creates an annual list of the most outstanding international literature published or distributed in the United States for children and young adults, maintains an active website, sponsors a biennial regional conference that features speakers of international interest, and cosponsors sessions held at annual conferences of ALA, ILA, and NCTE.

USBBY sponsors the publication of a series of annotated bibliographies of outstanding international literature for young people, the Bridges to Understanding series, published by Scarecrow Press. It also sponsors the creation of an annual

USBBY Outstanding International Books (OIB) list, published yearly in *School Library Journal*, and a bookmark listing the selected titles is distributed via the USBBY website (https://www.usbby.org/outstanding-international-books-list.html) and at meetings and conferences throughout the year. [Find the 2021 list on page 401 of this volume—*Ed.*]

The OIB committee selects international books that are deemed most outstanding of those published during the calendar year. Books selected for the list represent the best of children's literature from other countries, introduce American readers to outstanding authors and illustrators from other countries, help American children see the world from other points of view, provide a perspective or address a topic otherwise missing from children's literature in the United States, exhibit a distinct cultural flavor, and are accessible to American readers. Committee members judge the books based on artistic and literary merit, originality or creativity of approach, distinctiveness of topic, uniqueness of origin, and qualities that engage and appeal to children.

USBBY also submits nominations for the Hans Christian Andersen Award and prepares a biennial selection of outstanding recently published books for the IBBY Honour List, the Silent Books project, and the IBBY list of Outstanding Books for Young People with Disabilities. In addition, it nominates programs for the IBBY-Asahi Reading Promotion Award and the IBBY-iRead Outstanding Reading Promoter Award.

USBBY's Bridge to Understanding Award formally acknowledges the work of adults who use books to promote international understanding among children. The award was established in memory of Arlene Pillar, an educator who served USBBY as newsletter editor from 1984 until her death in 1990. Organizations eligible for this award include schools, libraries, Scout troops, clubs, and bookstores. The winning program may be a one-time event or an ongoing series that serves children ranging in age from kindergarten through tenth grade. The award carries a prize of $1,000 and a certificate. Recent winners include Promoting Global Awareness in Second Graders, a project in the Madeira City School District in Cincinnati that involved four second-grade teachers as well as the elementary art, music, library, gym, and computer teachers. The project was described as helping students to "make personal connections to the characters of the books, develop empathy, and relate to other children of the world through literature."

Other USBBY activities include support of IBBY's Hands across the Sea Fund, which gives assistance to underfunded IBBY sections.

USBBY has an active twinning relationship with four other IBBY national sections, allowing USBBY members to know and work closely with specific countries and to internationalize USBBY perspectives. Specific initiatives within the twinning program may include payment of IBBY dues for underfunded national sections; provision of funding to purchase books or other needed resources for classrooms and libraries; providing funding or training for writers, illustrators, editors, librarians, and publishers; facilitating fellowships for writers, illustrators, editors, librarians, publishers, or those who want to study children's literature; supporting cultural exchange and visits between members of USBBY and twinning national sections; developing reciprocal website postings of newsletters, information about projects, lists of children's books published in each country, and relevant websites; and including news about twinning partners in

Global Partnerships, a regular column in the USBBY newsletter, Bridges. Current USBBY twinning partners are Haiti, Lebanon, Palestine, and El Salvador.

The USBBY Secretariat is at the Center for Teaching through Children's Books at National Louis University, 1000 Capitol Drive, Wheeling, IL 60090. It can be reached by telephone at 224-233-2798, and its e-mail address is secretariat@usbby.org. Its website is http://www.usbby.org. USBBY's executive director is V. Ellis Vance, 5503 N. El Adobe Drive, Fresno, CA 93711-2363, e-mail: executive.director@usbby.org.

Part 2
Legislation, Funding, and Grants

Legislation

Legislation and Regulations Affecting Libraries in 2021: A Report from ALA's Public Policy and Advocacy Office

Kathi Kromer
Associate Executive Director

Shawnda Hines
Assistant Director, Communications

American Library Association
Public Policy and Advocacy Office

In 2021 libraries saw unprecedented levels of federal funding, beginning with the $1.9 trillion American Rescue Plan Act (ARPA). The largest spending bill ever approved by Congress, ARPA included $200 million for the Institute of Museum and Library Services (IMLS), the only source of federal funding dedicated to America's libraries. Of the $200 million for IMLS, 89 percent ($178 million) was allocated for state library administrative agencies.

In addition to the one-time influx of funding through ARPA, libraries won increases in annual congressional appropriations for fiscal year (FY) 2021. IMLS received an additional $5 million, a record eighth consecutive increase for the agency. Innovative Approaches to Literacy (IAL), a federal program administered by the Department of Education supporting school libraries and nonprofit literacy organizations, also saw a $1 million increase above FY 2020 appropriations.

The nation's libraries also benefited from significant investments in broadband funding through several new programs. ARPA provided more than $7 billion for libraries and schools to purchase and distribute technology necessary for remote learning, working from home, virtual healthcare visits, and more. The American Library Association (ALA) contributed rulemaking for the new Emergency Connectivity Fund and worked with the Federal Communications Commission (FCC) to promote the funding through the FCC's E-rate program. Participating libraries received 100 percent reimbursement for the cost of hotspots and other Wi-Fi-capable devices such as modems, routers, laptops, and tablets.

ALA advocates worked to ensure that libraries would be eligible for additional funding in any broadband provisions negotiated in proposed infrastructure spending throughout 2021. The Infrastructure Investment and Jobs Act, which was signed into law in November, included unparalleled funding for digital equity programs. Along with providing an additional $43 billion for broadband deployment, the legislation featured $2.75 billion in new investments in digital inclusion through the Digital Equity Act. The legislation would support libraries and other community organizations to help individuals develop the skills and the confidence to put that internet connection to use. ALA weighed in early to influence the design of the forthcoming grant programs and will provide guidance for libraries of all kinds to access the funds in 2022.

Libraries may be eligible to receive funding for library infrastructure through the Coronavirus Capital Projects Fund, another program established through ARPA. It provides $10 billion in available funding for eligible states, territories, and tribal communities to ensure individuals' access to high-quality broadband; the implementation of broadband infrastructure improvements; and the enhancement of the overall quality of education, work, and telehealth as a direct response to the ongoing public health emergency. Funds will be allocated from the U.S. Department of the Treasury to states. Through its new resources, ALA is promoting the federal program to assist state chapters and local libraries in accessing funds as the program develops in 2022.

Library workers also benefited significantly from the nation's response to the pandemic when the U.S. Department of Education announced a change to Public Service Loan Forgiveness (PSLF) program rules. For a limited period of time, borrowers could receive credit for past periods of repayment that would otherwise not qualify for PSLF. Library workers who were previously denied eligibility have received tens of thousands of dollars in loan forgiveness. Having long advocated with education coalition partners for changes to PSLF, ALA encouraged library workers in all contexts to explore their eligibility for the program before the waiver ends on October 31, 2022.

The continuing focus on digital inclusion resulted in the expansion of tribal libraries' eligibility for federal relief funding, which then led the FCC to address long-standing barriers to tribal library participation in the E-rate program. ALA, in partnership with the Association of Tribal Archives, Libraries, and Museums (ATALM), filed comments in this proceeding to affirm the proposed change in the definition of a tribal library and recommend additional changes to bolster the place of tribal libraries in the E-rate program.

ALA led a campaign throughout the year to garner support for federal legislation to provide funding exclusively for public library facilities for the first time since 1997. Library champions in the House of Representatives and Senate introduced the Build America's Libraries Act in early 2021 to designate funds for the construction of modern libraries in underserved and disadvantaged communities as well as for the renovation and enhancement of facilities to reduce the risk of COVID-19 and vulnerability to natural disasters. Although advocates garnered strong support for the Build America's Libraries Act, the bill was not included in the hotly debated congressional spending packages, which were significantly paired down.

Last year was also a pivotal time for library access to digital content, as ALA enlisted states in legislative efforts for fair pricing for e-books. In March the Maryland General Assembly was the first to pass bills requiring publishers who sell e-book licenses to Maryland consumers to also sell licenses to Maryland public libraries "on reasonable terms." That same month, libraries celebrated when e-book bills passed the New York state senate and assembly. Despite the overwhelming bipartisan support of lawmakers and advocates alike, the Maryland law was challenged when a lawsuit was filed against the state in December, and the governor of New York refused to sign that state's legislation into law. ALA will continue to support other states that are planning to introduce similar legislation in 2022 legislative sessions.

ALA continued its advocacy at the congressional staff level to change the "illegal aliens" subject heading. On November 12 the Library of Congress approved a change to replace the terms "aliens" and "illegal aliens" with the new subject headings "Noncitizens" and "Illegal immigration." ALA president Patty Wong applauded the replacement of the outdated and dehumanizing terms and acknowledged this important first step in aligning the Library of Congress's subject headings with the core values of social justice for ALA members and respecting members of the library community from all backgrounds.

Funding Programs and Grant-Making Agencies

National Endowment for the Humanities

400 7th St. S.W., Washington, DC 20506
202-606-8400, 800-634-1121
TDD (hearing impaired) 202-606-8282 or 866-372-2930 (toll free)
E-mail info@neh.gov, World Wide Web http://neh.gov

The National Endowment for the Humanities (NEH) is an independent federal agency created in 1965. It is one of the largest funders of humanities programs in the United States.

Because democracy demands wisdom, NEH serves and strengthens our republic by promoting excellence in the humanities and conveying the lessons of history to all Americans. It accomplishes this mission by awarding grants for top-rated proposals examined by panels of independent, external reviewers.

NEH grants typically go to cultural institutions, such as museums, archives, libraries, colleges, universities, public television, and radio stations, as well as to individual scholars. The grants do the following:

- Strengthen teaching and learning in schools and colleges
- Facilitate research and original scholarship
- Provide opportunities for lifelong learning
- Preserve and provide access to cultural and educational resources
- Strengthen the institutional base of the humanities

Since 1965 NEH has opened new worlds of learning for the American public with noteworthy projects such as the following:

- Seven thousand books, 16 of which have won Pulitzer Prizes and 20 of which have received the Bancroft Prize
- *The Civil War*, the landmark documentary by Ken Burns viewed by 38 million Americans
- The Library of America editions of novels, essays, and poems celebrating America's literary heritage
- The United States Newspaper Project, which cataloged and microfilmed 63.3 million pages of historic newspapers and paved the way for the National Digital Newspaper Program and its digital repository, Chronicling America

- Annual support for 56 states and territories to help support some 56,000 lectures, discussions, exhibitions, and other programs each year

For more than a half century, NEH has reached millions of people with projects and programs that preserve and study the nation's culture and history while providing a foundation for the future.

The endowment's mission is to enrich cultural life by promoting the study of the humanities. According to the National Foundation on the Arts and the Humanities Act, "The term 'humanities' includes, but is not limited to, the study of the following: language, both modern and classical; linguistics; literature; history; jurisprudence; philosophy; archaeology; comparative religion; ethics; the history, criticism, and theory of the arts; those aspects of social sciences which have humanistic content and employ humanistic methods; and the study and application of the humanities to the human environment with particular attention to reflecting our diverse heritage, traditions, and history and to the relevance of the humanities to the current conditions of national life."

The act, adopted by Congress in 1965, provided for the establishment of the National Foundation on the Arts and the Humanities in order to promote progress and scholarship in the humanities and the arts in the United States. The act included the following findings:

- The arts and the humanities belong to all the people of the United States.
- The encouragement and support of national progress and scholarship in the humanities and the arts, while primarily matters for private and local initiative, are also appropriate matters of concern to the federal government.
- An advanced civilization must not limit its efforts to science and technology alone but must give full value and support to the other great branches of scholarly and cultural activity in order to achieve a better understanding of the past, a better analysis of the present, and a better view of the future.
- Democracy demands wisdom and vision in its citizens. It must therefore foster and support a form of education, and access to the arts and the humanities, designed to make people of all backgrounds, and wherever located, masters of technology and not its unthinking servants.
- It is necessary and appropriate for the federal government to complement, assist, and add to programs for the advancement of the humanities and the arts by local, state, regional, and private agencies and their organizations. In doing so, the government must be sensitive to the nature of public sponsorship. Public funding of the arts and humanities is subject to the conditions that traditionally govern the use of public money. Such funding should contribute to public support and confidence in the use of taxpayer funds. Public funds provided by the federal government ultimately must serve public purposes the Congress defines.
- The arts and the humanities reflect the high place accorded by the American people to the nation's rich culture and history and to the fostering of mutual respect for the diverse beliefs and values of all persons and groups.

What NEH Grants Accomplish

Since its founding, NEH has awarded more than $5.6 billion for humanities projects through more than 64,000 grants.

Interpretive Exhibitions

Interpretive exhibitions provide opportunities for lifelong learning in the humanities for millions of Americans. Since 1967 NEH has awarded approximately $310 million in grants for interpretive exhibitions, catalogs, and public programs, which are among the most highly visible activities supported by the endowment. NEH support finances exhibitions; reading, viewing, and discussion programs; web-based programs; and other public education programs at venues across the country.

Renewing Teaching

Over NEH's history, more than 100,000 high school and college teachers have deepened their knowledge of the humanities through intensive summer study supported by the endowment; tens of thousands of students benefit from these better-educated teachers every year.

Reading and Discussion Programs

Since 1982 NEH has supported reading and discussion programs in the nation's libraries, bringing people together to discuss works of literature and history. Scholars in the humanities provide thematic direction for the discussion programs. Using selected texts and such themes as "Work," "Family," "Diversity," and "Not for Children Only," these programs have attracted more than 2 million Americans to read and talk about what they've read. Funded programs have included veterans' reading groups focused on classic Greek and Roman texts about the experience of war, community reading and discussion programs examining 200 years of Maine state history, and humanities-focused reading and discussion programs for at-risk youth. Most recently, NEH supported a national "Lift Every Voice" reading and discussion program on African American poetic traditions based around the Library of America anthology *African American Poetry: 250 Years of Struggle & Song*.

Chronicling America

NEH's National Digital Newspaper Program is supporting projects to convert microfilm of historically important U.S. newspapers into fully searchable digital files. Developed in partnership with the Library of Congress, this long-term project ultimately will make more than 30 million pages of newspapers accessible online. For more on this project, visit http://chroniclingamerica.loc.gov.

Stimulating Private Support

About $2 billion in humanities support has been generated by NEH challenge grants, which require grant recipients to match federal funds. NEH Infrastructure and Capacity Building Challenge grants leverage federal funding to spur private investment in capital projects and infrastructure upgrades to ensure the long-term health of our cultural institutions.

Presidential Papers

Ten presidential papers projects, from Washington to Eisenhower, have received support from NEH. Matching grants for the ten projects have leveraged millions of dollars in nonfederal contributions.

New Scholarship

NEH grants enable scholars to do in-depth study. Jack Rakove explored the making of the Constitution in his book *Original Meanings*, and James McPherson chronicled the Civil War in his book *Battle Cry of Freedom*.

History on Screen

Since 1967 NEH has awarded approximately $310 million to support the production of films for broad public distribution, including the Emmy Award-winning series *The Civil War*; the Oscar-nominated films *Brooklyn Bridge, The Restless Conscience,* and *Freedom on My Mind;* and film biographies of John and Abigail Adams, Eugene O'Neill, and Ernest Hemingway. Over seven successive nights on PBS, more than 33 million people watched Ken Burns's *The Roosevelts* (2014), which chronicles the lives of Teddy, Eleanor, and Franklin. The NEH-funded series *The Vietnam War* (2018), by Ken Burns and Lynn Novick, was seen by 39 million viewers. Other recent NEH-supported films include *The Vote*, on the women's suffrage movement; *Chasing the Moon*, on the U.S. Space Race; Stanley Nelson's *Freedom Riders* and *Freedom Summer* documentaries; and *Worlds of Ursula K. Le Guin.*

American Voices

NEH support for scholarly editions makes the writings of prominent and influential Americans accessible. Ten presidents are included, along with such key figures as Martin Luther King, Jr., George C. Marshall, and Eleanor Roosevelt. Papers of prominent writers—among them Emily Dickinson, Walt Whitman, Mark Twain, and Robert Frost—are also available.

Library of America

Millions of books have been sold as part of the Library of America series, a collection of the riches of the nation's literature. Begun with NEH seed money, the 303 volumes published to date include the works of such figures as Henry Adams, Edith Wharton, William James, Eudora Welty, and W.E.B. Du Bois.

The Library of America also received a $150,000 grant for the publication of *American Poetry: The Seventeenth and Eighteenth Centuries* (two volumes) and an expanded volume of selected works by Captain John Smith—a key figure in the establishment of the first permanent English settlement in North America, at Jamestown, Virginia—and other early exploration narratives.

Technical Innovation

NEH support for the digital humanities is fueling innovation and new tools for research in the humanities. Modern 3D technology allows students to visit sites ranging from ancient Egypt to the 1964–1965 New York World's Fair. Spectral imaging was used to create an online critical edition of explorer David Livingstone's previously unreadable field diary of 1871.

Science and the Humanities

The scientific past is being preserved with NEH-supported editions of the letters of Charles Darwin, the works of Albert Einstein, and the 14-volume papers of Thomas Edison. Additionally, NEH and the National Science Foundation have joined forces in Documenting Endangered Languages (DEL), a multiyear effort to preserve records of key languages that are in danger of becoming extinct.

EDSITEment

EDSITEment (http://edsitement.neh.gov) assembles the best humanities resources on the web, drawing more than 400,000 visitors each month. Incorporating these Internet resources, particularly primary documents, from more than 350 peer-reviewed websites, EDSITEment features more than 500 online lesson plans in all areas of the humanities. Teachers use EDSITEment's resources to enhance lessons and to engage students through interactive technology tools that hone critical-thinking skills.

Federal-State Partnership

The Office of Federal-State Partnership links NEH with the nationwide network of 56 humanities councils, which are located in each state, the District of Columbia, Puerto Rico, the U.S. Virgin Islands, the Northern Mariana Islands, American Samoa, and Guam. Each council funds humanities programs in its own jurisdiction.

Directory of State and Jurisdictional Humanities Councils

Alabama

Alabama Humanities Foundation
1100 Ireland Way, Suite 202
Birmingham, AL 35205
205-558-3980, fax 205-558-3981
http://www.alabamahumanities.org

Alaska

Alaska Humanities Forum
421 W. 1st Ave., Suite 200
Anchorage, AK 99501
907-272-5341, fax 907-272-3979
http://www.akhf.org

American Samoa

Amerika Samoa Humanities Council
P.O. Box 5800
Pago Pago, AS 96799
684-633-4870, fax 684-633-4873
http://ashcouncil.org

Arizona

Arizona Humanities Council
Ellis-Shackelford House
1242 N. Central Ave.
Phoenix, AZ 85004
602-257-0335, fax 602-257-0392
http://www.azhumanities.org

Arkansas

Arkansas Humanities Council
1400 W. Markham Street, Suite 400
Little Rock, AR 72201
501-353-0349
http://www.arkansashumanitiescouncil.org

California

California Humanities
538 9th St., #210
Oakland, CA 94607
415-391-1474, fax 510-808-7533
http://www.calhum.org

Colorado

Colorado Humanities
7935 E. Prentice Ave., Suite 450
Greenwood Village, CO 80111
303-894-7951, fax 303-864-9361
http://www.coloradohumanities.org

Connecticut

Connecticut Humanities Council
100 Riverview Center, Suite 209
Middletown, CT 06457
860-785-9640, fax 860-685-7597
http://cthumanities.org

Delaware

Delaware Humanities
100 W. Tenth St., Suite 509
Wilmington, DE 19801
302-657-0650, fax 302-657-0655
http://dehumanities.org

District of Columbia

Humanities D.C.
925 U St. N.W.
Washington, DC 20001
202-387-8391, fax 202-387-8149
http://wdchumanities.org

Florida

Florida Humanities Council
599 Second St. S.
St. Petersburg, FL 33701-5005
727-873-2000, fax 727-873-2014
http://www.floridahumanities.org

Georgia

Georgia Humanities Council
50 Hurt Plaza S.E., Suite 595
Atlanta, GA 30303-2915
404-523-6220, fax 404-523-5702
http://www.georgiahumanities.org

Guam

Humanities Guahan
Reflection Center
222 Chalan Santo Papa, Suite 106
Hagåtña, Guam 96910
671-472-4460, fax 671-646-2243
http://www.humanitiesguahan.org

Hawaii

Hawai'i Council for the Humanities
3599 Waialae Ave., Room 25
Honolulu, HI 96816
808-732-5402, fax 808-732-5432
http://www.hihumanities.org

Idaho

Idaho Humanities Council
217 W. State St.
Boise, ID 83702
208-345-5346, fax 208-345-5347
http://www.idahohumanities.org

Illinois

Illinois Humanities Council
125 S. Clark St., Suite 650
Chicago, IL 60603
312-422-5580, fax 312-422-5588
http://www.ilhumanities.org

Indiana

Indiana Humanities
1500 N. Delaware St.
Indianapolis, IN 46202
317-638-1500, fax 317-634-9503
http://www.indianahumanities.org

Iowa

Iowa Department of Cultural Affairs
State Historical Building
600 E. Locust Street

Des Moines, IA 50319
515-281-3223
www.Iowaculture.gov

Kansas

Humanities Kansas
112 S.W. 6th Ave., Suite 210
Topeka, KS 66603-3895
785-357-0359, fax 785-357-1723
https://www.humanitieskansas.org

Kentucky

Kentucky Humanities
206 E. Maxwell St.
Lexington, KY 40508
859-257-5932, fax 859-257-5933
http://www.kyhumanities.org

Louisiana

Louisiana Endowment for the Humanities
938 Lafayette St., Suite 300
New Orleans, LA 70113
504-523-4352, fax 504-529-2358
http://www.leh.org

Maine

Maine Humanities Council
674 Brighton Ave.
Portland, ME 04102-1012
207-773-5051, fax 207-773-2416
http://www.mainehumanities.org

Maryland

Maryland Humanities Council
108 W. Centre St.
Baltimore, MD 21201-4565
410-685-0095, fax 410-685-0795
http://www.mdhumanities.org

Massachusetts

Mass Humanities
66 Bridge St.
Northampton, MA 01060
413-584-8440, fax 413-584-8454
http://www.masshumanities.org

Michigan

Michigan Humanities

2364 Woodlake Drive, Suite 100
Okemos, MI 48864
517-372-7770, fax 517-372-0027
http://michiganhumanities.org

Minnesota

Minnesota Humanities Center
987 East Ivy Ave
St. Paul, MN 55106
651-774-0105, fax 651-774-0205
http://www.mnhum.org

Mississippi

Mississippi Humanities Council
3825 Ridgewood Rd., Room 311
Jackson, MS 39211
601-432-6752, fax 601-432-6750
http://www.mshumanities.org

Missouri

Missouri Humanities
105 N Main, Suite 108
St. Louis, MO 63301
314-781-9660
http://www.mohumanities.org

Montana

Humanities Montana
311 Brantly
Missoula, MT 59812-7848
406-243-6022, fax 406-243-4836
http://www.humanitiesmontana.org

Nebraska

Humanities Nebraska
215 Centennial Mall South
Lincoln, NE 68508
402-474-2131, fax 402-474-4852
http://www.humanitiesnebraska.org

Nevada

Nevada Humanities
1670-200 N. Virginia St.
P.O. Box 8029
Reno, NV 89507-8029
775-784-6587, fax 775-784-6527
http://www.nevadahumanities.org

New Hampshire

New Hampshire Humanities
117 Pleasant St.
Concord, NH 03301-3852
603-224-4071, fax 603-224-4072
http://www.nhhumanities.org

New Jersey

New Jersey Council for the Humanities
336 Friends Street
Camden, NJ 08102
609-695-4838, fax 609-695-4929
http://www.njhumanities.org

New Mexico

New Mexico Humanities Council
4115 Silver Ave. S.E.
Albuquerque, NM 87108
505-633-7370, fax 505-633-7377
http://www.nmhum.org

New York

Humanities New York
150 Broadway, Suite 1700
New York, NY 10038
212-233-1131, fax 212-233-4607
http://www.humanitiesny.org

North Carolina

North Carolina Humanities Council
320 East 9th St., Suite 414
Charlotte, NC 28202
704-687-1520
http://www.nchumanities.org

North Dakota

Humanities North Dakota
418 E. Broadway, Suite 8
P.O. Box 2191
Bismarck, ND 58502
701-255-3360, fax 701-223-8724
http://www.humanitiesnd.org

Northern Marianas Islands

Northern Marianas Humanities Council
P.O. Box 506437
Saipan, MP 96950

670-235-4785, fax 670-235-4786
http://www.nmhcouncil.org/

Ohio

Ohio Humanities Council
471 E. Broad St., Suite 1620
Columbus, OH 43215-3857
614-461-7802, fax 614-461-4651
http://www.ohiohumanities.org

Oklahoma

Oklahoma Humanities
424 Concord Dr., Suite E
Oklahoma City, OK 73102
405-235-0280, fax 405-235-0289
http://www.okhumanities.org

Oregon

Oregon Humanities
619 SW Alder Street
Suite 1111
Portland, OR 97205
503-241-0543, fax 503-241-0024
http://www.oregonhumanities.org

Pennsylvania

Pennsylvania Humanities Council
230 South Broad Street
Suite 403
Philadelphia, PA 19102
215-925-1005, fax 215-925-3054
http://www.pahumanities.org

Puerto Rico

Fundación Puertorriqueña de las Humanidades
109 San José St., 3rd floor
Box 9023920
San Juan, PR 00902-3920
787-721-2087, fax 787-721-2684
http://www.fphpr.org

Rhode Island

Rhode Island Council for the Humanities
131 Washington St., Suite 210
Providence, RI 02903
401-273-2250, fax 401-454-4872
http://www.rihumanities.org

South Carolina

South Carolina Humanities
2711 Middleburg Drive, Suite 203
Columbia, SC 29254
803-771-2477, fax 803-771-2487
http://www.schumanities.org

South Dakota

South Dakota Humanities Council
1215 Trail Ridge Rd., Suite A
Brookings, SD 57006
605-688-6113, fax 605-688-4531
http://sdhumanities.org

Tennessee

Humanities Tennessee
807 Main Street, Suite B
Nashville, TN 37206
615-770-0006, fax 615-770-0007
http://www.humanitiestennessee.org

Texas

Humanities Texas
1410 Rio Grande St.
Austin, TX 78701
512-440-1991, fax 512-440-0115
http://www.humanitiestexas.org

Utah

Utah Humanities
202 W. 300 North
Salt Lake City, UT 84103
801-359-9670, fax 801-531-7869
http://www.utahhumanities.org

Vermont

Vermont Humanities
11 Loomis St.
Montpelier, VT 05602
802-262-2626, fax 802-262-2620
http://www.vermonthumanities.org

U.S. Virginia Islands

Community Foundation of the Virginia Islands
PO Box 380
St. Thomas, VI 00804
340-774-6031, fax 340-774-3852
http://www.cfvi.net

Virginia

Virginia Humanities
946 Grady Ave., Suite 100
Charlottesville, VA 22903
434-924-3296
http://www.virginiahumanities.org

Washington

Humanities Washington
1015 8th Ave. N., Suite B
Seattle, WA 98109
206-682-1770, fax 206-682-4158
http://www.humanities.org

West Virginia

West Virginia Humanities Council
1310 Kanawha Blvd. East
Charleston, WV 25301
304-346-8500, fax 304-346-8504
http://wvhumanities.org/

Wisconsin

Wisconsin Humanities Council
3801 Regent St.
Madison, WI 53705
608-262-0706, fax 608-263-7970
http://www.wisconsinhumanities.org

Wyoming

Wyoming Humanities Council
1315 E. Lewis St.
Laramie, WY 82072-3459
307-721-9243, fax 307-742-4914
http://www.thinkwy.org

NEH Overview

Division of Education Programs

The Division of Education Programs supports humanities education through programs aimed primarily at program and curriculum development and through professional development opportunities for K–12 and higher education faculty. Intensive reading and discussion programs featuring recognized scholars bring together small communities of teachers at both the higher education and K–12 levels to investigate new themes and innovative approaches to humanities subjects. Largely residential and held during the summer, these programs encourage the study of common texts and other resources, include visits to collections in libraries and museums, and help faculty integrate what has been learned back into their classrooms. The division has several grant programs to support broad institutional endeavors. Community colleges, historically Black colleges and universities, tribal colleges and universities, and Hispanic-serving institutions receive grants to enhance the humanities content of existing programs, develop new programs, or lay the foundation for more extensive endeavors. The division also supports creative, integrative, collaborative curricular projects at two- and four-year postsecondary institutions between the humanities and STEM, pre-professional and professional programs in law, the health sciences, etc. Finally, the division's veterans-centered program supports institutions interested in designing and implementing discussions programs that explore the experiences of war and military service through the examination of humanities texts and other resources.

Contact: 202-606-8500, e-mail education@neh.gov.

Division of Preservation and Access

Grants are made for projects that will create, preserve, and increase the availability of resources important for research, education, and public programming in the humanities.

Support may be sought to preserve the intellectual content and aid bibliographic control of collections; to compile bibliographies, descriptive catalogs, and guides to cultural holdings; and to create dictionaries, encyclopedias, databases, and electronic archives. Applications also may be submitted for education and training projects dealing with issues of preservation or access; for research and development leading to improved preservation and access standards, practices, and tools; and for projects to digitize historic U.S. newspapers and to document endangered languages. Grants are also made to help smaller cultural repositories preserve and care for their humanities collections. Proposals may combine preservation and access activities within a single project.

Contact: 202-606-8570, e-mail preservation@neh.gov.

Division of Public Programs

Public humanities projects enable millions of Americans to explore significant humanities works, ideas, and events. They offer new insights into familiar subjects and invite reflection upon important questions about human life. The division supports a wide range of public humanities programming that reaches large and diverse public audiences and makes use of a variety of formats—interpretation at historic sites, television and radio productions, museum exhibitions, podcasts, short videos, digital games, websites, mobile apps, and other digital media. Examples of funded projects include Ken Burns's *Civil War* documentary, which increased public understanding of a pivotal point in American history; the Walters Art Museum exhibition The Book of Kings: Art, War; the Morgan Library's *Medieval Picture Bible*, which gave visitors insights into the role of religion in the Middle Ages; the reinterpretation of Historic Hudson Valley's Phillipsburg Manor, an 18th-century New York mill site, through which visitors learn about the contributions of enslaved African Americans in the North; and Walden, a free-to-educators digital game that allows players to spend a year at Walden Pond as Henry David Thoreau.

Program officers are prepared to answer a wide variety of questions from prospective applicants. They can provide information about the division's application guidelines and the eligibility or competitiveness of potential project ideas and provide tips about common proposal-writing mistakes to avoid. They will supply samples of successful application narratives in each grant category and even offer feedback for a preliminary draft of a proposal if it is submitted well before the deadline. All potential applicants are encouraged to contact a program officer early in their project conceptualization process.

Contact: 202-606-8269, e-mail publicpgms@neh.gov.

Division of Research Programs

The Division of Research Programs supports scholarly research that advances knowledge and understanding of the humanities. Through 12 annual funding opportunities, awards are made to scholars—individuals, collaborative teams, or institutions—working on research projects of significance to specific humanities fields and to the humanities as a whole. The projects that the division supports are as diverse as America itself: editions of the Dead Sea Scrolls, the history of "The Star Spangled Banner," and the autobiography of Mark Twain.

NEH's Fellowships program was established more than 50 years ago and was the first award offered by the endowment. Since then, approximately 7,000 books have been written by NEH fellows. In the academic world, "getting an NEH" is shorthand for receiving an NEH Fellowship, which indicates the award's widely respected reputation and prestige. Recognizing the specific needs of certain scholars, Awards for Faculty offer more flexible fellowships to those employed at historically Black colleges and universities, Hispanic-serving institutions, and tribal colleges and universities. Summer Stipends offer two-month awards to allow scholars to take a shorter break to pursue focused research. Public Scholar Awards encourage writing books for a wide readership. Placing NEH at the forefront of innovative methods in the humanities, NEH-Mellon Fellowships for Digital Publication support projects that require digital expression and digital publication. Books resulting from all of these grants regularly earn awards and recognition. NEH-funded work has been honored with Pulitzer Prizes and Bancroft Prizes, as well as awards from academic associations across the country and accolades from reviewers in major newspapers and literature journals.

While Research Programs is the only NEH division to make awards to individuals, institutional grants are also available. Collaborative Research supports projects by teams of scholars. Scholarly Editions and Scholarly Translations provides funding for time-intensive editing projects such as the Papers of George Washington, and Fellowship Programs at Independent Research Institutions provides American scholars with access to unique collections at American centers for humanities research around the world.

Teachers, too, make use of NEH-supported research in their classrooms—often with the aid of the web resources and books resulting from many projects. For example, the papers of William F. Cody (Buffalo Bill) and the Freedmen and Southern Society Project on the history of Emancipation are used in U.S. history classes, the papers of Albert Einstein in physics, and the literary works and letters of writers such Willa Cather, Ernest Hemingway, and Samuel Beckett in English classes. Archaeology projects unearth artifacts used by museum curators in mounting exhibitions that teach us about life in ancient civilizations. Translations of materials in other languages bring little-known foreign works such as ancient Roman graffiti in Pompeii, the letters of the Dakota people, and contemporary Ukrainian literature to American readers. Documentarians, artists, and producers of all sorts of fiction and nonfiction media rely on new research findings in many fields—American history, literature, music, and the history of science and technology—to inform and inspire their audiences. Projects like these add to the existing store of knowledge and reach every area of the humanities.

Contact: 202-606-8200, e-mail research@neh.gov.

Office of Challenge Grants

Challenge Grants programs strengthen institutional and organizational capacity for work in the humanities. Institutions and organizations in the United States support the humanities by preserving and providing access to collections, conducting scholarship and research, and developing educational programs for various audiences. Challenge Grants projects may involve building and renovating structures such as museums and libraries and updating the infrastructure that undergirds humanities work in its many forms.

Successful applicants will be awarded matching funds intended to stimulate additional private, state, and local support for humanities infrastructure. Recipients must raise cash contributions from nonfederal third parties and have them certified by NEH before matching funds are released.

NEH offers two Challenge Grants funding opportunities. Their purpose is to strengthen the institutional base of the humanities with grants that support infrastructure development and capacity-building or that support work to maintain, modernize, and sustain digital infrastructure. Both approaches should help institutions secure and sustain their core activities for the long term.

Contact: 202-606-8309, e-mail challenge@neh.gov.

Office of Digital Humanities

The Office of Digital Humanities (ODH) offers grant programs that fund project teams experimenting with digital technologies to develop new methodologies for humanities research, teaching and learning, public engagement, and scholarly communications. ODH funds those studying digital culture from a humanistic perspective and humanists seeking to create digital publications. Another major goal of ODH is to increase capacity of the humanities in applying digital methods.

To best tackle the broad, interdisciplinary questions that arise when studying digital technology, ODH works closely with the scholarly community and other funding agencies in the United States and abroad to encourage collaboration across national and disciplinary boundaries.

Funded digital projects contribute to humanities scholarship that serve carefully identified audiences, address issues of accessibility and usability, and are designed to be open, replicable, and sustainable. All projects funded in this division analyze their workflows and publish their results in white papers that are shared widely. This body of work contributes to the bibliography of digital humanities.

ODH staff members participate in conferences and workshops with the scholarly community to help foster understanding of issues in the digital humanities and to ensure they are meeting the needs of the field.

Contact: 202-606-8401, e-mail odh@neh.gov.

A full list of NEH grants programs and deadlines is available on the endowment's website at http://www.neh.gov/grants.

Institute of Museum and Library Services

955 L'Enfant Plaza North, S.W., Suite 4000, Washington, DC 20024-2135
202-653-4657, fax 202-653-4600
http://www.imls.gov

Crosby Kemper III
Director

The Institute of Museum and Library Services (IMLS) is an independent grant-making agency and the primary source of federal support for the nation's libraries and museums. The mission of IMLS is to advance, support, and empower America's museums, libraries, and related organizations through grant making, research, and policy development. Its vision is a nation where museums and libraries work together to transform the lives of individuals and communities.

IMLS was created with the passage of the Museum and Library Services Act of 1996, which was reauthorized on December 31, 2018. The agency has statutory authority to award financial assistance, collect data, form strategic partnerships, and advise policymakers and other federal agencies on museum, library, and information services.

The agency consolidates federal library programs dating back to 1956 with museum programs dating back to 1976.

IMLS helps to ensure that all Americans have access to museum, library, and information services. The agency invests in new and exploratory approaches, as well as proven and tested methods. IMLS funds work that advances collective knowledge, lifelong learning, and cultural and civic engagement. And the agency builds capacity within the museum and library fields to enable better service to communities and to enhance community decision making by sharing trends and data.

IMLS has an expansive reach. The agency is the largest source of federal funding for libraries in the nation, directing population-based funding to all 50 states, the District of Columbia, the U.S. territories, and Freely Associated States through its Grants to States program. The agency's discretionary grants are selected through a highly respected and competitive peer review process, drawing on professionals located across the nation. This work enables museums and libraries located in geographically and economically diverse areas to deliver essential services that make it possible for individuals and communities to flourish.

Strategic Goals

When IMLS was established, lawmakers recognized that U.S. libraries and museums are powerful national assets. They saw "great potential in an institute that is focused on the combined roles that libraries and museums play in our community life." The Museum and Library Services Act of 1996 charges IMLS with advising policymakers on library, museum, and information services and supporting a wide range of programs that improve the lives of individuals throughout the nation.

IMLS carries out this charge as the agency adapts to meet the changing needs of the nation's museums and libraries and their communities. IMLS's role—to advance, support, and empower America's museums and libraries through grant making, research, data collection, and policy development—is essential to helping these institutions navigate change and continue to improve their services.

IMLS goals and objectives are to:

- Promote Lifelong Learning. IMLS supports learning and literacy for people of all ages through museums and libraries.
- Build Capacity. IMLS strengthens the capacity of museums and libraries to improve the well-being of their communities.
- Increase Public Access. IMLS makes strategic investments that increase access to information, ideas, and networks through libraries and museums.
- Achieve Excellence. IMLS strategically aligns its resources and relationships to support libraries and museums nationwide.

COVID-19 Response

CARES Act Grants

On March 27, 2020, the president signed the Coronavirus Aid, Relief, and Economic Security (CARES) Act, Pub. L. 116-136, which authorized funding for IMLS to assist states, tribes, museums, and libraries to "prevent, prepare for, and respond to [the] coronavirus, ... expand digital network access, purchase internet accessible devices, and provide technical support services" for the benefit of communities impacted by the public health emergency.

IMLS CARES Act Grants Funding Opportunities

In fiscal year (FY) 2020 IMLS established two competitive funding opportunities to support libraries, museums, and Native American/Native Hawaiian communities in responding to the COVID-19 pandemic. A total of $13.8 million was awarded to 39 museums and 29 libraries, as well as an additional $1.2 million to 15 Native American Tribes and nonprofit organizations that primarily serve and represent Native Hawaiians. In FY 2021 IMLS funded 22 additional applications from museums and libraries in response to the IMLS CARES Act Grants for Museums and Libraries funding opportunity. These awards totaled $3,062,796.

American Rescue Plan (ARP) Act Grants

On March 11, 2021, the president signed the American Rescue Plan (ARP) Act, Pub. L. 117-2, which authorized funding for IMLS "to carry out museum and library services" for the benefit of communities impacted by the public health emergency. ARP designated $200 million in pandemic response funding for IMLS, enabling the agency to efficiently provide critical funding to State Library Administrative Agencies (SLAAs), located in every state and territory and with reach into local communities across the United States. In addition to the $178 million allocated to the SLAAs, IMLS also offered $15 million in grants to museums, libraries, and Native American and Native Hawaiian communities to provide direct support to address community needs created or exacerbated by the

COVID-19 pandemic and in assisting with recovery. Projects could continue, enhance, or expand existing programs and services, or the recipients could launch new ones to address emergent needs and unexpected hardships. IMLS received 572 applications for its ARP grant program, requesting over $22.8 million. These discretionary awards were made in October 2021 and will be included in IMLS's FY 2022 reporting. In FY 2021 IMLS applied a total of $4,644,267 of ARP funds to support awards for ARP-related projects that were submitted as applications to various FY 2021 agency grant programs.

ARP Allotments to SLAAs

Process

Using a population-based formula, the Grants to States program awarded $178 million in ARP funds to the 59 SLAAs in the 50 states, the District of Columbia, the U.S. Territories, and the Freely Associated States. IMLS distributed these awards on April 9, 2021, with funds remaining available until September 30, 2022. IMLS directed the SLAAs to use the funds in helping communities respond directly and immediately to the pandemic, as well as to related economic and community needs through equitable approaches.

Highlights

Early, informal ARP plans from the states indicated an emphasis on connectivity, including purchasing hotspots, devices with data plans, and wifi upgrades, as well as digital inclusion support to address gaps in digital literacy. States collectively anticipated reaching 14,410 libraries and other institutions with these investments. In just five months after SLAAs received the ARP awards, a national roll-up of publicly available information showed that 46 of 59 states and territories had already publicized their investments. High-level data as of September 30, 2021, pointed to the following:

- Funds have reached at least 3,900 libraries, 37 museums, and 10 tribal entities.
- Twenty-six SLAAs were offering competitive ARP subawards, and some with multiple opportunities, for a total of 42 programs.
- Nineteen SLAAs were offering noncompetitive ARP subawards, based on formulas of need or other distribution methods.
- SLAAs had already announced more than 2,600 subawards.
- SLAAs and their subrecipients had already announced the purchase of more than 5,300 devices, such as hotspots, laptops, and tablets.
- SLAAs and their subrecipients had already announced the purchase of more than 28 library vehicles to reach remote users, including bookmobiles and book bikes.
- Twenty-three SLAAs were offering statewide programs, and some with multiple offerings, for a total of 47 programs.
- Connectivity efforts remained the primary ARP focus among the states, with 37 of them investing in this area. But 23 states also prioritized supplies to help libraries safely reopen their physical spaces.

The ARP grants continued the new approaches for the Grants to States program that began with CARES Act. SLAAs found creative ways to reach museums and tribes, in addition to traditionally eligible libraries. And while not all had the flexibility to do so, as of September 30, 2021, five states had found ways to incorporate museums into their ARP grant making, and five states had done the same for tribes.

REopening Archives, Libraries, and Museums (REALM) Project

In late March 2020 IMLS took initial steps to help identify and respond to the needs of collecting institutions by hosting a webinar with the Centers for Disease Control (CDC) to provide information for libraries and museums and their staff and patrons to address the unique challenges of mitigating COVID-19 when managing their collections, spaces, and public interactions. The need to provide more information to libraries, archives, and museums about the important and existential problems facing them in the COVID-19 global pandemic was clear, and IMLS established a cooperative agreement with OCLC and Battelle. The REopening Archives, Libraries, and Museums (REALM) project has drawn upon scientific research and Battelle laboratory work to produce, widely disseminate, and periodically update evidence-based information that has informed operational considerations for reducing the risk of transmission of SARS-CoV-2 through libraries, archives, and museums to their staff and visitors.

IMLS exercised its authority to accept donations and enter into interagency relationships to fund the majority of the project. As such, the REALM project was made possible in part with support from IMLS, the Library of Congress, the Andrew W. Mellon Foundation, and the Carnegie Corporation of New York.

The project conducted laboratory tests to assess the attenuation of SARS-CoV-2 on materials common in libraries, archives, and museums. It evaluated emergent published research for applicable scientific information that can be applied to the risk-based decision making of the libraries, archives, and museums community and provides a website and toolkits in the form of webinars, infographics, videos, and other materials with the goal of informing local policies, operations, and space configuration decisions that support reopening and operations within a SARS-CoV-2 environment. The REALM project website (https://www.oclc.org/realm/about.html) details the status of the project and its publications.

Library Services

The Museum and Library Services Act (20 U.S.C. § 9171) authorizes the Office of Library Services to do the following:

- Enhance coordination among federal programs that relate to library, education, and information services
- Promote continuous improvement in library services in all types of libraries in order to better serve the people of the United States
- Facilitate access to resources in all types of libraries for the purpose of cultivating an educated and informed citizenry
- Encourage resource sharing among all types of libraries for the purpose of achieving economical and efficient delivery of library services to the public

- Promote literacy, education, and lifelong learning, including by building learning partnerships with school libraries in the nation's schools, including tribal schools, and developing resources, capabilities, and programs in support of state, tribal, and local efforts to offer a well-rounded educational experience to all students
- Enable libraries to develop services that meet the needs of communities throughout the nation, including people of diverse geographic, cultural, and socioeconomic backgrounds; individuals with disabilities; residents of rural and urban areas; Native Americans; military families; veterans; and caregivers
- Enable libraries to serve as anchor institutions to support community revitalization through enhancing and expanding the services and resources provided by libraries, including those services and resources relating to workforce development, economic and business development, critical-thinking skills, health information, digital literacy skills, financial literacy and other types of literacy skills, and new and emerging technology
- Enhance the skills of the current library workforce and recruit future professionals, including those from diverse and underrepresented backgrounds, to the field of library and information services
- Ensure the preservation of knowledge and library collections in all formats and enable libraries to serve their communities during disasters
- Enhance the role of libraries within the information infrastructure of the United States in order to support research, education, and innovation
- Promote library services that provide users with access to information through national, state, local, regional, and international collaborations and networks
- Encourage, support, and disseminate model programs of library and museum collaboration

Grants to States

The Grants to States program awards population-based formula grants to each SLAA in the 50 states; the District of Columbia; the U.S. territories of the Commonwealth of Puerto Rico; the U.S. Virgin Islands; American Samoa; Guam; and the Commonwealth of the Northern Mariana Islands; and the Freely Associated States of the Federated States of Micronesia, the Republic of the Marshall Islands, and the Republic of Palau (20 U.S.C. § 9131). Following the passage of the Museum and Library Services Act of 2018, FY 2020 was the first year that the three Freely Associated States submitted five-year plans, which IMLS approved before disseminating their allotments.

The formula consists of a minimum allotment set by law plus a supplemental amount based on population (dependent on annual appropriations). Population data are based on the information available from the U.S. Census Bureau.

The Museum and Library Services Act of 2018 increased minimum allotments for states from $680,000 to $1 million and for Pacific territories and Freely Associated States from $60,000 to $100,000. Increases to the minimum allotments depend on increases to the program's overall budget, which grew by $2 million in FY 2021. Although this increase did not fully enact the new statutory minimum allotments, it did raise the base to $833,845 for states, with $60,000 for other entities. The Museum and Library Services Act of 2018 limits administrative costs at the state level to 4 percent and requires a 34 percent match from nonfederal state or local funds.

Programs and services delivered by each SLAA support the purposes and priorities set forth in the Library Services and Technology Act (LSTA). SLAAs must complete five-year plans, conduct a five-year evaluation based on those plans, and report annually to IMLS on their progress in strengthening library services, which helps improve practice and inform policy. SLAAs set goals and objectives for their states regarding the use of Grants to States funds within the statutorily required five-year plan approved by IMLS. These goals and objectives are determined through a planning process that includes statewide needs assessments.

Use of Funds

States are subject to a statutory "maintenance of effort" requirement that helps ensure that federal funds do not supplant state investments. SLAAs may use their funding for the following:

- Expanding services for learning and access to information and educational resources in a variety of formats, including new and emerging technology, in all types of libraries, for individuals of all ages, in order to support such individuals' needs for education, lifelong learning, workforce development, economic and business development, health information, critical-thinking skills, digital literacy skills, and financial literacy and other types of literacy skills
- Establishing or enhancing electronic and other linkages and improved coordination among and between libraries and entities for the purpose of improving the quality of and access to library and information services
- Providing training and professional development, including continuing education, to enhance the skills of the current library workforce and leadership and advance the delivery of library and information services
- Enhancing efforts to recruit future professionals, including those from diverse and underrepresented backgrounds, to the field of library and information services
- Developing public and private partnerships with other agencies, tribes, and community-based organizations
- Targeting library services to individuals of diverse geographic, cultural, and socioeconomic backgrounds; to individuals with disabilities; and to individuals with limited functional literacy or information skills
- Targeting library and information services to persons having difficulty using a library and to underserved urban and rural communities, including children from families with incomes below the poverty line
- Developing library services that provide all users access to information through local, state, regional, national, and international collaborations and networks
- Carrying out other activities as described in the state library administrative agency's plan

Discretionary Grants

The Office of Library Services offered five funding opportunities in FY 2021: National Leadership Grants, Native American Library Services Basic Grants, Native American Library Services Enhancement Grants, Native Hawaiian Library Services Grants, and the Laura Bush 21st Century Librarian Program.

Museum Services

The Museum and Library Services Act (20 U.S.C. § 9171) authorizes the Office of Museum Services to do the following;

- Encourage and support museums in carrying out their educational role as core providers of learning and in conjunction with schools, families, and communities
- Encourage and support museums in carrying out their public service role of connecting the whole of society to the cultural, artistic, historical, natural, and scientific understandings that constitute our diverse heritage
- Encourage leadership, innovation, and applications of the most current technologies and practices to enhance museum services through international, national, regional, state, and local networks and partnership
- Assist, encourage, and support museums in carrying out their stewardship responsibilities to achieve the highest standards in conservation and care of the diverse cultural, historic, natural, and scientific heritage of the United States to benefit future generations
- Assist, encourage, and support museums in achieving the highest standards of management and service to the public and to ease the financial burden borne by museums as they serve their communities in new and different ways
- Support resource sharing and partnerships among museums, libraries, schools, and other community organizations
- Encourage and support museums as a part of economic development and revitalization in communities
- Ensure museums of various types and sizes in diverse geographic regions of the United States are afforded attention and support
- Support efforts at the state and regional levels to leverage museum resources and maximize museum services
- Assist museums in their civic engagement efforts to ensure that every person in the United States has access to high-quality museum services

IMLS also conducts a grant program with the purpose of improving operations, care of collections, and development of professional management at African American museums, pursuant to the National Museum of African American History and Culture Act (20 U.S.C. § 80r-5).

Discretionary Grants

The Office of Museum Services offered six competitive funding opportunities in FY 2021: Museums for America (MFA), Inspire! Grants for Small Museums,

Museums Empowered, National Leadership Grants for Museums, Native American/Native Hawaiian Museum Services, and Museum Grants for African American History and Culture.

Interagency Collaboration

The Museum and Library Services Act authorizes IMLS to enter into interagency agreements to promote or assist with the museum, library, and information services-related activities of other federal agencies (20 U.S.C. § 9103). Recognizing the role of museums and libraries as anchor institutions, the act directs the agency to coordinate and work jointly with other federal departments and agencies on the following:

- Initiatives, materials, technology, or research to support education, workforce development, economic and business development, and related activities and services undertaken by libraries
- Resource and policy approaches to eliminate barriers to fully leveraging the role of libraries and museums in supporting the early learning, literacy, lifelong learning, digital literacy, workforce development, and education needs of the people of the United States
- Initiatives, materials, technology, or research to support educational, cultural, historical, scientific, environmental, and other activities undertaken by museums

In addition to project support, the director of IMLS holds several statutory positions, including on the Federal Council on the Arts and the Humanities, in the American Folklife Center, and in connection with the nation's Semiquincentennial Commission.

Policy Research, Analysis, Data Collection, and Dissemination

The Museum and Library Services Act authorizes IMLS to support and conduct policy research, data collection, analysis and modeling, evaluation, and dissemination of information to extend and improve the nation's museum, library, and information services (20 U.S.C. § 9108). The act identifies the following objectives:

- To enhance and expand the capacity of museums, libraries, and information services to anticipate, respond to, and meet the evolving needs of communities and the public, including by identifying trends and developments that may impact the need for and delivery of services
- To provide information and data on the role, value, and impact of museum, library, and information resources, including the identification of trends and the potential gaps in the availability and use of museum and library services by their communities and the public
- To measure the effectiveness of museums, libraries, and information services throughout the United States, including the impact of federal programs authorized under the act

- To identify indicators and outcomes that can be used to create enhancements to the efficiency and efficacy of museum, library, and information services
- To promote advancement and growth in museum, library, and information services through the sharing of best practices and effective strategies in order to better serve the people of the United States
- To facilitate planning for, and the building of, institutional capacity in order to improve museum, library, and information services at the national, state, local, and regional levels and international communications and cooperative networks

In carrying out these objectives, IMLS engages with the SLAAs and networks of museums and libraries, as well as with national, state, tribal, and regional museum and library organizations.

Surveys

IMLS produces evaluations and performs data collection and analysis to inform policy decisions and support the museum and library fields of practice. These efforts identify trends, make important comparisons, and enable objective policy making at the national and state levels. The primary data products maintained by IMLS are the Public Libraries Survey (PLS) and the State Library Administrative Agency (SLAA) Survey.

The PLS has been conducted annually since 1988 and is a definitive source on the state of public libraries in the United States. PLS data provide key information on more than 9,000 public library systems and 17,000 public library outlets nationwide.

The SLAA Survey has been collected annually since 1994 and biennially after 2010. It is a definitive source on the state of state library agencies in the United States and provides key information on the state library agencies in all 50 states and the District of Columbia.

For IMLS surveys and data, visit https://www.imls.gov/research-tools/data-collection, and see the report "Highlights of IMLS Public Library Surveys" in Part 4 of this volume.

IMLS Website and Publications

The IMLS website (www.imls.gov) provides a wealth of information on the agency's activities, including IMLS-sponsored conferences, webinars, publications, and grant programs. Through an electronic newsletter, *IMLS News*, and its blog, IMLS provides information on grant deadlines, success stories, and opportunities.

IMLS is on Twitter (@US_IML) and Facebook (https://www.facebook.com/USIMLS).

EveryLibrary

P.O. Box 406, Riverside, IL 60546
312-574-0316; e-mail info@everylibrary.org
http://www.everylibrary.org | http://action.everylibrary.org | http://SaveSchoolLibrarians.org
Facebook https://www.facebook.com/EveryLibrary
LinkedIn https://www.linkedin.com/company/3801587
Twitter @EveryLibrary

John Chrastka
Executive Director

Founded in December 2012 as a political action committee for libraries, EveryLibrary focuses on building political power for libraries at all levels of government across all types of libraries. EveryLibrary is the first and only nationwide political action committee for libraries. It provides pro bono advising and consulting to libraries about their funding requests, either when they appears on a ballot or through a municipal funding partner. Its school library-focused digital activism platform SaveSchoolLibrarians.org works to support school librarian positions and budgets for school library programs. EveryLibrary's mission statement is "Building voter support for libraries." Its vision statement, and the inspiration for its name, is "Any library funding issue anywhere should matter to every library everywhere." It is chartered in the state of Illinois as a nonprofit and is designated as a 501(c)4 social welfare organization by the IRS, enabling it to raise and expend funds on political engagement, legislative and regulatory matters, and direct and indirect lobbying of elected or appointed officials.

Board and Advisors

EveryLibrary is administered by a board of directors and is run by staff. It has no members. Its 2021 board of directors were John Chrastka, president and executive director; Erica Findley, treasurer; Patrick "PC" Sweeney, board secretary and political director; and Brian D. Hart, Harmony V. Faust, Peter Bromberg, Jeannie Allen, Lori Ayers, Roberto Delgadillo, Gary Kirk, and Kathleen McEvoy, directors.

Organizational History

As a 501(c)4 organization, EveryLibrary works to support the funding formula for libraries at the local, state, and national levels along with focusing on policies and legislation that support and extend the future of library work. For library Election Days, EveryLibrary works with library boards and staff on informational communications campaigns and with local citizen ballot committees as they conduct "Get Out the Vote" and "Vote Yes" campaigns for local library ballot measures. Through 2021 EveryLibrary has helped take 121 libraries to their Election Days, winning 85 percent and securing more than $392 million (aggregated per annum) in stable funding for those libraries. For school libraries, EveryLibrary supports direct action and outreach across local districts on its SaveSchoolLibrarans.org platform. During state or federal policy campaigns, EveryLibrary's national network of more than 360,000 library activists are engaged and empowered via the action.everylibrary.org platform.

EveryLibrary is funded by individual donors, both monthly and annually, and corporate (vendor) donors. Being able to provide its services at no cost to libraries and committees allows EveryLibrary to focus on best practices for campaigns rather than revenue generation from direct consulting.

Library Ballot Measures

In 2021 EveryLibrary supported nine public library campaigns to establish, renew, or expand funding for operations, collections, programs, services, and staffing or to issue a bond for construction or remodeling of library facilities. It supported one statewide education funding coalition campaign to benefit among its provisions school library program budgets.

Library election wins in 2021 included a renewal of the basic operational levy for the New Orleans Public Library, which had been in place since 1986; a new operating levy for the Central Arkansas Library System in Little Rock; a first-ever local option levy for the Portage County (Ohio) Public Library; a renewal of the local option levy in St. Clairsville, Ohio; a bond in McCall, Indiana, to renovate and expand its library; a bond in Southington, Connecticut, to build a new library; and a bond in Carthage, Illinois, as a local matching fund to a state construction grant. There was a loss in Pearl River, New York, where voters rejected a construction bond question.

Direct Political Actions for Public Libraries

Funding libraries is always a political decision. How we choose to tax ourselves and how our collective values are expressed in the town, state, or federal budget is fundamentally what every fight for libraries is about. In 2021 EveryLibrary was able to support dozens of public libraries that were trying to face down a political problem or that were attempting to embrace a political opportunity. Each and every community situation is different, so EveryLibrary begins its work by listening to the local stakeholders, assessing if their involvement will serve the sector's best interests, and only then moving to build political power for the library.

EveryLibrary is uniquely focused on helping local libraries during political and funding crises, and state or national library organizational partners reach and activate the public about budgetary, legislative, or regulatory issues. Many direct actions are operationalized through the action.everylibrary.org platform. This digital advocacy and communications platform allows EveryLibrary to field petitions and e-mailing campaigns targeted at elected officials and to use social-influencing campaigns to effect positive change for libraries and their users. EveryLibrary can set up a direct action for a library in crisis in only a few hours. At the close of 2021 the EveryLibrary network of library activists included more than 220,000 individuals who had taken an active role in at least one pro-library campaign.

Highlights include a collaborative campaign to support the Save Niles-Maine Library Coalition, in which EveryLibrary worked alongside the coalition to expose the true impact of the library board's behavior to local elected officials, business and education interests, and neighbors across the district. This was an unusual campaign because it focused on the behavior and intent of the library board itself. However, EveryLibrary believes a board may have to be opposed when it has broken faith with the mission, vision, and values of libraries.

Other direct actions for public libraries include one in Ellsworth, Maine, where the city council cut the library budget. EveryLibrary helped create and field a strategy to activate the public for their library. In West Haven, Connecticut, EveryLibrary continued a campaign against a branch closure and further cuts proposed by the mayor and city council by bringing out hundreds of supporters through a digital campaign. The parish council in Lafayette Parish, Louisiana, forced the resignation of the library director and stacked the board with its allies in order to defund the library from within. EveryLibrary continues to support outreach alongside local stakeholders through digital campaigns to fight back.

The previous year was dynamic in state government and Congress. EveryLibrary was the only national library organization to support a vaccine plan that would include librarians in the Phase 1B or 1C definition. It was disappointed when libraries were dropped from the Economic Justice Plan as it moved to become the Infrastructure Plan under the Biden Administration. Its petition to support Section 230 of the Communications Decency Act was the first to connect libraries with this important platform protection. EveryLibrary's continued support for the Don't Block LGBTQ Act and its opposition to the Lawful Access to Encrypted Data (LAED) Act, which would erode privacy protections, were unique among national library organizations.

School Library and School Librarian Campaigns

Through an ongoing partnership with Follett Learning, EveryLibrary continues to support school library budgets and school librarians through its SaveSchool-Librarians.org digital action site and through advocacy partnerships with state school library associations and organizations.

In early 2021 before federal Elementary and Secondary School Emergency Relief stabilization funds were authorized under the American Rescue Plan, EveryLibrary fought against dozens of proposed cuts to school librarian positions from coast to coast. These included districts in New Jersey, where local administrators in The Chathams and Glen Ridge attempted to use the pandemic as cover for eliminating school librarians.

The highlight of EveryLibrary's 2021 advocacy campaigns was a reversal by the administration of the District of Columbia Public Schools to allow principals to "excess" school librarians and a new policy by the city council to instead fund a school librarian in every school. For two years, EveryLibrary had campaigned alongside the Washington Teachers Union and school library stakeholders to reverse cuts and restore school librarians. *Publishers Weekly* designated this campaign as a Top 10 Library News Story for 2021.

EveryLibrary helped several state library associations in the lead-up to local 2021 elections by hosting candidate surveys to engage school board candidates and legislative candidates directly during the campaign season. Both the Pennsylvania School Librarians Association (PSLA) and the New Jersey Association of

School Librarians (NJASL) designed and fielded nonpartisan candidate surveys with EveryLibrary's assistance. The goal was to learn about candidates' awareness and interest in school library issues and policies as a component of their overall advocacy strategy. EveryLibrary plans to support more school library communities with this unique service in 2022.

Other state and local partnerships were focused on building political power or influencing policy outcomes. In April 2021 EveryLibrary co-hosted a benefit event with the New York City School Librarians Association featuring authors and local elected officials, including Senator Kirsten Gillibrand, New York Attorney General Letitia James, and city council members. Of the 1,700 public schools in New York City, only 600 have a school librarian. This event was intended to kick off a concerted campaign to hire more school librarians in the city.

Through its SaveSchoolLibrarians.org digital campaign site, EveryLibrary supported policy issues for several state library associations, including the Michigan Association for Media in Education, which saw a new $800,000 grant program for collaboration between public libraries and certified school librarians in the budget; NJASL, in which its Information Literacy Standards Bill advanced in the state senate; and PSLA, in which more than 30 new cosponsors were added to its ratio bill.

Organizational Agenda

EveryLibrary will continue to work in 2022 to fulfill its core mission of building voter support for libraries of all types. EveryLibrary's six strategic priorities in 2022 continue to be:

- To deepen its efforts to support local library communities that go on the ballot to renew or extend their basic taxpayer-approved funding and cultivate opportunities for libraries that want to enhance services and facilities through municipal budgets or voter-approved measures
- To join and support coalitions that align with the mission of libraries as institutions; that promote and extend the rights and prosperity of the people whom libraries serve; and that protect the rights, employment, and pensions of the people who work in all types of libraries
- To continue to build a unique and extensive network of Americans who believe in the power of libraries to change lives and build communities and who are ready to become advocates and activists for libraries
- To support the role of library boards and commissions in governing libraries, making policy, and setting budgets that are responsive to diverse local priorities and create inclusive, prosperous, and vibrant communities
- To focus its support of school library programs as effective solutions for some of the biggest problems facing schools and districts around the country
- To be a leader and a listener in a national discussion about the role that public, academic, and school libraries have in people's lives and to work within the profession and across civil society to find the best ways to preserve, protect, and extend everyone's right to use libraries

Budget, Donor Transparency, and Reporting

EveryLibrary puts its donor funding to work in three ways: directly on local library campaigns—for both public libraries and school libraries—on building its national reach as an advocacy organization for libraries, and on staff and projects that run the organization. As the only national 501(c)4 for libraries, it "bundles" small donations from around the country and sends them to local Vote Yes committees where needed.

EveryLibrary is entirely supported by individual donors and library vendor donors. It does not ask for or receive any funding from grant-making, philanthropic, or charitable organizations. As an independent 501(c)4, EveryLibrary is ineligible for government grants (federal or state). EveryLibrary's operating budget allocates one-third to direct campaign expenditures, one-third to salaries and operations, and one-third to growing its organizational reach. To keep costs low, staff and interns collaborate across the country in a virtual office environment that has few fixed expenses. Its office environment is supported by G-Suite; Nation Builder hosts its public-facing webpages; and it utilizes PayPal, Stripe, and Act Blue as third-party donation processors.

EveryLibrary provides a high level of transparency about its donations and is one of only a few national political action groups that encourage donors to self-disclose. EveryLibrary voluntarily provides annual financial disclosure information to GuideStar, a large national nonprofit clearinghouse and rating service, where it currently holds a Gold Rate certification.

EveryLibrary Institute NFP

The EveryLibrary Institute NFP (http://everylibraryinstitute.org) is a public policy and tax policy think tank for libraries that is focused on the future of public library and school library funding in the United States and abroad. Its nonprofit 501(c)3 mission is to develop research, programmatic opportunities, trainings, fiscal sponsorships, and scholarship that advance the image and impact of libraries to the general public and policymakers. Domestically, this includes conducting training programs with state libraries and library associations, publishing its journal (*The Political Librarian*), supporting public outreach and education across the EveryLibrary network, and providing crowdfunding services through its FundLibraries .org platform. Its board members are K.C. Boyd, John Chrastka, Kyle Courtney, Trevor A. Dawes, Erica Findley, Britten Follett, Amy Garmer, Fran Glick, Kafi Kumasi, Steve Potter, Rivkah Sass, Cal Shepard, Maureen Sullivan, Patrick "PC" Sweeney, Jill Hurst-Wahl, and Lance Werner.

Part 3
Library/Information Science Education and Career Resources

Career Resources and Job Listings for Library and Information Professionals

Susanne Markgren

Job-seeking can, and should, be a job in and of itself. Fortunately, there are many resources and tools out there to help navigate a successful path to employment. These past few years have proven that we are all vulnerable to outside forces and that our statuses and circumstances can change quickly and, perhaps, permanently. Adaptability and creativity will most likely play key roles in all of our career paths going forward as we examine what the new normal looks like and prepare for more (certain) uncertainty.

Connectivity and community are essential components of job satisfaction and are equally important in the job search to help one another seek out new skills and opportunities to clinch that first, or next, position. It is also important to research the existing job market, to take note of changes and trends in job postings and job titles, to identify strengths and limitations, and to address needs and expectations in developing a personal job-search strategy.

Coverage from *Library Journal*'s "Placements and Salaries 2021" tells a story of a difficult and uncertain year for 2020 graduates, with fewer open positions, many rescinded offers, and modified (or entirely remote) work environments. Despite the hardships for these job seekers, there are some positives: Unemployment rose only slightly—just one percent—from 2019, starting salary levels showed a slight dip but did not plummet, most graduates who found employment landed full-time permanent positions, and gender-based salary disparity showed a slight improvement over the previous year.

The top five job-seeking resources that were mentioned in the *Library Journal* survey are Indeed, ALA JobLIST, city/state/regional websites, LinkedIn, and specific institution/employer websites. Some of these resources now include ways to narrow your search to "work from home" or "remote."

San José State University's annual "MLIS Skills at Work" (listed in the Career Advice Sites and Resources section) offers an overview of trends seen within the job postings themselves. Some notable ones, which clearly represent the times we live in, are the following: a demand for candidates who can successfully work remotely; a demand for candidates who are collaborative, forward-thinking, and open to uncertainty and ambiguity; and a push to ask candidates to think intentionally about what it means to serve diverse and historically excluded communities. They also offer some sage advice for job seekers: get started now, be resourceful, focus on intentional skill development, make the most of student and professional leadership opportunities, promote yourself, become known for adaptability and a positive attitude.

This article identifies a variety of relevant and current (at the time of publication) online resources and tools to assist students, recent graduates, and experienced library professionals in their journeys to a new or improved position. The

Susanne Markgren is co-author of the career guidance books *How to Thrive as a Library Professional: Achieving Success and Satisfaction* (Libraries Unlimited, 2019), with Linda Miles, and *Career Q&A: A Librarian's Real-Life, Practical Guide to Managing a Successful Career* (Information Today, Inc., 2013), with Tiffany Eatman Allen.

resources have been selected based on popularity, longevity, and influence. All are freely available online, and as with every online information source, users should employ critical analysis and judgment to determine currency, accuracy, and bias.

The Directory of Organizations in Part 6 of this volume may also prove useful for job seekers. Many of these organizations, institutions, libraries, and associations maintain their own job sites and social media accounts where active job listings can be found.

Organization of the Resources

The resources that follow are organized into three sections. The first, Career Advice Sites and Resources, lists informational websites that provide tips and strategies to assist those seeking advice on specific areas of librarianship and archive work. Many of these are association sites, and some offer materials and guidance on resume and cover letter writing and interviewing.

The second section, Podcasts, lists podcasts that provide listeners with current news, hot topics, interviews, and reviews, as well as real-world examples and narratives from library and informational professionals working in a variety of roles and settings. As a bonus, podcasts offer up an entertaining and insightful way to consume information and a popular platform to increase awareness about trends and issues in librarianship.

The third section is for the active job seeker and offers two lists of resources— the first list is specific to librarians, archivists, and information professionals; the second covers a broader range of resources that are not specific to library or information-related positions. The selected sites primarily post jobs in the United States, but some also list international opportunities. It is good practice to search a variety of job sites, systematically and routinely, to get the most comprehensive and current snapshot of available positions. It is also a good idea to seek out specific libraries, companies, institutions, and associations on their own websites, as well as on social media. Where available, Twitter handles have been included at the end of each listing.

Career Advice Sites and Resources

American Association of Law Libraries (AALL)—Career Center

https://www.aallnet.org/careers/career-center
Offers information on careers in law libraries, advice on how to find a job, and access to the *AALL Salary Survey*.　@aallnet

American Association of School Librarians (AASL)—Education and Careers

http://www.ala.org/aasl/about/ed ,
Career and education resources for those seeking to enter or advance in the school library field. Job listings are found at ALA JobLIST.　@aasl

American Library Association (ALA) JobLIST—Career Development Resources

http://www.ala.org/educationcareers/employment/career-resources
A wealth of resources from ALA to help with the job search as well as enhance career development efforts.　@ALA_JobLIST and @alaplacement

BCALA (Black Caucus of the American Library Association) Career Center

https://jobs.bcala.org/career-resources
Tools and resources to make your resume stand out, ace the interview, and advance your career. @BC_ALA

Bureau of Labor Statistics, U.S. Department of Labor, Occupational Outlook Handbook, Librarians

https://www.bls.gov/ooh/education-training-and-library/librarians.htm
Provides information on librarian jobs and salaries and insight into the growth and outlook of the profession.

HigherEdJobs

https://www.higheredjobs.com/career/resumes.cfm
Advice on writing cover letters, resumes, and CVs, as well as interviewing and developing job search strategies for landing a job in academe. @HigherEdJobs

Library Worklife—HR E-News for Today's Leaders

http://ala-apa.org/newsletter
Informs readers on issues such as career advancement, certification, pay equity, recruitment, research, and work/life balance. @alaapa

Medical Library Association (MLA) Career Center

http://www.mlanet.org/p/cm/ld/fid=352
Includes information, resources, and connections for students and job seekers alike. @MedLibAssn

MLIS SKILLS AT WORK—A Snapshot of Job Postings Spring 2021

https://ischool.sjsu.edu/sites/main/files/file-attachments/career_trends.pdf
Prepared annually by the M.L.I.S. online degree program at the San José State University School of Information. @SJSUiSchool

Public Library Association (PLA)—Careers in Public Librarianship

http://www.ala.org/pla/tools/careers
Information and career advice about public librarianship from a leading ALA division. Job listings are found at ALA JobLIST. @ALA_PLA

RBMS—Careers and Scholarships

http://rbms.info/careers-faq
Advice and resources for those interested in careers in special collections. @RBMSinfo

SAA (Society of American Archivists) Career Learning Center

https://careers.archivists.org/jobseekers/resources/blueskyLMS
Encourages an integrative career and professional development process that enhances your skill set. @archivists_org

Public Library Association (PLA)—Skilling for Employment Post COVID-19

http://www.ala.org/pla/initiatives/digitalskilling
PLA and Microsoft are helping libraries identify tools to assist members in gaining skills for jobs that are well-positioned to grow in the future.

Your Library Career: Career Q&A for Library People

http://yourlibrarycareer.com
A Q&A forum and career development archive of professional guidance and advice for librarians, library staff, and those thinking of entering the profession. Includes "How I Got My First Job" interviews.

Podcasts

Call Number with American Libraries Podcast

https://soundcloud.com/dewey-decibel-703453552
Each month, your host and *American Libraries* senior editor Phil Morehart will be your guide to conversations with librarians, authors, thinkers, and scholars about topics from the library world and beyond.

Circulating Ideas: The Librarian Interview Podcast

https://circulatingideas.com
Circulating Ideas facilitates conversations about the innovative people and ideas that are allowing libraries to thrive in the 21st century.

FYI: The Public Libraries Podcast

http://publiclibrariesonline.org/category/media/podcast
Covers current programs and initiatives in public libraries such as serving the homeless; equity, diversity, and inclusion; imposter syndrome; embedded librarianship; early literacy; social services; marketing; and much more

Library Pros

https://www.thelibrarypros.com
A librarian and information technology pro talking libraries, library tech, and everything in between

Linking Our Libraries

https://linkingourlibraries.libsyn.com
The hosts share information with all types of libraries, archives, and nonprofit staff and leaders working to build their skills.

Lost in the Stacks: The Research Library Rock'n'Roll Radio Show

https://lostinthestacks.libsyn.com
Each show features an hour of music, interviews, and library talk united by a common theme.

Not a Rocking Chair Librarian

https://podcasts.apple.com/us/podcast/not-a-rocking-chair-librarian
Conversations and ruminations on the shifts taking place in K–12 librarianship and libraries

School Librarians United

https://schoollibrariansunited.libsyn.com
A podcast dedicated to the nuts and bolts of running a successful school library

T Is for Training

https://tisfortraining.wordpress.com
A podcast dedicated to improvement through learning. It also covers training, presenting, learning, teaching, understanding, and compassion.

Job Listings for Librarians, Archivists, and Information Professionals

ALA JobLIST

http://joblist.ala.org | @ALA_JobLIST

American Association of Law Libraries (AALL) —Career Center

https://careers.aallnet.org/jobs | @aallnet

Archives Gig

https://archivesgig.wordpress.com | @archivesgig

ARLIS/NA JobList

https://www.arlisna.org/professional-resources/arlis-na-joblist | @ARLIS_NA

Association for Information Science and Technology (ASIS&T) Careers

https://asist-jobs.careerwebsite.com | @asist_org

Association of Research Libraries (ARL)—Job/Residency/Internship Listings

http://www.arl.org/leadership-recruitment/job-listings | @ARLnews

American Theological Library Association (ATLA) Job Board

https://www.atla.com/jobs | @YourAtla

BCALA Jobs

https://jobs.bcala.org | @BC_ALA

Metropolitan New York Library Council (METRO) Jobs

https://metro.org/jobs | @mnylc

Music Library Association Job Search

https://www.musiclibraryassoc.org/networking/opening_search.asp | @musiclibassoc

NASIG Jobs

http://nasigjobs.wordpress.com | @NASIG

Special Libraries Association (SLA) Jobs

https://careers.sla.org | @SLAhq

Job Listings Not Specific to Librarians, Archivists, and Information Professionals

Higher Education

Chronicle of Higher Education: Jobs
https://jobs.chronicle.com | @chronicle

EDUCAUSE Career Center

https://jobs.educause.edu/jobs | @educause

HigherEdJobs.com

http://www.higheredjobs.com | @insidehighered

Government

USAJobs.gov
https://www.usajobs.gov | @USAJOBS

Interdisciplinary (mega job sites)

Indeed

https://www.indeed.com | @indeed

LinkedIn Jobs

https://www.linkedin.com/jobs | @LinkedIn

Monster

https://www.monster.com | @Monster

SimplyHired

https://www.simplyhired.com | @SimplyHired

Zip Recruiter

https://www.ziprecruiter.com | @ZipRecruiter

Accredited Master's Programs in Library and Information Studies

This list of graduate programs accredited by the American Library Association is issued by the ALA Office for Accreditation. Regular updates and additional details appear on the Office for Accreditation's website at http://www.ala.org/CFApps/lisdir/index.cfm. A total of 128 U.S. and Canadian institutions offering both accredited and nonaccredited programs in librarianship are included in the 75th edition (2022–2023) of *American Library Directory* (Information Today, Inc.).

Northeast: Conn., D.C., Md., Mass., N.J., N.Y., Pa., R.I.

Catholic University of America, School of Arts and Sciences, Dept. of Lib. and Info. Science, 620 Michigan Ave. N.E., Washington, DC 20064. Renate Chancellor, chair. Tel. 202-319-5085, fax 319-5574, e-mail cualis@cua.edu, World Wide Web http://lis.cua.edu. Admissions contact: Louise Gray. Tel. 202-319-5085, fax 319-5574, e-mail cualis@cua.edu.

Clarion University of Pennsylvania, College of Business Admin. and Info. Sciences, Dept. of Info. and Lib. Science, 210 Carlson Lib. Bldg., Clarion, PA 16214. Linda L. Lillard, chair. Tel. 866-272-5612, fax 814-393-2150, e-mail libsci@clarion.edu, World Wide Web http://www.clarion.edu/libsci. Admissions contact: Michelle Ritzler. Tel. 866-393-2337, e-mail gradstudies@clarion.edu.

Drexel University, College of Computing and Informatics, Dept. of Info. Science, 3141 Chestnut St., Philadelphia, PA 19104-2875. Andrea Forte, dept. head. Tel. 215-895-2474, fax 215-895-2494, e-mail istinfo@drexel.edu, World Wide Web http://drexel.edu/cci/academics/graduate-programs/ms-In-information. Admissions contact: Matthew Lechtenburg. Tel. 215-895-1951, e-mail ml333@drexel.edu.

Long Island University, College of Education, Info. and Technology, Palmer School of Lib. and Info. Science, 720 Northern Blvd., Brookville, NY 11548-1300. Bea Baaden, dir. Tel. 516-299-3818, fax 516-299-4168, e-mail post-palmer@liu.edu, World Wide Web https://www.liu.edu/post/Academics/College-of-Education-Information-and-Technology/Palmer-School-of-Library-Information-Science/Academic-Programs/MS-Library-Informa-tion-Science. Admissions contact: Heather Ranieri. Tel. 516-299-4110, e-mail heather.ranieri@liu.edu.

Pratt Institute, School of Info. and Lib. Science, 144 W. 14 St., 6th Fl., New York, NY 10011. Anthony Cocciolo, dean. Tel. 212-647-7682, fax 212-367-2492, e-mail si@pratt.edu, World Wide Web https://www.pratt.edu/academics/information/degrees/library-and-information-science-mslis. Admissions contact: Quinn Lai. Tel. 212-647-7701, e-mail qlai@pratt.edu.

Queens College, Grad. School of Lib. and Info. Studies, Rm. 254, Rosenthal Lib., 65-30 Kissena Blvd., Flushing, NY 11367-1597. Kwong bor Ng, chair. Tel. 718-997-3790, fax 718-997-3797, e-mail qc_gslis@qc.cuny.edu, World Wide Web http://sites.google.com/a/qc.cuny.edu/gslis. Admissions contact: Roberta Brody. Tel. 718-997-3790, e-mail roberta_brody@qc.edu.

Rutgers University, School of Communication and Info., Dept. of Lib. and Info. Science, New Brunswick, NJ 08901-1071. Marie Radford, chair. Tel. 848-932-7602, e-mail mi@comminfo.rutgers.edu, World Wide Web http://comminfo.rutgers.edu. Admissions contact: Lilia Pavlovsky. Tel. 732-932-7576.

Saint John's University, College of Liberal Arts and Sciences, Div. of Library and Information Science, 8000 Utopia Parkway, Queens, NY 11439. James Vorbach, dir. Tel. 718-990-1834, fax 718-990-2071, e-mail vorbach@stjohns.edu, World Wide Web http://www.stjohns.edu/academics/programs/library-and-information-science-master-science. Admissions contact: Michael Crossfox. Tel. 718-990-6200, e-mail dlis@stjohns.edu.

Simmons University, School of Lib. and Info. Science, College of Organizational,

Computational and Info. Sci., 300 The Fenway, Boston, MA 02115. Sanda Erdelez, dir. Tel. 617-521-2868, e-mail slisadm@simmons.edu, World Wide Web http://simmons.edu/slis. Admissions contact: Kate Benson. Tel. 617-521-2868, e-mail slisadm@simmons.edu.

Southern Connecticut State University, College of Education, Dept. of Info. and Lib. Sci., 501 Crescent St., New Haven, CT 06515. Hak Joon Kim. Tel. 203-392-5781, fax 203-392-5780, e-mail ils@southernct.edu, World Wide Web http://inside.southernct.edu/information-and-library-science. Admissions contact: Dr. Arlene Bielefield. Tel. 203-392-5708, e-mail bielefielda1@southernct.edu.

Syracuse University, School of Info. Studies, 343 Hinds Hall, Syracuse, NY 13244. Jian Qin, MLIS program dir. Tel. 315-443-2911, fax 315-443-6886, e-mail ischool@syr.edu, World Wide Web http://ischool.syr.edu/academics/graduate/masters-degrees/ms-library-and-information-science. Admissions contact: Blythe Bennett. Tel. 315-443-2911, e-mail mslis@syr.edu.

University at Albany, State Univ. of New York, College of Emergency Preparedness, Homeland Security and Cybersecurity, Draper 015, Albany, NY 12222. Jennifer Goodall, vice dean. Tel. 518-442-5258, fax 518-442-5632, e-mail infosci@albany.edu, World Wide Web http://www.albany.edu/cehc/programs/ms-information-science. Admissions contact: Graduate Admissions. Tel. 518-442-3980, e-mail graduate@albany.edu.

University at Buffalo, State Univ. of New York, Graduate School of Educ., Dept. of Info. Sci, 534 Baldy Hall, Buffalo, NY 14260-1020. Dan Albertson, chair. Tel. 716-645-2412, fax 716-645-3775, e-mail ub-lis@buffalo.edu, World Wide Web http://ed.buffalo.edu/information/about.html. Admissions contact: Ryan Taughrin. Tel. 716-645-2110, e-mail gse-info@buffalo.edu.

University of Maryland, College of Info. Studies, 4121 Hornbake Bldg., College Park, MD 20742. Ursula Gorham, MLIS program dir. Tel. 301-405-2039, fax 301-314-9145, e-mail ischooladmission@umd.edu, World Wide Web http://ischool.umd.edu/academics/master-of-library-and-information-science. Admissions contact: Morgan Adle.

Tel. 301-405-2039, e-mail mlisprogram@umd.edu.

University of Pittsburgh, School of Computing and Info., Info. Culture and Data Stewardship, 135 N. Bellefield Ave., Pittsburgh, PA 15260. Mary K. Biagini, chair. Tel. 412-624-5230, fax 412-648-7001, e-mail sciadmit@pitt.edu, World Wide Web http://www.sci.pitt.edu/academics/masters/mlis. Admissions contact: Shabana Reza. Tel. 412-624-3988, e-mail shabana.reza@pitt.edu.

University of Rhode Island, Grad. School of Lib. and Info. Studies, Rodman Hall, 94 W. Alumni Ave., Kingston, RI 02881. Valerie Karno, dir. Tel. 401-874-2878, fax 401-874-4964, e-mail vkarno@uri.edu, World Wide Web http://www.uri.edu/artsci/lsc.

Southeast: Ala., Fla., Ga., Ky., La., Miss., N.C., S.C., Tenn., Va., P.R.

East Carolina University, College of Educ., Lib. Science Degree Program, Mailstop 172, ECU, Greenville, NC 27858. Barbara Miller Marson, MLIS program dir. Tel. 252-328-2347, fax 252-328-4368, e-mail marsonb@ecu.edu, World Wide Web http://bit.ly/ECUML. Admissions contact: Camilla King. Tel. 252-328-6012, e-mail gradschool@ecu.edu.

Florida State University, College of Communication and Info., School of Info., 142 Collegiate Loop, P.O. Box 3062100, Tallahassee, FL 32306-2100. Kathleen Burnett, dir. Tel. 850-644-5775, fax 850-644-9763, e-mail jb.mitchell@cci.fsu.edu, World Wide Web http://ischool.cci.fsu.edu. Admissions tel. 850-645-3280, e-mail ischooladvising@admin.fsu.edu.

Louisiana State University, College of Human Sciences and Education, School of Lib. and Info. Science, 267 Coates Hall, Baton Rouge, LA 70803. Carol Barry, dir. Tel. 225-578-3158, fax 225-578-4581, e-mail slis@lsu.edu, World Wide Web http://slis.lsu.edu. Admissions contact: LaToya Coleman Joseph. Tel. 225-578-3150, e-mail lcjoseph@lsu.edu.

North Carolina Central University, School of Lib. and Info. Sciences, P.O. Box 19586, Durham, NC 27707. Jon P. Gant, dean. Tel.

919-530-7585, fax 919-530-6402, e-mail slisadmissions@nccu.edu, World Wide Web http://www.nccuslis.org. Admissions contact: Nina Clayton. Tel. 919-530-5184.

Old Dominion University, Darden College of Educ. and Prof. Studies, Lib. and Info. Studies Program, STEM Educ. and Prof. Studies, 4301 Hampton Blvd., Norfolk, VA 23529. Dr. Sue C. Kimmel, contact. Tel. 757-683-4305, e-mail libraryscience@odu. edu, World Wide Web http://www.odu.edu/ stemps/academics/library-science.

University of Alabama, College of Communication and Info. Sciences, School of Lib. and Info. Studies, Box 870118, Tuscaloosa, AL 35487-0252. Jamie Naidoo, interim dir. Tel. 205-348-2719, fax 205-348-3746, e-mail info@slis.ua.edu, World Wide Web http:// www.slis.ua.edu. Admissions contact: Lita Shive. Tel. 205-348-1527, e-mail lmshive@ ua.edu.

University of Kentucky, College of Communication and Info., School of Info. Science, 320 Little Library, Lexington, KY 40506-0224. Jeffrey T. Huber, dir. Tel. 859-218-2290, fax 859-257-4205, e-mail sis@uky.edu, World Wide Web http://www.uky.edu/cis/slis. Admissions contact: Will Buntin. Tel. 859-257-3317, e-mail wjbunt0@uky.edu.

University of North Carolina at Chapel Hill, School of Info. and Lib. Science, CB 3360, 100 Manning Hall, Chapel Hill, NC 27599-3360. Gary Marchionini, dean. Tel. 919-962-8366, fax 919-962-8071, e-mail info@ ils.unc.edu, World Wide Web http://sils.unc. edu/programs/graduate/msls. Admissions contact: Lara Bailey.

University of North Carolina at Greensboro, School of Educ., Dept. of Lib. and Info. Studies, 446 School of Educ. Bldg., P.O. Box 26170, Greensboro, NC 27402-6170. Lisa O'Connor, chair. Tel. 336-334-3477, fax 336-334-4120, e-mail lis@uncg.edu, World Wide Web http://soe.uncg.edu/academics/departments/lis. Admissions contact: Nora Bird. Tel. 336-256-1313, e-mail njbird@uncg.edu.

University of Puerto Rico, Info. Sciences and Technologies, P.O. Box 21906, San Juan, PR 00931-1906. Noraida Dominguez-Flores, acting dir. Tel. 787-763-6199, fax 787-764-2311, e-mail egcti@uprrp. edu, World Wide Web http://egcti.upr.edu.

Admissions contact: Migdalia Dávila-Pérez. Tel. 787-764-0000 ext. 3530, e-mail migdalia.davila@upr.edu.

University of South Carolina, College of Info. and Communications, School of Lib. and Info. Science, 1501 Greene St., Columbia, SC 29208. Karen Gavigan, interim dir. Tel. 803-777-3858, fax 803-777-7938, e-mail kgavigan@sc.edu, World Wide Web http://www. libsci.sc.edu. Admissions contact: Tel. 803-777-3887, e-mail slisss@mailbox.sc.edu.

University of South Florida, College of Arts and Sciences, School of Info., 4202 E. Fowler Ave., CIS 1040, Tampa, FL 33620. Randy Borum, dir. Tel. 813-974-3520, fax 813-974-6840, e-mail si@usf.edu, World Wide Web https://www.usf.edu/arts-sciences/departments/information/programs/ graduate-programs/ma-in-library-and-information-sciences/index.aspx. Admissions contact: Alexis Shinawongse. Tel. 813-974-8022.

University of Southern Mississippi, College of Educ. and Health Sciences, School of Lib. and Info. Science, 118 College Dr., No. 5146, Hattiesburg, MS 39406-0001. Stacy Creel, interim dir. Tel. 601-266-4228, fax 601-266-5774, e-mail slis@usm.edu, World Wide Web http://www.usm.edu/slis. Admissions: tel. 601-266-5137, e-mail graduatestudies@usm.edu.

University of Tennessee, College of Communication and Info., School of Info. Sciences, 451 Communication Bldg., Knoxville, TN 37996. Abebe Rorissa, interim dir. Tel. 865-974-2148, fax 865-974-4967, e-mail sis@ utk.edu, World Wide Web http://www.sis. utk.edu, Admissions: Tel. 865-974-2148.

Valdosta State Univ., College of Education and Human Services, Dept. of Lib. and Info. Studies, 1500 N. Patterson St., Odum 4600, Valdosta, GA 31698-0133. Linda R. Most, dept. head. Tel. 229-333-5966, fax 229-259-5055, e-mail mlis@valdosta.edu, World Wide Web http://www.valdosta.edu/mlis. Admissions contact: Sheila Peacock.

Midwest: Ill., Ind., Iowa, Kan., Mich., Minn., Mo., Ohio, Wis.

Chicago State University, College of Arts & Sciences, Dept. of Computing, Information,

Mathematical Sciences and Technology, 9501 S. King Dr., Education Bldg., Room 208, Chicago, IL 60628-1598. Rae-Anne Montague, LIS program coordinator. Tel. 773-995-5016, e-mail montague@csu. edu, World Wide Web http://www.csu.edu/ cimst/infostudies/lib_info_science_ms.htm. Admissions contact: Gloria Adams. Tel. 773-995-2404, e-mail graduateprograms@ csu.edu.

Dominican Univ., School of Info. Studies, 7900 W. Division St., River Forest, IL 60305. Kate Marek, dean. Tel. 708-524-6983, fax 708-524-6657, e-mail sois@dom. edu, World Wide Web http://www.dom.edu/ academics/majors-programs/master-library-and-information-science. Admissions contact: Aracelis Sanchez. Tel. 708-524-6456, e-mail asanche2@dom.edu.

Emporia State University, School of Lib. and Info. Management, Campus Box 4025, 1 Kellogg Circle, Emporia, KS 66801-5415. Wooseob Jeong, dean. Tel. 620-341-5203, fax 620-341-5233, e-mail sliminfo@ emporia.edu, World Wide Web http:// www.emporia.edu/school-library-and-information-management/programs-certif-icates-licensures/master-library-science/. Admissions contact: Kathie Buckman. Tel. 620-341-5065.

Indiana University, School of Informatics, Computing and Engineering, Info. and Lib. Science, Luddy Hall, Suite 2999C, 700 N. Woodlawn Ave., Bloomington, IN 47408. Raj Achayra, dean. Tel. 812-855-2018, fax 812-855-6166, e-mail ilsmain@indiana.edu, World Wide Web http://www.ils.indiana. edu/about/accreditation.html. Admissions contact: Michelle Dunbar-Sims. Tel. 812-855-2018, e-mail GoLuddy@iu.edu.

Indiana University–Purdue University Indianapolis, School of Informatics and Computing, Dept. of Lib. and Info. Science, 535 W. Michigan St., IT 475, Indianapolis, IN 46202. Andrea Copeland, chair. Tel. 317-278-4636, fax 317-278-7669, e-mail soicindy@iupui.edu, World Wide Web http://soic.iupui.edu/lis. Admissions: e-mail soicapps@iupui.edu.

Kent State University, School of Info., P.O. Box 5190, Kent, OH 44242-0001. Meghan Harper, dir. Tel. 330-672-2782, fax 330-672-7965, e-mail ischool@kent.edu, World Wide Web http://www.kent.edu/iSchool/ master-library-information-science. Admissions contact: Janna Korzenko.

Saint Catherine University, Graduate College, School of Humanities, Arts, and Sciences, MLIS Program/Information Management Department, 2004 Randolph Ave. No. 4125, St. Paul, MN 55105. Joyce Yakawa, interim dir. Tel. 651-690-6802, fax 651-690-8724, e-mail imdept@stkate.edu, World Wide Web https://www.stkate.edu/academics/ academic-programs/gc-library-and-infor-mation-science. Admissions contact: Ashley Wells. Tel. 612-214-0741, e-mail aewells@ stkate.edu.

University of Illinois at Urbana-Champaign, School of Info. Science, 501 E. Daniel St., Champaign, IL 61820-6211. Emily Knox, interim assoc. dean for acad. affairs. Tel. 217-333-3280, fax 217-244-3302, e-mail ischool@illinois.edu, World Wide Web http://ischool.illinois.edu. Admissions contact: Moises Orozco Villicana. Tel. 217-300-5007, e-mail orozco6@illinois.edu.

University of Iowa, Graduate College, School of Lib. and Info. Science, 3087 Main Lib., Iowa City, IA 52242-1420. Lindsay Kistler Mattock, dir. Tel. 319-335-5707, fax 319-335-5374, e-mail slis@uiowa.edu, World Wide Web http://slis.grad.uiowa.edu. Admissions contact: Katie McCullough. Tel. 319-384-1538, e-mail katie-mccullough@ uiowa.edu.

University of Michigan, School of Info., 4322 North Quad, 105 S. State St., Ann Arbor, MI 48109-1285. Elizabeth Yakel, sr. assoc. dean. Tel. 734-763-2285, fax 734-764-2475, e-mail umsi.admissions@umich.edu, World Wide Web http://si.umich.edu/. Admissions contact: Laura Elgas.

University of Missouri, College of Educ., Info. Science and Learning Technologies, 303 Townsend Hall, Columbia, MO 65211. Cynthia Dudenhoffer, LIS program coord. Tel. 877-747-5868, fax 573-884-0122, e-mail sislt@missouri.edu, World Wide Web http:// lis.missouri.edu. Admissions tel. 573-882-4546.

University of Wisconsin–Madison, College of Letters and Sciences, Info. School, 600 N. Park St., Madison, WI 53706. Alan Rubel, dir. Tel. 608-263-2900, fax 608-263-4849, e-mail info@ischool.wisc.edu, World Wide

Web http://ischool.wisc.edu. Admissions contact: Tanya Hendricks Cobb. Tel. 608-263-2909, e-mail student-services@slis.wisc.edu.

University of Wisconsin–Milwaukee, School of Info. Studies, P.O. Box 413, Milwaukee, WI 53201. Dietmar Wolfram, senior assoc. dean. Tel. 414-229-4707, fax 414-229-6699, e-mail soisinfo@uwm.edu, World Wide Web http://uwm.edu/informationstudies/.

Wayne State University, School of Info. Science, 106 Kresge Lib., Detroit, MI 48202. Hermina Anghelesco, interim dir. Tel. 313-577-1825, fax 313-577-7563, e-mail ask-lis@wayne.edu, World Wide Web http://sis.wayne.edu/mlis/index.php. Admissions contact: Matthew Fredericks. Tel. 313-577-2446, e-mail mfredericks@wayne.edu.

Southwest: Ariz., Okla., Texas

Texas Woman's University, School of Lib. and Info. Studies, P.O. Box 425769, Denton, TX 76204-5438. Ling Hwey Jeng, dir. Tel. 940-898-2602, fax 940-898-2611, e-mail slis@twu.edu, World Wide Web http://www.twu.edu/slis. Admissions contact: Mary Honard. E-mail slis@twu.edu.

University of Arizona, College of Social and Behavioral Sciences, School of Info., 1103 E. Second St., Tucson, AZ 85721. Catherine Brooks, dir. Tel. 520-621-3565, fax 520-621-3279, e-mail si-info@email.arizona.edu, World Wide Web http://ischool.arizona.edu/master-arts-library-and-information-science. Admissions contact: Holly Brown. Tel. 520-621-3567, e-mail brownhb@email.arizona.edu.

University of North Texas, College of Info., Dept. of Info. Science, 1155 Union Circle, No. 311068, Denton, TX 76203-5017. Jiangping Chen, chair. Tel. 940-565-2445, fax 940-369-7600, e-mail lis-chair@unt.edu, World Wide Web http://informationscience.unt.edu./master-science. Admissions contact: Caley Barnhart. Tel. 940-891-6861, e-mail ci-admissions@unt.edu.

University of Oklahoma, School of Lib. and Info. Studies, College of Arts and Sciences, 401 W. Brooks, Norman, OK 73019-6032. Susan Burke, dir. Tel. 405-325-3921, e-mail slisinfo@ou.edu, World Wide Web http://slis.ou.edu. Admissions contact: Sarah Connelly.

University of Texas at Austin, School of Info., Suite 5.202, 1616 Guadalupe St., Austin, TX 78701-1213. Eric T. Meyer, dean. Tel. 512-471-3821, fax 512-471-3971, e-mail info@ischool.utexas.edu, World Wide Web http://www.ischool.utexas.edu. Admissions contact: Carla Criner. Tel. 512-471-5654, e-mail criner@ischool.utexas.edu.

West: Calif., Colo., Hawaii, Wash.

San José State University, School of Info., College of Professional and Global Education, One Washington Sq., San Jose, CA 95192-0029. Anthony Chow, dir. Tel. 408-924-2490, fax 408-924-2476, e-mail sjsuischool@gmail.com, World Wide Web http://ischool.sjsu.edu/master-library-and-information-science. Admissions contact: Linda Main. Tel. 408-924-2494, e-mail linda.main@sjsu.edu.

University of California, Los Angeles, Graduate School of Educ. and Info. Studies, Dept. of Info. Studies, Box 951520, Los Angeles, CA 90095-1520. Michelle Caswell, chair. Tel. 310-825-8799, fax 310-206-3076, e-mail info@gseis.ucla.edu, World Wide Web http://is.gseis.ucla.edu. Admissions contact: Michelle Maye. Tel. 310-825-5269, e-mail maye@gseis.ucla.edu.

University of Denver, Morgridge College of Educ., Research Methods and Info. Science, 1999 E. Evans Ave., Denver, CO 80208-1700. Nicholas Cutforth, chair. Tel. 303-871-3587, fax 303-871-4456, e-mail mce@du.edu, World Wide Web http://www.du.edu/education. Admissions contact: Rachel Riley. Tel. 303-871-2508, e-mail rachel.riley@du.edu.

University of Hawaii, College of Natural Sciences, Lib. and Info. Science Program, 2550 McCarthy Mall, Honolulu, HI 96822. Rich Gazan, chair. Tel. 808-956-7321, fax 808-956-5835, e-mail slis@hawaii.edu, World Wide Web http://www.hawaii.edu/lis.

University of Southern California, Marshall School of Business, 3550 Trousdale Parkway, DML 312, Los Angeles, CA 90089-0183. Christopher Stewart. Tel.

213-764-4593, e-mail info@libraryscien-
cedegree.usc.edu, World Wide Web http://
librarysciencedegree.usc.edu. Admissions:
tel. 213-740-2741, e-mail mmlis.admis-
sions@marshall.usc.edu.

University of Washington, The Information
School, 370 Mary Gates Hall, Seattle,
WA 98195-2840. Anind Dey, dean. Tel.
206-685-9937, fax 206-616-3152, e-mail
ischool@uw.edu, World Wide Web http://
ischool.uw.edu. Admissions contact: Tel.
206-543-1794, e-mail mlis@uw.edu.

Canada

Dalhousie University, School of Info. Management, Kenneth C. Rowe Management Bldg.,
Halifax, NS B3H 4R2. Vivian Howard,
interim dir. Tel. 902-494-3656, fax 902-494-
2451, e-mail sim@dal.ca, World Wide Web
http://www.sim.management.dal.ca. Admissions contact: JoAnn Watson. Tel. 902-494-
2471, e-mail joann.watson@dal.ca.

McGill University, School of Info. Studies,
3661 Peel St., Montreal, QC H3A 1X1.
Kimiz Dalkir, dir. Tel. 514-398-4204, fax
514-398-7193, e-mail sis@mcgill.ca, World
Wide Web http://www.mcgill.ca/sis. Admissions contact: Kathryn Hubbard. Tel. 514-
398-4204 ext. 0742, e-mail sis@mcgill.ca.

University of Alberta, School of Library and
Information Studies, Faculty of Education,
7-104 Education North, Edmonton, AB T6G
2G5. Kathleen De Long, interim chair. Tel.
780-492-3932, fax 780-492-2024, e-mail
slis@ualberta.ca, World Wide Web http://
www.ualberta.ca/school-of-library-and-
information-studies/programs. Admissions
contact: Joan White. Tel. 780-492-3679,
e-mail slis@ualberta.ca.

University of British Columbia, School of
Information, Irving K. Barber Learning
Centre, Suite 470, 1961 East Mall, Vancouver, BC V6T 1Z1. Erik Kwakkel, dir.
Tel. 604-822-2404, fax 604-822-6006,
e-mail ischool.info@ubc.ca, World Wide
Web http://www.slais.ubc.ca. Admissions
contact: Sandra Abah. Tel. 604-822-3459,
e-mail ischool.program@ubc.ca.

Université de Montréal, École de bibliothécon-
omie et des sciences de l'information, C.P.
6128, Succursale Centre-Ville, Montreal,
QC H3C 3J7. Lyne Da Sylva, acting dir.
Tel. 514-343-6044, fax 514-343-5753,
e-mail ebsiinfo@ebsi.umontreal.ca, World
Wide Web http://www.ebsi.umontreal.ca.
Admissions contact: Alain Tremblay. Tel.
514-343-6044, e-mail alain.tremblay.1@
umontreal.ca.

University of Ottawa, School of Info. Studies,
Desmarais Bldg., Ottawa, ON K1N 6N5.
Mary Cavanagh, dir. Tel. 613-562-5130,
fax 613-562-5854, e-mail esis@uOttawa.ca,
World Wide Web http://arts.uottawa.ca/sis.
Admissions contact: Catherine Bernard. Tel.
613-562-5800 ext. 1324, e-mail artsgrad@
uottawa.ca.

University of Toronto, Faculty of Info., 140
George St., Toronto, ON M5S 3G6. Wendy
Duff, dean. Tel. 416-978-3202, fax 416-
978-5762, e-mail inquire.ischool@utoronto.
ca, World Wide Web http://www.ischool.
utoronto.ca. Admissions contact: Barbara
Brown. Tel. 416-978-8589, e-mail barb.
brown@utoronto.ca.

University of Western Ontario, Grad. Programs in Lib. and Info. Science, Faculty of
Info. and Media Studies, Room 240, North
Campus Bldg., London, ON N6A 5B7.
Pam McKenzie, associate dean of graduate and postdoctoral programs (acting). Tel.
519-661-4017, fax 519-661-3506, e-mail
mlisinfo@uwo.ca, World Wide Web http://
www.fims.uwo.ca. Admissions contact:
Shelley Long.

Library Scholarship Sources

For a more complete list of scholarships, fellowships, and assistantships offered for library study, see *Financial Assistance for Library and Information Studies,* published annually by the American Library Association (ALA). The document is also available on the ALA website at http://www.ala.org/educationcareers/scholarships.

American Association of Law Libraries (AALL). (1) Degree Candidates Scholarships are available for individuals studying to become law librarians as either a library or law school student or to library school graduates seeking an advanced degree in a related field. Preference is given to AALL members, but scholarships are not restricted to members. Applicants with law library experience are also given preference, but it is not required. Evidence of financial need must be submitted. (2) The AALL Scholarship is awarded annually to individuals seeking a degree from an accredited library or law school and who intend to have a career in legal information or to a library school graduate seeking an advanced degree in a related field. (3) The LexisNexis John R. Johnson Memorial Scholarship is awarded annually to individuals seeking a degree from an accredited library or law school and who intend to have a career in legal information or to a library school graduate seeking an advanced degree in a related field. (4) The George A. Strait Minority Scholarship & Fellowship is awarded annually to students enrolled in an ALA-accredited library graduate school or a law school and who are members of a minority group as defined by current U.S. guidelines and are degree candidates in an accredited library or law school and intend to have a career in law librarianship. (5) The Marcia J. Koslov Scholarship supports AALL members who work in a government law library by providing funding to attend continuing education programs. For information, write to AALL Scholarship Committee, 230 W. Monroe St., Suite 2650, Chicago, IL 60606.

American Library Association (ALA). (1) The ALA Century Scholarship of $2,500 funds services or accommodation for a library school student(s) with disabilities admitted to an ALA-accredited library school. (2) The David A. Clift Scholarship of $3,000 goes to a U.S./Canadian citizen or permanent resident who is pursuing an M.L.S. in an ALA-accredited program. (3) The Tom and Roberta Drewes Scholarship of $3,000 goes to a library support-staff member who is a U.S./Canadian citizen or permanent resident and is pursuing an M.L.S. in an ALA-accredited program. (4) The deg farrelly Memorial/Alexander Street Press AMIA/FMRT Media Librarian Scholarship is given once a year to a master's degree candidate in library science who intends to work professionally with media collections in libraries. (5) The Mary V. Gaver Scholarship of $3,000 is awarded to a U.S./Canadian citizen or permanent resident who is pursuing an M.L.S. specializing in youth services in an ALA-accredited program. (6) The Miriam L. Hornback Scholarship of $3,000 is given to an ALA or library support staffer who is a U.S./Canadian citizen or permanent resident and is pursuing an M.L.S. in an ALA-accredited program. (7) The Christopher Hoy/ERT Scholarship of $5,000 goes to a U.S./Canadian citizen or permanent resident who is pursuing an M.L.S. in an ALA-accredited program. (8) The Julia J. Brody Public Librarian Scholarship of $4,000 is awarded to a U.S./Canadian citizen or permanent resident who is pursuing an M.L.S. specializing public library services in an ALA-accredited program. (9) The Tony B. Leisner Scholarship of $3,000 goes to a library support-staff member who is a U.S./Canadian citizen or permanent resident pursuing an M.L.S. in an ALA-accredited program. (10) The Peter Lyman Memorial/SAGE Scholarship in New Media supports a student in an ALA-accredited master's program in library and information studies pursuing a specialty in new media. (11) The Regina U. Minudri Young Adult Scholarship of $3,000 is given once a year to a master's degree candidate in library science who intends to work professionally with young adults in public libraries. (12) The W. David Rozkuszka Scholarship of $3,000 goes to an individual who is currently working with government documents in a library and is working toward a master's degree in library science. (13) The Spectrum Scholarship Program is ALA's national diversity and recruitment effort designed to address the specific issue of underrepresentation of critically needed ethnic librarians within the profession while serving as a model for ways to bring attention to larger diversity issues in the future. For information, write to ALA Scholarship Clearinghouse, 225 N. Michigan Ave., Suite 1300, Chicago, IL 60601, or see http://www.ala.org/scholarships.

ALA/Association for Library Service to Children. (1) The Bound to Stay Bound Books Scholarship provides financial assistance for the education of individuals who intend to pursue an M.L.S. or advanced degree and who plan to work in the area of library service to children. (2) The Frederic G. Melcher Scholarship provides financial assistance for individuals who intend to pursue an M.L.S. degree and who plan to work in children's librarianship. For information, write to ALA Scholarship Clearinghouse, 225 N. Michigan Ave., Suite 1300, Chicago, IL 60611, or see http://www.ala.org/scholarships.

ALA/Association of College and Research Libraries. The ESS De Gruyter European Librarianship Study Grant supports research in European studies with an emphasis on librarianship, the book trade, resource documentation, and similar information-science-related topics. An award of €2,500 is given to cover travel to and from Europe and transportation, room, and board in Europe, for up to 30 consecutive days. The application is electronic only. Note: The 2022 grant is temporarily on hold due to funding suspension from the sponsor, and submissions are not currently being accepted.

ALA International Relations Committee. The Bogle Pratt International Library Travel Fund of $1,000 is given to an ALA personal member to attend their first international conference. Applications should be submitted via e-mail to the ALA International Relations Office, intl@ala.org.

ALA/Library and Information Technology Association (LITA). (1) The LITA/Christian (Chris) Larew Memorial Scholarship of $3,000 is given for study in an ALA-accredited M.L.S. program to encourage the entry of qualified persons into the library and information technology field. (2) The LITA/OCLC Spectrum Scholarship of $5,000 goes to a U.S. or Canadian citizen who is a qualified member of a principal minority group (American Indian or Alaska native, Asian or Pacific Islander, African American, or Hispanic) for study in an ALA-accredited M.L.S. program, has a strong commitment to the use of automated systems in libraries, and plans to follow a career in the library and automation field. (3) The LITA/LSSI Minority Scholarship of $2,500 is awarded to a U.S. or Canadian citizen who is a qualified member of a principal minority group (American Indian or Alaska native, Asian or Pacific Islander, African American, or Hispanic) for study in an ALA-accredited M.L.S. program, has a strong commitment to the use of automated systems in libraries, and plans to follow a career in the library and automation field. For information, write to ALA Scholarship Clearinghouse, 225 N. Michigan Ave., Suite 1300, Chicago, IL 60611, or see http://www.ala.org/scholarships.

ALA/Public Library Association (PLA). The Demco New Leaders Travel Grant of up to $1,500 goes to a varying number of PLA members to enhance their professional development by making possible their attendance at major professional development activities. For information, write to PLA Awards Program, ALA/PLA, 225 N. Michigan Ave., Suite 1300, Chicago, IL 60611, or see http://www.ala.org/pla/awards. Note: PLA announced it would not accept nominations for awards and travel grants while it revisits the number, purpose, and impact of the awards.

American-Scandinavian Foundation. Fellowships (up to $23,000) and grants (up to $5,000) are given to pursue research, study, or creative arts projects in Denmark, Finland, Iceland, Norway, or Sweden. For information, write to Fellowships and

Grants, American-Scandinavian Foundation, 58 Park Ave., New York, NY 10026, or see http://www.amscan.org/fellowships-and-grants.

Association for Library and Information Science Education (ALISE). (1) The ALISE Community conn@CT mini-grants of $750 for ALISE members are given to address a library and information need of a social justice organization through community engagement (in a collaborative manner). (2) A varying number of research grants totaling $5,000 are awarded to members of ALISE. For information, write to ALISE, 4 Lan Drive, Suite 310, Westford, MA 01886.

Association of Bookmobile and Outreach Services (ABOS). (1) The Bernard Vavrek Scholarship of $1,000 is awarded to a student who is currently enrolled and has completed at least one semester in a library and/or information science graduate degree program and who is interested in becoming an outreach/bookmobile librarian. (2) The John Philip Excellence in Outreach Award recognizes outstanding contributions and leadership by an individual in bookmobile and outreach services. (3) The Carol Hole Conference Attendance Award consists of ten awards of free conference registration and $500 stipends for the winners' travel expenses and/or accommodations for a conference. For information, write to Chair, ABOS Awards Committeee, at awards@abos-outreach.com.

Association of Jewish Libraries. (1) One academic scholarship of $1,000 is given to a student enrolled or accepted in a graduate school of library and information science. Additionally, free full-conference registration is included and encouraged. (2) A conference subvention award is given for attending the Association of Jewish Libraries annual conference. Free full-conference registration, travel, and (shared) room are included. For information, see https://jewishlibraries.org/student-scholarship-award.

Association of Seventh-Day Adventist Librarians (ASDAL). The D. Glenn Hilts Scholarship goes to a member of the Seventh-Day Adventist Church in an ALA-accredited graduate library program or, if attending outside the United States or Canada, a program recognized by the International Federation of Library Associations and Institutions (IFLA). The recipient must be enrolled as a full-time student and use the scholarship only for tuition and books. For information, write to ASDAL Scholarship and Awards Committee, McKee Library, Southern Adventist University, P.O. Box 629, Collegedale, TN 37315.

Beta Phi Mu. (1) The Sarah Rebecca Reed Scholarship consists of two $2,250 awards for individuals beginning LIS studies at an ALA-accredited school. Note: Due to budgetary constraints, the Reed Scholarship will not be awarded in 2022. (2) The Frank B. Sessa Scholarship provides ten $150 awards for Beta Phi Mu members' continuing education. (3) The Harold Lancour Scholarship of $1,750 goes to a librarian conducting foreign research. (4) The Blanche E. Woolls Scholarship for School Library Media Service of $2,250 is awarded to an individual beginning LIS studies with a concentration in school library media. (5) The Eugene Garfield Doctoral Dissertation Scholarship of up to six $3,000 awards goes to doctoral students who are working on their dissertations in LIS and related fields. For information, write to Beta Phi Mu Honor Society, P.O. Box 42139, Philadelphia, PA 19101, or see https://www.betaphimu.org/scholarships_overview.html.

Canadian Association of Law Libraries (CALL). (1) The Diana M. Priestly Scholarship of $2,500 is for a student enrolled in an approved Canadian law school or accredited Canadian library school. (2) The CALL/ACBD Research Grant of up to $3,000 is for research in areas of interest to members and to the association. (3) The CALL/ACBD Education Reserve Fund Grants are for CALL members to further their education in pursuits that do not fit the guidelines of already established scholarships. (4) The James D. Lang Memorial Scholarship supports attendance at a continuing education program. (5) The Eunice Beeson Memorial Travel Fund assists members of the association who wish to attend the annual meeting but, for financial reasons, are unable to do so. (6) The Northern Exposure to Leadership Grant identifies individuals who demonstrate an aspiration to lead libraries, information service organizations, or programs in the 21st century and motivates them to develop their leadership potential. (7) The Janine Miller Fellowship of $2,500 goes to one CALL member to attend the Law via the Internet Conference. For information, see https://www.callacbd.ca/Awards.

Canadian Federation of University Women (CFUW). (1) The Aboriginal Women's Award of $10,000–$25,000 is for studies in specific programs of law, medicine, or nurse practitioners or a master of Aboriginal studies. (2) The Ruth Binnie Fellowship of $6,000 is for a student in master's studies that focus on one or more aspect(s) of the field of human ecology/home economics/family and consumer sciences. (3) The Canadian Home Economics Association Fellowship of $6,000 is for a student enrolled in a postgraduate program in the field of human ecology/home economics/family and consumer sciences in Canada. (4) The CFUW Memorial Fellowship of $8,000 is for a student who is currently enrolled in a master's program in science, mathematics, or engineering in Canada or abroad. (5) The Bourse Georgette LeMoyne award of $5,000 is for graduate study in any field at a Canadian university (the candidate must be studying in French). (6) The Elizabeth and Rachel Massey Award of $5,000 is for postgraduate studies in the visual arts or in music. (7) The Margaret McWilliams Pre-Doctoral Fellowship of $11,000 is for a female student who has completed at least one full year as a full-time student in doctoral-level studies. (8) The 1989 Ecole Polytechnique Commemorative Award of $7,000 is for graduate studies in any field at the doctoral level, and there is one award of $5,000 for master's study. The applicant must justify the relevance of her work to women. (9) The Linda Souter Humanities Award of $6,000 is for a master's or doctoral student studying in the area of the humanities. (10) The Alice E. Wilson Award of $5,000 each is for four mature students returning to graduate studies in any field after at least three years. (11) The CFUW 100th Anniversary Legacy Fellowship of one $5,000 award goes to a woman who has completed one calendar year of a doctoral program. For information, write to Fellowships Program Manager, Canadian Federation of University Women, fellowships@cfuw-fcfdu.ca.

Chinese American Librarians Association (CALA). (1) The Sheila Suen Lai Scholarship of $1,000 is awarded to a Chinese descendant who has been accepted in an ALA-accredited program. (2) The CALA Scholarship of Library and Information Science of $1,000 goes to a Chinese descendant who has been accepted in an ALA-accredited program. (3) The Huang Tso-ping and Wu Yao-yu Research and Scholarship awards faculty and students at Wuhan University in China; one award is for a library school faculty member ($400) and two awards go to library school students ($200 each). (4) The Lisa Zhao Scholarship of $400 each goes to one student and one new librarian with less than five years' experience. For information, write to Jen Woo at jennifer.woo@sfpl.org.

Massachusetts Black Librarians' Network. $500 for students of African descent entering an ALA-accredited master's program in library science. For information, write to Massachusetts Black Librarians' Network, P.O. Box 400504, Cambridge, MA 02140.

Medical Library Association (MLA). (1) The Cunningham Memorial International Fellowship is given to health sciences librarians from countries other than the United States and Canada. (2) A scholarship of up to $5,000 is awarded to a person entering an ALA-accredited library program, with no more than one-half of the program yet to be completed. (3) A scholarship of up to $5,000 goes to a minority student studying health sciences librarianship. (4) A varying number of Research, Development, and Demonstration Project Grants of $100–$1,000 go U.S. or Canadian citizens, preferably MLA members. (5) The MLA Doctoral Fellowship of $2,000 is for doctoral work in medical librarianship or information science. (6) The Librarians without Borders Ursula Poland International Scholarship of $1,000 funds an international project by a U.S. or Canadian health sciences librarian. For information, write to MLA Grants and Scholarships Coordinator, awards@mlahq.org, or see http://www.mlanet.org/page/awards.

Mountain Plains Library Association (MPLA). A varying number of grants of up to $600 are for applicants who are members of the association and have been for the preceding two years. For information, write to Judy Kulp, Executive Secretary, MPLA, 14293 W. Center Drive, Lakewood, SD 80228, or see https://mpla.us/about/professional-development-grants.html.

Society of American Archivists (SAA). (1) The F. Gerald Ham and Elsie Ham Scholarship of $10,000 is for graduate students in archival education at a U.S. university that meets the society's criteria for graduate education. (2) The Mosaic Scholarship of $5,000 is for up to two U.S. or Canadian minority students enrolled in a graduate program in archival administration. (3) The Josephine Foreman Scholarship of $10,000 is for a U.S. citizen or permanent resident who is a minority graduate student enrolled in a program in archival administration. (4) The Oliver Wendell Holmes Travel Award of $1,000 enables foreign students involved in archival training in the United States or Canada to attend the SAA Annual Meeting. (5) The Donald Peterson Student Travel Award of up to $1,500 enables graduate students or recent graduates to attend the meeting. (6) The Harold T. Pinkett Student of Color Awards enables minority students or graduate students to attend the meeting. (7) The Brenda S. Banks Travel Award recognizes and acknowledges individuals of color who have demonstrated professional archival experience and who manifest an interest in becoming active members of the Society of American Archivists. For details, write to Society of American Archivists, 17 N. State St., Suite 1425, Chicago, IL 60607, or see https://www2.archivists.org/governance/handbook/section12-ham.

Special Libraries Association (SLA). The Leadership Symposium Scholarship of $1,000 is for travel expenses and registration at the symposium (value $395) for members who demonstrate a desire and commitment to advance their leadership skills and abilities within SLA units. For information, write to Special Libraries Association, 7918 Jones Branch Dr., Suite 300, McLean, VA 22102.

Library Scholarship and Award Recipients, 2021

Compiled by the staff of *Library and Book Trade Almanac*

Scholarships and awards are listed by organization.

American Association of Law Libraries (AALL)

AALL Educational Scholarships. To assist individuals studying to become law librarians with their educational expenses. *Winners:* (college graduate seeking library degree) Jan Lah; (law school graduate seeking library degree) Adrienne J. Flory, Natasha Landon, Michael Muehe.

AALL Grants. To enable law librarians to participate in professional educational opportunities at the AALL Annual Meeting or to engage in original research on topics important to law librarianship. *Winners:* (annual meeting grants) Sara McMahon, Angela Reaux, Gail Wechsler; (AALL Management Institute grant) Jocelyn Stilwell-Tong; (Equal Justice Conference grant) Sabrina Davis.

AALL Hall of Fame Award. Recognizes significant, substantial, and long-standing contributions to the profession and service to the association. *Winners:* John D. Edwards, Michele Finerty, Kevin M. Marmion.

AALL Marcia J. Koslov Scholarship. To an AALL member to finance conference or seminar attendance. Not awarded in 2021.

AALL New Product Award. For new commercial information products that enhance or improve existing law library services or procedures or innovative products that improve access to legal information, the legal research process, or procedures for technical processing of library materials. *Winner:* Compose by Casetext.

AALL Spectrum Article of the Year Award. *Winners:* Edna L. Lewis and Clanitra Stewart Nejdl for "Academic Law Libraries and the Early Days of the COVID-19 Pandemic" (September/October 2020).

AALL George A. Strait Minority Scholarship & Fellowship. *Winners:* (scholarship and fellowship) Arianna Alcaraz, Juan Fuentes, Olivia Yvette Kane-Cruz, Jane Lah, Diona Layden, and Michael Teresa Mellifera; (scholarship) Lee Barber, Carla Bywaters, Nadia Montenegro, and Alice Perez Ververa.

Joseph L. Andrews Legal Literature Award. *Winners:* Melissa Beck and Melody Busse Lembke for *Cataloging Legal Literature, Fifth Edition*; Joan S. Howland, Scott B. Pagel, and Michelle M. Wu (co-editors) for *Academic Law Libraries within the Changing Landscape of Legal Education: A Primer for Deans and Provosts*; Douglas W. Lind and Stacia Stein for *The Leaven of Sympathy: A Bio-Bibliography of Frederick C. Hicks*.

Emerging Leader Award. To recognize newer members who have made significant contributions to AALL and/or to the profession and have demonstrated the potential for leadership and continuing service. *Winners:* Ashley Ames Ahlbrand, Elizabeth S. Graham, and Clanitra Stewart Nejdl.

Excellence in Community Engagement Award. For outstanding achievement in public relations activities. *Winners:* George W. Hopper Law Library, University of Wyoming College of Law in Laramie, Wyoming, for "Access to Justice: Legal Research on the Road"; San Diego Law Library in San Diego, California, for "Preparing Our Community for COVID-19 Legal Issues."

Marian Gould Gallagher Distinguished Service Award. To recognize extended and sustained service to law librarianship. *Winners:* Daniel L. Wade and Mary Whisner.

Innovations in Technology Award. To recognize an AALL member, special interest section, chapter, or library for innovative use of technology in the development and creation of an application or resource for law librarians or legal professionals. *Winner:* Tarlton Law Library, University of Texas–Austin in Austin, Texas, for *The Thomas Woodward Houghton 50 State Ethics Guide*.

Law Library Advocate Award. To an AALL member who has been a strong advocate of private law librarianship through service to the Special Interest Sections, their organization, or the larger legal community and demonstrates outstanding potential for continued service and leadership within the profession. *Winner:* Sandra Levin, executive director of Los Angeles Law Library in Los Angeles, California.

Law Library Journal Article of the Year. *Winners:* Julie Graves Krishnaswami and Shawn G. Nevers for "The Shadow Code: Statutory Notes in the United States Code" (Spring 2020).

LexisNexis Call for Papers Awards. To promote the scholarship of AALL members and of students on any subject relevant to law librarianship. *Winners:* (new member) Matthew L. Timko for "Applying Universal Design into the Legal Academy"; (short form) Ingrid Mattson for "Billie Holiday's Legacy Walks the Halls of 55 Fifth Avenue"; (open) Amanda Bolles Watson for "The Report of My Death Was an Exaggeration—The Legal Treatise"; (student) John L. Moreland for "Organized for Service: The Hicks Classification System and the Evolution of Law School Curriculum."

LexisNexis/John R. Johnson Memorial Scholarships. *Winners:* (college graduate seeking library degree) Bailey DeSimone, Deja Jenkins, and Yana Verenich; (college graduate seeking dual law/library degree) Andrew Wisniewsky; (law school graduate seeking library degree) Sophie Le and Alex Clay Hutchings; (library school graduate seeking law degree) Lee Barber.

LexisNexis Research Fund Grants. *Winners:* Casandra Laskowski and Andrew Christensen for "Building Data Infrastructures for Bespoke Faculty Services."

Minority Leadership Development Award. *Winner:* Mandy Lee, research and instructional services librarian at Chicago-Kent College of Law Library in Chicago, Illinois.

Robert L. Oakley Advocacy Award. To recognize an AALL member who has been an outstanding advocate and has contributed significantly to the AALL policy agenda at the federal, state, local, or international level. *Winner:* Mariann Sears, director of Harris County Robert W. Hainsworth Law Library in Houston, Texas.

Public Access to Government Information Award. Recognizes individuals or organizations that have made significant contributions to protect and promote greater access to government information. *Winner:* Mike Lissner, executive director of the Free Law Project in Oakland, California.

Volunteer Service Award. Honors volunteers who have made significant contributions to the work of AALL. Not awarded in 2021.

American Library Association (ALA)

ALA Excellence in Library Programming Award ($5,000). For a cultural/thematic library program or program series that engages the community in planning, sponsorship, and/or active participation; addresses an identified community need; and has a measurable impact. *Donor:* ALA Cultural Communities Fund. Not awarded in 2021.

ALA Honorary Membership. To recognize outstanding contributions of lasting importance to libraries and librarianship. *Honoree:* Robert Wedgeworth.

ALA/Information Today, Inc. Library of the Future Award ($1,500). For a library, consortium, group of librarians, or support organization for innovative planning for,' applications of, or development of patron training programs about information technology in a library setting. *Donors:* Information Today, Inc. and IIDA. *Winner:* Plano Public Library in Texas for its innovative use of technology to provide one-on-one tech training to seniors, Brain Injury Network of Dallas club members, and ESL students.

ALA Medal of Excellence. For creative leadership and professional achievement in library management, training, cataloging, and classification and the tools and techniques of librarianship. *Donor:* OCLC. Not awarded in 2021.

Hugh C. Atkinson Memorial Award. For outstanding achievement (including risk taking) by academic librarians that has contributed significantly to improvements in library automation, management, and/or development or research. *Offered by:* ACRL, ALCTS, LITA, and LLAMA. *Winner:* Mark E. Phillips, University of North Texas.

Beta Phi Mu Award ($1,000). For distinguished service in library education. *Donor:* Beta

Phi Mu International Library and Information Science Honorary Society. *Winner:* Marcia Rapchak, teaching assistant professor at the School of Computing and Information, University of Pittsburgh.

Bogle-Pratt International Library Travel Fund Award ($1,000). To ALA members to attend their first international conference. *Donors:* Bogle Memorial Fund and Pratt Institute School of Information and Library Science. Not awarded in 2021.

W.Y. Boyd Literary Award for Excellence in Military Fiction. See "Literary Prizes, 2021" in Part 5.

Julia J. Brody Public Librarian Scholarship ($4,000). To a U.S. or Canadian citizen or permanent resident who is pursuing an M.L.S. specializing in public library services in an ALA-accredited program. *Winner:* Ellen Rose Avis.

David H. Clift Scholarship ($3,000). To worthy U.S. or Canadian citizens enrolled in an ALA-accredited program toward an M.L.S. degree. *Winner:* Bria Victoria Harris.

Tom and Roberta Drewes Scholarship ($3,000). To a library support staff member pursuing a master's degree in an ALA-accredited program. *Donor:* Quality Books. *Winner:* Melissa Grasso.

EBSCO/ALA Conference Sponsorship Award ($1,000). To enable librarians to attend the ALA Annual Conference. *Donor:* EBSCO. Not awarded in 2021.

EBSCO Library Staff Development Grant ($3,500). To a library organization for a program to further its staff development goals and objectives. *Donor:* EBSCO. *Winner:* Burlington County Library System in New Jersey.

Equality Award ($1,000). To an individual or group for an outstanding contribution that promotes equality in the library profession. *Donor:* Rowman & Littlefield. *Winner:* Joint Council of Librarians of Color.

Elizabeth Futas Catalyst for Change Award ($1,000). A biennial award to recognize a librarian who invests time and talent to make positive change in the profession of librarianship. *Donor:* Elizabeth Futas Memorial Fund. *Winner (2020):* Nora Wiltse.

Gale, a Cengage Company, Financial Development Award ($2,500). To a library organization for a financial development project to secure new funding resources for a public or academic library. *Donor:* Gale, a Cengage company. Not awarded in 2021.

Mary V. Gaver Scholarship ($3,000). To a student pursuing an M.L.S. degree and specializing in youth services. *Winner:* Monet Raquel Hardison.

Ken Haycock Award for Promoting Librarianship ($1,000). For significant contribution to public recognition and appreciation of librarianship through professional performance, teaching, or writing. *Winner:* Steven Yates, assistant director and assistant professor at the School of Library and Information Studies (SLIS), University of Alabama.

Miriam L. Hornback Scholarship ($3,000). To an ALA or library support staff person pursuing a master's degree in library science. *Winner:* Tiffany Hien Ly.

Paul Howard Award for Courage ($1,000). A biennial award to a librarian, library board, library group, or individual for exhibiting unusual courage for the benefit of library programs or services. *Donor:* Paul Howard Memorial Fund. *Winner (2021):* Amy Dodson, Douglas County Public Library in Minden, New York.

John Ames Humphry/OCLC/Forest Press Award ($1,000). To one or more individuals for significant contributions to international librarianship. *Donor:* OCLC/Forest Press. *Winner:* Janet Lee.

Tony B. Leisner Scholarship ($3,000). To a library support staff member pursuing a master's degree. *Donor:* Tony B. Leisner. *Winner:* Meaghan E. Davidson.

Joseph W. Lippincott Award ($1,500). For distinguished service to the library profession. *Donor:* Joseph W. Lippincott III. *Winner:* Newlen Robert.

Peter Lyman Memorial/Sage Scholarship in New Media. To support a student seeking an M.L.S. degree in an ALA-accredited program and pursing a specialty in new media. *Donor:* Sage Publications. *Winner:* Mia Ines Glionna.

James Madison Award. To recognize efforts to promote government openness. Not awarded in 2021.

Schneider Family Book Awards. See "Literary Prizes, 2021" in Part 5.

Scholastic Library Publishing Award ($1,000). To a librarian whose "unusual contributions to the stimulation and guidance of reading by children and young people exemplifies achievement in the profession." *Sponsor:* Scholastic Library Publishing. *Winner:* Barbara Stripling.

Lemony Snicket Prize for Noble Librarians Faced with Adversity ($3,000 plus a $1,000 travel stipend to enable attendance at the ALA Annual Conference). To honor a librarian who has faced adversity with integrity and dignity intact. *Sponsor:* Lemony Snicket (author Daniel Handler). *Winner:* Janet Eldred, Hollidaysburg Area Public Library in Pennsylvania.

Spectrum Scholarships ($5,000). To minority students admitted to ALA-accredited library schools. *Donors:* ALA and Institute of Museum and Library Services. *Winners:* Israa Abbas, Precious Abujana, Selena Aguilera, Saba Al-Hachami, Josselyn Atahualpa, Ashley Bolger, Nikole Brown, Brittany Butler, Karina Cardenas, Isabel Carlin, Sheridan Cazarez, Okunyi Chol, Helen Christian, Diana Dawson, Beatrice Downey, Bonita Dyess, Laila El Mugammar, Philip Espe, Laquanda M. Fields, River Freemont, Whitney Garcia, Zahra Garrett, James Glenn, Andrea Gutmann Fuentes, Brandi Hart, Cordiah Hayes, Randy Dantrell Heath, Truc Ho, Hikaru Ikeda, Leslie Lopez Holder, Diona Eberhart Layden, Vidhya Jagannathan, Jerrell Jones, Ikaika Keliiliki, Kathryn Kuppens, Elizabeth Lafont-Hurtado, Jessica Lee, Tina (Tianyi) Liu, Kimberly Nguyen, Jessica Nombrano Larsen, Amrita Patel, Deborah Alejandra Popowski, Valerie Salazar, Isaac San Miguel, Kristina Santiago, David Satten-López, Kaitlin Srader, Victoria Sun, Lily Susman, Berenice Sylverain, Patricia Ledesma Villon, Chantra Tham, Kaila Thomas, Ide Thompson, Celina Tirona, Lauren Turner, Cynthia Wade, Kelly West, Kellie Willis, Ryan Zohar.

Sullivan Award for Public Library Administrators Supporting Services to Children. To a library supervisor/administrator who has shown exceptional understanding and support of public library services to children. *Donor:* Peggy Sullivan. *Winner:* Patricia Uttaro, director of the Monroe County Library System and Rochester Public Library in Rochester, New York.

American Association of School Librarians (AASL)

AASL/ABC-CLIO Leadership Grant (up to $1,750). To AASL affiliates for planning and implementing leadership programs at state, regional, or local levels. *Donor:* ABC-CLIO. *Winner:* Oklahoma School Librarians, a division of the Oklahoma Library Association.

AASL Chapter of the Year ($1,000). In recognition of the AASL Chapter most active and dynamic in achieving the goals of AASL at the state and local level. *Winner:* Maryland Association of School Librarians.

AASL Collaborative School Library Award ($2,500). For expanding the role of the library in elementary and/or secondary school education. *Donor:* Scholastic Book Fairs. *Winners:* Amanda Hurley and Sarah Zehnder, Fayette County Public Schools in Kentucky.

AASL Distinguished School Administrator Award ($2,000). For expanding the role of the library in elementary and/or secondary school education. *Donor:* ProQuest. *Winner:* Dr. April Grace, Shawnee Public Schools in Oklahoma.

AASL/Frances Henne Award ($1,250). To a school library media specialist with five or fewer years in the profession to attend an AASL regional conference or ALA Annual Conference for the first time. *Donor:* Libraries Unlimited. *Winner:* Maria Frederick of John Read Middle School in Redding, Connecticut.

AASL Innovative Reading Grant ($2,500). To support the planning and implementation of an innovative program for children that motivates and encourages reading, especially for struggling readers. *Sponsor:* Capstone. *Winner:* Karen Snay of South Elementary School in St. Peter, Minnesota.

AASL President's Crystal Apple Award. To an individual, individuals, or group for a significant impact on school libraries and students. Not awarded in 2021.

Distinguished Service Award ($3,000). For outstanding contributions to librarianship and school library development. *Donor:* Rosen Publishing Group. Not awarded in 2021.

Intellectual Freedom Award ($2,000 plus $1,000 to the media center of the recipient's choice). To a school library media specialist and AASL member who has upheld the principles of intellectual freedom. *Donor:* ProQuest. Not awarded in 2021.

National School Library of the Year Award ($10,000). Honors school libraries exemplifying implementation of AASL's National School Library Standards for Learners, School Librarians, and School Libraries. *Donor:* Follett Library Resources. *Winner:* Calvert County Public Schools in Maryland.

Association for Library Collections and Technical Services (ALCTS)

ALCTS Presidential Citations for Outstanding Service. Not awarded in 2021.

Hugh C. Atkinson Memorial Award. See under American Library Association.

Ross Atkinson Lifetime Achievement Award ($3,000). To recognize the contribution of an ALCTS member and library leader who has demonstrated exceptional service to ALCTS and its areas of interest. *Donor:* EBSCO. Not awarded in 2021.

Paul Banks and Carolyn Harris Preservation Award ($1,500). To recognize the contribution of a professional preservation specialist who has been active in the field of preservation and/or conservation for library and/or archival materials. *Donor:* Preservation Technologies. Not awarded in 2021.

George Cunha and Susan Swartzburg Preservation Award ($1,250). To recognize cooperative preservation projects and/or individuals or groups that foster collaboration for preservation goals. *Sponsor:* Hollinger Metal Edge. Not awarded in 2021.

First Step Award (Wiley Professional Development Grant) ($1,500). To enable librarians new to the serials field to attend the ALA Annual Conference. *Donor:* John Wiley & Sons. Not awarded in 2021.

Harrassowitz Award for Leadership in Library Acquisitions ($1,500). For significant contributions by an outstanding leader in the field of library acquisitions. *Donor:* Harrassowitz. Not awarded in 2021.

Margaret Mann Citation (includes $2,000 scholarship award to the U.S. or Canadian library school of the winner's choice). To a cataloger or classifier for achievement in the areas of cataloging or classification. *Donor:* OCLC. Not awarded in 2021.

Outstanding Collaboration Citation. For outstanding collaborative problem-solving efforts in the areas of acquisition, access, management, preservation, or archiving of library materials. Not awarded in 2021.

Outstanding Publication Award ($250). To honor the year's outstanding monograph, article, or original paper in the field of acquisitions, collection development, and related areas of resource development in libraries. Not awarded in 2021.

Esther J. Piercy Award ($1,500). To a librarian with no more than ten years' experience for contributions and leadership in the field of library collections and technical services. *Donor:* YBP Library Services. Not awarded in 2021.

ProQuest Award for Innovation ($2,000). To recognize significant and innovative contributions to electronic collections management and development practice. *Donor:* ProQuest. Not awarded in 2021.

Edward Swanson Memorial Best of *LRTS* Award ($250). To the author(s) of the year's best paper published in the division's official journal. Not awarded in 2021.

Ulrich's Serials Librarianship Award ($1,500). For distinguished contributions to serials librarianship. *Sponsor:* ProQuest. Not awarded in 2021.

Association for Library Service to Children (ALSC)

ALSC/Baker & Taylor Summer Reading Program Grant ($3,000). For implementation of an outstanding public library summer reading program for children. *Donor:* Baker & Taylor. *Winner:* New Brunswick Free Public Library in New Jersey.

ALSC/Booklist/YALSA Odyssey Award. To the producer of the best audiobook for children and/or young adults available in English in the United States. See Odyssey Award in "Literary Prizes, 2021" in Part 5.

ALSC/Candlewick Press "Light the Way" Grant ($3,000). To a library conducting exemplary outreach to underserved populations. *Donor:* Candlewick Press. *Winner:* Madison Public Library in Ohio.

ALSC Spectrum Scholarships. To a Spectrum applicant who expresses an interest in library service to children. *Winners:* Chantra Tham, San Jose State University (in honor of Ellen Fader); Elizabeth Lafont-Hurtado, University of North Texas; and Kimberly Nguyen, University of California.

May Hill Arbuthnot Honor Lectureship. To an author, critic, librarian, historian, or teacher of children's literature who prepares a paper considered to be a significant contribution to the field of children's literature. Lecture postponed.

Mildred L. Batchelder Award. See "Literary Prizes, 2021" in Part 5.

Louise Seaman Bechtel Fellowship ($4,000). For librarians with 12 or more years of professional-level work in children's library collections, to read and study at Baldwin Library, University of Florida. *Donor:* Bechtel Fund. Not awarded in 2021.

Pura Belpré Awards. See "Literary Prizes, 2021" in Part 5.

Bound to Stay Bound Books Scholarships ($7,000). For men and women who intend to pursue an M.L.S or other advanced degree and who plan to work in the area of library service to children. *Donor:* Bound to Stay Bound Books. *Winners:* Molly Boehm, Dana Fanslow, Lindsay Michelle Robins, and Scott Shaffer.

Randolph Caldecott Medal. See "Literary Prizes, 2021" in Part 5.

Carnegie-Whitney Awards (up to $5,000). For the preparation of print or electronic reading lists, indexes, or other guides to library resources that promote reading or the use of library resources at any type of library. *Donors:* James Lyman Whitney and Andrew Carnegie Funds. *Winners:* Grace Enriquez and Meg Burns for "A Bibliography of Children's Literature to Celebrate Multilingualism and Facilitate Translanguaging Pedagogies"; Jennifer Embree and Neyda Gilman for "Equitable Sustainability Literacy: A Resource Guide for Environmental Justice & Activism"; Keren Dali for "Mainstreaming Stories from Around the World: Reviews of Children's International Literature in English Translation"; Lauren Hays and Jenna Kammer for "Digital Citizenship: An Annotated Bibliography"; Rae-Anne Montague for "Fifty Years of ALA Stonewall Book Awards: An Annotated Guide"; Robin Moeller for "We're All Orchids Now:

A Bibliography of Children's Picture Books about Dealing with Anxiety, 2010–2022"; and Shu Wan for "A Trilingual Bibliography of LGBTQ History Books (2000–2020)."

Century Scholarship ($2,500). For a library school student or students with disabilities admitted to an ALA-accredited library school. *Winner:* Mary Catherine Elisabeth Franks.

Children's Literature Legacy Award. See "Literary Prizes, 2021," in Part 5.

Distinguished Service Award ($1,000). To recognize significant contributions to, and an impact on, library services to children and/or ALSC. *Winner:* Elizabeth (Liz) McChesney.

Theodor Seuss Geisel Award. See "Literary Prizes, 2021" in Part 5.

Maureen Hayes Author/Illustrator Visit Award (up to $4,000). For an honorarium and travel expenses to make possible a library talk to children by a nationally known author/illustrator. *Sponsor:* Simon & Schuster Children's Publishing. *Winner:* Virginia Beach Library Foundation in Virginia on behalf of the Virginia Beach Public Library.

Frederic G. Melcher Scholarships ($6,000). To two students entering the field of library service to children for graduate work in an ALA-accredited program. *Winners:* Jeremiah Henderson, San Jose State University, and Brianna King, University of North Carolina–Greensboro.

John Newbery Medal. See "Literary Prizes, 2021" in Part 5.

Penguin Random House Young Readers Group Awards ($600). To children's librarians in school or public libraries with ten or fewer years of experience to attend the ALA Annual Conference. *Donor:* Penguin Young Readers Group and Random House Children's Books. Not awarded in 2021.

Robert F. Sibert Medal. See "Literary Prizes, 2021" in Part 5.

Association of College and Research Libraries (ACRL)

ACRL Academic or Research Librarian of the Year Award ($5,000). For outstanding contribution to academic and research librarianship and library development. *Donor:* YBP Library Services. *Winner:* Julia M. Gelfand, University of California–Irvine.

ACRL/CLS Innovation in College Librarianship Award ($3,000). To academic librarians who show a capacity for innovation in the areas of programs, services, and operations; or creating innovations for library colleagues that facilitate their ability to better serve the library's community. Not awarded in 2021.

ACRL/Routledge Distance Learning Librarian Conference Sponsorship Award ($1,200). To an ACRL member working in distance-learning librarianship in higher education. *Sponsor:* Routledge/Taylor & Francis. *Winner:* Natalie Haber, online services librarian at the University of Tennessee–Chattanooga.

ACRL/EBSS Distinguished Education and Behavioral Sciences Librarian Award. To an academic librarian who has made an outstanding contribution as an education and/or behavioral sciences librarian through accomplishments and service to the profession. *Donor:* John Wiley & Sons. *Winner:* Kaya van Beynen, associate dean of library research and instruction at the University of South Florida.

ACRL/STS Oberly Award for Bibliography in the Agricultural or Natural Sciences. Awarded biennially for the best English-language bibliography in the field of agriculture or a related science in the preceding two-year period. *Donor:* Eunice Rockwood Oberly. *Winners (2021):* Jen Kirk, government information librarian at Utah State University, and Helen F. Smith, agricultural sciences librarian at Pennsylvania State University, for "An Inventory of Published Soil Surveys of the United States."

ACRL/WGSS Award for Career Achievement in Women and Gender Studies Librarianship ($750). To a distinguished academic librarian who has made outstanding contributions to women and gender studies through accomplishments and service to the profession. *Donor:* Duke University Press. *Winner:* Jane Nichols, associate professor and head of the Teaching and Engagement Department at Oregon State University.

ACRL/WGSS Award for Significant Achievement in Women and Gender Studies Librarianship ($750). To a distinguished academic librarian who has made outstanding contributions to women and gender studies through accomplishments and service to the

profession. *Donor:* Duke University Press. *Winner:* Nicola Andrews, instruction and first year experience librarian at the University of San Francisco.

Hugh C. Atkinson Memorial Award. See under American Library Association.

CJCL/EBSCO Community College Learning Resources Leadership Award ($750). Recognizes significant achievement in community college programs. *Donor:* EBSCO. *Winner:* Yumi Shin of Lamar State College in Port Arthur, Texas.

CJCLS/EBSCO Community College Learning Resources Program Award ($750). Recognizes significant achievement in community college programs. *Donor:* EBSCO. *Winners:* Anjali Parasnis-Samar and Alice Wilson of Monroe Community College in Brighton, New York.

Miriam Dudley Instruction Librarian Award ($1,000). For a contribution to the advancement of bibliographic instruction in a college or research institution. *Winner:* Nicole Pagowsky, associate research and learning librarian and information literacy instruction program manager at the University of Arizona.

ESS De Gruyter European Librarianship Study Grant (€2,500). Supports research pertaining to European studies, librarianship, or the book trade. *Sponsor:* Walter de Gruyter Foundation for Scholarship and Research. Not awarded in 2021.

Excellence in Academic Libraries Awards ($3,000). To recognize outstanding college and university libraries. *Donor:* YBP Library Services. *Winners:* (university) Loyola Marymount University in Santa Clara, California; (college) Davidson College in North Carolina; (community college) Tulsa Community College in Oklahoma.

Instruction Section Innovation Award ($3,000). To librarians or project teams in recognition of a project that demonstrates creative, innovative, or unique approaches to information literacy instruction or programming. *Donor:* ProQuest. *Winners:* Alexandria Chisholm and Sarah Hartman-Caverly, reference and instruction librarians at Penn State Berks, for their Digital Shred Privacy Literacy Initiative project.

Marta Lange/Sage-CQ Press Award. To recognize an academic or law librarian for contributions to bibliography and information service in law or political science. *Donor:* Sage-CQ Press. *Winner:* Jill Severn, archivist and head of access and outreach at the University of Georgia and director of the Russell Forum for Civic Life in Georgia.

Katharine Kyes Leab and Daniel J. Leab American Book Prices Current Exhibition Catalog Awards (citations). For the best catalogs published by American or Canadian institutions in conjunction with exhibitions of books and/or manuscripts. *Sponsor:* Leab Endowment. *Winners:* (catalogs) Getty Research Institute in Los Angeles, California, for *Käthe Kollwitz: Prints, Process, Politics*; (brochures) Rosenbach Museum in Philadelphia, Pennsylvania, for *Chart Your Own Voyage*; (digital) University of Delaware's Library Special Collections for *Votes for Delaware Women*; (innovation) Free Library of Philadelphia for *Our 5 Senses Activity Booklet and Seek & Find*; (student) Haverford College in Pennsylvania for *Crossing Borders: From Slavery to Abolition, 1670-1865*.

Ilene F. Rockman Instruction Publication of the Year Award ($3,000). To recognize an outstanding publication relating to instruction in a library environment. *Sponsor:* Emerald Group. *Winners:* Alison J. Head, Barbara Fister, and Margy MacMillan for *Information Literacy in the Age of Algorithms: Student Experiences with News and Information, and the Need for Change* for Project Information Literacy.

Black Caucus of the American Library Association (BCALA)

Baker & Taylor Support Staff Award. For dedicated and outstanding performance by a library support staff member. Not awarded in 2021.

BCALA Book Literary Award. *Winners:* (first novelist) Lisa Moore Ramée for *A Good Kind of Trouble* (Balzer + Bray/HarperCollins); (fiction) by Lamar Giles for *Not So Pure and Simple* (Quill Tree Books/HarperCollins); (nonfiction) Wade Hudson and Cheryl Willis Hudson for *The Talk: Conversations about Race, Love & Truth* (Yearling/Penguin Random House); (graphic novel) Varian Johnson and Shannon Wright for *Twins* (Scholastic/Graphix).

BCALA Trailblazers Award. Presented once every five years in recognition of outstanding and unique contributions to librarianship. *Winners (2015):* Thomas Alford and Mary Biblo.

DEMCO/BCALA Excellence in Librarianship Award. To a librarian who has made significant contributions to promoting the status of African Americans in the library profession. *Winner:* Not awarded in 2021.

E.J. Josey Scholarship Award ($2,000). To African American students enrolled in or accepted by ALA-accredited programs who submit a three-to-five page essay on social justice, voting rights and civic engagement, immigration, or diversity and inclusion, designing a program for your local community and including objectives and desired outcomes. *Winners:* Alice Conyers, Drexel University; Monet Hardison, University of North Carolina–Greensboro; Jade Vaughn, Clarion University of Pennsylvania; and Rena Barlow, San Jose State University.

Ethnic and Multicultural Information and Exchange Round Table (EMIERT)

David Cohen Multicultural Award ($300). A biennial award to recognize articles of significant research and publication that increase understanding and promote multiculturalism in North American libraries. *Donor:* Routledge. *Winners (2020):* Denice Adkins, Jenny Bossaller, and Heather Moulaison Sandy, School of Information Science & Learning Technologies at the University of Missouri.

EMIERT Distinguished Librarian Award. Given biennially to recognize significant accomplishments in library services that are national or international in scope and that include improving, spreading, and promoting multicultural librarianship. *Winner:* K.C. Boyd.

Coretta Scott King Book Awards. See "Literary Prizes, 2021" in Part 5.

Exhibits Round Table (ERT)

Christopher J. Hoy/ERT Scholarship ($5,000). To an individual or individuals who will work toward an M.L.S. degree in an ALA-accredited program. *Donor:* Family of Christopher Hoy. *Winner:* Patricia Concepcion.

Freedom to Read Foundation

Freedom to Read Foundation Gordon M. Conable Conference Scholarship. To enable a library school student or new professional to attend the ALA Annual Conference. Not awarded in 2021.

Freedom to Read Foundation Roll of Honor (citation): To recognize individuals who have contributed substantially to the foundation. *Winner:* Robie H. Harris.

Judith Krug Fund Banned Books Week Event Grants ($1,000 to $2,500). To support activities that raise awareness of intellectual freedom and censorship issues during the annual Banned Books Week celebration. *Winners:* Acadia Parish Library in Louisiana for a parish-wide poster contest for K–12 students to increase awareness about censorship and book challenges; Highland County District Library in Ohio for a weeklong Banned Book Festival featuring a "Dear Banned Author" Day when patrons can write letters to their favorite authors who have had their books challenged; New Madrid County Library in Missouri will hold an essay contest for middle and high school students with cash prizes for the first, second, and third place winners; Patchogue-Medford Library in New York for a discussion with author Suzanne Nossel, CEO of PEN America, on free speech and the importance of debate and dialogue in a democratic society; West Lake Middle School and Northglenn Middle School in Broomfield, Colorado, to teach students about banned books by pairing them with primary sources in order to understand what was going on in the world at the time the books were published and events that followed their publication..

Gay, Lesbian, Bisexual, and Transgender Round Table (GLBTRT)

Larry Romans Mentorship Award ($1,000). To recognize librarians who, through their sustained mentoring efforts, have made a difference in our profession. Not awarded in 2021.

Stonewall Book Awards. See "Literary Prizes, 2021" in Part 5.

Government Documents Round Table (GODORT)

James Bennett Childs Award. To a librarian or other individual for distinguished lifetime contributions to documents librarianship. *Winner:* Janet Fisher of the Arizona Talking Book Library at Arizona State Library.

GODORT-Sponsored ALA Emerging Leader Award. A leadership development program that enables newer library workers from across the country to participate in problem-solving work groups, network with peers, gain an inside look into ALA structure, and have an opportunity to serve the profession in a leadership capacity. *Winner:* Not awarded in 2021.

Bernadine Abbott Hoduski Founders Award. To recognize documents librarians who may not be known at the national level but who have made significant contributions to the field of local, state, federal, or international documents. Not awarded in 2021.

Margaret T. Lane/Virginia F. Saunders Memorial Research Award. *Winners:* Amanda Wakaruk and Sam-chin Li for *Government Information in Canada: Access and Stewardship* (University of Alberta Press).

NewsBank/Readex/GODORT/ALA Catharine J. Reynolds Research Grant. To documents librarians for travel and/or study in the field of documents librarianship or an area of study benefiting their performance. *Donor:* NewsBank and Readex Corporation. *Winner:* Susanne Caro of the Main Library at North Dakota State University.

ProQuest/GODORT/ALA Documents to the People Award. To an individual, library, organization, or noncommercial group that most effectively encourages or enhances the use of government documents in library services. *Winner:* Kelly Smith of the University of California–San Diego Library.

Larry Romans Mentorship Award ($1,000). To recognize librarians who, through their sustained mentoring efforts, have made a difference in our profession. Not awarded in 2021.

W. David Rozkuszka Scholarship ($3,000). To provide financial assistance to individuals currently working with government documents in a library while completing a master's program in library science. Not awarded in 2021.

Intellectual Freedom Round Table (IFRT)

Gerald Hodges Intellectual Freedom Chapter Relations Award. *Winner:* Missouri Library Association.

John Phillip Immroth Memorial Award for Intellectual Freedom ($500). For notable contribution to intellectual freedom fueled by personal courage. *Winner:* Martin Garner of Amherst College Library.

Eli M. Oboler Memorial Award. See "Literary Prizes, 2021" in Part 5.

Library and Information Technology Association (LITA)

Hugh C. Atkinson Memorial Award. See under American Library Association.

Ex Libris Student Writing Award ($1,000 and publication in *Information Technology and Libraries*). For the best unpublished manuscript on a topic in the area of libraries and information technology written by a student or students enrolled in an ALA-accredited library and information studies graduate program. *Donor:* Ex Libris. Not awarded in 2021.

LITA/Christian Larew Memorial Scholarship in Library and Information Technology ($3,000). To encourage the entry of qualified persons into the library and information technology field. *Sponsor:* Informata.com. Not awarded in 2021.

LIT/Library Hi Tech Award for Outstanding Communication for Continuing Education in Library and Information Science. To an individual or institution for outstanding communication in library and information technology. *Donor:* Emerald Group. Not awarded in 2021.

LITA/OCLC Frederick G. Kilgour Award for Research in Library and Information Technology ($2,000 and expense-paid attendance at the ALA Annual Conference). To bring attention to research relevant to the development of information technologies.

Donor: OCLC. *Winner:* Trevor Owens of the Library of Congress.

Library History Round Table (LHRT)

Phyllis Dain Library History Dissertation Award. Given irregularly in odd-numbered years to the author of a dissertation treating the history of books, libraries, librarianship, or information science. *Winner (2021):* Dr. Cindy Anh Nguyen for "Reading and Misreading: The Social Life of Libraries and Colonial Control in Vietnam, 1865–1958."

Donald G. Davis Article Award (certificate). Awarded biennially for the best article written in English in the field of U.S. and Canadian library history. *Winner (2020):* Laura E. Helton for "On Decimals, Catalogs, and Racial Imaginaries of Reading" (PMLA).

Eliza Atkins Gleason Book Award. Presented every third year to the author of a book in English in the field of library history. *Winners (2019):* Wayne Wiegand and Shirley Wiegand for *The Desegregation of Public Libraries in the Jim Crow South: Civil Rights and Local Activism* (Louisiana State University Press).

Justin Winsor Library History Essay Award ($500). To the author of an outstanding essay embodying original historical research on a significant subject of library history. *Winner:* Dr. Jennifer Burek Pierce for "More Than a Room with Books: The Development of Author Visits for Young People in Mid-Century U.S. Public Libraries."

Library Leadership and Management Association (LLAMA)

Hugh C. Atkinson Memorial Award. See under American Library Association.

John Cotton Dana Library Public Relations Awards ($10,000). To libraries or library organizations of all types for public relations programs or special projects ended during the preceding year. *Donors:* H.W. Wilson Foundation and EBSCO. *Winners:* Anchorage Public Library in Alaska for the "Books Get Our Vote" campaign that tackled declining civic engagement, declining reading test scores in school-age children, and a community disconnected by COVID-19; Chicago Public Library in Illinois for its "Live from the Library" series, a virtual story time to help combat the effects of closing libraries and schools due to COVID-19 in spring 2020; Cincinnati & Hamilton County Public Library in Ohio for a media campaign titled "Visit the Cincinnati & Hamilton County Public Library: For Minds of All Kinds" to increase awareness that all 41 locations were open for in-person services; Edmonton Public Library in Alberta, Canada, for a virtual open house promoting services offered by the Stanley A. Milner Library; Fort Worth Public Library in Texas for a local artist music-streaming service, Amplify 817, aimed to establish brand awareness and reiterate the value and relevance of the library; Los Angeles County Library in California for efforts to bridge the digital divide during the pandemic, including Park & Connect, allowing customers to park in branch parking lots to access free Internet; Spartanburg County Public Libraries in South Carolina for encouraging their community to complete the 2020 Census, resulting in effectively counting 5,000 more households in the 2020 Census than in the 2010 effort; and Whatcom County Library System in Washington for their Library Card Sign-up Month campaign that abandoned traditional approaches and relied on equal parts whimsy and fact to drive new enrollments.

Library Research Round Table (LRRT)

Jesse H. Shera Award for Excellence in Published Research. For a research article on library and information studies published in English during the calendar year. Not awarded in 2021.

Jesse H. Shera Award for Support of Dissertation Research. To recognize and support dissertation research employing exemplary research design and methods. Not awarded in 2021.

Map and Geospatial Information Round Table (MAGIRT)

MAGIRT Honors Award. To recognize outstanding achievement and major contributions to map and geospatial librarianship. *Winners:* Carol McAuliffe, University of

Florida, and David Bertuca, University of Buffalo.

New Members Round Table (NMRT)

NMRT ALA Student Chapter of the Year Award. To an ALA student chapter for outstanding contributions to the association. *Winner:* University of Hawaii–Manoa.

NMRT Annual Conference Professional Development Attendance Award (formerly the Marshall Cavendish Award). Provides tickets to the ALA Annual Conference event of the winners' choice. Not awarded in 2021.

NMRT Professional Development Grant. To new NMRT members to encourage professional development and participation in national ALA and NMRT activities. Not awarded in 2021.

Shirley Olofson Memorial Award ($1,000). To an individual to help defray costs of attending the ALA Annual Conference. Not awarded in 2021.

Office for Diversity

Achievement in Library Diversity Research Honor. To an ALA member who has made significant contributions to diversity research in the profession. Not awarded in 2021.

Diversity Research Grants ($2,500). To the authors of research proposals that address critical gaps in the knowledge of diversity issues within library and information science. Not awarded in 2021.

Office for Information Technology Policy

L. Ray Patterson Copyright Award. To recognize an individual who supports the constitutional purpose of U.S. copyright law, fair use, and the public domain. *Sponsor:* Freedom to Read Foundation. Not awarded in 2021.

Office for Literacy and Outreach Services (OLOS)

Jean E. Coleman Library Outreach Lecture. *Sponsor:* OLOS Advisory Committee. *Lecturer:* Aaron LaFromboise of Medicine

Spring Library at Blackfeet Community College in Browning, Montana.

Public Library Association (PLA)

Baker & Taylor Entertainment Audio Music/ Video Product Grant ($2,500 worth of audio music or video products). To help a public library to build or expand a collection of either or both formats. *Donor:* Baker & Taylor. Not awarded in 2021.

Gordon M. Conable Award ($1,500). To a public library staff member, library trustee, or public library for demonstrating a commitment to intellectual freedom and the Library Bill of Rights. *Sponsor:* LSSI. Not awarded in 2021.

EBSCO Excellence in Rural Library Service Award ($1,000). Honors a library serving a population of 10,000 or fewer that demonstrates excellence of service to its community as exemplified by an overall service program or a special program of significant accomplishment. *Donor:* EBSCO. Not awarded in 2021.

Helping Communities Come Together Award recognizes a public library's ability to identify community needs specifically in times of crisis and division and respond in creative and exemplary ways. *Donor:* The Singer Group. Not awarded in 2021.

John Iliff Award ($1,000). To a library worker, librarian, or library for the use of technology and innovative thinking as a tool to improve services to public library users. *Sponsor:* Innovative. Not awarded in 2021.

Allie Beth Martin Award ($3,000). To honor a public librarian who has demonstrated extraordinary range and depth of knowledge about books or other library materials and has distinguished ability to share that knowledge. *Donor:* Baker & Taylor. Not awarded in 2021.

New Leaders Travel Grants (up to $1,500). To PLA members who have not attended a major PLA continuing education event in the past five years. Not awarded in 2021.

PLA Library Innovation Award ($2,000). To recognize a public library's innovative achievement in planning and implementing a creative community service program. Not awarded in 2021.

Charlie Robinson Award ($1,000). To honor a public library director who, over a period of seven years, has been a risk taker, an innovator, and/or a change agent in a public library. *Donor:* Baker & Taylor. Not awarded in 2021.

Romance Writers of America Library Grant ($4,500). To a library to build or expand a fiction collection and/or host romance fiction programming. *Donor:* Romance Writers of America. Not awarded in 2021.

Public Programs Office

Sara Jaffarian School Library Program Award for Exemplary Humanities Programming ($4,000). To honor a K–8 school library that has conducted an outstanding humanities program or series. *Donors:* Sara Jaffarian and ALA Cultural Communities Fund. *Winner:* Shawnee Middle School in Oklahoma for "Teaching the Tulsa Race Massacre with Guided Inquiry Design."

Reference and User Services Association (RUSA)

Award for Excellence in Reference and Adult Library Services ($1,500). To recognize a library or library system for developing an imaginative and unique library resource to meet patrons' reference needs. *Donor:* Data Axle. *Winners:* Sarah Qronfleh and Allison Ryall from Genealogy Services at the Orange County Library System in Windermere, Florida.

BRASS Academic Business Librarianship Travel Award ($1,250). To recognize a librarian who is new to the field of academic business librarianship and support his or her attendance at the ALA Annual Conference. *Donor:* Global Financial Data. *Winner:* Blake Robinson of Rollins College in Winter Park, Florida.

BRASS Excellence in Business Librarianship Award ($4,000). For distinguished activities in the field of business librarianship *Donor:* Mergent by FTSE Russell. *Winner:* Mark Pond of Spokane Public Library in Washington.

BRASS Public Librarian Support Award ($1,250). To support attendance at the ALA Annual Conference of a public librarian who has performed outstanding business reference service. *Donor:* Morningstar. *Winner:* Alexander Blend of Middle Country Public Library in Centereach, New York.

BRASS Research Grant Award ($2,500). To an ALA member seeking support to conduct research in business librarianship. *Donor:* Emerald Publishing. Not awarded in 2021.

BRASS Student Travel Award ($1,250). To enable a student enrolled in an ALA-accredited master's program to attend the ALA Annual Conference. *Donor:* Simply Analytics. *Winner:* Rashida C. Scott of Maricopa County Library District in Arizona.

Sophie Brody Medal. See "Literary Prizes, 2021" in Part 5.

Federal Rising Stars Initiative. To a member who is new to the profession in a federal or armed forces library or government information management setting. *Winner:* Mariah Antoinette Lovick.

Francis Joseph Campbell Award. For a contribution of recognized importance to library service for the blind and physically handicapped. *Winner:* David J. Kelsey.

CODES Zora Neale Hurston Award. To recognize the efforts of RUSA members in promoting African American literature. *Donor:* HarperCollins. Not awarded in 2021.

CODES Louis Shores Award (citation). To an individual, team, or organization in recognition of excellence in reviewing of books and other materials for libraries. *Winner:* Terry Hong of Booklist.

ETS Achievement Award. To recognize excellence in service to RUSA's Emerging Technologies Section (ETS). *Winner:* Jason Coleman of Kansas State University Libraries in Manhattan, Kansas.

Federal Achievement Award. For achievement in the promotion of library and information service and the information profession in the federal community. Not awarded in 2021.

HS Genealog/History Achievement Award ($1,500). To encourage and commend professional achievement in historical reference and research librarianship. *Donor:* ProQuest. *Winner:* DeeDee Baldwin, history research librarian at Mississippi State University Libraries in Starkville, Mississippi.

HS History Research and Innovation Award ($2,500). To an M.L.S.-degreed librarian from an ALA-accredited school to facilitate and further research relating to history and history librarianship. *Donor:* Gale Cengage. *Winner:* Jennifer Daugherty from the North Carolina Collection in Academic

Library Services at East Carolina University in Greenville, North Carolina.

Margaret E. Monroe Library Adult Services Award ($1,250). To a librarian for his or her impact on library service to adults. *Donor:* NoveList. *Winner:* Kelvin Watson of Broward County Library in Florida.

Isadore Gilbert Mudge Award ($5,000). For distinguished contributions to reference librarianship. *Donor:* EBSCO. *Winner:* R. David Lankes of the School of Information Science at the University of South Carolina.

RSS Service Achievement Award. To an RSS member who has made either a sustained contribution toward attaining the goals of the Reference Services Section or a single significant contribution that has resulted in a positive impact on the work of the section. Not awarded in 2021.

RUSA Exceptional Service Award. To recognize exceptional service to patients, to the homebound, to people of all ages who live in group homes or residences, and to inmates and to recognize professional leadership, effective interpretation of programs, pioneering activity, and significant research of experimental projects. *Winner:* Catherine G. Zimmerman.

RUSA/Keystone Library Automation System (KLAS) & National Organization on Disability (NOD) Award ($1,000). To a library organization to recognize an innovative project to benefit people with disabilities. *Donor:* Keystone Systems. Not awarded in 2021.

John Sessions Memorial Award (plaque). To a library or library system in recognition of work with the labor community. *Donor:* Department for Professional Employees, AFL/CIO. *Winner:* Labor Archives of Washington, University of Washington Libraries Special Collections in Seattle, Washington.

STARS Mentoring Award ($1,250). To a library practitioner who is new to the field of interlibrary loan, resource sharing, or electronic reserves, to attend the ALA Annual Conference. *Donor:* Atlas Systems. *Winners:* Carla Lasky of Rosalind Franklin University of Medicine and Science in North Chicago, Illinois, and Jacob E. Lotter of Wheaton College in Norton, Massachusetts.

STARS Virginia Boucher Distinguished ILL Librarian Award ($2,000). To a librarian for outstanding professional achievement, leadership, and contributions to interlibrary loan and document delivery. *Winner:* Melissa Eighmy Brown, manager of interlibrary loan and digital delivery and co-interim director of Content Services.

United for Libraries

Trustee Citation. To recognize public library trustees for individual service to library development on the local, state, regional, or national level. Not awarded in 2021.

United for Libraries/Baker & Taylor Awards. To recognize library friends groups for outstanding efforts to support their libraries. *Donor:* Baker & Taylor. Not awarded in 2021.

United for Libraries Major Benefactors Citation. To individuals, families, or corporate bodies that have made major benefactions to public libraries. Not awarded in 2021.

United for Libraries Public Service Award. To a legislator who has been especially supportive of libraries. Not awarded in 2021.

United for Libraries/Thrift Books Friends Grant ($850 plus free conference registration). Enables one member of a Friends of the Library group at a public library to attend the ALA Annual Conference. *Donor:* Thrift Books. Not awarded in 2021.

Young Adult Library Services Association (YALSA)

Baker & Taylor/YALSA Collection Development Grants ($1,000). To YALSA members who represent a public library and work directly with young adults, for collection development materials for young adults. *Donor:* Book Wholesalers, Inc. *Winners:* Karen Bilton from Franklin Township Public Library in Somerset, New Jersey, and Emily Mazzoni from Monroe Township Public Library in New Jersey.

Baker & Taylor/YALSA Conference Scholarship Grants ($1,000). To young adult librarians in public or school libraries to attend the ALA Annual Conference for the first time. *Donor:* Baker & Taylor. Not awarded in 2021.

Dorothy Broderick Student Scholarship ($1,000). To enable a graduate student to attend the ALA Conference for the first time. *Sponsor:* YALSA Leadership Endowment. Not awarded in 2021.

Margaret A. Edwards Award. See "Literary Prizes, 2021" in Part 5.

Great Books Giveaway (approximately 3,000 books, videos, CDs, and audiocassettes). *Winners:* Belfast Area High School in Maine; Franklin Township Public Library in Somerset, New Jersey; and Townsend Harris High School in Flushing, New York.

Frances Henne/YALSA Research Grant ($1,000). To provide seed money to an individual, institution, or group for a project to encourage research on library service to young adults. *Donor:* Greenwood Publishing Group. *Winner:* Emily Booth from the University of Technology Sydney (UTS) in New South Wales, Australia.

William C. Morris YA Debut Award. See "Literary Prizes, 2021" in Part 5.

Michael L. Printz Award. See "Literary Prizes, 2021" in Part 5.

YALSA/MAE Award for Best Literature Program for Teens ($500 for the recipient plus $500 for his or her library). For an exemplary young adult reading or literature program. *Sponsor:* Margaret A. Edwards Trust. *Winner:* Amanda Cawthon of the Pflugerville Public Library in Texas.

YALSA Service to Young Adults Outstanding Achievement Award ($2,000). Biennial award to a YALSA member who has demonstrated unique and sustained devotion to young adult services. *Winner (2020):* Mega Subramaniam of the College of Information Studies (iSchool) at the University of Maryland.

Art Libraries Society of North America (ARLIS/NA)

ARLIS/NA Distinguished Service Award. To honor an individual whose exemplary service in art librarianship, visual resources curatorship, or a related field has made an outstanding national or international contribution to art information. *Winner:* Deborah Kempe.

ARLIS/NA Wolfgang M. Freitag Internship Award ($3,000). To provide financial support for students preparing for a career in art librarianship or visual resource librarianship. Not awarded in 2021.

Melva J. Dwyer Award. To the creators of exceptional reference or research tools relating to Canadian art and architecture. *Winner:* Nancy Campbell for *Itee Pootoogook: Hymns to the Silence* (Goose Lane Editions/McMichael Canadian Art Collection).

Gerd Muehsam Award. To one or more graduate students in library science programs to recognize excellence in a graduate paper or project. Not awarded in 2021.

H.W. Wilson Foundation Research Award ($3,000). For research activities by ARLIS/NA individual members in the fields of librarianship, visual resources curatorship, and the arts. *Winner:* Janelle Rebel for "Bibliographic Performances & Surrogate Readings."

George Wittenborn Memorial Book Awards. See "Literary Prizes, 2021" in Part 5.

Asian/Pacific Americans Libraries Association (APALA)

APALA Scholarship ($1,000). For a student of Asian or Pacific background who is enrolled in, or has been accepted into, a master's or doctoral degree program in library and/or information science at an ALA-accredited school. *Winner:* Amrita S. Patel.

APALA Travel Grant ($500). To a U.S. or Canadian citizen or permanent resident enrolled in a master's or doctoral degree program in library and/or information science at an ALA-accredited school or a professional possessing a master's degree or doctoral degree in library and/or information science to enable attendance at the ALA Annual Conference. *Winners:* Hana Kim, Andrew Carlos, and Mitsuko Brooks.

Emerging Leaders Sponsorship. To enable newer library workers to participate in problem-solving work groups, network with peers, gain an inside look into ALA's structure, and have an opportunity to serve the profession. Not awarded in 2021.

Association for Information Science and Technology (ASIS&T)

ASIS&T Award of Merit. For an outstanding contribution to the field of information science. *Winner:* Steve Sawyer.

ASIS&T Best Information Science Book. *Winner:* Christina Dunbar-Hester for *Hacking Diversity: The Politics of Inclusion in Open Technology Cultures* (Princeton University Press).

ASIS&T Doctoral Dissertation Proposal Scholarship ($2,000). *Winner:* Rongqian Ma for "Bridging Sight and Insight: Visualization in Action among Digital Humanists."

ASIS&T Outstanding Information Science Teacher Award ($1,500). To recognize the unique teaching contribution of an individual as a teacher of information science. *Winner:* Colin Rhinesmith of the School of Library and Information Science at Simmons University.

ASIS&T ProQuest Doctoral Dissertation Award ($1,000 plus expense-paid attendance at ASIS&T Annual Meeting). *Winner:* Dr. Laura Molloy for "Creative Connections: The Value of Digital Information and Its Effective Management for Sustainable Contemporary Visual Art Practice."

ASIS&T Research in Information Science Award. For a systematic program of research in a single area at a level beyond the single study, recognizing contributions in the field of information science. *Winner:* Chun Wei Choo of the Faculty of Information at the University of Toronto.

James M. Cretsos Leadership Award. To recognize new ASIS&T members who have demonstrated outstanding leadership qualities in professional ASIS&T activities. *Winner:* Md. Anwarul Islam.

Watson Davis Award for Service. For outstanding continuous contributions and dedicated service to the society. *Winner:* Dr. Abebe Rorissa.

Louise Lunin Award. To recognize individuals who have made noteworthy contributions to the practice of information science and technology through leadership, mentoring, and innovation. *Winner:* Prodip Roy.

Pratt Severn Best Masters Student Paper Award. To encourage student research and writing in the field of information science. Not awarded in 2021.

John Wiley Best *JASIST* Paper Award. *Winners:* Drs. Joshua Introne, Ingrid Erickson, Bryan Semaan, and Sean Goggins for "Designing Sustainable Online Support: Examining the Effects of Design Change in Forty-Nine Online Health Support Communities"

(*Journal of the Association for Information Science & Technology*, Vol. 71, Issue 4).

Bob Williams Research Grant Award. Not awarded in 2021.

Bob Williams Research Paper Award. Not awarded in 2021.

Association for Library and Information Science Education (ALISE)

ALISE Award for Professional Contribution. Not awarded in 2021.

ALISE Best Conference Paper Award. *Winners:* Melissa Gross and Don Latham of Florida State University for "Is There a Social Worker in Your Library?" and Joseph Winberry of the University of Tennessee–Knoxville for "Student Perspectives of LIS Education in an Aging Society."

ALISE Community conn@CT Mini-Grants. *Winners:* Travis Wagner and Vanessa Kitzie of the University of South Carolina for "Creating Sustainable Digital Spaces for Sharing Health Information with South Carolina Transgender and Non-Binary Communities."

ALISE Diversity Travel Award ($750 for travel expenses, complimentary registration to the ALISE Annual Conference, and one-year student membership). To increase diversity in LIS education/research for an individual who wishes to address issues of diversity through doctoral study or teaching. *Winner:* Shannon Williams of Florida State University.

ALISE Excellence in Teaching Award. *Winner:* Beth Brendler from the University of Missouri–Columbia.

ALISE/Eugene Garfield Doctoral Dissertation Competition. *Winner:* Darra Hofman from San Jose State University, for "Between Knowing and Not Knowing: Privacy, Transparency, and Digital Records."

ALIS/Norman Horrocks Leadership Award. To recognize a new ALISE member who has demonstrated outstanding leadership qualities in professional ALISE activities. *Winner:* Michele Villagran of San Jose State University.

ALISE/Pratt-Severn Faculty Innovation Award. To recognize innovation by full-time faculty members in incorporating evolving information technologies in the curricula of accredited master's degree programs in library and information studies. *Winners:* Heather Moulaison-Sandy and Felicity Dykas of the University of Missouri for "Organizing Information in Information Agencies."

ALISE/ProQuest Methodology Paper Competition. Not awarded in 2021.

ALISE Research Grant Competition (one or more grants totaling $5,000). *Winners:* Michele Villagran and Darra Hofman of San Jose State University for "Educating for Equity?: Sexual and Gender Minority Privacy in Library and Information Studies Education."

ALISE Service Award. *Winner:* Heidi E. Julien of the University at Buffalo.

ALISE/Jean Tague Sutcliffe Doctoral Student Research Poster Competition. *Winners:* (first place) Schenita Floyd of the University of North Texas; Travis Wagner of the University of South Carolina; (second place) Ly Dinh from the University of Illinois–Urbana-Champaign.

ALISE/University of Washington Information School Youth Services Graduate Student Travel Award. To support the costs associated with travel to and participation in the ALISE Annual Conference. *Winner:* Kerry Townsend of the University of Missouri.

ALISE/Connie Van Fleet Award for Research Excellence in Public Library Services to Adults. To recognize LIS research concerning services to adults in public libraries. *Winner:* Noah Lenstra of the University of North Carolina–Greensboro.

ALISE/Bohdan S. Wynar Research Paper Competition. *Winners:* Joseph Winberry and Devendra Potnis of the University of Tennessee–Knoxville for "Social Innovations in Public Libraries: Types and Challenges."

Doctoral Students to ALISE Grant. To support the attendance of one or more promising LIS doctoral students at the ALISE Annual Conference. *Sponsor:* Libraries Unlimited/Linworth. *Winners:* Maria Ortiz-Myers of Rutgers University and Jieun Yeon of Syracuse University.

Association of Jewish Libraries (AJL)

AJL Scholarships ($1,000). For students enrolled in accredited library schools who plan to work as Judaica librarians. Not awarded in 2021.

Fanny Goldstein Merit Award. To honor loyal and ongoing contributions to the association and to the profession of Jewish librarianship. *Winner:* Rachel Kamin.

Life Membership Award. To recognize outstanding leadership and professional contributions to the association and to the profession of Jewish librarianship. Not awarded in 2021.

Association of Research Libraries

ARL Diversity Scholarships (stipend of up to $10,000). To a varying number of M.L.S. students from underrepresented groups who are interested in careers in research libraries. *Sponsors:* ARL member libraries and the Institute of Museum and Library Services. *Winners:* Karen Adjei of the University of Maryland; Lyndon J. Batiste of the University of Alabama; danielle luz Belanger of the University of Illinois–Urbana-Champaign; Isabel Carlin of the University of British Columbia; Genevia M. Chamblee-Smith of North Carolina Central University; Cora Coady of the University of Toronto; Sylvia Figueroa-Ortiz of the University of Illinois–Urbana-Champaign; Aparna Ghosh of the University of South Florida; Sarah M. Henry of Wayne State University; Alexis Herrera of the University of Michigan; Taya Reece Jardine of the University of British Columbia; Jessica Nombrano Larsen of San José State University; Francisco J. López-Huerta of San José State University; Krystal Madkins of the University of Illinois–Urbana-Champaign; Anthony Martinez of the University of Illinois–Urbana-Champaign; Rosemary N. Medrano of the University of Missouri; Ari Negovschi of the University of Illinois–Urbana-Champaign; and Adira-Danique Philyaw of Florida State University.

Association of Seventh-Day Adventist Librarians

D. Glenn Hilts Scholarship ($1,500) for a member or members of the Seventh-Day Adventist Church who are enrolled in a graduate library program. *Winner:* Aaron Wilson of the University of Maryland.

Beta Phi Mu

Beta Phi Mu Award. See under American Library Association.

Eugene Garfield Doctoral Dissertation Fellowships ($3,000). *Winners:* Stephen Abrams of Queensland University of Technology/San José State University for "A Communicological Critique of Evaluative Norms for Digital Preservation Success"; Elizabeth Campbell of Drexel University for "A Framework for Measuring and Mitigating Bias in Electronic Health Record Data: A Case Study in Childhood Obesity Incident"; Yi-Yun Cheng of the University of Illinois–Urbana-Champaign for "Agreeing to Disagree: Applying a Logic Based Approach to Reconciling and Merging Multiple Taxonomies"; Julaine Clunis of Kent State University for "Semantic Analysis Mapping Framework for Clinical Coding Schemes"; Lo Lee of the University of Illinois–Urbana-Champaign for "Exploring Information Behavior of Hobbyists and the Making Process of Arts and Crafts"; Rongquian Ma of the University of Pittsburgh for "Bridging Sight and Insight: Visualization in Action among Digital Humanists."

Harold Lancour Scholarship for Foreign Study ($1,750). For graduate study in a country related to the applicant's work or schooling. Not awarded in 2021.

Sarah Rebecca Reed Scholarship ($2,250). For study at an ALA-accredited library school. Not awarded in 2021.

Frank B. Sessa Scholarship for Continuing Professional Education ($1,500). For continuing education for a Beta Phi Mu member. *Winners:* Ariel Barnes of Simmons University, Beta Beta Chapter; Lori Bello of the Rutgers School of Communication & Information, Omicron Chapter; Amanda Click, Beta Beta Zeta Chapter; Heather Healy of Emporia State University, Beta Epsilon Chapter; Araceli Hintermeister of Simmons University, Beta Beta Chapter; Jamie Luedtke, Alpha Chapter; Regina Pagani of Simmons University, Beta Beta Chapter; Liza Palmer, Beta Beta Epsilon

Chapter; Jennifer Taylor, Beta Psi Chapter; and Cindy Tian, Alpha Chapter.

Blanche E. Woolls Scholarship ($2,250). For a beginning student in school library media services. Not awarded in 2021.

Bibliographical Society of America (BSA)

BSA Fellowships ($1,500–$6,000). For scholars involved in bibliographical inquiry and research in the history of the book trades and in publishing history. *Winners:* (Fredson Bowers Award) Meghan Constantinou for "The Library Catalogues of the Elliots of Minto: A Scottish Aristocratic Library in Context, 1738–1938"; (BSA-ASECS Fellowship for Bibliographical Studies in the Eighteenth Century) Julie Park for "Writing's Maker: Inscribing the Self in the Eighteenth Century"; (BSA Peck-Stacpoole Fellowship for Early Career Collections Professionals) Ostap Kin for "Poet's Choice: Bohdan Boychuk's Lost Anthology of Ukrainian Modernist Poetry"; Lucy Mookerjee for "The Itinerary of a Cookbook: Mapping the Cultural Routes of Morgan MS B.36 (An Edition and Analysis)"; (BSA-Pine Tree Foundation Fellowship in Culinary Bibliography) Ellen Barth for "Women as Producers of American Community Cookbooks, 1950s to 1990s: Motivations and Materials"; (BSA-Pine Tree Foundation Fellowship in Hispanic Bibliography) Carlos Diego Arenas Pacheco for "Indigenous Latinists: 16th-Century Books from Santa Cruz de Tlatelolco at the Sutro Library, San Francisco"; (BSA-St. Louis Mercantile Library Fellowship for Research in North American Bibliography) Mark Mattes for "Archival Apocrypha: Indigenous Writing and the Figure of Logan in Colonial and Native American History"; (BSA Short Term Fellowships) Amanda Arceneaux for "To Know an Herbe: Vernacular Herbal Manuscripts, 1570–1750"; James P. Ascher for "Seventeenth-Century Printer's Copy and Records at the Royal Society"; Paulina Banas for "Visualizing Egypt: European Travel, Book Illustration, and the Marketing of the East in the 19th Century"; Patricia Andrea Dosio for "Sketching Connections: Reconstruction of the Rioplatense Cultural Scene through the Editions of Aquilino Fernández (1880–1930)"; Cecilia Sideri for "Reconstructing the Library and Reading Habits of the Renaissance Manuscript Collector and Calligraphist Marco Antonio Altieri (1450–1532)"; Jessica Terekhov for "The Life Cycle of the Part-Issued Victorian Novel"; Laura Viaut for "Production and Circulation of Educational Manuscripts of Roman-Barbarian Law in the Early Middle Ages"; (Caxton Club Fellowship for Midwestern Bibliographers) William Little for "The Latin Poetry of Nallio Rainaldi of Tagliacozzo"; (The Katharine Pantzer Junior Fellowship in the British Book Trades) Yelda Nasifoglu for "Mathematics in Circulation in Late Seventeenth-Century London: Evidence from Hammer Copies of Auction Catalogues"; (Katharine F. Pantzer Senior Fellow in the British Book Trades) Sandro Jung for "Eighteenth-Century British Regional Book Illustrations of Literature: Models, Production, and Commercial Use in the North of England"; (Reese Fellowship for American Bibliography and the History of the Book in the Americas) Fabián Vega for "Books from the Guaraní Missions. Jesuit Libraries and Circulation of Knowledge in the South American Borderlands (18th Century)"; (Charles J. Tanenbaum Fellowship in Cartographical Bibliography) Anne Garner for "Recovering Feminine Cartographies: Women Wayfinders and 'Vanishing Monuments' in the Canadian Territories, 1795–1990"; (Dorothy Porter Wesley Fellowship) Jacinta Saffold for "Independent Hip Hop Production as Freedom Dreaming."

William L. Mitchell Prize for Research on Early British Serials ($1,000). Awarded triennially for the best single work published in the previous three years. *Winner (2021):* Dr. Megan Peiser for "William Lane and the Minerva Press in the Review Periodical, 1790–1820" in *Romantic Textualities* (Summer 2020).

New Scholars Program. To promote the work of scholars who are new to the field of bibliography. *Winners:* (Pantzer New Scholar) Mathieu D.S. Bouchard for "A Revised Account of the 1714 Works of Mr. William Shakespear"; (Malkin New Scholar) Dr. Sophia Brown for "Paratexts and Prize Culture: A Case Study of Contemporary Arab

Writing in the Anglophone Market"; (BSA New Scholar) Ryan Low for "Community of the Written Word: The Spread of Notarial Registers in Medieval Provence."

St. Louis Mercantile Library Prize ($2,000). Awarded triennially for outstanding scholarship in the bibliography of American history and literature. *Sponsor:* St. Louis Mercantile Library, University of Missouri, St. Louis. *Winners (2020):* Dr. Lindsay DiCuirci for *Colonial Revivals: The Nineteenth-Century Lives of Early American Books* (University of Pennsylvania Press) and Dr. Derrick R. Spires for *The Practice of Citizenship: Black Politics and Print Culture in the Early United States* (University of Pennsylvania Press).

Justin G. Schiller Prize for Bibliographical Work on Pre-20th Century Children's Books ($2,000). A triennial award to encourage scholarship in the bibliography of historical children's books. *Winner (2019):* Maroussia Oakley for *The Book and Periodical Illustrations of Arthur Hughes: A Spark of Genius 1832–1914* (Oak Knoll Press & Private Libraries Association).

Catholic Library Association

Regina Medal. For continued, distinguished contribution to the field of children's literature. *Winner:* Jan Brett.

Chinese American Librarians Association (CALA)

CALA Conference Travel Grant. Not awarded in 2021.

CALA Distinguished Service Award. To a librarian who has been a mentor, role model, and leader in the fields of library and information science. Not awarded in 2021.

CALA Outstanding Library Leadership Award in Memory of Dr. Margaret Chang Fung. Not awarded in 2021.

CALA President's Recognition Award. Not awarded in 2021.

CALA Scholarship of Library and Information Science ($1,000). *Winner:* Shengang Wang.

Sheila Suen Lai Scholarship ($500). *Winner:* Tiffany Cheung.

Lisa Zhao Scholarship ($500). Not awarded in 2021.

Coalition for Networked Information (CNI)

Paul Evan Peters Award. Awarded biennially to recognize notable and lasting international achievements relating to high-performance networks and the creation and use of information resources and services that advance scholarship and intellectual productivity. *Sponsors:* Association of Research Libraries, CNI, EDUCAUSE. *Winner (2020):* Francine Berman from Rensselaer Polytechnic University and Radcliffe Institute at Harvard University.

Paul Evan Peters Fellowship ($5,000 a year for two years). Awarded biennially to a student or students pursuing a graduate degree in librarianship or the information sciences. *Sponsors:* Association of Research Libraries, CNI, EDUCAUSE. *Winners (2020):* Jen Liu and Jake Tompins.

Council on Library and Information Resources (CLIR)

CLIR Postdoctoral Fellowships in Scholarly Information Resources. *Current fellows (2020):* Portia D. Hopkins, Luling Huang, Petrouchka Moise, Jennifer Ross, Synatra Smith, Francena Turner, Laura Wilson, and Rebecca Pickens.

Digitizing Hidden Special Collections and Archives Awards. *Sponsor:* Andrew W. Mellon Foundation. *Winners (2020):* Burke Museum of the University of Washington, the University of Alaska–Fairbanks, and Western Washington University for "Digitizing and Creating Online Access to Vascular Plant Specimens from the Russian Far East"; Cal State Los Angeles and the University of Southern California for "Restoring the Visual Record of Mesoamerican and Spanish Colonial Cultures: Hidden Artifacts, Rare Books, and Photography Collections at Cal State LA and the USC Libraries"; College of Charleston for "Southern Roots of American Judaism"; Fisk University John Hope and Aurelia E. Franklin Library for "Fisk Forever: Digitizing Materials by and about Fisk University"; FIT (Fashion Institute of Technology) for "The Ruth Finley Collection: Digitizing 70 Years of the Fashion Calendar";

Georgia State University and the University of Maryland for "Advancing Workers Rights in the American South: Digitizing the Records of the AFL-CIO's Civil Rights Division"; KVZK-TV, WGBH, and the Library of Congress for "KVZK/American Samoa Public Media Digitization Project"; Media Burn Archive, University of Chicago, Appalshop, Community TV Network, Rose Golden Archive of New Media Art at Cornell University, Kartemquin Films, and New Orleans Video Access Center for "Resurrecting the 1970s Guerrilla Television Movement"; Mount Mary University for "Mount Mary University Fashion Archive Digitization Project"; Museum of Pop Culture for "Digitizing Early Hip-Hop Materials from the Museum of Pop Culture (MoPOP) Permanent Collection"; Northeast Historic Film for "More Than the News: The Local Television Programs of WCVB Boston"; Recovering the US Hispanic Literary Heritage (University of Houston) for "Periodicals in the US-Mexico Border Region"; Science History Institute for "Science and Survival: Digitizing the Papers of Georg and Max Bredig"; University of Idaho for "Digitizing the Donald E. Crabtree Lithic Comparative Collection in 2D and 3D"; University of Utah and Ocean Alliance for "What Giant Moms Can Tell Us: Digital Rescue and Distribution of a Photo Collection Documenting the Lifetime Reproductive Histories of Right Whales, Revealing the Effects of Climate Change on the Southern Ocean Ecosystem and Supporting a Sustainable Ecotourism Industry"; University of Wisconsin–Madison for "Digitizing Egypt's Historic Geography."

Mellon Fellowships for Dissertation Research in Original Sources. *Sponsor:* Andrew W. Mellon Foundation. Award discontinued.

EDUCAUSE

EDUCAUSE Community Leadership Award. *Winner:* Marcia L. Dority Baker, assistant director for academic technologies at the University of Nebraska–Lincoln.

EDUCAUSE DEI Leadership Award. To acknowledge and celebrate exemplary leadership in advancing equity, diversity, and inclusion. *Winner:* Michael Cato, senior vice-president and chief information officer at Bowdoin College.

EDUCAUSE Leadership Award. To acknowledge leadership in higher education information technology. *Winner:* Michele Norin, senior vice-president and chief information officer at Rutgers, The State University of New Jersey.

EDUCAUSE Rising Star Award. To recognize early-career information technology professionals who demonstrate exceptional achievement in the area of information technology in higher education. *Winners:* Tonya Bennett, director of educational technology at the University of Pennsylvania School of Veterinary Medicine, and Kyle Shachmut, assistant director of digital accessibility services at Harvard University.

Friends of the National Library of Medicine

Michael E. DeBakey Librarian Outreach and Community Collaboration Award. To recognize outstanding service and contributions to rural and underserved communities by a practicing health sciences librarian. Not awarded in 2021.

Institute of Museum and Library Services

National Medal for Museum and Library Service. For extraordinary civic, educational, economic, environmental, and social contributions ($5,000). *Winners:* (libraries) Cabell County Public Library in West Virginia; Highwood Public Library in Illinois; Memphis Public Libraries in Tennessee; (museums) High Desert Museum in Bend, Oregon; Mississippi Children's Museum in Jackson, Mississippi; and Museo de Arte de Ponce in Ponce, Puerto Rico.

International Association of School Librarians (IASL)

Ken Haycock Leadership Development Grant ($1,000). Awarded in odd-numbered years to enable applicants from any nation to attend their first IASL Annual Conference. Not awarded in 2021.

Jean Lowrie Leadership Development Grant ($1,000). Awarded in even-numbered years to enable applicants from developing nations to attend their first IASL Annual Conference. *Winner:* Ifunanya Evangel Obim, Nigeria.

Takeshi Murofushi Research Award ($500). For funding a research project, preferably of international interest. *Winners:* Dr. Lucilia Green and Dr. Jenna Spiering from the University of South Carolina.

Diljit Singh Leadership Development Grant ($1,000). To enable applicants from developing nations to attend their first IASL conference. Not awarded in 2021.

International Board on Books for Young People (IBBY)

IBBY-Asahi Reading Promotion Award ($10,000). Awarded biennially to projects that are making a lasting contribution to reading promotion for young people. *Offered by:* International Board on Books for Young People. *Sponsor:* Asahi Shimbun. *Winner (2020):* Casa Cuna Cuenteros, a volunteer group that carries out reading and storytelling activities in a children's hospital in Buenos Aires, Argentina.

International Federation of Library Associations and Institutions (IFLA)

International Federation of Library Associations and Institutions (IFLA) Honorary Fellow. For distinguished service to IFLA. *Winner:* Glòria Pérez-Salmerón.

IFLA Medal. To a person or organization for a distinguished contribution either to IFLA or to international librarianship. Not awarded in 2021.

Jay Jordan IFLA/OCLC Early Career Development Fellowships. To library and information science professionals from countries with developing economies who are in the early stages of their careers. Not awarded in 2021.

Dr. Shawky Salem Conference Grant (up to $1,900). To enable an expert in library and information science who is a national of an Arab country to attend the IFLA Conference for the first time. Not awarded in 2021.

Library Journal

DEMCO/*Library Journal* Paralibrarian of the Year Award. Not awarded in 2021.

Gale/*Library Journal* Library of the Year. *Sponsor:* Gale Cengage Learning. *Winner:* Anaheim Public Library in California.

Library Journal/ALISE Excellence in Teaching Award. See under Association for Library and Information Science Education (ALISE).

Library Journal Best Small Library in America ($20,000). To honor a public library that profoundly demonstrates outstanding service to populations of 25,000 or less. *Cosponsors: Library Journal* and the Bill and Melinda Gates Foundation. Not awarded in 2021.

Library Journal Librarian of the Year. *Winners:* Elaine R. Hicks, research, education, and public health librarian at Tulane University; Stacy Brody, reference and instruction librarian at George Washington University School of Medicine and Health Sciences in Bethesda, Maryland; and Sara Loree, medical librarian at St. Luke's Health System in Boise, Idaho.

Library of Congress

Kluge Fellowships in Digital Studies. To promote examination of the impact of the digital revolution on society, culture, and international relations using the library's collections and resources. *Fellow:* Joshua Lauer.

Library of Congress Literacy Awards. *Sponsor:* David M. Rubenstein. *Winners:* (David M. Rubenstein Prize, $150,000, for a groundbreaking or sustained record of advancement of literacy by any individual or entity) Dolly Parton's Imagination Library in Pigeon Forge, Tennessee; (American Prize, $50,000, for a project developed and implemented successfully during the past decade for combating illiteracy and or aliteracy) The Parents as Teachers National Center in St. Louis, Missouri; (International Prize,

$50,000, for the work of an individual, nation, or nongovernmental organization working in a specific country or region) The Luminos Fund, Boston, Massachusetts.
Library of Congress Prize for American Fiction. See "Literary Prizes, 2021" in Part 5.

Medical Library Association (MLA)

Virginia L. and William K. Beatty MLA Volunteer Service Award. To recognize a medical librarian who has demonstrated outstanding, sustained service to the Medical Library Association and the health sciences library profession. *Winner:* Nancy Schaefer.
Estelle Brodman Award for the Academic Medical Librarian of the Year. To honor significant achievement, potential for leadership, and continuing excellence at midcareer in the area of academic health sciences librarianship. *Winner:* Karen Gutzman.
Lois Ann Colaianni Award for Excellence and Achievement in Hospital Librarianship. To a member of MLA who has made significant contributions to the profession in the area of overall distinction or leadership in hospital librarianship. *Winner:* Nancy A. Clark.
Consumer Health Librarian of the Year Award. To recognize those who demonstrate excellence in consumer health information services, promote innovation and collaboration, and provide examples to follow for other consumer health librarians. *Winner:* Shari Clifton.
Cunningham Memorial International Fellowships. For health sciences librarians from countries outside the United States and Canada, to provide for attendance at the MLA Annual Meeting and observation and supervised work in one or more medical libraries. *Winner:* Mercy Wamunyima Monde.
Louise Darling Medal. For distinguished achievement in collection development in the health sciences. *Winner:* Collection Development Caucus of the Medical Library Association.
Janet Doe Lectureship. *Winner:* Sandra G. Franklin for "Diversity That Defines Us: The View through a Crystal Lens."
EBSCO/MLA Annual Meeting Grants (up to $1,000). To enable four health sciences

librarians to attend the MLA Annual Meeting. Not awarded in 2021.
Ida and George Eliot Prize. To recognize a work published in the preceding calendar year that has been judged most effective in furthering medical librarianship. *Winners:* Bethany S. McGowan, Laureen P. Cantwell, Jamie L. Conklin, Rebecca Raszewski, Julie Planchon Wolf, Maribeth Slebodnik, Sandra McCarthy, and Shannon Johnson for "Evaluating Nursing Faculty's Approach to Information Literacy Instruction: A Multi-Institutional Study."
Carla J. Funk Governmental Relations Award ($500). To recognize a medical librarian who has demonstrated outstanding leadership in the area of governmental relations at the federal, state, or local level and who has furthered the goal of providing quality information for improved health. *Sponsor:* Kent A. Smith. *Winner:* Barbara A. Epstein.
Murray Gottlieb Prize. See under Erich Meyerhoff Prize.
T. Mark Hodges International Service Award. To honor outstanding achievement in promoting, enabling, or delivering improved health information internationally. *Winner:* Bethany S. McGowan.
David A. Kronick Traveling Fellowship ($2,000). *Sponsor:* Bowden-Massey Foundation. Not awarded in 2021.
Joseph Leiter NLM/MLA Lectureship. *Winner:* Mitzi Baum for "The Culture of Public Health and Food Safety."
Donald A.B. Lindberg Research Fellowship ($10,000). To fund research aimed at expanding the research knowledge base, linking the information services provided by librarians to improved healthcare and advances in biomedical research. *Winners:* Brandon Patterson and Kerri Shaffer for "Implicit Bias in Health Care: Exploring the Upstream and Downstream Effects with Virtual Reality."
Lucretia W. McClure Excellence in Education Award. To an outstanding educator in the field of health sciences librarianship and informatics. *Winner:* Jodi L. Philbrick.
John P. McGovern Award Lectureship. *Winner:* Damon Tweedy, M.D., for "Black Man in a White Coat."
Medical Informatics Section Career Development Grant ($1,500). To support a career

development activity that will contribute to advancement in the field of medical informatics. Not awarded in 2021.

Erich Meyerhoff Prize (formerly the Murray Gottlieb Prize). For the best unpublished essay on the history of medicine and allied sciences written by a health sciences librarian. *Sponsor:* MLA History of the Health Sciences Section. *Winner:* Aidy Weeks for "Proving the Proverbial Gadfly: Situating the Historical & Racial Context of Southern Medical Works by Mary Louise Marshall through a Critical Librarianship Framework."

MLA Award for Distinguished Public Service. *Winner:* Anthony S. Fauci, M.D., director of the National Institute of Allergy and Infectious Diseases.

MLA Chapter Project of the Year Award. *Winner:* Northern California and Nevada Medical Library Group for their sponsorship, mentorship, and financial support of ALA Spectrum Scholars.

MLA Continuing Education Grant ($100–$500). *Winners:* Alanna Campbell and Alessia Zanin-Yost.

MLA Scholarship (up to $5,000). For graduate study at an ALA-accredited library school. *Winner:* Claudio Garcia.

MLA Scholarship for Under-Represented Students (up to $5,000). For graduate study at an ALA-accredited library school. *Winner:* Laurier Lynette Cress.

Marcia C. Noyes Award. For an outstanding contribution to medical librarianship. *Winner:* Beverly Murphy.

President's Award. To an MLA member for a notable or important contribution made during the past association year. *Winner:* Carolyn E. Lipscomb.

Rittenhouse Award. For the best unpublished paper on medical librarianship submitted by a student enrolled in, or having been enrolled in, a course for credit in an ALA-accredited library school or a trainee in an internship program in medical librarianship. *Donor:* Rittenhouse Book Distributors. *Winner:* Robert Browder for "Blockchain Technologies in Health Information Management."

Frank Bradway Rogers Information Advancement Award. To recognize outstanding contributions to the application of technology to the delivery of health science information, to the science of information, or to the facilitation of the delivery of health science information. *Sponsor:* Thomson Reuters. Not awarded in 2021.

Music Library Association

Vincent H. Duckles Award. For the best book-length bibliography or other tool in music. *Winner:* Laura Stokes for *Fanny Hensel: A Research and Information Guide* (Routledge).

Dena Epstein Award for Archival and Library Research in American Music. To support research in archives or libraries internationally on any aspect of American music. *Winners:* John Bimbiras for "Invisible Labor: Transnational Dominican Musicians in New York City during the Early to Mid-Twentieth Century"; Clifton Boyd for "The Role of Vernacular Music Theory in the Institution of Barbershop Music"; and Marc Rice on the relationship between Black jazz and dance bands in Kansas City during the 1920s and the African-American business, social, and political organizations that supported them.

Kevin Freeman Travel Grants. To colleagues who are new to the profession to enable them to attend the MLA Annual Meeting. Not awarded in 2021.

Walter Gerboth Award. To members of the association who are in the first five years of their professional library careers, to assist research in progress in music or music librarianship. Not awarded in 2021.

Richard S. Hill Award. For the best article on music librarianship or article of a music-bibliographic nature. *Winner:* Holling Smith-Borne for "Creating a Welcoming and Inclusive Environment for Transgender and Gender Fluid Music Library Users" in *Music Reference Services Quarterly* 22, no. 1–2 (2019): 18–29.

MLA Citation. Awarded in recognition of contributions to the profession over a career. *Winners:* Beth Christensen, Jean Harden, and Vincent Pelote.

MLA Diversity Scholarship ($3,000). Provides candidates from underrepresented groups the opportunity to pursue a master's degree in library and information science. *Winner:* Mia Watts.

Eva Judd O'Meara Award. For the best review published in *Notes*. *Winner:* Marci Cohen for review of *Bloomsbury Popular Music,* in *Notes* 76, no. 1 (September 2019): 159–161.

A. Ralph Papakhian Special Achievement Award. To recognize extraordinary service to the profession of music librarianship over a relatively short period of time. *Winner:* Katie Buehner.

National Library Service for the Blind and Print Disabled, Library of Congress

Library of the Year Awards ($1,000). *Winner:* (Regional Library of the Year) Iowa Library for the Blind and Print Disabled in Des Moines, Iowa; (Subregional Library/ Advisory and Outreach Center of the Year) Bayside Area and Special Services Library in Virginia Beach, Virginia.

REFORMA (National Association to Promote Library and Information Services to Latinos and the Spanish-Speaking)

Elizabeth A. Martinez Lifetime Achievement Award. To recognize those who have achieved excellence in librarianship over an extended period of service and who have made significant and lasting contributions to REFORMA and the Latino community. *Winner:* Patrick Sullivan.

REFORMA scholarships (up to $1,500). To students who qualify for graduate study in library science and who are citizens or permanent residents of the United States. (Rose Trevino Memorial Scholarship) *Winner:* Maria Dones. (REFORMA Scholarship) *Winners:* Andrea Domínguez and Jennifer Larsen.

Arnulfo D. Trejo Librarian of the Year Award. To recognize a librarian who has promoted and advocated services to the Spanish-speaking and Latino communities and made outstanding contributions to REFORMA. *Winners:* Maria Estrella and Michele Villagran.

Society of American Archivists (SAA)

Brenda S. Banks Travel Award. For individuals of color (such as those of African, Asian, Latinx, Middle Eastern/North African, Native American, Alaska Native, or Pacific Islander descent) who have demonstrated professional archival experience and manifest an interest in becoming active members of the Society of American Archivists. *Winner:* Shelly Black, Cyma Rubin Library Fellow at North Carolina State University.

C.F.W. Coker Award for Description. To recognize creators of tools that enable archivists to produce more effective finding aids. *Winner:* Museum of Indian Arts and Culture and the Indigenous Digital Archives, in partnership with the National Archives and Records Administration's Office of Innovation and the Conservation Department, and Digirati for Indigenous Digital Archives DigiTreaties Treaties Explorer.

Distinguished Service Award. To recognize an archival institution, education program, nonprofit organization, or governmental organization that has given outstanding service to its public and has made an exemplary contribution to the archives profession. *Winner:* Knox County Archives in Tennessee.

Diversity Award. To an individual, group, or institution for outstanding contributions to advancing diversity within the archives profession, SAA, or the archival record. *Winner:* Judy Tyrus, cofounder and CEO of ChromaDiverse, Inc.

Fellows' Ernst Posner Award. For an outstanding essay dealing with a facet of archival administration, history, theory, or methodology published in *American Archivist*. *Winner:* Katherine Fisher for "Copyright and Preservation of Born-Digital Materials: Persistent Challenges and Selected Strategies" (Fall/Winter 2020, Vol. 83.2).

Josephine Forman Scholarship ($10,000). *Sponsor:* General Commission on Archives and History of the United Methodist Church. *Winner:* Hinaikawaihi'ilei Keala from the University of Hawaii–Manoa.

Mark A. Greene Emerging Leader Award. To recognize early-career archivists who have completed archival work of broad merit, demonstrated significant promise of leadership, performed commendable service to the archives profession, or accomplished a combination of these requirements. *Winner:* Dorothy Berry of Houghton Library at Harvard University.

F. Gerald Ham and Elsie Ham Scholarship ($7,500). To recognize an individual's past performance in a graduate archival studies program and his or her potential in the field. *Winner:* aems emswiler of the University of Arizona School of Information.

Philip M. Hamer and Elizabeth Hamer Kegan Award. For individuals and/or institutions that have increased public awareness of a specific body of documents. *Winner:* Japanese American Digitization Project at California State University.

Oliver Wendell Holmes Travel Award. To enable overseas archivists already in the United States or Canada for training to attend the SAA Annual Meeting. *Winner:* Jiarui Sun.

J. Franklin Jameson Archival Advocacy Award. For individuals and/or organizations that promote greater public awareness of archival activities and programs. Not awarded in 2021.

Sister M. Claude Lane, O.P., Memorial Award. For a significant contribution to the field of religious archives. *Winner:* Mary Grace Kosta, congregational archivist at the Sisters of St. Joseph in Canada.

Waldo Gifford Leland Award. To encourage and reward writing of superior excellence and usefulness in the field of archival history, theory, or practice. *Winner:* Cheryl Oestreicher for *Reference and Access for Archives and Manuscripts* (Society of American Archivists).

Theodore Calvin Pease Award. For the best student paper ($100 and publication in *American Archivist*). *Winner:* Ferrin Evans for "Love (and Loss) in the Time of COVID-19: Translating Trauma into an Archive of Embodied Immediacy" (Spring/Summer 2022, Vol. 85, No. 1).

Donald Peterson Student Travel Award (up to $1,000). To enable a student or recent graduate to attend the SAA Annual Meeting. *Winner:* Sidney Louie from the Library and Information Science Program at the University of Hawaii–Manoa.

Harold T. Pinkett Student of Color Award. To encourage minority students to consider careers in the archival profession and to promote minority participation in SAA. *Winner:* Aparna Subramanian from the Moving Image Archiving and Preservation Program at New York University.

Preservation Publication Award. To recognize an outstanding work published in North America that advances the theory or the practice of preservation in archival institutions. *Winners:* Alexandra Chassanoff and Colin Post for *OSSArcFlow Guide to Documenting Born-Digital Archival Workflows* (Educopia Institute).

SAA Archival Innovator Award. To an archivist, group of archivists, repository, or organization that demonstrates the greatest overall current impact on the profession or their communities. *Winner:* National Archives and Records Administration's History Hub.

SAA Fellows. To a limited number of members for their outstanding contribution to the archival profession. *Honored:* Tamar Chute of Ohio State University in Columbus, Ohio, and Katherine Wisser of Simmons University in Boston, Massachusetts.

SAA Mosaic Scholarship ($5,000). To minority students pursuing graduate education in archival science. *Winner:* Christopher Castro of the University of California–Los Angeles.

SAA Spotlight Award. To recognize the contributions of individuals who work for the good of the profession and of archival collections and whose work would not typically receive public recognition. *Winner:* Lee Price, director of development at the Conservation Center for Art and Historic Artifacts.

Special Libraries Association (SLA)

SLA James M. Matarazzo Rising Star Award. To SLA members in the first five years of membership who demonstrate exceptional promise of leadership. *Winners:* Emma Antobam-Ntekudzi and Amy Stubbing.

SLA John Cotton Dana Award. For exceptional support and encouragement of special librarianship. *Winner:* Jill Hurst-Wahl.

SLA Fellows. *Honored*: Parveen Babbar, Clara Cabrera, John DiGilio, Michael Sholinbeck, and Laura Walesby.

SLA Hall of Fame Award. For outstanding performance and distinguished service to SLA. *Winners:* James King (posthumous) and Penny Leach.

Rose L. Vormelker Award. To SLA members for exceptional service through the education and mentoring of students and working professionals. Not awarded in 2021.

Theatre Library Association (TLA)

Brooks McNamara Performing Arts Librarian Scholarship ($500 and a one-year TLA membership). A biennial award acknowledging the outstanding professional accomplishments of a promising student currently enrolled in a M.L.I.S. or archival training program specializing in performing arts librarianship. *Winner (2020):* Megan Ralston-Munger.

Louis Rachow Distinguished Service in Performing Arts Librarianship Award. For extraordinary contributions to performing arts. *Winner:* Alan Jones, Performing Arts Librarian at the Royal Conservatoire of Scotland.

George Freedley Memorial Award. *Winner:* Marlis Schweitzer for *Bloody Tyrants and Little Pickles: Stage Roles of Anglo-American Girls in the Nineteenth Century* (University of Iowa Press).

Richard Wall Memorial Award. See "Literary Prizes, 2021" in Part 5.

Other Awards of Distinction

Robert B. Downs Intellectual Freedom Award. To recognize individuals or groups that have furthered the cause of intellectual freedom, particularly as it affects libraries and information centers and the dissemination of ideas. *Offered by:* Graduate School of Library and Information Science at the University of Illinois–Urbana-Champaign. *Sponsor:* Sage Publications. *Winner:* Amy Dodson from the Douglas County Public

Library in Nevada for supporting the value and necessity of equity, diversity, and inclusion as a part of her library's mission and service.

I Love My Librarian Awards ($5,000, a plaque, and a $500 travel stipend to attend the awards ceremony). To recognize librarians for service to their communities, schools, and campuses. Winners are nominated by library patrons. *Sponsors:* Carnegie Corporation of New York and the *New York Times*. *Winners:* Jayanti Addleman of the Hayward Public Library in California; Jessica Bell of the Bellack Library at the MGH Institute of Health Professions in Boston, Massachusetts; Sean C. Bird of the Mabee Library at Washburn University in Topeka, Kansas; Naomi Bishop from the Arizona Health Science Library at the Phoenix Biomedical Campus in Phoenix, Arizona; Jesse Braun from the Beverly Vista Middle School Library in Beverly Hills, California; Adeline Estrada-Huerta from the Sacramento Public Library in California; Jianye He from the C.V. Starr East Asian Library at the University of California–Berkeley; Jane E. Martellino from the International School at Dundee in Greenwich, Connecticut; Jennifer L. Newcome from Northeastern High School in Manchester, Pennsylvania; and Elizabeth Moreau Nicolai from Anchorage Public Library in Alaska.

RWA Cathie Linz Librarian of the Year. To a librarian who demonstrates outstanding support of romance authors and the romance genre. *Offered by:* Romance Writers of America. Not awarded in 2021.

USBBY Bridge to Understanding Award ($1,000). To acknowledge the work of adults who use books to promote international understanding among children. *Offered by:* United States Board on Books for Young People. *Winner:* To be announced.

Women's National Book Association Award. Awarded biennially to a living American woman who derives part or all of her income from books and allied arts and who has done meritorious work in the world of books. *Offered by:* Women's National Book Association (WNBA). *Winners (2021):* Hannah Oliver Depp of Loyalty Bookstores in Washington, D.C., and Silver Spring, Maryland.

Part 4
Research and Statistics

Library Research and Statistics

Number of Libraries in the United States and Canada

Statistics are from the *American Library Directory (ALD)* 2022–2023 (Information Today, Inc., 2022). Data are exclusive of elementary and secondary school libraries.

Libraries in the United States

Public Libraries	16,967*
Public libraries, excluding branches	9,638
Main public libraries that have branches	1,439
Public library branches	7,329
Academic Libraries	3,501*
Community college	1,082
Departmental	243
Medical	5
Religious	5
University and college	2,419
Departmental	1,137
Law	190
Medical	238
Religious	247
Armed Forces Libraries	225*
Air Force	62
Medical	3
Army	103
Medical	21
Marine Corps	12
Navy	48
Law	1
Medical	9
Government Libraries	801*
Law	349
Medical	108

Special Libraries (excluding public, academic, armed forces, and government)	4,396*
Law	626
Medical	778
Religious	349
Total Special Libraries (including public, academic, armed forces, and government)	5,572
Total law	1,166
Total medical	1,162
Total religious	762
Total Libraries Counted (*)	25,890

Libraries in Regions Administered by the United States

Public Libraries	18*
Public libraries, excluding branches	9
Main public libraries that have branches	3
Public library branches	9
Academic Libraries	38*
Community college	3
Departmental	1
University and college	35
Departmental	18
Law	3
Medical	3
Religious	1
Armed Forces Libraries	2*
Air Force	1
Army	1
Government Libraries	3*
Law	1
Medical	1
Special Libraries (excluding public, academic, armed forces, and government)	4*
Law	3
Religious	1
Total Special Libraries (including public, academic, armed forces, and government)	13
Total law	7
Total medical	4
Total religious	2
Total Libraries Counted (*)	65

Libraries in Canada

Public Libraries	2,216*
Public libraries, excluding branches	799
Main public libraries that have branches	159
Public library branches	1,417
Academic Libraries	316*
Community college	75
Departmental	14
Religious	1
University and college	241
Departmental	169
Law	16
Medical	11
Religious	31
Government Libraries	154*
Law	25
Medical	4
Special Libraries (excluding public, academic, armed forces, and government)	501*
Law	85
Medical	117
Religious	20
Total Special Libraries (including public, academic, armed forces, and government)	589
Total law	126
Total medical	132
Total religious	66
Total Libraries Counted (*)	3,187

Summary

Total U.S. Libraries	25,890
Total Libraries Administered by the United States	65
Total Canadian Libraries	3,187
Grand Total of Libraries Listed	29,142

Note: Numbers followed by an asterisk are added to find "Total libraries counted" for each of the three geographic areas (United States, U.S.-administered regions, and Canada). The sum of the three totals is the "Grand total of libraries listed" in *ALD*. For details on the count of libraries, see the preface to the 75th edition of *ALD—Ed.*

Highlights of IMLS Public Library Surveys

The Institute of Museum and Library Services (IMLS) collects and disseminates statistical information about public libraries in the United States and its outlying areas. This article presents highlights from two recent IMLS surveys of public libraries and state library administrative agencies. For further information, see "Institute of Museum and Library Services" in Part 2 of this volume and visit https://www.imls.gov/research-tools/data-collection for the most current and comprehensive IMLS survey data and reports.

Public Libraries Survey

Following are highlights from the IMLS report "Characteristics of Public Libraries in the United States: Results from the FY2019 Public Libraries Survey," released in 2021. Based on an annual public library survey (PLS), the report collected data from approximately 9,000 public library systems comprising more than 17,000 individual main libraries, library branches, and bookmobiles in all 50 states, the District of Columbia, and U.S. territories.

Public Library Indicators

Table S1 summarizes 12 indicators on public library financial health; public library resources, services, and usage; and public library staffing. Table S2 shows information about the collections and circulation at public libraries in all 50 states and the District of Columbia.

To enable comparability across states, indicators are computed per person based on the unduplicated population but are sometimes reported as per person, per 1,000 people, per 5,000 people, or per 25,000 people to obtain estimates that are most easily understood by a general audience.

As shown in Table S1, Americans visited public libraries 1.2 billion times, with 124.7 million attending one of the more than 5.9 million programs offered by public libraries in fiscal year (FY) 2019. The 1.8 billion items in public libraries' collections were circulated 2.2 billion times, representing 6.9 items checked out per person in FY 2019. Moreover, 143,883 full-time equivalent (FTE) library staffers answered 219.7 million questions for patrons (reference transactions).

Public libraries addressed the persistent digital divide by providing 299,445 public access Internet computers. These computers logged 224 million user sessions, and patrons accessed wifi services more than 485.2 million times. These public library resources and services cost an average of $44.88 per person for the nearly 316 million Americans who lived in a public library service area in FY 2019 (Table S1).

Table S2 shows that the electronic collection items available from America's public libraries now exceed the number of physical items. There were 3 e-books and downloadable audio and video items for each person compared to 2.5 print materials and physical audio and video items per person. Print item use exceeded that of the electronic items, with 5.8 physical items circulated per person and 1.1 electronic items circulated per person.

S1. Summary: Public Libraries in the United States, FY 2019

PLS Indicators	FY 2019 Total	FY 2019 Indicator
Public Library Financial Health		
1. Total Operating Revenue	$14.2 billion	$44.88 per person
2. Total Operating Expenditures	$13.3 billion	$41.90 per person
Public Library Resources, Services, and Usage		
3. Collection Materials	1.8 billion	5.6 per person
4. Circulation	2.2 billion	6.9 per person
5. Library Visits[1]	1.2 billion	3.9 per person
6. Reference Transactions	219.7 million	0.7 per person
7. Programs Offered	5.9 million	18.7 per 1,000 people
8. Program Attendance	124.7 million	394.3 per 1,000 people
9. Public Access Internet Computers	299,445	4.7 per 5,000 people
10. Public Access Internet Computer User Sessions	224 million	0.7 per person
11. Wireless Sessions	485.2 million	1.7 per person
Public Library Staffing		
12. Staffing	143,883 FTE[2]	11.4 FTE2 per 25,000 people

[1] This is the number of in-person visits to public libraries; the FY 2019 PLS did not count digital visits to libraries.
[2] FTE = full-time equivalent

S2. Summary: Collection Materials and Circulation Detail, FY 2019

Type	Total, FY 2019	Number of Items per Person
Total Collection Materials	**1,765.5 million**	**5.6**
Print Materials	686.9 million	2.2
E-Books	615.7 million	1.9
Audio: Physical	40.9 million	0.1
Audio: Downloadable	326.1 million	1
Video: Physical	68.5 million	0.2
Video: Downloadable	27.5 million	0.1
Circulation	**2,171.9 million**	**6.9**
Physical Circulation	1,829.0 million	5.8
Electronic Circulation	342.9 million	1.1

NOTE: Detail may not sum to totals due to rounding.

Public Library Organization and Size

- Nearly 97 percent of people lived within the service area of one of America's 9,057 public libraries and their 17,278 outlets.
- More than three-fourths of public libraries serve areas with fewer than 25,000 people.

- The nation's 671 bookmobiles brought physical materials with staff support on a regular schedule to meet patrons where they are. Many of these mobile libraries also bring Internet service to remote areas.
- The average library (stationary point of service) is 12,792.4 sq. ft. in size. Size ranges from an average of 2,148.6 sq. ft. for libraries that serve fewer than 1,000 people to 19,922.4 sq. ft. for those that serve 1 million or more people.

Public Library Finances

- Public libraries' $14.2 billion in revenues were predominantly derived (85.9 percent) from local funding sources. Staff salaries and benefits were the largest expense category for public libraries, accounting for two-thirds (66.7 percent) of their operating expenditures.
- Libraries spent $44.88 per person in FY 2019, with variations based on the size of the population served by the library. While libraries that served 1 million or more people spent $41.28 per person, those that served fewer than 1,000 people spent $74.29 per person.

Public Library Services, Resources, and Programs

- Overall, public libraries spent $4.51 per person on collection materials. Almost one-third (31.1 percent) of the collection materials spending was for electronic materials.
- America's public libraries provided more than 67.5 million items obtained via interlibrary loan to their patrons in FY 2019.
- Children's programs accounted for 53 percent of all public library programs, and there were more than 81 million attendees to the more than 3.1 million children's programs.
- Approximately 10 percent, or 596,106, of all young adult programs offered by America's public libraries were attended by nearly 8.9 million people.
- The average public library point of service (outlet) provided more than 29,000 wireless internet sessions during FY 2019.
- There was an average of just more than 18 public access Internet computers per point of service (outlet) at America's public libraries. Libraries that served larger population sizes had more computers per stationary outlet than those serving smaller populations.

Public Library Staffing

- Nearly half (46 percent) of public libraries have at least one FTE librarian on staff with a master's degree accredited by the American Library Association, and fewer than a quarter (24 percent) of all library staffers are librarians with such degrees.
- More than two-thirds (72 percent) of public libraries have fewer than 10 FTE staffers.

- All libraries that served populations of 1 million or more had at least 100 FTE staffers. In contrast, 77 percent of libraries that served fewer than 1,000 people had less than one FTE staff member.

State Ranking

To make comparisons across states, indicators are computed per person, per 1,000 people, per 5,000 people, or per 25,000 people based on each state's unduplicated population. Because both Hawaii and the District of Columbia have one administrative entity for the entire jurisdiction, care must be exercised in making comparisons of these jurisdictions to others.

- Staff salaries and benefits as a percentage of total public library expenditures in FY 2019 ranged from about 58 percent for Missouri to 75 percent for New Hampshire.
- Nationwide, 37 states reported that half or more of people who live in a given library service area had library cards in FY 2019.
- The average Ohio resident visited a public library 5.9 times in FY 2019 (the highest number of visits per person), while the average Mississippi resident visited 2.3 times.
- Nationwide, each person checked out an average of 6.9 items from the library, but two states had more than twice this national rate: Ohio (15.6) and Oregon (15.4).
- The number of public access Internet computers per 5,000 people and the utilization of these resources show an inverse relationship. For example, Vermont had the most public access Internet computers (8.9 per 5,000 people), and each computer was used 415 times in FY 2019. However, Nevada had the fewest public access Internet computers (2.4 per 5,000 people), with each one logging more than 1,700 uses.
- E-book availability varied greatly among the states. At the national level, there were 1.9 e-books per person, but six states had more than twice this national rate: Kansas (16.6), Wisconsin (10.3), Ohio (9.6), Iowa (7.2), West Virginia (4.9), and New Hampshire (4.8).
- Attendance at public library programs was highest in Vermont (750.6 per 1,000 people) and lowest in Georgia (236.7 per 1,000 people).
- The number of FTE library staff per 25,000 people also varied among the states. Ohio had more than 20 FTE staff for every 25,000 people (20.6), and Georgia had 6.3.

Pre-Pandemic Trends

According to IMLS's "The Use and Cost of Public Library Materials: Trends before the COVID-19 Pandemic," between FY 2014 and FY 2018:

- The percentage of libraries offering electronic collection materials increased from 80 percent to 90 percent.

- Median per-person spending on physical materials decreased by 6 percent, while median per-person spending on electronic materials increased by 31 percent.
- Median cost for physical items circulated increased by 11 percent, while median cost for e-circulation decreased by 26 percent.

In FY 2018 libraries in rural areas and libraries serving smaller populations paid less per electronic circulation than libraries situated in other locales or serving larger populations.

State Library Administrative Agencies Survey

Following are executive summary highlights from the IMLS report "State Library Administrative Agencies Survey, Fiscal Year 2018," released in April 2020. Based on a survey that has been conducted annually or biennially since 1994, the report collected data from State Library Administrative Agencies (SLAAs) throughout the 50 states and the District of Columbia. For additional context and supplemental information or to read the full report, visit www.imls.gov.

Introduction

An SLAA is the official state agency charged with the extension and development of public library services throughout the state. It has the authority to administer state plans in accordance with the provisions of the federal Library Services and Technology Act (LSTA).

Across the 50 states and the District of Columbia, SLAAs are located in various state government agencies and report to different authorities. They coordinate and distribute federal funds from the IMLS Grants to States program in addressing statewide and local needs.

Although all SLAAs coordinate and distribute federal funds authorized by the administration of the LSTA, not all share the same function and role within their respective states. Most SLAAs provide important reference and information services to the state government, administer the state library or serve as the state archives, operate libraries for people who are blind or physically handicapped, and support the State Center for the Book. In some states, the SLAA may also function as the public library at large, providing library services to the general public.

Revenues and Expenditures

In FY 2018 SLAAs reported the following:

- Revenues totaled more than $1.1 billion across federal, state, and other revenue sources; 83 percent of this revenue was from states, and 14 percent was from federal sources.
- Expenditures also totaled more than $1.1 billion, with 67 percent spent on financial assistance to libraries and 32 percent on operations.

Over the 14-year period from FY 2004–FY 2018:

- Revenues and expenditures of funds through the LSTA decreased by 20 percent.
- Per-person revenues decreased from $4.66 in FY 2004 (in dollars adjusted for 2018) to $3.47 per person in FY 2012, a 26 percent decrease. The $3.38 per-person revenues in FY 2018 represent a moderate decrease since FY 2012.

A closer review of SLAA revenues and expenditures over this period reveals a more nuanced picture:

- Between FY 2004–FY 2008 SLAA expenditures increased 3 percent, with revenues decreasing less than 3 percent.
- From FY 2008–FY 2012, which includes the Great Recession, SLAA revenues and expenditures declined sharply and continuously, falling by about 22 percent.
- Since FY 2012 SLAA revenues and expenditures have fundamentally leveled out.

The revenues and expenditures for SLAAs based on administrative structures also varied across this period:

- All four categories of administrative structures reported declines over the 14-year period, ranging from 9 percent–14 percent.
- In the most recent two-year period, between FY 2016–FY 2018, there was a continued decline in revenues and expenditures for SLAAs that were part of the state's Department of Education or in the "Other Agency" category.

Agency Workforce

- In FY 2018 there were 2,524 FTE staffers across all SLAAs.
- Nearly half (48 percent) of FTE staff were in library services, followed by library development (20 percent), other services (18 percent), and administration (14 percent).
- Overall, the number of FTE staff at SLAAs has declined by 27 percent over the 12-year period from FY 2006–FY 2018.
- In the most recent two-year period between FY 2016–FY 2018, there were no meaningful changes (i.e., less than 3 percent) in FTEs per million residents for the eight SLAAs in the "Other Agency" category and the 20 SLAAs housed in Independent Agencies/Legislative Branch.
- During the same two-year period, there was a 22 percent increase in FTEs per 1 million residents for the ten SLAAs located in Departments of State/ Administration and a 22 percent decline for the 13 SLAAs in Departments of Education.

Services

The proportion of SLAAs providing services to libraries and library cooperatives varied in FY 2018:

- Forty-nine of the 51 SLAAs (96 percent) provided consulting services, most commonly for library management/organizational development, continuing education, and youth services.
- Thirty-six SLAAs (71 percent) provided some form of literacy support.
- Forty-two SLAAs (82 percent) reported having statewide reading programs.

Due to reorganization of the survey questionnaire in FY 2014, trend comparisons for services offered by SLAAs to libraries and library cooperatives are limited to the most recent four years, from FY 2014–FY 2018. During this time:

- The number of SLAAs providing the various types of services in FY 2018 remained largely unchanged from FY 2014.
- All SLAAs provided LSTA statewide services, and almost all reported offering consulting services in FY 2014, FY 2016, and FY 2018.
- The percent of SLAAs providing LSTA statewide grant programs and administrative library system support remained relatively consistent over these four years, returning in FY 2018 to FY 2014 levels.
- The percent of SLAAs providing statewide reading programs increased from 69 percent in FY 2014 to 86 percent in FY 2016, then decreased slightly to 82 percent in FY 2018.

In FY 2018 SLAAs varied in the types of services provided to libraries and library cooperatives based on administrative structure. While nearly all SLAAs provided continuing education support, there were differences in other services provided based on a state's administrative structure, such as the following:

- Administrative library support services—While 70 percent of SLAAs in Independent Agency/Legislative Branch and Departments of State/Administration provided such services, only 50 percent or fewer of those in Departments of Education or in the "Other Agency" category did so.
- Program assistance services—While 85 percent of SLAAs in Independent/ Legislative agencies provided literacy program support, only 50 percent of those housed in Departments of Education did so.
- Coordination and integration services—About 70 percent of SLAAs in Departments of State/Administration and Departments of Education provided statewide coordination of digital programs and services, while half or fewer of those in Independent/Legislative and the "Other Agency" category did so.

Functions and Roles of State Libraries: 2000 and 2020

The following are highlights from the IMLS report "Functions and Roles of State Libraries: 2000 and 2020," released in November 2021.

In 2000 the 51 state libraries had a total revenue of $1.45 billion, which decreased to $1.27 billion by 2020. The Great Recession of 2008–2009 had an impact on state libraries, as it did on many other state agencies. In the 2014 and 2016 IMLS SLAA reports, five long-term cluster analyses of the trends in state library financial data showed that states could be characterized in one of three groups in the post-recession period:

- Some recovery: Nine state libraries had slight post-recession gains to revenues and expenditures (AK, AR, CO, DE, DC, HI, MN, MT, and ND).
- Post-recession decline: 27 state libraries had level or increases in finances prior to the recession and various levels of decline after the recession (AZ, GA, ID, IN, IA, KS, KY, ME, MD, MA, MS, NE, NV, NY, NC, OH, OR, RI, SC, SD, TN, TX, UT, VT, VA, WV, and WI).
- Long-term decline: 15 states' finances were already in decline prior to the recession, with continuing declines after the recession (AL, CA, CT, FL, IL, LA, MI, MO, NH, NJ, NM, OK, PA, WA, and WY).

Increases in revenues and expenditures in FY 2020 over FY 2018 were due to an increase in funds from both federal sources ($12.9 million additional funds) and states ($169.1 million additional funds), as state libraries responded to the coronavirus pandemic. State libraries received funding from a host of federal agencies beyond the LSTA awards, six of which generally account for 97 percent or more of the federal funds reported by the state libraries. In contrast, in FY 2020 LSTA awards accounted for 91 percent of federal funds reported by state libraries. Another report later this year will provide more details about the impacts of the pandemic on state libraries.

School Librarian Employment in the United States

Debra E. Kachel and Keith Curry Lance
The School Librarian Investigation—Decline or Evolution?

The SLIDE Project

The status of school librarianship is the subject of a three-year research project funded by a Laura Bush 21st Century Librarian grant from the Institute of Museum and Library Services (IMLS) to Antioch University Seattle. The School Librarian Investigation—Decline or Evolution? (SLIDE) began in September 2020. Debra E. Kachel (dkachel@antioch.edu) is the project director, and Keith Curry Lance, Ph.D. (keithlance@comcast.net), is the principal investigator. For the latest information about the SLIDE study, visit its website—https://libSLIDE.org—which provides access to its reports and infographics, videos and PowerPoint files for conference and workshop presentations, external links to news articles and editorials citing the study, and access to a powerful set of interactive data tools providing on-demand access to user-selected data about school librarian employment from 2009–2010 to the present. Embedded, step-by-step tutorials make it possible to use these tools quickly and easily.

The Latest on School Librarian Employment

As every year, the only possible source of comparable data on school librarian employment in U.S. public schools is the National Center for Education Statistics's (NCES) Common Core of Data (CCD). The latest available data from this source is for the 2020–2021 school year. For the first time in at least two decades, this project's state data file did not include data on school librarians for all 50 states and the District of Columbia. No data were reported for Illinois and Utah. The missing Utah figure, however, was obtainable from the Utah State Board of Education. For the purposes of this status report, the totals for the 50 states and the District of Columbia include an estimate of school librarian FTEs for Illinois for 2020–2021, extrapolating from the change that state reported from 2018–2019 to 2019–2020.

Differential Impact of the COVID-19 Pandemic on School Librarian Employment by State, 2018–2019 to 2020–2021

In July 2021 the SLIDE project released an in-depth analysis titled "Perspectives on School Librarian Employment in the United States, 2009-10 to 2018-19." It examined the most recent decade of data available when that analysis began. Among many types of inequity in access to school librarians, this report documented the very dramatic geographic inequities from state to state and region to region. Not surprisingly, the COVID-19 pandemic has had an extremely variable impact on school librarian employment from state to state. To assess that impact, we compared school librarian full-time equivalents (FTEs) in 2018–2019 (the school year before the pandemic began) and 2020–2021 (the first full school year since the pandemic began).

Table 1 / School Librarians in Full-Time Equivalents (FTEs) and Ratios to Schools, Students, and Teachers, by State, 2020–2021 School Year

State	School Librarians in Full-Time Equivalents (FTEs)	Total Schools	Ratio of School Librarian FTEs to Schools	Total Student Enrollment	Ratio of Students to School Librarian FTEs	Teachers in FTEs	Ratio of Teacher FTEs to School Librarian FTEs
AK	132.35	503	0.26	129,872	981	7,558.21	57
AL	1,305.34	1,542	0.85	734,559	563	42,335.96	32
AR	894.33	1,080	0.83	486,305	544	38,542.66	43
AZ	415.46	2,357	0.18	1,111,500	2,675	49,546.93	119
CA	620.94	10,328	0.06	6,064,504	9,767	269,850.03	435
CO	468.60	1,927	0.24	883,199	1,885	54,318.97	116
CT	668.10	1,001	0.67	509,058	762	42,580.20	64
DC	88.00	235	0.37	89,883	1,021	7,678.30	87
DE	105.30	225	0.47	138,092	1,311	9,849.93	94
FL	1,923.52	4,219	0.46	2,791,707	1,451	161,413.31	84
GA	2,033.30	2,311	0.88	1,730,015	851	118,059.10	58
HI	114.00	294	0.39	176,441	1,548	12,145.40	107
IA	376.73	1,309	0.29	506,656	1,345	36,048.38	96
ID	41.67	774	0.05	307,581	7,381	17,582.26	422
IL	no data	4,384	no data	1,886,137	no data	no data	no data
IN	522.54	1,902	0.27	1,033,964	1,979	65,758.31	126
KS	602.99	1,310	0.46	481,750	799	38,007.33	63
KY	1,010.54	1,532	0.66	658,809	652	42,458.13	42
LA	926.54	1,353	0.68	693,150	748	38,368.88	41
MA	555.45	1,845	0.30	921,712	1,659	75,146.72	135
MD	1,132.73	1,421	0.80	882,527	779	62,276.32	55
ME	181.70	595	0.31	172,455	949	15,142.94	83
MI	479.96	3,526	0.14	1,434,137	2,988	84,317.37	176
MN	433.52	2,541	0.17	872,083	2,012	54,535.32	126
MO	1,302.60	2,444	0.53	882,477	677	68,923.84	53
MS	725.03	1,042	0.70	442,627	610	31,479.63	43
MT	362.42	826	0.44	146,252	404	10,941.68	30
NC	2,023.42	2,683	0.75	1,513,677	748	101,057.02	50
ND	174.58	488	0.36	114,955	658	9,472.82	54
NE	532.99	1,086	0.49	324,697	609	23,943.47	45
NH	325.80	496	0.66	169,027	519	14,799.90	45
NJ	1,216.14	2,565	0.47	1,373,960	1,130	116,530.03	96
NM	190.57	886	0.22	316,840	1,663	21,576.65	113
NV	258.00	736	0.35	482,348	1,870	23,746.00	92
NY*	2,459.00	4,807	0.51	2,606,748	1,060	213,537.44	87
OH	722.72	3,531	0.20	1,645,412	2,277	101,147.65	140
OK	879.82	1,789	0.49	694,113	789	43,110.11	49
OR	146.70	1,263	0.12	560,917	3,824	30,785.93	210
PA	1,521.78	2,947	0.52	1,704,396	1,120	125,028.25	82
RI	176.16	314	0.56	139,184	790	10,669.04	61
SC	1,086.40	1,266	0.86	766,819	706	53,702.97	49
SD	66.38	706	0.09	139,566	2,103	10,020.18	151
TN	1,333.19	1,880	0.71	985,207	739	64,667.05	49

Table 1 / School Librarians in Full-Time Equivalents (FTEs) and Ratios to Schools, Students, and Teachers, by State, 2020–2021 School Year

State	School Librarians in Full-Time Equivalents (FTEs)	Total Schools	Ratio of School Librarian FTEs to Schools	Total Student Enrollment	Ratio of Students to School Librarian FTEs	Teachers in FTEs	Ratio of Teacher FTEs to School Librarian FTEs
TX	4,485.48	9,002	0.50	5,372,806	1,198	370,718.50	83
UT*	235.30	1,088	0.22	680,659	2,893	no data	no data
VA	1,779.53	2,125	0.84	1,251,639	703	87,049.37	49
VT	202.80	305	0.66	82,401	406	7,989.43	39
WA	792.59	2,506	0.32	1,087,354	1,372	61,810.07	78
WI	898.67	2,240	0.40	830,066	924	60,091.66	67
WV	200.59	710	0.28	253,930	1,266	18,629.99	93
WY	77.11	364	0.21	92,772	1,203	7,521.73	98
50 States + DC Total**	40,566.12	98,609	0.41	49,356,945	1,217	3,196,445.73	79
State Average***	784.19	1,934	0.44	967,783	1,538	61,887.17	95
State Median***	544.22	1,353	0.45	693,150	1,041	42,458.13	82

* Figures for Librarians in FTEs for NY and UT are from their state education departments.
** Includes librarian estimate for Illinois, extrapolating from 2018–2019 to 2019–2020 change
*** State averages and medians exclude Illinois, except for Total Student Enrollment and Total Schools and Utah for Teachers in FTEs and Ratio of Teacher FTEs to School Librarian FTEs.

Three states—Washington, Tennessee, and Texas—each lost more than 100 FTEs of school librarians between the 2018–2019 and 2020–2021 school years. Thirteen additional states lost 50 or more and fewer than 80 school librarian FTEs during the same period. Those states are Minnesota, Colorado, Pennsylvania, New Jersey, Kansas, Arkansas, Connecticut, Massachusetts, Florida, Ohio, Missouri, Indiana, and Louisiana. (See Table 2.)

Between 2018–2019 and 2020–2021, South Dakota lost the largest percentage of school librarians, at almost 45 percent. Washington, D.C., and Washington state lost three out of ten school librarians during that period. At the same time, Minnesota, Hawaii, and Colorado lost one out of six school librarians. One out of seven school librarians were lost in Tennessee, and one out of eight in Oregon, Kansas, Idaho, and Massachusetts. West Virginia lost one out of nine school librarians. And one out of ten school librarians were lost by New Mexico, Indiana, and Rhode Island.

Only three states—Nevada, Utah, and Vermont—gained school librarian FTEs between the 2018–2019 and 2020–2021 school years. Nevada gained a mere half FTE, giving it a total of 258 by 2020–2021, Utah gained 7.59 FTEs, giving it a total of 235.3 by that time, and Vermont gained 5.56 FTEs, giving it a total of 202.8. All other states experienced smaller numerical and percentage losses than those previously mentioned.

Table 2 / States with the Largest Numerical Losses of School Librarians in Full-Time Equivalents (FTEs), 2018–2019 to 2020–2021

State	School Librarians (FTEs)		
	2020–2021 (NCES)	2018–2019 (SLIDE)	Numerical Change
WA	792.59	1,031.83	-239.24
TN	1,333.19	1,532.00	-198.81
TX	4,485.48	4,604.80	-119.32
MN	433.52	512.66	-79.14
CO	468.60	546.26	-77.66
PA	1,521.78	1,599.38	-77.60
NJ	1,216.14	1,289.97	-73.83
KS	602.99	676.40	-73.41
AR	894.33	967.49	-73.16
CT	668.10	733.95	-65.85
MA	555.45	621.15	-65.70
FL	1,923.52	1,986.85	-63.33
OH	722.72	785.87	-63.15
MO	1,302.60	1,359.63	-57.03
IN	522.54	575.38	-52.84
LA	926.54	978.39	-51.85

Between 2018–2019 and 2020–2021, South Dakota lost the largest percentage of school librarians at 31 percent. Washington, D.C., and Washington state each lost just under a quarter of their school librarians during that period. At the same time, Minnesota, Hawaii, and Colorado lost one out of seven school librarians. One out of eight school librarians were lost in Tennessee, and one out of ten by Oregon, Kansas, Idaho, Massachusetts, and West Virginia.

Table 3 / States with the Largest Percentage Losses of School Librarians in Full-Time Equivalents, 2018–2019 to 2020–2021

State	School Librarians (FTEs)		
	2020–2021 (NCES)	2018–2019 (SLIDE)	Percent Change
SD	66.38	96.18	-31.0%
DC	88.00	114.75	-23.3%
WA	792.59	1,031.83	-23.2%
MN	433.52	512.66	-15.4%
HI	114.00	134.50	-15.2%
CO	468.60	546.26	-14.2%
TN	1,333.19	1,532.00	-13.0%
OR	146.70	164.73	-10.9%
KS	602.99	676.40	-10.9%
ID	41.67	46.71	-10.8%
MA	555.45	621.15	-10.6%
WV	200.59	223.24	-10.1%

Need for Better Data

Because NCES's CCD project is the only annual source of district, state, and national data on school librarian employment, it is important that improvements be made at district, state, and national levels. Although most states and districts do a laudable job in this data collection process, a few—unfortunately including some of the largest—submit incomplete or inconsistent data or no data at all, making accurate totals and averages impossible.

The SLIDE project offers the following recommendations for ensuring that better data on school librarian employment will be available in the future:

1. Incentives for data compliance—Technically, local school districts are required to report data to their state education departments, which, in turn, are responsible for vetting and compiling the data before passing it on to NCES. In reality, however, there are few, if any, incentives for compliance and no consequences for failure to comply. Incentives for collecting and reporting quality data at all levels could improve data quality tremendously.

2. Imputation—If states do not report complete data, NCES should impute, or estimate, missing data, as was done in the past. The accuracy and precision of imputation at the state level would also be improved if NCES imputed missing data at the district level.

3. Update educator positions and definitions—NCES's CCD project collects FTE data for positions that were selected and defined decades ago. Many of these definitions—not just the one for school librarian—are outdated. Also, FTE data are not collected for many positions that are now commonplace—such as educational technology staff and testing and reading coaches. The continuation of this practice is not defensible either conceptually or statistically. Indeed, continued reliance on a dated set of positions with outdated definitions means that many newer positions are likely being lumped into the FTE counts of district or school administrators, teachers, or instructional coordinators.

4. Update the definition of "school librarian"—The definition of school librarian reflects that of a 1980s librarian, not the current role of a school librarian. As defined by the American Association of School Librarians (AASL), a school librarian "serves as a leader, instructional partner, information specialist, teacher, and program administrator" (AASL 2018).

   (a) Those in district offices who report CCD data to their states should be aware of the variety of job titles and job descriptions that might be used by school librarians. While "school librarian," "library media specialist," and "teacher librarian" are commonly used, some districts have invented other titles, such as "educational technology and information literacy coordinator" and "digital learning specialist."

   (b) District data reporters should also understand that both certified and non-certified librarians are to be reported since NCES does not consider state certification in its definitions.

The SLIDE project is making CCD data about school librarian employment at all levels more accessible and usable with the interactive data tools at libslide.org. As a result, many are seeing the data for the first time and questioning its accuracy. Responsibility for data accuracy lies with NCES, state departments of education, and local school districts where the data originates.

Inevitably, improving the quality of NCES data on school librarian employment—its completeness, consistency, and accuracy—will require a wholesale review of the entire staff FTE data collection that is part of CCD. Such a review is long overdue. While the SLIDE project did what it could to address data-quality issues, it is only a three-year project with limited resources. Resolving the previously identified issues systemically will require a long-term commitment and closer collaboration among local, state, and federal education agencies.

Library Acquisition Expenditures, 2021–2022 U.S. Public, Academic, Special, and Government Libraries

The information in these tables is taken from the 2021–2022 edition of *American Library Directory* (*ALD*) (Information Today, Inc.). The tables report acquisition expenditures by public, academic, special, and government libraries.

Understanding the Tables

Number of libraries includes only those U.S. libraries in *ALD* that reported annual acquisition expenditures. Libraries that reported annual income but not expenditures are not included in the count. Academic libraries include university, college, and community college libraries. Special academic libraries, such as law and medical libraries, that reported acquisition expenditures separately from the institution's main library are counted as independent libraries.

The amount in the *total acquisition expenditures* column for a given state is generally greater than the sum of the categories of expenditures. This is because the total acquisition expenditures amount also includes the expenditures of libraries that did not itemize by category.

Figures in *categories of expenditures* columns represent only those libraries that itemized expenditures. Libraries that reported a total acquisition expenditure amount but did not itemize are only represented in the total acquisition expenditures column.

Table 1 / Public Library Acquisition Expenditures

State	Number of Libraries	Total Acquisition Expenditures	Books	Other Print Materials	Periodicals/ Serials	Manuscripts & Archives	AV Equipment	AV Materials	Microforms	Electronic Reference	Preservation
										Category of Expenditures (in U.S. dollars)	
Alabama	8	2,221,824	455,038	11,091	6,087	0	4,700	15,004	0	113,541	20,000
Alaska	9	1,783,625	833,852	17,876	78,963	43,021	1,500	288,379	0	225,519	175
Arizona	14	16,862,682	2,482,763	88,424	91,230	575	0	1,083,644	0	374,884	0
Arkansas	6	705,549	263,433	250	21,274	500	0	39,307	0	42,186	0
California	35	58,847,021	19,528,527	126,895	1,491,985	2,500	34,987	7,747,922	39,578	16,925,973	63,997
Colorado	10	13,001,916	3,928,364	434,162	363,980	0	15,000	1,960,352	0	2,352,326	0
Connecticut	28	14,472,906	1,826,763	6,238	578,109	4,705	0	469,153	1,080	831,091	39,362
Delaware	3	453,811	55,000	0	8,000	0	0	5,200	0	1,400	0
District of Columbia	0	0	0	0	0	0	0	0	0	0	0
Florida	24	20,875,347	9,654,638	786,484	780,951	0	52,514	3,437,680	35,480	4,721,131	0
Georgia	6	1,787,947	680,580	42,253	58,488	0	0	201,223	1,850	212,223	0
Hawaii	1	4,242,675	2,491,491	43,698	120,461	0	0	0	43,895	1,120,394	0
Idaho	6	536,487	116,220	1,736	82	0	0	6,261	0	11,360	0
Illinois	60	85,445,311	8,962,699	150,600	373,828	0	10,900	2,279,775	9,049	4,286,423	2,500
Indiana	32	21,710,093	8,300,900	800	876,198	0	127,040	3,306,121	13,485	5,129,769	0
Iowa	36	4,498,284	1,711,336	55,504	120,093	4,000	1,840	554,067	5,757	503,061	0
Kansas	21	5,091,500	1,034,146	0	115,559	0	4,300	338,117	5,000	99,649	3,600
Kentucky	18	11,856,949	2,278,812	109,345	292,249	0	30,224	923,068	0	1,806,910	40,776
Louisiana	7	11,636,290	3,669,432	58,554	429,384	0	175,561	1,582,866	0	3,283,814	0
Maine	16	889,950	307,533	1,000	72,748	2,000	5,000	69,803	800	237,035	1,000
Maryland	2	7,791,058	0	0	0	0	0	0	0	0	0
Massachusetts	41	10,179,303	1,895,815	35,966	240,428	5,000	7,717	649,661	11,484	505,420	5,500
Michigan	46	23,880,671	2,077,248	178,982	215,048	0	450	728,867	5,038	890,000	0
Minnesota	16	78,019,948	1,707,284	64,813	20,738	0	83	323,916	3,898	415,231	516
Mississippi	4	783,270	441,264	0	77,664	0	0	26,722	26,000	149,093	2,162
Missouri	17	17,244,571	4,175,760	183,329	295,840	0	10,045	2,040,512	32,651	2,803,517	0
Montana	12	875,079	337,380	98,472	45,874	200	4,373	107,159	0	84,994	7,302

Table 1 / Public Library Acquisition Expenditures (cont.)

State	Number of Libraries	Total Acquisition Expenditures	Books	Other Print Materials	Periodicals/ Serials	Manuscripts & Archives	AV Equipment	AV Materials	Microforms	Electronic Reference	Preservation
Nebraska	17	11,358,802	193,609	119,000	16,736	0	47	42,550	440	756,484	0
Nevada	3	374,744	127,003	0	9,621	0	0	33,388	0	20,000	894
New Hampshire	22	649,919	386,279	900	20,918	0	0	97,930	2,980	54,432	400
New Jersey	29	17,349,134	7,134,287	34,614	559,759	500	21,500	1,194,456	13,000	843,900	6,956
New Mexico	10	3,393,577	815,673	7,084	46,938	0	1,000	143,070	9,013	208,441	0
New York	73	46,686,300	12,002,386	50,465	739,024	0	219,015	2,017,826	29,053	2,015,030	3,950
North Carolina	6	855,075	449,090	0	32,082	0	0	186,666	4,707	21,812	0
North Dakota	8	3,575,588	514,592	300	26,700	0	0	98,121	2,000	94,354	1,000
Ohio	37	49,194,244	9,668,705	183,106	1,071,668	133	43,960	4,267,051	6,277	8,053,775	8,013
Oklahoma	11	12,944,716	4,757,458	3,708	852,429	0	0	2,272,584	3,725	1,917,092	0
Oregon	15	5,308,356	1,486,557	133,530	135,877	0	3,500	678,938	150	1,411,499	0
Pennsylvania	37	20,547,270	3,279,482	848,370	642,650	156,260	1,686	2,066,434	158,127	1,433,290	219,661
Rhode Island	4	533,104	277,219	0	12,654	0	0	110,200	0	128,669	650
South Carolina	8	29,726,229	2,646,583	31,426	114,500	0	0	4,858,473	0	647,398	0
South Dakota	7	1,416,958	690,098	15,756	11,000	0	16,846	198,843	0	480,415	0
Tennessee	12	469,767,171	23,777,299	276,606	738,854	1,000	2,438,770	8,659,606	0	18,428,323	12,107
Texas	51	12,549,125	3,676,230	3,561	200,401	0	3,000	733,004	8,915	1,100,595	46,700
Utah	6	1,210,147	244,079	0	7,000	0	0	20,406	0	12,120	0
Vermont	15	458,371	243,740	90	14,017	215	0	77,967	0	33,122	0
Virginia	20	10,166,239	3,663,301	5,037	293,351	21,260	22,043	1,100,320	16,244	2,170,420	1,336,701
Washington	11	4,451,298	766,083	65,834	53,768	0	1,975	191,382	511	307,165	400
West Virginia	4	408,644	230,458	1,000	8,600	0	0	59,366	0	67,356	0
Wisconsin	38	4,958,524	1,809,644	72,833	83,617	0	12,952	631,539	2,746	282,280	0
Wyoming	5	7,044,180	97,878	0	4,710	0	0	15,727	0	0	0
Puerto Rico	0	0	0	0	0	0	0	0	0	0	0
Total	927	1,130,621,782	158,154,011	4,349,692	12,472,135	241,869	3,272,528	57,940,626	492,933	87,614,916	1,824,322
Estimated % of Acquisition Expenditures			13.98	0.38	1.10	0.02	0.28	5.12	0.04	7.74	0.16

Category of Expenditures (in U.S. dollars)

Table 2 / Academic Library Acquisition Expenditures

State	Number of Libraries	Total Acquisition Expenditures	Category of Expenditures (in U.S. dollars)								
			Books	Other Print Materials	Periodicals/ Serials	Manuscripts & Archives	AV Equipment	AV Materials	Microforms	Electronic Reference	Preservation
Alabama	7	4,578,090	350,471	5,899	2,091,716	0	0	20,322	0	1,029,810	21,307
Alaska	2	1,900,000	200,000	20,000	1,600,000	0	0	17,500	2,500	50,000	0
Arizona	3	3,122,553	42,897	0	34,152	0	0	60	0	211,245	0
Arkansas	6	9,920,924	979,276	419,834	5,626,174	34,264	2,000	28,472	426,218	511,257	6,187
California	26	29,956,795	2,443,898	350,271	2,897,463	101,910	6,772	126,850	26,433	8,829,205	108,288
Colorado	9	6,700,154	1,140,926	25,081	487,366	0	100	121,339	0	5,075,903	27,747
Connecticut	7	10,371,628	948,589	15,690	2,640,282	0	80,000	34,922	0	960,490	18,429
Delaware	2	12,839,012	0	0	0	0	0	0	0	0	0
District of Columbia	2	6,803,069	439,600	110,000	1,803,000	0	0	3,267	34,380	1,409,960	47,000
Florida	9	19,923,212	1,605,008	5,538	7,255,147	0	0	149,816	0	5,977,415	43,406
Georgia	10	16,798,018	491,793	0	77,733	0	98	26,300	0	1,745,558	300
Hawaii	0	0	0	0	0	0	0	0	0	0	0
Idaho	1	4,318,101	0	0	0	0	0	0	0	0	0
Illinois	22	49,936,743	1,280,626	7,000	1,889,182	0	0	57,599	17,741	1,677,238	67,721
Indiana	10	15,886,978	1,233,233	20,385	4,369,449	0	0	44,306	4,496	2,745,794	21,033
Iowa	11	20,459,261	2,356,516	391,576	4,101,707	0	6,000	53,222	30,353	3,391,954	51,962
Kansas	10	7,338,555	415,031	800	6,012,610	3,000	0	17,181	1,000	640,605	26,150
Kentucky	6	17,508,971	138,841	17,945	1,341,620	0	2,886	1,562	14,722	385,628	4,969
Louisiana	6	3,870,416	240,500	2,935	688,369	500	0	4,935	36,508	2,673,487	23,182
Maine	3	4,567,909	867,921	0	2,374,955	0	0	0	0	475,000	16,000
Maryland	12	166,150,569	1,434,259	34,648	8,337,193	12,434	0	37,469	6,642	1,266,762	49,919
Massachusetts	10	23,497,430	939,483	0	2,453,728	36,000	19,011	57,882	1,550	7,410,764	132,781
Michigan	20	22,055,034	1,909,644	65,821	8,919,141	5,203	0	144,896	1,358,172	6,433,775	41,856
Minnesota	7	3,553,441	516,011	10,000	1,354,400	8,200	53,955	52,964	0	991,220	34,939
Mississippi	1	96,040	10,000	0	2,700	0	0	0	0	83,340	0
Missouri	14	9,409,804	428,143	0	1,740,564	8,767	4,120	101,474	102,359	804,275	31,576
Montana	1	83,000	30,000	0	53,000	0	0	0	0	0	0

Table 2 / Academic Library Acquisition Expenditures *(cont.)*

State	Number of Libraries	Total Acquisition Expenditures	Books	Other Print Materials	Periodicals/ Serials	Manuscripts & Archives	AV Equipment	AV Materials	Microforms	Electronic Reference	Preservation
Nebraska	6	15,403,953	387,037	89,831	2,135,772	15,000	0	62,021	66,665	1,844,618	16,812
Nevada	0	0	0	0	0	0	0	0	0	0	0
New Hampshire	0	0	0	0	0	0	0	0	0	0	0
New Jersey	8	59,984,769	895,345	0	2,564,716	1,000	0	21,329	0	2,014,247	4,732
New Mexico	3	3,315,114	133,311	0	2,684,913	11,802	0	15,878	16,450	107,334	27,574
New York	29	36,535,561	6,071,133	237,527	9,039,294	29,596	66,463	219,248	46,351	8,646,487	235,248
North Carolina	18	70,468,015	408,217	82,542	920,541	0	1,106,546	112,551	126,798	1,026,945	13,000
North Dakota	2	2,965,537	365,806	0	2,011,935	0	0	30,752	684	539,766	16,594
Ohio	17	32,004,891	1,584,084	0	3,015,398	1,605	9,998	99,557	10,213	718,157	19,388
Oklahoma	5	4,572,162	188,784	575	2,533,231	1,000	0	2,433	0	970,780	4,986
Oregon	6	21,683,521	742,555	0	2,418,862	0	32,779	70,337	0	625,837	18,704
Pennsylvania	17	8,005,845	1,281,930	8,603	2,356,921	1,688	0	77,600	23,791	2,293,507	25,026
Rhode Island	3	1,855,603	439,983	0	925,966	5,840	0	23,270	3,000	450,870	6,674
South Carolina	6	6,381,487	1,021,816	289,130	769,178	20,000	137,300	87,153	60,264	2450,960	47,510
South Dakota	2	4,684,675	37,161	0	1,760,530	0	718	18,515	2,816	106,460	22,060
Tennessee	7	6,205,711	260,691	0	711,552	0	0	38,530	8,900	791,265	1,613
Texas	22	38,939,608	3,779,876	263,714	14,474,506	0	78,340	81,156	34,820	4,410,633	95,434
Utah	2	7,142,967	159,582	0	6,188	0	0	5,458	0	182,205	21,249
Vermont	2	773,460	161,235	0	550,487	0	0	22,323	0	35,202	4,213
Virginia	7	13,897,281	2,986,538	0	5,407,631	0	0	212,306	11,903	4,244,379	50,658
Washington	6	8,553,006	902,925	0	5,680,423	0	27,400	32,250	0	645,252	0
West Virginia	7	2,611,839	140,867	57	69,386	6,750	14,300	11,792	11,017	411,206	7,500
Wisconsin	6	9,524,768	243,750	238	810,373	0	0	65,917	24,505	1,275,580	140
Wyoming	0	0	0	0	0	0	0	0	0	0	0
Puerto Rico	3	285,002	67,807	4,000	10,276,234	0	1,263	1,025,926	0	39,691,149	300
Total	401	827,440,482	42,703,099	2,479,640	139,275,688	304,559	1,650,049	3,438,640	2,511,251	128,263,524	1,414,167
Estimated % of Acquisition Expenditures			5.16	0.30	16.83	0.03	0.20	0.41	0.30	15.50	0.17

Category of Expenditures (in U.S. dollars)

Table 3 / Special Library Acquisition Expenditures

State	Number of Libraries	Total Acquisition Expenditures	Books	Other Print Materials	Periodicals/ Serials	Manuscripts & Archives	AV Equipment	AV Materials	Microforms	Electronic Reference	Preservation
								Category of Expenditures (in U.S. dollars)			
Alabama	0	0	0	0	0	0	0	0	0	0	0
Alaska	0	0	0	0	0	0	0	0	0	0	0
Arizona	3	83,324	55,500	0	26,324	0	0	0	0	0	1,000
Arkansas	0	0	0	0	0	0	0	0	0	0	0
California	5	278,964	117,834	0	49,122	600	0	24,090	0	86,588	730
Colorado	0	0	0	0	0	0	0	0	0	0	0
Connecticut	2	46,000	5,000	0	40,000	0	0	0	0	0	0
Delaware	0	0	0	0	0	0	0	0	0	0	0
District of Columbia	2	71,000	48,000	0	20,000	0	0	0	2,000	0	1,000
Florida	0	0	0	0	0	0	0	0	0	0	0
Georgia	0	0	0	0	0	0	0	0	0	0	0
Hawaii	0	0	0	0	0	0	0	0	0	0	0
Idaho	0	0	0	0	0	0	0	0	0	0	0
Illinois	3	4,202,300	52,000	0	55,300	4,000	0	0	0	49,000	5,000
Indiana	1	95,000	0	0	0	0	0	0	0	0	0
Iowa	1	10,000	0	0	0	0	0	0	0	0	0
Kansas	1	6,000	3,000	0	3,000	0	0	0	0	0	0
Kentucky	0	0	0	0	0	0	0	0	0	0	0
Louisiana	1	18,000	5,000	0	13,000	0	0	0	0	0	0
Maine	0	0	0	0	0	0	0	0	0	0	0
Maryland	1	1,000	500	0	300	100	0	0	0	0	100
Massachusetts	0	0	0	0	0	0	0	0	0	0	0
Michigan	0	0	0	0	0	0	0	0	0	0	0
Minnesota	1	50,000	20,000	5,000	9,000	0	0	0	0	16,000	0
Mississippi	0	0	0	0	0	0	0	0	0	0	0
Missouri	0	0	0	0	0	0	0	0	0	0	0

Table 3 / Special Library Acquisition Expenditures (cont.)

State	Number of Libraries	Total Acquisition Expenditures	Books	Other Print Materials	Periodicals/ Serials	Manuscripts & Archives	AV Equipment	AV Materials	Microforms	Electronic Reference	Preservation
Montana	0	0	0	0	0	0	0	0	0	0	0
Nebraska	0	0	0	0	0	0	0	0	0	0	0
Nevada	0	0	0	0	0	0	0	0	0	0	0
New Hampshire	1	43,000	1,000	8,000	2,000	0	0	0	0	32,000	0
New Jersey	2	4,200	1,000	0	0	0	0	0	0	0	200
New Mexico	1	2,500	1,000	0	1,000	0	0	0	0	0	500
New York	7	495,948	251,900	0	43,300	0	4,000	0	0	38,350	152,500
North Carolina	0	0	0	0	0	0	0	0	0	0	0
North Dakota	1	8,098	2,660	0	3,975	0	0	0	0	0	1,463
Ohio	2	572,701	10,666	0	782	1,066	0	100	0	5,832	0
Oklahoma	1	160,000	8,000	0	45,000	0	0	0	0	0	0
Oregon	0	0	0	0	0	0	0	0	0	0	0
Pennsylvania	0	0	0	0	0	0	0	0	0	0	0
Rhode Island	0	0	0	0	0	0	0	0	0	0	0
South Carolina	0	0	0	0	0	0	0	0	0	0	0
South Dakota	1	105,000	0	0	0	0	0	0	0	0	0
Tennessee	0	0	0	0	0	0	0	0	0	0	0
Texas	3	1,381,886	2,026	12,000	2,261	0	188	411	0	805,000	0
Utah	1	75,000	5,000	5,000	10,000	0	5,000	0	0	50,000	0
Vermont	0	0	0	0	0	0	0	0	0	0	0
Virginia	3	54,787	17,055	0	2,110	3,026	0	0	0	30,000	2,596
Washington	1	19,800	7,000	0	10,200	0	0	0	0	0	2,600
West Virginia	0	0	0	0	0	0	0	0	0	0	0
Wisconsin	2	85,500	4,000	0	20,000	0	0	0	0	60,000	0
Wyoming	0	0	0	0	0	0	0	0	0	0	0
Puerto Rico	0	0	0	0	0	0	0	0	0	0	0
Total	47	7,870,008	618,141	30,000	356,674	8,792	9,188	24,601	2,000	1,172,770	167,689
Estimated % of Acquisition Expenditures			7.85	0.38	4.53	0.11	0.11	0.31	0.02	14.90	2.13

Category of Expenditures (in U.S. dollars)

Table 4 / Government Library Acquisition Expenditures

State	Number of Libraries	Total Acquisition Expenditures	Books	Other Print Materials	Periodicals/ Serials	Manuscripts & Archives	AV Equipment	AV Materials	Microforms	Electronic Reference	Preservation
Alabama	0	0	0	0	0	0	0	0	0	0	0
Alaska	0	0	0	0	0	0	0	0	0	0	0
Arizona	1	2,012	2,000	0	12	0	0	0	0	0	0
Arkansas	0	0	0	0	0	0	0	0	0	0	0
California	4	539,005	234,264	0	1,442	0	0	0	0	145,582	0
Colorado	0	0	0	0	0	0	0	0	0	0	0
Connecticut	0	0	0	0	0	0	0	0	0	0	0
Delaware	0	0	0	0	0	0	0	0	0	0	0
District of Columbia	0	0	0	0	0	0	0	0	0	0	0
Florida	0	0	0	0	0	0	0	0	0	0	0
Georgia	0	0	0	0	0	0	0	0	0	0	0
Hawaii	0	0	0	0	0	0	0	0	0	0	0
Idaho	0	0	0	0	0	0	0	0	0	0	0
Illinois	0	0	0	0	0	0	0	0	0	0	0
Indiana	0	0	0	0	0	0	0	0	0	0	0
Iowa	0	0	0	0	0	0	0	0	0	0	0
Kansas	1	515,260	26,852	0	396,491	0	0	0	0	85,690	6,227
Kentucky	0	0	0	0	0	0	0	0	0	0	0
Louisiana	1	1,627,826	524,121	0	11,796	0	0	0	887	221,858	8,034
Maine	1	380,116	0	0	0	0	0	0	0	0	0
Maryland	1	37,000	5,000	0	32,000	0	0	0	0	0	0
Massachusetts	0	0	0	0	0	0	0	0	0	0	0
Michigan	0	0	0	0	0	0	0	0	0	0	0
Minnesota	1	74,500	10,000	0	45,500	0	0	0	0	19,000	0
Mississippi	0	0	0	0	0	0	0	0	0	0	0
Missouri	0	0	0	0	0	0	0	0	0	0	0
Montana	0	0	0	0	0	0	0	0	0	0	0

Table 4 / Government Library Acquisition Expenditures (cont.)

State	Number of Libraries	Total Acquisition Expenditures	Category of Expenditures (in U.S. dollars)								
			Books	Other Print Materials	Periodicals/ Serials	Manuscripts & Archives	AV Equipment	AV Materials	Microforms	Electronic Reference	Preservation
Nebraska	0	0	0	0	0	0	0	0	0	0	0
Nevada	0	0	0	0	0	0	0	0	0	0	0
New Hampshire	0	0	0	0	0	0	0	0	0	0	0
New Jersey	0	0	0	0	0	0	0	0	0	0	0
New Mexico	0	0	0	0	0	0	0	0	0	0	0
New York	0	0	0	0	0	0	0	0	0	0	0
North Carolina	0	0	0	0	0	0	0	0	0	0	0
North Dakota	0	0	0	0	0	0	0	0	0	0	0
Ohio	0	0	0	0	0	0	0	0	0	0	0
Oklahoma	0	0	0	0	0	0	0	0	0	0	0
Oregon	0	0	0	0	0	0	0	0	0	0	0
Pennsylvania	1	125,000	0	0	0	0	0	0	0	0	0
Rhode Island	0	0	0	0	0	0	0	0	0	0	0
South Carolina	0	0	0	0	0	0	0	0	0	0	0
South Dakota	0	0	0	0	0	0	0	0	0	0	0
Tennessee	0	0	0	0	0	0	0	0	0	0	0
Texas	0	0	0	0	0	0	0	0	0	0	0
Utah	0	0	0	0	0	0	0	0	0	0	0
Vermont	0	0	0	0	0	0	0	0	0	0	0
Virginia	0	0	0	0	0	0	0	0	0	0	0
Washington	0	0	0	0	0	0	0	0	0	200,000	0
West Virginia	1	650,000	50,000	0	400,000	0	0	0	0	0	0
Wisconsin	1	10,000	0	0	0	0	0	0	0	0	0
Wyoming	0	0	0	0	0	0	0	0	0	0	0
Puerto Rico	0	0	0	0	0	0	0	0	0	0	0
Total	13	3,960,719	852,237	0	887,241	0	0	0	887	672,130	14,261
Estimated % of Acquisition Expenditures			21.52	0.00	22.40	0.00	0.00	0.00	0.02	16.97	0.36

Public Library State Rankings, 2019

State	Library visits per capita[1]	Registered users per capita[1]	Total circulation[2] per capita[1]	Reference transactions per capita[1]
Alabama	41	30	47	13
Alaska	23	19	18	31
Arizona	38	41	27	51
Arkansas	37	14	41	12
California	35	23	37	46
Colorado	12	7	5	23
Connecticut	3	44	21	7
Delaware	28	51	34	9
District of Columbia	8	7	26	4
Florida	43	16	42	5
Georgia	49	47	50	29
Hawaii	49	3	48	46
Idaho	6	16	6	21
Illinois	13	47	13	13
Indiana	16	40	7	26
Iowa	10	10	16	39
Kansas	11	6	8	13
Kentucky	34	11	29	10
Louisiana	36	35	44	6
Maine	7	31	28	35
Maryland	29	27	10	3
Massachusetts	4	19	15	19
Michigan	26	41	20	16
Minnesota	33	4	12	31
Mississippi	51	34	51	50
Missouri	27	16	9	31
Montana	30	44	32	34
Nebraska	25	5	14	45
Nevada	40	41	36	48
New Hampshire	14	23	23	28
New Jersey	20	39	33	18
New Mexico	24	1	31	25
New York	17	19	35	2
North Carolina	45	14	43	20
North Dakota	42	49	39	36
Ohio	1	2	1	1
Oklahoma	31	11	17	36
Oregon	5	11	2	39
Pennsylvania	39	44	40	26
Rhode Island	17	49	30	42
South Carolina	44	29	38	30
South Dakota	22	38	22	43
Tennessee	46	35	46	39
Texas	48	23	45	36
Utah	21	23	4	8
Vermont	2	31	25	22

State	Library visits per capita[1]	Registered users per capita[1]	Total circulation[2] per capita[1]	Reference transactions per capita[1]
Virginia	32	19	24	16
Washington	19	27	3	44
West Virginia	47	35	49	49
Wisconsin	15	31	11	24
Wyoming	8	7	19	11

State	Public-access Internet computers per 5,000 population[3]	Public-access Internet computers per stationary outlet	Print materials per capita[1]	E-books per capita[1]
Alabama	30	27	37	22
Alaska	11	40	15	19
Arizona	45	7	51	31
Arkansas	26	37	29	30
California	49	13	46	41
Colorado	17	5	39	37
Connecticut	15	23	6	38
Delaware	24	3	43	40
District of Columbia	9	1	47	51
Florida	42	2	49	44
Georgia	39	9	45	49
Hawaii	51	41	32	50
Idaho	8	32	21	41
Illinois	10	12	14	11
Indiana	13	21	10	20
Iowa	3	45	6	4
Kansas	5	43	11	1
Kentucky	22	6	30	7
Louisiana	14	25	25	23
Maine	6	49	1	17
Maryland	37	4	40	44
Massachusetts	27	29	3	14
Michigan	16	18	23	28
Minnesota	28	28	28	33
Mississippi	35	38	35	47
Missouri	40	35	20	26
Montana	20	44	27	18
Nebraska	2	42	9	10
Nevada	50	26	50	48
New Hampshire	21	50	4	6
New Jersey	32	20	19	29
New Mexico	19	29	22	43
New York	29	24	12	21
North Carolina	47	19	44	35
North Dakota	25	46	16	27
Ohio	18	17	13	3
Oklahoma	31	31	34	24

State	Public-access Internet computers per 5,000 population[3]	Public-access Internet computers per stationary outlet	Print materials per capita[1]	E-books per capita[1]
Oregon	41	34	26	16
Pennsylvania	48	36	33	34
Rhode Island	12	15	18	9
South Carolina	34	11	37	36
South Dakota	7	48	8	12
Tennessee	38	14	41	8
Texas	43	8	47	46
Utah	43	16	31	32
Vermont	1	51	2	13
Virginia	33	10	35	24
Washington	36	22	42	39
West Virginia	46	47	24	5
Wisconsin	23	33	17	2
Wyoming	4	39	5	15

State	Audio physical materials per capita[1]	Audio downloadable materials per capita[1]	Video physical materials per capita[1]	Video downloadable materials per capita[1]
Alabama	38	27	43	14
Alaska	17	22	3	21
Arizona	41	24	40	21
Arkansas	38	28	29	21
California	41	42	45	26
Colorado	20	30	24	12
Connecticut	5	37	9	41
Delaware	27	45	37	38
District of Columbia	51	50	49	47
Florida	41	7	40	31
Georgia	50	48	49	41
Hawaii	41	50	47	47
Idaho	21	40	21	47
Illinois	4	14	12	13
Indiana	10	32	9	19
Iowa	8	6	5	41
Kansas	14	2	5	28
Kentucky	32	25	25	19
Louisiana	35	17	14	7
Maine	10	16	11	10
Maryland	21	39	35	31
Massachusetts	6	26	12	21
Michigan	14	29	15	7
Minnesota	25	43	32	41
Mississippi	48	47	44	41
Missouri	17	35	21	28
Montana	32	11	25	21

State	Audio physical materials per capita[1]	Audio downloadable materials per capita[1]	Video physical materials per capita[1]	Video downloadable materials per capita[1]
Nebraska	21	9	20	41
Nevada	41	49	32	35
New Hampshire	10	3	5	2
New Jersey	8	21	18	4
New Mexico	27	38	21	31
New York	21	34	15	35
North Carolina	48	46	51	38
North Dakota	27	13	29	14
Ohio	2	4	1	1
Oklahoma	35	33	35	26
Oregon	14	15	15	5
Pennsylvania	27	36	37	7
Rhode Island	25	18	18	31
South Carolina	38	31	37	17
South Dakota	17	19	25	47
Tennessee	41	10	47	14
Texas	47	43	45	38
Utah	13	23	25	28
Vermont	6	8	4	47
Virginia	35	20	40	6
Washington	27	40	32	35
West Virginia	34	1	31	3
Wisconsin	3	5	5	17
Wyoming	1	12	2	10

State	Total paid full-time-equivalent (FTE) staff[4] per 25,000 population[6]	Paid full-time-equivalent (FTE) librarians per 25,000 population[6]	Percentage of total full-time-equivalent (FTE) librarians with ALA-MLS[5]
Alabama	42	31	35
Alaska	29	25	29
Arizona	45	48	13
Arkansas	35	36	37
California	47	47	5
Colorado	11	29	20
Connecticut	7	4	19
Delaware	39	38	28
District of Columbia	2	28	1
Florida	43	46	10
Georgia	51	51	1
Hawaii	37	41	3
Idaho	17	32	33
Illinois	3	10	21
Indiana	4	14	24
Iowa	15	3	46
Kansas	5	7	38
Kentucky	25	6	47

State	Total paid full-time-equivalent (FTE) staff[4] per 25,000 population[6]	Paid full-time-equivalent (FTE) librarians per 25,000 population[6]	Percentage of total full-time-equivalent (FTE) librarians with ALA-MLS[5]
Louisiana	12	13	40
Maine	16	5	36
Maryland	19	18	30
Massachusetts	18	8	23
Michigan	27	26	18
Minnesota	36	33	25
Mississippi	48	21	51
Missouri	13	33	41
Montana	34	17	43
Nebraska	24	12	48
Nevada	49	50	15
New Hampshire	10	1	34
New Jersey	21	30	4
New Mexico	30	27	31
New York	8	19	14
North Carolina	45	49	6
North Dakota	40	24	39
Ohio	1	15	16
Oklahoma	28	11	42
Oregon	20	35	12
Pennsylvania	38	39	17
Rhode Island	14	16	7
South Carolina	32	40	9
South Dakota	31	20	49
Tennessee	44	45	32
Texas	50	44	22
Utah	33	37	27
Vermont	9	2	45
Virginia	26	42	8
Washington	23	43	11
West Virginia	41	23	50
Wisconsin	22	22	26
Wyoming	6	9	44

State	Total operating revenue[7] per capita[1]	State operating revenue per capita[1]	Local operating revenue per capita[1]	Other operating revenue per capita[1]
Alabama	46	29	45	30
Alaska	8	25	6	31
Arizona	42	41	38	48
Arkansas	38	16	40	25
California	25	33	20	26
Colorado	9	38	7	13
Connecticut	10	41	12	3
Delaware	37	9	41	37
District of Columbia	1	46	1	51
Florida	39	28	36	44

State	Total operating revenue[7] per capita[1]	State operating revenue per capita[1]	Local operating revenue per capita[1]	Other operating revenue per capita[1]
Georgia	50	11	48	42
Hawaii	43	2	51	39
Idaho	26	21	24	21
Illinois	5	12	3	16
Indiana	7	8	9	11
Iowa	23	30	19	22
Kansas	11	19	11	7
Kentucky	21	21	16	33
Louisiana	12	27	8	28
Maine	29	39	34	2
Maryland	16	3	26	8
Massachusetts	18	18	18	12
Michigan	20	24	17	24
Minnesota	27	20	27	18
Mississippi	51	13	50	36
Missouri	15	32	14	17
Montana	40	40	37	34
Nebraska	31	37	25	29
Nevada	35	5	42	40
New Hampshire	19	46	15	20
New Jersey	13	35	10	27
New Mexico	34	26	33	23
New York	3	10	4	1
North Carolina	45	21	44	46
North Dakota	41	14	39	35
Ohio	2	1	29	5
Oklahoma	30	33	23	38
Oregon	4	43	2	15
Pennsylvania	44	7	49	9
Rhode Island	17	4	30	6
South Carolina	36	15	35	47
South Dakota	32	46	31	43
Tennessee	49	44	46	45
Texas	48	46	43	49
Utah	28	36	22	41
Vermont	24	46	28	4
Virginia	33	17	32	50
Washington	6	44	5	19
West Virginia	47	6	47	32
Wisconsin	22	31	21	10
Wyoming	14	46	13	14

State	Total operating expenditures[8] per capita[1]	Salaries and benefits	Total collection expenditures[9]	Other operating expenditures[10]
Alabama	46	20	48	45
Alaska	11	27	21	8
Arizona	43	49	34	33
Arkansas	42	31	39	38
California	26	42	36	14
Colorado	8	38	3	10
Connecticut	6	3	14	15
Delaware	37	43	46	23
District of Columbia	1	4	13	1
Florida	40	50	41	26
Georgia	50	11	50	51
Hawaii	44	30	38	42
Idaho	27	46	27	16
Illinois	5	35	5	3
Indiana	9	48	2	6
Iowa	21	17	16	29
Kansas	10	45	10	4
Kentucky	31	36	19	28
Louisiana	17	44	12	11
Maine	24	16	37	22
Maryland	15	2	8	37
Massachusetts	16	10	9	27
Michigan	22	47	20	13
Minnesota	25	36	29	17
Mississippi	51	24	51	50
Missouri	19	51	6	9
Montana	41	12	42	43
Nebraska	29	25	17	30
Nevada	35	28	21	41
New Hampshire	18	1	25	32
New Jersey	13	9	18	19
New Mexico	34	41	23	34
New York	2	7	15	7
North Carolina	45	14	45	49
North Dakota	36	34	33	35
Ohio	4	39	1	5
Oklahoma	28	29	11	30
Oregon	3	32	7	2
Pennsylvania	39	22	44	36
Rhode Island	14	6	40	18
South Carolina	38	15	30	44
South Dakota	33	19	28	39
Tennessee	49	26	49	46
Texas	47	18	47	48
Utah	30	40	24	23
Vermont	20	13	31	21
Virginia	32	8	35	40
Washington	7	23	4	12

State	Total operating expenditures[8] per capita[1]	Salaries and benefits	Total collection expenditures[9]	Other operating expenditures[10]
West Virginia	48	33	43	47
Wisconsin	23	21	31	25
Wyoming	12	5	26	20

1 Per capita is based on the total unduplicated population of legal service areas. The determination of the unduplicated figure is the responsibility of the state library agency and should be based on the most recent state population figures for jurisdictions in the state.

2 Total circulation is the sum of physical materials circulation and electronic materials circulation.

3 Per 5,000 population is based on the total unduplicated population of legal service areas. The determination of the unduplicated figure is the responsibility of the state library agency and should be based on the most recent state population figures for jurisdictions in the state.

4 Paid staff were reported in FTEs. To ensure comparable data, 40 hours was set as the measure of full-time employment (for example, 60 hours per week of part-time work by employees in a staff category divided by the 40-hour measure equals 1.50 FTEs). FTE data were reported to two decimal places but rounded to one decimal place in the table.

5 ALA-MLS: A master's degree from a graduate library education program accredited by the American Library Association (ALA). Librarians with an ALA-MLS are also included in total librarians.

6 Per 25,000 population is based on the total unduplicated population of legal service areas. The determination of the unduplicated figure is the responsibility of the state library agency and should be based on the most recent state population figures for jurisdictions in the state.

7 Total revenue includes federal, state, local, and other revenue.

8 Total operating expenditures includes total staff expenditures, collection expenditures, and other operating expenditures.

9 Total collection expenditures includes expenditures for print, electronic, and other materials.

10 Other operating expenditures not included in staff or collections.

Note: The District of Columbia, although not a state, is included in the state rankings. Special care should be used in comparing its data to state data. Caution should be used in making comparisons with the state of Hawaii, as Hawaii reports only one public library for the entire state. Additional information on nonsampling error, response rates, and definitions may be found in Data File Documentation Public Libraries Survey: Fiscal Year 2019.

Source: IMLS, Public Libraries Survey, FY 2019. Data users who create their own estimates using data from these tables should cite the Institute of Museum and Library Services as the source of the original data only.

Book Trade Research and Statistics

Prices of U.S. and Foreign Published Materials

George Aulisio

Editor, ALA Core Library Materials Price Index Editorial Board

The Library Materials Price Index (LMPI) Editorial Board of Core, a division of the American Library Association, continues to monitor prices for a range of library materials from sources within North America and other key publishing centers worldwide.

The U.S. Consumer Price Index (CPI) increased by 7.0 percent in 2021. CPI figures are obtained from the Bureau of Labor Statistics at http://www.bls.gov/.

In 2017 all tables that utilized a base index price increase reset their base year to 2010. All indexes continue to utilize the 2010 base year. Percent changes in average prices from 2018–2022 are conveniently noted in Chart 1.

Index	Average Price Percent Change				
	2018	2019	2020	2021	2022
U.S. Consumer Price Index	1.9	2.3	1.4	7.0	n.a.
U.S. Periodicals (Table 1)	5.7	6.7	6.7*	2.3	5.6
Legal Serials Services (Table 2)	21.8	10.9	21.4	20.4	21.7
Hardcover Books (Table 3)	-8.4*	-2.5	-2.5	-3.3	1.5
Academic Books (Table 4)	0.0	-0.9	8.3	-0.9	n.a.
Academic E-Books (Table 4A)	5.3	0.3	4.9	-1.8	n.a.
Academic Textbooks (Table 4B)	-3.2	2.0	2.8	6.8	n.a.
U.S. College Books (Table 5)	-0.7	1.3	13.5	6.1	n.a.
U.S. Mass Market Paperback Books (Table 6)	1.2*	1.9	3.5	3.3	1.8
U.S. Paperbacks (Table 7)	23.0	-8.5	-6.7	-0.1	n.a.
U.S. Audiobooks (Table 7A)	13.8*	1.6	-1.1	-26.8	n.a.
U.S. E-Books (Table 7B)	16.7	12.7*	7.0*	-13.2	n.a.
+Serials (Table 8)	6.1*	6.1	5.9*	3.6	3.8
+Online Serials (Table 8A)	6.0	6.5*	6.2*	3.8	3.3
British Academic Books (Table 9)	7.0	-1.8	-1.4	8.2	n.a.

* = figures revised from previous editions based on new data
+Dataset changes each year.

U.S. Published Materials

Tables 1 through 7B indicate average prices and price indexes for library materials published primarily in the United States. These indexes are U.S. Periodicals (Table

1), Legal Serials Services (Table 2), U.S. Hardcover Books (Table 3), North American Academic Books (Table 4), North American Academic E-Books (Table 4A), North American Academic Textbooks (Table 4B), U.S. College Books (Table 5), U.S. Mass Market Paperback Books (Table 6), U.S. Paperbacks (Excluding Mass Market) (Table 7), U.S. Audiobooks (Table 7A), and U.S. E-Books (Table 7B).

Periodical and Serials Prices

The U.S. Periodical Price Index (USPPI) (Table 1) was reestablished in 2014 by Stephen Bosch, University of Arizona, and is here updated for 2022 using data supplied by EBSCO Information Services. This report includes 2018–2022 data indexed to the base year of 2010. Table 1 is derived from a selected set of titles that, as much as possible, will remain as the sample base for the index for future comparisons. The data in Table 1 are from a print preferred data pull, but more than 52 percent of the titles in the index are based on online pricing, and only 22 percent are print only. The data provide a strong mix of both print and online pricing, characteristic of a current academic library's serials collection. The subscription prices used are publishers' list prices, excluding publisher discounts or vendor service charges. The pricing data for 2010–2014, the base years for the new USPPI, published in 2014, were created from one report that pulled pricing information for a static set of titles for the five years. The pricing data for 2018–2022 are based on that same sampling of titles but are not an exact match due to changes that occur with serial titles. Some titles fell off the list due to pricing not being available, while others for which pricing had not been available in 2014 now have pricing available.

The new USPPI treats a little more than 6,000 titles compared to the original title list, which covered only about 3,700 titles. The previous versions of USPPI treated Russian translations as a separate category. Russian translations are no longer a focus of this index and are not tracked as a category. These were once seen as a major cost factor, but this is no longer the case, and therefore, their inclusion in or exclusion from the index no longer makes sense. There are Russian translation titles in the index, but they are not reported separately.

The main barrier to creating this index is maintaining the title list and obtaining standard retail pricing for titles on the list. Changes in serials titles due to ceased publication, movement to open access, mergers, combining titles in packages, moving to direct orders, and publication delays are a few of the situations that can affect compilers' ability to obtain current pricing information. The new index retained that part of the title list from the previous index that remained viable and added new titles to that list based on data from EBSCO on the most frequently ordered serials in their system. From that list of serials, titles were selected for the new index to ensure that the distribution by subject was similar to the distribution in the original index. There are more titles in the selected title set than the number of titles that produced prices over the past six years. This should allow the current index to be sustainable into the future as titles fall off the list and pricing becomes available for titles that may have been delayed or are no longer in memberships.

The first five years of data, published in 2014, showed consistent price changes across subject areas because the pricing data was a historical look at the prices of the same set of journals. The data for 2018–2022 are based on the same sample list but is not the same list of titles as the data for 2010–2014 due to the aforementioned issues that can impact pricing availability. Across subject areas, the price changes were greater this year, showing an overall 5.6 percent increase compared to the 2.3 percent increase in 2021. This is slightly higher than price changes seen in other pricing studies (see Table 8), which showed a 3–4 percent increase. The 2.3 percent increase for 2021 was a marked decrease from the 6.7 percent increase seen in 2020, but as the economy moves away from the pandemic mode, prices are trending up again. The impact of current increases in the CPI may have contributed to part of this increase. The sample sizes are smaller at the subject level, so a few changes can cause a large swing in the overall price for that area. In 2022 price increases were consistent across subjects. There was a variation from 2.8–9.4 percent compared to the 2021 variance from -3.6–4.3 percent. The outliers in 2022 were subjects with few titles, so the changes in price in a few titles can drop or raise the average price from the norm.

Direct comparisons between Table 1 and Table 8 should be avoided, especially at the subject level. Both tables show the overall rate of increase in serial prices to be around 3 percent; however, there is little that makes a statistically valid comparison beyond that point. Table 8 has slightly higher average prices and higher prices in most subject areas. This is due to Table 8's larger dataset coming from a broad mix of sources, including a much larger set of journals from foreign sources and a higher mix of STM titles. Table 1 is a mix of journals that attempts to reflect the journal collections in an average U.S. library, so the mix of journals contains more trade and popular titles than would be found in Table 8, but Table 8 has more foreign titles, and prices for those can be impacted by the strength of the U.S. dollar. Differences in the two datasets yield different results.

The most important trend seen in this data (Table 1) is that the consistent increase in prices that had averaged around 6 percent before 2021 and had been subdued due to the impact of the pandemic on library budgets has now rebounded. In 2022 we saw prices increase at a higher rate, 5.6 percent, which is close to recent years. This year, titles from a broad mix of social science and STM subjects dominate the list of areas with larger price increases. Average prices for journals in the science and technology area are still far higher than in other areas. That trend continues, with the average cost of chemistry journals being $6,271 and physics journals being $5,174.

In this price index, like similar price indexes, the data are less accurate at describing price changes the smaller the sample becomes. For that reason, drawing conclusions about price changes in subject areas with a limited number of titles is less accurate than for large areas or the broader price index. Price changes are far more volatile where smaller datasets are used. Technology journals went up 6.1 percent this year, but concluding that all journals in the technology area will increase by 6.1 percent in the coming year is incorrect. If a specific inflation figure for a small subject area were needed, it would be better to look at an average over a longer period or the overall number for the price study (5.6 percent) than to use the actual numbers year by year. The variation in pricing is too volatile in smaller sample sizes to be comparable on a year-to-year basis. In a small sample size, the change in just one or two titles could easily have a large impact on the overall price for an area.

(text continues on page 318)

Table 1 / U.S. Periodicals: Average Prices and Price Indexes, 2018–2022

Index Base 2010 = 100

Subject	LC Class	Titles	2010 Average Price	2018 Average Price	2019 Average Price	2020 Average Price	2021 Average Price	2022 Average Price	Percent Change 2021–2022	Index
Agriculture	S	239	$579.48	$1,057.11	$1,130.08	$1,196.79	$1,239.19	$1,288.64	4.0%	222.4
Anthropology	GN	54	373.64	567.65	604.61	632.59	652.36	684.57	4.9	183.2
Arts and Architecture	N	100	112.39	252.56	265.50	278.55	284.72	295.07	3.6	262.5
Astronomy	QB	25	1,793.08	3,036.83	3,164.64	3,381.71	3,246.54	3,408.96	5.0	190.1
Biology	QH	426	2,053.06	3,216.41	3,417.54	3,593.19	3,655.53	3,846.76	5.2	187.4
Botany	QK	71	1,361.09	2,087.20	2,184.71	2,286.57	2,324.35	2,424.17	4.3	178.1
Business and Economics	HA-HJ	453	351.29	657.23	703.22	750.83	765.75	799.67	4.4	227.6
Chemistry	QD	158	3,396.26	5,066.08	5,421.00	5,802.85	5,894.79	6,271.51	6.4	184.7
Education	L	222	354.92	689.83	743.84	795.58	830.65	878.79	5.8	247.6
Engineering	T	559	1,244.39	2,153.86	2,310.50	2,485.50	2,548.97	2,722.04	6.8	218.7
Food Science	TX	47	356.17	940.82	989.04	1,069.29	1,105.16	1,166.40	5.5	327.5
General Science	Q	97	998.51	1,832.80	1,956.50	2,073.75	2,129.94	2,236.80	5.0	224.0
General Works	A	107	85.84	128.50	137.08	142.83	156.20	170.84	9.4	199.0
Geography	G-GF	89	670.60	1,292.06	1,385.17	1,481.24	1,533.40	1,614.21	5.3	240.7
Geology	QE	76	1,368.79	1,938.38	2,102.23	2,239.77	2,304.87	2,411.70	4.6	176.2
Heath Sciences	R	917	1,009.55	1,731.51	1,852.19	1,992.94	2,056.14	2,191.50	6.6	217.1

Subject	LC Class									
History	C,D,E,F	316	202.39	340.32	361.89	383.33	395.79	414.77	4.8	204.9
Language and Literature	P	296	168.12	262.98	277.57	295.55	297.21	307.57	3.5	182.9
Law	K	207	214.01	395.22	412.63	433.26	445.35	480.01	7.8	224.3
Library Science	Z	85	290.02	467.41	501.34	537.90	548.92	578.59	5.4	199.5
Math and Computer Science	QA	353	1,242.13	1,943.21	2,062.45	2,231.21	2,282.99	2,424.14	6.2	195.2
Military and Naval Science	U,V	26	239.90	461.57	485.80	507.62	512.71	527.29	2.8	219.8
Music	M	48	82.18	179.33	188.74	199.87	205.22	211.24	2.9	257.0
Philosophy and Religion	B-BD, BH-BX	220	232.37	377.19	395.77	418.13	423.61	445.77	5.2	191.8
Physics	QC	163	2,845.54	4,308.39	4,591.19	4,897.95	4,989.24	5,173.78	3.7	181.8
Political Science	J	100	312.76	799.27	856.61	927.19	960.98	995.47	3.6	318.3
Psychology	BF	126	648.21	1,201.78	1,284.52	1,383.81	1,423.09	1,498.84	5.3	231.2
Recreation	GV	62	69.79	190.36	202.37	211.91	218.04	232.15	6.5	332.6
Social Sciences	H	45	351.40	846.48	896.93	945.01	946.78	993.47	4.9	282.7
Sociology	HM-HX	250	482.59	910.33	976.45	1,045.67	1,076.98	1,132.47	5.2	234.7
Technology	TA-TT	124	535.73	1,023.00	1,098.98	1,194.01	1,242.47	1,318.81	6.1	246.2
Zoology	QL	135	1,454.26	2,338.06	2,482.80	2,561.01	2,537.57	2,621.53	3.3	180.3
Total		6,196	$843.46	$1,483.87	$1,583.17	$1,689.42	$1,728.22	$1,824.84	5.6%	216.4

Compiled by Stephen Bosch, University of Arizona, based on subscription information supplied by EBSCO Information Services

(continued from page 315)

More extensive reports from the periodical price index have been published annually in the mid-April issue of *Library Journal* through 1992, in the May issue of *American Libraries* from 1993–2002, and in the October 2003 issue of *Library Resources and Technical Services*.

The Legal Serials Services Index (Table 2) is compiled by Ajaye Bloomstone, Louisiana State University Law Center Library, using data collected from various legal serials vendors. The base year for this index is 2010. This index presents price data covering the years 2010–2022.

As in past years, vendors were asked to provide cost data on particular titles with the assumption that the title or set has been held as an active subscription over a period of time by a large academic research law library. The cost recorded in the index is intended to be based on the upkeep cost of a particular title, not necessarily the cost incurred in purchasing a new set, though sometimes the cost is the same, and often the cost of updates can be more expensive than purchasing a new set. A nuance of legal publishing is that for some of the larger legal publishers, hard prices for a calendar year are not set at the beginning of that year but halfway through, so only gross price estimates may be available in time for publication of this article. In addition to titles issued on a "regular" basis (e.g., journals and law reviews published monthly, quarterly, etc.), legal serials may also be updated throughout the year with regular and irregular updates or releases, new editions, and new or revised volumes. If a title is updated irregularly, the price for its renewal may increase or decrease from one year to the next, depending on the publisher's plans for keeping the title current. It is noteworthy that although legal serials in print format are still produced, titles seem to be migrating, albeit slowly, to an electronic-only format.

Table 2 / Legal Serials Services:
Average Prices and Price Indexes, 2010–2022
Index Base: 2010 = 100

Year	Titles	Average Price	Percent Change	Index
2010	217	$1,714.96	3.5	100.0
2011	217	1,904.69	11.1	111.1
2012	219	2,058.66	8.1	120.0
2013	218	2,241.42	8.9	130.7
2014	219	2,473.44	10.4	144.2
2015	218	2,818.02	13.9	164.3
2016	217	3,085.34	9.5	179.9
2017	218	3,446.12	11.7	200.9
2018	185	4,195.99	21.8	244.7
2019	191	4,653.97	10.9	271.4
2020	187	5,648.39	21.4	329.4
2021	186	6,802.39	20.4	396.6
2022	183	8,277.79	21.7	482.7

Compiled by Ajaye Bloomstone, Louisiana State University Law Center Library

Some prices were provided to the compiler with the caveat "no longer available for new sales," meaning that a print subscription can continue to be ordered in that format if it is currently an existing subscription of the purchaser. There is also a trend for print titles to come with an electronic component. The purchasing library may have no choice but to accept both formats for such titles, even if the print is preferred. If one could purchase the print format without the electronic component, the cost might conceivably change. This leads one to believe that if the publication is not to be phased out immediately, then the title might, at some point soon, no longer be available in print, and this process will serve to wean the print subscriber to an electronic format if the publication doesn't cease. More than 20 titles used in Table 2 ceased publication in 2019. To compensate for the loss of titles, new titles were added. The new titles were added with the intent to match the previous year's cost of the ceased publications plus the average percentage of an increase for the remainder of the titles from 2018–2019. Further substitutions occurred between 2019–2020 due to titles discontinuing print and migrating to an electronic format or ceasing altogether, though, in terms of the titles tracked in this list over time, the number that has ceased seems to have been curtailed, at least temporarily, for 2021 and now 2022. With this 2022 survey, it was decided that there would be no substitutions made for the two titles indicated as ceased or discontinued by the vendor; it is assumed that there would be little or no variance in the three ultimate determinants for the annual survey: average cost per title, percent of change, and index.

Book Prices

U.S. Hardcover Books (Table 3), U.S. Mass Market Paperback Books (Table 6), U.S. Paperbacks (Excluding Mass Market) (Table 7), U.S. Audiobooks (Table 7A), and U.S. E-Books (Table 7B) were prepared by Narda Tafuri, retired, from the University of Scranton. These tables are derived from data provided by Baker & Taylor. Figures for 2019 have been revised again to reflect additional late updates to the Baker & Taylor database. Data for 2018 should now be considered finalized. The 2020 figures given here may be similarly revised in next year's tables and should be considered preliminary, as are the 2021 figures. The figures for this edition of the *Library and Book Trade Almanac* were provided by Baker & Taylor and are based on the Book Industry Study Group's BISAC categories. The BISAC juvenile category (fiction and nonfiction) has been divided into children and young adult. An additional category, Non-classified, has been added to Table 7B (e-books). For more information on the BISAC categories, visit http://www.bisg.org.

Average book prices overall saw both increases and decreases in 2021. List prices for hardcover books (Table 3) and mass market paperback books (Table 6) showed slight increases of 1.5 percent and 1.8 percent, respectively. Trade paperbacks (Table 7) exhibited an insignificant decrease of -0.1 percent. Audiobooks (Table 7A) and e-books (Table 7B) exhibited substantial price decreases of -26.8 percent and -13.2 percent, respectively.

North American Academic Books (Table 4), North American Academic E-Books (Table 4A), and North American Academic Textbooks (Table 4B) were prepared by Stephen Bosch. The current version of North American Academic Books: Average Prices and Price Indexes 2019–2021 (Table 4) has been stable for the past

(text continues on page 328)

Table 3 / Hardcover Books: Average Prices and Price Indexes, 2018–2021

Index Base: 2010 = 100

BISAC Category	2010 Average Price	2018 Final Volumes	2018 Final Average Price	2018 Final Index	2019 Final Volumes	2019 Final Average Price	2019 Final Index	2020 Preliminary Volumes	2020 Preliminary Average Price	2020 Preliminary Index	2021 Preliminary Volumes	2021 Preliminary Average Price	2021 Preliminary Index
Antiques and Collectibles	$51.44	103	$72.96	141.8	101	$66.07	128.4	96	$77.73	151.1	78	$77.22	150.1
Architecture	85.52	908	95.80	112.0	928	94.78	110.8	902	93.92	109.8	836	91.37	106.8
Art	71.53	2,041	75.20	105.1	2,247	74.24	103.8	2,051	82.03	114.7	1,834	83.89	117.3
Bibles	37.50	251	44.42	118.5	188	57.63	153.7	201	50.38	134.3	191	67.50	180.0
Biography and Autobiography	53.41	1,727	46.09	86.3	1,575	41.72	78.1	1,520	42.92	80.4	1,767	41.20	77.1
Body, Mind and Spirit	36.91	214	25.60	69.4	291	25.78	69.9	307	22.84	61.9	308	29.18	79.1
Business and Economics	134.61	4,612	162.44	120.7	4,346	142.57	105.9	4,164	136.60	101.5	4,408	133.97	99.5
Children	24.63	16,782	26.30	106.8	16,335	25.42	103.2	15,438	24.01	97.5	14,376	24.97	101.4
Comics and Graphic Novels	31.51	668	43.57	138.3	689	48.59	154.2	651	46.70	148.2	637	48.71	154.6
Computers	138.53	1,155	179.43	129.5	1,118	162.78	117.5	1,027	151.81	109.6	1,046	180.28	130.1
Cooking	30.91	1,158	29.85	96.6	1,110	30.26	97.9	927	31.70	102.5	947	33.55	108.5
Crafts and Hobbies	33.28	188	31.04	93.3	158	32.38	97.3	143	32.45	97.5	137	31.33	94.1
Design	76.59	359	66.91	87.4	365	68.60	89.6	305	69.75	91.1	258	70.40	91.9
Drama	42.91	67	85.39	199.0	84	111.60	260.1	76	104.22	242.9	81	91.89	214.2
Education	117.59	2,822	271.54	230.9	2,556	168.75	143.5	2,315	157.28	133.8	2,326	140.45	119.4
Family and Relationships	32.24	223	47.90	148.6	225	46.85	145.3	223	49.93	154.9	242	67.13	208.2
Fiction	32.20	4,964	29.46	91.5	5,055	29.73	92.3	4,523	29.93	93.0	5,081	29.21	90.7
Foreign Language Study	132.47	277	125.96	95.1	216	121.91	92.0	236	119.53	90.2	237	116.73	88.1
Games and Activities	52.07	183	44.44	85.4	145	38.50	73.9	136	40.39	77.6	122	56.91	109.3
Gardening	36.42	124	37.87	104.0	121	39.28	107.9	110	38.07	104.5	118	36.22	99.5
Health and Fitness	48.51	343	69.30	142.9	393	83.96	173.1	352	83.97	173.1	351	73.15	150.8
History	82.65	5,866	94.37	114.2	6,222	103.28	125.0	5,658	108.94	131.8	5,654	101.63	123.0
House and Home	44.61	123	39.01	87.4	131	42.17	94.5	116	39.19	87.9	122	43.44	97.4
Humor	21.94	349	22.89	104.4	298	19.45	88.7	250	20.50	93.4	225	23.64	107.7

Category													
Language Arts and Disciplines	117.67	1,385	143.93	122.3	1,476	139.58	118.6	1,319	131.06	111.4	1,347	135.22	114.9
Law	174.48	2,384	182.75	104.7	2,272	175.77	100.7	2,295	182.18	104.4	2,396	174.72	100.1
Literary Collections	83.49	253	86.96	104.2	272	135.18	161.9	252	112.35	134.6	258	84.16	100.8
Literary Criticism	117.63	2,403	127.02	108.0	2,649	125.12	106.4	2,574	127.67	108.5	2,671	128.00	108.8
Mathematics	133.23	1,037	155.50	116.7	994	148.16	111.2	844	139.81	104.9	829	138.89	104.2
Medical	171.13	3,050	185.97	108.7	3,547	175.16	102.4	2,855	183.52	107.2	2,567	190.40	111.3
Music	87.84	603	90.93	103.5	675	96.38	109.7	653	96.38	109.7	586	96.87	110.3
Nature	74.89	424	85.60	114.3	466	94.56	126.3	453	83.42	111.4	523	85.36	114.0
Performing Arts	76.27	822	102.14	133.9	775	121.13	158.8	795	101.68	133.3	834	101.11	132.6
Pets	24.66	70	21.65	87.8	56	27.34	110.9	60	22.77	92.4	51	26.52	107.5
Philosophy	108.93	1,668	109.55	100.6	1,899	115.44	106.0	1,762	120.30	110.4	1,710	112.30	103.1
Photography	107.99	651	71.38	66.1	825	69.86	64.7	790	59.24	54.9	607	121.99	113.0
Poetry	40.76	295	37.01	90.8	320	36.98	90.7	259	35.44	87.0	331	33.07	81.1
Political Science	110.32	3,482	114.34	103.6	5,551	127.46	115.5	3,642	112.81	102.3	3,403	117.27	106.3
Psychology	109.85	1,449	149.40	136.0	2,736	144.60	131.6	1,187	146.13	133.0	1,148	152.43	138.8
Reference	302.69	340	382.33	126.3	311	280.56	92.7	231	368.29	121.7	219	317.20	104.8
Religion	80.88	3,126	79.06	97.7	2,746	87.44	108.1	2,820	84.31	104.2	2,895	87.83	108.6
Science	192.20	3,902	177.18	92.2	4,144	189.21	98.4	3,549	188.48	98.1	3,457	191.92	99.9
Self-help	27.11	425	25.98	95.8	438	24.20	89.2	418	23.48	86.6	459	24.31	89.7
Social Science	100.47	4,709	127.86	127.3	5,354	128.55	127.9	4,014	123.81	123.2	4,053	127.24	126.6
Sports and Recreation	41.23	503	56.24	136.4	541	52.27	126.8	492	55.35	134.2	515	59.88	145.2
Study Aids	101.54	14	103.31	101.7	9	177.87	175.2	30	125.04	123.1	10	160.89	158.5
Technology and Engineering	164.66	3,155	204.94	124.5	3,007	185.86	112.9	3,171	182.08	110.6	3,389	192.23	116.7
Transportation	84.28	289	62.23	73.8	301	86.46	102.6	219	89.48	106.2	238	91.22	108.2
Travel	41.32	482	40.52	98.1	238	41.78	101.1	215	36.80	89.1	176	42.17	102.0
True Crime	34.83	84	33.53	96.3	107	37.37	107.3	82	60.90	174.8	97	39.71	114.0
Young Adult	35.99	2,122	35.79	99.4	1,995	37.65	104.6	1,489	29.99	83.3	1,191	26.73	74.3
Totals and Averages	$89.54	84,934	$101.47	113.3	88,601	$99.74	111.4	78,197	$96.49	107.8	77,342	$97.90	109.3

Compiled by Narda Tafuri, Retired, University of Scranton, from data supplied by Baker & Taylor

Table 4 / North American Academic Books: Average Prices and Price Indexes, 2019–2021

Index Base: 2010 = 100

Subject Area	LC Class	2010		2019		2020		2021			Index
		Titles	Average Price	Titles	Average Price	Titles	Average Price	Titles	Average Price	Percent Change 2020–2021	
Agriculture	S	1,139	$107.44	1,915	$115.92	1,969	$127.89	2,035	$129.89	1.6%	120.9
Anthropology	GN	609	91.96	857	94.56	918	103.45	882	100.17	-3.2	108.9
Botany	QK	260	125.84	456	136.82	525	156.64	561	149.49	-4.6	118.8
Business and Economics	H	10,916	97.31	14,431	107.54	15,110	113.58	15,341	107.22	-5.6	110.2
Chemistry	QD	667	223.03	918	191.15	926	215.75	883	240.41	11.4	107.8
Education	L	4,688	86.47	7,122	93.01	7,488	102.26	7,279	97.83	-4.3	113.1
Engineering and Technology	T	6,913	133.45	11,202	153.75	12,737	155.18	12,835	158.54	2.2	118.8
Fine and Applied Arts	M-N	5,535	57.17	7,694	74.66	7,456	82.74	8,186	81.83	-1.1	143.2
General Works	A	80	75.60	290	98.42	295	103.92	295	99.47	-4.3	131.6
Geography	G	1,144	104.98	1,900	123.05	2,005	123.77	2,064	113.49	-8.3	108.1
Geology	QE	276	114.34	429	133.49	404	119.64	427	131.35	9.8	114.9
History	C-D-E-F	10,079	65.29	15,105	73.36	14,357	85.45	15,103	79.78	-6.6	122.2
Home Economics	TX	812	44.35	1,170	63.04	901	72.68	774	67.31	-7.4	151.8
Industrial Arts	TT	265	52.60	297	57.59	207	77.94	169	71.96	-7.7	136.8
Language and Literature	P	19,364	57.31	30,452	58.25	30,316	66.40	7,859	139.91	4.2	111.6

Subject	LC										
Law	K	4,596	125.35	6,728	128.39	7,039	134.26	889	96.59	-4.8	107.1
Library and Information science	Z	636	90.18	921	99.72	912	101.49	30,006	67.07	1.0	117.0
Mathematics and Computer Science	QA	3,965	103.85	5,318	116.20	6,724	120.42	6,757	121.38	0.8	116.9
Medicine	R	8,679	112.66	12,452	137.62	12,982	135.98	12,447	137.47	1.1	122.0
Military and Naval Science	U-V	773	79.99	1,391	78.80	1,429	78.83	1,412	75.78	-3.9	94.7
Philosophy and Religion	B	7,386	81.75	12,153	80.10	12,020	85.98	12,830	88.07	2.4	107.7
Physical Education and Recreation	GV	1,788	56.03	2,983	71.12	3,028	76.19	2,957	71.82	-5.7	128.2
Physics and Astronomy	QB	1,627	128.36	2,342	127.36	2,297	131.51	2,444	130.20	-1.0	101.4
Political Science	J	3,549	99.70	5,991	96.67	5,919	103.36	5,639	102.67	-0.7	103.0
Psychology	BF	1,730	76.65	2,944	82.11	2,965	94.77	2,898	94.85	0.1	123.8
Science (general)	Q	631	108.4	1,175	112.86	1,696	134.16	1,717	133.26	-0.7	122.9
Sociology	HM	6,666	88.75	11,518	89.35	11,870	100.38	11,471	97.02	-3.3	109.3
Zoology	QH, QL-QR	3,029	140.26	3,916	133.28	3,843	137.87	3,794	134.61	-2.4	96.0
Totals and Averages		107,802	$89.15	164,070	$95.87	168,338	$103.87	169,954	$102.98	-0.9%	115.5

Compiled by Stephen Bosch, University of Arizona, from electronic data provided by ProQuest (formerly Ingrams Content Group-Coutts Information Services) and GOBI Library Solutions from EBSCO (formerly YBP Library Services). The data represent all titles (includes e-books, hardcover, trade & paperback books, as well as annuals) treated for all approval plan customers serviced by the vendors. This table covers titles published or distributed in the United States and Canada during the calendar years listed. This index does include paperback editions and electronic books. The inclusion of these items does impact pricing in the index.

Table 4A / North American Academic E-Books: Average Prices and Price Indexes, 2019–2021

Index Base: 2010 = 100

Subject Area	LC Class	2010		2019		2020		2021			
		Titles	Average Price	Titles	Average Price	Titles	Average Price	Titles	Average Price	Percent Change 2020–2021	Index
Agriculture	S	697	$168.73	874	$132.96	961	$146.83	971	$147.63	0.5%	87.5
Anthropology	GN	385	109.96	393	103.92	435	114.52	429	107.84	-5.8	98.1
Botany	QK	190	175.23	193	159.51	257	168.72	261	165.04	-2.2	94.2
Business and Economics	H	8,481	102.87	6,797	118.09	7,625	123.43	7931	115.69	-6.3	112.5
Chemistry	QD	521	232.57	446	186.38	499	228.23	453	267.56	17.2	115.0
Education	L	2,852	99.96	3,231	101.52	3,660	114.12	3627	106.42	-6.7	106.5
Engineering and Technology	T	4,976	152.33	5,281	165.33	6,404	165.47	6471	170.13	2.8	111.7
Fine and Applied Arts	M-N	1,493	83.35	2,338	96.52	2,822	106.81	3047	104.18	-2.5	125.0
General Works	A	53	89.13	132	97.67	148	108.32	139	112.94	4.3	126.7
Geography	G	829	117.83	828	141.23	993	135.83	1045	123.54	-9.1	104.8
Geology	QE	178	146.85	186	152.31	171	133.30	197	151.11	13.4	102.9
History	C-D-E-F	5,189	89.42	6,233	87.41	6,582	94.95	7126	90.81	-4.4	101.6
Home Economics	TX	211	78.08	435	81.29	407	92.92	323	84.86	-8.7	108.7
Industrial Arts	TT	23	46.11	77	66.08	77	109.80	67	93.09	-15.2	201.9
Language and Literature	P	7,664	103.12	10,276	81.88	11,922	92.77	3911	154.66	5.9	104.7
Law	K	2,433	147.66	2,650	147.22	3,256	146.01	377	108.73	-3.9	121.6

Library and Information Science	Z	387	89.43	378	111.23	383	113.09	12413	89.81	-3.2	87.1
Mathematics and Computer Science	QA	5,000	112.65	2,231	128.80	3,376	131.14	3422	133.85	2.1	118.8
Medicine	R	6,404	134.60	5,741	164.83	6,297	153.95	6154	154.54	0.4	114.8
Military and Naval Science	U-V	487	105.07	598	93.88	663	89.29	634	89.45	0.2	85.1
Philosophy and Religion	B	4,262	110.31	5,189	94.03	5,983	96.13	6599	97.18	1.1	88.1
Physical Education and Recreation	GV	791	76.57	1,257	89.00	1,437	91.84	1433	82.64	-10.0	107.9
Physics and Astronomy	QB	1,288	147.50	1,078	145.53	1,154	148.24	1171	157.26	6.1	106.6
Political Science	J	2,638	110.10	2,738	110.76	2,944	114.09	2938	111.17	-2.6	101.0
Psychology	BF	1,062	91.35	1,342	95.97	1,460	110.12	1466	108.17	-1.8	118.4
Science (general)	Q	462	122.51	495	125.52	874	140.77	893	139.98	-0.6	114.3
Sociology	HM	4,520	103.73	5,140	103.29	5,803	113.97	5838	107.97	-5.3	104.1
Zoology	QH; QL-R	2,336	164.82	1,655	152.48	1,803	160.50	1707	153.42	-4.4	93.1
Totals and Averages		63,812	$116.25	68,212	$114.95	78,396	$120.64	81043	$118.50	-1.8%	101.9

Compiled by Stephen Bosch, University of Arizona, from electronic data provided by ProQuest (formerly Ingrams Content Group-Coutts Information Services) and GOBI Library Solutions from EBSCO (formerly YBP Library Services). The data represent all e-book titles treated for all approval plan customers serviced by the vendors. This table covers titles published or distributed in the United States and Canada during the calendar years listed. It is important to note that e-books that were released in a given year may have been published in print much earlier.

Table 4B / North American Academic Textbooks: Average Prices and Price Indexes, 2019–2021
(Index Base: 2010 = 100)

Subject Area	LC Class	2010		2019		2020		2021			
		Titles	Average Price	Titles	Average Price	Titles	Average Price	Titles	Average Price	Percent Change 2020–2021	Index
Agriculture	S	49	$115.80	65	$133.22	98	$138.63	59	$132.09	-4.7%	97.1
Anthropology	GN	35	90.65	54	103.15	47	99.66	39	92.46	-7.2	102.0
Botany	QK	11	109.52	8	119.10	21	143.66	18	144.38	0.5	131.8
Business and Economics	H	694	121.36	1,058	121.32	1,073	117.37	972	130.19	10.9	107.3
Chemistry	QD	94	134.59	109	130.15	131	157.96	92	174.76	10.6	129.8
Education	L	271	87.75	525	83.92	419	95.97	334	101.64	5.9	115.8
Engineering and Technology	T	744	116.38	1,142	141.11	1,229	146.31	936	143.21	-2.1	123.1
Fine and Applied Arts	M-N	73	93.33	171	104.39	142	96.90	112	115.12	18.8	123.4
General Works	A	0	0.00	6	114.52	7	109.84	7	85.84	-21.9	110.2
Geography	G	78	105.21	127	121.51	101	128.18	109	117.91	-8.0	112.1
Geology	QE	36	117.97	46	165.25	36	152.19	37	165.20	8.6	140.0
History	C-D-E-F	81	81.49	158	91.78	133	96.79	145	103.14	6.6	126.6
Home Economics	TX	39	89.52	39	145.85	35	146.18	20	178.06	21.8	198.9
Industrial Arts	TT	14	84.72	6	99.87	8	87.86	7	36.82	-58.1	43.5
Language and Literature	P	309	77.71	559	89.22	561	103.08	352	129.18	4.7	126.5

Subject	LC Class										
Law	K	242	102.09	464	120.14	393	123.34	31	77.47	-9.2	110.2
Library and Information Science	Z	19	70.30	33	70.01	26	85.31	425	103.43	0.3	133.1
Mathematics and Computer Sscience	QA	683	96.11	997	117.72	1,073	119.49	914	128.81	7.8	134.0
Medicine	F	1512	126.75	2,153	138.65	1,832	138.27	1,620	157.76	14.1	124.5
Military and Naval Science	U-V	3	122.65	27	138.42	25	154.76	14	115.39	-25.4	94.1
Philosophy and Religion	B	101	72.13	179	70.29	141	69.93	149	81.22	16.1	112.6
Physical Education and Recreation	GV	51	79.39	129	96.87	98	110.60	110	112.72	1.9	142.0
Physics and Astronomy	QB	243	107.38	402	131.64	390	130.44	392	129.12	-1.0	120.2
Political Science	J	110	80.09	267	92.27	216	93.41	205	116.91	25.2	146.0
Psychology	BF	138	95.95	210	120.23	167	109.64	150	143.00	30.4	149.0
Science (general)	Q	33	97.14	79	95.33	100	111.17	74	126.97	14.2	130.7
Sociology	HM	353	86.97	674	102.18	507	104.30	427	112.75	8.1	129.6
Zoology	QH, QL-QR	227	109.82	354	139.56	335	138.44	267	136.79	-1.2	124.6
Totals and Averages		6,243	$107.94	10,041	$120.16	9,344	$123.49	8,017	$131.87	6.8%	122.2

Compiled by Stephen Bosch, University of Arizona, from electronic data provided by ProQuest (formerly Ingrams Content Group-Coutts Information Services) and GOBI Library Solutions from EBSCO (formerly YBP Library Services). The data represent all textbook titles treated for all approval plan customers serviced by the vendors. This table covers titles published or distributed in the United States and Canada during the calendar years listed.

(continued from page 319)

several years, so it is a good summary of changes in the academic book market since 2010. Direct comparisons with earlier versions published before 2014 show variations since the number of titles treated and their average prices have changed. This is especially true for those versions published before 2009. The data for the current indexes are supplied by ProQuest Books (formerly Ingrams Content Group-Coutts Information Services) and by GOBI Library Solutions from EBSCO (formerly YBP Library Services). Prior to ProQuest/Coutts supplying data, the book pricing data were obtained from Blackwell Book Services and YBP.

Over time, the data and the data suppliers have changed due to changes in the industry. Compared with earlier versions, the North American Academic Books Price Index now contains many more titles in the source data, affecting the index considerably. ProQuest Books treats far more titles in its approval programs than Blackwell Book Services. For indexes published before 2009, Blackwell was a supplier of data for the index. Blackwell was purchased in 2009 by YBP, and the vendor data used to create the index changed. After 2009 the data came from Ingram (Coutts) and YBP. Prior to 2009 the data came from Blackwell and YBP. With recent changes at both ProQuest and GOBI, there have been changes to how the annual price data are pulled for books. Starting in 2016 each vendor supplied data in separate files for print, e-books, and textbooks. Before 2016 this was not the case, and this change caused large variations in the numbers of titles in the tables and the average prices. The data for 2014 were normalized in 2016 to conform to the current sets of data, so the numbers of titles and prices have changed from those published in 2015 and previous years. In the future, this approach to gathering the data, separate data files for print, electronic, and texts, will improve the consistency of the data, especially for e-books. Another major change was made in 2017, when the base index year was moved to 2010 to provide consistency across the various indexes published by the Library Materials Price Index Committee.

The average price for books in the North American Academic Books Price Index (Table 4) saw a small decrease in 2021, dropping by close to 1 percent. The previous year showed a spike after several years of relatively flat increases, mainly due to the index's growth in the number of e-books in the index. In 2021 there were not similar large swings in the number of print books/e-books, so the price changes were less pronounced. The overall number of titles has been volatile, going from 147,108 in 2018 and jumping up to 164,070 in 2019 and at 168,338 in 2020. The number of titles in 2021 was just slightly higher, 169,954. The overall growth in available titles and increasing prices are pressure points for library budgets. The decrease in price in 2021 was primarily due to increases in the number of titles available in the lower price ranges. These areas showed growth in numbers, 3,500, while the number of books in the highest price ranges decreased by close to 2,000 titles. Overall, the ratio of print to electronic has been growing, with e-books being 43 percent of the titles in 2018, dropping slightly to 42 percent in 2019 and increasing to 47 percent in 2020 and 48 percent in 2021.

Since 2008 two additional indexes have been available, one for e-books only (Table 4A) and another for textbooks (Table 4B). Based on users' high interest, the indexes continue to be published. In 2017 the base index was set to 2010. It has always been assumed that e-books are more expensive than their print counterparts in the academic market. The cheaper versions of e-books available to consumers through such channels as Amazon and Google Books are not available to libraries at comparable prices if they are available at all in the library market. At best, the academic pricing will match the print price for single-user license models, with multiuser models far more expensive than print. The e-book index points out this price difference: The average price of an e-book in 2021 was $118.50, while the average price for all books was $102.98. The average price of a print book drops to $88.07 if the e-books are removed from the overall index. The high price for e-books is not that surprising, as most pricing models for academic e-books generally charge a higher price than the list print price for access to the e-books. Another factor is that STEM publishing has migrated more quickly to electronic formats for books, with social science and humanities slower to adopt digital publishing. STEM books have always been more expensive than other subjects, contributing to the higher cost of e-books.

Over the past two years, it is becoming common practice for single-user licenses to be priced at the same price as print. Multiuser licenses are still significantly more expensive than print. Responding to customer demands, publishers and vendors offer e-books on multiple platforms with multiple pricing models; consequently, there can be multiple prices for the same title. Only the first license level (normally single user) is included in the data for these indexes. Where multiple prices are available for different use models, the lowest price is included in the index. Because electronic access is a major market trend, it is appropriate to have e-books as a separate index. It is important to note that the e-book market is rapidly changing. It is also important to note that by using the lowest price available for e-books, this approach may artificially keep the average price of e-books low for libraries that generally buy multiuser licenses. As with the overall market, prices declined for e-books in 2021, -1.8 percent, driven by a decline in the number of titles in the high end of the price range.

The cost of textbooks has been a hot topic on many college campuses. The index for textbooks (Table 4B) documents price changes in this area. The data show that textbooks tend to be more expensive than other books, with an average price of $131.87 in 2021. This represents a 6.8 percent increase. Over the past two years, the price has increased from $117.79–$131.87. This price increase is bad news for students, as textbooks remain more expensive than regular print or e-books, and the prices are not moderating. Please note that this index does not measure the impact of new programs like inclusive access for textbooks. This index measures only publishers' retail prices. The flat increases in previous years seemed to be a positive trend as it seemed textbook publishers were responding to market pressure and scaled back large price increases. That ended in 2020 as the pandemic market showed close to a 5 percent increase and then nearly a 7 percent increase in 2021. Textbooks are expensive, and the prices are not dropping significantly to make required reading less expensive for students. Pressure on the textbook market from alternative sources like rental services for either print or electronic versions or resales of used copies may have slowed price increases but has not resulted in an overall significant price drop. Electronic versions are included in the textbook index, so migration to the electronic format does not seem to be lowering costs. This is not much consolation for cash-strapped students.

The average price of North American academic books in 2021 (Table 4) decreased by 0.9 percent compared with the 2020 average price. This is mainly due to a 3,500 increase in books treated in the lower part of the price bands (below $60) and a decrease of -2,000 of the most expensive books (see Figure 1). In other words, fewer titles costing more than $120 and greater numbers of titles costing less than $60 helped to drive prices down in 2021.

One thing that stands out when looking at the data by price band is that the highest end of the price bands ($120 and up) continues to have a huge impact on the costs for books. The impact on pricing from the titles in the $120 and up price band is confirmed when looking at the actual dollar values in groups (sum of all prices for titles in the group). The increase in the top end of the index was the main component in the overall changes for 2017–2020, and the minimal growth led to a decrease in 2021. In 2021 the impact of the highest range could not offset the greater growth in the lower ranges. In 2020 the drop in the low-priced books and the increase in the most expensive books resulted in an 8.3 percent increase that year. Although the $0–$30 price area has the second largest number of titles, the total cost remains the smallest portion as far as total cost (sum of all prices) in the index. Again, changes in the number of titles available are a significant driver in increasing or decreasing costs. The average price remains constant within the price bands except for the area with prices over $120. Unlike serials, where inflation in price drives higher costs, the data show that changes in the number of titles were the primary driver in escalating costs, not inflationary price increases. See Figures 2 and 3.

The data used for this index are derived from all titles treated by the ProQuest Books (formerly Ingrams Content Group-Coutts Information Services)

(text continues on page 332)

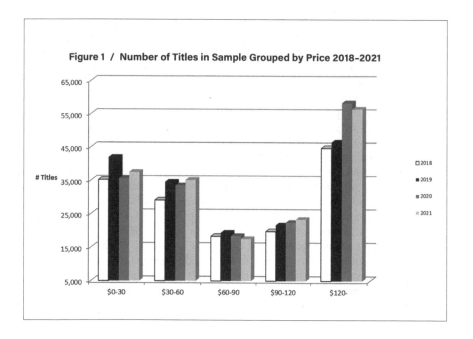

Figure 1 / Number of Titles in Sample Grouped by Price 2018–2021

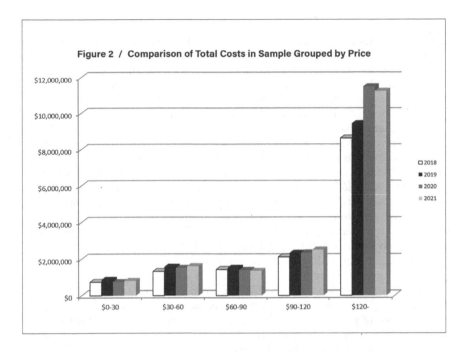

Figure 2 / Comparison of Total Costs in Sample Grouped by Price

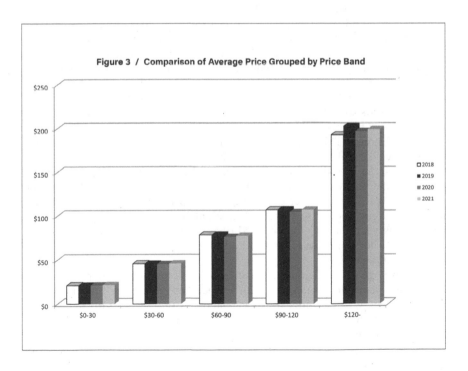

Figure 3 / Comparison of Average Price Grouped by Price Band

(continued from page 330)

and GOBI Library Solutions in their approval plans during the calendar years listed. The index includes e-books and paperback editions as supplied by these vendors, and this inclusion of paperbacks and e-books as distributed as part of the approval plans has influenced the prices reflected in the index figures. The index includes the broadest categories of materials, as that is the marketplace in which academic libraries operate, and the index attempts to chart price changes impacting that market.

Price changes vary, as always, among subject areas. There were several double-digit increases in subject areas this year, and two areas showed price decreases. The 2021 data indicate that those with the largest increases were not concentrated in one area but included all broad subject areas. Overall, prices for books in the STM subjects are still more expensive than the humanities. STM publishers have tended to be early adopters of e-books and have been publishing e-books for a while. The high average prices in the sciences reflect the availability and higher pricing of e-books and the overall high cost of STM books.

It is good to remember that price indexes become less accurate at describing price with smaller samples. Industrial arts is a small sample (169 titles) and showed a very large price drop of 7.7 percent in 2021, but to conclude that all books in that area decreased at like amounts is incorrect. In small samples, inclusion/exclusion of just a few expensive items or low-priced items can have a major impact on prices for the category. The decreases in industrial arts, for example, were due to fewer expensive titles. Because the sample is very small, fewer expensive books changed, causing the overall price to decline.

The U.S. College Books Price Index (Table 5), prepared by Narda Tafuri, contains average price and index number data for 2019–2021 and the percentage change in price between 2020–2021. The index base year was reset to 2010 in 2017. Previous instances of this table have an index base year of 1989.

Data for the index were compiled from 3,623 reviews of books published in *Choice* during 2021. An additional nine print titles reviewed in *Choice* were omitted from the analysis due to price ($500 or more). These books were removed from the analysis so that the average prices were not skewed. The total number of books reviewed for this analysis has increased by 3.46 percent from the previous year's 3,502 books. This index includes some paperback prices; as a result, the average price of books is less than if only hardcover books were included.

In 2021 the overall average price for books in the humanities, sciences, and social and behavioral sciences (including reference books) was $88.04, an increase of 6.10 percent over the average 2020 price of $82.98. The average price of reference books was $125.97, a slight increase of 5.38 percent from the previous year's average price of $119.54. Excluding reference books, the average 2021 book price was $86.85, or a 6.30 percent increase over the average 2020 price of $81.70.

The average 2021 price for humanities titles increased by 6.92 percent over the previous year. The average price for science and technology titles increased by 6.54 percent, while the price for social and behavioral sciences titles increased by 7.52 percent. Since 2010 an overall book price increase of 32.85 percent when reference books are included.

(text continues on page 344)

Table 5 / U.S. College Books: Average Prices and Price Indexes, 2019–2021
Index Base: 2010 = 100

Subject	2010		2019				2020				2021				% Change 2020–2021
	Titles	Average Price	Titles	Average Price	Indexed to 2010	Indexed to 2018	Titles	Average Price	Indexed to 2010	Indexed to 2019	Titles	Average Price	Indexed to 2010	Indexed to 2020	
HUMANITIES	91	$58.99	47	$81.60	138.33	114.05	43	$72.40	122.73	88.73	41	$89.23	151.26	123.25	23.25%
Art and Architecture	149	61.69	117	70.57	114.39	106.91	90	67.44	109.32	95.56	73	77.62	125.82	115.09	15.09
Fine Arts	92	67.13	54	61.24	91.23	100.81	51	59.71	88.95	97.50	41	58.23	86.74	97.52	-2.48
Architecture	48	61.53	39	75.49	122.69	115.25	20	76.47	124.28	101.29	26	80.99	131.63	105.91	5.91
Photography	28	53.02	6	73.33	138.31	118.48	15	58.98	111.24	80.43	13	60.52	114.15	102.61	2.61
Communication	112	59.97	52	72.94	121.63	104.92	48	78.05	130.15	107.01	63	95.56	159.35	122.43	22.43
Language and Literature	94	68.66	82	82.60	120.30	93.88	58	84.00	122.34	101.69	69	82.56	120.24	98.29	-1.71
African and Middle Eastern	24	62.28	6	64.17	103.03	82.98	8	80.49	129.24	125.43	9	84.88	136.29	105.45	5.45
Asian and Oceanian	24	71.99	17	78.53	109.08	102.20	12	70.08	97.35	89.24	10	91.40	126.96	130.42	30.42
Classical	24	78.76	28	89.41	113.52	95.43	19	72.96	92.64	81.60	26	108.41	137.65	148.59	48.59
English and American	394	61.96	227	80.68	130.21	102.18	167	80.17	129.39	99.37	181	80.65	130.16	100.60	0.60
Germanic	22	70.36	21	87.55	124.43	107.91	13	84.28	119.78	96.26	23	85.47	121.48	101.41	1.41
Romance	70	59.00	32	79.94	135.49	98.84	25	74.03	125.47	92.61	26	78.61	133.24	106.19	6.19
Slavic	32	35.95	17	81.60	226.98	102.00	14	62.91	174.99	77.10	13	84.22	234.27	133.87	33.87
Performing Arts	30	61.97	14	84.45	136.28	109.85	8	83.74	147.14	99.16	13	76.83	123.98	91.75	-8.25
Film	130	64.13	114	89.53	139.61	109.14	73	91.18	123.34	101.84	69	85.17	132.81	93.41	-6.59
Music	123	61.01	93	76.14	124.80	111.61	61	79.10	153.01	103.89	108	79.95	131.04	101.07	1.07
Theater and Dance	45	62.38	44	80.01	128.26	105.65	21	93.35	146.55	116.67	26	104.41	167.38	111.85	11.85
Philosophy	198	63.45	232	74.13	116.83	97.78	119	91.42	122.47	123.32	167	92.74	146.16	101.44	1.44
Religion	272	57.18	196	69.99	122.40	105.37	150	77.71	137.83	111.03	149	82.72	144.67	106.45	6.45
TOTAL HUMANITIES	2,002	$61.60	1,438	$76.90	124.84	104.61	1,015	$78.81	127.94	102.48	1,146	$84.26	136.79	106.92	6.92

Table 5 / U.S. College Books: Average Prices and Price Indexes, 2019–2021
Index Base: 2010 = 100 (cont.)

Subject	2010		2019				2020				2021				
	Titles	Average Price	Titles	Average Price	Indexed to 2010	Indexed to 2018	Titles	Average Price	Indexed to 2010	Indexed to 2019	Titles	Average Price	Indexed to 2010	Indexed to 2020	% Change 2020–2021
SCIENCE AND TECHNOLOGY	110	$58.09	95	$60.44	104.05	102.77	35	$65.26	112.34	107.97	28	$85.68	147.50	131.29	31.29
History of Science and Technology	78	54.10	59	57.41	106.12	98.29	42	74.00	136.78	128.90	25	67.12	124.07	90.70	-9.30
Astronautics and Astronomy	63	55.58	41	54.00	97.16	104.01	21	69.65	125.31	128.98	14	63.52	114.29	91.20	-8.80
Biology	151	72.74	95	72.01	99.00	120.92	60	98.09	134.85	136.22	49	78.80	108.33	80.33	-19.67
Botany	85	85.09	70	56.79	66.74	94.68	20	94.43	110.98	166.28	7	139.41	163.84	147.63	47.63
Zoology	121	64.33	96	62.41	97.02	102.63	43	84.71	131.68	135.73	39	91.09	141.60	107.53	7.53
Chemistry	42	115.42	13	102.74	89.01	100.94	12	141.21	122.34	137.44	17	152.56	132.18	108.04	8.04
Earth Science	102	63.33	68	74.46	117.57	112.16	36	78.65	124.19	105.63	34	118.49	187.10	150.65	50.65
Engineering	103	88.38	43	80.28	90.84	85.85	56	136.71	154.68	170.29	35	143.04	161.85	104.63	4.63
Health Sciences	146	56.14	195	69.78	124.30	104.51	129	98.85	176.08	141.66	99	98.24	174.99	99.38	-0.62
Information and Computer Science	83	73.50	66	77.36	105.25	130.21	45	92.86	126.34	120.04	44	120.23	163.58	129.47	29.47
Mathematics	108	61.97	74	81.00	130.71	104.23	51	94.45	152.41	116.60	56	110.54	178.38	117.04	17.04
Physics	50	54.74	39	63.49	115.98	91.33	34	127.39	232.72	200.65	38	94.96	173.47	74.54	-25.46
Sports and Physical Education	67	54.06	87	62.40	115.43	112.62	43	71.78	132.78	115.03	27	76.63	141.75	106.76	6.76
TOTAL SCIENCE	1,309	$67.13	1,041	$67.83	101.04	104.11	627	$95.09	141.65	140.19	512	$101.31	150.92	106.54	6.54
SOCIAL AND BEHAVIORAL SCIENCES	129	$66.32	43	$70.20	105.85	90.55	118	$83.26	125.54	118.60	115	$82.53	124.44	99.12	-0.88
Anthropology	139	63.60	95	89.67	140.99	112.96	117	93.06	146.32	103.78	113	96.14	151.16	103.31	3.31
Business Management and Labor	150	58.00	69	53.52	92.28	103.86	68	68.31	117.78	127.63	84	85.98	148.24	125.87	25.87
Economics	270	61.16	105	60.99	99.72	107.99	70	69.38	113.44	113.76	41	82.80	135.38	119.34	19.34
Education	158	62.56	43	72.74	116.27	98.06	123	82.02	131.11	112.76	144	88.41	141.32	107.79	7.79
History, Geography and Area Studies	154	58.16	63	58.55	100.67	88.69	89	84.21	144.79	143.83	115	76.84	132.12	91.25	-8.75
Africa	38	69.05	17	72.77	105.39	106.70	37	91.73	132.85	126.05	40	98.23	142.26	107.09	7.09

Ancient History	49	57.90	39	86.19	148.86	100.22	37	79.90	138.00	92.70	32	87.34	150.85	109.31	9.31
Asia and Oceania	72	60.88	71	64.47	105.90	87.65	75	84.90	139.45	131.69	81	91.83	150.84	108.16	8.16
Central and Eastern Europe	56	66.53	31	67.21	101.02	88.24	38	80.53	121.04	119.82	56	91.64	137.74	113.80	13.80
Latin America and Caribbean	54	59.31	49	76.56	129.08	101.75	44	80.26	135.32	104.83	44	90.58	152.72	112.86	12.86
Middle East and North Africa	43	65.57	28	66.12	100.84	95.00	69	81.47	124.25	123.22	56	91.08	138.90	111.80	11.80
North America	444	45.50	245	48.96	107.60	89.64	184	58.60	128.79	119.69	201	55.86	122.77	95.32	-4.68
United Kingdom	80	69.56	39	56.44	81.14	79.85	46	75.65	108.76	134.04	52	71.82	103.25	94.94	-5.06
Western Europe	138	59.14	74	61.88	104.63	72.69	65	78.91	133.43	127.52	74	80.57	136.24	102.10	2.10
Political Science	4	84.36	58	74.12	87.86	118.67	26	81.20	96.25	109.55	59	96.39	114.26	118.71	18.71
Comparative Politics	183	66.34	115	71.06	107.11	105.07	38	89.07	134.26	125.34	26	97.31	146.68	109.25	9.25
International Relations	213	65.64	91	57.20	87.14	92.89	67	98.19	149.59	171.66	90	100.15	152.57	102.00	2.00
Political Theory	73	56.74	104	72.32	127.46	97.76	45	79.02	139.27	109.26	48	95.42	168.17	120.75	20.75
U.S. Politics	253	53.03	125	60.62	114.31	95.52	122	61.61	116.18	101.63	82	65.84	124.16	106.87	6.87
Psychology	126	60.55	189	81.34	134.34	113.05	82	77.96	128.75	95.84	90	86.19	142.35	110.56	10.56
Sociology	226	60.71	167	71.12	117.15	97.81	181	83.50	137.54	117.41	212	93.78	154.47	112.31	12.31
TOTAL BEHAVIORAL SCIENCES	3,052	$59.09	1,860	$66.73	112.93	99.18	1,741	$78.56	132.95	117.73	1,855	$84.47	142.95	107.52	7.52
TOTAL GENERAL, HUMANITIES, SCIENCE AND SOCIAL SCIENCE (without Reference)	6,363	$61.53	4,339	$70.36	114.35	102.45	3,383	$81.70	132.78	116.12	3,513	$86.85	141.15	106.30	6.30
REFERENCE															
General	29	$61.17	17	$118.52	193.76	76.60	13	$131.30	214.65	110.78	4	$52.74	86.22	40.17	-59.83
Humanities	128	117.12	45	104.93	89.59	79.10	32	107.96	92.18	102.89	23	125.43	107.10	116.18	16.18
Library and Information Sciences	n.a.	n.a.	32	80.48	n.a.	n.a.	21	75.32	n.a.	n.a.	25	68.14	n.a.	90.47	-9.53
Science and Technology	76	133.19	34	140.05	105.15	84.93	7	186.00	139.65	132.81	8	98.11	73.66	52.75	-47.25
Social and Behavioral Sciences	216	152.91	86	156.80	102.54	105.11	46	134.35	87.86	85.68	50	165.44	108.19	123.14	23.14
TOTAL REFERENCE	449	$133.44	214	$128.78	96.51	87.75	119	$119.54	89.58	92.82	110	$125.97	94.40	105.38	5.38
GRAND TOTALS	6,812	$66.27	4,553	$73.11	110.32	101.26	3,502	$82.98	125.22	113.50	3,623	$88.04	132.85	106.10	6.1%

Compiled by Narda Tafuri, Retired, University of Scranton

Table 6 / U.S. Mass Market Paperback Books: Average Prices and Price Indexes, 2018–2021

Index Base: 2010 = 100

BISAC Category	2010 Average Price	2018 Final			2019 Final			2020 Preliminary			2021 Preliminary		
		Volumes	Average Price	Index	Volumes	Average Price	Index	Volumes	Average Price	Index	Volumes	Average Price	Index
Antiques and Collectibles	$8.77	n.a.	n.a.	n.a.	n.a.	n.a.	n.a.	n.a.	n.a.	n.a.	n.a.	n.a.	n.a.
Architecture	n.a.	n.a.	n.a.	n.a.	n.a.	n.a.	n.a.	n.a.	n.a.	n.a.	n.a.	n.a.	n.a.
Art	n.a.	n.a.	n.a.	n.a.	n.a.	n.a.	n.a.	n.a.	n.a.	n.a.	n.a.	n.a.	n.a.
Bibles	n.a.	n.a.	n.a.	n.a.	n.a.	n.a.	n.a.	n.a.	n.a.	n.a.	n.a.	n.a.	n.a.
Biography and Autobiography	7.51	8	$9.87	131.4	3	$9.99	133.0	3	$9.32	124.1	3	$10.32	137.4
Body, Mind and Spirit	7.99	n.a.	n.a.	n.a.	n.a.	n.a.	n.a.	n.a.	n.a.	n.a.	n.a.	n.a.	n.a.
Business and Economics	9.32	3	8.99	96.5	n.a.	n.a.	n.a.	n.a.	n.a.	n.a.	n.a.	n.a.	n.a.
Children	6.22	230	8.05	129.4	187	8.58	137.9	222	8.78	141.2	213	9.04	145.3
Comics and Graphic Novels	n.a.	n.a.	n.a.	n.a.	n.a.	n.a.	n.a.	n.a.	n.a.	n.a.	n.a.	n.a.	n.a.
Computers	n.a.	n.a.	n.a.	n.a.	n.a.	n.a.	n.a.	n.a.	n.a.	n.a.	n.a.	n.a.	n.a.
Cooking	n.a.	n.a.	n.a.	n.a.	n.a.	n.a.	n.a.	n.a.	n.a.	n.a.	n.a.	n.a.	n.a.
Crafts and Hobbies	n.a.	n.a.	n.a.	n.a.	n.a.	n.a.	n.a.	n.a.	n.a.	n.a.	n.a.	n.a.	n.a.
Design	n.a.	n.a.	n.a.	n.a.	n.a.	n.a.	n.a.	n.a.	n.a.	n.a.	n.a.	n.a.	n.a.
Drama	6.30	n.a.	n.a.	n.a.	n.a.	n.a.	n.a.	n.a.	n.a.	n.a.	n.a.	n.a.	n.a.
Education	n.a.	n.a.	n.a.	n.a.	n.a.	n.a.	n.a.	n.a.	n.a.	n.a.	n.a.	n.a.	n.a.
Family and Relationships	7.99	n.a.	n.a.	n.a.	n.a.	n.a.	n.a.	2	9.49	118.8	n.a.	n.a.	n.a.
Fiction	6.80	2,737	7.27	106.9	2,468	7.45	109.6	2,256	7.65	112.5	2,228	7.81	114.9
Foreign Language Study	7.08	n.a.	n.a.	n.a.	n.a.	n.a.	n.a.	n.a.	n.a.	n.a.	n.a.	n.a.	n.a.
Games and Activities	n.a.	1	8.50	n.a.	n.a.	n.a.	n.a.	n.a.	n.a.	n.a.	n.a.	n.a.	n.a.
Gardening	n.a.	n.a.	n.a.	n.a.	n.a.	n.a.	n.a.	n.a.	n.a.	n.a.	n.a.	n.a.	n.a.
Health and Fitness	7.92	3	8.66	109.3	1	13.99	176.6	n.a.	n.a.	n.a.	2	8.99	113.5
History	9.95	3	9.99	100.4	4	8.99	90.4	4	9.99	100.4	2	9.99	100.4
House and Home	n.a.	n.a.	n.a.	n.a.	n.a.	n.a.	n.a.	n.a.	n.a.	n.a.	n.a.	n.a.	n.a.
Humor	n.a.	2	12.49	n.a.	n.a.	n.a.	n.a.	n.a.	n.a.	n.a.	n.a.	n.a.	n.a.

Language Arts and Disciplines	13.25	n.a.	n.a.	n.a.	1	7.99	60.3	n.a.	n.a.	n.a.	n.a.	n.a.	n.a.
Law	n.a.	n.a.	n.a.	n.a.	n.a.	n.a.	n.a.	n.a.	n.a.	n.a.	n.a.	n.a.	n.a.
Literary Collections	5.95	n.a.	n.a.	n.a.	n.a.	n.a.	n.a.	n.a.	n.a.	n.a.	n.a.	n.a.	n.a.
Literary Criticism	7.99	n.a.	n.a.	n.a.	n.a.	n.a.	n.a.	n.a.	n.a.	n.a.	n.a.	n.a.	n.a.
Mathematics	n.a.	n.a.	n.a.	n.a.	n.a.	n.a.	n.a.	n.a.	n.a.	n.a.	n.a.	n.a.	n.a.
Medical	8.99	n.a.	n.a.	n.a.	n.a.	n.a.	n.a.	n.a.	n.a.	n.a.	n.a.	n.a.	n.a.
Music	n.a.	n.a.	n.a.	n.a.	n.a.	n.a.	n.a.	n.a.	n.a.	n.a.	n.a.	n.a.	n.a.
Nature	n.a.	n.a.	n.a.	n.a.	n.a.	n.a.	n.a.	n.a.	n.a.	n.a.	n.a.	n.a.	n.a.
Performing Arts	9.99	n.a.	n.a.	n.a.	1	n.a.	n.a.	n.a.	n.a.	n.a.	n.a.	n.a.	n.a.
Pets	7.99	n.a.	n.a.	n.a.	n.a.	8.99	89.99	n.a.	n.a.	n.a.	n.a.	n.a.	n.a.
Philosophy	6.47	n.a.	n.a.	n.a.	n.a.	n.a.	n.a.	2	3.99	61.7	n.a.	n.a.	n.a.
Photography	n.a.	n.a.	n.a.	n.a.	n.a.	n.a.	n.a.	n.a.	n.a.	n.a.	n.a.	n.a.	n.a.
Poetry	7.95	n.a.	n.a.	n.a.	1	n.a.	n.a.	n.a.	n.a.	n.a.	1	3.99	50.2
Political Science	7.97	1	9.99	125.3	1	9.99	125.3	n.a.	n.a.	n.a.	n.a.	n.a.	n.a.
Psychology	n.a.	1	13.99	n.a.	n.a.	4.99	n.a.	n.a.	n.a.	n.a.	n.a.	n.a.	n.a.
Reference	7.99	n.a.	n.a.	n.a.	n.a.	n.a.	n.a.	1	8.99	112.5	3	7.5	93.9
Religion	7.99	n.a.	n.a.	n.a.	n.a.	n.a.	n.a.	n.a.	n.a.	n.a.	n.a.	n.a.	n.a.
Science	n.a.	n.a.	n.a.	n.a.	n.a.	n.a.	n.a.	n.a.	n.a.	n.a.	n.a.	n.a.	n.a.
Self-help	7.99	6	13.99	175.1	4	12.74	159.4	n.a.	n.a.	n.a.	3	7.99	100.0
Social Science	n.a.	n.a.	n.a.	n.a.	n.a.	n.a.	n.a.	n.a.	n.a.	n.a.	n.a.	n.a.	n.a.
Sports and Recreation	7.99	n.a.	n.a.	n.a.	n.a.	n.a.	n.a.	n.a.	n.a.	n.a.	1	9.99	125
Study Aids	n.a.	n.a.	n.a.	n.a.	n.a.	n.a.	n.a.	n.a.	n.a.	n.a.	n.a.	n.a.	n.a.
Technology and Engineering	n.a.	n.a.	n.a.	n.a.	n.a.	n.a.	n.a.	n.a.	n.a.	n.a.	n.a.	n.a.	n.a.
Transportation	n.a.	n.a.	n.a.	n.a.	n.a.	n.a.	n.a.	n.a.	n.a.	n.a.	n.a.	n.a.	n.a.
Travel	n.a.	n.a.	n.a.	n.a.	n.a.	n.a.	n.a.	n.a.	n.a.	n.a.	n.a.	n.a.	n.a.
True Crime	7.64	7	8.42	110.2	6	8.82	115.4	5	8.99	117.7	4	9.74	127.5
Young Adult	8.13	26	11.80	145.1	36	9.71	119.4	47	11.97	147.2	33	10.93	134.4
Totals and Averages	$6.83	3,028	$7.40	108.3	2,713	$7.58	111.0	2,542	$7.83	114.6	2,493	$7.97	116.7

Compiled by Narda Tafuri, Retired, University of Scranton, from data supplied by Baker & Taylor

n.a. = not available

Table 7 / U.S. Paperback Books (Excluding Mass Market): Average Prices and Price Indexes, 2018–2021

Index Base: 2010 = 100

BISAC Category	2010 Average Price	2018 Final Volumes	2018 Final Average Price	2018 Final Index	2019 Final Volumes	2019 Final Average Price	2019 Final Index	2020 Preliminary Volumes	2020 Preliminary Average Price	2020 Preliminary Index	2021 Preliminary Volumes	2021 Preliminary Average Price	2021 Preliminary Index
Antiques and Collectibles	$25.53	89	$42.24	165.5	87	$41.73	163.5	79	$44.04	172.5	70	$43.41	170.0
Architecture	45.31	742	49.36	108.9	914	50.45	111.3	892	49.03	108.2	797	51.76	114.2
Art	38.25	1,734	40.36	105.5	1,759	39.55	103.4	1,581	39.75	103.9	1,450	40.56	106.1
Bibles	38.66	709	45.42	117.5	630	48.55	125.6	485	56.61	146.4	515	58.74	151.9
Biography and Autobiography	20.35	2,581	20.67	101.6	2,424	20.81	102.3	2,290	21.11	103.7	2,415	21.48	105.6
Body, Mind and Spirit	18.03	761	18.22	101.1	826	19.05	105.7	819	18.93	105.0	843	19.92	110.5
Business and Economics	69.30	7,064	84.06	121.3	6,730	73.39	105.9	6,123	68.71	99.2	5,985	69.98	101.0
Children	10.42	11,651	12.82	123.1	12,027	12.86	123.4	10,428	11.64	111.7	10,035	12.19	117.0
Comics and Graphic Novels	16.11	2,331	19.13	118.8	2,196	20.64	128.1	1,903	18.87	117.2	2,336	18.52	115.0
Computers	70.42	3,408	104.73	148.7	3,387	102.85	146.0	2,958	80.96	115.0	2,660	79.68	113.1
Cooking	19.95	932	21.17	106.1	832	22.13	110.9	805	21.34	106.9	754	21.36	107.1
Crafts and Hobbies	19.34	693	21.54	111.4	577	22.39	115.8	573	21.68	112.1	495	22.14	114.5
Design	63.98	234	41.19	64.4	253	46.01	71.9	210	36.81	57.5	221	38.94	60.9
Drama	18.95	555	20.72	109.3	463	23.02	121.5	393	21.72	114.6	399	19.60	103.4
Education	42.98	4,511	63.10	146.8	4,852	131.68	306.4	3,716	104.47	243.1	3,364	52.97	123.2
Family and Relationships	18.72	590	22.15	118.3	635	21.97	117.4	610	21.26	113.6	605	21.17	113.1
Fiction	17.99	10,427	17.59	97.8	10,014	17.59	97.8	9,107	17.64	98.1	10,683	17.74	98.6
Foreign Language Study	31.33	836	45.05	143.8	1,012	42.09	134.3	923	42.84	136.7	478	46.06	147.0
Games and Activities	16.57	699	17.41	105.1	635	18.04	108.9	671	17.98	108.5	691	18.17	109.7
Gardening	23.45	120	21.39	91.2	126	22.45	95.7	99	23.30	99.4	115	24.64	105.1
Health and Fitness	26.95	1,057	31.05	115.2	968	32.89	122.0	928	32.02	118.8	932	32.23	119.6
History	35.79	6,347	40.05	111.9	6,654	40.45	113.0	6,500	39.82	111.3	5,918	39.24	109.6
House and Home	21.19	87	22.50	106.2	109	24.31	114.7	66	22.98	108.4	74	25.33	119.5
Humor	14.37	263	15.50	107.9	268	15.69	109.2	210	16.95	117.9	208	16.83	117.1

Category													
Language Arts and Disciplines	64.46	1,627	61.43	95.3	1,704	57.54	89.3	1,435	55.45	86.0	1,454	55.58	86.2
Law	72.07	3,423	90.56	125.7	3,146	86.04	119.4	3,198	87.40	121.3	3,408	83.85	116.3
Literary Collections	36.42	440	29.88	82.1	464	24.92	68.4	429	28.58	78.5	458	30.02	82.4
Literary Criticism	36.57	2,149	50.56	138.2	2,352	44.69	122.2	2,228	41.90	114.6	2,249	44.54	121.8
Mathematics	86.13	1,540	105.18	122.0	1,373	76.41	88.7	1,131	67.56	78.4	1,091	73.76	85.6
Medical	90.22	5,282	115.14	127.6	4,470	87.02	96.4	3,581	81.20	90.0	3,937	84.47	93.6
Music	22.83	1,816	27.87	122.1	2,056	30.41	133.2	3,556	27.37	119.9	1,564	31.92	139.8
Nature	37.28	590	45.59	122.3	668	42.20	113.2	696	35.03	94.0	749	41.13	110.3
Performing Arts	33.53	948	42.79	127.6	972	38.50	114.8	833	36.74	109.6	895	39.91	119.0
Pets	17.34	113	18.71	107.9	123	20.37	117.5	100	18.58	107.2	95	20.13	116.1
Philosophy	52.66	1,902	52.75	100.2	1,947	42.39	80.5	1,808	42.24	80.2	1,823	47.55	90.3
Photography	31.30	292	34.06	108.8	319	40.11	128.1	296	36.28	115.9	235	44.39	141.8
Poetry	16.73	2,161	17.22	102.9	2,062	17.35	103.7	1,896	17.42	104.2	1,858	17.78	106.3
Political Science	41.00	4,395	58.93	143.7	4,398	50.66	123.6	4,797	46.94	114.5	4,470	48.04	117.2
Psychology	47.98	2,058	61.04	127.2	2,130	51.87	108.1	1,804	53.52	111.6	1,706	50.41	105.1
Reference	84.85	425	184.68	217.7	399	128.42	151.3	254	208.22	245.4	226	228.88	269.8
Religion	22.08	6,753	27.36	123.9	6,867	28.09	127.2	5,798	27.41	124.2	5,167	29.81	135.0
Science	116.37	4,873	127.83	109.8	4,172	94.71	81.4	3,361	93.86	80.7	3,887	96.20	82.7
Self-help	17.84	1,136	17.18	96.3	1,310	17.90	100.4	1,220	17.87	100.2	1,232	17.88	100.2
Social Science	45.05	5,592	60.10	133.4	5,640	49.65	110.2	5,910	47.58	105.6	4,761	46.78	103.8
Sports and Recreation	22.30	913	26.52	118.9	996	26.95	120.9	837	27.09	121.5	809	26.94	120.8
Study Aids	49.24	690	43.12	87.6	2,593	43.61	88.6	2,449	43.55	88.4	768	46.70	94.8
Technology and Engineering	111.20	3,995	143.34	128.9	3,099	118.63	106.7	2,918	126.78	114.0	3,380	133.72	120.2
Transportation	36.26	498	34.76	95.9	388	37.99	104.8	337	34.07	94.0	259	35.00	96.5
Travel	20.93	1,615	21.17	101.1	1,545	21.50	102.7	909	20.86	99.7	750	21.57	103.1
True Crime	20.94	221	19.96	95.3	248	20.01	95.6	209	19.56	93.4	244	20.39	97.3
Young Adult	14.86	2,949	18.09	121.7	2,889	18.70	125.8	2,254	16.30	109.7	1,938	15.99	107.6
Totals and Averages	$42.06	116,817	$52.81	125.6	116,708	$48.30	114.8	106,613	$45.05	107.1	101,456	$45.00	107.0

Compiled by Narda Tafuri, Retired, University of Scranton, from data supplied by Baker & Taylor

Table 7A / U.S. Audiobooks: Average Prices and Price Indexes, 2018–2021

Index Base: 2010 = 100

BISAC Category	2010 Average Price	2018 Final Volumes	2018 Final Average Price	2018 Final Index	2019 Final Volumes	2019 Final Average Price	2019 Final Index	2020 Preliminary Volumes	2020 Preliminary Average Price	2020 Preliminary Index	2021 Preliminary Volumes	2021 Preliminary Average Price	2021 Preliminary Index
Antiques and Collectibles	$36.66	n.a.	n.a.	n.a.	n.a.	n.a.	n.a.	3	$40.99	111.8	9	$19.66	53.6
Architecture	41.24	2	$22.99	55.7	8	$33.12	80.3	5	41.99	101.8	12	25.82	62.6
Art	58.21	16	31.54	54.2	8	31.05	53.3	13	33.37	57.3	47	21.94	37.7
Bibles	43.28	2	49.99	115.5	3	76.31	176.3	12	32.17	74.3	8	52.15	120.5
Biography and Autobiography	50.79	1,242	42.79	84.2	1,376	43.63	85.9	1,209	42.78	84.2	3,052	29.57	58.2
Body, Mind and Spirit	32.98	147	35.88	108.8	180	35.17	106.6	163	35.81	108.6	401	25.85	78.4
Business and Economics	49.70	799	35.66	71.7	656	36.87	74.2	656	40.56	81.6	1,147	26.99	54.3
Children	37.80	1,333	36.52	96.6	1,555	37.14	98.2	1,846	33.17	87.7	1,372	32.04	84.8
Comics and Graphic Novels	n.a.	n.a.	n.a.	n.a.	66	37.57	n.a.	31	36.44	n.a.	4	29.49	n.a.
Computers	45.00	27	42.32	94.0	33	38.05	84.6	12	34.73	77.2	106	26.21	58.2
Cooking	44.97	58	39.69	88.3	16	37.30	82.9	34	38.92	86.6	144	26.72	59.4
Crafts and Hobbies	24.98	3	22.32	89.4	5	39.79	159.3	3	39.99	160.1	13	17.02	68.1
Design	n.a.	6	51.31	n.a.	1	39.99	n.a.	4	41.24	n.a.	6	21.49	n.a.
Drama	33.21	163	18.48	55.6	98	22.32	67.2	36	25.65	77.2	124	29.14	87.7
Education	45.71	41	33.58	73.5	39	38.20	83.6	26	38.29	83.8	181	24.59	53.8
Family and Relationships	41.17	183	34.16	83.0	185	37.01	89.9	150	36.29	88.1	620	21.79	52.9
Fiction	50.38	9,918	39.33	78.1	11,455	40.16	79.7	12,254	41.51	82.4	19,599	31.25	62.0
Foreign Language Study	45.11	100	207.23	459.4	147	86.40	191.5	39	52.70	116.8	3	33.64	74.6
Games and Activities	n.a.	5	39.99	n.a.	2	22.49	n.a.	4	42.49	n.a.	23	25.44	n.a.
Gardening	47.82	n.a.	n.a.	n.a.	1	14.99	31.3	9	37.55	78.5	10	26.39	55.2
Health and Fitness	43.09	264	38.61	89.6	242	40.17	93.2	222	42.98	99.7	502	28.35	65.8
History	58.07	809	47.41	81.6	811	46.40	79.9	720	47.05	81.0	2,179	28.35	48.8
House and Home	n.a.	20	35.48	n.a.	13	34.45	n.a.	17	39.52	n.a.	28	23.31	n.a.
Humor	36.62	93	41.75	114.0	74	35.78	97.7	85	39.67	108.3	316	20.18	55.1

Subject													
Language Arts and Disciplines	38.34	29	34.50	90.0	47	38.01	99.1	26	42.33	110.4	107	25.18	65.7
Law	64.49	34	34.16	53.0	25	31.15	48.3	30	38.82	60.2	110	23.99	37.2
Literary Collections	52.07	69	42.97	82.5	66	42.00	80.7	34	38.98	74.9	100	30.72	59.0
Literary Criticism	42.53	34	41.10	96.6	27	32.61	76.7	36	34.54	81.2	118	27.43	64.5
Mathematics	n.a.	4	26.99	n.a.	7	46.70	n.a.	2	32.49	n.a.	27	27.51	n.a.
Medical	40.13	36	41.82	104.2	31	32.70	81.5	36	40.37	100.6	168	25.91	64.6
Music	35.67	61	30.91	86.6	64	41.50	116.4	51	36.94	103.6	204	26.56	74.5
Nature	41.20	53	35.10	85.2	93	41.92	101.8	109	42.58	103.3	238	25.44	61.7
Performing Arts	40.60	99	40.52	99.8	116	41.09	101.2	177	42.87	105.6	375	32.58	80.2
Pets	38.33	29	38.02	99.2	18	42.77	111.6	18	37.44	97.7	107	21.11	55.1
Philosophy	53.05	54	37.87	71.4	74	34.24	64.5	51	39.07	73.6	252	26.69	50.3
Photography	n.a.	n.a.	n.a.	n.a.	n.a.	n.a.	n.a.	1	29.99	n.a.	7	18.99	n.a.
Poetry	33.59	56	27.17	80.9	106	28.89	86.0	137	30.61	91.1	122	18.40	54.8
Political Science	48.04	377	39.29	81.8	368	43.14	89.8	395	45.19	94.1	866	28.83	60.0
Psychology	45.42	162	37.25	82.0	99	35.16	77.4	118	46.30	101.9	464	27.71	61.0
Reference	59.99	8	46.62	77.7	7	30.70	51.2	8	36.24	60.4	32	28.03	46.7
Religion	33.94	1,152	30.52	89.9	930	35.14	103.5	812	37.64	110.9	1,158	30.54	90.0
Science	51.89	212	38.97	75.1	168	41.25	79.5	220	40.55	78.2	613	30.24	58.3
Self-help	39.43	427	36.21	91.8	517	35.41	89.8	501	37.52	95.2	811	27.77	70.4
Social Science	48.07	322	35.98	74.9	265	41.89	87.1	274	39.58	82.3	776	26.09	54.3
Sports and Recreation	48.48	111	38.35	79.1	142	42.11	86.9	145	38.40	79.2	350	25.22	52.0
Study Aids	19.41	3	41.63	214.5	2	63.00	324.5	3	38.66	199.2	6	24.73	127.4
Technology and Engineering	53.33	31	45.18	84.7	13	39.29	73.7	16	38.74	72.6	111	26.22	49.2
Transportation	46.28	10	46.49	100.5	2	49.99	108.0	3	46.66	100.8	42	17.47	37.8
Travel	50.96	32	43.67	85.7	49	42.42	83.2	35	40.99	80.4	143	27.03	53.0
True Crime	52.58	189	36.65	69.7	193	43.11	82.0	147	45.60	86.7	445	27.63	52.6
Young Adult	44.81	1,118	44.63	99.6	1,224	43.81	97.8	1,162	43.16	96.3	1,210	34.13	76.2
Totals and Averages	$48.00	19,943	$39.69	82.7	21,627	$40.32	84.0	22,100	$40.75	84.9	38,868	$29.84	62.2

Compiled by Narda Tafuri, Retired, University of Scranton, from data supplied by Baker & Taylor

Table 7B / U.S. E-Books: Average Prices and Price Indexes, 2018–2021

Index Base: 2010 = 100

BISAC Category	2010 Average Price	2018 Final Volumes	2018 Final Average Price	2018 Final Index	2019 Final Volumes	2019 Final Average Price	2019 Final Index	2020 Preliminary Volumes	2020 Preliminary Average Price	2020 Preliminary Index	2021 Preliminary Volumes	2021 Preliminary Average Price	2021 Preliminary Index
Antiques and Collectibles	$30.24	174	$10.85	35.9	147	$11.97	39.6	123	$28.34	93.7	123	$20.97	69.3
Architecture	66.57	467	48.45	72.8	498	50.78	76.3	397	55.45	83.3	358	58.21	87.4
Art	41.56	1,456	36.47	87.8	1,724	36.27	87.3	1,138	47.24	113.7	1,013	42.14	101.4
Bibles	6.11	444	10.00	163.6	300	14.33	234.5	367	16.90	276.5	358	15.63	255.8
Biography and Autobiography	15.47	7,380	19.74	127.6	7,127	23.27	150.4	7,529	30.17	195.0	9,586	26.34	170.3
Body, Mind and Spirit	13.95	3,047	11.41	81.8	3,575	13.22	94.7	3,888	17.10	122.6	4,087	18.86	135.2
Business and Economics	44.82	28,520	51.31	114.5	24,398	68.27	152.3	20,318	57.27	127.8	11,269	38.94	86.9
Children	13.82	28,927	15.72	113.8	28,490	19.62	141.9	23,945	20.02	144.8	25,219	19.39	140.3
Comics and Graphic Novels	11.39	1,371	8.11	71.2	1,062	11.85	104.0	2,365	9.72	85.3	1,650	13.10	115.0
Computers	62.09	4,026	75.10	121.0	2,448	63.22	101.8	2,009	59.20	95.3	1,808	59.57	95.9
Cooking	16.79	3,228	13.35	79.5	2,935	14.17	84.4	2,635	18.97	113.0	3,193	18.91	112.6
Crafts and Hobbies	17.63	652	15.07	85.5	563	15.66	88.8	746	17.33	98.3	907	15.97	90.6
Design	37.03	131	24.03	64.9	139	43.68	118.0	147	38.36	103.6	152	26.57	71.7
Drama	4.86	1,137	10.97	225.8	989	15.09	310.6	738	22.71	467.2	611	18.21	374.8
Education	45.95	4,578	43.77	95.3	5,349	42.81	93.2	3,603	45.92	99.9	3,393	46.18	100.5
Family and Relationships	14.79	2,393	12.65	85.5	2,304	15.37	103.9	2,609	19.12	129.3	3,241	18.62	125.9
Fiction	7.06	83,090	11.26	159.5	85,303	13.64	193.1	78,038	24.64	349.0	70,689	21.54	305.1
Foreign Language Study	46.68	2,321	22.16	47.5	1,560	34.05	72.9	4,719	20.29	43.5	979	45.23	96.9
Games and Activities	12.85	1,518	6.85	53.3	342	20.13	156.6	448	31.77	247.2	350	27.76	216.0
Gardening	17.41	339	15.12	86.8	290	18.83	108.2	385	18.67	107.2	525	18.46	106.0
Health and Fitness	18.78	3,229	13.73	73.1	3,002	17.12	91.1	3,646	19.75	105.2	4,155	21.04	112.1
History	48.20	9,693	42.23	87.6	9,283	56.72	117.7	12,645	46.07	95.6	8,133	53.60	111.2
House and Home	21.57	279	16.19	75.1	245	19.92	92.3	259	22.88	106.1	316	21.24	98.5
Humor	11.15	1,101	14.44	129.5	822	16.23	145.5	888	17.46	156.6	849	20.71	185.7

Language Arts and Disciplines	75.61	2,987	67.54	89.3	3,164	101.77	134.6	2,333	104.61	138.3	1,568	78.30	103.6
Law	112.19	3,121	112.45	100.2	2,804	139.87	124.7	2,671	146.68	130.7	2,114	154.81	138.0
Literary Collections	20.27	1,633	14.86	73.3	6,169	5.18	25.6	1,189	23.88	117.8	1,166	25.60	126.3
Literary Criticism	87.17	3,895	79.64	91.4	3,266	97.71	112.1	3,029	107.84	123.7	2,286	88.10	101.1
Mathematics	112.32	1,150	81.08	72.2	910	97.07	86.4	614	111.23	99.0	360	114.65	102.1
Medical	135.71	3,631	104.48	77.0	2,739	128.56	94.7	2,295	99.66	73.4	2,090	95.25	70.2
Music	32.65	3,014	16.79	51.4	1,785	30.06	92.1	1,604	35.60	109.0	1,572	35.29	108.1
Nature	59.48	891	27.58	46.4	784	30.04	50.5	785	32.14	54.0	1,022	31.24	52.5
Performing Arts	32.17	2,125	25.84	80.3	2,000	28.86	89.7	1,166	38.97	121.2	1,455	41.90	130.3
Pets	14.50	451	10.52	72.5	438	14.41	99.4	390	16.89	116.5	497	18.41	126.9
Philosophy	71.43	2,938	48.73	68.2	2,847	52.54	73.6	3,489	46.69	65.4	1,992	61.51	86.1
Photography	27.23	342	18.80	69.1	259	22.67	83.3	322	24.42	89.7	265	25.98	95.4
Poetry	9.54	5,015	8.11	85.0	4,621	9.84	103.2	3,939	10.75	112.7	4,322	11.18	117.2
Political Science	59.74	4,982	51.98	87.0	3,882	54.40	91.1	3,574	54.80	91.7	3,380	51.55	86.3
Psychology	56.42	2,157	44.82	79.4	1,883	50.01	88.6	2,322	40.29	71.4	2,087	39.50	70.0
Reference	22.92	1,083	44.46	194.0	871	74.31	324.2	753	65.37	285.2	783	28.48	124.3
Religion	27.81	12,123	25.91	93.2	11,169	30.63	110.1	12,354	34.05	122.5	12,512	26.60	95.7
Science	155.80	4,197	98.62	63.3	3,715	105.24	67.5	2,812	109.66	70.4	2,754	113.30	72.7
Self-help	14.06	5,229	12.69	90.2	6,550	13.05	92.8	6,590	17.81	126.7	10,402	15.77	112.1
Social Science	56.83	5,095	48.42	85.2	4,445	58.86	103.6	3,711	54.51	95.9	3,956	55.88	98.3
Sports and rRecreation	19.22	1,669	20.77	108.1	1,437	21.84	113.6	1,304	25.68	133.6	1,486	23.92	124.5
Study Aids	13.94	2,660	19.57	140.4	3,206	31.77	227.9	929	16.18	116.0	758	18.31	131.4
Technology and eEngineering	158.44	3,191	121.41	76.6	2,588	123.84	78.2	1,407	111.96	70.7	1,319	119.25	75.3
Transportation	33.12	333	27.66	83.5	294	30.43	91.9	616	29.02	87.6	344	29.51	89.1
Travel	15.84	2,223	16.62	104.9	2,785	12.64	79.8	1,300	21.84	137.9	1,216	22.77	143.7
True Crime	10.37	534	21.54	207.7	559	25.87	249.5	649	26.80	258.4	1,235	17.71	170.7
Young Adult	11.96	6,601	17.82	149.0	6,672	19.83	165.8	6,784	23.38	195.5	6,985	21.80	182.2
Totals and Averages	$41.61	272,771	$29.51	70.9	264,737	$33.25	79.9	242,516	$35.59	85.5	222,890	$30.88	74.2

Compiled by Narda Tafuri, Retired, University of Scranton, from data supplied by Baker & Taylor

(continued from page 332)

Calculated separately, the average 2021 reference book price increased slightly by 5.38 percent over the previous year. Previous years had seen declining costs of reference books. The overall price of reference books has seen large fluctuations over the past several years.

Questions regarding this index should be addressed to the author at her email address: narda.tafuri@scranton.edu.

Foreign Prices

As shown in the chart below, in 2021 the U.S. dollar retained parity with the Canadian dollar, British pound sterling (1.4 percent), and Euro (7.3 percent). The U.S. dollar strengthened against the Japanese Yen (11.6 percent).

	12/31/2017	12/31/2018	12/31/2019	12/31/2020	12/31/2021
Canada	1.26	1.36	1.30	1.28	1.28
Euro	0.83	0.87	0.89	0.82	0.88
U.K.	0.74	0.78	0.76	0.73	0.74
Japan	112.55	109.85	108.53	103.08	115.04

Data from the Bureau of Fiscal Services. U.S. Treasury Department (https://fiscaldata.treasury.gov)

Serials Prices

Average Price of Serials (Table 8) and Average Price of Online Serials (Table 8A), compiled by Stephen Bosch, provide the average prices and percent increases for serials based on titles in select serials' abstracting and indexing products. The serials in this price survey are published in the United States as well as overseas and are indexed in the Clarivate Analytics (formerly ISI) Arts and Humanities Citation Index, Science Citation Index, and Social Sciences Citation Index, as well as EBSCO's Academic Search Ultimate and Masterfile Premier and Elsevier's Scopus. This is the third year when titles indexed in Scopus are included in the data. Adding Scopus expands this price survey from about 11,000 priced titles in 2015 to the current 30,160. The increase in the sample size makes the results more likely to reflect pricing trends accurately.

Tables 8 and 8A cover prices for periodicals and serials for five years, 2018–2022. The 2022 pricing is the renewal pricing for serial titles indexed in the selected products. These tables were derived from pricing data supplied by EBSCO Information Services and reflect broad pricing changes aggregated from serials indexed in the six major products previously mentioned. USPPI (Table 1) is based on price changes seen in a static set of approximately 6,000 serial titles. The Average Price of Serials (Table 8) is based on a much broader set of titles, approximately 30,160; however, the indexed titles are not static year to year, so this pricing study does not rise to the level of a price index. This study is still useful in showing price changes for periodicals. The indexes selected for this price survey were deemed representative of serials that are frequently purchased in academic and public libraries. There are some foreign titles in the indexes, so the scope is broader, and this may give a better picture of the overall price pressures experienced in libraries. Table 8 contains both print and online serials pricing. Table 8A is a subset of the titles treated in Table 8 and contains only online serials pricing.

The most important trend seen in the data in Table 8 is that increases in serial prices have continued to be lower than the increases over the past 10 years due to the impact of the pandemic. In previous years, the price increases had remained constant since the economic recovery began in 2010. Since that time, price increases hovered around 6 percent annually. The increase for 2021 was 3.4 percent and for 2022 it was 3.8 percent. For titles with online availability (Table 8A), the increase for 2021 was 3.5 percent and dipped slightly to 3.3 percent in 2022. For online serials, rates of increase in previous years had also averaged around 6 percent over the past five years. There is a difference between the average prices for print serials and online serials, so, at least for this set of data, print formats do cost less than their online counterparts. Several large publishers have made online pricing only available through custom quotes, so there is no standard retail price. Those publishers' pricing data are not available for this survey. Consequently, the number of titles covered in the online survey (Table 8A) is less than the number of titles in Table 8, but titles with print-only pricing are now 38 percent of the overall dataset.

Another interesting trend is that the science areas do not dominate the list of subjects with the largest price increases. The subject areas that displayed large increases were quite varied. Military and naval science, arts and architecture, health sciences, geography, engineering, psychology, social sciences, recreation, and law saw higher increases than most areas. Some of these same areas showed the highest increases in the online table (Table 8A). Average prices of journals in the science and technology areas are far higher than average prices in other areas. That trend continues, with the average cost of chemistry and physics journals being $5,696 and $4,406, respectively. Online journals (Table 8A) showed similar average prices for chemistry ($5,779) and physics ($4,653).

In this price study, as in similar price surveys, the data become less accurate at describing price changes as the sample size becomes smaller. For that reason, drawing conclusions about price changes in subject areas with a limited number of titles will be less accurate than for large areas or the broader price survey. Price changes are far more volatile where smaller datasets are used. For example, recreation (212 titles) showed a price change of 5.8 percent in 2022, greater than most other areas. To calculate inflation, librarians are encouraged to look at an average price change over the period or the overall number for the price study (3.8 percent). Year-to-year price changes in small subject areas are too unstable for budgeting purposes to be reliable indicators of future prices.

Foreign Book Prices

British Academic Books (Table 9), compiled by George Aulisio, University of Scranton, indicates the average prices and price indexes from 2018–2021. The percent change in titles and the average price is calculated for 2020–2021, and the index price shows the percent change between 2021 and the base year of 2010.

(text continues on page 352)

Table 8 / Average Price of Serials, Based on Titles in Select Serial Indexes, 2018–2022

Subject	LC Class	Titles	2018 Average Price	2019 Average Price	Percent Change 2018–2019	2020 Average Price	Percent Change 2019–2010	2021 Average Price	Percent Change 2020–2021	2022 Average Price	Percent Change 2021–2022
Agriculture	S	724	$1,301.99	$1,384.78	6.4%	$1,466.22	5.9%	$1,527.95	4.2%	$1,591.63	4.2%
Anthropology	GN	240	620.00	652.58	5.3	687.50	5.4	717.27	4.3	739.67	3.1
Arts and Architecture	N	391	462.80	487.41	5.3	523.95	7.5	545.64	4.1	571.78	4.8
Astronomy	QB	104	1,962.28	2,059.12	4.9	2,180.41	5.9	2,139.28	-1.9	2,223.93	4.0
Biology	QH	1,787	2,764.47	2,924.33	5.8	3,072.62	5.1	3,170.54	3.2	3,297.30	4.0
Botany	QK	233	1,691.76	1,787.37	5.7	1,876.36	5.0	1,931.23	2.9	1,992.92	3.2
Business and Economics	HA-HJ	2,631	1,529.82	1,605.85	5.0	1,690.92	5.3	1,755.09	3.8	1,748.14	-0.4
Chemistry	QD	647	4,762.67	5,047.90	6.0	5,293.87	4.9	5,448.46	2.9	5,695.89	4.5
Education	L	964	898.69	962.69	7.1	1,026.16	6.6	1,077.03	5.0	1,110.41	3.1
Engineering	T	2,812	2,183.28	2,330.53	6.7	2,480.36	6.4	2,573.94	3.8	2,703.28	5.0
Food Science	TX	153	1,852.67	1,955.83	5.6	2,063.56	5.5	2,159.62	4.7	2,119.76	-1.8
General Science	Q	391	1,492.28	1,583.91	6.1	1,669.08	5.4	1,731.76	3.8	1,801.85	4.0
General Works	A	313	298.85	311.68	4.3	324.57	4.1	337.06	3.8	349.19	3.6
Geography	G-GF	487	1,302.71	1,395.97	7.2	1,489.00	6.7	1,544.79	3.7	1,622.25	5.0
Geology	QE	336	2,026.69	2,162.02	6.7	2,292.62	6.0	2,377.58	3.7	2,475.82	4.1
Health Sciences	R	5,952	1,492.12	1,583.14	6.1	1,692.40	6.9	1,764.74	4.3	1,851.36	4.9
History	C,D,E,F	1,556	426.69	457.60	7.2	484.11	5.8	506.67	4.7	525.42	3.7

Subject	LC Class	No. of Titles	Avg. Price	Avg. Price	% Change	Avg. Price	% Change	Avg. Price	% Change	Avg. Price	% Change
Language and Literature	P	1,742	416.04	440.67	5.9	465.55	5.6	483.22	3.8	503.32	4.2
Law	K	680	495.15	521.57	5.3	550.40	5.5	571.42	3.8	635.33	11.2
Library Science	Z	297	1,024.08	1,077.06	5.2	1,132.09	5.1	1,174.06	3.7	1,145.29	-2.5
Math and Computer Science	QA	1,524	1,544.71	1,634.34	5.8	1,734.58	6.1	1,788.52	3.1	1,873.29	4.7
Military and Naval Science	U,V	140	672.79	734.75	9.2	781.06	6.3	818.28	4.8	857.15	4.8
Music	M	249	294.67	309.06	4.9	327.06	5.8	338.20	3.4	348.63	3.1
Philosophy and Religion	B-BD, BH-BX	1,027	394.85	414.81	5.1	432.90	4.4	448.19	3.5	466.62	4.1
Physics	QC	762	3,722.95	3,942.14	5.9	4,148.76	5.2	4,270.71	2.9	4,406.16	3.2
Political Science	J	507	771.24	826.98	7.2	885.37	7.1	921.85	4.1	960.13	4.2
Psychology	BF	614	915.44	987.39	7.9	1,059.10	7.3	1,091.60	3.1	1,146.53	5.0
Recreation	GV	212	691.58	741.80	7.3	790.60	6.6	837.82	6.0	886.52	5.8
Social Sciences	H	251	847.89	903.55	6.6	959.14	6.2	965.95	0.7	1,017.09	5.3
Sociology	HM-HX	1,439	931.64	997.37	7.1	1,062.55	6.5	1,103.69	3.9	1,146.66	3.9
Technology	TA-TT	566	1,916.01	2,040.77	6.5	2,160.47	5.9	2,243.54	3.8	2,244.02	0.0
Zoology	QL	429	1,855.96	1,952.78	5.2	2,030.61	4.0	2,034.95	0.2	2,097.69	3.1
Totals and Averages		30,160	$1,472.39	$1,562.21	6.1	$1,654.78	5.9	$1,714.59	3.6	$1,780.38	3.8

Compiled by Stephen Bosch, University of Arizona. Data on serial pricing supplied by EBSCO and are based on titles indexed in EBSCO Academic Search Ultimate, EBSCO Masterfile Complete, Clarivate Analytics (formerly ISI) Arts and Humanities Citation Index, Clarivate Analytics Science Citation Index, Clarivate Analytics Social Sciences Citation Index, and Elsevier's Scopus.

Table 8A / Changes in the Average Price of Online Serials 2018–2022, Based on Titles in Select Serial Indexes

Subject	LC Class	Titles	2018 Average Price	2019 Average Price	Percent Change 2018–2019	2020 Average Price	Percent Change 2019–2020	2021 Average Price	Percent Change 2020–2021	2022 Average Price	Percent Change 2021–2022
Agriculture	S	380	$1,282.82	$1,374.34	7.1%	$1,454.13	5.8%	$1,530.17	5.2%	$1,582.82	3.4%
Anthropology	GN	165	710.22	753.35	6.1	795.83	5.6	831.81	4.5	861.69	3.6
Arts and Architecture	N	213	629.14	673.13	7.0	719.58	6.9	750.98	4.4	782.41	4.2
Astronomy	QB	66	2,174.33	2,281.70	4.9	2,429.09	6.5	2,345.46	-3.4	2,445.49	4.3
Biology	QH	953	2,514.10	2,676.89	6.5	2,802.21	4.7	2,897.43	3.4	3,026.24	4.4
Botany	QK	144	1,727.31	1,815.60	5.1	1,893.17	4.3	1,947.62	2.9	2,023.61	3.9
Business and Economics	HA-HJ	1,686	1,858.09	1,946.33	4.7	2,046.27	5.1	2,130.52	4.1	2,087.33	-2.0
Chemistry	QD	368	4,712.24	5,050.71	7.2	5,320.63	5.3	5,504.29	3.5	5,778.72	5.0
Education	L	775	990.15	1,062.97	7.4	1,132.31	6.5	1,190.87	5.2	1,222.64	2.7
Engineering	T	1,597	2,153.84	2,310.38	7.3	2,465.69	6.7	2,566.65	4.1	2,682.94	4.5
Food Science	TX	103	2,048.80	2,153.09	5.1	2,263.68	5.1	2,376.00	5.0	2,251.15	-5.3
General Science	Q	246	1,687.09	1,787.80	6.0	1,871.29	4.7	1,940.39	3.7	2,009.40	3.6
General Works	A	81	786.04	818.44	4.1	857.94	4.8	893.71	4.2	931.71	4.3
Geography	G-GF	327	1,181.93	1,277.96	8.1	1,368.81	7.1	1,432.29	4.6	1,506.65	5.2
Geology	QE	189	1,734.81	1,852.02	6.8	1,962.74	6.0	2,033.44	3.6	2,118.04	4.2

Subject	LC Class	Titles	Price	Price	%	Price	%	Price	%	Price	%
Health Sciences	R	2,968	1,532.48	1,622.99	5.9	1,743.05	7.4	1,811.16	3.9	1,894.27	4.6
History	C,D,E,F	882	551.05	596.50	8.2	634.03	6.3	668.61	5.5	693.37	3.7
Language and Literature	P	975	528.81	565.08	6.9	600.01	6.2	627.50	4.6	654.58	4.3
Law	K	314	654.83	690.39	5.4	727.65	5.4	756.98	4.0	805.59	6.4
Library Science	Z	205	1,176.24	1,236.61	5.1	1,297.27	4.9	1,351.21	4.2	1,286.66	-4.8
Math and Computer Science	QA	1,058	1,537.45	1,638.71	6.6	1,756.94	7.2	1,825.90	3.9	1,921.67	5.2
Military and Naval Science	U,V	98	746.26	819.49	9.8	872.41	6.5	918.65	5.3	965.08	5.1
Music	M	126	430.71	456.94	6.1	480.30	5.1	495.79	3.2	512.03	3.3
Philosophy and Religion	B-BD, BH-BX	527	537.15	568.31	5.8	595.96	4.9	618.81	3.8	642.93	3.9
Physics	QC	454	3,867.55	4,127.32	6.7	4,366.38	5.8	4,504.46	3.2	4,653.27	3.3
Political Science	J	375	863.06	929.47	7.7	997.42	7.3	1,041.44	4.4	1,079.58	3.7
Psychology	BF	386	962.77	1,039.34	8.0	1,123.70	8.1	1,155.73	2.9	1,212.45	4.9
Recreation	GV	143	847.53	910.66	7.4	969.35	6.4	1,026.73	5.9	1,086.19	5.8
Social Sciences	H	151	980.71	1,038.70	5.9	1,106.61	6.5	1,120.17	1.2	1,176.74	5.0
Sociology	HM-HX	1,066	1,033.77	1,109.83	7.4	1,184.75	6.8	1,231.32	3.9	1,277.55	3.8
Technology	TA-TT	336	2,400.17	2,563.35	6.8	2,712.51	5.8	2,821.64	4.0	2,784.76	-1.3
Zoology	QL	223	1,950.21	2,074.47	6.4	2,181.71	5.2	2,183.84	0.1	2,241.69	2.6
Totals and Averages		17,620	$1,546.95	$1,647.03	6.5%	1,748.45	6.2%	$1,815.52	3.8%	$1,875.23	3.3%

Compiled by Stephen Bosch, University of Arizona Data on serial pricing supplied by EBSCO and are based on titles indexed in EBSCO Academic Search Ultimate, EBSCO Masterfile Complete, Clarivate Analytics (formerly ISI) Arts and Humanities Citation Index, Clarivate Analytics Science Citation Index, Clarivate Analytics Social Sciences Citation Index, and Elsevier's Scopus.

Table 9 / British Academic Books: Average Prices and Price Indexes, 2018–2021

Index Base: 2010 = 100

Subject	LC Class	2010		2018		2019		2020		2021			
		Titles	Average Price (£)	Titles	Average Price (£)	Titles	Average Price (£)	Titles	Average Price (£)	Titles	Average Price (£)	Percent Change 2020–2021	Index
Agriculture	S	154	£63.97	142	£85.45	154	£84.11	613	£87.95	716	£91.59	4.1%	143.2
Anthropology	GN	154	50.85	150	65.47	173	74.65	294	70.16	311	80.89	15.3	159.1
Botany	QK	45	66.08	30	77.10	36	89.13	162	115.45	220	103.98	-9.9	157.4
Business and Economics	H-HJ	1,913	60.54	2,185	84.35	2,185	80.42	4,409	78.68	5,120	81.31	3.3	134.3
Chemistry	QD	96	105.68	58	127.93	61	121.99	309	130.53	370	161.17	23.5	152.5
Education	L	558	52.21	723	77.96	731	78.83	2,315	69.15	2,183	82.00	18.6	157.0
Engineering and Technology	T-TS	742	61.84	654	86.12	693	90.24	3,845	109.15	5,088	111.55	2.2	180.4
Fine and Applied Arts	M, N	1,037	35.95	974	59.66	989	60.88	3,601	50.02	3,646	53.18	6.3	147.9
General Works	A	30	60.03	33	108.43	37	85.11	90	91.85	94	93.72	2.0	156.1
Geography	G-GF, GR-GT	276	65.69	317	86.29	342	81.01	798	82.65	908	83.64	1.2	127.3
Geology	QE	33	52.28	30	74.38	51	58.66	123	106.49	160	104.12	-2.2	199.2
History	C,D,E,F	1,822	42.55	2,051	60.70	2,215	57.95	4,813	62.73	5,257	60.38	-3.7	141.9
Home Economics	TX	46	30.48	36	78.58	37	91.70	333	46.16	326	44.88	-2.8	147.3
Industrial Arts	TT	41	28.47	36	53.10	23	51.59	105	55.50	77	41.34	-25.5	145.2

Subject	LC Class												
Language and Literature	P	3,987	31.58	3,112	55.95	3,219	55.93	7,444	47.93	8,155	54.26	13.2	171.8
Law	K	1,°53	83.10	1,276	101.89	1,313	99.48	2,050	89.98	2,487	95.18	5.8	114.5
Library and Information Science	Z	100	53.58	93	68.03	85	79.97	269	73.66	389	76.09	3.3	142.0
Mathematics and Computer Science	QA	207	48.29	195	71.84	222	78.73	2,189	77.88	2,784	82.18	5.5	170.2
Medicine	R	1,182	55.12	931	73.90	1,081	76.98	3,880	94.36	4,890	101.92	8.0	184.9
Military and Naval Sciences	U, V	184	40.95	181	65.54	165	57.91	520	55.82	532	51.91	-7.0	126.7
Philosophy and Religion	B-BD, BH-BX	1,336	48.17	1,364	73.64	1,505	69.70	3,998	53.46	4,362	60.49	13.2	125.6
Physics and Astronomy	QB, QC	214	64.83	206	73.19	200	75.70	751	93.42	859	89.66	-4.0	138.3
Political Science	J	737	71.88	787	87.59	1,107	77.96	1,670	73.37	1,874	77.61	5.8	108.0
Psychology	BF	265	39.69	378	76.47	414	80.74	854	63.66	875	72.99	14.7	183.9
Science (general)	Q	60	40.70	82	67.59	99	71.83	521	85.30	634	94.97	11.3	233.3
Sociology	HM-HX	1,169	58.24	1,649	78.65	1,685	73.91	3,367	66.26	3,685	73.82	11.4	126.8
Sports and Recreation	GV	192	36.76	207	84.02	216	80.04	645	51.38	748	51.05	-0.6	138.9
Zoology	QH, QL-QR	382	65.79	262	80.40	321	85.51	1,203	101.95	1,525	106.18	4.1	161.4
Totals and Averages		18,115	£50.50	18,142	£73.94	19,350	£72.61	51,171	£71.56	58,275	£77.44	8.2%	153.3

Compiled by George Aulisio, University of Scranton, based on information provided by GOBI Library Solutions

(continued from page 345)

This index is compiled using data from GOBI Library Solutions and utilizes prices from cloth editions except when not available. The data also draw from select titles from continental Europe and Africa. The index does not separate more expensive reference titles. Small numbers of titles that include higher-priced reference sets may not be reliable indicators of price changes. This table does not include e-book prices.

Data in the "Totals and Averages" row include the total of the LC Classes profiled in this table, not the total of all books profiled by GOBI Library Solutions. In 2021 total British academic books profiled by GOBI increased substantially for the second year in a row to 58,275 titles. This is the fifth year the table has recorded an increase in titles. Notably, this is a 13.8 percent increase in titles profiled from 2020.

In 2021 British academic books experienced an overall price increase of 8.2 percent, bringing the average price for all books profiled to £77.44. The 2021 price decrease comes when the United Kingdom's Consumer Price Index saw high inflation of 4.8 percent as of December 2021 (http://www.ons.gov.uk).

Table 9 shows how average prices have increased or decreased compared to the 2010 base year. For 2021 the overall index price for all LC subjects profiled in this table is 153.3 percent. All LC classes listed are currently above their 2010 base prices. The highest increases in comparison with the 2010 base prices are science (general) (233.3 percent), geology (199.2 percent), and industrial arts (145.2 percent). There are currently no known reliable indicators for a 2022 industry forecast.

Using the Price Indexes

Librarians are encouraged to monitor publishing industry trends and changes in economic conditions when preparing budget forecasts and projections. The Library Materials Price Index (LMPI) Editorial Board endeavors to make information on publishing trends readily available by sponsoring the annual compilation and publication of price data contained in our published tables. The indexes cover newly published library materials and document prices and rates of percent changes at the national and international levels. They are useful benchmarks to compare against local costs. Still, because they reflect retail prices in the aggregate, they are not a substitute for cost data that reflect the collecting patterns of individual libraries. They are not a substitute for specific cost studies.

Differences between local prices and those found in national indexes arise partially because these indexes exclude discounts, service charges, shipping and handling fees, and other discounts or costs that a library might see. Discrepancies may also relate to a library's subject coverage, its mix of titles purchased—including both current and backfiles—and the proportion of the library's budget expended on domestic or foreign materials. These variables can affect the average price paid by an individual library, although the individual library's rate of increase may not differ greatly from the national indexes.

Closing Note

The LMPI Editorial Board is interested in pursuing studies that correlate a particular library's costs with the national prices. The group welcomes interested parties to its meeting at ALA Annual. The LMPI Editorial Board consists of compilers George Aulisio, Ajaye Bloomstone, Stephen Bosch, and Narda Tafuri. Sylvia Orner, University of Scranton, serves as assistant editor. This edition marks the completion of George Aulisio's second term as editor.

Book Title Output and Average Prices: 2019–2021

Constance Harbison

Baker & Taylor

The figures appearing in this report were provided for publication in *Library and Book Trade Almanac* by book wholesaler Baker & Taylor and are based on the Book Industry Study Group's BISAC Subject Headings. Figures for 2019 and 2020 have been revised since the previous edition was published, reflecting updates to the Baker & Taylor database. Figures for 2021 are considered preliminary at the time of this report.

Annual book title output in the United States took a significant downturn from 2019–2020, decreasing over 10 percent, followed by an additional drop in 2021 (see Table 1). After increasing to 209,892 volumes (up from 2018's 206,591), revised total production figures for 2020 were 188,412, with preliminary 2021 results dropping even more to 182,015. This continuing drop in output is not surprising, as the country entered quarantine in March 2020 due to the COVID-19 pandemic. Throughout 2020 and 2021 publishers faced challenges such as being understaffed and issues throughout the supply chain, including rising freight and fuel costs and shortages of necessary materials. The popular subject category of Fiction saw a significant drop from 2019–2020 but trended upward for 2021—perhaps indicating that publishers held off on releasing Fiction titles in 2020, instead releasing them in 2021, as the year saw people getting out more to visit bookstores and libraries. Other popular subjects, such as Children and Young Adults, continue to trend downward from 2019. Not surprisingly, the subject Travel has seen one of the most significant drops—dropping 48 percent from 2019–2021 as people had been limiting unnecessary travel during the pandemic.

Typically, preliminary figures are revised upward as late-arriving materials are added to the database, suggesting that the final "total" 2021 output shown in Table 1 may increase and show less dramatic changes between 2020–2021.

Output and Prices by Format and Category

The output and pricing of titles overall peaked in 2019, but then dropped in 2020 and again in 2021, with the average price of titles in 2021 dropping about 1.09 percent below 2020 (Table 2).

For some categories, such as Bibles, Photography, and Games and Activities, the average price of titles increased, suggesting that publishers were raising prices on those titles related to prayer, hobbies, and recreation. A 22 percent increase on the average prices of Study Aids suggests that publishers may be raising prices on titles within this category, as standardized testing for colleges begins to be required again. The greatest drop in average price was in True Crime, which had a

53.34 percent decrease since 2020, but became more inline with the average price of that category in 2019 from which there was only a 5.91 percent increase.

The average price of hardcover titles remained consistent from 2019–2021, though output dropped within that period (Table 3). The period from 2020–2021 shows a 1.09 percent decrease in average price. The average price of hardcover fiction has been trending downward since 2019, down almost 3 percent from 2019–2021. Categories showing significant price increases or decreases (greater than 5 percent) from 2020–2021 all have fewer than 1,000 titles published in hardcover for each year. So, though Drama shows a 32.38 percent decrease in average price, the category had only 25 hardcover titles in 2020 and 26 in 2021. The History category remained the most consistent, showing the same average price of $43.84 in both 2019 and 2021.

Mass market titles had a slight average price increase from 2019–2020, and the preliminary 2021 average price is moving in the same direction with an increase of 1.68 percent over 2020; however, the preliminary 2021 figures show mass market output dropping 1.97 percent from 2020 and 8.82 percent from 2019 (Table 4). In addition to the drop in output of mass market titles, there was also a drop in categories having mass market titles. In 2019 mass market titles were published in 12 categories, nine categories in 2020, and 11 categories in 2021. This suggests that publishers are concentrating the focus of mass market titles into only specific, more consumer-focused categories. As with most years, mass market titles were dominated by the Fiction category, making up 89.30 percent of the output; many of the STEM titles, as categorized by such subjects as Mathematics, Science, and Technology and Engineering, do not have any titles published as mass market.

The preliminary 2021 counts show a decrease in output from 2019–2021 for trade paperbacks at 15.03 percent less (Table 5). The average price of trade paperbacks has remained steady between 2020–2021—with only a 5-cent difference between the two. The category of Nature saw the greatest increase in output for 2021. After showing little variant in output between 2019–2020, the category grew by 10.81 percent in 2021. After trending downward from 2019–2020, the categories Foreign Language Study and Travel showed the most dramatic drops in output from 2020 2021, with the former dropping 111.72 percent and the latter dropping 106 percent. It will be interesting to see if these categories trend upward once there is a demand for them as people start traveling again.

The preliminary output figure for 2021 shows the output of physically packaged audiobooks increasing beyond the high-water mark reached in 2016, when more than 32,000 volumes were produced; since then, total annual output for the format has remained in the 20,000 range but shows a 43.14 percent increase so far for 2021 (Table 6). Average pricing of audiobooks looks to be trending downward in 2021, as the preliminary numbers show the average price to be 36.5 percent under the 2020 average. Like trade paperbacks, the category showing the greatest drop in output is Foreign Language Study—showing only three audiobooks in 2021. This suggests that publishers are moving these titles to a digital format, so that people can listen from their phones.

(text continues on page 368)

Table 1 / American Book Production 2019–2021

BISAC Category	2019	2020	2021
Antiques and Collectibles	188	175	148
Architecture	1,843	1,794	1,633
Art	4,022	3,637	3,288
Bibles	820	688	706
Biography and Autobiography	4,002	3,813	4,186
Body, Mind and Spirit	1,117	1,126	1,151
Business and Economics	11,424	10,474	10,518
Children	28,586	26,124	24,644
Comics and Graphic Novels	2,884	2,554	2,975
Computers	4,762	4,046	3,727
Cooking	1,946	1,733	1,701
Crafts and Hobbies	748	734	659
Design	618	515	479
Drama	553	469	480
Education	7,529	6,106	5,718
Family and Relationships	860	836	849
Fiction	17,537	15,885	17,993
Foreign Language Study	1,289	1,188	717
Games and Activities	782	808	813
Gardening	247	209	233
Health and Fitness	1,375	1,294	1,294
History	12,966	12,199	11,610
House and Home	240	182	196
Humor	566	460	433
Language Arts and Disciplines	3,250	2,812	2,834
Law	5,500	5,580	5,890
Literary Collections	736	684	716
Literary Criticism	5,002	4,803	4,920
Mathematics	2,596	2,064	1,960
Medical	8,057	6,468	6,557
Music	2,740	4,222	2,154
Nature	1,134	1,151	1,276
Performing Arts	1,756	1,629	1,734
Pets	179	160	146
Philosophy	3,865	3,582	3,541
Photography	1,145	1,086	842
Poetry	2,382	2,155	2,191
Political Science	9,982	8,449	7,892
Psychology	4,941	3,036	2,903
Reference	711	489	451
Religion	9,645	8,626	8,062
Science	8,513	7,032	7,427
Self-help	1,752	1,641	1,694
Social Science	11,053	9,984	8,850
Sports and Recreation	1,542	1,332	1,326
Study Aids	2,602	2,480	778
Technology and Engineering	6,152	6,132	6,790
Transportation	689	556	497
Travel	1,783	1,124	926
True Crime	361	296	345
Young Adult	4,920	3,790	3,162
Totals	209,892	188,412	182,015

Table 2 / Hardcover Output and Average Per-Volume Prices, 2019–2021

BISAC Category	2019 Vols.	2019 $ Total	2019 Avg.	2020 Vols.	2020 $ Total	2020 Avg.	2021 Vols.	2021 $ Total	2021 Avg.
Antiques and Collectibles	101	$6,672.84	$66.07	96	$7,462.19	$77.73	78	$6,023.44	$77.22
Architecture	928	$87,959.88	$94.78	902	$84,717.91	$93.92	836	$76,382.05	$91.37
Art	2,247	$166,818.37	$74.24	2,051	$168,247.85	$82.03	1,834	$153,851.67	$83.89
Bibles	188	$10,833.86	$57.63	201	$10,125.81	$50.38	191	$12,892.07	$67.50
Biography and Autobiography	1,575	$65,706.47	$41.72	1,520	$65,233.64	$42.92	1,767	$72,802.48	$41.20
Body, Mind and Spirit	291	$7,503.38	$25.78	307	$7,011.60	$22.84	308	$8,987.15	$29.18
Business and Economics	4,346	$619,599.19	$142.57	4,164	$568,807.25	$136.60	4,408	$590,530.47	$133.97
Children	16,335	$415,227.03	$25.42	15,438	$370,615.78	$24.01	14,376	$359,032.94	$24.97
Comics and Graphic Novels	689	$33,481.14	$48.59	651	$30,401.72	$46.70	637	$31,031.10	$48.71
Computers	1,118	$181,987.82	$162.78	1,027	$155,911.23	$151.81	1,046	$188,570.85	$180.28
Cooking	1,110	$33,590.95	$30.26	927	$29,382.06	$31.70	947	$31,767.21	$33.55
Crafts and Hobbies	158	$5,116.25	$32.38	143	$4,640.27	$32.45	137	$4,291.55	$31.33
Design	365	$25,039.38	$68.60	305	$21,272.43	$69.75	258	$18,164.32	$70.40
Drama	84	$9,374.02	$111.60	76	$7,920.69	$104.22	81	$7,443.34	$91.89
Education	2,556	$431,333.43	$168.75	2,315	$364,108.85	$157.28	2,326	$326,692.01	$140.45
Family and Relationships	225	$10,540.24	$46.85	223	$11,134.22	$49.93	242	$16,245.55	$67.13
Fiction	5,055	$150,272.42	$29.73	4,523	$135,395.85	$29.93	5,081	$148,390.91	$29.21
Foreign Language Study	216	$26,333.58	$121.91	236	$28,208.89	$119.53	237	$27,663.91	$116.73
Games and Activities	145	$5,582.89	$38.50	136	$5,493.22	$40.39	122	$6,943.34	$56.91
Gardening	121	$4,753.20	$39.28	110	$4,187.24	$38.07	118	$4,274.48	$36.22
Health and Fitness	393	$32,995.25	$83.96	352	$29,556.34	$83.97	351	$25,675.16	$73.15
History	6,222	$642,620.32	$103.28	5,658	$616,355.69	$108.94	5,654	$574,612.82	$101.63
House and Home	131	$5,524.16	$42.17	116	$4,546.32	$39.19	122	$5,300.18	$43.44
Humor	298	$5,796.25	$19.45	250	$5,125.36	$20.50	225	$5,317.94	$23.64
Language Arts and Disciplines	1,476	$206,026.26	$139.58	1,319	$172,870.92	$131.06	1,347	$182,145.97	$135.22
Law	2,272	$399,359.29	$175.77	2,295	$418,112.99	$182.18	2,396	$418,622.41	$174.72
Literary Collections	272	$36,768.61	$135.18	252	$28,311.59	$112.35	258	$21,713.51	$84.16
Literary Criticism	2,649	$331,447.62	$125.12	2,574	$328,614.62	$127.67	2,671	$341,896.71	$128.00
Mathematics	994	$147,273.05	$148.16	844	$118,000.81	$139.81	829	$115,137.01	$138.89

Table 2 / Hardcover Output and Average Per-Volume Prices, 2019–2021 (cont.)

BISAC Category	2019 Vols.	2019 $ Total	2019 Avg.	2020 Vols.	2020 $ Total	2020 Avg.	2021 Vols.	2021 $ Total	2021 Avg.
Medical	3,547	$621,285.30	$175.16	2,855	$523,950.52	$183.52	2,567	$488,750.23	$190.40
Music	675	$65,058.93	$96.38	653	$62,933.31	$96.38	586	$56,766.66	$96.87
Nature	466	$44,065.62	$94.56	453	$37,788.26	$83.42	523	$44,642.85	$85.36
Performing Arts	775	$93,878.58	$121.13	795	$80,836.91	$101.68	834	$84,322.73	$101.11
Pets	56	$1,531.13	$27.34	60	$1,366.47	$22.77	51	$1,352.52	$26.52
Philosophy	1,899	$219,211.69	$115.44	1,762	$211,974.53	$120.30	1,710	$192,026.50	$112.30
Photography	825	$57,631.20	$69.86	790	$46,803.33	$59.24	607	$74,045.42	$121.99
Poetry	320	$11,832.92	$36.98	259	$9,179.73	$35.44	331	$10,946.12	$33.07
Political Science	5,551	$707,555.20	$127.46	3,642	$410,868.68	$112.81	3,403	$399,069.85	$117.27
Psychology	2,736	$395,627.13	$144.60	1,187	$173,459.19	$146.13	1,148	$174,993.71	$152.43
Reference	311	$87,253.15	$280.56	231	$85,075.39	$368.29	219	$69,467.13	$317.20
Religion	2,746	$240,103.78	$87.44	2,820	$237,753.26	$84.31	2,895	$254,261.84	$87.83
Science	4,144	$784,096.60	$189.21	3,549	$668,906.22	$188.48	3,457	$663,469.59	$191.92
Self-help	438	$10,597.56	$24.20	418	$9,814.93	$23.48	459	$11,157.40	$24.31
Social Science	5,354	$688,258.22	$128.55	4,014	$496,988.83	$123.81	4,053	$515,697.15	$127.24
Sports and Recreation	541	$28,277.44	$52.27	492	$27,230.50	$55.35	515	$30,835.86	$59.88
Study Aids	9	$1,600.82	$177.87	30	$3,751.13	$125.04	10	$1,608.91	$160.89
Technology and Engineering	3,007	$558,885.28	$185.86	3,171	$577,385.97	$182.08	3,389	$651,475.43	$192.23
Transportation	301	$26,023.10	$86.46	219	$19,595.05	$89.48	238	$21,710.36	$91.22
Travel	238	$9,943.59	$41.78	215	$7,912.00	$36.80	176	$7,421.36	$42.17
True Crime	107	$3,998.22	$37.37	82	$4,993.72	$60.90	97	$3,852.34	$39.71
Young Adult	1,995	$75,114.20	$37.65	1,489	$44,662.20	$29.99	1,191	$31,839.16	$26.73
Totals	88,601	$8,837,366.81	$99.74	78,197	$7,545,003.47	$96.49	77,342	$7,572,115.67	$97.90

Table 3 / Hardcover Output and Average Per-Volume Prices, Less than $81, 2019–2021

BISAC Category	2019 Vols.	2019 $ Total	2019 Avg.	2020 Vols.	2020 $ Total	2020 Avg.	2021 Vols.	2021 $ Total	2021 Avg.
Antiques and Collectibles	79	$3,721.91	$47.11	67	$3,017.20	$45.03	56	$2,838.45	$50.69
Architecture	509	$25,058.14	$49.23	535	$27,312.05	$51.05	491	$25,791.87	$52.53
Art	1,629	$75,128.41	$46.12	1,433	$66,850.05	$46.65	1,243	$58,291.20	$46.90
Bibles	165	$6,645.06	$40.27	186	$8,099.96	$43.55	151	$6,338.42	$41.98
Biography and Autobiography	1,453	$45,165.37	$31.08	1,391	$42,849.16	$30.80	1,617	$50,947.51	$31.51
Body, Mind and Spirit	279	$5,411.03	$19.39	298	$5,824.61	$19.55	293	$6,696.30	$22.85
Business and Economics	1,397	$58,279.72	$41.72	1,464	$61,683.96	$42.13	1,546	$63,995.32	$41.39
Children	15,895	$338,715.53	$21.31	15,124	$316,143.78	$20.90	14,081	$282,133.03	$20.04
Comics and Graphic Novels	592	$19,552.57	$33.03	555	$18,361.96	$33.08	527	$17,846.36	$33.86
Computers	182	$10,271.44	$56.44	188	$11,310.88	$60.16	205	$12,203.02	$59.53
Cooking	1,097	$30,340.95	$27.66	900	$24,938.54	$27.71	918	$27,115.29	$29.54
Crafts and Hobbies	154	$4,643.75	$30.15	141	$4,390.27	$31.14	134	$3,891.55	$29.04
Design	267	$12,020.65	$45.02	208	$9,096.49	$43.73	179	$7,911.43	$44.20
Drama	27	$1,392.32	$51.57	25	$1,237.91	$49.52	26	$972.50	$37.40
Education	568	$29,699.18	$52.29	510	$27,472.89	$53.87	431	$24,395.49	$56.60
Family and Relationships	183	$4,405.48	$24.07	188	$4,840.58	$25.75	200	$5,188.67	$25.94
Fiction	5,024	$146,621.69	$29.18	4,476	$129,642.02	$28.96	5,033	$142,660.05	$28.34
Foreign Language Study	72	$4,208.03	$58.44	76	$4,552.88	$59.91	79	$4,710.35	$59.62
Games and Activities	134	$4,182.95	$31.22	125	$3,961.27	$31.69	100	$3,450.45	$34.50
Gardening	113	$3,898.20	$34.50	104	$3,332.29	$32.04	111	$3,601.53	$32.45
Health and Fitness	259	$7,430.52	$28.69	225	$6,257.27	$27.81	264	$7,597.55	$28.78
History	2,864	$125,561.09	$43.84	2,605	$114,423.39	$43.92	2,438	$106,871.70	$43.84
House and Home	125	$4,979.16	$39.83	110	$3,960.33	$36.00	115	$4,460.73	$38.79
Humor	297	$5,646.25	$19.01	247	$4,720.36	$19.11	219	$4,432.99	$20.24
Language Arts and Disciplines	275	$15,402.30	$56.01	227	$12,991.93	$57.23	233	$13,162.90	$56.49
Law	297	$16,586.71	$55.85	275	$15,469.83	$56.25	285	$15,728.92	$55.19
Literary Collections	128	$4,491.28	$35.09	121	$4,714.39	$38.96	148	$4,861.80	$32.85
Literary Criticism	648	$36,600.66	$56.48	630	$36,162.11	$57.40	592	$33,911.00	$57.28
Mathematics	125	$7,316.57	$58.53	133	$8,127.31	$61.11	138	$8,272.05	$59.94

Table 3 / Hardcover Output and Average Per-Volume Prices, Less than $81, 2019–2021 (cont.)

BISAC Category	2019 Vols.	2019 $ Total	2019 Avg.	2020 Vols.	2020 $ Total	2020 Avg.	2021 Vols.	2021 $ Total	2021 Avg.
Medical	332	$18,715.29	$56.37	267	$14,732.61	$55.18	295	$16,212.81	$54.96
Music	299	$12,405.30	$41.49	299	$13,443.42	$44.96	262	$11,564.79	$44.14
Nature	261	$8,679.64	$33.26	269	$8,997.16	$33.45	311	$10,079.32	$32.41
Performing Arts	280	$12,138.39	$43.35	244	$10,019.59	$41.06	282	$12,095.21	$42.89
Pets	53	$1,236.13	$23.32	59	$1,261.52	$21.38	50	$1,152.52	$23.05
Philosophy	489	$24,684.90	$50.48	507	$25,836.54	$50.96	446	$23,277.02	$52.19
Photography	719	$33,159.59	$46.12	704	$32,826.53	$46.63	529	$25,137.52	$47.52
Poetry	291	$7,950.10	$27.32	236	$6,549.98	$27.75	303	$8,270.32	$27.29
Political Science	1,102	$51,294.69	$46.55	1,097	$48,235.27	$43.97	919	$43,070.66	$46.87
Psychology	241	$11,378.29	$47.21	229	$10,596.33	$46.27	245	$11,354.85	$46.35
Reference	119	$3,520.25	$29.58	96	$2,619.67	$27.29	82	$2,047.73	$24.97
Religion	1,554	$54,212.69	$34.89	1,571	$55,123.56	$35.09	1,570	$54,312.89	$34.59
Science	620	$29,074.99	$46.90	566	$26,128.29	$46.16	576	$25,476.88	$44.23
Self-help	436	$10,120.57	$23.21	415	$9,404.93	$22.66	456	$10,811.46	$23.71
Social Science	1,069	$53,446.02	$50.00	1,036	$49,932.90	$48.20	933	$45,180.21	$48.42
Sports and Recreation	444	$14,061.11	$31.67	397	$13,076.28	$32.94	400	$12,993.08	$32.48
Study Aids	4	$200.94	$50.24	22	$1,206.77	$54.85	4	$159.93	$39.98
Technology and Engineering	235	$12,773.21	$54.35	244	$14,014.84	$57.44	239	$13,163.76	$55.08
Transportation	219	$8,996.67	$41.08	163	$7,753.43	$47.57	169	$7,924.71	$46.89
Travel	222	$7,344.84	$33.08	199	$6,202.05	$31.17	160	$5,233.96	$32.71
True Crime	104	$3,728.28	$35.85	79	$2,364.72	$29.93	92	$3,038.34	$33.03
Young Adult	1,907	$54,059.60	$28.35	1,456	$36,503.37	$25.07	1,173	$27,055.57	$23.07
Totals	45,837	$1,486,558.41	$32.43	42,722	$1,378,575.43	$32.27	41,349	$1,319,891.97	$31.92

Table 4 / Mass Market Paperbacks Output and Average Per-Volume Prices, 2019–2021

BISAC Category	2019 Vols.	2019 $ Total	2019 Avg.	2020 Vols.	2020 $ Total	2020 Avg.	2021 Vols.	2021 $ Total	2021 Avg.
Biography and Autobiography	3	$29.97	$9.99	3	$27.97	$9.32	3	$30.97	$10.32
Children	187	$1,603.89	$8.58	222	$1,949.54	$8.78	213	$1,924.61	$9.04
Family and Relationships				2	$18.98	$9.49			
Fiction	2,468	$18,386.96	$7.45	2,256	$17,253.02	$7.65	2,228	$17,410.05	$7.81
Health and Fitness	1	$13.99	$13.99				2	$17.98	$8.99
History	4	$35.96	$8.99	4	$39.96	$9.99	2	$19.98	$9.99
Language Arts and Disciplines	1	$7.99	$7.99						
Performing Arts	1	$8.99	$8.99						
Philosophy				2	$7.98	$3.99			
Poetry							1	$3.99	$3.99
Political Science	1	$9.99	$9.99						
Psychology	1	$4.99	$4.99						
Reference				1	$8.99	$8.99	3	$22.50	$7.50
Self-help	4	$50.96	$12.74				3	$23.97	$7.99
Sports and Recreation							1	$9.99	$9.99
True Crime	6	$52.94	$8.82	5	$44.95	$8.99	4	$38.96	$9.74
Young Adult	36	$349.64	$9.71	47	$562.50	$11.97	33	$360.67	$10.93
Totals	2,713	$20,556.27	$7.58	2,542	$19,913.89	$7.83	2,493	$19,863.67	$7.97

Table 5 / Trade Paperbacks Output and Average Per-Volume Prices, 2019–2021

BISAC Category	2019 Vols.	2019 $ Total	2019 Avg.	2020 Vols.	2020 $ Total	2020 Avg.	2021 Vols.	2021 $ Total	2021 Avg.
Antiques and Collectibles	87	$3,630.56	$41.73	79	$3,479.39	$44.04	70	$3,038.82	$43.41
Architecture	914	$46,109.54	$50.45	892	$43,733.41	$49.03	797	$41,252.95	$51.76
Art	1,759	$69,559.73	$39.55	1,581	$62,846.97	$39.75	1,450	$58,818.16	$40.56
Bibles	630	$30,585.85	$48.55	485	$27,458.11	$56.61	515	$30,252.85	$58.74
Biography and Autobiography	2,424	$50,450.01	$20.81	2,290	$48,346.30	$21.11	2,415	$51,886.22	$21.48
Body, Mind and Spirit	826	$15,734.25	$19.05	819	$15,501.64	$18.93	843	$16,791.40	$19.92
Business and Economics	6,730	$493,922.04	$73.39	6,123	$420,726.17	$68.71	5,985	$418,807.59	$69.98
Children	12,027	$154,689.48	$12.86	10,428	$121,393.76	$11.64	10,035	$122,305.38	$12.19
Comics and Graphic Novels	2,196	$45,325.95	$20.64	1,903	$35,917.85	$18.87	2,336	$43,259.25	$18.52
Computers	3,387	$348,339.37	$102.85	2,958	$239,484.39	$80.96	2,660	$211,944.10	$79.68
Cooking	832	$18,412.69	$22.13	805	$17,175.00	$21.34	754	$16,107.56	$21.36
Crafts and Hobbies	577	$12,920.85	$22.39	573	$12,424.34	$21.68	495	$10,959.47	$22.14
Design	253	$11,639.29	$46.01	210	$7,729.88	$36.81	221	$8,606.72	$38.94
Drama	463	$10,657.66	$23.02	393	$8,535.84	$21.72	399	$7,820.72	$19.60
Education	4,852	$638,931.70	$131.68	3,716	$388,217.45	$104.47	3,364	$178,188.87	$52.97
Family and Relationships	635	$13,953.46	$21.97	610	$12,968.95	$21.26	605	$12,807.40	$21.17
Fiction	10,014	$176,182.19	$17.59	9,107	$160,666.47	$17.64	10,683	$189,471.47	$17.74
Foreign Language Study	1,012	$42,593.22	$42.09	923	$39,538.09	$42.84	478	$22,016.41	$46.06
Games and Activities	635	$11,456.85	$18.04	671	$12,067.01	$17.98	691	$12,555.49	$18.17
Gardening	126	$2,828.09	$22.45	99	$2,307.14	$23.30	115	$2,833.87	$24.64
Health and Fitness	968	$31,838.43	$32.89	928	$29,713.30	$32.02	932	$30,038.30	$32.23
History	6,654	$269,157.33	$40.45	6,500	$258,839.33	$39.82	5,918	$232,233.81	$39.24
House and Home	109	$2,649.43	$24.31	66	$1,516.69	$22.98	74	$1,874.32	$25.33
Humor	268	$4,205.52	$15.69	210	$3,559.28	$16.95	208	$3,500.21	$16.83
Language Arts and Disciplines	1,704	$98,048.14	$57.54	1,435	$79,573.88	$55.45	1,454	$80,817.00	$55.58

Law	3,146	$270,687.66	$86.04	3,198	$279,495.07	$87.40	3,408	$285,756.22	$83.85
Literary Collections	464	$11,560.63	$24.92	429	$12,262.44	$28.58	458	$13,748.40	$30.02
Literary Criticism	2,352	$105,102.29	$44.69	2,228	$93,347.98	$41.90	2,249	$100,181.13	$44.54
Mathematics	1,373	$104,914.05	$76.41	1,131	$76,412.63	$67.56	1,091	$80,474.61	$73.76
Medical	4,470	$338,959.14	$87.02	3,581	$290,776.58	$81.20	3,937	$332,577.06	$84.47
Music	2,056	$62,529.02	$30.41	3,556	$97,321.51	$27.37	1,564	$49,920.82	$31.92
Nature	668	$28,188.82	$42.20	696	$24,379.95	$35.03	749	$30,803.57	$41.13
Performing Arts	972	$37,426.58	$38.50	833	$30,607.28	$36.74	895	$35,721.51	$39.91
Pets	123	$2,505.87	$20.37	100	$1,858.26	$18.58	95	$1,912.69	$20.13
Philosophy	1,947	$82,529.80	$42.39	1,808	$76,370.10	$42.24	1,823	$86,681.68	$47.55
Photography	319	$12,794.85	$40.11	296	$10,737.96	$36.28	235	$10,431.72	$44.39
Poetry	2,062	$35,766.67	$17.35	1,896	$33,036.49	$17.42	1,858	$33,041.48	$17.78
Political Science	4,398	$222,822.89	$50.66	4,797	$225,148.83	$46.94	4,470	$214,750.19	$48.04
Psychology	2,130	$110,491.81	$51.87	1,804	$96,554.28	$53.52	1,706	$85,999.19	$50.41
Reference	399	$51,238.64	$128.42	254	$52,887.03	$208.22	226	$51,727.79	$228.88
Religion	6,867	$192,895.33	$28.09	5,798	$158,949.73	$27.41	5,167	$154,036.57	$29.81
Science	4,172	$395,127.15	$94.71	3,361	$315,473.81	$93.86	3,887	$373,944.21	$96.20
Self-help	1,310	$23,455.25	$17.90	1,220	$21,805.61	$17.87	1,232	$22,025.63	$17.88
Social Science	5,640	$280,031.44	$49.65	5,910	$281,178.69	$47.58	4,761	$222,714.34	$46.78
Sports and Recreation	996	$26,844.51	$26.95	837	$22,670.15	$27.09	809	$21,793.09	$26.94
Study Aids	2,593	$113,082.09	$43.61	2,449	$106,651.82	$43.55	768	$35,866.23	$46.70
Technology and Engineering	3,099	$367,630.74	$118.63	2,918	$369,940.40	$126.78	3,380	$451,962.95	$133.72
Transportation	388	$14,740.19	$37.99	337	$11,481.70	$34.07	259	$9,065.55	$35.00
Travel	1,545	$33,213.64	$21.50	909	$18,960.36	$20.86	750	$16,179.52	$21.57
True Crime	248	$4,962.89	$20.01	209	$4,047.31	$19.56	244	$4,973.96	$20.39
Young Adult	2,889	$54,028.08	$18.70	2,254	$36,749.42	$16.30	1,938	$30,994.05	$15.99
Totals	116,708	$5,637,351.66	$48.30	106,613	$4,802,866.03	$45.05	101,456	$4,565,472.50	$45.00

Table 6 / Audiobook Output and Average Per-Volume Prices, 2019–2021

BISAC Category	2019 Vols.	2019 $ Total	2019 Avg.	2020 Vols.	2020 $ Total	2020 Avg.	2021 Vols.	2021 $ Total	2021 Avg.
Antiques and Collectibles				3	$122.97	$40.99	9	$176.91	$19.66
Architecture	8	$264.92	$33.12	5	$209.95	$41.99	12	$309.81	$25.82
Art	8	$248.43	$31.05	13	$433.87	$33.37	47	$1,030.97	$21.94
Bibles	3	$228.94	$76.31	12	$386.00	$32.17	8	$417.23	$52.15
Biography and Autobiography	1,376	$60,030.60	$43.63	1,209	$51,721.76	$42.78	3,052	$90,244.54	$29.57
Body, Mind and Spirit	180	$6,330.91	$35.17	163	$5,837.55	$35.81	401	$10,364.89	$25.85
Business and Economics	656	$24,186.05	$36.87	656	$26,609.86	$40.56	1,147	$30,952.01	$26.99
Children	1,555	$57,747.79	$37.14	1,846	$61,230.36	$33.17	1,372	$43,962.45	$32.04
Comics and Graphic Novels	66	$2,479.34	$37.57	31	$1,129.69	$36.44	4	$117.96	$29.49
Computers	33	$1,255.59	$38.05	12	$416.74	$34.73	106	$2,778.47	$26.21
Cooking	16	$596.84	$37.30	34	$1,323.43	$38.92	144	$3,847.90	$26.72
Crafts and Hobbies	5	$198.96	$39.79	3	$119.97	$39.99	13	$221.25	$17.02
Design	1	$39.99	$39.99	4	$164.96	$41.24	6	$128.94	$21.49
Drama	98	$2,187.60	$22.32	36	$923.49	$25.65	124	$3,613.24	$29.14
Education	39	$1,489.67	$38.20	26	$995.64	$38.29	181	$4,450.33	$24.59
Family and Relationships	185	$6,846.41	$37.01	150	$5,442.96	$36.29	620	$13,506.79	$21.79
Fiction	11,455	$459,993.90	$40.16	12,254	$508,658.92	$41.51	19,599	$612,432.62	$31.25
Foreign Language Study	147	$12,700.41	$86.40	39	$2,055.34	$52.70	3	$100.93	$33.64
Games and Activities	2	$44.98	$22.49	4	$169.96	$42.49	23	$585.22	$25.44
Gardening	1	$14.99	$14.99	9	$337.91	$37.55	10	$263.86	$26.39
Health and Fitness	242	$9,720.66	$40.17	222	$9,541.71	$42.98	502	$14,231.08	$28.35
History	811	$37,631.72	$46.40	720	$33,875.78	$47.05	2,179	$61,765.56	$28.35
House and Home	13	$447.85	$34.45	17	$671.82	$39.52	28	$652.73	$23.31
Humor	74	$2,648.06	$35.78	85	$3,371.76	$39.67	316	$6,375.96	$20.18

Category								
Language Arts and Disciplines	47	$1,786.29	$38.01	26	$1,100.70	$42.33	107	$2,693.81	$25.18
Law	25	$778.68	$31.15	30	$1,164.57	$38.82	110	$2,639.40	$23.99
Literary Collections	66	$2,771.90	$42.00	34	$1,325.45	$38.98	100	$3,071.53	$30.72
Literary Criticism	27	$880.59	$32.61	36	$1,243.50	$34.54	118	$3,236.44	$27.43
Mathematics	7	$326.87	$46.70	2	$64.98	$32.49	27	$742.74	$27.51
Medical	31	$1,013.62	$32.70	36	$1,453.43	$40.37	168	$4,352.25	$25.91
Music	64	$2,656.28	$41.50	51	$1,883.92	$36.94	204	$5,417.90	$26.56
Nature	93	$3,898.76	$41.92	109	$4,641.13	$42.58	238	$6,054.82	$25.44
Performing Arts	116	$4,766.81	$41.09	177	$7,588.29	$42.87	375	$12,217.35	$32.58
Pets	18	$769.77	$42.77	18	$673.83	$37.44	107	$2,258.25	$21.11
Philosophy	74	$2,533.89	$34.24	51	$1,992.38	$39.07	252	$6,726.30	$26.69
Photography			#Div/0!	1	$29.99	$29.99	7	$132.93	$18.99
Poetry	106	$3,062.75	$28.89	137	$4,193.07	$30.61	122	$2,244.35	$18.40
Political Science	368	$15,875.83	$43.14	395	$17,849.29	$45.19	866	$24,969.68	$28.83
Psychology	99	$3,480.81	$35.16	118	$5,463.37	$46.30	464	$12,856.58	$27.71
Reference	7	$214.91	$30.70	8	$289.93	$36.24	32	$897.05	$28.03
Religion	930	$32,676.52	$35.14	812	$30,564.72	$37.64	1,158	$35,366.75	$30.54
Science	168	$6,930.04	$41.25	220	$8,921.98	$40.55	613	$18,536.66	$30.24
Self-help	517	$18,306.19	$35.41	501	$18,798.93	$37.52	811	$22,522.96	$27.77
Social Science	265	$11,101.54	$41.89	274	$10,844.15	$39.58	776	$20,246.75	$26.09
Sports and Recreation	142	$5,979.59	$42.11	145	$5,568.47	$38.40	350	$8,826.27	$25.22
Study Aids	2	$125.99	$63.00	3	$115.97	$38.66	6	$148.38	$24.73
Technology and Engineering	13	$510.80	$39.29	16	$619.77	$38.74	111	$2,910.52	$26.22
Transportation	2	$99.98	$49.99	3	$139.97	$46.66	42	$733.86	$17.47
Travel	49	$2,078.45	$42.42	35	$1,434.59	$40.99	143	$3,865.48	$27.03
True Crime	193	$8,321.18	$43.11	147	$6,703.77	$45.60	445	$12,296.66	$27.63
Young Adult	1,224	$53,623.73	$43.81	1,162	$50,153.19	$43.16	1,210	$41,296.76	$34.13
Totals	21,627	$871,906.38	$40.32	22,100	$900,575.74	$40.75	38,868	$1,159,794.08	$29.84

Table 7 / E-Book Output and Average Per-Volume Prices, 2019–2021

BISAC Category	2019 Vols.	2019 $ Total	2019 Avg.	2020 Vols.	2020 $ Total	2020 Avg.	2021 Vols.	2021 $ Total	2021 Avg.
Antiques and Collectibles	147	$1,759.81	$11.97	123	$3,485.28	$28.34	123	$2,578.90	$20.97
Architecture	498	$25,289.29	$50.78	397	$22,015.12	$55.45	358	$20,837.94	$58.21
Art	1,724	$62,535.06	$36.27	1,138	$53,753.86	$47.24	1,013	$42,687.64	$42.14
Bibles	300	$4,297.62	$14.33	367	$6,200.92	$16.90	358	$5,596.12	$15.63
Biography and Autobiography	7,127	$165,833.11	$23.27	7,529	$227,164.69	$30.17	9,586	$252,489.44	$26.34
Body, Mind and Spirit	3,575	$47,243.71	$13.22	3,888	$66,479.14	$17.10	4,087	$77,068.49	$18.86
Business and Economics	24,398	$1,665,752.54	$68.27	20,318	$1,163,671.93	$57.27	11,269	$438,827.92	$38.94
Children	28,490	$558,886.35	$19.62	23,945	$479,297.48	$20.02	25,219	$488,948.85	$19.39
Comics and Graphic Novels	1,062	$12,579.45	$11.85	2,365	$22,983.93	$9.72	1,650	$21,612.53	$13.10
Computers	2,448	$154,762.19	$63.22	2,009	$118,937.80	$59.20	1,808	$107,700.58	$59.57
Cooking	2,935	$41,599.49	$14.17	2,635	$49,979.37	$18.97	3,193	$60,378.75	$18.91
Crafts and Hobbies	563	$8,813.94	$15.66	746	$12,930.87	$17.33	907	$14,483.74	$15.97
Design	139	$6,071.16	$43.68	147	$5,638.45	$38.36	152	$4,038.41	$26.57
Drama	989	$14,927.44	$15.09	738	$16,758.30	$22.71	611	$11,128.62	$18.21
Education	5,349	$229,008.47	$42.81	3,603	$165,443.76	$45.92	3,393	$156,690.25	$46.18
Family and Relationships	2,304	$35,412.28	$15.37	2,609	$49,892.18	$19.12	3,241	$60,359.40	$18.62
Fiction	85,303	$1,163,141.11	$13.64	78,038	$1,922,612.85	$24.64	70,689	$1,522,596.08	$21.54
Foreign Language Study	1,560	$53,119.61	$34.05	4,719	$95,759.90	$20.29	979	$44,278.25	$45.23
Games and Activities	342	$6,882.78	$20.13	448	$14,231.62	$31.77	350	$9,715.45	$27.76
Gardening	290	$5,461.12	$18.83	385	$7,187.59	$18.67	525	$9,691.15	$18.46
Health and Fitness	3,002	$51,385.01	$17.12	3,646	$71,998.69	$19.75	4,155	$87,435.59	$21.04
History	9,283	$526,524.45	$56.72	12,645	$582,493.00	$46.07	8,133	$435,944.78	$53.60
House and Home	245	$4,879.98	$19.92	259	$5,926.41	$22.88	316	$6,711.22	$21.24
Humor	822	$13,339.13	$16.23	888	$15,506.28	$17.46	849	$17,580.78	$20.71
Language Arts and Disciplines	3,164	$322,015.73	$101.77	2,333	$244,045.45	$104.61	1,568	$122,771.71	$78.30

Category									
Law	2,804	$392,199.39	$139.87	2,671	$391,783.82	$146.68	2,114	$327,274.11	$154.81
Literary Collections	6,169	$31,959.32	$5.18	1,189	$28,391.80	$23.88	1,166	$29,852.54	$25.60
Literary Criticism	3,266	$319,110.17	$97.71	3,029	$326,641.10	$107.84	2,286	$201,395.53	$88.10
Mathematics	910	$88,338.05	$97.07	614	$68,294.70	$111.23	360	$41,274.51	$114.65
Medical	2,739	$352,126.86	$128.56	2,295	$228,711.04	$99.66	2,090	$199,066.73	$95.25
Music	1,785	$53,664.35	$30.06	1,604	$57,105.69	$35.60	1,572	$55,479.15	$35.29
Nature	784	$23,554.24	$30.04	785	$25,227.66	$32.14	1,022	$31,924.87	$31.24
Performing Arts	2,000	$57,719.81	$28.86	1,166	$45,443.93	$38.97	1,455	$60,969.15	$41.90
Pets	438	$6,310.42	$14.41	390	$6,586.58	$16.89	497	$9,147.84	$18.41
Philosophy	2,847	$149,573.76	$52.54	3,489	$162,910.02	$46.69	1,992	$122,518.12	$61.51
Photography	259	$5,872.48	$22.67	322	$7,862.54	$24.42	265	$6,885.12	$25.98
Poetry	4,621	$45,491.44	$9.84	3,939	$42,343.43	$10.75	4,322	$48,337.83	$11.18
Political Science	3,882	$211,166.36	$54.40	3,574	$195,855.29	$54.80	3,380	$174,224.22	$51.55
Psychology	1,883	$94,161.55	$50.01	2,322	$93,546.19	$40.29	2,087	$82,444.24	$39.50
Reference	871	$64,724.04	$74.31	753	$49,222.35	$65.37	783	$22,300.85	$28.48
Religion	11,169	$342,065.90	$30.63	12,354	$420,712.45	$34.05	12,512	$332,871.82	$26.60
Science	3,715	$390,957.18	$105.24	2,812	$308,375.60	$109.66	2,754	$312,039.97	$113.30
Self-help	6,550	$85,456.65	$13.05	6,590	$117,375.52	$17.81	10,402	$163,995.33	$15.77
Social Science	4,445	$261,636.37	$58.86	3,711	$202,301.39	$54.51	3,956	$221,070.15	$55.88
Sports and Recreation	1,437	$31,381.95	$21.84	1,304	$33,486.96	$25.68	1,486	$35,544.59	$23.92
Study Aids	3,206	$101,849.51	$31.77	929	$15,028.23	$16.18	758	$13,879.42	$18.31
Technology and Engineering	2,588	$320,501.63	$123.84	1,407	$157,531.29	$111.96	1,319	$157,290.10	$119.25
Transportation	294	$8,947.30	$30.43	616	$17,874.40	$29.02	344	$10,153.02	$29.51
Travel	2,785	$35,192.85	$12.64	1,300	$28,390.69	$21.84	1,216	$27,683.67	$22.77
True Crime	559	$14,460.95	$25.87	649	$17,391.30	$26.80	1,235	$21,867.01	$17.71
Young Adult	6,672	$132,326.71	$19.83	6,784	$158,614.55	$23.38	6,985	$152,239.53	$21.80
Totals	264,737	$8,802,270.06	$33.25	242,516	$8,631,403.39	$35.59	222,890	$6,883,882.02	$30.88

(continued from page 355)

Average e-book pricing can be seen to fluctuate from 2019–2021 (Table 7), with 2020 being up from 2019 and then 2021 being down from both 2019 and 2020. E-book output has steadily decreased since 2019, dropping 9.13 percent from 2019–2021 and then again dropping 8.83 percent from 2020–2021. Every category has a healthy output in e-book format, with Self Help and True Crime showing the greatest increase in output during that period.

As with most years, Children's Books is the dominant category represented in Table 1, with 26.99 percent more output in 2021 than the next highest category, Fiction. Though this category ranks highly in most of the individual publication formats, it is the highest ranked among hardcovers, overtaking Fiction by 64.26 percent more titles in 2021. The average price of Children's titles is consistent across all formats, varying by plus or minus one dollar, with the only outlier being audiobooks, which dropped almost $4 between 2019–2020. The Young Adult category appears stable in both output and pricing for most publication formats, though it's worth noting that there are very few mass market titles published for the Young Adult market. The Young Adult market exploded around 2008, when *Twilight* was released; more recently, the total output of Young Adult titles has been decreasing slightly each year as from 2019–2020 when it decreased 22.97 percent.

Fiction, consistently a major category across all publication formats, dropped in output for 2020, but the preliminary 2021 figures show that it is already making a giant comeback in all formats except mass market and e-books. However, the mass market format in general has had declining output over the past few years overall. Fiction prices remained stable in most formats—increasing or decreasing by about 2 percent; the outliers being audiobooks and e-books, which saw more dramatic drops in average prices from 2020–2021.

The two topics most often in the spotlight in 2020 and 2021—Health and Fitness and Political Science—did now show the rise in output one might expect. The former maintained a similar output amount for all print categories, while the latter actually saw a drop in output for print categories. This suggests that consumers were looking to books as a way to escape these two heated topics; publishers replied to those needs by increasing output in more enjoyable topics, such as Biography and Autobiography, Nature, and Self-Help.

It will be interesting to see what categories begin to trend in 2022 as we emerge from COVID-19 and fall back into a more regular way of life. We may see surges in output amongst Political Science books, focusing on relations with Russia, or Social Science books, focusing on diversity, equity, and inclusion—two highly discussed current topics.

Number of Book Outlets in the United States and Canada

The *American Book Trade Directory* (Information Today, Inc.) has been published since 1915. Revised annually, it features lists of booksellers, wholesalers, periodicals, reference tools, and other information about the U.S. and Canadian book markets. The data shown in Table 1, the most current available, are from the 2022–2023 edition of the directory.

The 10,414 stores of various types shown are located throughout the United States, Canada, and regions administered by the United States. "General" bookstores stock trade books and children's books in a general variety of subjects. "College" stores (both general and specified) carry college-level textbooks. "Educational" outlets handle school textbooks up to and including the high school level. "Mail order" outlets (both general and specified) sell general trade books by mail and are not book clubs; all others operating by mail are classified according to the kinds of books carried.

"Antiquarian" dealers sell old and rare books. Stores handling secondhand books are classified as "used." "Paperback" stores have more than 80 percent of their stock in paperbound books. Stores with paperback departments are listed under the appropriate major classification ("general," "department store," "stationer," and so forth). Bookstores with at least 50 percent of their stock on a particular subject are classified by subject.

Table 1 / Bookstores in the United States and Canada, 2021

Category	United States	Canada
Antiquarian General	365	37
Antiquarian Mail Order	114	4
Antiquarian Specialized	67	1
Art Supply Store	12	1
College General	1,578	111
College Specialized	82	5
Comics	180	26
Computer Software	2	0
Cooking	194	7
Department Store	193	17
Educational	107	6
Federal Sites	305	1
Foreign Language	10	2
General	2,025	392
Gift Shop	77	6
Juvenile	44	11
Mail Order General	34	3
Mail Order Specialized	137	5

Table 1 / Bookstores in the United States and Canada, 2021
(cont.)

Category	United States	Canada
Metaphysics, New Age and Occult	93	12
Museum Store and Art Gallery	367	26
Nature and Natural History	27	5
Newsdealer	7	1
Office Supply	5	1
Other	2,115	267
Paperback	16	1
Religious	753	66
Self Help / Development	11	3
Stationer	3	2
Toy Store	36	73
Used	320	43
Totals	9,279	1,135

Part 5
Reference Information

Ready Reference

How to Obtain an ISBN

Beat Barblan
United States ISBN/SAN Agency

The International Standard Book Numbering (ISBN) system was introduced into the United Kingdom by J. Whitaker & Sons Ltd. in 1967 and into the United States in 1968 by R. R. Bowker. The Technical Committee on Documentation of the International Organization for Standardization (ISO TC 46) is responsible for the international standard.

The purpose of this standard is to "establish the specifications for the International Standard Book Number (ISBN) as a unique international identification system for each product form or edition of a monographic publication published or produced by a specific publisher." The standard specifies the construction of an ISBN, the rules for assignment and use of an ISBN, and all metadata associated with the allocation of an ISBN.

Types of monographic publications to which an ISBN may be assigned include printed books and pamphlets (in various product formats); electronic publications (either on the Internet or on physical carriers such as CD-ROMs or diskettes); educational/instructional films, videos, and transparencies; educational/instructional software; audiobooks on cassette or CD or DVD; braille publications; and microform publications.

Serial publications, printed music, and musical sound recordings are excluded from the ISBN standard as they are covered by other identification systems.

The ISBN is used by publishers, distributors, wholesalers, bookstores, and libraries, among others, in more than 200 countries and territories as an ordering and inventory system. It expedites the collection of data on new and forthcoming editions of monographic publications for print and electronic directories used by the book trade. Its use also facilitates rights management and the monitoring of sales data for the publishing industry.

As of January 1, 2007, a revision to the ISBN standard substantially increased the numbering capacity of the system. The 10-digit ISBN identifier (ISBN-10) was replaced by the ISBN 13-digit identifier (ISBN-13). All facets of book publishing are now expected to use the ISBN-13, and the ISBN agencies throughout the world are now issuing only ISBN-13s to publishers. Publishers with existing ISBN-10s need to convert their ISBNs to ISBN-13s by the addition of the EAN prefix 978 and recalculation of the new check digit:

ISBN-10: 0-8352-8235-X
ISBN-13: 978-0-8352-8235-2

As the inventory of 978 prefixes has started to exhaust, ISBN agencies have begun assigning ISBN-13s with the "979" prefix. There is no 10-digit equivalent for 979 ISBNs.

Construction of an ISBN

An ISBN currently consists of 13 digits separated into the following parts:

1 A prefix of "978" for an ISBN-10 converted to an ISBN-13 and a prefix of "979" for ISBN-13s without a 10-digit equivalent
2 Group or country identifier, which identifies a national or geographic grouping of publishers
3 Publisher identifier, which identifies a particular publisher within a group
4 Title identifier, which identifies a particular title or edition of a title
5 Check digit, the single digit at the end of the ISBN that validates the ISBN-13

For more information regarding ISBN-13 conversion services provided by the U.S. ISBN Agency at R. R. Bowker, LLC, visit the ISBN Agency website at http://www.isbn.org, or contact the U.S. ISBN Agency at isbn-san@bowker.com.

Publishers requiring their ISBNs to be converted from the ISBN-10 to ISBN-13 format can use the U.S. ISBN Agency's free ISBN-13 online converter at http://isbn.org/converterpub.asp. Publishers can also view their ISBNs online by accessing their personal account at http://www.myidentifiers.com.

Displaying the ISBN on a Product or Publication

When an ISBN is written or printed, it should be preceded by the letters ISBN, and each part should be separated by a space or hyphen. In the United States, the hyphen is used for separation, as in the following example: ISBN 978-0-8352-8235-2. In this example, 978 is the prefix that precedes the ISBN-13, 0 is the group identifier, 8352 is the publisher identifier, 8235 is the title identifier, and 2 is the check digit. The group of English-speaking countries, which includes the United States, Australia, Canada, New Zealand, and the United Kingdom, uses the group identifiers 0 and 1. The 979 assignments by the United States ISBN Agency will start with 979-8. The 8 will be unique to the United States. Of course, as with the 978-0 and 978-1, an ISBN starting with 979-8 will allow U.S. publishers and self-publishers to market their books anywhere in the world.

The ISBN Organization

The administration of the ISBN system is carried out at three levels—through the International ISBN Agency in the United Kingdom, through the national agencies, and through the publishing houses themselves. The International ISBN Agency, which is responsible for assigning country prefixes and for coordinating the worldwide implementation of the system, has an advisory panel that represents the

International Organization for Standardization (ISO), publishers, and libraries. The International ISBN Agency publishes the *Publishers International ISBN Directory,* which is a listing of all national agencies' publishers with their assigned ISBN publisher prefixes. R. R. Bowker, as the publisher of *Books in Print,* with its extensive and varied database of publishers' addresses, was the obvious place to initiate the ISBN system and to provide the service to the U.S. publishing industry. To date, the U.S. ISBN Agency has entered more than 450,000 publishers into the system.

ISBN Assignment Procedure

Assignment of ISBNs is a shared endeavor between the U.S. ISBN Agency and the publisher. Publishers can apply online through the ISBN Agency's website www.myidentifiers.com. Once the order is processed, an e-mail confirmation will be sent with instructions for managing the account. The publisher then has the responsibility of assigning an ISBN to each title, keeping an accurate record of each number assigned, and registering each title in the *Books in Print* database at www. myidentifiers.com. It is the responsibility of the ISBN Agency to validate assigned ISBNs and keep a record of all ISBN publisher prefixes in circulation.

ISBN implementation is very much market-driven. Major distributors, wholesalers, retailers, and so forth recognize the necessity of the ISBN system and request that publishers register with the ISBN Agency. Also, the ISBN is a mandatory bibliographic element in the International Standard Bibliographical Description (ISBD). The Library of Congress Cataloging in Publication (CIP) Division directs publishers to the agency to obtain their ISBN prefixes.

Location and Display of the ISBN

On books, pamphlets, and other printed material, the ISBN shall be printed on the verso of the title leaf or, if this is not possible, at the foot of the title leaf itself. It should also appear on the outside back cover or on the back of the jacket if the book has one (the lower right-hand corner is recommended). The ISBN shall also appear on any accompanying promotional materials following the provisions for location according to the format of the material.

On other monographic publications, the ISBN shall appear on the title or credit frames and any labels permanently affixed to the publication. If the publication is issued in a container that is an integral part of the publication, the ISBN shall be displayed on the label. If it is not possible to place the ISBN on the item or its label, then the number should be displayed on the bottom or the back of the container, box, sleeve, or frame. It should also appear on any accompanying material, including each component of a multitype publication.

Printing of ISBN in Machine-Readable Coding

All books should carry ISBNs in the EAN-13 bar code machine-readable format. All ISBN EAN-13 bar codes start with the EAN prefixes 978 and 979 for books. As of January 1, 2007, all EAN bar codes should have the ISBN-13 appearing immediately above the bar code in eye-readable format, preceded by the acronym

"ISBN." The recommended location of the EAN-13 bar code for books is in the lower right-hand corner of the back cover (see Figure 1).

Figure 1 / Printing the ISBN in Bookland/EAN Symbology

Five-Digit Add-On Code

In the United States, a five-digit add-on code is used for additional information. In the publishing industry, this code is used for price information. The lead digit of the five-digit add-on has been designated a currency identifier, when the add-on is used for price. Number 5 is the code for the U.S. dollar, while 6 denotes the Canadian dollar. Publishers that do not want to indicate price in the add-on should print the code 90000 (see Figure 2).

Figure 2 / Printing the ISBN Bookland/EAN Number in Bar Code with the Five-Digit Add-On Code

978 = ISBN Bookland/EAN prefix   90000 means no information
5 = Code for U.S. $ in the add-on code
2499 = $24.99

Reporting the Title and the ISBN

After the publisher reports a title to the ISBN Agency, the number is validated and the title is listed in the many R. R. Bowker hard-copy and electronic publications, including *Books in Print*; *Forthcoming Books*; *Paperbound Books in Print*; *Books in Print Supplement*; *Books Out of Print*; *Books in Print Online*; *Books in Print Plus-CD ROM*; *Children's Books in Print*; *Subject Guide to Children's Books in*

Print; *Books Out Loud: Bowker's Guide to AudioBooks*; *Bowker's Complete Video Directory*; *Software Encyclopedia*; *Software for Schools*; and other specialized publications.

For an ISBN application and information, visit the ISBN Agency website at www.myidentifiers.com, call the toll-free number 877-310-7333, fax 908-623-8508, or write to the United States ISBN Agency, 26 Main Street, Suite 102, Chatham, NJ 07928.

The ISSN, and How to Obtain One

U.S. ISSN Center
Library of Congress

In the early 1970s the rapid increase in the production and dissemination of information and an intensified desire to exchange information about serials in computerized form among different systems and organizations made it increasingly clear that a means to identify serial publications at an international level was needed. The International Standard Serial Number (ISSN) was developed and became the internationally accepted code for identifying serial publications.

The ISSN is an international standard. ISO 3297:2020, the sixth edition of the standard, was published in 2020. This edition expands on the role of the ISSN for digital resources, provides detailed information on implementing the standard in various technical environments, and explains the concept of "cluster ISSNs."

The scope of the ISSN is "continuing resources," a concept that was introduced with the 2007 edition. Continuing resources include not only serials such as journals, magazines, open-ended series, and blogs but also open-ended publications such as updating databases, updating loose-leaf services, and certain types of updating websites.

The number itself has no significance other than as a brief, unique, and unambiguous identifier. The ISSN consists of eight digits in the Arabic numerals 0 to 9, except for the last ("check") digit, which is calculated using Modulus 11 and uses an "X" in place of the numeral 10 to maintain the ISSN at 8 digits. The numbers appear as two groups of four digits separated by a hyphen and preceded by the letters ISSN—for example, ISSN 1234-5679.

The ISSN is not self-assigned by publishers. Administration of the ISSN is coordinated through the ISSN Network, an intergovernmental organization within the UNESCO/UNISIST program. The ISSN Network consists of national ISSN centers, coordinated by the ISSN International Centre, located in Paris. National ISSN Centers are responsible for registering serials published in their respective countries. Responsibility for the assignment of ISSN to titles from multinational publishers is allocated among the ISSN Centers in which the publisher has offices. A list of these publishers and the corresponding ISSN centers is located on the ISSN International Centre's website, http://www.issn.org.

The ISSN International Centre handles ISSN assignments for international organizations and for countries that do not have a national center. It also maintains and distributes the ISSN Register and makes it available in a variety of products, most commonly via the ISSN Portal, an online subscription database containing full metadata records for each ISSN as well as other features and functionality. In January 2018, a new ISSN Portal was released that includes free look-up and access to a subset of ISSN metadata. The ISSN Register is also available via Z39.50 access, and as a data file. Selected ISSN data can also be obtained in customized files or database extracts that can be used, for example, to check the accuracy or completeness of a requestor's list of titles and ISSN. Another available ISSN service is OAI-PMH, a customizable "harvesting" protocol through which external applications can automatically and regularly gather new and updated metadata on a defined schedule. The ISSN Register contains bibliographic records corresponding to each ISSN assignment as reported by national ISSN centers. The database contains records for more than 2.5 million ISSNs.

The ISSN is used all over the world by serials publishers to identify their serials and to distinguish their titles from others that are the same or similar. It is used by subscription services and libraries to manage files for orders, claims, and back issues. It is used in automated check-in systems by libraries that wish to process receipts more quickly. Copyright centers use the ISSN as a means to collect and disseminate royalties. It is also used as an identification code by postal services and legal deposit services. The ISSN is included as a verification element in interlibrary lending activities and for union catalogs as a collocating device. The ISSN is also incorporated into bar codes for optical recognition of serial publication identification and metadata and into the standards for the identification of issues and articles in serial publications. A key use of the ISSN is as an identifier in online systems, where it can serve to connect catalog records or citations in abstracting and indexing databases with full-text journal content via OpenURL resolvers or reference linking services, and as an identifier and link in archives of electronic and print serials.

Because serials are generally known and cited by title, assignment of the ISSN is inseparably linked to the key title, a standardized form of the title derived from information in the serial issue. Only one ISSN can be assigned to a title in a particular medium. For titles issued in multiple media—e.g., print, online, CD-ROM—a separate ISSN is assigned to each medium version. If a major title change occurs or the medium changes, a new ISSN must be assigned. Centers responsible for assigning ISSNs also construct the key title and create an associated bibliographic record.

A significant new feature of the 2007 ISSN standard was the Linking ISSN (ISSN-L), a mechanism that enables collocation or linking among different media versions of a continuing resource. The Linking ISSN allows a unique designation (one of the existing ISSNs) to be applied to all media versions of a continuing resource while retaining the separate ISSN that pertains to each version. When an ISSN is functioning as a Linking ISSN, the eight digits of the base ISSN are prefixed with the designation "ISSN-L." The Linking ISSN facilitates search, retrieval, and delivery across all medium versions of a serial or other continuing resource for improved ISSN functionality in OpenURL linking, search engines, library catalogs, and knowledge bases.

The ISSN standard also supports interoperability by specifying the use of ISSN and ISSN-L with other systems such as DOI, OpenURL, URN, and EAN bar codes. ISSN-L was implemented in the ISSN Register in 2008. To help ISSN users implement the ISSN-L in their databases, two free tables are available from the ISSN International Centre's home page: one lists each ISSN and its corresponding ISSN-L; the other lists each ISSN-L and its corresponding ISSNs. The Linking ISSN is the first example of a cluster ISSN; in 2020, the sixth edition of the standard introduced the potential for additional cluster ISSNs.

In the United States, the U.S. ISSN Center at the Library of Congress is responsible for assigning and maintaining the ISSNs for all U.S. serial and other continuing resource publications. Publishers wishing to have an ISSN assigned should follow the instructions on the U.S. ISSN Center's website. Although some of the more than 90 ISSN centers worldwide charge for ISSNs, ISSN assignment by the U.S. ISSN Center is free.

To obtain an ISSN for a U.S. publication by using the new application system, ISSN Uplink, or for more information about ISSNs in the United States, libraries, publishers, and other ISSN users should visit the U.S. ISSN Center's website, http://www.loc.gov/issn, or contact the U.S. ISSN Center, U.S. Programs, Law, and Literature, Library of Congress, 101 Independence Ave. S.E., Washington, DC 20540-4284; e-mail issn@loc.gov.

For information about ISSN products and services, and for application procedures that non-U.S. parties should use to apply for an ISSN, visit the ISSN International Centre's website, http://www.issn.org, or contact the International Centre at 45 rue de Turbigo, 75003 Paris, France (telephone 33-1-44-88-22-20, e-mail issnic@issn.org).

How to Obtain an SAN

Beat Barblan

United States ISBN/SAN Agency

SAN stands for Standard Address Number. The SAN system, an American National Standards Institute (ANSI) standard, assigns a unique identification number that is used to positively identify specific addresses of organizations in order to facilitate buying and selling transactions within the industry. It is recognized as the identification code for electronic communication within the industry.

For purposes of this standard, the book industry includes book publishers, book wholesalers, book distributors, book retailers, college bookstores, libraries, library binders, and serial vendors. Schools, school systems, technical institutes, and colleges and universities are not members of this industry, but are served by it and therefore included in the SAN system.

The purpose of the SAN is to ease communications among these organizations, of which there are several hundreds of thousands that engage in a large volume of separate transactions with one another. These transactions include purchases of books by book dealers, wholesalers, schools, colleges, and libraries from publishers and wholesalers; payments for all such purchases; and other communications between participants. The objective of this standard is to establish an identification code system by assigning each address within the industry a unique code to be used for positive identification for all book and serial buying and selling transactions.

Many organizations have similar names and multiple addresses, making identification of the correct contact point difficult and subject to error. In many cases, the physical movement of materials takes place between addresses that differ from the addresses to be used for the financial transactions. In such instances, there is ample opportunity for confusion and errors. Without identification by SAN, a complex record-keeping system would have to be instituted to avoid introducing errors. In addition, problems with the current numbering system—such as errors in billing, shipping, payments, and returns—are significantly reduced by using the SAN system. The SAN also eliminates one step in the order fulfillment process: the "look-up procedure" used to assign account numbers. Previously a store or library dealing with 50 different publishers was assigned a different account number by each of the suppliers. The SAN solved this problem. If a publisher prints its SAN on its stationery and ordering documents, vendors to whom it sends transactions do not have to look up the account number, but can proceed immediately to process orders by SAN.

Libraries are involved in many of the same transactions as book dealers, such as ordering and paying for books and charging and paying for various services to other libraries. Keeping records of transactions—whether these involve buying, selling, lending, or donations—entails operations suited to SAN use. SAN stationery speeds up order fulfillment and eliminate errors in shipping, billing, and crediting; this, in turn, means savings in both time and money.

History

Development of the Standard Address Number began in 1968, when Russell Reynolds, general manager of the National Association of College Stores (NACS), approached R. R. Bowker and suggested that a "Standard Account Number" system be implemented in the book industry. The first draft of a standard was prepared by an American National Standards Institute (ANSI) Committee Z39 subcommittee, which was co-chaired by Reynolds and Emery Koltay of Bowker. After Z39 members proposed changes, the current version of the standard was approved by NACS on December 17, 1979.

Format

The SAN consists of six digits plus a seventh *Modulus 11* check digit; a hyphen follows the third digit (XXX-XXXX) to facilitate transcription. The hyphen is to be used in print form, but need not be entered or retained in computer systems. Printed on documents, the Standard Address Number should be preceded by the identifier "SAN" to avoid confusion with other numerical codes (SAN XXXXXXX).

Check Digit Calculation

The check digit is based on *Modulus 11,* and can be derived as follows:

1. Write the digits of the basic number.   2 3 4 5 6 7
2. Write the constant weighting factors associated with each position by the basic number.   7 6 5 4 3 2
3. Multiply each digit by its associated weighting factor.   14 18 20 20 18 14
4. Add the products of the multiplications.   14 + 18 + 20 + 20 + 18 + 14 = 104
5. Divide the sum by Modulus 11 to find the remainder.   104 ÷ 11 = 9 plus a remainder of 5
6. Subtract the remainder from the Modulus 11 to generate the required check digit. If there is no remainder, generate a check digit of zero. If the check digit is 10, generate a check digit of X to represent 10, since the use of 10 would require an extra digit.   11 − 5 = 6
7. Append the check digit to create the standard seven-digit Standard Address Number.   SAN 234-5676

SAN Assignment

R. R. Bowker accepted responsibility for being the central administrative agency for SAN, and in that capacity assigns SANs to identify uniquely the addresses of organizations. No SANs can be reassigned; in the event that an organization should cease to exist, for example, its SAN would cease to be in circulation entirely. If an organization using an SAN should move or change its name with no change in ownership, its SAN would remain the same, and only the name or address would be updated to reflect the change.

The SAN should be used in all transactions; it is recommended that the SAN be imprinted on stationery, letterheads, order and invoice forms, checks, and all other documents used in executing various book transactions. The SAN should always be printed on a separate line above the name and address of the organization, preferably in the upper left-hand corner of the stationery to avoid confusion with other numerical codes pertaining to the organization, such as telephone number, zip code, and the like.

SAN Functions

The SAN is strictly a Standard Address Number, becoming functional only in applications determined by the user; these may include activities such as purchasing, billing, shipping, receiving, paying, crediting, and refunding. It is the method used by Pubnet and PubEasy systems and is required in all electronic data interchange communications using the Book Industry Systems Advisory Committee (BISAC) EDI formats. Every department that has an independent function within an organization could have an SAN for its own identification.

For additional information or to make suggestions, write to ISBN/SAN Agency, R. R. Bowker, LLC, 26 Main Street, Suite 102, Chatham, NJ 07928, call 877-310-7333, or fax 908-623-8508. The e-mail address is san@bowker.com. An SAN can be ordered online through the website www.myidentifiers.com, or an application can be requested by e-mail through san@bowker.com.

Distinguished Books

The Year's Notable Books

The Notable Books Council of the Reference and User Services Association (RUSA), a division of the American Library Association (ALA), released its annual list of notable books on January 23, 2022. These titles were selected for their significant contributions to the expansion of knowledge or for the pleasure they can provide to adult readers.

Fiction

Afterparties by Anthony Veasna So (Ecco, an imprint of HarperCollins)

Cloud Cuckoo Land by Anthony Doerr (Schribner, an imprint of Simon & Schuster, Inc.)

Gordo by Jaime Cortez (Black Cat, an imprint of Grove Atlantic)

Hell of a Book by Jason Mott (Dutton, an imprint of Penguin Random House, LLC)

Klara and the Sun by Kazuo Ishiguro (A Borzoi book published by Alfred A. Knopf)

Matrix by Lauren Groff (Riverhead Books, an imprint of Penguin Random House, LLC)

Painting Time by Maylis de Kerangal (Farrar, Straus and Giroux)

The Five Wounds by Kirstin Valdez Quade (W. W. Norton & Company)

The Love Songs of W.E.B. Du Bois by Honorée Fanonne Jeffers (Harper, an imprint of HarperCollins Publishers)

The Wrong End of the Telescope by Rabih Alameddine (Grove Press, an imprint of Grove Atlantic)

When We Cease to Understand the World by Benjamín Labatut (New York Review Books published by The New York Review of Books)

Nonfiction

A Little Devil in America: Notes in Praise of Black Performance by Hanif Abdurraqib (Random House, an imprint and division of Penguin Random House, LLC)

A World on the Wing: The Global Odyssey of Migratory Birds by Scott Weidensaul (W.W. Norton & Company)

Beyond: The Astonishing Story of the First Human to Leave Our Planet and Journey into Space by Stephen Walker (Harper, an imprint of HarperCollins Publishers)

Chasing Me to My Grave: An Artist's Memoir of the Jim Crow South by Winfred Rembert as told to Erin I. Kelly (Bloomsbury Publishing)

Empire of Pain: The Secret History of the Sackler Dynasty by Patrick Radden Keefe (Doubleday, a division of Penguin Random House, LLC)

Four Hundred Souls: A Community History of African America, 1619-2019 Edited by Ibram X. Kendi and Keisha N. Blain (One World, an imprint of Random House, a division of Penguin Random House, LLC)

How the Word Is Passed: A Reckoning with the History of Slavery Across America by Clint Smith (Little, Brown and Company, a division of Hachette Book Group, Inc.)

Pastoral Song: A Farmer's Journey by James Rebanks (Custom House, an imprint of HarperCollins Publishers)

People Love Dead Jews: Reports from a Haunted Present by Dara Horn (W.W. Norton & Company)

Poet Warrior by Joy Harjo (W.W. Norton & Company)

The Hospital: Life, Death, and Dollars in a Small American Town by Brian Alexander (St. Martin's Press, an imprint of St. Martin's Publishing Group)

Poetry

Playlist for the Apocalypse by Rita Dove (W.W. Norton & Company)

The Renunciations by Donika Kelly (Graywolf Press)

Winter Recipes from the Collective by Louise Glück (Farrar, Straus & Giroux)

The Reading List

Established in 2007 by the CODES section of the Reference and User Services Association (RUSA), this list highlights outstanding genre fiction that merits special attention by general adult readers and the librarians who work with them.

The winners were selected by the Reading List Council, whose members include 12 librarians who are experts in readers' advisory and collection development. The eight genres currently included in the council's considerations are adrenaline titles (suspense, thrillers, and action adventure), fantasy, historical fiction, horror, mystery, romance, science fiction, and relationship fiction. The RUSA website provides additional details on each of the winning titles along with shortlists of "Readalikes" and runners-up.

Adrenaline

Razorblade Tears by S.A. Cosby (Flatiron Books)

Fantasy

A Master of Djinn by P. Djèlí Clark (A Tordotcom Book, published by Tom Doherty Associates)

Historical Fiction

The Sweetness of Water by Nathan Harris (Little, Brown and Company, a division of Hachette Book Group, Inc.)

Horror

Nothing But Blackened Teeth by Cassandra Khaw (A Nightfire Book, published by Tom Doherty Associates)

Mystery

Arsenic and Adobo by Mia P. Manansala (Berkley Prime Crime, published by Berkley, an imprint of Penguin Random House LLC)

Relationship Fiction

The Guncle: A Novel by Steven Rowley (G.P. Putnam's Sons, an imprint of Penguin Random House LLC)

Romance

One Last Stop by Casey McQuiston (St. Martin's Griffin, an imprint of St. Martin's Publishing Group)

Science Fiction

A Psalm for the Wild-Built by Becky Chambers (A Tordotcom Book, published by Tom Doherty Associates)

The Listen List

Established in 2010 by the CODES section of the Reference and User Services Association (RUSA), The Listen List: Outstanding Audiobook Narration seeks to highlight outstanding audiobook titles that merit special attention by general adult listeners and the librarians who work with them. The Listen List Council selects a list of 12 titles, including fiction, nonfiction, poetry, and plays. To be eligible, titles must be available for purchase and circulation by libraries. The council consists of seven librarians who are experts in readers' advisory and collection development.

An annotated version of the list on the RUSA website includes more information on each choice and lists additional audiobooks of interest.

Black Water Sister by Zen Cho, narrated by Catherin Ho (Recorded Books)

Broken Horses by Brandi Carlile, narrated by Brandi Carlile (Books on Tape)

The Final Revival of Opal and Nev by Dawnie Walton, narrated by Janina Edwards, Bahni Turpin, James Langton, Andre De Shields, Dennis Boutsikaris, Steve West, Gabra Zackman and a full cast (Simon & Schuster Audio)

Four Hundred Souls: A Community History of African America edited by Ibram X. Kendi and Keisha N. Blain, narrated by a full cast (Books on Tape)

Gold Diggers by Sanjena Sathian, narrated by Rama Vallury (Books on Tape)

The Office of Historical Corrections: A Novella and Stories by Danielle Evans, narrated by Joniece Abbott-Pratt, Nicole Lewis, Brittany Pressley, Shayna Small, January LaVoy, Adenrele Oho, and Janina Edwards (Books on Tape)

Razorblade Tears by S.A. Cosby, narrated by Adam Lazerre-White (Books on Tape)

Remote Control by Nnedi Okorafor, narrated by Adjoa Andoh (Macmillian Audio)

The Secret Lives of Church Ladies by Deesha Philyaw, narrated by Janina Edwards (Tantor Media)

Seven Days in June by Tia Williams, narrated by Mela Lee (Hachette Audio)

This Is Ear Hustle by Nigel Poor and Earlonne Woods, narrated by Nigel Poor, Earlonne Woods, Lt. Sam Robinson, Chayna Hampton, Andrew Eiden, Gary Tiedemann, Landon Woodson, Ary Hite, Debi Tinsley, Joniece Abbot Pratt, Curt Bonnem, Teri Clark Linden, and Pierce Cravens (Books on Tape)

When Women Invented Television by Jennifer Keishin Armstrong, narrated by Nan McNamara (HarperAudio)

Best Fiction for Young Adults

Each year a committee of the Young Adult Library Services Association (YALSA), a division of the American Library Association, compiles a list of the best fiction appropriate for young adults ages 12 to 18. Selected on the basis of each book's proven or potential appeal and value to young adults, the titles span a variety of subjects as well as a broad range of reading levels. An asterisk denotes the title was selected as a top ten.

Ace of Spades by Faridah Àbíké-Íyímídé (Macmillan/Feiwel & Friends). 978-1250800817.

Amari and the Night Brothers by B.B. Alston (HarperCollins/Balzer + Bray). 978-0062975164.

American Betiya by Anuradha D. Rajurkar (Penguin Random House/Knopf Books for Young Readers). 978-1984897152.

The Awakening of Malcolm X by Ilyasah Shabazz and Tiffany D. Jackson (Macmillan/ Farrar, Straus & Giroux Books for Young Readers). 978-0374313296.

The Barren Grounds by David A. Robertson (Penguin Random House Canada/Puffin). 978-0735266100.

Beasts of Prey by Ayana Gray (Penguin Random House/G.P. Putnam's Sons Books for Young Readers). 978-0593405680.

*Blackout by Dhonielle Clayton, Tiffany D. Jackson, Nic Stone, Angie Thomas, Ashley Woodfolk, and Nicola Yoon (HarperCollins/ Quill Tree Books). 978-0063088092.

The Block by Ben Oliver (Scholastic Press/ Chicken House). 978-1338589337.

Bluebird by Sharon Cameron (Scholastic Press). 978-1338355963.

*The City Beautiful by Aden Polydoros (Harlequin/Inkyard Press). 978-1335402509.

*Concrete Rose by Angie Thomas (HarperCollins/Balzer + Bray). 978-0062846716.

The Corpse Queen by Heather M. Herrman (Penguin Random House/G.P. Putnam's Sons Books for Young Readers). 978-1984816702.

The Cost of Knowing by Brittney Morris (Simon & Schuster Books for Young Readers). 978-1534445451.

A Cuban Girl's Guide to Tea and Tomorrow by Laura Taylor Namey (Simon & Schuster/ Atheneum Books for Young Readers). 978-1534471245.

Curses by Lish McBride (Penguin Random House/G.P. Putnam's Sons Books for Young Readers). 9781984815590.

The Darkness outside Us by Eliot Schrefer (HarperCollins/Katherine Tegen Books). 978-0062888280.

Don't Hate the Player by Alexis Nedd (Bloomsbury YA). 978-1547605026.

Donuts and Other Proclamations of Love by Jared Reck (Penguin Random House/ Knopf Books for Young Readers). 978-1524716110.

Dustborn by Erin Bowman (HarperCollins/ Clarion Books). 978-0358244431.

*Electric Kingdom by David Arnold (Penguin Random House/Viking Books for Young Readers). 978-0593202227.

Excuse Me While I Ugly Cry by Joya Goffney (HarperCollins/HarperTeen). 978-0063024793.

Fat Chance, Charlie Vega by Crystal Maldonado (Holiday House). 978-0823447176.

Fierce as the Wind by Tara Wilson Redd (Random House/Wendy Lamb Books). 978-1524766917.

Fifteen Hundred Miles`from the Sun by Jonny Garza Villa (Amazon/Skyscape). 978-1542027052.

*Firekeeper's Daughter by Angeline Boulley (Macmillan/Henry Holt and Co. Books for Young Readers). 978-1250766564.

The Forest of Stolen Girls by June Hur (Macmillan/Feiwel and Friends). 978-1250229588.

Gilded by Marissa Meyer (Macmillan/Feiwel & Friends). 978-1250618849.

The Girls I've Been by Tess Sharpe (Penguin Random House/G.P. Putnam's Sons Books for Young Readers). 978-0593353806.

The Great Bear by David A. Robertson (Penguin Random House Canada/Puffin). 978-0735266131.

The Heartbreak Bakery by A.R. Capetta (Candlewick Press). 978-1536216530.

Hold Back the Tide by Melinda Salisbury (Scholastic Press). 978-1338681307.

Home Is Not a Country by Safia Elhillo (Random House/Make Me a World). 978-0593177051.

How Moon Fuentez Fell in Love with the Universe by Raquel Vasquez Gilliland (Simon & Schuster Books for Young Readers). 978-1534448667.

Hunting by Stars by Cherie Dimaline (ABRAMS/Amulet Books). 978-1419753473.

Hurricane Summer by Asha Bromfield (Macmillan/Wednesday Books). 978-1250622235.

In the Wild Light by Jeff Zentner (Penguin Random House/Crown Books for Young Readers). 978-1524720247.

Indestructible Object by Mary McCoy (Simon & Schuster Books for Young Readers). 978-1534485051.

Indivisible by Daniel Aleman (Hachette/Little, Brown Books for Young Readers). 978-0759556058.

The Initial Insult by Mindy McGinnis (HarperCollins/Katherine Tegen Books). 978-0062982421.

Kate in Waiting by Becky Albertalli (HarperCollins/Balzer + Bray). 978-0062643834.

Kneel by Candace Buford (Harlequin/Inkyard Press). 978-1335402516.

Last Night at the Telegraph Club by Malinda Lo (Penguin Random House/Dutton Books). 978-0525555254.

The Life I'm In by Sharon G. Flake (Scholastic Press). 978-1338573176.

Like Other Girls by Britta Lundin (Hyperion/Freeform Books). 978-1368039925.

List of Ten by Halli Gomez (Union Square & Co.). 978-1454940142.

Little Thieves by Margaret Owen (Macmillan/Henry Holt & Co. Books for Young Readers). 978-1250191908.

Love in English by Maria E. Andreu (HarperCollins/Balzer + Bray). 978-0062996510.

Luck of the Titanic by Stacey Lee (Penguin Random House/G.P. Putnam's Sons Books for Young Readers). 978-1524740986.

Margot Mertz Takes It Down by Carrie McCrossen and Ian McWethy (Penguin Random House/Philomel). 978-0593205259.

Me (Moth) by Amber McBride (Macmillan/Feiwel & Friends). 978-1250780362.

The Mirror Season by Anna-Marie McLemore (Macmillan/Feiwel & Friends). 978-1250624123.

Mister Impossible by Maggie Stiefvater (Scholastic Press). 978-1338188363.

My Contrary Mary by Cynthia Hand, Brodi Ashton, and Jodi Meadows (HarperCollins/HarperTeen). 978-0062930040.

Not My Problem by Ciara Smyth (HarperCollins/HarperTeen). 978-0062957146.

Off the Record by Camryn Garrett (Penguin Random House/Knopf Books for Young Readers). 978-1984829993.

One of the Good Ones by Maika Moulite and Maritza Moulite (Harlequin/Inkyard Press). 978-1335145802.

The Ones We're Meant to Find by Joan He Macmillan (Roaring Brook Press). 978-1250258564.

The Other Merlin by Robyn Schneider (Penguin Random House/Viking Books for Young Readers) 978-0593351024.

The Other Side of Perfect by Mariko Turk (Little, Brown Books for Young Readers/Poppy). 978-0316703406.

Perfect on Paper by Sophie Gonzales (Macmillan/Wednesday Books). 978-1250769787.

Perfectly Parvin by Olivia Abtahi (Penguin Random House/G.P. Putnam's Sons Books for Young Readers). 978-0593109427.

Pumpkin by Julie Murphy (HarperCollins/Balzer + Bray). 978-0062880451.

The River Has Teeth by Erica Waters (HarperCollins/HarperTeen). 978-0062894250.

Rural Voices: 15 Authors Challenge Assumptions About Small-Town America edited by Nora Shalaway Carpenter. 2020. (Candlewick Press). 978-1536212105.

She Drives Me Crazy by Kelly Quindlen (Macmillan/Roaring Brook Press). 978-1250209153.

A Sitting in St. James by Rita Williams-Garcia (HarperCollins/Quill Tree Books). 978-0062367297.

Six Crimson Cranes by Elizabeth Lim (Penguin Random House/Knopf Books for Young Readers). 978-0593300916.

The Sky Blues by Robbie Couch (Simon & Schuster Books for Young Readers). 978-1534477858.

A Snake Falls to Earth by Darcie Little Badger (Levine Querido). 978-1646140923.

Some Girls Do by Jennifer Dugan (Penguin Random House/G.P. Putnam's Sons Books for Young Readers). 978-0593112533.

Somewhere between Bitter and Sweet by Laekan Zea Kemp (Hachette/Little, Brown Books for Young Readers). 978-0316460279.

Starfish by Lisa Fipps (Penguin Random House/ Nancy Paulsen Books). 978-1984814500.

Sugar Town Queens by Malla Nunn (Penguin Random House/G.P. Putnam's Sons Books for Young Readers). 978-0525515609.

The Surprising Power of a Good Dumpling by Wai Chim. 2020. (Scholastic Press). 978-1338656114.

Sway with Me by Syed M. Masood (Hachette/ Little, Brown Books for Young Readers). 978-0316492416.

Switch by A.S. King (Penguin Random House/ Dutton Books for Young Readers). 978-0525555513.

This Poison Heart by Kalynn Bayron (Bloomsbury YA). 978-1547603909.

This Will Be Funny Someday by Katie Henry (HarperCollins/Katherine Tegen Books). 978-0062955708.

The Way Back by Gavriel Savit. 2020. (Penguin Random House/Knopf Books for Young Readers). 978-1984894625.

We Are the Ashes, We Are the Fire by Joy McCullough (Penguin Random House/Dutton Books). 978-0525556053.

What About Will by Ellen Hopkins (Penguin Random House/G.P. Putnam's Sons Books for Young Readers). 978-0593108642.

What Beauty There Is by Cory Anderson (Macmillan/Roaring Brook Press). 978-1250268099.

When We Make It by Elisabet Velasquez (Penguin Random House/Dial Books). 978-0593324486.

Where the Rhythm Takes You by Sarah Dass (HarperCollins/Balzer + Bray). 978-0063018525.

Who I Was with Her by Nita Tyndall. 2020. (HarperCollins/HarperTeen). 978-0062978387.

With You All the Way by Cynthia Hand (HarperCollins/HarperTeen). 978-0062693198.

The Words in My Hands by Asphyxia (Annick Press). 978-1773215280.

Year of the Reaper by Makiia Lucier (HarperCollins/Clarion Books). 978-0358272090.

Your Heart, My Sky: Love in a Time of Hunger by Margarita Engle (Simon & Schuster/ Atheneum Books for Young Readers). 978-1534464964.

Quick Picks for Reluctant Young Adult Readers

The Young Adult Library Services Association (YALSA), a division of the American Library Association, annually chooses a list of outstanding titles that may stimulate the interest of reluctant teen readers. The list is intended to attract teens who are not inclined to read, for whatever reason. This year's list includes 55 fiction and nonfiction titles published from late 2020 through 2021. An asterisk denotes the title was selected as a top ten.

Across the Tracks: Remembering Greenwood, Black Wall Street, and the Tulsa Race Massacre. By Alverne Ball. Art by Stacey Robinson. Abrams/Megascope. $15.99 (9781419755170). Greenwood—also known as Black Wall Street—was a bustling district in Tulsa, Oklahoma, with many successful Black-owned businesses. In 1921 a white mob descended on Greenwood, destroying businesses and devastating the community. One hundred years later, *Across the Tracks* pays homage to Greenwood.

Alone. By Megan E. Freeman. 2020, Aladdin/Simon and Shuster. $17.99 (9780593176399). Maddie finds herself completely, totally alone when she wakes up from a secret sleepover and discovers that everyone was evacuated overnight from her town, her state, and maybe her whole half of the country. She has to survive natural disasters, the elements, looters, wild animals, and her own crushing loneliness.

*Amari and the Night Brothers. By B.B. Alston. Harper Collins/Balzer + Bray. $17.99 (9781725418295). Amari knows her brother isn't dead. A briefcase in his closet leads her to a magical world—and the Bureau of Supernatural Affairs, the place Quinton was working when he disappeared. Amari must use all her smarts and her heart to find out what really happened.

A-Okay. By Jarad Greene. HarperCollins Children's Books/Harper Alley. $12.99 (9780063032859). Jay deals with acne, acne medicine side effects, friend drama, and figuring out romantic feelings during a tumultuous eighth-grade year.

Artie and the Wolf Moon. By Olivia Stephens. Lerner Publishing Group/Graphic Universe. $16.99 (9781728420202). After Artie finds out her mother is a werewolf and that she lost her father to vampires, she must then battle vampires to save her friends and new wolf family while trying to practice her own potential wolf abilities.

Becoming Muhammad Ali. By James Patterson and Kwame Alexander. Illustrated by Dawud Anyabwile. 2020, Little, Brown and Company/JIMMY Patterson Books. $16.99 (9780316498166). James Patterson and Kwame Alexander tackle the life of Cassius Clay before he became Muhammad Ali in this novel that mixes prose and verse.

Blackout. By Dhonielle Clayton, Tiffany D. Jackson, Nic Stone, Angie Thomas, Ashley Woodfolk, and Nicola Yoon. HarperCollins/Quill Tree Books. $19.99 (9780063088092). Six distinct but connected stories highlight black resilience and love in the midst of a New York City-wide blackout.

*The Canyon's Edge. By Dusti Bowling. Little Brown and Company/Little, Brown Books for Young Readers. $16.99 (9780316494694). One year after a tragedy changed their family forever, Nora and her father set off to explore an isolated canyon. Disaster strikes, bringing with it a struggle for survival punctuated by flashbacks of the horrible events from a year earlier."

*Cheer Up! Love and Pompoms. By Crystal Fraiser. Art by Val Wise. Letterer Oscar O. Jupiter. Oni Press. $14.95 (9781620109557). Smart, antisocial Annie is pressured by her mom and college counselor to join the cheerleading squad. To her surprise, not only does she enjoy the sport, but she also rekindles a friendship (and maybe more) with BeBe, who is experiencing support but also microaggressions as the state's first trans cheerleader.

Chlorine Sky. By Mahogany L. Browne. Penguin Random House/Crown. $17.99

(9780593176399). In this novel in verse, Mahogany Browne explores what it's like to lose a best friend but find yourself.

Cool for the Summer. By Dahlia Adler. Macmillan/Wednesday Books. $18.99 (9781250765826). When Lara returns to her hometown after a surprising summer fling in the Outer Banks, she's even more shocked that the most popular guy in school is suddenly interested in her. Everyone expects her to be interested in him, too, but she can't forget about what happened last summer.

*The Crossroads at Midnight. By Abby Howard. Iron Circus Comics. $18.00 (9781945820687). What happens in that dark fuzzy place in the middle of the night? What happens when you are desperate enough to reach out and accept the supernatural? These beautifully drawn short stories attempt to answer these questions and more in this creepy graphic story collection.

Don't Stand So Close to Me. By Eric Walters. 2020, Orca Book Publishers. $10.95 (9781459827875). Quinn, Isaac, Reese, and the rest of their eighth-grade class react to the quickly evolving COVID-19 pandemic with the help of Quinn's physician father and their very helpful teacher.

Every Single Lie. By Rachel Vincent. Bloomsbury/Bloomsbury YA. $17.99 (9781547605231). 16-year-old Beckett Bergen's life completely changes the moment she discovers a dead baby in the girls' locker room. Beck is then targeted with violent threats and rumors that she's the #BabyKiller. Hunting for the truth only uncovers more secrets but none so shattering as discovering what really happened.

Fast Pitch. By Nic Stone. Penguin Random House/Crown Books for Young Readers. $17.99 (9781984893017). For softball player and team captain Shenice "Lightning" Lockwood, playing ball runs in the family. When Shenice uncovers a family mystery in the middle of her softball season, she must decide how far she'll go to clear her family's name.

*The Girl from the Sea. By Molly Knox Ostertag. Scholastic/Graphix. $14.99 (9781338540581). Teenage Morgan is ready to leave her island home and start living her real life. One summer, Morgan meets Keltie, a mysterious girl from the sea, and starts keeping secrets.

Goosebumps: Secrets of the Swamp. By Marieke Nijkamp. Art by Yasmin Flores Montanez and Bill Underwood. IDW/Scholastic. $12.99 (9781684058136). Blake is an expert hunter in her favorite video game, but will that translate when she finds herself in Fever Swamp with actual monsters?

Hide and Don't Seek: And Other Very Scary Stories. By Anica Mrose Rissi. Art By Carolina Godina. 2020, HarperCollins Publishers/Quill Tree Books. $16.99 (9780063026957). A collection of dark and scary stories, including a sinister summer camp and creepy animals, that will keep you up at night.

Hide and Seeker. By Daka Hermon. Scholastic. $18.99 (9781338583625). Justin and his friends play an innocent game of hide-and-seek at their friend Zee's coming-home party, but the game, and Zee himself, are more dangerous than they seem. Zee came back different from his mysterious missing year, and soon party guests start disappearing.

I Dare You. By Jeff Ross. Orca Book Publishers. $10.95 (9781459828018). When a video of a fight goes viral, Rainy and two classmates, Jordan and Rowen, convince him to create a prank video. When that video sparks rumors that in turn cause a horrible accident, will Rainy admit to being behind it all? Or was the video true?

In the Shadow of the Fallen Towers: The Seconds, Minutes, Hours, Days, Weeks, Months, and Years after the 9/11 Attacks. By Don Brown. Etch/Houghton Mifflin Harcourt. $19.99 (9780358223573). A beautifully illustrated review of the events on 9/11 and the far-reaching effects of that terrible day.

Karma Moon: Ghost Hunter. By Melissa Savage. Penguin Random House/Crown Books for Young Readers. $16.99 (9780593302804). Karma Moon and her best friend join her father's film crew at a famously haunted hotel, which isn't a great place for someone with a bad case of the "what-ifs" to spend spring break, especially because her dad won't get paid unless they get a real ghost on camera.

Last Gate of the Emperor. By Kwame Mbalia and Prince Joel Makonnen. Scholastic, Inc. $17.99 (9781338665857). Yared Heywat is a loner, and his uncle forces him to keep a low profile. When Yared's favorite game forces him to log in under his real name, an attack rocks the city. Now, Yared must find his missing uncle and the truth of his place in the galaxy.

The Lost Girls: A Vampire Revenge Story. By Sonia Hartl. Macmillan/Page Street Publishing Co. $17.99 (9781645673149). Holly Liddell has been trapped as a 16-year-old girl since she was turned into a vampire in 1987. After Elton ditches her after 30 years together, she learns that she was not his first. Holly and his other girls, Ida and Rose, team up to end Elton once and for all—before he can turn another girl.

Love Is a Revolution. By Renée Watson. Bloomsbury/Bloomsbury YA. $18.99 (9781547600601). Nala is learning about love—most significantly, how important it is to love yourself. Her relationship with her cousin-sister-friend Imani is strained, and Nala can't stop lying and pretending she's something she's not to the boy she likes. In the Harlem heat, Nala has to figure out her best path.

Martin Ghost Centaur. By Mat Heagerty. Art By Steph Mided. Oni Press. $19.99 (9781620108499). Southborough used to be a major tourist destination for folks, ever since a Sasquatch was spotted there. However, fewer and fewer people started coming. Now, a tech start-up is buying up the town so it can build its headquarters. Can Louie and Felix find a way to save the town?

Mine. By Delilah S. Dawson. Penguin Random House/Delacorte Press. $16.99 (9780593373224). After moving to Florida, Lily is horrified to discover that the former owner of their house was a hoarder. While cleaning out the mess, Lily realizes there is more in the house than junk and that the ghosts that reside there may not want her to stay.

The Missing Passenger. By Jack Heath. Simon & Schuster/Simon & Schuster Books for Young Readers. $18.99 (9781534449893). A plane with no passengers crashes in his hometown, and Jarli quickly finds himself in the middle of a mystery. When he learns that no one can be trusted, Jarli allies himself with his best option: his former bully. Together they attempt to outwit a secretive criminal known as Viper.

Muted. By Tami Charles. Scholastic, Inc./ Scholastic Press. $18.99 (9781338673524). Denver and her best friends are taken under the wing of music legend Sean "Mercury" Jones to become the next big thing, but at what price? As Merc becomes more controlling and cuts the girls off from family and friends, will they even make it out alive?

My Epic Spring Break (Up). By Kristin Rockaway. Penguin Random House/Underlined. $9.99 (9780593180112). When Ashley's carefully planned spring break that was supposed to be focused on winning the NYC Hackathon takes an expected turn, she must decide what she wants. Is it her crush whom she has nothing in common with? Or her longtime friend she is starting to see as something more?

Noelle: The Mean Girl. By Ashley Woodfolk. Penguin Random House/Penguin Workshop. $15.99 (9780593096079). Noelle is losing control. First, she has a crush on her friend Tobyn. Next, her younger brother Pierre keeps getting beat up. Then, when her father loses his job, she agrees to work more hours at her grandparent's restaurant. Can Noelle figure out how to handle all of these changes?

*Nubia: The Real One. By L.L. McKinney. Art by Robyn Smith. DC Comics. $16.99 (9781401296407). Nubia, an Amazon with superhuman powers, has to decide what is more important: protecting the ones she loves or keeping her identity secret.

Off the Record. By Camryn Garrett. Penguin Random House/Knopf Books for Young Readers. $17.00 (9781984829993). When Josie Wright wins the chance to profile a major up-and-coming movie star for a press tour, she finds another story worth following, one of a big director who has sexually assaulted numerous others and gotten away with it for years.

Oh My Gods! By Stephanie Cooke and Insha Fitzpatrick. Art by Juliana Moon. Etch/ Clarion Books. $12.99 (9780358299523). After her mom gets a new job, 13-year-old Karen moves to Greece to live with her dad Zed. Her new home and school, Mt. Olympus Junior High, seem a little strange, but fun, until people mysteriously start turning into stone statues. Can Karen figure out the secrets of her new home?

*The Passing Playbook. By Isaac Fitzsimons. Dial Books. $18.99 (9781984815408). Spencer is starting a brand-new school and

wants a fresh start where no one knows he's trans. But as he develops feelings for another boy on the soccer team and comes face-to-face with a discriminatory rule stopping him from playing soccer, he considers what he's losing by not coming out.

Playing with Fire. By April Henry. Macmillian/Henry Holt and Co. $17.99 (9781250234063) When a fast-moving wildfire traps Natalia, Wyatt, and a group of other hikers, they must do whatever it takes to survive, which means hiking farther into the forest and potential danger to get to safety. This is not what Natalia had in mind for her and Wyatt's first date.

Poison Ivy: Thorns. By Kody Keplinger. Art by Sara Kipin. DC Comics. $16.99 (9781401298425). Pamela Isley is keeping secrets, including what's really going on in her family's creepy mansion late at night. When a cute goth girl comes into Pamela's life, it seems like there's hope for a real connection, but it also sets in motion a series of dangerous occurrences.

*The Power of Style: How Fashion and Beauty Are Being Used to Reclaim Cultures. By Christian Allaire. Annick Press. $19.95 (9781773214900). Authored by the fashion and style writer for *Vogue*, this look at current elements of style focuses on social justice, culture, and politics and their connection to how underrepresented communities use fashion to proudly claim these identities.

The Prom House. By Chelsea Mueller. Delacorte Press/ Underline. $9.99 (9780593180051). When a group of ten friends decide to keep the party going after their prom by renting a house on the Jersey Shore and they end up murdered one by one, which one is behind it all, and who will make it out alive?

Recommended for You. By Laura Silverman. 2020, Simon & Schuster/Margaret K. McElderry Books. $17.99 (9781534474192). Shoshanna Greenberg loves working at her local indie bookstore—and knows her love of books and readers will help her win the store's holiday bookselling contest. Only one person stands in her way: new employee Jake Kaplan, who rubs Shoshanna the wrong way. But the more they get to know each other, the more they realize that they aren't so annoying after all.

Rivals. By Tommy Greenwald. Abrams/ Amulet Books. $17.99 (9781419748271). Walthorne takes their basketball seriously, so when rivaling North and South middle schools play each other, the competition gets fierce. Student-reporter Alfie Jenks provides commentary on the matchups as well as the controversies off the court. Teams will have to learn whether morality is more important than winning.

She Drives Me Crazy. By Kelly Quindlen. Macmillan/Roaring Brook Press. $17.99 (9781250209160). Athlete Scottie's ex-girlfriend now plays for their rival basketball team. She wants to get back at her toxic ex-girlfriend and hatches a fake dating plan with popular cheerleader Irene, but the plan gets complicated the longer the scheme carries on.

Sink or Swim. By Tash McAdam. Orca Book Publishers. $10.95 (9781459828513). When Bass sneaks away on a boat trip with his girlfriend Rosie, things take a turn for the worst when their boat capsizes in a storm and they find themselves stranded and with severe injuries, fighting for survival.

Starfish. By Lisa Fipps. Penguin Random House/Nancy Paulsen Books. $17.99 (9781984814500) Ellie has been bullied for her weight for as long as she remembers. Through new friendships and a helpful therapist, she feels confident being herself for the very first time. Written in verse from Ellie's perspective, readers follow the mental and emotional evolution of a girl striving to fit in.

Stranded. By Jocelyn Shipley. 2020, Orca Publishing. $10.95 (9781459823891). Kipp, a troubled teen trying to do right despite obstacles, finds himself working for a wealthy woman with a secret: She's had troubled teens work for her before, but they've gone missing. Could Kipp be next?

Sunkissed. By Kasie West. Penguin Random House/Delacorte Press. $18.99 (9780593176269). Avery is spending this summer with her family at a remote resort/ camp. She's happy to leave some troubling drama at home, but embraces a chance to really discover herself. She also meets Brooks, the staff musician who might be as frustrating as he is handsome, but also completely off-limits.

Sunny Song Will Never Be Famous. By Suzanne Park. Sourcebooks/Sourcebooks Fire. $10.99 (9781728209425). Sunny Song is an aspiring influencer, but those plans come derailed when she accidentally makes an inappropriate livestream. Her parents respond by sending Sunny to a technology detox camp at a working farm. Will Sunny be able to decide between the cute farm boy or her desire to go viral?

Take Back the Block. By Chrystal D. Giles. Penguin Random House/Random House Books for Young Readers. $16.99 (9780593175170). Wes doesn't want to go to all the protests his mom keeps dragging him to. But when developers swoop in and try to gentrify the neighborhood he loves, he finds that some things are worth fighting for.

Teen Killers Club. By Lily Sparks. 2020, Penguin Random House/Crooked Lane Books. $18.99 (9781643852294). Signal Deere was deemed a "Class A" criminal and sent to a special camp to be trained as an assassin. Everyone else there is a stone-cold teen killer, so Signal should fit right in. But the thing is, she's never actually killed anyone—she was framed.

That Weekend. By Kara Thomas. Penguin Random House/Delacorte Press. $18.99 (9781524718367). When Claire wakes up in the hospital and finds out her two best friends have gone missing while they were all on a camping trip, she is determined to find out exactly what happened to them, even though she has amnesia and can't remember that weekend.

They Better Call Me Sugar: My Journey from the Hood to the Hardwood. By Sugar Rodgers. Black Sheep/Akashic Books. $14.95 (9781617759291). WNBA All-Star Sugar Rodgers shares her story of growing up, poverty, family life, school, sports, friends, and how she eventually shaped a successful career as a professional basketball player.

Tobyn: The It Girl. By Ashley Woodfolk. Penguin Random House/Penguin Workshop. $15.99 (9780593096109). High school is wrapping up for Tobyn. All she wants for her future is to sing, but her mother wants her to go to college. Will she be able to balance what she wants and what her mother wants while also dealing with her absentee sister?

Too Bright to See. By Kyle Lukoff. Penguin Random House/Dial Books for Young Readers. $16.99 (9780593111154). Bug has always been a bit odd. The 11-year-old lives in a haunted house. But when Bug's beloved uncle dies and starts haunting the home he used to live in, Bug seeks to figure out why—and ends up unraveling an even bigger mystery.

The Truth Project. By Dante Medema. 2020, Harper Collins/Quill Tree Books. $17.99 (9780062954404). High school senior Cordelia gets her DNA test results as part of a senior writing project and is jarred to learn something scandalous about her family's past.

Yesterday Is History. By Kosoko Jackson. Sourcebooks/Sourcebooks Fire. $17.99 (9781492694359). After a life-saving liver transplant, Andre gains the ability to time travel. He finds himself tethered to Michael in the year 1969, and the two quickly build a bond. Andre must balance this version of reality with life in 2021, which holds its own complicated relationships.

The Alex Awards

The Young Adult Library Services Association (YALSA), a division of the American Library Association, has selected ten adult books with special appeal to teen readers to receive the 2022 Alex Awards. The award is sponsored by the Margaret A. Edwards Trust.

The 100 Years of Lenni and Margot by Marianne Cronin, published by Harper Perennial, an imprint of HarperCollins (9780063017504).

Crossing the Line: A Fearless Team of Brothers and the Sport That Changed Their Lives Forever by Kareem Rosser, published by St. Martin's Press, a division of Macmillan (9781250270863).

How Lucky by Will Leitch, published by Harper, an imprint of HarperCollins (978-0063073098).

The Library of the Dead by T.L. Huchu, published by Tor Books, an imprint of Tom Doherty Associates, a division of Macmillan (9781250767769).

Light from Uncommon Stars by Ryka Aoki, published by Tor Books, an imprint of Tom Doherty Associates, a division of Macmillan (9781250789068).

Lore Olympus, Vol. 1 by Rachel Smythe, published by Del Rey, an imprint of Penguin Random House (ISBN 9780593160299).

Malice by Heather Walter, published by Del Rey, an imprint of Penguin Random House (ISBN 9781984818652).

The Rose Code by Kate Quinn, published by William Morrow, an imprint of HarperCollins (9780062943477).

Winter's Orbit by Everina Maxwell, published by Tor Books, an imprint of Tom Doherty Associates, a division of Macmillan (9781250758835).

The Witch's Heart by Genevieve Gornichec, published by ACE, an imprint of Berkley, a division of Penguin Random House (9780593099940).

Amazing Audiobooks for Young Adults

Each year, the Amazing Audiobooks Blogging Team of the Young Adult Library Services Association (YALSA), a division of the American Library Association, selects and annotates a list of notable audio recordings significant to young adults from among those released in the past two years. This year's list comprises 76 titles selected from among 123 nominations that were posted and discussed on YALSA's teen collection blog, The Hub. While the list as a whole addresses the interests and needs of young adults, individual titles need not appeal to this entire age range but rather to parts of it. An asterisk denotes the title was selected as a top ten.

Ace of Spades. By Faridah Àbíké-Íyímídé. Read by Jeanette Illidge and Tapiwa Mugweni. Macmillan Audio, $59.99 (9781250808332).

All Thirteen: The Incredible Cave Rescue of the Thai Boys' Soccer Team. By Christina Soontornvat. Read by Quincy Surasmith and Christina Soontornvat. 2020. Brilliance Audio, $35.99 (9781713547792).

Any Way the Wind Blows, Simon Snow Trilogy, Book 3. By Rainbow Rowell. Read by Euan Morton. Macmillan Young Listeners, $69.99 (9781250803122).

*Apple: Skin to the Core. By Eric Gansworth. Read by Eric Gansworth. 2020. Dreamscape Media, LLC, $64.99 (9781662039706).

Between Perfect and Real. By Ray Stoeve. Read by MW Cartozian Wilson. Recorded Books, Inc., $70 (9781705028339).

The Bitterwine Oath. By Hanna West. Read by Reba Buhr. Tantor Media, $63 (9781705222911).

The Cat I Never Named: A True Story of Love, War and Survival. By Amra Sabic-El-Rayess and Laura L. Sullivan. Read by Leila Buck. 2020. Recorded Books, LLC, $98 (9781705017708).

*Chlorine Sky. By Mahogany L. Browne. Read by Mahogany L. Browne. Listening Library, $28 (9780593343784).

Cinderella Is Dead. By Kalynn Bayron. Read by Bahni Turpin. 2020. Bloomsbury USA/ Bloomsbury YA, $76 (9781547605590).

City of the Plague God. By Sarwat Chadda. Read by Vikas Adam. Listening Library, $63 (9780593291160).

Class Act. By Jerry Craft. Read by Nile Bullock, Jesus Del Orden, Guy Lockard, Marc Thompson, Peyton Lusk, Rebecca Soler, Dan Bittner, January LaVoy, Phoebe Strole, Jordan Cobb, A.J. Beckles, Robin Miles, Ron Butler, Miles Harvey, Kim Mai Guest, Kyla Garcia and Soneela Nankani. Harper-Collins Publishers, Inc./Quill Tree Books, $34.98 (9780063032057).

A Complicated Love Story Set in Space. By Shaun David Hutchinson. Read by Gibson Frazier, Candace Thaxton, and Kevin R. Free. Simon & Schuster Audio, $79.99 (9781797118222).

*Concrete Rose. By Angie Thomas. Read by Dion Graham. HarperCollins Publishers, Inc./ Balzer + Bray, $59.98 (9780063043817).

The Cost of Knowing. By Brittney Morris. Read by Kevin R. Free. Simon & Schuster Audio, $59.99 (9781797117898).

The Cousins. By Karen M. McManus. Read by Sarah Skaer, Kate Reinders, David Garelik and Julia Whelan. 2020. Listening Library, $69 (9781984842152).

Crownchasers. By Rebecca Coffindaffer. Read by Reba Buhr. 2020. Harper Audio, $69.50 (9780063033160).

A Cuban Girl's Guide to Tea and Tomorrow. By Laura Taylor Namey. Read by Frankie Corzo. 2020. Simon & Schuster Audio, $59.99 (9781797123912).

The Darkness Outside Us. By Eliot Schrefer. Read by James Fouhey. HarperAudio, $26.99 (9780063089358).

Dawn Raid. By Pauline Vaeluaga Smith. Read by Tameka Sowman Vahatau. Dreamscape Media, LLC, $64.99 (9781662083228).

Donuts and Other Proclamations of Love. By Jared Reck. Read by Kirby Heyborne. Listening Library, $63 (9780593398968).

The Electric Kingdom. By David Arnold. Read by Thérèse Plummer. Listening Library, $75 (9780593342572).

Firekeeper's Daughter. By Angeline Boulley. Read by Isabella Star LeBlanc. Macmillan Young Listeners, $49.99 (9781250779519).

Flash Fire. By TJ Klune. Read by Michael Lesley. Macmillan Audio, $63 (9781250807755).

Flyy Girls. By Ashley Woodfolk. *Noelle: The Mean Girl* Book #3. Read by Shayna Small. Listening Library, $28.00 (9780593340660).*Tobyn: The It Girl* Book #4. Read by Nicole Lewis. Listening Library, $28 (9780593397596).

From a Whisper to a Rallying Cry: The Killing of Vincent Chin and the Trial that Galvanized the Asian American Movement. By Paula Yoo. Read by Catherine Ho. Recorded Books, $24.99 (9781705028384).

Game Changer. By Neal Shusterman. Read by Andrew Eiden and Jennifer Jill Araya. HarperCollins Publishers, Inc./Quill Tree Books, $67.48 (9780063033061).

The Gilded Ones, Deathless, Book 1. By Namina Forna. Read by Shayna Small. Listening Library, $75 (9780593207833).

The Girl from the Sea. By Molly Knox Ostertag. Read by Shannon Tyo, Kristen Sieh, M.J. Kang, Raymond Lee, Grant Beck, and others. Scholastic Audio, $74.99 (9781338773699).

The Girls I've Been. By Tess Sharpe. Read by Tess Sharpe. Listening Library, $63 (9780593400401).

A Good Girl's Guide to Murder. By Holly Jackson. *Good Girl, Bad Blood* Book 2. Read by MacLeod Andrews, Donte Bonner, James Fouhey, Neil Hellegers, Cary Hite, Amy Landon, Raymond J. Lee, Keylor Leigh, Maggi-Meg Reed, Shezi Sardar, and Bailey Carr. Listening Library, $69 (9780593342398). *As Good as Dead* Book 3. Read by Bailey Carr, Kristen DiMercurio, Robert Fass, Lauren Fortgang, Johnny Heller, Barrett Leddy, Shezi Sardar, Vassilea Terzaki and Megan Tusing. Listening Library, $75 (9780593416761).

The Hill We Climb. By Amanda Gorman. Read by Amanda Gorman and Oprah Winfrey. Books on Tape, $22 (9780593460900).

Hold Back the Tide. By Melinda Salisbury. Read by Elle Newlands. Scholastic Audio, $74.99 (9781338751086).

Home Is Not a Country. By Safia Elhillo. Read by Safia Elhillo, intro by Christopher Myers. Listening Library, $38 (9780593343715).

How Moon Fuentez Fell in Love with the Universe. By Raquel Vasquez Gilliland. Read by Kyla Garcia. Simon & Schuster Audio, $63 (9781797125497).

In the Shadow of the Moon: America, Russia, and the Hidden History of the Space Race. By Amy Cherrix. Read by Josh Horowitz. HarperCollins Publishers, Inc./Balzer+Bray, $52.48 (9780063058224).

In the Wild Light. By Jeff Zentner. Read by Michael Crouch. Listening Library, $69 (9780593399040).

The Initial Insult. By Mindy McGinnis. Read by Lisa Flanagan, Brittany Pressley and Tim Campbell. HarperCollins Publishers, Inc./Katherine Tegen Books, $52.48 (9780063064232).

K-Pop Confidential. By Stephan Lee. Read by Joy Osmanski. 2020. Scholastic Audio, $74.99 (9781338673401).

Last Night at the Telegraph Club. By Malinda Lo. Read by Emily Woo Zeller. Listening Library, $75 (9780593341650).

The Love Curse of Melody McIntyre. By Robin Talley. Read by Jennifer Jill Araya. 2020. HarperTeen, $67.48 (9780063033641).

Love in English. By Maria E. Andreu. Read by Frankie Corzo. HarperCollins Publishers, Inc./Balzer + Bray, $52.48 (9780063058118).

Middletown. By Sarah Moon. Read by Hope Newhouse. Dreamscape Media, LLC, $64.99 (9781662083211).

The Mirror Season. By Anna-Marie McLemore. Read by Jennifer Jill Araya. Recorded Books, LLC, $79 (9781705039366).

Off the Record. By Camryn Garrett. Read by Joniece Abbott-Pratt. Listening Library, $63 (9780593399460).

Once Upon a Quinceañera. By Monica Gomez-Hira. Read by Frankie Corzo. HarperTeen, $67.48 (9780063061415).

One Last Stop. By Casey McQuiston. Read by Natalie Naudus. Macmillan Audio, $59.99 (9781250803184).

One Two Three. By Laurie Frankel. Read by Emma Galvin, Jesse Vilinsky, and Rebecca

Soler. Macmillan Audio Production from St. Martin's Press, $69.99 (9781250790958).

Out: How to Be Your Authentic Self. By Miles McKenna and Tyler Oakley. Read by Miles McKenna. 2020. Tantor Audio, $47.95 (9781494532796).

Perfect on Paper. By Sophie Gonzalez. Read by Barrie Kreinik. Macmillan Audio, $63 (9781250805386).

Pocket Change Collective. By Amyra Leon and Chella Man. *Concrete Kids.* Read by Amyra Leon. 2020. Listening Library, $22 (9780593294833). *Continuum.* Read by Chella Man. Listening Library, $22 (9780593411452).

Pumpkin. By Julie Murphy. Read by Chad Burris. HarperCollins Publishers, Inc/Balzer + Bray, $54.05 (9780063088764).

Rent a Boyfriend. By Gloria Chao. Read by Feodor Chin and Emily Woo Zeller. 2020. Simon & Schuster/Simon & Schuster Audio, $59.99 (9781797113210).

Sasha Masha. By Agnes Borinsky. Read by Agnes Borinsky. 2020. Tantor Audio, $47.95 (9781705234839).

She's Too Pretty to Burn. By Wendy Heard. Read by Frankie Corzo, Bailey Carr, and Stephen Dexter. Dreamscape Media, LLC, $64.99 (9781662051333).

*Singled Out: The True Story of Glenn Burke. By Andrew Maraniss. Read by Kevin R. Free. Listening Library, $50 (9780593346211).

Six Crimson Cranes. By Elizabeth Lim. Read by Emily Woo Zeller. Listening Library, $75 (9780593398883).

Sixteen Scandals. By Sophie Jordan. Read by Moira Quirk. Recorded Books, LLC, $60 (9781980077589).

Some Girls Do. By Jennifer Dugan. Read by Nora Hunter and Bailey Carr. Listening Library, $63 (9780593397879).

Starfish. By Lisa Fipps. Read by Jenna Lamia. Listening Library, $34 (9780593341674).

Sugar Town Queens. By Malla Nunn. Read by Bahni Turpin. Listening Library, $63 (9780593397893).

These Violent Delights. By Chloe Gong. Read by Cindy Kay. Tantor Audio, $54.95 (9781705283837).

They'll Never Catch Us. By Jessica Goodman. Read by Jesse Vilinsky, Phoebe Strole, and Kristen Sieh. Listening Library, $69 (9780593398012).

This Is Not the Jess Show. By Anna Carey. Read by Suzy Jackson. Blackstone Audio, Inc., $47.95 (9781094032528).

Time Travel for Love and Profit. By Sarah Lariviere. Read by Kristen Sieh. Listening Library, $56 (9780593294024).

Tokyo Ever After. By Emiko Jean. Read by Ali Ahn. Macmillan Young Listeners, $49.99 (9781250804167).

Unspeakable: The Tulsa Race Massacre. By Carole Boston Weatherford. Read by January LaVoy and Carole Boston Weatherford. Dreamscape Media, LLC, $28 (9781666501940).

We Must Not Forget: Holocaust Stories of Survival and Resistance. By Deborah Hopkinson. Read by Rosie Jones. Scholastic Audio, $83.99 (9781338739299).

What Beauty There Is. By Cory Anderson. Read by Dan Bittner and Emma Galvin. Macmillan Young Listeners, $49.99 (9781250780447).

What I Like About Me. By Jenna Guillaume. Read by Candice Moll. Listening Library, $56 (9780593400296).

*When You Look Like Us. By Pamela N. Harris. Read by Preston Butler, III. HarperCollins Publishers, Inc./Quill Tree Books, $67.48 (9780063064317).

White Smoke. By Tiffany D. Jackson. Read by Marcella Cox. HarperAudio, $26.99 (9780063029125).

The Witch King. By H.E. Edgmon. Read by Dani Martineck. HarperCollins Publishers, Inc./Harlequin, $69.50 (9781488211249).

You Have a Match. By Emma Lord. Read by Eva Kaminsky. Macmillan Audio, $44.99 (9781250792280).

Outstanding International Books for Young Readers

Since 2006, the United States Board on Books for Young People (USBBY) has selected an annual honor list of international books for young people. The 42 titles on this year's Outstanding International Books (OIB) list, all published or released in 2021, have been identified as significant for both their exceptional quality and globe-spanning origins.

Preschool to Grade 2

Atinuke. *Too Small Tola.* Illus. by Onyinye Iwu. Candlewick Press. (Nigeria)

Baek, Heena. *Moon Pops.* Trans. from Korean by Jieun Kiaer. Illus. by author. Owlkids Books. (South Korea)

Flett, Julie. *We All Play/Kimêtawânaw.* Trans. by The Cree Literacy Network. Illus. by author. Greystone Kids. (Canada)

Kontoleon, Anna and Kontoleon, Manos. *Comings and Goings.* Illus. by Fontini Tikkou. Star Bright Books. (Greece)

Lam, Thao. *Thao.* Illus. by author. Owlkids Books. (Vietnam/Canada)

Larsen, Marit. *Agnes's Place.* Trans. from Norwegian by Kari Dickson. Illus. by Jenny Løvlie. Amazon Crossing Kids. (Norway)

Luby, Brittany. *Mii Maanda Ezhi-Gkendmaanh: This Is How I Know.* Trans. from Anishinaabemowin by Alvin Ted Corbiere and Alan Corbiere. Illus. by Joshua Mangeshig Pawis-Steckley. Groundwood Books. (Canada: Anishinaabewaking)

Morgan, Sally. *Little Bird's Day.* Illus. by Johnny Warrkatja Malibirr. Blue Dot Kids Press. (Australia)

Motum, Markus. *Ducks Overboard! A True Story of Plastic in Our Oceans.* Illus. by author. Candlewick Press. (UK: England)

Pearson, Debora. *My Words Flew Away Like Birds.* Illus. by Shrija Jain. Kids Can Press. (Canada)

Perrin, Clotilde. *Inside the Suitcase.* Trans. from French by Daniel Hahn. Illus. by author. Gecko Press. (France)

Robert, Nadine. *On the Other Side of the Forest.* Trans. from French by Paula Ayer. Illus. by Gérard Dubois. Greystone Kids. (Canada)

Soundar, Chitra. *Sona Sharma, Very Best Big Sister?* Illus. by Jen Khatun. Candlewick Press. (India)

Grades 3 to 5

Abery, Julie. *Sakamoto's Swim Club: How a Teacher Led an Unlikely Team to Victory.* Illus. by Chris Sasaki. Kids Can Press. (Canada)

Ahn, Angela. *Peter Lee's Notes from the Field.* Illus. by Julie Kwon. Tundra Books. (Canada)

Atinuke. *Africa, Amazing Africa: Country by Country.* Illus. by Mouni Feddag. Candlewick Press. (African Continent)

Birkjær, Betina. *Coffee, Rabbit, Snowdrop, Lost.* Trans. from Danish by Sinéad Quirke Køngerskov. Illus. by Anna Margrethe Kjærgaard. Enchanted Lion. (Denmark)

Böge, Dieter. *189 Canaries.* Trans. from German by Laura Watkinson. Illus. by Elsa Klever. Eerdmans Books For Young Readers. (Germany)

Boivin, Lisa. *We Dream Medicine Dreams.* Illus. by author. Highwater Press. (Canada: Northwest Territories)

Buitrago, Jairo. *Wounded Falcons.* Trans. from Spanish by Elisa Amado. Illus. by Rafael Yockteng. Groundwood Books. (Mexico)

Carmona, Hannah. *Anita and the Dragons.* Illus. by Anna Cunha. Lantana. (Dominican Republic)

Fried, Hédi. *The Story of Bodri.* Trans. from Swedish by Linda Schenck. Illus. by Stina Wirsén. Eerdmans Books For Young Readers. (Sweden)

Fontaine, Valérie. *The Big Bad Wolf in My House.* Trans. from French by Shelley Tanaka. Illus. by Nathalie Dion. Groundwood Books. (Canada)

Hrab, Naseem. *The Sour Cherry Tree.* Illus. by Nahid Kazemi. Owlkids Books. (Canada)

Manrique, María Eugenia. *The Caiman.* Trans. from Spanish by Amy Brill. Illus. by Ramón París. Amazon Crossing Kids. (Venezuela)

Morstad, Julie. *Time Is a Flower.* Illus. by author. Tundra Books. (Canada)

Pang, Hannah. *Seasons: A Year in Nature.* Illus. by Clover Robin. Tiger Tales/360 Degrees. (UK)

Raúf, Onjali Q. *The Star Outside My Window.* Illus. by Pippa Curnick. Delacorte Press. (UK: England)

Osada, Hiroshi. *Almost Nothing, yet Everything: A Book about Water.* Trans. from Japanese by David Boyd. Illus. by Ryōji Arai. Enchanted Lion. (Japan)

Waters, Fiona. *Tiger, Tiger, Burning Bright! An Animal Poem for Each Day of the Year.* Illus. by Britta Teckentrup. Candlewick Press/Nosy Crow. (UK)

Grades 6 to 8

Cheng, Eugenia. *Molly and the Mathematical Mysteries: Ten Interactive Adventures in Mathematical Wonderland.* Illus. by Aleksandra Artymowska. Candlewick Press/Big Picture Press. (UK)

Fung, Rosena. *Living with Viola.* Illus. by author. Annick Press. (Canada)

Kuzki, Shaw. *Soul Lanterns.* Trans. from Japanese by Emily Balistrieri. Delacorte Press. (Japan)

Mckay, Hilary. *The Swallows' Flight.* Simon & Schuster/Margaret K. McElderry Books. (England/Germany)

Poulin, Andrée. *Burying the Moon.* Illus. by Sonali Zohra. Groundwood Books. (India)

Romanyshyn, Romana and Lesiv, Andriy. *How War Changed Rondo.* Trans. from Ukrainian by Oksana Lushchevska. Illus. by authors. Enchanted Lion. (Ukraine)

Grades 9 to 12

Aisato, Lisa. *All the Colors of Life.* Trans. from Norwegian by Olivia Lasky. Illus. by author. W1-Media/Arctis Books. (Norway)

Boulerice, Simon. *Carry On: Poetry by Young Immigrants.* Trans. from French by Susan Ouriou. Illus. by Rogé. Owlkids Books. (Canada)

Chim, Wai. *Freedom Swimmer.* Scholastic Press. (China)

Kessler, Liz. *When the World Was Ours.* Simon & Schuster/Aladdin. (Austria/Poland/England)

Kinew, Wab. *Walking in Two Worlds.* Penguin Teens. (Canada)

Letria, José Jorge. *War.* Trans. from Portuguese by Elisa Amado. Illus. by André Letria. Greystone Kids. (Portugal)

Notable Children's Books

Each year a committee of the Association for Library Service to Children (ALSC) identifies the best of the best in children's books. According to the Notables Criteria, "notable" is defined as: Worthy of note or notice, important, distinguished, outstanding. As applied to children's books, notable should be thought to include books of especially commendable quality, books that exhibit venturesome creativity, and books of fiction, information, poetry, and pictures for all age levels (birth through age 14) that reflect and encourage children's interests in exemplary ways. [See "Literary Prizes, 2021" later in Part 5 for Caldecott, Newbery, and other award winners—*Ed.*]

Younger Readers

Alaina and the Great Play. By Eloise Greenfield. Illus. by Colin Bootman. Alazar.

Amira's Picture Day. By Reem Faruqi. Illus. by Fahmida Azim. Holiday.

Areli Is a Dreamer. By Areli Morales. Illus. by Luisa Uribe. Random House Studio.

Beak & Ally #1: Unlikely Friends. By Norm Feuti. Illus. by the author. HarperAlley.

The Big Bath House. By Kyo Maclear. Illus. by Gracey Zhang. Random House Studio.

Bodies Are Cool. By Tyler Feder. Illus. by the author. Dial.

Boogie Boogie, Y'all. By C.G. Esperanza. Illus. by the author. HarperCollins/Katherine Tegen.

Bright Star. By Yuyi Morales. Illus. by the author. Holiday/Neal Porter.

Coffee, Rabbit, Snowdrop, Lost. By Betina Birkjær. Illus. by Anna Margrethe Kjærgaard. Tr. by Sinéad Quirke Køngerskov. Enchanted Lion.

Coquí in the City. By Nomar Perez. Illus. by the author. Tr. by Farah Perez. Dial.

The Cot in the Living Room. By Hilda Eunice Burgos. Illus. by Gaby D'Alessandro. Penguin/Kokila.

A Day for Rememberin': Inspired by the True Events of the First Memorial Day. By Leah Henderson. Illus. by Floyd Cooper. Abrams.

Don't Hug Doug: (He Doesn't Like It). By Carrie Finison. Illus. by Daniel Wiseman. Putnam.

Dream Street. By Tricia Elam Walker. Illus. by Ekua Holmes. Random/Anne Schwartz.

Except Antarctica. By Todd Sturgell. Illus. by the author. Sourcebooks/eXplore.

Eyes that Kiss in the Corners. By Joanna Ho. Illus. by Dung Ho. Harper.

The First Blade of Sweetgrass: A Native American Story. By Suzanne Greenlaw and Gabriel Frey. Illus. by Nancy Baker. Tilbury.

Fox at Night. By Corey R. Tabor. Illus. by the author. HarperCollins/Balzer+Bray.

From the Tops of the Trees. By Kao Kalia Yang. Illus. by Rachel Wada. Carolrhoda.

The Great Stink: How Joseph Bazalgette Solved London's Poop Pollution Problem. By Colleen Paeff. Illus. by Nancy Carpenter. Simon & Schuster/Margaret K. McElderry.

Have You Ever Seen a Flower? By Shawn Harris. Illus. by the author. Chronicle.

I Am Smoke. By Henry Herz. Illus. by Mercè López. Tilbury.

I Dream of Popo. By Livia Blackburne. Illus. by Julia Kuo. Roaring Brook.

I Hop: An I Like to Read® Book. By Joe Cepeda. Illus. by the author. Holiday.

I Sang You Down from the Stars. By Tasha Spillett-Sumner. Illus. by Michaela Goade. Little Brown.

In the Meadow of Fantasies. By Hadi Mohammadi. Illus. by Nooshin Safakhoo. Tr. by Sara Khalili. Archipelago/Elsewhere Editions.

In My Mosque. By M.O. Yuksel. Illus. by Hatem Aly. Harper.

King of Ragtime: The Story of Scott Joplin. By Stephen Costanza. Illus. by the author. Atheneum.

Laxmi's Mooch. By Shelly Anand. Illus. by Nabi H. Ali. Penguin/Kokila.

Let Me Fix You a Plate: A Tale of Two Kitchens. By Elizabeth Lilly. Illus. by the author. Holiday/Neal Porter.

The Little Wooden Robot and the Log Princess. By Tom Gauld. Illus. by the author. Holiday/Neal Porter.

The Longest Storm. By Dan Yaccarino. Illus. by the author. Astra/mineditionUS.

The Lost Package: A Lot Can Happen Between the Post Office and the Destination. By Richard Ho. Illus. by Jessica Lanan. Roaring Brook.

May Your Life Be Deliciosa. By Michael Genhart. Illus. by Loris Lora. Cameron Kids.

Mel Fell. By Corey R. Tabor. Illus. by the author. HarperCollins/Balzer+Bray.

Milo Imagines the World. By Matt de la Peña. Illus. by Christian Robinson. Putnam.

Mornings with Monet. By Barb Rosenstock. Illus. by Mary GrandPré. Knopf.

The Most Beautiful Story. By Brynjulf Jung Tjønn. Illus. by Øyvind Torseter. Tr. by Kari Dickson. Enchanted Lion.

My First Day. By Phùng Nguyên Quang & Huỳnh Kim Liên. Illus. by the authors. Random/Make Me a World.

My Two Border Towns. By David Bowles. Illus. by Erika Meza. Penguin/Kokila.

Nina: A Story of Nina Simone. By Traci N. Todd. Illus. by Christian Robinson. Putnam.

Not Little. By Maya Myers. Illus. by Hyewon Yum. Holiday/Neal Porter.

Nothing Fits a Dinosaur. By Jonathan Fenske. Illus. by the author. Simon & Schuster/Simon Spotlight.

Odd Beasts: Meet Nature's Weirdest Animals. By Laura Gehl. Illus. by Gareth Lucas. Abrams/Appleseed.

Osnat and Her Dove: The True Story of the World's First Female Rabbi. By Sigal Samuel. Illus. by Vali Mintzi. Levine Querido.

Our Skin: A First Conversation about Race. By Megan Madison and Jessica Ralli. Illus. by Isabel Roxas. Penguin Workshop/RISE.

Outside, Inside. By LeUyen Pham. Illus. by the author. Roaring Brook.

Over the Shop. By JonArno Lawson. Illus. by Qin Leng. Candlewick.

The People Remember. By Ibi Zoboi. Illus. by Loveis Wise. HarperCollins/Balzer+Bray.

The People's Painter: How Ben Shahn Fought for Justice with Art. By Cynthia Levinson. Illus. by Evan Turk. Abrams.

Room for Everyone. By Naaz Khan. Illus. by Mercè López. Atheneum/Caitlyn Dlouhy.

Sato the Rabbit. By Yuki Ainoya. Illus. by the author. Tr. by Michael Blaskowsky. Enchanted Lion.

Someone Builds the Dream. By Lisa Wheeler. Illus. by Loren Long. Dial.

A Song of Frutas. By Margarita Engle. Illus. by Sara Palacios. Atheneum.

Soul Food Sunday. By Winsome Bingham. Illus. by C.G. Esperanza. Abrams.

Summertime Sleepers: Animals that Estivate. By Melissa Stewart. Illus. by Sarah S. Brannen. Charlesbridge.

Sunrise Summer. By Matthew Swanson. Illus. by Robbi Behr. Macmillan/Imprint.

Ten Beautiful Things. By Molly Beth Griffin. Illus. by Maribel Lechuga. Charlesbridge.

Too Small Tola. By Atinuke. Illus. by Onyinye Iwu. Candlewick.

¡Vamos! Let's Cross the Bridge. By Raúl the Third. Illus. by Raúl the Third and Elaine Bay. HarperCollins/Versify.

Watercress. By Andrea Wang. Illus. by Jason Chin. Holiday/Neal Porter.

The Water Lady: How Darlene Arviso Helps a Thirsty Navajo Nation. By Alice B. McGinty. Illus. by Shonto Begay. Random/Schwartz & Wade.

What I Am. By Divya Srinivasan. Illus. by the author. Viking.

When Lola Visits. By Michelle Sterling. Illus. by Aaron Asis. HarperCollins/Katherine Tegen.

Wishes. By Mượn Thị Văn. Illus. by Victo Ngai. Scholastic/Orchard.

Wonder Walkers. By Micha Archer. Illus. by the author. Penguin/Nancy Paulsen.

Middle Readers

The 1619 Project: Born on the Water. By Nikole Hannah-Jones and Renée Watson. Illus. by Nikkolas Smith. Penguin/Kokila.

Amari and the Night Brothers. By B.B. Alston. HarperCollins/Balzer+Bray.

Ancestor Approved: Intertribal Stories for Kids. Ed. by Cynthia Leitich Smith. HarperCollins/Heartdrum.

Bad Sister. By Charise Mericle Harper. Illus. by Rory Lucey. First Second.

Barefoot Dreams of Petra Luna. By Alda P. Dobbs. Sourcebooks.

The Beatryce Prophecy. By Kate DiCamillo. Illus. by Sophie Blackall. Candlewick.

Borders. By Thomas King. Illus. by Natasha Donovan. Little, Brown.
Cece Rios and the Desert of Souls. By Kaela Rivera. Harper.
Child of the Flower-Song People: Luz Jiménez, Daughter of the Nahua. By Gloria Amescua. Illus. by Duncan Tonatiuh. Abrams.
Healer of the Water Monster. By Brian Young. HarperCollins/Heartdrum.
How to Become a Planet. By Nicole Melleby. Algonquin.
How to Find What You're Not Looking For. By Veera Hiranandani. Penguin/Kokila.
The Leak. By Kate Reed Petty. Illus. by Andrea Bell. First Second.
The One Thing You'd Save. By Linda Sue Park. Illus. by Robert Sae-Heng. Clarion.
Playing the Cards You're Dealt. By Varian Johnson. Scholastic.
Red, White, and Whole. By Rajani LaRocca. HarperCollins/Quill Tree.
Root Magic. By Eden Royce. HarperCollins/Walden Pond.
Runaway: The Daring Escape of Ona Judge. By Ray Anthony Shepard. Illus. by Keith Mallett. Farrar.
Saving American Beach: The Biography of African American Environmentalist MaVynee Betsch. By Heidi Tyline King. Illus. by Ekua Holmes. Putnam.
The Sea in Winter. By Christine Day. HarperCollins/Heartdrum.
Sharice's Big Voice: A Native Kid Becomes a Congresswoman. By Sharice Davids and Nancy K. Mays. Illus. by Joshua Mangeshig Pawis-Steckley. Harper.
Sona Sharma, Very Best Big Sister? By Chitra Soundar. Illus. by Jen Khatun. Candlewick.
Stamped (For Kids): Racism, Antiracism, and You. By Sonja Cherry-Paul, Jason Reynolds, and Ibram X. Kendi. Illus. by Rachelle Baker. Little, Brown.
Starfish. By Lisa Fipps. Penguin/Nancy Paulsen.
Survivor Tree. By Marcie Colleen. Illus. by Aaron Becker. Little, Brown.
Temple Alley Summer. By Sachiko Kashiwaba. Illus. by Miho Satake. Tr. by Avery Fischer Udagawa. Restless.
Ten Thousand Tries. By Amy Makechnie. Atheneum.
This Very Tree: A Story of 9/11, Resilience, and Regrowth. By Sean Rubin. Illus. by the author. Holt.

Too Bright to See. By Kyle Lukoff. Dial.
Twenty-One Steps: Guarding the Tomb of the Unknown Soldier. By Jeff Gottesfeld. Illus. by Matt Tavares. Candlewick.
Unspeakable: The Tulsa Race Massacre. By Carole Boston Weatherford. Illus. by Floyd Cooper. Carolrhoda.
We Are Still Here! Native American Truths Everyone Should Know. By Traci Sorell. Illus. by Frané Lessac. Charlesbridge.

Older Readers

Amber and Clay. By Laura Amy Schlitz. Illus. by Julia Iredale. Candlewick.
Boy, Everywhere. By A.M. Dassu. Lee & Low/Tu.
Call and Response: The Story of Black Lives Matter. By Veronica Chambers. HarperCollins/Versify.
Dawn Raid. By Pauline Vaeluaga Smith. Illus. by Mat Hunkin. Levine Querido.
Fallout: Spies, Superbombs, and the Ultimate Cold War Showdown. By Steve Sheinkin. Roaring Brook.
The Genius under the Table: Growing Up behind the Iron Curtain. By Eugene Yelchin. Illus. by the author. Candlewick.
The In-Between. By Rebecca K.S. Ansari. HarperCollins/Walden Pond.
The Last Cuentista. By Donna Barba Higuera. Levine Querido.
The Legend of Auntie Po. By Shing Yin Khor. Illus. by the author. Penguin/Kokila.
A Place to Hang the Moon. By Kate Albus. Holiday/Margaret Ferguson.
Race Against Time: The Untold Story of Scipio Jones and the Battle to Save Twelve Innocent Men. By Sandra Neil Wallace and Rich Wallace. Astra/Calkins Creek.
Recognize!: An Anthology Honoring and Amplifying Black Life. Ed. by Wade Hudson and Cheryl Willis Hudson. Crown.
Revolution in Our Time: The Black Panther Party's Promise to the People. By Kekla Magoon. Candlewick.
Salt Magic. By Hope Larson. Illus. by Rebecca Mock. Holiday/Margaret Ferguson.
Six Crimson Cranes. By Elizabeth Lim. Knopf.
A Snake Falls to Earth. By Darcie Little Badger. Levine Querido.

Thanks a Lot, Universe. By Chad Lucas. Abrams/Amulet.
While I Was Away. By Waka T. Brown. Harper-Collins/Quill Tree.

All Ages

Hear My Voice/Escucha mi voz: The Testimonies of Children Detained at the Southern Border of the United States. By Warren Binford for Project Amplify. Workman.
I Am an American: The Wong Kim Ark Story. By Martha Brockenbrough and Grace Lin. Illus. by Julia Kuo. Little, Brown.
Legacy: Women Poets of the Harlem Renaissance. By Nikki Grimes. Bloomsbury.

Make Meatballs Sing: The Life and Art of Corita Kent. By Matthew Burgess. Illus. by Kara Kramer. Enchanted Lion.
¡Mambo Mucho Mambo! The Dance that Crossed Color Lines. By Dean Robbins. Illus. by Eric Velasquez. Candlewick.
Nano: The Spectacular Science of the Very (Very) Small. By Jess Wade. Illus. by Melissa Castrillón. Candlewick.
Niños: Poems for the Lost Children of Chile. By María José Ferrada. Illus. by María Elena Valdez. Tr. by Lawrence Schimel. Eerdmans.
The Sea-Ringed World: Sacred Stories of the Americas. By María García Esperón. Illus. by Amanda Mijangos. Tr. by David Bowles. Levine Querido.

Notable Recordings for Children

This annual listing of notable compact disc (CD) and digital download (DD) recordings for children 14 years and younger is produced by the Association for Library Service to Children (ALSC), a division of the American Library Association (ALA). Chosen by children's librarians and educators, the list includes recordings deemed to be of especially commendable quality that demonstrate respect for young people's intelligence and imagination, exhibit venturesome creativity, and reflect and encourage the interests of children and young adolescents in exemplary ways.

All Because You Matter. By Tami Charles. Read by the author. 2020. 9m. Weston Woods Studios, CD and book (9781338750294). Gr. PreS–2. Narrated by the author, the poetic text is enhanced by background music and sound effects that add depth to both the words and Bryan Collier's beautiful illustrations.

Allergic. By Megan Wagner Lloyd. Read by a full cast. 2021. 1.75hr. Scholastic Audio, DD (9781338751031). Gr. 2+. This graphic novel about Maggie, who desperately wants a dog, but is allergic, is brought to life by a stellar full-cast performance complete with scene-setting sound effects.

At the Mountain's Base. By Traci Sorell. Read by Kimberly Guerrero. 2020. 6m. Listening Library, DD (9780593342077). Gr. K–3. A Cherokee family separated by war waits for a cherished loved one to return in this lyrical story celebrating family and bravery.

Be You! By Peter H. Reynolds. Read by the author. 2021. 6m. Weston Woods Studios, CD and book (9781338803822). Gr. PreS–1. Reynolds encourages kids to be themselves in this inspirational story that features his signature whimsical illustration style, engaging narration, and lively music and sound effects.

Boogie, Boogie, Y'all. By C.G. Esperanza. Read by the author. 2021. 3m. HarperAudio, DD (9780063112865). PreS–3. With a hip-hop beat and perfect timing and cadence, this celebration of the city matches the energy of the often-overlooked art that illustrates public spaces. (The 2022 Odyssey Award winner for children)

Because of Winn-Dixie. By Kate DiCamillo. Read by Jenna Lamia. 2021. 3hr. Listening Library, DD (9780593456378). Gr. 3–7.

With authentic feeling and distinct characters, Lamia brings a classic story to life in this exceptional updated edition.

The Cat Man of Aleppo. By Karim Shamsi-Basha and Irene Latham. Read by Ramsey Faragallah. 2020. 15m. Listening Library, DD (9780593342022). Gr. K–4. Set against a lush soundscape, complete with many meows, Faragallah's quiet narration tells the story of Alaa, who stayed in Syria at the start of the war to work as an ambulance driver.

City of the Plague God. By Sarwat Chadda. Read by Vikas Adam. 2021. 10.5h. Listening Library, DD (9780593291160). Gr. 3+. Chadda's tale of demons and disease comes to life with distinct characters and emotions. Listeners will find themselves caught up in the story of Sik and his battle to rid the world of evil.

Class Act. By Jerry Craft. Read by a full cast. 2021. 2hr. HarperAudio, DD (9780063032057). Gr. 3–8. In this graphic novel sequel to "New Kid," a full cast gives Jordan and his friends distinct voicing set against a vivid soundscape as they face microaggressions from middle school teachers and peers.

Emmanuel's Dream: The True Story of Emmanuel Ofosu Yeboah. By Laurie Ann Thompson Read by Adjoa Andoh. 2021. 12m. Listening Library, DD (9780593396681). Gr. PreS–3. Andoh's expressive voice, working in tandem with the warm musical score, brings out the joy and triumph in this uplifting story. (A 2022 Odyssey Honor Audiobook)

Grandma's Purse. By Vanessa Brantley-Newton. Read by the author. 2021. 5m. Listening Library, DD (9780593399903). Gr. PreS–1. With warm and engaging narration, Brantley-Newton tells the story of a grandmother sharing the exciting items found in her purse with her granddaughter.

I and I Bob Marley. By Tony Medina. Read by Jamie Lincoln Smith. 2021. Live Oak, CD and book (9781430144632). Gr. 3–8. Smith's authentic narration transports the listener to Marley's Jamaica through the use of Marley's own music, poetry, and creative sound effects.

I Talk Like a River. By Jordan Scott. Read by the author. 2020. 19m. Dreamscape, DD (9781662052392). Gr. K–3. Scott's stuttering narration of this autobiographical story gives an immersive experience unmatched by the picture book alone. (A 2022 Odyssey Honor Audiobook)

Ivy. By Katherine Coville. Read by Carmen Viviano Crafts. 2021. 2h. Full Cast Audio, DD (9781936223947). Gr. K–5. A full cast of narrators successfully conjures dragons, griffins, trolls, and more in this exceptional recording the whole family can enjoy.

Kaleidoscope. By Brian Selznick. Read by Gwendoline Christie with music by Robert Een. 2021. 3hr. Scholastic Audio, DD (9781338794151). Gr. 5+. Christie's perfectly paced narration and ethereal voice, paired with Een's unique, discordant music, tie together Selznick's haunting short stories about a pair of friends bound to each other across time and space.

Max and the Midknights: Battle of the Bodkins. By Lincoln Peirce. Read by a full cast. 2020. 2.75h. Listening Library, DD (9780593339435). Gr. 2–6. Medieval music sets the scene, along with humorous sound effects and exemplary voicing from a full cast led by Kristen DiMercurio.

A Mind of Your Own. By The Bright Siders. 2021. 45m. Smithsonian Folkways Recordings, DD. Gr. PreS–2. Through a mixture of singable lyrics and full-cast skits, *A Mind of Your Own* highlights important topics for social emotional learning in this fun, family-friendly recording.

Ohana Means Family. By Ilima Loomis. Read by Lois Leinani Whitney. 2021. 12m. Live Oak, CD and book (9781430144595). Gr. PreS–4. Soothing music and rhythmic description capture the lush natural beauty of Hawaii through the process of farming taro and creating the traditional dish of poi for a family luau.

Okay to Be Different. By SaulPaul. 2021. 15m. 8 Pound Gorilla Records, DD. Gr. PreS–3. Grammy-nominated SaulPaul delivers a dynamic album featuring a plethora of music genres, centered on themes of self-confidence, hope, and individuality.

The Oldest Student: How Mary Walker Learned to Read. By Rita Lorraine Hubbard. Read by Nikki M. James. 2021. 14m. Weston Woods Studios, CD and book (9781338751857). Gr. K–5. The story of tenacious Mary Walker, who learned to read at the age of 116, is presented through an engaging, emotional, and honest narration highlighted by vivid illustrations by Oge More.

Playing the Cards You're Dealt. By Varian Johnson. Read by Dion Graham. 2021. 6h. Scholastic Audio, DD (9781338780949). Gr. 4–7. Graham's nuanced performance allows each character to shine in this poignant tale of community, family history, and spades.

Ricky Ricotta's Mighty Robot. By Dav Pilkey. Read by Oliver Wyman. 2021. 15m. Scholastic Audio, DD (9781338750072). Gr. K–3. With non-stop sound effects and Wyman's squeaktastic performance, Ricky Ricotta's adventure is an uproarious good time.

Rise of the Slippery Sea Monster. By Gareth P. Jones. Read by David Thorpe. 2021. 2 hr. Listening Library, DD (9780593344286). Gr. 1–4. In this installment of Adventures of the Steampunk Pirates, Thorpe delivers a side-splitting performance featuring spunky voices for an entire cast of characters.

The Strawberry Band. By Story Pirates. 2021. 30m. Face Cake Records, DD. Gr. PreS–3. Inspired by stories written by children, this vibrant and zany mix of songs pays hilarious homage to concept albums.

The Sun Is Kind of a Big Deal. By Nick Seluk. Read by a full cast. 2021. 14m. Weston Woods Studios, CD and book (9781338810240). Gr. 1–4. An enthusiastic full cast humorously introduces the wonders of our solar system to children, focusing on the significance of the sun and all its amazing characteristics.

Twins. By Varian Johnson and Shannon Wright. Read by a full cast. 2021. 1.5h. Scholastic Audio, DD (9781338785210). Gr. 2–6. In this full-cast performance, Johnson's popular graphic novel is reinvented as an energetic and engaging audiobook.

The Way Back. By Gavriel Savit. Read by Allan Corduner. 2020. 11hr. Listening Library, DD (9780593286135). Gr. 7+. Corduner's narration dazzles in this tale, inspired by Jewish folklore, giving each character a highly distinctive voice and switching between English, Hebrew, and Yiddish with ease.

We Are Still Here! Native American Truths Everyone Should Know. By Traci Sorell. Read by a full cast. 2021. 45m. Live Oak Media, CD and Book (9781430144670). Gr. 2+. Presented by a full cast of children and featuring a robust soundscape, this recording realizes the full potential of Sorell's powerful, illustrated nonfiction title.

We Are Water Protectors. By Carole Lindstrom. Read by the author. 2021. 7m. Weston Woods Studios, CD and book (9781338784107). Gr. PreS+. This Caldecott Medal-winning book, illustrated by Michaela Goade, is enhanced by Lindstrom's authentic, steady voice; immersive music; and sound effects.

Notable Children's Digital Media

The Association for Library Service to Children (ALSC), a division of the American Library Association, produces this annual list covering a diverse array of digital media for children 14 and younger. The Notable Children's Digital Media list recognizes real-time, dynamic, and interactive media content that enables and encourages active engagement and social interaction while informing, educating, and entertaining in exemplary ways. This list represents the titles selected by the committee for the first half of 2021, and titles added in January 2022.

4-H at Home. Website. All Ages. Parents/Caregivers. 4-H at Home is a free website full of fun and educational activities kids and teens can try at home. Organized by grade range and topic, projects explore the hands-on nature-based STEM learning for which the organization and its cooperative extension programs are known. Available in English.

Animal Antics (for Families). App: iOS and Android. Younger. Parents/Caregivers. Animal Antics is a free app designed to give children and their caregivers the opportunity to create a story together. Each participant chooses a character and records their voice. Prompts are given along the way to model conversation between child and caregiver and to encourage joint media engagement while building early literacy skills. Available in English.

Civics! An American Musical. Elementary, Middle School. Teacher. Civics! A Hollywood Musical is a game created by Fablevision, an educational website aimed at classrooms to teach research methods. Civics! allows an educator to select one of four American history topics, then students learn how to conduct research by assisting various theater employees in selecting correct primary sources, studying each resource carefully, and offering observations and reflections. The result is a musical, complete with a song, costumes, and reviews. Available in English.

Duolingo ABC: Learn to Read. App: iOS, Android. PreK, Elementary. Parent/Teacher/Caregiver. Duolingo ABC: Learn to Read is a free app designed to help beginning readers explore the alphabet and build early literacy skills. The app's games focus on letter recognition, writing skills, and comprehension skills. High-quality graphics and user-friendly gameplay make this app a fun and engaging way to learn the alphabet. Available in English.

Google Arts & Culture. Website and app: iOS, Android. Elementary, Middle School. Parent/Teacher/Caregiver. Google Arts & Culture is a comprehensive, high-quality resource of primary source materials for families, students, and teachers. The website, and its companion app, allow for the exploration of a wide range of content from more than 2,000 museums and archives across 80 countries. Music, art, and culture from around the world are accessible through interactive exhibits, tours, and games. Enjoy a wide range of activities in 3D and augmented and virtual reality. Available in English.

Grasshopper: Learn to Code for Free. App: iOS and Android. PreK, Elementary, Middle School. Parent/Teacher/Caregiver. Grasshopper is a free coding app for beginners developed by a team of passionate coders from Google. Using your smartphone, learn JavaScript coding fundamentals like functions, variables, "if" statements, operators, and more in progressively challenging levels. With a few taps, get started programming with these fun, quick games. Available in English, Spanish, and Portuguese.

How Do Animals Work? App: iOS and Android. Younger, Middle School. Parents/Caregivers. Interactively explore the biology of seven animals from the Amazon Rainforest and learn what makes each animal unique, from the pink river dolphin's use of echolocation to the extraordinary night vision of the jaguar. Available in 17 languages.

Mindful Powers. App: iOS and Android. All Ages. Parents/Caregivers. Mindful Powers is a free, kid-first, holistic approach to building social-emotional learning through play. Through mindful play and focus time, the Mindful Powers app allows kids (PreK-Middle School) to bring calm to their lives and build a healthier relationship with life, stress, and anxiety. Available in English.

NFL Play 60. Website and app: iOS and Android. Middle School. Parents/Caregivers. NFL Play 60 is a free app that encourages and challenges kids to get at least 60 minutes of physical activity per day. Kids can choose their own avatars and then earn coins to buy cool avatar gear by jumping, running, and turning while holding onto a device to log their movements. Available in English.

Pango Musical March (Studio Pango). App: iOS and Android. Kindle Fire. Younger. Pango Musical March is a paid app that allows users to create their own marching band parade. Kids choose from four different styles of music and have a wide variety of instruments within that style as options to add to an animated, fun, musical parade. Available in English.

Procreate. App: iOS for iPad. All ages. A powerful digital drawing app for iPad used by amateurs and professionals, Procreate offers an impressive range of tools like hundreds of handmade brushes, an advanced layering system, and a rich palette of colors of pens and pencils for simple sketching. The language setting in Procreate is based on the language used on the iPad.

Seek by iNaturalist. App: iOS and Android. Website. PreK, Elementary, Middle School. Parent/Teacher/Caregiver. Seek by iNaturalist is a free, family-friendly nature identification and exploration app. Children and families will learn about commonly recorded species in their area and can use the Seek Camera to identify organisms themselves. With earnable badges and monthly observation challenges, this app encourages everyone to get outside and learn. Available in English.

Sesame Street Family Play: Caring for Each Other. App: iOS and Android. Amazon. PreK, Elementary. Parent/Teacher/Caregiver. Sesame Street Family Play: Caring for Each Other is a free app that guides parents and caregivers through suggested games and songs to keep kids entertained and learning while offline. Users choose from activities by location in a home or outside within three categories: Keep Busy, Move Your Body,

or Calm Down. Available in English and Spanish.

Small Wonders (for Families). App: iOS and Android. Younger. Parents/Caregivers. Small Wonders is a free app designed to encourage children and their caregivers to learn together by exploring various topics. Each topic has a song and some simple games with questions for the caregiver to read, encouraging dialogue between child and caregiver. Available in English.

Smithsonian Fun Stuff for Kids and Teens. Elementary, Middle School. Parent/Teacher/Caregiver. Smithsonian's Fun Stuff for Kids and Teens is a curated collection of interactive activities, games, and exhibits. Discover and explore art, history, culture, nature, and science with many of the Smithsonian's museums: Meet the Zoo's animals, create with the Learning Lab, bring a treasured object "home" through the wonders of augmented reality, and play and learn through games from the Smithsonian Science Education Center.

Tayasui Sketches. App: iOS and Android. All ages. Tayasui Sketches is a user-friendly, versatile drawing app for mobile devices that uses your finger or stylus to create fun doodles, paintings, or illustrations for storytelling. With pens, pencils, and watercolor brushes, this realistic digital drawing tool will spark the imagination of all ages. Available in English, French, and traditional Chinese.

Tinybop: The Human Body. iOS and Android. PreK, Elementary, Middle School. Parent/Teacher/Caregiver. The Human Body by Tinybop supports children's curiosity in how the human body works. In this interactive app, children will discover how hearing works, how food travels through the intestines, and how the eye sees when they dive into the skeletal, muscular, nervous, circulatory, and digestive systems with seven interactive, animated, layered models. To learn how to play, Tinybop's website offers instructions and ideas on how to use this app effectively, or you can download the free handbook within the app. Available in multiple languages.

Wonder Weeks. App: iOS and Android. Younger. Parents/Caregivers. The Wonder Weeks app helps parents and caregivers understand their baby's developmental leaps and provides tips for how they can support and stimulate their baby's development. The app allows parents and caregivers to track their baby's milestones (noting that not every baby accomplishes every skill or shows all the signals at that specific age), personalize schedules, and look back on past moments through the diary feature. Available in 16 languages.

Wonder Woollies: Play World. iOS and Android. Amazon. PreK. Wonder Woollies: Play World is carefully designed for the youngest audience. As it allows for multitouch play, children and caregivers can explore the beautifully crafted world together, checking out different tools and interactive content. Of note are the beautiful, handmade graphic elements that give this game a unique visual quality that stands in stark contrast to other games with bright, possibly overstimulating colors. With no points or pre-set goals, this wordless, open-ended world allows children to independently direct how they want to play and to pursue their own interests and curiosities. Directions are available in multiple languages, including English.

Zigazoo. App: iOS and Android. Elementary, Middle School. Parent/Teacher/Caregiver. Zigazoo is a free, safety-focused social streaming app for kids. It offers many different prompts for kids to respond to in video format. Zigazoo is a fun, safe way for kids to experience healthy online relationships in an appropriate social media-type platform. Available in English.

Top Ten Book Lists, 2021

Sources included in this roundup of 2021's bestselling and most popular books are *Publishers Weekly*, *USA Today*, Barnes & Noble, Amazon, and Goodreads for print titles and Amazon for Kindle. Library-centric lists include the top ten adult print book checkouts reported by two major U.S. public library systems—New York Public Library and San Diego County Library—and the ten most popular library e-books and audiobooks as reported by OverDrive. [Due to varying selection criteria among the sources, apples-to-apples comparisons are not practicable.—*Ed.*]

Print Bestsellers

Publishers Weekly

1. *Assembly*, Natasha Brown
2. *Second Place*, Rachel Cusk
3. *A Shock*, Keith Ridgway
4. *The War for Gloria*, Atticus Lish
5. *Wayward*, Dana Spiotta
6. *All That She Carried: The Journey of Ashley's Sack, a Black Family Keepsake*, Tiya Miles
7. *All the Frequent Troubles of Our Days: The True Story of the American Woman at the Heart of the German Resistance to Hitler*, Rebecca Donner
8. *Dirty Work: Essential Jobs and the Hidden Toll of Inequality in America*, Eyal Press
9. *A Little Devil in America: Notes in Praise of Black Performance*, Hanif Abdurraqib
10. *Somebody's Daughter: A Memoir*, Ashley C. Ford

USA Today

1. *The Lincoln Highway*, Amor Towles
2. *Crying in H Mart*, Michelle Zauner
3. *The Plot*, Jean Hanff Korelitz
4. *How the Word Is Passed: A Reckoning with the History of Slavery Across America*, Clint Smith
5. *The Four Winds*, Kristin Hannah
6. *Empire of Pain: The Secret History of the Sackler Dynasty*, Patrick Radden Keefe
7. *Harlem Shuffle*, Colson Whitehead
8. *Great Circle*, Maggie Shipstead
9. *Project Hail Mary*, Andy Weir
10. *Klara and the Sun*, Kazuo Ishiguro

Barnes & Noble

1. *The 1619 Project: A New Origin Story*, Nikole Hannah-Jones
2. *Crying in H Mart*, Michelle Zauner
3. *Under the Whispering Door*, TJ Klune
4. *Cloud Cuckoo Land*, Anthony Doerr
5. *The Sentence*, Louise Erdrich
6. *Call Us What We Carry*, Amanda Gorman
7. *The Lyrics: 1956 to the Present*, Paul McCartney
8. *Harlem Shuffle*, Colson Whitehead
9. *Pony*, R.J. Palacio
10. *You Will Get through This Night*, Daniel Howell

Amazon

1. *The Lincoln Highway*, Amor Towles
2. *Crying in H Mart*, Michelle Zauner
3. *The Plot*, Jean Hanff Korelitz
4. *How the Word Is Passed: A Reckoning with the History of Slavery Across America*, Clint Smith
5. *The Four Winds*, Kristin Hannah
6. *Empire of Pain: The Secret History of the Sackler Dynasty*, Patrick Radden Keefe
7. *Harlem Shuffle*, Colson Whitehead
8. *Great Circle*, Maggie Shipstead
9. *Project Hail Mary*, Andy Weir
10. *Klara and the Sun*, Kazuo Ishiguro

Goodreads Most Popular Books Added by Readers

1. *People We Meet on Vacation*, Emily Henry
2. *The Love Hypothesis*, Ali Hazelwood
3. *Malibu Rising*, Taylor Jenkins Reid

4. *Beautiful World, Where Are You*, Sally Rooney
5. *The Four Winds*, Kristin Hannah
6. *The Last Thing He Told Me*, Laura Dave
7. *Project Hail Mary*, Andy Weir
8. *The Lost Apothecary*, Sarah Penner
9. *The Spanish Love Deception*, Elena Armas
10. *A Court of Silver Flames*, Sarah J. Maas

Digital Bestsellers

Amazon Kindle

1. *The Four Winds: A Novel*, Kristin Hannah
2. *If You Tell: A True Story of Murder, Family Secrets, and the Unbreakable Bond of Sisterhood*, Gregg Olsen
3. *The Moonlight Child*, Karen McQuestion
4. *The Last Thing He Told Me*, Laura Dave
5. *When We Believed in Mermaids*, Barbara O'Neal
6. *The Midnight Library: A Novel*, Matt Haig
7. *Harry Potter and the Sorcerer's Stone*, J.K. Rowling
8. *The Shadow Box*, Luanne Rice
9. *The Bad Seed*, Jory John
10. *Temptation*, Ivy Smoak

Top Print, Digital, and Audiobook Titles from the Library

New York Public Library Top Ten Print Checkouts System-Wide†

1. *The Vanishing Half*, Brit Bennett
2. *Mexican Gothic,* Silvia Moreno-Garcia
3. *Klara and the Sun*, Kazuo Ishiguro
4. *A Promised Land*, Barack Obama
5. *Caste: The Origins of Our Discontents*, Isabel Wilkerson
6. *The Guest List*, Lucy Foley
7. *Where the Crawdads Sing*, Delia Owens
8. *Maybe You Should Talk to Someone: A Therapist, Her Therapist, and Our Lives Revealed*, Lori Gottlieb
9. *The Other Black Girl*, Zakiya Dalila Harris
10. *Malibu Rising*, Taylor Jenkins Reid

San Diego County Library Top Ten Print Checkouts System-wide†

1. *A Slow Fire Burning*, Paula Hawkins
2. *Where the Crawdads Sing*, Delia Owens
3. *The Four Winds*, Kristin Hannah
4. *The Madness of Crowds*, Louise Penny
5. *Apples Never Fall*, Liane Moriarty
6. *The Judge's List*, John Grisham
7. *Sooley*, John Grisham
8. *The Midnight Library*, Matt Haig
9. *A Time for Mercy*, John Grisham
10. *Better Off Dead*, Lee Child

† Lists include adult fiction and nonfiction checkouts only.

OverDrive's Top Ten Most Popular Library E-Books and Audiobooks

E-Books

1. *The Four Winds*, Kristin Hannah
2. *The Midnight Library*, Matt Haig
3. *The Vanishing Half*, Brit Bennett
4. *The Guest List*, Lucy Foley
5. *Nomadland*, Jessica Bruder
6. *Bridgerton Collection, Volume 1*, Julia Quinn
7. *The Invisible Life of Addie LaRue*, V.E. Schwab
8. *The Last Thing He Told Me,* Laura Dave
9. *Anxious People*, Fredrik Backman
10. *A Time for Mercy,* John Grisham

Audiobooks

1. *A Promised Land*, Barack Obama
2. *Where the Crawdads Sing*, Delia Owens
3. *Cold Mourning*, Brenda Chapman
4. *The Four Winds*, Kristin Hannah
5. *Greenlights*, Matthew McConaughey
6. *Talking to Strangers*, Malcolm Gladwell
7. *The Midnight Library*, Matt Haig
8. *The Guest List*, Lucy Foley
9. *Harry Potter and the Chamber of Secrets,* J.K. Rowling
10. *Becoming*, Michelle Obama

Literary Prizes, 2021

Compiled by the staff of *Library and Book Trade Almanac*

Academy of American Poets Fellowship ($25,000). For outstanding poetic achievement. *Offered by:* Academy of American Poets. *Winner:* Camille T. Dungy.

Academy of American Poets Laureate Fellowships ($50,000 each). Marcus Amaker, Poet Laureate of Charleston, SC; Semaj Brown, Poet Laureate of Flint, MI; Roscoe Burnems, Poet Laureate of Richmond, VA; Aileen Cassinetto, Poet Laureate of San Mateo County, CA; Magdalena Gómez, Poet Laureate of Springfield, MA; Georgina Marie Guardado, Poet Laureate of Lake County, CA; Chasity Gunn, Poet Laureate of Elgin, IL; Kari Gunter-Seymour, Poet Laureate of Ohio; Dasha Kelly Hamilton, Poet Laureate of Milwaukee, WI and Wisconsin state; Luisa A. Igloria, Poet Laureate of Virginia; Angela Jackson, Poet Laureate of Illinois; Melissa Kwasny and M.L. Smoker, Poets Laureate of Montana; Bobby LeFebre, Poet Laureate of Colorado; Debra Marquart, Poet Laureate of Iowa; Trapeta B. Mayson, Poet Laureate of Philadelphia, PA; Anis Mojgani, Poet Laureate of Oregon; Chelsea Rathburn, Poet Laureate of Georgia; Andrea "Vocab" Sanderson, Poet Laureate of San Antonio, TX; Leslie Contreras Schwartz, Poet Laureate of Houston, TX; Lloyd Schwartz, Poet Laureate of Somerville, MA; M. Bartley Seigel, Poet Laureate of Upper Peninsula, MI; Brian Sonia-Wallace, Poet Laureate of West Hollywood, CA.

Jane Addams Children's Book Awards. For children's books that effectively promote the cause of peace, social justice, world community, and equality. *Offered by:* Jane Addams Peace Association. *Winners:* (younger children) Carole Lindstrom for *We Are Water Protectors*, illustrated by Michaela Goade (Roaring Books Press); (older children) Christina Soontornvat for *A Wish in the Dark* (Candlewick Press).

Aesop Prize. For outstanding illustrated children's publications utilizing folkloric themes. *Offered by:* American Folklore Society. *Winner:* Duncan Tonatiuh for *Feathered Serpent and the Five Suns: A Mesoamerican Creation Myth* (Harry N. Abrams).

Agatha Awards. For mystery writing in the method exemplified by author Agatha Christie. *Offered by:* Malice Domestic Ltd. *Winners:* (contemporary novel) Louise Penny for *All the Devils Are Here* (Minotaur Books); Erica Ruth Neubauer for *Murder at the Mena House* (Kensington Books); (historical) Rhys Bown for *The Last Mrs. Summers* (Berkeley); (young adult) Richard Narvaez for *Holly Hernandez and the Death of Disco* (Piñata Books); (nonfiction) Christina Lane for *Phantom Lady: Hollywood Producer Joan Harrison, the Forgotten Woman Behind Hitchcock* (Chicago Review Press); (short story) Barb Goffman for "Dear Emily Etiquette" in *Ellery Queen Mystery Magazine* (September/October 2020).

Ambroggio Prize ($1,000 and publication by the University of Arizona Press). *Offered by:* Academy of American Poets. For a book-length poetry manuscript originally written in Spanish and with an English translation. *Winner:* Carlos Aguasaco for *Cardenal en mi ventana con una máscara en el pico / Cardinal in My Window with a Mask on Its Beak.*

American Academy of Arts and Letters Award of Merit ($25,000). Given annually, in rotation, for the short story, sculpture, novel, poetry, drama, and painting. *Offered by:* American Academy of Arts and Letters. *Winner:* Chang-rae Lee (literature).

American Academy of Arts and Letters Awards in Literature ($10,000 each). To honor eight writers for exceptional accomplishment in any genre. *Offered by:* American Academy of Arts and Letters. *Winners:* Katori Hall, Saskia Hamilton, Yiyun Li, Jana Prikryl, Adam Rapp, Kathryn Scanlan, Layli Long Soldier, Benjamin Taylor.

American Academy of Arts and Letters Blake-Dodd Prize ($25,000). Triennial prize to a nonfiction writer. *Offered by:* American Academy of Arts and Letters. *Winner (2020):* Janine Di Giovanni.

American Academy of Arts and Letters Benjamin H. Danks Award ($20,000). Given annually, in rotation, to a composer of ensemble works, a playwright, and a writer. *Offered by:* American Academy of Arts and Letters. *Winner:* Yotam Haber (music).

American Academy of Arts and Letters E.M. Forster Award ($20,000). To a young writer from the United Kingdom or Ireland for a stay in the United States. *Offered by:* American Academy of Arts and Letters. Not awarded in 2021.

American Academy of Arts and Letters Gold Medal in Poetry. For distinguished achievement. *Offered by:* American Academy of Arts and Letters. *Winner:* Rita Dove.

American Academy of Arts and Letters William Dean Howells Medal. Given once every five years in recognition of the most distinguished American novel published during that period. *Offered by:* American Academy of Arts and Letters. *Winner (2020):* Richard Powers for *The Overstory* (W.W. Norton & Company).

American Academy of Arts and Letters Sue Kaufman Prize for First Fiction ($5,000). For a work of first fiction (novel or short stories). *Offered by:* American Academy of Arts and Letters. *Winner:* Douglas Stuart for *Shuggie Bain* (Grove Press).

American Academy of Arts and Letters Addison M. Metcalf Award ($10,000). Given biennially to a young writer of fiction, nonfiction, drama, or poetry. *Offered by:* American Academy of Arts and Letters. *Winner (2021):* Kali Fajardo-Anstine.

American Academy of Arts and Letters Katherine Anne Porter Award ($20,000). Awarded biennially to a prose writer of demonstrated achievement. *Offered by:* American Academy of Arts and Letters. *Winner (2020):* Christine Schutt.

American Academy of Arts and Letters Arthur Rense Poetry Prize ($20,000). Triennial prize to an exceptional poet. *Offered by:* American Academy of Arts and Letters. *Winner (2020):* Mary Ruefle.

American Academy of Arts and Letters Rosenthal Family Foundation Award ($10,000). To a young writer of considerable literary talent for a work of fiction. *Offered by:* American Academy of Arts and Letters. *Winner:* C Pam Zhang for *How Much of These Hills Is Gold* (Riverhead Books).

American Academy of Arts and Letters John Updike Award ($10,000). Biennial prize to a writer in midcareer whose work has demonstrated consistent excellence. *Offered by:* American Academy of Arts and Letters. *Winners (2021):* Stephen Adly Guirgis and Diane Seuss.

American Academy of Arts and Letters Harold D. Vursell Memorial Award ($20,000). To a writer whose work merits recognition for the quality of its prose style. *Offered by:* American Academy of Arts and Letters. *Winner:* Garth Greenwell.

American Academy of Arts and Letters Christopher Lightfoot Walker Award ($100,000). Biennial award to a writer of fiction or nonfiction who has made a significant contribution to American literature. *Offered by:* American Academy of Arts and Letters. *Winner (2020):* Leslie Marmon Silko.

American Academy of Arts and Letters E.B. White Award ($10,000). Biennial award to a writer for achievement in children's literature. *Offered by:* American Academy of Arts and Letters. *Winner (2021):* Kate DiCamillo.

American Book Awards. For literary achievement by people of various ethnic backgrounds. *Offered by:* Before Columbus Foundation. *Winners:* Ayad Akhtar for *Homeland Elegies* (Little, Brown and Company); Maisy Card for *These Ghosts Are Family* (Simon & Schuster); Anthony Cody for *Borderland Apocrypha* (Omnidawn Press); Ben Ehrenreich for *Desert Notebooks: A Road Map for the End of Time* (Counterpoint); Johanna Fernández for *The Young Lords: A Radical History* (University of North Carolina Press); Carolyn Forché for *In the Lateness of the World: Poems* (Penguin Press); John Giorno for *Great Demon Kings: A Memoir of Poetry, Sex, Art, Death, and Enlightenment* (Farrar, Straus and Giroux); Cathy Park Hong for *Minor Feelings: An Asian American Reckoning* (One World); Randall Horton for *{#289-128}: Poems* (University Press of Kentucky); Gerald Horne for *The Dawning of the Apocalypse: The Roots of Slavery, White Supremacy, Settler Colonialism, and Capitalism in the Long Sixteenth Century* (Monthly Review Press); Robert P Jones for *White Too Long: The Legacy of White Supremacy in American Christianity* (Simon & Schuster); Judy Juanita for *Manhattan*

My Ass, You're In Oakland (Equidistance Press); William Melvin Kelley for *Dunfords Travels Everywhere*, illustrated by Aiki Kelley (Anchor); (lifetime achievement) Maryemma Graham; (Walter & Lillian Lowenfels Criticism Award) Shana Redmond for *Everything Man: The Form and Function of Paul Robeson* (Duke University Press); (anti-censorship award) Jacob Soboroff for *Separated: Inside an American Tragedy* (HarperCollins).

American Indian Youth Literature Awards. Offered biennially to recognize excellence in books by and about American Indians. *Offered by:* American Indian Library Association. *Winners (2022):* (picture book) Daniel W. Vandever (author) and Corey Begay (illustrator) for *Herizon* (South of Sunrise Creative); (middle school) Brian Young for *Healer of the Water Monster* (Heartdrum, an imprint of HarperCollins); (young adult) Eric Gansworth for *Apple Skin to the Core* (Levine Querido).

American Poetry Review/Honickman First Book Prize in Poetry ($3,000 and publication of the book). To encourage excellence in poetry and to provide a wide readership for a deserving first book of poems. *Winner:* Natasha Rao for *Latitude* (Copper Canyon Press).

Américas Book Award for Children's and Young Adult Literature. To recognize U.S. works of fiction, poetry, folklore, or selected nonfiction that authentically and engagingly portray Latin America, the Caribbean, or Latinos in the United States. *Sponsor:* Consortium of Latin American Studies Programs (CLASP). *Winners:* Angela Burke Kunkel (author) and Paola Escobar (illustrator) for *Digging for Words* (Schwartz & Wade); Aida Salazar for *Land of the Cranes* (Scholastic).

Hans Christian Andersen Literature Award (500,000 Danish kroner, about $90,000). Biennial prize to a writer whose work can be compared with that of Andersen. *Offered by:* Hans Christian Andersen Literary Committee. *Winner (2020):* Karl Ove Knausgård.

Anthony Awards. For superior mystery writing. *Offered by:* Boucheron World Mystery Convention. *Winners:* (novel) S.A. Cosby for *Blacktop Wasteland* (Flatiron Books); (first novel) David Heska Wanbli Weiden

for *Winter Counts* (Ecco Press); (paperback original/e-book/audiobook original novel) Jess Lourey for *Unspeakable Things* (Thomas & Mercer); (short story) Alex Segura for "90 Miles" in *Both Sides: Stories from the Border* (Agora Books); (critical/nonfiction) Sarah Weinman (editor) for *Unspeakable Acts: True Tales of Crime, Murder, Deceit, and Obsession* (Ecco Press); (juvenile/young adult) Richie Narvaez for *Holly Hernandez and the Death of Disco* (Piñata Books); (anthology/collection) Heather Graham (editor) for *Shattering Glass: A Nasty Woman Press Anthology* (Nasty Woman Press).

Asian/Pacific American Awards for Literature. For books that promote Asian/Pacific American culture and heritage. Sponsor: Asian/Pacific American Librarians Association (APALA). Winners: (adult fiction) C. Pam Zhang for *How Much of These Hills Is Gold* (Riverhead Books); (adult nonfiction) Erika Lee for *America for Americans: A History of Xenophobia in the United States* (Basic Books); (young adult) Andrew Fukuda for *This Light Between Us* (Tor Teen); (children's) Tae Keller for *When You Trap a Tiger* (Random House Children's Books for Young Readers); (picture book) Julie Leung (author) and Chris Sasaki (illustrator) for *Paper Son: The Inspiring Story of Tyrus Wong, Immigrant and Artist* (Schwartz & Wade).

Aspen Words Literary Prize ($35,000). For a work of fiction that illuminates a vital contemporary issue and demonstrates the transformative power of literature on thought and culture. *Winner:* Louise Erdrich for *The Night Watchman* (HarperCollins).

Astounding Award for Best New Writer (formerly the John W. Campbell Award for Best New Writer). For the best new science fiction or fantasy writer whose first work of science fiction or fantasy was published in a professional publication in the previous two years. *Offered by:* Dell Magazines. *Winner:* Emily Tesh for *Silver in the Wood* (Tordotcom).

Atwood Gibson Writers' Trust Prize for Fiction (C$60,000) (Canada). *Offered by:* Writers' Trust of Canada. *Winner:* Katherena Vermete for *The Strangers* (Hamish Hamilton).

Audio Publishers Association Awards (Audies). To recognize excellence in audiobooks.

Winners: (audiobook of the year) *Piranesi* by Susanna Clarke, narrated by Chiwetel Ejiofor (Bloomsbury PLC); (drama) *Doctor Who-Stranded 1* by Matt Fitton, David K. Barnes, Lisa McMullin, and John Dorney, performed by Paul McGann, Nicola Walker, Hattie Morahan, Rebecca Root, Tom Price, and Tom Baker (Big Finish Productions); (autobiography/memoir) *The Autobiography of Malcolm X: As Told to Alex Haley* by Malcolm X and Alex Haley, narrated by Laurence Fishburne (Audible Studios); (best female narrator) *The City We Became* by N.K. Jemisin, narrated by Robin Miles (Hachette Audio); (best male narrator) *The Autobiography of Malcolm X: As Told to Alex Haley* by Malcolm X and Alex Haley, narrated by Laurence Fishburne (Audible Studios); (business/personal development) *The Gift: 12 Lessons to Save Your Life* by Dr. Edith Eva Eger, narrated by Tovah Feldshuh (Simon & Schuster Audio); (faith-based fiction and nonfiction) *Fierce, Free, and Full of Fire* by Jen Hatmaker, narrated by Jen Hatmaker (Thomas Nelson); (fantasy) *The City We Became* by N.K. Jemisin, narrated by Robin Miles (Hachette Audio); (fiction) *Such a Fun Age* by Kiley Reid, narrated by Nicole Lewis (Penguin Random House Audio); (history/biography) *His Truth Is Marching On: John Lewis and the Power of Hope* by Jon Meacham, narrated by JD Jackson (Penguin Random House Audio); (humor) *A Very Punchable Face* by Colin Jost, narrated by Colin Jost (Penguin Random House Audio); (literary fiction and classics) *The Death of Vivek Oji* by Akwaeke Emezi, narrated by Yetide Badaki and Chukwudi Iwuji (Penguin Random House Audio); (middle grade) *The Good Hawk* by Joseph Elliott, narrated by Gary Furlong and Fiona Hardingham (Brilliance Publishing); (multi-voiced performance) *Clap When You Land* by Elizabeth Acevedo, narrated by Elizabeth Acevedo and Melania-Luisa Marte (Harper-Audio); (mystery) *Fair Warning* by Michael Connelly, narrated by Peter Giles and Zach Villa (Hachette Audio); (narration by the author or authors) *More Myself* written and narrated by Alicia Keys (Macmillan Audio); (nonfiction) *Fire in Paradise* by Alastair Gee and Dani Anguiano, narrated by T. Ryder Smith (Recorded Books); (original work)

When You Finish Saving the World by Jesse Eisenberg, narrated by Kaitlyn Dever, Jesse Eisenberg, and Finn Wolfhard (Audible Originals); (romance) *Dirty Letters* by Vi Keeland and Penelope Ward, narrated by Andi Arndt and Jacob Morgan (Brilliance Publishing); (science fiction) *The Deep* by Rivers Solomon, Daveed Diggs, William Hutson, and Jonathan Snipes, narrated by Daveed Diggs (Simon & Schuster Audio); (short stories/collections) *The Chekhov Collection of Short Stories* by Anton Chekhov, narrated by Richard Armitage (Audible Studios); (Spanish language) *El Laberinto del Fauno* by Guillermo del Toro and Cornelia Funke, narrated by Kerygma Flores and Luis Ávila (Penguin Random House Grupo Editorial México); (thriller/suspense) *When No One Is Watching* by Alyssa Cole, narrated by Susan Dalian and Jay Aaseng (HarperCollins Publishers); (young adult) *Clap When You Land* by Elizabeth Acevedo, narrated by Elizabeth Acevedo and Melania-Luisa Marte (HarperAudio); (young listeners up to age eight) *The Overground Railroad* by Lesa Cline-Ransome, narrated by Shayna Small and Dion Graham (Live Oak Media).

Authors Guild Distinguished Service to the Literary Community Award. *Sponsor:* Authors Guild Foundation. *Winner:* Louise Erdrich.

Authors Guild Literature That Inspires Change Award. *Sponsor:* Authors Guild Foundation. *Winners:* (author) Ibram X. Kendi; (publisher) Chris Jackson.

Bad Sex in Fiction Award (United Kingdom). To "draw attention to the crude, badly written, often perfunctory use of redundant passages of sexual description in the modern novel, and to discourage it." *Sponsor: Literary Review.* Not awarded in 2021.

Bailey's Women's Prize for Fiction. See Women's Prize for Fiction.

Baillie Gifford Prize for Non-Fiction (£50,000). For a nonfiction work published in the United Kingdom in English. *Offered by:* Board of Directors of The Samuel Johnson Prize for Non-fiction Limited. *Sponsor:* Baillie Gifford. *Winner:* Patrick Radden Keefe for *Empire of Pain* (Doubleday/Picador).

Bancroft Prizes ($10,000). For books of exceptional merit and distinction in American history, American diplomacy, and the international relations of the United States.

Offered by: Columbia University. *Winners:* Andy Horowitz for *Katrina: A History, 1915–2015* (Harvard University Press); Claudio Saunt for *Unworthy Republic: The Dispossession of Native Americans and the Road to Indian Territory* (W.W. Norton & Company).

Barnes & Noble Book of the Year. To honor the book that B&N booksellers nominate as the book they are most proud to sell. *Offered by:* Barnes & Noble. *Winner:* Paul McCartney with Paul Muldoon (editor) for *Lyrics: 1956 to the Present* (Liveright).

Mildred L. Batchelder Award. To the American publisher of a children's book originally published in a language other than English and subsequently published in English in the United States. *Offered by:* American Library Association, Association for Library Service to Children. *Winner:* Enchanted Lion Books for *Telephone Tales,* written by Gianni Rodari, illustrated by Valerio Vidali, and translated by Antony Shugaar.

BBC National Short Story Award (United Kingdom) (£15,000). *Winner:* Lucy Caldwell for "All the People Were Mean and Bad."

Pura Belpré Awards. To a Latino/Latina writer and illustrator whose work portrays, affirms, and celebrates the Latino cultural experience in an outstanding work of literature for children and youth. *Offered by:* American Library Association, Association for Library Service to Children. *Winners:* (children's narrative) Ernesto Cisneros for *Efrén Divided* (Harper, an imprint of HarperCollins Publishers); (youth illustration) Raúl Gonzalez for *¡Vamos! Let's Go Eat* (Versify, an imprint of Houghton Mifflin Harcourt); (young adult narrative) Yamile Saied Méndez for *Furia* (Algonquin Young Readers, an imprint of Algonquin Books of Chapel Hill).

Helen B. Bernstein Book Award for Excellence in Journalism ($15,000). To a journalist who has written at book length about an issue of contemporary concern. *Offered by:* New York Public Library. Not awarded in 2021.

The Black Caucus of the American Library Association (BCALA) and BiblioLabs E-book Literary Awards. For the best self-published e-books in fiction and poetry by an African American author in the U.S. *Winners:* (fiction) Nikesha Elise Williams for *Beyond Bourbon Street* (NEW Reads Publications);

(poetry) Rahman Johnson for *Living, Loving, Letting Go* (Namhar Publishing).

Black Caucus of the American Library Association (BCALA) and *School Library Journal* Children and Youth Literary Awards. Honoring works by Black authors highlighting the diversity of the Black experience. *Winners:* (first novelist) Lisa Moore Ramée for *A Good Kind of Trouble* (Balzer + Bray/HarperCollins); (fiction) Lamar Giles for *Not So Pure and Simple* (Quill Tree Books/HarperCollins); (nonfiction) Wade Hudson and Cheryl Willis Hudson for *The Talk: Conversations about Race, Love & Truth* (Yearling/Penguin Random House); (graphic novel) Varian Johnson and Shannon Wright for *Twins* (Scholastic/Graphix).

Black Caucus of the American Library Association (BCALA) Literary Awards. *Winners:* (first novelist) Gabriel Bump for *Everywhere You Don't Belong* (Algonquin Books of Chapel Hill, a division of Workman Publishing) and Asha Lemme for *Fifty Words for Rain* (Dutton); (poetry) Kevin Young (editor) for *African American Poetry: 250 Years of Struggle and Song* (Library of America); (fiction) Brit Bennett for *The Vanishing Half* (Riverhead Books); (nonfiction) Eddie S. Glaude, Jr. for *Being Again: James Baldwin's America and Its Urgent Lessons for Our Own* (Crown, an imprint of Random House); (outstanding contribution to publishing) Candacy Taylor for *Overground Railroad: The Green Book and the Roots of Black Travel in America* (Abrams Press).

Irma Simonton Black and James H. Black Award for Excellence in Children's Literature. To a book for young children in which the text and illustrations work together to create an outstanding whole. *Offered by:* Bank Street College of Education. *Winner:* Nelly Buchet (author) and Andrea Zuill (illustrator) for *Cat Dog Dog: The Story of a Blended Family* (Schwartz & Wade).

James Tait Black Memorial Prize (United Kingdom) (£10,000). To recognize literary excellence in fiction and biography. *Offered by:* University of Edinburgh. *Winners:* (fiction) Shola von Reinhold for *Lote* (Jacaranda); (biography) Doireann Ní Ghríofa for *A Ghost in the Throat* (Tramp Press).

James Tait Black Prize for Drama (United Kingdom) (£10,000). *Offered by:* University of Edinburgh in partnership with the National Theatre of Scotland and in association with the Traverse Theatre. Not awarded in 2021.

Blue Peter Book of the Year (United Kingdom). To recognize excellence in children's books. Winners are chosen by a jury of viewers, ages eight–12, of the BBC television children's program *Blue Peter. Winners:* (best story) Elle McNicoll for *A Kind of Spark* (Knights Of); (best book with facts) Mike Barfield (author) and Jess Bradley (illustrator) for *A Day in the Life of a Poo, a Gnu, and You* (Buster Books).

Rebekah Johnson Bobbitt National Prize for Poetry ($10,000). A biennial prize for the most distinguished book of poetry written by an American and published during the preceding two years. *Offered by:* Library of Congress. *Donor:* Family of Rebekah Johnson Bobbitt. *Winners (2020):* Terrance Hayes for *American Sonnets for My Past and Future Assassin* (Penguin Books); (lifetime achievement) Natasha Trethewey.

Booker Prize for Fiction (United Kingdom) (£50,000). For the best English language novel. *Offered by:* Crankstart. *Winner:* Damon Galgut for *The Promise* (Europa).

Bookseller/Diagram Prize for Oddest Title of the Year. *Sponsor: The Bookseller* magazine. *Winner:* Roy Schwartz for *Is Superman Circumcised?* (McFarland & Company).

Boston Globe/Horn Book Awards. For excellence in children's literature. *Winners:* (fiction and poetry) Rita Williams-Garcia for *A Sitting in St. James* (Quill Tree Books/HarperCollins); (nonfiction) Paula Yoo for *From a Whisper to a Rallying Cry: The Killing of Vincent Chin and the Trial That Galvanized the Asian American Movement* (Norton Young Readers); (picture book) Jordan Scott (author) and Sydney Smith (illustrator) for *I Talk Like a River* (Neal Porter Books/Holiday House).

W.Y. Boyd Literary Award for Excellence in Military Fiction ($5,000). For a military novel that honors the service of American veterans during a time of war. *Offered by:* American Library Association. *Donor:* W.Y. Boyd II. *Winner:* Mark Treanor for *A Quiet Cadence* (Naval Institute Press).

Branford Boase Award (United Kingdom). To the author and editor of an outstanding novel for young readers by a first-time writer. *Winners:* Struan Murray (author) and Ben Horslen (editor) for *Orphans of the Tide* (Puffin).

Bridport International Creative Writing Prizes (United Kingdom). For poetry and short stories. *Offered by:* Bridport Arts Centre. *Winners:* (poetry, £5,000) Emma Walton Hamilton for "Over the Tannoy"; (short story, £5,000) Charlin McIsaac for "Manischewitz Night"; (flash fiction, 250-word maximum, £1,000) P.C. Verrone for "What to Watch"; (Peggy Chapman-Andrews Award for a First Novel) Fiona Williams for *The House of Broken Bricks.*

British Book Awards (aka the Nibbies) (United Kingdom). *Offered by: The Bookseller. Winners:* (book of the year) Douglas Stuart for *Shuggie Bain* (Pan Macmillan/Picador); (fiction) Maggie O'Farrell for *Hamnet* (Tinder Press); (debut) Douglas Stuart for *Shuggie Bain* (Pan Macmillan/Picador); (crime & thriller) Robert Galbraith for *Troubled Blood* (Sphere); (children's fiction) M.G. Leonard and Sam Sedgman (authors) and Lisa Paganelli (illustrator) for *The Highland Falcon Thief* (Macmillan Children's Books); (children's nonfiction and illustrated) David Olusoga for *Black and British: A Short, Essential History* (Macmillan Children's Books); (nonfiction narrative) Dara McAnulty for *Diary of a Young Naturalist* (Little Toller Books); (nonfiction lifestyle) Caroline Hirons for *Skincare* (HQ); (page-turner book of the year) Delia Owens for *Where the Crawdads Sing* (Putnam); (audio) Jay Shetty for *Think Like a Monk* (HarperCollins); (illustrator of the year) Charlie Mackesy; (author of the year) Richard Osman.

British Fantasy Awards. *Offered by:* British Fantasy Society. *Winners:* (Karl Edward Wagner Award) Alasdair Stuart; (Sydney J Bounds Award for a newcomer) Kathleen Jennings; (magazine/periodical) *Strange Horizons*; (nonfiction) Alison Peirse (ed.) for *Women Make Horror: Filmmaking, Feminism, Genre* (Rutgers University Press); (comic/graphic novel) Kieron Gillen and Stephanie Hans for *Die, Vol. 2: Split the Party* (Image); (independent press) Luna; (artist) Daniele Serra; (anthology) Zelda Knight and Ekpeki Oghenechovwe Donald (eds.) for *Dominion: An Anthology of Speculative Fiction from Africa and the African Diaspora* (Aurelia Leo); (collection) Charlotte Bond for *The Watcher in the Woods* (Black Shuck); (film/television production) *The Boys: "What I Know"* (Sony Pictures Television/Amazon Studios); (audio) *The Magnus Archives* (podcast); (novella) P. Djèlí Clark for Ring Shout (Tordotcom); (short story) Ida Keogh for "Infinite Tea in the Demara Café" in *London Centric: Tales of Future London* (NewCon Press); (August Derleth Award for horror novel) Silvia Moreno-Garcia for *Mexican Gothic* (Jo Fletcher); (Robert Holdstock Award for fantasy novel) Alix E. Harrow for *The Once and Future Witches* (Redhook).

Sophie Brody Medal. For the U.S. author of the most distinguished contribution to Jewish literature for adults, published in the preceding year. *Donors:* Sophie and Arthur Brody Foundation. *Offered by:* American Library Association, Reference and User Services Association. *Winner:* Yishai Sarid for *The Memory Monster* (Restless Books).

AKO Caine Prize for African Writing (£10,000). For a short story by an African writer, published in English. *Winner:* Meron Hadero for "The Street Sweep" in *ZYZZYVA* (Winter 2018, number 114).

Randolph Caldecott Medal. For the artist of the most distinguished picture book. *Offered by:* American Library Association, Association for Library Service to Children. *Winner:* Michaela Goade for *We Are Water Protectors,* written by Carole Lindstrom (Roaring Brook Press).

California Book Awards. To California residents to honor books of fiction, nonfiction, and poetry published in the previous year. *Offered by:* Commonwealth Club of California. *Winners:* (fiction) Daniel Mason for *A Registry of My Passage Upon the Earth* (Little, Brown and Company); (first fiction) C. Pam Zhang for *How Much of These Hills Is Gold* (Riverhead Books); (nonfiction) Alice L. Baumgartner for *South to Freedom: Runaway Slaves to Mexico and the Road to the Civil War* (Basic Books); (poetry) Nathalie Khankan for *Quiet Orient Riot* (Omnidawn); (juvenile) Ernesto Cisneros for *Efrén Divided* (Quill Tree Books); (young adult) Cynthia Salaysay for *Private Lessons* (Candlewick Press); (contribution to publishing) Sunbelt Publications for *A Natural History of the Anza-Borrego Region* by Marie Simovich and Mike Wells; (Californiana) Richard White and Jesse Amble White for *California Exposures: Envisioning Myth and History* (W.W. Norton & Company).

Eleanor Cameron Notable Middle Grade Books List. See LITA Excellence in Children's and Young Adult Science Fiction.

John W. Campbell Award for Best New Writer. See *Astounding* Award for Best New Writer.

John W. Campbell Memorial Award. For science fiction writing. *Offered by:* Gunn Center for the Study of Science Fiction. Not awarded in 2021.

Andrew Carnegie Medal for Excellence in Fiction and Nonfiction. For adult books published during the previous year in the United States. *Sponsors:* Carnegie Corporation of New York, ALA/RUSA, and *Booklist*. *Winners:* (fiction) James McBride for *Deacon King Kong* (Riverhead Books); (nonfiction) Rebecca Giggs for *Fathoms: The World in the Whale* (Simon & Schuster).

Carnegie Medal (United Kingdom). See CILIP Carnegie Medal.

Center for Fiction First Novel Prize ($10,000). *Offered by:* Center for Fiction, Mercantile Library of New York. *Winner:* Kirstin Valdez Quade for *The Five Wounds* (W.W. Norton & Company).

Chicago Folklore Prize. For the year's best folklore book. *Offered by:* American Folklore Society. *Winner:* Tom Mould for *Overthrowing the Queen: Telling Stories of Welfare in America* (Indiana University Press).

Chicago Tribune Nelson Algren Short Story Award ($3,500). For unpublished short fiction. *Offered by: Chicago Tribune.* Not awarded in 2021.

Chicago Tribune Heartland Prize for Fiction ($7,500). *Offered by: Chicago Tribune.* Not awarded in 2021.

Chicago Tribune Heartland Prize for Nonfiction ($7,500). *Offered by: Chicago Tribune.* Not awarded in 2021.

Chicago Tribune Literary Award. To recognize lifetime achievement of a prominent writer, usually someone with strong connections to the Midwest. *Offered by: Chicago Tribune.* Not awarded in 2021.

Chicago Tribune Young Adult Literary Prize. *Offered by: Chicago Tribune.* To recognize a distinguished literary career. Not awarded in 2021.

Children's Africana Book Awards. To recognize and encourage excellence in children's books about Africa. *Offered by:* Africa Access, African Studies Association. *Winners:* (young readers) Tricia Elam Walker (author) and April Harrison (illustrator) for *Nana Akua Goes to School* (Schwartz & Wade) and Ekiuwa Aire (author) and Alina Shabelnyk (illustrator) for *Idia of the Benin Kingdom* (Our Ancestors); (older readers) Jordan Ifueko for *Raybearer* (Amulet Books); (new adult) Tendai Huchu for *The Hairdresser of Harare* (Weaver Press).

Children's Literature Legacy Award (formerly the Laura Ingalls Wilder Award). Awarded to an author or illustrator whose books have made a substantial and lasting contribution to children's literature. *Offered by:* American Library Association, Association for Library Service to Children. *Winner:* Mildred D. Taylor.

Cholmondeley Awards for Poets (United Kingdom) (£1,680). For a poet's body of work and contribution to poetry. *Winners:* Kei Miller, Paula Claire, Maurice Riordan, Susan Wicks, and Katrina Porteous.

CILIP Carnegie Medal (United Kingdom). For the outstanding children's book of the year. *Offered by:* CILIP: The Chartered Institute of Library and Information Professionals. *Winner:* Jason Reynolds for *Look Both Ways* (Knights Of).

CILIP Kate Greenaway Medal and Colin Mears Award (United Kingdom) (£5,000 plus £500 worth of books donated to a library of the winner's choice). For children's book illustration. *Offered by:* CILIP: The Chartered Institute of Library and Information Professionals. *Winner:* Sydney Smith for *Small in the City* (Walker Books).

Arthur C. Clarke Award. For the best science fiction novel published in the United Kingdom. *Offered by:* British Science Fiction Association. *Winner:* Laura Jean McKay for *The Animals in That Country* (Scribe UK).

Hal Clement Notable Young Adult Books List. See LITA Excellence in Children's and Young Adult Science Fiction.

David Cohen Prize for Literature (United Kingdom) (£40,000). Awarded biennially to a living British writer, novelist, poet, essayist, or dramatist in recognition of an entire body of work written in the English language. *Offered by:* David Cohen Family Charitable Trust. *Winner (2021):* Colm Tóibín.

Matt Cohen Award: In Celebration of a Writing Life (C$20,000). To a Canadian author whose life has been dedicated to writing as a primary pursuit, for a body of work. *Offered by:* Writers' Trust of Canada. *Sponsors:* Marla and David Lehberg. *Winner:* Frances Itani.

Commonwealth Short Story Prize (United Kingdom) (£5,000 for overall winner; £2,500 for each regional winner). To reward and encourage new short fiction by Commonwealth writers. *Offered by:* Commonwealth Institute. *Winners:* (regional winner, Africa) Rémy Ngamije (Namibia) for "Granddaughter of the Octopus"; (regional winner, Asia, and overall winner) Kanya D'Almeida (Sri Lanka) for "I Cleaned the—"; (regional winner, Canada and Europe) Carol Farrelly (United Kingdom) for "Turnstones"; (regional winner, Caribbean) Roland Watson-Grant (Jamaica) for "The Disappearance of Mumma Dell"; (regional winner, Pacific) Katerina Gibson (Australia) for "Fertile Soil."

Jeanne Córdova Prize for Lesbian/Queer Nonfiction. *Offered by:* Lambda Literary Foundation. *Winner:* Nancy Agabian.

Costa Book Awards (United Kingdom) (£5,000 plus an additional £25,000 for Book of the Year). For literature of merit that is readable on a wide scale. *Offered by:* Booksellers Association of Great Britain and Costa Coffee. *Winners:* (biography) John Preston for *Fall: The Mystery of Robert Maxwell* (Viking); (novel) Claire Fuller for *Unsettled Ground* (Penguin/Fig Tree); (first novel) Caleb Azumah Nelson for *Open Water* (Viking); (children's) Manjeet Mann for *The Crossing* (Penguin); (poetry and Book of the Year) Hannah Lowe for *The Kids* (Bloodaxe Books).

Costa Short Story Award (United Kingdom). *Winner:* (first place, £3,500) L.E. Yates for "Sunblock."

Crime Writers' Association (CWA) Dagger Awards (United Kingdom). *Winners:*

(diamond dagger, for significant contribution to crime writing) Martina Cole; (gold dagger, for best novel) Chris Whitaker for *We Begin at the End* (Zaffre); (gold dagger, for nonfiction) Sue Black for *Written in Bone: Hidden Stories in What We Leave Behind* (Doubleday); (Ian Fleming steel dagger, for best thriller) Michael Robotham for *When She Was Good* (Sphere); (John Creasey dagger, for best debut crime novel) Eva Björg Ægisdóttir for *The Creak on the Stairs* (Orenda); (CWA historical dagger, for the best historical crime novel) Vaseem Khan for *Midnight at Malabar House* (Hodder & Stoughton); (CWA short story dagger) Clare Mackintosh for "Monsters" in *First Edition: Celebrating 21 Years of Goldsboro Books* (The Dome Press); (international dagger, for a work translated into English) Yun Ko-eun for *The Disaster Tourist*, translated by Lizzie Buehler (Serpent's Tail); (CWA dagger in the library, for a body of work) Peter May; (debut dagger, for a previously unpublished crime writer) Hannah Redding for *Deception: Two Women, Twelve Hours, One Dead Body. What Really Happened?*

Cundill History Prize ($75,000). For a book that embodies historical scholarship, originality, literary quality, and broad appeal. *Administered by:* McGill University. *Winner:* Marjoleine Kars for *Blood on the River: A Chronicle of Mutiny and Freedom on the Wild Coast* (The New Press).

Benjamin H. Danks Award ($20,000). Given annually, in rotation, to a composer of ensemble works, a playwright, and a writer. *Offered by:* American Academy of Arts and Letters. *Winner:* Yotam Haber (ensemble works).

Dartmouth Medal. For creating current reference works of outstanding quality and significance. *Donor:* Dartmouth College. *Offered by:* American Library Association, Reference and User Services Division. *Winner:* Spencer C. Tucker (editor) for *The Cold War: The Definitive Encyclopedia and Document Collection* (ABC-CLIO).

Derringer Awards. To recognize excellence in short crime and mystery fiction. *Sponsor:* Short Mystery Fiction Society. *Winners:* (flash story, up to 1,000 words) C.W. Blackwell for "Memories of Fire" in *Pulp Modern Flash* (August 3, 2020) and Travis Richardson for "War Words" in *Punk Noir Magazine* (December 3, 2020); (short story, 1,001–4,000 words) Eleanor Cawood Jones for "The Great Bedbug Incident and the Invitation of Doom" in *Chesapeake Crimes: Invitation to Murder* (Wildside Press) and Stacy Woodson for "River" in *The Beat of Black Wings: Crime Fiction Inspired by the Songs of Joni Mitchell* (Untreed Reads Publishing); (long story, 4,001–8,000 words) Sarah M. Chen for "Hotelin" in *Shotgun Honey Presents Volume #4: RECOIL*, edited by Ron Earl Phillips (Shotgun Honey); (novelette, 8,001–20,000 words) Art Taylor for "The Boy Detective and the Summer of '74" in *Alfred Hitchcock's Mystery Magazine* (January/February 2020).

Diagram Prize for Oddest Title of the Year. See Bookseller/Diagram Prize for Oddest Title of the Year.

Philip K. Dick Award. For a distinguished science fiction paperback published in the United States. *Sponsor:* Philadelphia Science Fiction Society and the Philip K. Dick Trust. *Winner:* Alison Stine for *Road Out of Winter: An Apocalyptic Thriller* (MIRA).

Digital Book Awards. To recognize high-quality digital content available to readers as e-books and enhanced digital books. *Sponsor:* Digital Book World. Not awarded in 2021.

DSC Prize for South Asian Literature ($50,000). To recognize outstanding literature from or about the South Asian region and raise awareness of South Asian culture around the world. *Sponsor:* DSC Limited. Not awarded in 2021.

Dublin Literary Award (Ireland) (€100,000). For a book of high literary merit, written in English or translated into English; if translated, the author receives €75,000 and the translator €25,000. *Offered by:* City of Dublin. *Winner:* Valeria Luiselli for *Lost Children Archive* (Fourth Estate).

Jim Duggins, PhD Outstanding Mid-Career Novelist Prize. *Offered by:* Lambda Literary Foundation. *Winners:* Sarah Gerard and Brontez Purnell.

Dundee Picture Book Award (Scotland) (£1,000). To recognize excellence in storytelling for children. The winner is chosen by the schoolchildren of Dundee. Not awarded in 2021.

Edgar Awards. For outstanding mystery, suspense, and crime writing. *Offered by:* Mystery Writers of America. *Winners:* (novel) Deepa Anappara for *Djinn Patrol on the Purple Line* (Random House); (first novel) Caitlin Mullen for *Please See Us* (Gallery Books/Simon & Schuster); (paperback original) Alyssa Cole for *When No One Is Watching* (William Morrow); (fact crime) Eric Eyre for *Death in Mud Lick: A Coal Country Fight Against the Drug Companies that Delivered the Opioid Epidemic* (Scribner); (critical/biographical) Christina Lane for *Phantom Lady: Hollywood Producer Joan Harrison, the Forgotten Woman Behind Hitchcock* (Chicago Review Press); (short story) Maaza Mengiste for "Dust, Ash, Flight" in *Addis Ababa Noir* (Akashic Books); (juvenile) Elizabeth C. Bunce for *Premeditated Myrtle* (Algonquin Young Readers); (young adult) Katie Alender for *The Companion* (G.P. Putnam's Sons Books for Young Readers); (television episode) John Morton (teleplay) for "Episode 1, Photochemistry" of *Dead Still* (Acorn TV); (Robert L. Fish Memorial Award) Colette Bancroft for "The Bite" in *Tampa Bay Noir* (Akashic Books); (grand masters) Charlaine Harris and Jeffery Deaver; (Raven Award) Malice Domestic; (Ellery Queen Award) Kelley Ragland; (Mary Higgins Clark Award) Elsa Hart for *The Cabinets of Barnaby Mayne* (Minotaur Books); (Sue Grafton Memorial Award) Rosalie Knecht for *Vera Kelly Is Not a Mystery* (Tin House Books).

Educational Writers' Award (United Kingdom) (£2,000). For noteworthy educational nonfiction for children. *Offered by:* Authors' Licensing and Collecting Society. *Winner:* Sarah Maycock for *Sometimes I Feel: A Menagerie of Feelings Big and Small* (Big Picture Press).

Margaret A. Edwards Award ($2,000). To an author whose book or books have provided young adults with a window through which they can view their world and which will help them to grow and to understand themselves and their role in society. *Donor: School Library Journal. Winner:* Kekla Magoon for *X: A Novel* (Candlewick Press), *How It Went Down* (Henry Holt and Co.), *The Rock and the River* (Aladdin), and *Fire in the Streets* (Aladdin).

T.S. Eliot Prize for Poetry (United Kingdom) (£20,000). *Offered by:* Poetry Book Society. *Winner:* Joelle Taylor for *C+nto & Othered Poems* (Westbourne Press).

Encore Award (United Kingdom) (£10,000). Awarded for the best second novel. *Offered by:* Royal Society of Literature. *Winner:* Caoilinn Hughes for *The Wild Laughter* (Oneworld Publications).

European Union Prize for Literature (€5,000). To recognize outstanding European writing. *Sponsors:* European Commission, European Booksellers Federation, European Writers' Council, Federation of European Publishers. *Winners:* Tom Kuka (Albania), Aram Pachyan (Armenia), Georgi Bardarov (Bulgaria), Lucie Faulerová (Czech Republic), Sigrún Pálsdóttir (Iceland), Laura Vinogradova (Latvia), Lara Calleja (Malta), Gerda Blees (the Netherlands), Frederico Pedreira (Portugal), Dejan Tiago Stanković (Serbia), Anja Mugerli (Slovenia), Maxim Grigoriev (Sweden), Amine Al Ghozzi (Tunisia).

FIL Literary Award in Romance Languages (formerly the Juan Rulfo International Latin American and Caribbean Prize) (Mexico) ($150,000). For lifetime achievement in any literary genre. *Offered by:* Juan Rulfo International Latin American and Caribbean Prize Committee. *Winner:* Diamela Eltit.

Financial Times and McKinsey Business Book of the Year Award (£30,000). To recognize books that provide compelling and enjoyable insight into modern business issues. *Winner:* Nicole Perlroth for *This Is How They Tell Me the World Ends: The Cyberweapons Arms Race* (Bloomsbury).

Sid Fleischman Humor Award. See Golden Kite Awards.

ForeWord Reviews Book of the Year Awards ($1,500). For independently published books. *Offered by: ForeWord Reviews* magazine. *Winners:* (editor's choice prize, fiction) Fowzia Karimi for *Above Us the Milky Way: An Illuminated Alphabet* (Deep Vellum); (editor's choice prize, nonfiction) R.E. Burrillo for *Behind the Bears Ears: Exploring the Cultural and Natural Histories of a Sacred Landscape* (Torrey House Press).

E.M. Forster Award ($20,000). To a young writer from the United Kingdom or Ireland for a stay in the United States. *Offered by:*

American Academy of Arts and Letters. Not awarded in 2021.

Forward Prizes (United Kingdom). For poetry. *Offered by: The Forward. Winners:* (best collection, £10,000) Luke Kennard for *Notes on the Sonnets* (Penned in the Margins); (Felix Dennis Prize for best first collection, £5,000) Caleb Femi for *Poor* (Penguin); (best single poem, £1,000) Nicole Sealey for "Pages 22-29, An Excerpt from The Ferguson Report: An Erasure" published in *Poetry London.*

Josette Frank Award. For a work of fiction in which children or young people deal in a positive and realistic way with difficulties in their world and grow emotionally and morally. *Offered by:* Bank Street College of Education and the Florence M. Miller Memorial Fund. *Winners:* Victoria Jamieson and Omar Mohamed (authors), Victoria Jamieson (illustrator), Imam Geddy (color) for *When Stars Are Scattered* (Dial Books).

George Freedley Memorial Award. For the best English-language work about live theater published in the United States. *Offered by:* Theatre Library Association. *Winner:* Marlis Schweitzer for *Bloody Tyrants and Little Pickles: Stage Roles of Anglo-American Girls in the Nineteenth Century* (University of Iowa Press).

French-American Foundation Translation Prize ($10,000). For a translation or translations from French into English of works of fiction and nonfiction. *Offered by:* French-American Foundation. *Donor:* Florence Gould Foundation. *Winners:* (fiction) Chris Andrews for his translation of *Our Riches* by Kaouther Adimi (New Directions Publishing); (nonfiction) Hoyt Rogers for his translation of *Rome, 1630: The Horizon of the Early Baroque, Followed by Five Essays on Seventeenth-Century Art* by Yves Bonnefoy (Seagull Books/University of Chicago Press).

Frost Medal. To recognize achievement in poetry over a lifetime. *Offered by:* Poetry Society of America. *Winner:* N. Scott Momaday.

Lewis Galantière Award. Awarded biennially for a literary translation into English from any language other than German. *Offered by:* American Translators Association. *Winner (2020):* Michael Meigs for his translation of *All This I Will Give to You* by Dolores Redondo (Amazon Crossing).

Theodor Seuss Geisel Award. For the best book for beginning readers. *Offered by:* American Library Association, Association for Library Service to Children. *Winners:* David LaRochelle (author) and Mike Wohnoutka (illustrator) for *See the Cat: Three Stories About a Dog* (Candlewick Press).

Giller Prize (Canada). See Scotiabank Giller Prize.

Gival Press Novel Award ($3,000 and publication by Gival Press). Given biennially. *Winner (2020):* Jordan Silversmith for *Redshift, Blueshift.*

Gival Press Oscar Wilde Award ($500 and publication by Gival Press). Given annually to an original, unpublished poem that relates LGBTQ life by a poet who is 18 or older. *Winner:* Brian Cronwall for "In the Brackish Place Where We Come to Love."

Gival Press Poetry Award ($1,000 and publication by Gival Press). Given biennially. Not awarded in 2021.

Gival Press Short Story Award ($1,000 and publication by Gival Press). Given annually. *Winner:* Leah Eichler for "My Pompeii."

Giverny Award. For an outstanding children's science picture book. *Offered by:* 15 Degree Laboratory. *Winner:* Becky Davies (author) and Jennie Poh (illustrator) for *Little Turtle and the Changing Sea: A Story of Survival in Our Polluted Oceans* (Tiger Tales).

Alexander Gode Medal. To an individual or institution for outstanding service to the translation and interpreting professions. *Offered by:* American Translators Association. *Winner:* InterpretAmerica.

Golden Duck Notable Picture Books List. See LITA Excellence in Children's and Young Adult Science Fiction.

Golden Kite Awards. For children's books. *Offered by:* Society of Children's Book Writers and Illustrators. *Winners:* (young reader and middle grade fiction) Renée Watson for *Ways to Make Sunshine* (Bloomsbury Children's Books); (young adult fiction) Sherri L. Smith for *The Blossom and the Firefly* (G.P. Putnam's Sons Books for Young Readers); (nonfiction text for younger readers) Don Tate for *William Still and His Freedom Stories* (Peachtree); (nonfiction text for older readers) Christina Soontornvat for *All Thirteen: The Incredible Cave Rescue of the Thai Boys' Soccer Team* (Candlewick Press);

(picture book illustration) Catia Chien for *The Bear and the Moon* (Chronicle Books); (picture book text) Tami Charles for *All Because You Matter* (Orchard Books); (illustrated book for older readers) Uri Shulevitz for *Chance: Escape from the Holocaust: Memories of a Refugee Childhood* (Farrar, Straus and Giroux Books for Young Readers; (Sid Fleischman Humor Award) Donna Barba Higuera for *Lupe Wong Won't Dance* (Levine Querido).

Governor General's Literary Awards (Canada) (C$25,000, plus C$3,000 to the publisher). For works, in English and French, of fiction, nonfiction, poetry, and drama and for translation. *Offered by:* Canada Council for the Arts. *Winners:* (fiction, English) Norma Dunning for *Tainna: The Unseen Ones* (Douglas & McIntyre); (nonfiction, English) Sadiqa de Meijer for *alfabet/alphabet: A Memoir of First Language* (Palimpsest Press); (poetry, English) Tolu Oloruntoba for *The Junta of Happenstance* (Anstruther); (drama, English) Hannah Moscovitch for *Sexual Misconduct of the Middle Classes* (Playwrights Canada Press); (young people's literature—text, English) Philippa Dowding for *Firefly* (DCB); (young people's literature—illustrated) David A. Robertson (author) and Julie Flett (illustrator) for *On the Trapline* (Tundra Books); (translation from French to English) Erín Moure for *This Radiant Life*, translation of *La vie radieuse* by Chantal Neveu (Book*hug Press); (fiction, French) Fanny Britt for *Faire les sucres* (Le Cheval d'août); (nonfiction, French) Serge Bouchard and Mark Fortier for *Du diesel dans les veines* (Lux Editeur); (poetry, French) Tania Langlais for *Pendant que Perceval tombait* (Les Herbes rouges); (drama, French) Mishka Lavigne for *Copeaux* (L'Interligne); (young people's literature—text, French) Jean-François Sénéchal for *Les avenues* (Lemeac); (young people's literature—illustrated, French) Mario Brassard and Gérard DuBois for *À qui appartiennent les nuages?* (La Pasteque); (translation from English to French) Marie Frankland for *Poèmes 1938–1984* from *The Collected Poems* by Elizabeth Smart (Du Noroît).

Dolly Gray Children's Literature Awards. Presented biennially for fiction or biographical children's books with positive portrayals of individuals with developmental disabilities. *Offered by:* Council for Exceptional Children, Division on Autism and Developmental Disabilities. *Winner (2020):* Gill Lewis for *Scarlet Ibis* (Simon & Schuster).

Kate Greenaway Medal and Colin Mears Award. See CILIP Kate Greenaway Medal and Colin Mears Award.

Eric Gregory Awards (United Kingdom) (£4,000). For a published or unpublished collection by poets under the age of 30. *Winners:* Michael Askew, Dominic Hand, Cynthia Miller, Gboyega Odubanjo, Kandance Siobhan Walker, Phoebe Walker, Milena Williamson.

Griffin Poetry Prizes (Canada) (C$65,000). To a living Canadian poet or translator and a living poet or translator from any country, which may include Canada. *Offered by:* Griffin Trust. *Winners:* (international) Valzhyna Mort for *Music for the Dead and Resurrected* (Farrar, Straus and Giroux); (Canadian) Canisia Lubrin for *The Dyzgraphxst* (McClelland & Stewart).

Gryphon Award ($1,000). To recognize a noteworthy work of fiction or nonfiction for younger children. *Offered by:* The Center for Children's Books. *Winners:* David LaRochelle (author) and Mike Wohnoutka (illustrator) for *See the Cat: Three Stories About a Dog* (Candlewick Press).

Hadada Award. To a distinguished member of the writing community who has made a strong and unique contribution to literature. Offered by: *The Paris Review. Winner:* N. Scott Momaday.

Dashiell Hammett Prize. For a work of literary excellence in the field of crime writing by a U.S. or Canadian writer. *Offered by:* North American Branch, International Association of Crime Writers. *Winner (2021):* To be announced. *Winner (2020):* David Joy for *When These Mountains Burn* (G.P. Putnam's Sons).

R.R. Hawkins Award. For the outstanding professional/scholarly work of the year. *Offered by:* Association of American Publishers. *Winner:* Cambridge University Press for *Ancient Maya Politics: A Political Anthropology of the Classic Period 150–900 CE* by Simon Martin.

Anthony Hecht Poetry Prize ($3,000 and publication by Waywiser Press). For an unpublished first or second book-length poetry collection. *Winner (2021):* Danielle Blau for *peep* (Waywiser Press).

Drue Heinz Literature Prize ($15,000 and publication by University of Pittsburgh Press). For short fiction. *Winner:* Joanna Pearson for *Now You Know It All* (University of Pittsburgh Press).

O. Henry Awards. See PEN/O. Henry Prize.

William Dean Howells Medal. Given once every five years in recognition of the most distinguished American novel published during that period. *Offered by:* American Academy of Arts and Letters. *Winner (2020):* Richard Powers for *The Overstory* (W.W. Norton & Company).

Hugo Awards. For outstanding science fiction writing. *Offered by:* World Science Fiction Convention. *Winners:* (novel) Martha Wells for *Network Effect* (Tordotcom); (novella) Nghi Vo for *The Empress of Salt and Fortune* (Tordotcom); (novelette) Sarah Pinsker for "Two Truths and a Lie" (Tordotcom); (short story) T. Kingfisher for "Metal Like Blood in the Dark" (*Uncanny Magazine,* September/October 2020); (series) Martha Wells for *The Murderbot Diaries* (Tordotcom); (related work) Maria Dahvana Headley for *Beowulf: A New Translation* (Farrar, Straus and Giroux); (graphic story or comic) Octavia Butler (author), Damian Duffy (adapted by), John Jennings (illustrator) for *The Parable of the Sower* (Harry N. Abrams); (dramatic presentation, long form) Greg Rucka (screenplay) and Gina Prince-Bythewood (director) for *The Old Guard* (Netflix/Skydance Media); (dramatic presentation, short form) Michael Schur (writer and director) for *The Good Place:* "Whenever You're Ready" (Fremulon/3 Arts Entertainment/Universal Television, a division of Universal Studio Group); (Lodestar Award for Best Young Adult Book) T. Kingfisher for *A Wizard's Guide to Defensive Baking* (Argyll Productions); (*Astounding* Award for Best New Writer) Emily Tesh.

ILA Children's and Young Adults' Book Awards. For first or second books in any language published for children or young adults. *Offered by:* International Literacy Association. *Winners:* (primary fiction) Samara Cole Doyon for *Magnificent Homespun Brown: A Celebration* (Tilbury House); (primary nonfiction) Cassandra Federman for *This Is a Seahorse* (Albert Whitman & Co); (intermediate fiction) Julie Lee for *Brother's Keeper* (Holiday House); (intermediate nonfiction) Lucinda Robb and Rebecca Boggs Roberts for *The Suffragist Playbook: Your Guide to Changing the World* (Candlewick Press); (young adult fiction) Trung Le Nguyen for *The Magic Fish* (Random House Children's Books); (young adult nonfiction) Frederick Joseph for *The Black Friend: On Being a Better White Person* (Candlewick Press).

Independent Publisher Book Awards (IPPY). Created to recognize exemplary independent, university, and self-published titles across a wide spectrum of genres. *Sponsor:* Jenkins Group/Independent Publisher Online. *Winners:* (fine art) by James Prosek for *James Prosek: Art, Artifact, Artifice* (Yale University Art Gallery); (performing arts) (tie) Kenneth Womack for *John Lennon 1980: The Last Days in the Life* (Omnibus Press) and Ben Sidran for *The Ballad of Tommy LiPuma* (Nardis Books); (photography) (tie) Stephen Marc for *American/True Colors* (George F. Thompson) and Ian Shive for *Refuge: America's Wildest Places—Exploring the National Wildlife Refuge System* (Earth Aware Editions); (architecture) Steven Keylon for *The Modern Architecture of Hugh Michael Kaptur* (Palm Springs Preservation Foundation); (coffee table books) David Freese for *Mississippi River: Headwaters and Heartland to Delta and Gulf* (George F. Thompson); (popular fiction) Nemo James for *A Single Tear* (Derek Newark Publishing); (literary fiction) Amy Shearn for *Unseen City* (Red Hen Press); (short story fiction) Joan Frank for *Where You're All Going: Four Novellas* (Sarabande Books); (poetry—standard) (tie) Lauren Berry for *The Rented Altar* (C&R Press) and Megan Denton Ray for *Mustard, Milk, and Gin* (Hub City Press); (poetry—specialty) Lisa Dolby Chadwick and Sierra Nguyen (editors) for *Stay Inspired: Shelter in Place 2020* (Dolby Chadwick Gallery); (anthologies) Joe Mackall and Daniel W. Lehman (editors) for *River Teeth: 20 Years of Creative NonFiction* (University of New Mexico Press); (juvenile fiction) Bess Kercher for *Now and at the Hour* (Warren

Publishing); (young adult fiction) (tie) Adam Sass for *Surrender Your Sons* (Flux) and Martha Engber for *Winter Light* (Vine Leaves Press); (fantasy) ML Spencer for *Dragon Mage: An Epic Fantasy Adventure* (Stoneguard Publications); (science fiction) Sarah Lahey for *Gravity Is Heartless* (She Writes Press); (LGBT+ fiction) Corey Sobel for *The Redshirt* (University Press of Kentucky); (erotica) Emerald for *Initiative: Tales of Erotic Boldness* (Midnight Gleam Press); (historical fiction) Linda Kass for *A Ritchie Boy* (She Writes Press); (military/wartime fiction) Travis Klempan for *Have Snakes, Need Birds* (Köehler Books); (horror) Polly Hall for *The Taxidermist's Lover* (CamCat Publishing); (multicultural fiction) Lauren J. Sharkey for *Inconvenient Daughter* (Akashic Books); (multicultural fiction—juvenile/young adult) Marisa de Jesus Paolicelli (author) and Susan E. Daly (illustrator) for *A Jibaro's Miracle* (A Caribbean Experience Con Amor); (mystery) Jeff Nania for *Spider Lake: A Northern Lakes Mystery* (Little Creek Press); (suspense/thriller) Susan Ouellette for *The Wayward Spy* (CamCat Publishing); (religious fiction) Linda Thompson for *The Mulberry Leaf Whispers* (Mountain Brook Ink); (romance) Kristin Gleeson for *Highland Lioness* (An Tig Beag Press); (urban fiction) Lisa Braxton for *The Talking Drum* (Inanna Publications); (visionary/new age fiction) Caroline Allen for *Water* (Art of Storytelling); (true crime) Alan C. Logan for *The Greatest Hoax on Earth: Catching Truth, While We Can* (Alan Logan); (graphic novel/drawn book) Julian Peters for *Poems to See By: A Comic Artist Interprets Great Poetry* (Plough Publishing House); (humor) Ann McMan for *The Big Tow: An Unlikely Romance* (Bywater Books); (children's picture book—age seven and under) (tie) Mila Coxon (author) and Karen Bentley (illustrator) for *A Tale for a Sleepy Bunny* (From You to Me) and Johnny DePalma (author) and Kyle Brown (illustrator) for *52—A Tale of Loneliness* (Umbrelly Books Publishing); (children's picture book—all ages) (tie) Paddy Donnelly for *The Vanishing Lake* (YeeHoo Press) and Richard Brehm (author) and Rogerio Coelho (illustrator) for *You Be You* (BeeZeus Publishing); (children's interactive) Sophia Fox and Carrie Fox (authors) and Nichole Wong Forti (illustrator) for *Adventures in Kindness* (Mission Partners Press).

International Booker Prize (United Kingdom) (£50,000). To the author and translator of a work translated into English. *Offered by:* Crankstart. *Winner:* David Diop for *At Night All Blood Is Black*, translated from the French by Anna Moschovakis (Pushkin Press).

International Prize for Arabic Fiction ($50,000 and publication in English). To reward excellence in contemporary Arabic creative writing. *Sponsors:* Booker Prize Foundation, Emirates Foundation for Philanthropy. *Winner:* Jalal Barjas (Jordan) for *Notebooks of the Bookseller* (Arabic Institute for Research and Publishing).

Rona Jaffe Foundation Writers' Awards ($30,000 each). To identify and support women writers of exceptional talent in the early stages of their careers. *Offered by:* Rona Jaffe Foundation. Award discontinued.

Jerusalem Prize (Israel). Awarded biennially to a writer whose works best express the theme of freedom of the individual in society. *Offered by:* Jerusalem International Book Fair. *Winner (2021):* Julian Barnes.

Jewish Book Council Awards. *Winners:* (Jewish Book of the Year) Dvora Hacohen for *To Repair a Broken World: The Life of Henrietta Szold, Founder of Hadassah* (Harvard University Press); (American Jewish studies) Nathaniel Deutsch and Michael Casper for *A Fortress in Brooklyn: Race, Real Estate, and the Making of Hasidic Williamsburg* (Yale University Press); (autobiography and memoir) Sherry Turkle for *The Empathy Diaries: A Memoir* (Penguin); (biography) Dvora Hacohen for *To Repair a Broken World: The Life of Henrietta Szold, Founder of Hadassah* (Harvard University Press); (book club award) Helene Wecker for *The Hidden Palace* (HarperCollins Publishers); (children's picture book) Nancy Churnin (author) and Bethany Stancliffe (illustrator) for *Dear Mr. Dickens* (Albert Whitman & Co.); (contemporary Jewish life and practice) Dara Horn for *People Love Dead Jews* (W.W. Norton & Company); (debut fiction) Jai Chakrabarti for *A Play for the End of the World* (Alfred A. Knopf); (education and Jewish identity) Simon J. Bronner for *Jewish Cultural Studies* (Wayne State University Press); (fiction) Joshua Cohen for *The Netanyahus: An Account of a Minor and Ultimately Even Negligible Episode in the History of a Very Famous Family* (New York Review Books); (food writing and cookbooks) Esther David for *Bene Appétit: The Cuisine of Indian Jews* (HarperCollins Publishers India); (history) James McAuley for *The House of Fragile Things* (Yale University Press); (Holocaust) Wendy Lower for *The Ravine: A Family, a Photograph, a Holocaust Massacre Revealed* (Mariner Books); (middle grade literature) Gordon Korman for *Linked* (Scholastic); (modern Jewish thought and experience) Erin Leib Smokler (editor) for *Torah in a Time of Plague: Historical and Contemporary Jewish Responses* (Ben Yehuda Press); (poetry) Joy Ladin for *The Book of Anna* (EOAGH Books); (scholarship) Katell Berthelot for *Jews and Their Roman Rivals: Pagan Rome's Challenge to Israel* (Princeton University Press); (Sephardic culture) Daniela Flesler and Adrián Pérez Melgosa for *The Memory Work of Jewish Spain* (Indiana University Press); (women's studies) Judy Batalion for *The Light of Days* (William Morrow); (writing based on archival material) Jaclyn Granick for *International Jewish Humanitarianism in the Age of the Great War* (Cambridge University Press); (young adult literature) Lori Banov Kaufmann for *Rebel Daughter* (Delacorte Press).

Sue Kaufman Prize for First Fiction ($5,000). For a work of first fiction (novel or short stories). *Offered by:* American Academy of Arts and Letters. *Winner:* Douglas Stuart for *Shuggie Bain* (Grove Press).

Ezra Jack Keats Awards. For children's picture books. *Offered by:* New York Public Library and the Ezra Jack Keats Foundation. *Winners:* (writer award) Tricia Elam Walker for *Nana Akua Goes to School*, illustrated by April Harrison (Schwartz & Wade); (illustrator award) Heidi Woodward Sheffield (author and illustrator) for *Brick by Brick* (Nancy Paulsen Books).

Randall Kenan Prize for Black LGBTQ Fiction. *Offered by:* Lambda Literary Foundation. *Winner:* Ana-Maurine Lara.

Kerlan Award. To recognize singular attainments in the creation of children's literature and in appreciation for generous donation of unique resources to the Kerlan Collection for the study of children's literature. *Offered by:* Kerlan Children's Literature Research Collections, University of Minnesota. *Winner:* Ariane Dewey.

Coretta Scott King Book Awards ($1,000). To an African American author and illustrator of outstanding books for children and young adults. *Offered by:* American Library Association, Ethnic and Multicultural Exchange Round Table (EMIERT). *Winners:* (author) Jacqueline Woodson for *Before the Ever After* (Nancy Paulsen Books); (illustrator) Frank Morrison for *R-E-S-P-E-C-T: Aretha Franklin, the Queen of Soul*, written by Carole Boston Weatherford (Atheneum Books for Young Readers).

Coretta Scott King/Virginia Hamilton Award for Lifetime Achievement. Given in even-numbered years to an African American author, illustrator, or author/illustrator for a body of books for children or young adults. In odd-numbered years, the award honors substantial contributions through active engagement with youth, using award-winning African American literature for children or young adults. *Winner:* Dorothy Guthrie.

Coretta Scott King/John Steptoe Award for New Talent. To offer visibility to a writer and illustrator at the beginning of their careers. *Sponsor:* Coretta Scott King Book Award Committee. *Winners:* (author) Tracy Deonn for *Legendborn* (Margaret K. McElderry Books); (illustrator) Not awarded in 2021.

Kirkus Prize ($50,000). For outstanding fiction, nonfiction, and young readers literature. *Offered by:* Kirkus Reviews. *Winners:* (fiction) Joy Williams for *Harrow* (Knopf); (nonfiction) Brian Broome for *Punch Me Up to the Gods* (Mariner Books); (young readers) Christina Soontornvat for *All Thirteen* (Candlewick Press).

Lambda Literary Awards. To honor outstanding lesbian, gay, bisexual, transgender, and queer (LGBTQ) literature. *Offered by:* Lambda Literary Foundation. *Winners:* (lesbian fiction) Juli Delgado Lopera for *Fiebre Tropical* (Feminist Press); (gay fiction) Joon Oluchi Lee for *Neotenica* (Nightboat Books); (bisexual fiction) Zaina Arafat for *You Exist Too Much* (Catapult); (transgender fiction) Zeyn Joukhadar for

The Thirty Names of Night (Atria Books); (bisexual nonfiction) Samantha Irby for *Wow, No Thank You.: Essays* (Vintage); (transgender nonfiction) J Mase III & Dane Figueroa Edidi for *The Black Trans Prayer Book* (Lulu.com); (LGBTQ nonfiction) Ashon T. Crawley for *The Lonely Letters* (Duke University Press); (lesbian poetry) Pamela Sneed for *Funeral Diva* (City Lights Books); (gay poetry) Eduardo C. Corral for *Guillotine* (Graywolf Press); (bisexual poetry) Aricka Foreman for *Salt Body Shimmer* (YesYes Books); (transgender poetry) Sade LaNay for *I love you and I'm not dead* (Argos Books); (lesbian memoir/biography) Jenn Shapland for *My Autobiography of Carson McCullers* (Tin House Books); (gay memoir/biography) Mohsin Zaidi for *A Dutiful Boy: A Memoir of a Gay Muslim's Journey to Acceptance* (Square Peg); (lesbian romance) Alexandria Bellefleur for *Written in the Stars* (Avon Books); (gay romance) Felice Stevens for *The Ghost and Charlie Muir* (self-published); (LGBTQ anthology) Joshua Whitehead (editor) for *Love after the End: An Anthology of Two-Spirit and Indigiqueer Speculative Fiction* (Arsenal Pulp Press); (LGBTQ children's/middle grade) Kacen Callender for *King and the Dragonflies* (Scholastic); (LGBTQ young adult) Mike Curato for *Flamer* (Henry Holt Books for Young Readers); (LGBTQ comics) Bishakh Som for *Apsara Engine* (Feminist Press); (LGBTQ drama) Yilong Liu for *The Book of Mountains and Seas* (New Conservatory Theatre Center); (LGBTQ erotica) Lee Suksi for *The Nerves* (Metatron Press); (LGBTQ mystery) Tom Ryan for *I Hope You're Listening* (Albert Whitman & Company); (LGBTQ science fiction/fantasy/horror) Julian K. Jarboe for *Everyone on the Moon Is Essential Personnel* (Lethe Press); (LGBTQ studies) Zakiyyah Iman Jackson for *Becoming Human: Matter and Meaning in an Antiblack World* (NYU Press).

Harold Morton Landon Translation Award ($1,000). For a book of verse translated into English. *Offered by:* Academy of American Poets. *Winner:* Maria Dahvana Headley for *Beowulf: A New Translation by Maria Dahvana Headley* (Farrar, Straus and Giroux).

David J. Langum, Sr. Prize in American Historical Fiction ($1,000). To honor a book of historical fiction published in the previous year. *Offered by:* Langum Foundation. *Winner:* (2020) Jess Walter for *The Cold Millions* (Harper).

David J. Langum, Sr. Prize in American Legal History or Biography ($1,000). For a university press book that is accessible to the educated general public, rooted in sound scholarship, with themes that touch upon matters of general concern. *Offered by:* Langum Foundation. *Winner:* (2020) Sara Mayeux for *Free Justice: A History of the Public Defender in Twentieth-Century America* (University of North Carolina Press).

Latner Writers' Trust Poetry Prize (C$25,000) (Canada). To a writer with an exceptional body of work in the field of poetry. *Offered by:* Writers' Trust of Canada. *Sponsor:* Latner Family Foundation. *Winner:* Weyman Chan.

James Laughlin Award ($5,000). To commend and support a second book of poetry. *Offered by:* Academy of American Poets. *Winner:* James Cagney for *Martian: The Saint of Loneliness* (Nomadic Press).

Library of Congress Prize for American Fiction. To an author for a body of extraordinary work. *Winner:* Joy Williams.

Claudia Lewis Award. For the best poetry book. *Offered by:* Bank Street College of Education. *Winner:* Derrick Barnes (author) and Gordon C. James (illustrator) for *I Am Every Good Thing* (Nancy Paulsen Books).

Ruth Lilly and Dorothy Sargent Rosenberg Poetry Fellowships ($25,800). To emerging poets to support their continued study and writing of poetry. *Offered by:* The Poetry Foundation. *Winners:* Bryan Byrdlong, Steven Espada Dawson, Noor Hindi, Natasha Rao, and Simon Shieh.

Ruth Lilly Poetry Prize ($100,000). To a U.S. poet in recognition of lifetime achievement. *Offered by:* The Poetry Foundation. *Winner:* Patricia Smith.

Astrid Lindgren Memorial Award (Sweden) (5 million kroner, more than $575,000). In memory of children's author Astrid Lindgren, to honor outstanding children's literature and efforts to promote it. *Offered by:* Government of Sweden and the Swedish Arts Council. *Winner:* Jean-Claude Mourlevat.

LITA Excellence in Children's and Young Adult Science Fiction. *Sponsor:* Library and Information Technology Association. *Winners:* (Golden Duck Notable Picture Books List) Terry Fan, Eric Fan, and Devin Fan for *The Barnabus Project* (Tundra Books); John Hare for *Field Trip to the Ocean Deep* (Margaret Ferguson Books); Preeti Chhibber (author) and Mike Deas (illustrator) for *A Jedi You Will Be* (Disney Lucasfilm Press); Jonathan Stutzman (author) and Heather Fox (illustrator) for *Llama Unleashes the Alpacalypse* (Henry Holt & Co.); An Leysen for *Mara the Space Traveler* (Clavis); Susanna Leonard Hill (author) and Elisa Paganelli (illustrator) for *Mars' First Friends: Come on Over, Rovers!* (Sourcebooks Wonderland); David Wiesner for *Robobaby* (Clarion Books); Molly Ruttan for *The Stray* (Nancy Paulsen Books); (Eleanor Cameron Notable Middle Grade Books List) Dave Whamond for *Alien Nate* (Kids Can Press); Kenneth Oppel for *Bloom* (Knopf Books for Young Readers); Jake Burt for *Cleo Porter and the Body Electric* (Feiwel & Friends); Mari Mancusi for *Dragon Ops* (Little, Brown Books for Young Readers); Michael Buckley for *Finn and the Intergalactic Lunchbox* (Delacorte Books for Young Readers); Damian Campanario, Mike Kennedy, and Alex Fuentes for *GenPet* (Magnetic Press); Laura Martin for *Glitch* (HarperCollins); Christopher Swiedler for *In the Red* (HarperCollins); Amy McCulloch for *Jinxed* (Sourcebooks Young Readers); Jason Walz for *Last Pick* (series) (First Second); Dan Jolley and Jacques Khouri for *Mega-Dogs of New Kansas* (Graphic Universe); Carlos Hernandez for *Sal and Gabi Fix the Universe* (Rick Riordan Presents); (Hal Clement Notable Young Adult Books List) Naomi Kritzer for *Catfishing on Catnet* (Tor Teen); Garth Stein and Matthew Southworth for *The Cloven: Book One* (Fantagraphics); Rebecca Coffindaffer for *Crown Chasers* (Harper Teen); Glen Zipper and Elaine Mongeon for *Devastation Class* (Blink); Alicia Ellis for *Girl of Flesh and Metal* (Figmented Ink); Len Vlahos for *Hard Wired* (Bloomsbury YA); Ben Oliver for *The Loop* (Chicken House); Pintip Dunn for *Malice* (Entangled); Jeremy Whitley and Jamie Noguchi for *School for Extraterrestrial Girls #1: Girl on Fire* (Papercutz); Raquel Vasquez Gilliland for *Sia Martinez and the Moonlit Beginning of Everything* (Simon & Schuster Books for Young Readers); Alechia Dow for *The Sound of Stars* (Inkyard Press); Maggie Stiefvater and Morgan Beem for *Swamp Thing: Twin Branches* (DC Comics).

Locus Awards. For science fiction writing. *Offered by:* Locus Publications. *Winners:* (science fiction) Martha Wells for *Network Effect* (Tordotcom); (fantasy) N.K. Jemisin for *The City We Became* (Orbit); (horror) Silvia Moreno-Garcia for *Mexican Gothic* (Del Rey/Jo Fletcher); (young adult) T. Kingfisher for *A Wizard's Guide to Defensive Baking* (Argyll); (first novel) Darcie Little Badger for *Elatsoe* (Levine Querido); (novella) P. Djèlí Clark for *Ring Shout* (Tordotcom); (novelette) Meg Elison for "The Pill" in *Big Girl* (PM Press); (short story) Naomi Kritzer for "Little Free Library" (Tordotcom Original, released April 8, 2020); (anthology) Jonathan Strahan (editor) for *The Book of Dragons* (Harper Voyager); (collection) Ken Liu for *The Hidden Girl and Other Stories* (Gallery/Saga Press); (nonfiction) Marc Burrows for *The Magic of Terry Pratchett* (White Owl); (art book) Piers Bizony for *The Art of NASA: The Illustrations that Sold the Missions* (Motorbooks).

Elizabeth Longford Prize for Historical Biography (United Kingdom) (£5,000). *Sponsors:* Flora Fraser and Peter Soros. *Winner:* Fredrik Logevall for *JFK, Volume One* (Viking).

Los Angeles Times Book Prizes. To honor literary excellence. *Offered by:* Los Angeles Times. *Winners:* (Art Seidenbaum Award for First Fiction) Deesha Philyaw for *The Secret Lives of Church Ladies* (West Virginia University Press); (biography) William Souder for *Mad at the World: A Life of John Steinbeck* (W.W. Norton & Company); (Christopher Isherwood Prize for Autobiographical Prose) Andrew O'Hagan for *Mayflies* (Faber & Faber); (current interest) Isabel Wilkerson for *Caste: The Origins of Our Discontents* (Random House); (fiction) David Diop for *At Night All Blood Is Black*, translated by Anna Moschovakis (Farrar, Straus and Giroux); (graphic novel/

comics) Bishakh Som for *Apsara Engine* (Feminist Press at CUNY); (history) Martha S. Jones for *Vanguard: How Black Women Broke Barriers, Won the Vote, and Insisted on Equality for All* (Basic Books); (mystery/thriller) S.A. Cosby for *Blacktop Wasteland* (Flatiron Books); (poetry) Victoria Chang for *Obit* (Copper Canyon Press); (Ray Bradbury Prize for Science Fiction, Fantasy & Speculative Fiction) Stephen Graham Jones for *The Only Good Indians* (Gallery/Saga Press); (science & technology) Sara Seager for *The Smallest Lights in the Universe: A Memoir* (Crown); (young adult literature) Ibi Zoboi and Dr. Yusef Salaam for *Punching the Air* (Balzer + Bray).

Amy Lowell Poetry Traveling Scholarship. For one or two U.S. poets to spend one year outside North America in a country the recipients feel will most advance their work. *Offered by:* Amy Lowell Poetry Traveling Scholarship. *Winners:* Tiana Clark and Ama Codjoe.

Walter & Lillian Lowenfels Criticism Award. *Offered by:* Before Columbus Foundation. *Winner:* Shana Redmond for *Everything Man: The Form and Function of Paul Robeson* (Duke University Press).

J. Anthony Lukas Awards. For nonfiction writing that demonstrates literary grace, serious research, and concern for an important aspect of American social or political life. *Offered by:* Columbia University Graduate School of Journalism and the Nieman Foundation for Journalism at Harvard. *Winners:* (Lukas Book Prize, $10,000) Jessica Goudeau for *After the Last Border: Two Families and the Story of Refuge in America* (Viking); (Mark Lynton History Prize, $10,000) William G. Thomas III for *A Question of Freedom: The Families Who Challenged Slavery from the Nation's Founding to the Civil War* (Yale University Press); (Work-in-Progress Award, two prizes of $25,000 each) Emily Dufton for *Addiction, Inc.: How the Corporate Takeover of America's Treatment Industry Created a Profitable Epidemic* (University of Chicago Press) and Casey Parks for *Diary of a Misfit: A Memoir and a Mystery* (Knopf).

Macavity Awards. For excellence in mystery writing. *Offered by:* Mystery Readers International. *Winners:* (mystery novel) S.A. Cosby for *Blacktop Wasteland* (Flatiron Books); (first mystery) David Heska Wanbli Weiden for *Winter Counts* (Ecco Press); (critical/biography) Sheila Mitchell for *H.R.F. Keating: A Life of Crime* (Level Best Books); (short story) Gabriel Valjan for "Elysian Fields" in *California Schemin': The 2020 Bouchercon Anthology*, edited by Art Taylor (Wildside Press); (Sue Feder Historical Mystery Award) James Ziskin for *Turn to Stone* (Seventh Street Books).

McKitterick Prize (United Kingdom) (£4,000). To an author over the age of 40 for a first novel, published or unpublished. *Winner:* Elaine Feeney for *As You Were* (Harvill Secker).

Judith A. Markowitz Award for Emerging LGBTQ Writers. *Offered by:* Lambda Literary Foundation. *Winners:* Taylor Johnson and T. Kira Madden.

Lenore Marshall Poetry Prize ($25,000). For an outstanding book of poems published in the United States. *Offered by:* Academy of American Poets. *Winner:* Honorée Fanonne Jeffers for *The Age of Phillis: Poems* (Wesleyan University Press).

Somerset Maugham Awards (United Kingdom) (£2,500). For works in any genre except drama by a writer under the age of 35, to enable young writers to enrich their work by gaining experience of foreign countries. *Winners:* Lamorna Ash for *Dark, Salt, Clear* (Bloomsbury Publishing); Isabelle Baafi for *Ripe* (Ignition Press); Akeem Balogun for *The Storm* (Okapi Books); Graeme Armstrong for *The Young Team* (Pan Macmillan/Picador).

Medal for Editorial Excellence (formerly the Maxwell E. Perkins Award). To honor an editor, publisher, or agent who has discovered, nurtured, and championed writers of fiction in the United States. *Offered by:* Center for Fiction, Mercantile Library of New York. *Winner:* Alvina Ling.

Addison M. Metcalf Award in Literature ($2,000). Awarded biennially to a writer of great promise. *Winner (2021):* Kali Fajardo-Anstine.

Vicky Metcalf Award for Literature for Young People (C$25,000) (Canada). To a Canadian writer of children's literature for a body of work. *Offered by:* Writers' Trust of Canada. *Sponsor:* Metcalf Foundation. *Winner:* Linda Bailey.

Midwest Booksellers Choice Awards. *Offered by:* Midwest Independent Publishers Association. *Winners:* (anthology nonfiction) Chad Allen Goldberg for *Education for Democracy: Renewing the Wisconsin Idea* (University of Wisconsin Press); (arts/photography/coffee table) Zaylore Stout for *Our Gay History* (Wise Ink); (autobiography/memoir) Jill Sisson Quinn for *Sign Here If You Exist and Other Essays* (Mad Creek Books/Ohio State University Press); (biography) Dennis Dresang for *Patrick J. Lucey: A Lasting Legacy* (Wisconsin Historical Society Press); (business) (tie) George C. Murray for *Hired* (Kirk House Publishers) and Sara Krisher for *The Confidence to Speak* (Kirk House Publishers); (children's fiction) Matthew Cody for *Cat Ninja* (Andrews McMeel Publishing); (children's nonfiction) Lucy Bell for *You Can Change the World* (Andrews McMeel Publishing); (children's picture) (tie) Michael Arndt for *My Heart Grows* (Andrews McMeel Publishing) and Bob Allen for *Monica the Muskie* (Beaver's Pond Press); (cookbooks/crafts/hobbies) Amy Zitelman for *The Tahini Table: Go Beyond Hummus with 100 Recipes for Every Meal* (Agate Publishing); (education/learning) Zaylore Stout for *Our Gay History* (Wise Ink); (family/parenting) Kimberly Ewertz for *Family Redefined* (Little Creek Press); (fantasy/sci-fi/horror/paranormal fiction) Geoffrey Carter for *Thicker than Water* (HenschelHAUS); (graphic novel) Matthew Cody for *Cat Ninja* (Andrews McMeel Publishing); (health) Deborah Day Laxson for *The Fog Zone* (Beaver's Pond Press); (history) Not awarded in 2021; (regional history) Phil Christman for *Midwest Futures* (Belt Publishing); (humor nonfiction) Lisa Smith Molinari for *The Meat and Potatoes of Life: My True Lit Com* (Elva Resa Publishing); (inspiration) Barb Greenberg for *The Seasons of Divorce* (Kirk House Publishers); (literary/contemporary/historical fiction) David Benjamin for *They Shot Kennedy* (Last Kid Books); (mystery/thriller fiction) Michael Prelee for *Lost Little Sister* (North Star Press of St. Cloud); (nature) Robert Seabloom for *Mammals of North Dakota* (North Dakota State University Press); (poetry) Carlos Andrés Gomez for *Fractures* (University of Wisconsin Press); (poetry anthology) Margaret Hasse and Athena Kildegaard for *Rocked by the Waters* (Nodin Press); (debut poetry) Adam Falkner for *The Willies* (Button Poetry); (regional poetry) Denise Lajimodiere for *His Feathers Were Chains* (North Dakota State University Press); (recreation/sports/travel) Patrick Mader (with Joel Rippel) for *More Minnesota Gold* (self-published); (religion/philosophy) Titus Burckhardt for *A Living Islamic City: Fez and Its Preservation* (World Wisdom); (romance fiction) Stacey Potter for *The Project* (Hadleigh House Publishing); (short story/anthology fiction) Joseph Harris for *You're in the Wrong Place* (Wayne State University Press); (social science/political science/culture) R. Richard Wagner for *Coming Out, Moving Forward: Wisconsin's Recent Gay History* (Wisconsin Historical Society Press); (young adult fiction) Julie Stielstra for *Opulence, Kansas* (Meadowlark Press).

William C. Morris YA Debut Award. To honor a debut book published by a first-time author writing for teens and celebrating impressive new voices in young adult literature. *Offered by:* American Library Association, Young Adult Library Services Association. *Donor:* William C. Morris Endowment. *Winner:* Kyrie McCauley for *If These Wings Could Fly* (Katherine Tegen Books/HarperCollins).

Mythopoeic Fantasy Awards. To recognize fantasy or mythic literature for children and adults that best exemplifies the spirit of the Inklings, a group of fantasy writers that includes J.R.R. Tolkien, C.S. Lewis, and Charles Williams. *Offered by:* Mythopoeic Society. *Winners:* (adult literature) TJ Klune for *The House in the Cerulean Sea* (Tor); (children's literature) T. Kingfisher for *A Wizard's Guide to Defensive Baking* (Argyll); (Mythopoeic Scholarship Award in Inklings Studies) John M. Bowers for *Tolkien's Lost Chaucer* (Oxford University Press); (Mythopoeic Scholarship Award in Myth and Fantasy Studies) Anna Vaninskaya for *Fantasies of Time and Death: Dunsany, Eddison, Tolkien* (Palgrave).

National Book Awards. To celebrate the best in American literature. *Offered by:* National Book Foundation. *Winners:* (fiction) Jason Mott for *Hell of a Book* (Dutton);

(nonfiction) Tiya Miles for *All That She Carried* (Random House); (poetry) Martín Espada for *Floaters* (W.W. Norton & Company); (translated literature) Elisa Shua Dusapin for *Winter in Sokcho*, translated from the French by Aneesa Abbas Higgins (Open Letter); (young people's literature) Malinda Lo for *Last Night at the Telegraph Club* (Dutton Books for Young Readers).

National Book Critics Circle Awards (March 17). For literary excellence. *Offered by:* National Book Critics Circle. *Winners:* (fiction) Honorée Fanonne Jeffers for *The Love Songs of W.E.B. DuBois* (Harper); (nonfiction) Clint Smith for *How the Word Is Passed* (Little, Brown); (biography) Rebecca Donner for *All the Frequent Troubles of Our Days: The True Story of the American Woman at the Heart of the German Resistance to Hitler* (Little, Brown); (autobiography) Jeremy Atherton Lin for *Gay Bar: Why We Went Out* (Little, Brown); (poetry) Diane Seuss for *frank: sonnets* (Graywolf); (criticism) Melissa Febos for *Girlhood* (Bloomsbury); (John Leonard Prize) Anthony Veasna So for *Afterparties* (Ecco); (Nona Balakian Citation for Excellence in Reviewing) Merve Emre; (Ivan Sandrof Lifetime Achievement Award) Percival Everett; (Toni Morrison Achievement Award) Cave Canem Foundation.

National Book Foundation Literarian Award for Outstanding Service to the American Literary Community. *Offered by:* National Book Foundation. *Winner:* Nancy Pearl.

National Book Foundation Medal for Distinguished Contribution to American Letters ($10,000). To a person who has enriched the nation's literary heritage over a life of service or corpus of work. *Offered by:* National Book Foundation. *Winner:* Karen Tei Yamashita.

National Translation Awards ($5,000). To honor translators whose work has made a valuable contribution to literary translation into English. *Offered by:* American Literary Translators Association. *Winners:* (prose) Tejaswini Niranjana, translator from Kannada, for *No Presents Please: Mumbai Stories* by Jayant Kaikini (Catapult); (poetry) Geoffrey Brock, translator from Italian, for *Allegria* by Giuseppe Ungaretti (Archipelago).

Nebula Awards. For science fiction writing. *Offered by:* Science Fiction and Fantasy Writers of America (SFWA). *Winners:* (novel) Martha Wells for *Network Effect* (Tordotcom); (novella) P. Djèlí Clark for *Ring Shout* (Tordotcom); (novelette) Sarah Pinsker for *Two Truths and a Lie* (Tordotcom); (short story) John Wiswell for "Open House on Haunted Hill" (Diabolical Plots); (Ray Bradbury Award for dramatic presentation) Michael Schur for "Whenever You're Ready" episode of *The Good Place* (NBC and Fremulon/3 Arts Entertainment/Universal); (Andre Norton Award for young adult science fiction and fantasy) T. Kingfisher for *A Wizard's Guide to Defensive Baking* (Argyll).

John Newbery Medal. For the most distinguished contribution to literature for children. *Offered by:* American Library Association, Association for Library Service to Children. *Winner:* Tae Keller for *When You Trap a Tiger* (Random House Children's Books).

Next Generation Indie Book Awards ($1,500). *Offered by:* Independent Book Publishing Professionals Group. *Winner:* (fiction) Beverley Brenna (author) and Tara Anderson (illustrator) for *Sapphire the Great and the Meaning of Life* (Pajama Press); (nonfiction) Nina Ansary (author) and Petra Dufkova (illustrator) for *Anonymous Is a Woman: A Global Chronicle of Gender Inequality* (Revela Press).

Nibbies (United Kingdom). See British Book Awards.

Nimrod Literary Awards ($2,000 plus publication). *Offered by:* Nimrod International Journal of Prose and Poetry. *Winners:* (Pablo Neruda Prize in Poetry) Emily Rose Cole for "Spell for Patience" and other poems; (Katherine Anne Porter Prize in Fiction) Celine Aenlle-Rocha for "White Black People."

Nobel Prize in Literature (Sweden). For the total literary output of a distinguished career. *Offered by:* Swedish Academy. *Winner:* Abdulrazak Gurnah.

Eli M. Oboler Memorial Award. Given biennially to an author of a published work in English or in English translation dealing with issues, events, questions, or controversies in the area of intellectual freedom. *Offered by:* Intellectual Freedom Round Table, American Library Association. *Winner*

(2020): Henry Reichman for *The Future of Academic Freedom* (Johns Hopkins University Press).

Flannery O'Connor Award for Short Fiction. For collections of short fiction. *Offered by:* University of Georgia Press. *Winner:* Toni Ann Johnson for *Light Skin Gone to Waste* (University of Georgia Press).

Oddest Book Title of the Year Award. See Bookseller/Diagram Prize for Oddest Title of the Year.

Scott O'Dell Award for Historical Fiction ($5,000). *Offered by: Bulletin of the Center for Children's Books,* University of Chicago. *Winner:* Helen Frost for *All He Knew* (Farrar, Straus and Giroux).

Odyssey Award. To the producer of the best audiobook for children and/or young adults available in English in the United States. *Sponsors:* American Library Association, ALSC/Booklist/YALSA. *Winner:* Scholastic Audio for *Kent State* written in verse by Deborah Wiles and narrated by Christopher Gebauer, Lauren Ezzo, Christina Delaine, Johnny Heller, Roger Wayne, Korey Jackson, and David de Vries, produced by Paul R. Gagne.

Seán Ó Faoláin Short Story Competition (€2,000 and publication in the literary journal *Southword*). *Offered by:* Munster Literature Centre, Cork, Ireland. *Winner:* Shelley Hastings for "Am I Helping?"

Dayne Ogilvie Prize (C$4,000) (Canada). To an emerging Canadian writer from the LGBT community who demonstrates promise through a body of quality work. *Offered by:* Writers' Trust of Canada. *Winner:* Jillian Christmas.

Orbis Pictus Award for Outstanding Nonfiction for Children. *Offered by:* National Council of Teachers of English. *Winner:* Jen Bryant (author) and Frank Morrison (illustrator) for *Above the Rim: How Elgin Taylor Changed Basketball* (Harry N. Abrams).

Oxford-Weidenfeld Translation Prize. *Winner:* Nichola Smalley for her translation from Swedish of Andrzej Tichý's *Wretchedness (And Other Stories).*

PEN Award for Poetry in Translation ($3,000). For a book-length translation of poetry from any language into English, published in the United States. *Offered by:* PEN American Center. *Winners:* Steve Bradbury for his translation from Chinese of *Raised by Wolves: Poems and Conversations* by Amang (Phoneme Media).

PEN/Saul Bellow Award for Achievement in American Fiction ($25,000). Awarded biennially to a distinguished living American author of fiction. *Offered by:* PEN American Center. *Winner (2020):* Not awarded in 2020.

PEN/Bellwether Prize for Socially Engaged Fiction ($25,000). Awarded biennially to the author of a previously unpublished novel that addresses issues of social justice and the impact of culture and politics on human relationships. *Founder:* Barbara Kingsolver. *Winner (2021):* Jamila Minnicks Gleason for *Hydrangeas of New Jessup.*

PEN Beyond Margins Awards. See PEN Open Book Awards.

PEN/Robert W. Bingham Prize ($25,000). To a writer whose first novel or short story collection represents distinguished literary achievement and suggests great promise. *Offered by:* PEN American Center. *Winner:* Michael X. Wang for *Further News of Defeat: Stories* (Autumn House Press).

PEN/Robert J. Dau Short Story Prize for Emerging Writers ($2,000 to 12 writers). To recognize 12 emerging fiction writers for their debut short stories. *Offered by:* PEN American Center. *Winners:* Heather Aruffo for "Force, Mass, Acceleration" in *The Southern Review*; Lindsay Ferguson for "Good Girls" in *Barrelhouse*; Isaac Hughes Green for "The First Time I Said It" in *The Georgia Review*; Amy Haejung for "Maria" in *Waxwing Magazine*; Nishanth Injam for "The Math of Living" in *Virginia Quarterly Review*; Khaddafina Mbabazi for "Transit" in *Virginia Quarterly Review*; Mackenzie McGee for "Re:Frankie" in *Porter House Review*; Mathapelo Mofokeng for "The Strong-Strong Winds" in *adda*; Alberto Reyes Morgan for "Salt" in *Michigan Quarterly Review*; Stanley Patrick Stocker for "The List" in *Kestrel: A Journal of Literature and Art*; Pardeep Toor for "Taxi" in *Midwest Review*; Qianze Zhang for "Mandy's Mary Sue" in *Sine Theta Magazine.*

PEN/Diamonstein-Spielvogel Award for the Art of the Essay ($10,000). For a book of essays by a single author that best exemplifies the dignity and esteem of the essay form. *Winner:* Barbara Ehrenreich for *Had I Known: Collected Essays* (Twelve).

PEN/Faulkner Award for Fiction ($15,000). To honor the year's best work of fiction published by an American. *Winner:* Deesha Philyaw for *The Secret Lives of Church Ladies* (West Virginia University Press).

PEN/John Kenneth Galbraith Award for Nonfiction ($10,000). Given biennially for a distinguished book of general nonfiction. *Offered by:* PEN American Center. *Winner (2021):* Saidiya Hartman for *Wayward Lives, Beautiful Experiments: Intimate Histories of Riotous Black Girls, Troublesome Women, and Queer Radicals* (W.W. Norton & Company).

PEN Grant for the English Translation of Italian Literature ($5,000). *Winner:* Brian Robert Moore for his translation of *A Silence Shared* by Lalla Romano.

PEN/Heim Translation Fund Grants ($2,000–$4,000). To support the translation of book-length works of fiction, creative nonfiction, poetry, or drama that have not previously appeared in English or have appeared only in an egregiously flawed translation. *Winners:* Natascha Bruce, Rohan Chhetri, Rachael Daum, Katharine Halls, Banibrata Mahanta, Adrian Minckley, Lara Norgaard, Ekaterina Petrova, Jake Syersak, Vala Thorodds.

PEN/Ernest Hemingway Foundation Award. For a distinguished work of first fiction by an American. *Offered by:* PEN New England. *Winner:* Kawai Strong Washburn for *Sharks in the Time of Saviors* (MCD/Farrar, Straus and Giroux).

PEN/O. Henry Prize. For short stories of exceptional merit, in English, published in U.S. and Canadian magazines. *Winners:* Daphne Palasi Andreades for "Brown Girls" in *Kenyon Review*; David Means for "Two Nurses, Smoking" in *The New Yorker*; Sindya Bhanoo for "Malliga Homes" in *Granta*; Crystal Wilkinson for "Endangered Species: Case 47401" in *Story*; Alice Jolly for "From Far around They Saw Us Burn" in *Ploughshares*; David Rabe for "Things We Worried About When I Was Ten" in *The New Yorker*; Karina Sainz Borgo for "Scissors," translated by Elizabeth Bryer, in *Granta*; Jamel Brinkley for "Witness" in *The Paris Review*; Tessa Hadley for "The Other One" in *The New Yorker*; Adachioma Ezeano for "Becoming the Baby Girl" in *McSweeneys Quarterly Concern*; Anthony Doerr for "The Master's Castle" in *Tin House*; Tiphanie Yanique for "The Living Sea" in *Harvard Review*; Joan Silber for "Freedom from Want" in *Tin House*; Jowhor Ile for "Fisherman's Stew" in *The Sewanee Review*; Emma Cline for "White Noise" in *The New Yorker*; Asali Solomon for "Delandria" in *McSweeney's Quarterly Concern*; Ben Hinshaw for "Antediluvian" in *Harvard Review*; Caroline Albertine Minor for "Grief's Garden," translated by Caroline Waight, in *Granta*; Jianan Qian for "To the Dogs" in *Granta Online*; Sally Rooney for "Color and Light" in *The New Yorker*.

PEN/Nora Magid Award ($2,500). Awarded biennially to honor a magazine editor who has contributed significantly to the excellence of the publication he or she edits. *Winner (2021):* Kwame Dawes for *Prairie Schooner*.

PEN/Malamud Award. To recognize a body of work that demonstrates excellence in the art of short fiction. *Winner:* Charles Baxter.

PEN/Ralph Manheim Medal for Translation. Given triennially to a translator whose career has demonstrated a commitment to excellence. *Winner (2021):* Pierre Joris.

PEN/Nabokov Award for Achievement in International Literature ($50,000). To a writer of any genre and of any nationality for their exceptional body of work. *Winner:* Anne Carson.

PEN/Phyllis Naylor Grant for Children's and Young Adult Novelists ($5,000). To a published author of children's or young adult fiction to aid in completing a book-length work in progress. *Offered by:* PEN American Center. *Winner:* Arno Bohlmeijer for *Scared—Mad—More!* (work-in-progress).

PEN/Mike Nichols Writing for Performance Award ($25,000). To a writer whose work exemplifies excellence and influence in the world of theater, television, or film. *Winner:* George C. Wolfe.

PEN Open Book Award (formerly PEN Beyond Margins Award) ($5,000). For book-length writings by authors of color, published in the United States during the current calendar year. *Offered by:* PEN American Center. *Winner:* Asako Serizawa for *Inheritors* (Doubleday).

PEN/Joyce Osterweil Award for Poetry ($5,000). A biennial award given in odd-numbered years to recognize a new and emerging American poet. *Offered by:* PEN American Center. Award discontinued.

PEN/Laura Pels International Foundation for Theater Award. To a playwright working at the highest level of achievement in mid-career. *Offered by:* PEN American Center. *Winner:* Daniel Alexander Jones.

PEN/Jean Stein Book Award ($75,000). To recognize a book-length work of any genre for its originality, merit, and impact. *Winner:* Ross Gay for *Be Holding: A Poem* (University of Pittsburgh Press).

PEN/Jean Stein Grant for Literary Oral History ($15,000 each). Two awards for literary works of nonfiction that use oral history to illuminate an event, individual, place, or movement. *Winners:* Helen Benedict for *Map of Hope and Sorrow: Stories of Refugees Trapped in Greece* (work-in-progress) and Brett Ashley Robinson for *Re-Enactment* (work-in-progress).

PEN Translation Prize ($3,000). To promote the publication and reception of translated world literature in English. *Winner:* Emma Ramadan for her translation from French of *A Country for Dying: A Novel* by Abdellah Taïa (Seven Stories Press).

PEN/Edward and Lily Tuck Award for Paraguayan Literature ($3,000 author and $3,000 translator). Given in even-numbered years to the living author of a major work of Paraguayan literature. *Winner (2020):* Liz Haedo for *Pieles de Papel* (Arandura).

PEN/Voelcker Award for Poetry Collection. Given annually to a poet for a distinguished collection that represents a notable and accomplished literary presence, expanding the scope of American poetry. *Offered by:* PEN American Center. *Winner:* Victoria Chang for *Obit* (Copper Canyon Press).

PEN/Jacqueline Bograd Weld Award for Biography ($5,000). To the author of a distinguished biography published in the United States during the previous calendar year. *Offered by:* PEN American Center. *Winner:* Amy Stanley for *Stranger in the Shogun's City: A Japanese Woman and Her World* (Scribner).

PEN/E.O. Wilson Literary Science Writing Award ($10,000). For a book of literary nonfiction on the subject of the physical and biological sciences. *Winner:* Jonathan C. Slaght for *Owls of the Eastern Ice: A Quest to Find and Save the World's Largest Owl* (Farrar, Straus and Giroux).

Maxwell E. Perkins Award. See Medal for Editorial Excellence.

Aliki Perroti and Seth Frank Most Promising Young Poet Award ($1,000). For a student poet 23 years old or younger. *Offered by:* Academy of American Poets. *Winner:* Edwin Williamson for "Life As We Know It."

Phoenix Awards. To the authors of English-language children's books that failed to win a major award at the time of publication 20 years earlier. *Offered by:* Children's Literature Association. *Winner:* Alyssa Brugman for *Finding Grace* (Allen & Unwin).

Plimpton Prize for Fiction ($10,000). For an outstanding story published by an emerging writer in *The Paris Review* in the previous calendar year. *Offered by: The Paris Review.* *Winner:* Eloghosa Osunde.

Edgar Allan Poe Awards. See Edgar Awards.

Poets Out Loud Prize ($1,000 and publication by Fordham University Press). For a book-length poetry collection. *Sponsor:* Poetic Justice Institute at Fordham University. Not awarded in 2021.

Katherine Anne Porter Award. See American Academy of Arts and Letters Katherine Anne Porter Award.

Michael L. Printz Award. For excellence in literature for young adults. *Offered by:* American Library Association, Young Adult Library Services Association. *Winner:* Daniel Nayeri for *Everything Sad Is Untrue* (Arthur A. Levine/Levine Querido).

V.S. Pritchett Short Story Prize (United Kingdom) (£1,000). For a previously unpublished short story. *Offered by:* Royal Society of Literature. *Winner:* Leeor Ohayon for "Gahnun on Shabbat."

Pritzker Military Library Literature Award ($100,000). To recognize a living author for a body of work that has profoundly enriched the public understanding of American military history. *Sponsor:* Tawani Foundation. *Winner:* Margaret Macmillan.

Prix Aurora Awards (Canada). For science fiction. *Offered by:* Canadian SF & Fantasy Association. *Winners:* (novel) Silvia Moreno-Garcia for *Mexican Gothic* (Del Rey); (young adult novel) Susan Forest for *Flights of Marigold* (Laksa Media Groups);

(novelette/novella) Derek Künsken for "Tool Use by the Humans of Danzhai County" in *Asimov's Science Fiction Magazine* (July/August 2020); (short story) Chadwick Ginther for "All Cats Go to Valhalla" in *Swashbuckling Cats: Nine Lives on the Seven Seas* (Tyche Books); (related work) Diane L. Walton (managing ed.) for *On Spec* magazine; (graphic novel) Kari Maaren for *It Never Rains* (webcomic); (poem/song) Jo Walton for "Nidhog" in *The Book of Dragons* (Harper Voyager); (artist) Samantha M. Beiko; (visual presentation) Steve Blackman for *The Umbrella Academy* (Dark Horse Entertainment).

Prix Goncourt (France). For "the best imaginary prose work of the year." *Offered by:* Société des Gens des Lettres. *Winner:* Mohamed Mbougar Sarr for *La plus secrète mémoire des hommes* (Philippe Rey).

PROSE Awards. For outstanding professional and scholarly works. *Offered by:* Association of American Publishers. *Winners:* (biological and life sciences) Harvard University Press for *Desert Navigator: The Journey of an Ant* by Rüdiger Wehner; (humanities) Cambridge University Press for *Ancient Maya Politics: A Political Anthropology of the Classic Period 150–900 CE* by Simon Martin; (physical sciences and mathematics) Cambridge University Press for *A Philosophical Approach to MOND: Assessing the Milgromian Research Program in Cosmology* by David Merritt; (reference works) Johns Hopkins University Press for *Frogfishes: Biodiversity, Zoogeography, and Behavioral Ecology* by Theodore W. Pietsch and Rachel J. Arnold; (social sciences) W.W. Norton & Company for *Mind Over Media: Propaganda Education for a Digital Age* by Renee Hobbs, foreword by Douglas Rushkoff.

Publishing Triangle Awards. For the best LGBTQ fiction, nonfiction, poetry, and trans literature. *Offered by:* Publishing Triangle. (Ferro-Grumley Award for LGBTQ Fiction) Juliana Delgado Lopera for *Fiebre Tropical* (Feminist Press); (Edmund White Award for Debut Fiction) Julia Serano for *99 Erics* (Switch Hitter Press); (Thom Gunn Award for Gay Poetry) Mark Bibbins for *13th Balloon* (Copper Canyon Press); (Audre Lorde Award for Lesbian Poetry) Natalie Diaz for *Postcolonial Love Poem* (Graywolf Press); (Publishing Triangle Award for Trans and Gender-Variant Literature) Hil Malatino for *Trans Care* (University of Minnesota Press); (Judy Grahn Award for Lesbian Nonfiction) Jenn Shapland for *My Autobiography of Carson McCullers* (Tin House); (Randy Shilts Award for Gay Nonfiction) Eric Cervini for *The Deviant's War* (Farrar, Straus and Giroux).

Pulitzer Prizes in Letters ($10,000). To honor distinguished work dealing preferably with American themes. *Offered by:* Columbia University Graduate School of Journalism. *Winners:* (fiction) Louise Erdrich for *The Night Watchman* (Harper); (drama) Katori Hall for *The Hot Wing King*; (history) Marcia Chatelain for *Franchise: The Golden Arches in Black America* (Liveright/W.W. Norton & Company); (biography/autobiography) Les Payne and Tamara Payne for *The Dead Are Arising: The Life of Malcolm X* (Liveright/W.W. Norton & Company); (poetry) Natalie Diaz for *Postcolonial Love Poem* (Graywolf Press); (general nonfiction) David Zucchino for *Wilmington's Lie: The Murderous Coup of 1898 and the Rise of White Supremacy* (Atlantic Monthly Press).

Raiziss/De Palchi Translation Award ($10,000 book award and a $25,000 fellowship, awarded in alternate years). For a translation into English of a significant work of modern Italian poetry by a living translator. *Offered by:* Academy of American Poets. *Winner:* (book) Paula Bohince for her translation of selected poems by Corrado Govoni.

RBC Bronwen Wallace Award for Emerging Writers (C$10,000) (Canada). For writers under the age of 35 who are unpublished in book form. *Offered by:* Writers' Trust of Canada. *Sponsor:* Royal Bank of Canada. *Winner:* (short story) Anna Ling Kaye for "East City"; (poetry) Zehra Naqvi for "The Knot of My Tongue."

Arthur Rense Poetry Prize ($20,000). Awarded triennially to an exceptional poet. *Offered by:* American Academy of Arts and Letters. *Winner (2020):* Mary Ruefle.

Rita Awards. See Vivian Awards.

Sami Rohr Prize for Jewish Literature ($100,000). For emerging writers of Jewish literature. *Offered by:* Family of Sami Rohr.

Winner: (Inspiration Award for Fiction) Nicole Krauss.

Rosenthal Family Foundation Award ($10,000). To a young writer of considerable literary talent for a work of fiction. *Offered by:* American Academy of Arts and Letters. *Winner:* C Pam Zhang for *How Much of These Hills Is Gold* (Riverhead Books).

Royal Society of Literature Benson Medal (United Kingdom). To recognize meritorious works in poetry, fiction, history, and belles lettres, honoring an entire career. The recipient may be someone who is not a writer but has done conspicuous service to literature. *Winner:* Alastair Niven.

Royal Society of Literature Giles St Aubyn Awards for Non-Fiction (United Kingdom). For first-time writers of nonfiction. *Offered by:* Royal Society of Literature. *Winners:* (£10,000) Tomiwa Owolade for *This Is Not America* (Atlantic Books); (£5,000) Tom Ireland for *The Good Virus* (Hodder & Stoughton); (£2,500) David Veevers for *A New History of the World at the Dawn of British Expansion* (Penguin Random House/Ebury).

Royal Society of Literature Ondaatje Prize (United Kingdom) (£10,000). For a distinguished work of fiction, nonfiction, or poetry evoking the spirit of a place. *Offered by:* Royal Society of Literature. *Winner:* Ruth Gilligan for *The Butchers* (Atlantic Books).

Saltire Society Scotland Literary Awards. To recognize noteworthy work by writers of Scottish descent or living in Scotland, or by anyone who deals with the work or life of a Scot or with a Scottish problem, event, or situation. *Offered by:* Saltire Society. *Winners:* (fiction and book of the year) Ely Percy for *Duck Feet* (Monstrous Regiment Publishing); (debut) Roddy Murray for *Bleak: The Mundane Comedy* (Saraband); (nonfiction) Peter Ross for *A Tomb with a View* (Headline Publishing Group); (poetry) Daisy Lafarge for *Life without Air* (Granta); (history) Maria Hayward for *Stuart Style Monarchy, Dress and the Scottish Male Elite* (Yale University Press); (research) Ian Armit and Lindsey Buster for *Darkness Visible: The Sculptor's Cave, Covesa, from the Bronze Age to the Picts* (Society of Antiquaries of Scotland).

Carl Sandburg Literary Awards. *Sponsor:* Chicago Public Library Foundation. *Winner:* Amy Tan; (21st Century Award, for an early career author with ties to Chicago) J. Nicole Brooks.

Schneider Family Book Awards ($5,000). To honor authors and illustrators for books that embody artistic expressions of the disability experience of children and adolescents. *Offered by:* American Library Association. *Donor:* Katherine Schneider. *Winners:* (young children) Jordan Scott (author) and Sydney Smith (illustrator) for *I Talk Like a River* (Neal Porter Books); (middle school) Ann Clare LeZotte for *Show Me a Sign* (Scholastic); (teen) I.W. Gregorio for *This Is My Brain in Love* (Little, Brown Books for Young Readers).

Scotiabank Giller Prize (Canada) (C$100,000 first place, C$10,000 to each of the finalists). For the best Canadian novel or short story collection written in English. *Offered by:* Giller Prize Foundation and Scotiabank. *Winner:* Omar El Akkad for *What Strange Paradise* (Penguin Random House); (finalists) Angélique Lalonde for *Glorious Frazzled Beings* (Astoria); Cheluchi Onyemelukwe-Onuobia for *The Son of the House* (Dundurn Press); Jordan Tannahill for *The Listeners* (HarperAvenue); Miriam Toews for *Fight Night* (Knopf Canada).

Shamus Awards. To honor mysteries featuring independent private investigators. *Offered by:* Private Eye Writers of America. *Winners:* (hardcover novel) Matt Coyle for *Blind Vigil* (Oceanview); (original paperback) Richard Helms for *Brittle Karma* (Black Arch Books); (short story) John M. Floyd for "Mustang Sally" in *Black Cat Mystery Magazine* (Volume 2, No. 3, Issue #7); (debut) Kwei Quartey for *The Missing American* (Soho).

Shelley Memorial Award ($6,000–$9,000). To a poet or poets living in the United States, chosen on the basis of genius and need. *Offered by:* Poetry Society of America. *Winner:* Arthur Sze.

Robert F. Sibert Medal. For the most distinguished informational book for children. *Offered by:* American Library Association, Association for Library Service to Children. *Winners:* Candace Fleming (author) and Eric Rohmann (illustrator) for *Honeybee: The Busy Life of Apis Mellifera* (Neal Porter Books/Holiday House).

Society of Authors Traveling Scholarships (United Kingdom) (£1,600). *Winners:* Yara Rodrigues Fowler, Guy Gunaratne, Lola Okolosie, Clare Pollard, and Tom Stevenson.

Spur Awards. *Offered by:* Western Writers of America. *Winners:* (contemporary novel) David Heska Wanbli Weiden for *Winter Counts* (Ecco); (historical novel) James Wade for *All Things Left Wild* (Blackstone Publishing); (traditional novel) Tyler Enfield for *Like Rum Drunk Angels* (Goose Lane); (historical nonfiction) Robert M. Utley for *The Last Sovereigns* (University of Nebraska Press); (contemporary nonfiction) Hustin Farrell for *Billionaire Wilderness* (Princeton University Press); (biography) Peter Cozzens for *Tecumseh and the Prophet* (Alfred A. Knopf); (original mass market paperback novel) Johnny D. Boggs for *A Thousand Texas Longhorns* (Pinnacle/Kensington); (romance novel) Tom Lowe for *Midnight's Whisperer* (Kingsbridge Entertainment); (juvenile fiction) Matthew P. Mayo for *Dilly* (Five Star Publishing); (storyteller—illustrated children's book) Cami Carlson (author) and Greg White (illustrator) for *Run Cow Run* (self-published); (short fiction) Kevin Wolf for *Belthanger* (Western Fictioneers); (short nonfiction) Ted Franklin Belue for "Daniel Boone's Life in the Far West: An Inquiry into His Alleged Yellowstone Hunt" in *Muzzleloader Magazine* (January/February, March/April, and May/June 2020); (poem) Patricia Frolander for "Baptism" (High Plains Press); (documentary script) Gus Chambers and Paul Zalis for *Charlie Russell's Old West* (Montana PBS); (first nonfiction book) Laura J. Arata for *Race and the Wild West* (University of Oklahoma Press); (first novel) David Heska Wanbli Weiden for Winter Counts (Ecco).

Stella Prize (A$50,000). For the best fiction or nonfiction book by an Australian woman. *Sponsor:* Wilson Foundation. *Winner:* Evie Wyld for *The Bass Rock* (Vintage).

Wallace Stevens Award ($100,000). To recognize outstanding and proven mastery in the art of poetry. *Offered by:* Academy of American Poets. *Winner:* Toi Derricotte.

Bram Stoker Awards. For superior horror writing. *Offered by:* Horror Writers Association. *Winners (2021):* To be announced. *Winners (2020):* (novel) Stephen Graham Jones for *The Only Good Indians* (Gallery/Saga Press); (first novel) E.V. Knight for *The Fourth Whore* (Raw Dog Screaming Press); (young adult novel) Adam Cesare for *Clown in a Cornfield* (HarperTeen); (graphic novel) Nancy Holder (author), Chiara Di Francia (artist), Amelia Woo (artist), Laurie Foster (inker), Sandra Molina (colorist), and Saida Temofonte (letterer) for *Mary Shelley Presents* (Kymera Press); (long fiction) Stephen Graham Jones for *Night of the Mannequins* (Tordotcom); (short fiction) Josh Malerman for "One Last Transformation" in *Miscreations: Gods, Monstrosities & Other Horrors* (Written Backwards); (fiction collection) Lee Murray for *Grotesque: Monster Stories* (Things in the Well); (screenplay) Leigh Whannell for *The Invisible Man* (Universal Pictures, Blumhouse Productions, Goalpost Pictures, Nervous Tick Productions); (anthology) Lee Murray and Geneve Flynn for *Black Cranes: Tales of Unquiet Women* (Omnium Gatherum Media); (nonfiction) Tim Waggoner for *Writing in the Dark* (Guide Dog Books/Raw Dog Screaming Press); (short nonfiction) Tim Waggoner for "Speaking of Horror" in *The Writer* (November 2020); (poetry collection) Christina Sng for *A Collection of Dreamscapes* (Raw Dog Screaming Press).

Stonewall Book Awards. *Offered by:* Gay, Lesbian, Bisexual, and Transgender Round Table, American Library Association. *Winners:* (Barbara Gittings Literature Award) Zeyn Joukhadar for *The Thirty Names of Night* (Atria Books); (Israel Fishman Nonfiction Award) Bonnie Ruberg for *Queer Games Avant-Garde: How LGBTQ Game Makers Are Reimagining the Medium of Video Games* (Duke University Press); (Mike Morgan and Larry Romans Children's and Young Adult Literature Award) Lindsey Blakely (designer) and Archaa Shrivastay (author) for *We Are Little Feminists: Families* (Little Feminist).

Story Prize ($20,000). For a collection of short fiction. *Offered by: Story* magazine. *Winner (2020–2021):* Deesha Philyaw for *The Secret Lives of Church Ladies* (West Virginia University Press).

Flora Stieglitz Straus Awards. For nonfiction books that serve as an inspiration to young readers. *Offered by:* Bank Street College of Education and the Florence M. Miller Memorial Fund. *Winners:* (older readers) Christina Soontornvat for *All Thirteen: The Incredible Cave Rescue of the Thai Boys' Soccer Team* (Candlewick Press); (younger readers) Beth Anderson (author) and E.B. Lewis (illustrator) for *Lizzie Demands a Seat!: Elizabeth Jennings Fights for Streetcar Rights* (Calkins Creek).

Theodore Sturgeon Memorial Award. For the year's best short science fiction. *Offered by:* Gunn Center for the Study of Science Fiction. *Winner:* Rebecca Campbell for "An Important Failure" in *Clarkesworld* (Issue 167, August 2020).

Sunburst Awards for Canadian Literature of the Fantastic (C$1,000). To Canadian writers with a speculative fiction novel or book-length collection of speculative fiction published any time during the previous calendar year. Not awarded in 2021.

Sunday Times Audible Short Story Award (United Kingdom) (£30,000). To an author from any country for an English-language story of 6,000 words or fewer. *Winner:* Susan Choi for "Flashlight."

Sunday Times Charlotte Aitken Young Writer of the Year Award (United Kingdom) (£5,000). For a full-length published or self-published (in book or e-book format) work of fiction, nonfiction, or poetry by a British or Irish author age 18–35 years. *Winner:* Cal Flyn for *Islands of Abandonment* (William Collins).

Tanizaki Prize (Japan) (1 million yen, approximately $8,450). For a full-length work of fiction or drama by a professional writer. *Offered by:* Chuokoron-Shinsha, Inc. *Winner:* Kanehara Hitomi for *Unsocial Distance.*

RBC Taylor Prize (Canada). Award discontinued.

Sydney Taylor Book Awards. For a distinguished contribution to Jewish children's literature. *Offered by:* Association of Jewish Libraries. *Winners:* (picture book) Susan Kusel (author) and Sean Rubin (illustrator) for *The Passover Guest* (Neal Porter Books/ Holiday House); (middle grade) Veera Hiranandani for *How to Find What You're Not Looking For* (Kokila/Penguin Random House); (young adult) Aden Polydoros for *The City Beautiful* (Inkyard Press).

Sydney Taylor Manuscript Award ($1,000). For the best fiction manuscript appropriate for readers ages 8–13, both Jewish and non-Jewish, revealing positive aspects of Jewish life and written by an unpublished author. *Winner:* Noah Weisz for *Echo of Light.*

Theatre Library Association Award. See Richard Wall Memorial Award.

Dylan Thomas Prize (United Kingdom) (£30,000). For a published or produced literary work in the English language, written by an author under 30. *Offered by:* Swansea University. *Winner:* Raven Leilani for *Luster* (Farrar, Straus and Giroux).

Henry David Thoreau Prize for Literary Excellence in Nature Writing. *Offered by:* Thoreau Society of Concord. *Winner:* Robin Wall Kimmerer.

Thriller Awards. *Offered by:* International Thriller Writers. *Winners:* (hardcover novel) S.A. Cosby for *Blacktop Wasteland* (Flatiron Books); (first novel) David Heska Wanbli Weiden for *Winter Counts* (Ecco); (paperback original) John Marrs for *What Lies Between Us* (Thomas & Mercer); (short story) Alan Orloff for "Rent Due" (Down & Out Books); (young adult) Andrea Contos for *Throwaway Girls* (Kids Can Press); (e-book original novel) Jeff Buick for *Killing Game* (Novel Words).

Thurber Prize for American Humor ($5,000). For a humorous book of fiction or nonfiction. *Offered by:* Thurber House. *Winner (2020):* Damon Young for *What Doesn't Kill You Makes You Blacker* (Ecco).

Tom-Gallon Trust Award (United Kingdom) (£1,000). For a short story. *Offered by:* Society of Authors. *Sponsor:* Authors' Licensing and Collecting Society. *Winner:* D.M. O'Connor for "I Told You Not to Fly So High."

Paul Torday Memorial Prize (United Kingdom) (£1,000). For a first novel by an author age 60 or older. *Offered by:* Society of Authors. *Winner:* Kathy O'Shaughnessy for *In Love with George Eliot* (Scribe UK).

Betty Trask Prize and Awards (United Kingdom). To Commonwealth writers under the age of 35 for "romantic or traditional" first novels. *Offered by:* Society of Authors. *Winners:* (Betty Trask Prize, £10,000) Thomas McMullan for *The Last Good Man* (Bloomsbury); (Betty Trask Awards, £5,000) Maame

Blue for *Bad Love* (Jacaranda Books); Eley Williams for *The Liar's Dictionary* (William Heinemann); Kiran Millwood Hargrave for *The Mercies* (Picador); Nneoma Ike-Njoku for *The Water House*; Graeme Armstrong for *The Young Team* (Pan Macmillan/Picador).

Kate Tufts Discovery Award ($10,000). For a first or very early book of poetry by an emerging poet. *Offered by:* Claremont Graduate University. *Winner:* Jake Skeets for *Eyes Bottle Dark with a Mouthful of Flowers* (Milkweed Editions).

Kingsley Tufts Poetry Award ($100,000). For a book of poetry by a midcareer poet. *Offered by:* Claremont Graduate School. *Winner:* John Murillo for *Kontemporary Amerikan Poetry* (Four Way Books).

21st Century Award. See Carl Sandburg Literary Awards.

UKLA Children's Book Awards (United Kingdom). Sponsor: United Kingdom Literacy Association. *Winners:* (ages 3–6+) Nathan Bryon (author) and Dapo Adeola (illustrator) for *Look Up!* (Puffin); (ages 7–10+) Stewart Foster for *Check Mates* (Simon & Schuster); (ages 11–14+) (tie) Manjeet Mann for *Run Rebel* (Penguin) and Kerry Drewery for *The Last Paper Crane* (Hot Key); (information, ages 3-14+) Kwame Alexander (author) and Kadir Nelson (illustrator) for *The Undefeated* (Andersen).

Ungar German Translation Award ($1,000). Awarded biennially for a distinguished literary translation from German into English that has been published in the United States. *Offered by:* American Translators Association. *Winner (2021):* Philip Boehm.

John Updike Award ($10,000). Biennial prize to a writer. in midcareer whose work has demonstrated consistent excellence. *Offered by:* American Academy of Arts and Letters. *Winners (2021):* Stephen Adly Guirgis and Diane Seuss.

VCU/Cabell First Novelist Award ($5,000). For a first novel published in the previous year. *Offered by:* Virginia Commonwealth University. *Winner:* Raven Leilani for *Luster* (Farrar, Straus and Giroux).

Vivian Awards. *Offered by:* Romance Writers of America. *Winners:* (first book) Annmarie Boyle for *Love Me Like a Love Song* (Dahlia Media); (long contemporary romance) Jessica Ruddick for *False Start* (Peake Ink Press); (mid-length contemporary romance) Sara Whitney for *Tempting Taste* (LoveSpark Press); (short contemporary romance) Reese Ryan for *Engaging the Enemy* (Mills & Boon); (erotic romance) Rebecca Hunter for *Pure Satisfaction* (Harlequin Dare); (long historical romance) Loretta Chase for *Ten Things I Hate About the Duke* (Avon); (mid-length historical romance) Louisa Cornell for *A Study in Passion* (Scarsdale Publishing); (mainstream fiction with a central romance) Laura Trentham for *An Everyday Hero* (Griffin); (most anticipated romance) Janet Oppedisano for *Burning Caine* (Janet Oppedisano); (romance with religious or spiritual elements) Karen Witemeyer for *At Love's Command* (Bethany House) (award rescinded); (long romantic suspense) Hope Anika for *Hail Mary* (self-published); (mid-length romantic suspense) Janie Crouch for *Storm* (Aces Press); (long speculative romance) Kelley Armstrong for *A Stitch in Time* (Subterranean Press); (mid-length speculative romance) Darynda Jones for *Betwixt* (self-published).

Harold D. Vursell Memorial Award ($20,000). To a writer whose work merits recognition for the quality of its prose style. *Offered by:* American Academy of Arts and Letters. *Winner:* Garth Greenwell.

Amelia Elizabeth Walden Award ($5,000). To honor a book relevant to adolescents that has enjoyed a wide teenage audience. *Sponsor:* Assembly on Literature for Adolescents, National Council of Teachers of English. *Winner:* Elizabeth Acevedo for *Clap When You Land* (HarperCollins/Quill Tree Books).

Richard Wall Memorial Award (formerly the Theatre Library Association Award). To honor an English-language book of exceptional scholarship in the field of recorded performance, including motion pictures, television, and radio. *Offered by:* Theatre Library Association. *Winner:* Steven C. Smith for *Music by Max Steiner: The Epic Life of Hollywood's Most Influential Composer* (Oxford University Press).

George Washington Book Prize ($50,000). To recognize an important new book about America's founding era. *Offered by:* Washington College and the Gilder Lehrman Institute of American History. *Winner:* Mary

Beth Norton for *1774: The Long Year of Revolution* (Alfred A. Knopf).

Hilary Weston Writers' Trust Prize for Nonfiction (C$60,000) (Canada). *Offered by:* Writers' Trust of Canada. *Winner:* Tomson Highway for *Permanent Astonishment: A Memoir* (Doubleday Canada).

E.B. White Award. See American Academy of Arts and Letters E.B. White Award.

E.B. White Read-Aloud Awards. For children's books with particular appeal as read-aloud books. *Offered by:* American Booksellers Association/Association of Booksellers for Children. Not awarded in 2021.

Whiting Writers' Awards ($50,000). For emerging writers of exceptional talent and promise. *Offered by:* Mrs. Giles Whiting Foundation. *Winners:* (poetry) Marwa Helal, Ladan Osman, Xandria Phillips; (fiction) Steven Dunn, Tope Folarin; (nonfiction) Joshua Bennett, Sarah Stewart Johnson; (drama) Sylvia Khoury, Donnetta Lavinia Grays, Jordan E. Cooper.

Walt Whitman Award ($5,000). To a U.S. poet who has not published a book of poems in a standard edition. *Offered by:* Academy of American Poets. *Winner:* Kemi Alabi for *Against Heaven* (Graywolf Press).

Richard Wilbur Award ($1,000 and publication by University of Evansville Press). For a book-length poetry collection. *Winner:* M.B. Smith for "Midlife."

Laura Ingalls Wilder Award. See Children's Literature Legacy Award.

Thornton Wilder Prize for Translation ($20,000). Awarded every two years to a practitioner, scholar, or patron who has made a significant contribution to the art of literary translation. *Offered by:* American Academy of Arts and Letters. *Winner (2020):* Linda Asher.

Robert H. Winner Memorial Award ($2,500). To a midcareer poet older than 40 who has published no more than one book of poetry. *Offered by:* Poetry Society of America. *Winner:* Melissa Crowe.

George Wittenborn Memorial Book Awards. To North American art publications that represent the highest standards of content, documentation, layout, and format. *Offered by:* Art Libraries Society of North America (ARLIS/NA). *Winner:* Nathaniel Silver (editor) for *Boston's Apollo: Thomas McKeller*

and John Singer Sargent (Isabella Stewart Gardner Museum/Yale University Press).

Thomas Wolfe Prize and Lecture. To honor writers with distinguished bodies of work. *Offered by:* Thomas Wolfe Society and University of North Carolina–Chapel Hill. *Winner:* Frank Bruni.

Thomas Wolfe Fiction Prize ($1,000). For a short story that honors Thomas Wolfe. *Offered by:* North Carolina Writers Network. *Winner:* Louis Schlesinger for "Post-Traumatic MoonPie."

Helen and Kurt Wolff Translator's Prize ($10,000). For an outstanding translation from German into English, published in the United States. *Offered by:* Goethe Institut Inter Nationes, New York. *Winner:* Jackie Smith for *An Inventory of Losses* by Judith Schalansky (New Directions).

Women's Prize for Fiction (United Kingdom) (formerly the Bailey's Women's Prize for Fiction) (£30,000). For the best novel written by a woman and published in the United Kingdom. *Winner:* Susanna Clarke for *Piranesi* (Bloomsbury).

World Fantasy Awards. For outstanding fantasy writing. *Offered by:* World Fantasy Convention. *Winners:* (novel) Alaya Dawn Johnson for *Trouble the Saints* (Tor); (novella) Tochi Onyebuchi for *Riot Baby* (Tordotcom); (short fiction) Celeste Rita Baker for "Glass Bottle Dancer" in *Lightspeed* (April 2020); (anthology) Ann and Jeff VanderMeer (editors) for *The Big Book of Modern Fantasy* (Vintage Books); (collection) Aoka Matsuda for *Where the Wild Ladies Are*, translated by Polly Barton (Soft Skull Press); (best artist) Rovina Cai; (special award, professional) C.C. Finlay for *The Magazine of Fantasy & Science Fiction*; (special award, nonprofessional) Brian Attebery for *Journal of the Fantastic in the Arts.*

Writers' Trust Engel/Findley Award (C$25,000) (Canada). To a Canadian writer predominantly of fiction, for a body of work. *Offered by:* Writers' Trust of Canada. *Sponsors:* Writers' Trust Board of Directors, Pitblado Family Foundation, and Michael Griesdorf Fund. *Winner:* Cherie Dimaline.

Writers' Trust Fiction Prize. See Atwood Gibson Writers' Trust Fiction Prize.

Writers' Trust/McClelland & Stewart Journey Prize (C$10,000) (Canada). To a new, developing Canadian author for a short story first published in a Canadian literary journal during the previous year. *Offered by:* Writers' Trust of Canada. *Sponsor:* McClelland & Stewart. *Winner:* To be awarded.

Writers' Trust Shaughnessy Cohen Prize for Political Writing (C$25,000) (Canada). For literary nonfiction that captures a political subject of relevance to Canadian readers. *Offered by:* Writers' Trust of Canada. *Winner:* Ronald J. Deibert for *Reset: Reclaiming the Internet for Civil Society* (House of Anansi Press).

YALSA Award for Excellence in Nonfiction. For a work of nonfiction published for young adults (ages 12–18). *Offered by:* American Library Association, Young Adult Library Services Association. *Winner:* Candace Fleming for *The Rise and Fall of Charles Lindbergh* (Schwartz and Wade/Random House Children's Books).

Young Lions Fiction Award ($10,000). For a novel or collection of short stories by an American under the age of 35. *Offered by:* Young Lions of the New York Public Library. *Winner:* Catherine Lacey for *Pew* (Farrar, Straus and Giroux).

Young People's Poet Laureate ($25,000). For lifetime achievement in poetry for children. Honoree holds the title for two years. *Offered by:* Poetry Foundation. *Winner (2019):* Naomi Shihab Nye.

Morton Dauwen Zabel Award ($10,000). Awarded biennially, in rotation, to a progressive and experimental poet, writer of fiction, or critic. *Offered by:* American Academy of Arts and ·Letters. *Winner (2020):* Brenda Hillman (poetry).

Zoetrope Short Fiction Prizes. *Offered by: Zoetrope: All-Story. Winners:* (first, $1,000) Jack Gain for "Port-Bou"; (second, $500) T.S. Zupancis for "The Burr"; (third, $250) Eugenia Borkowski for "View."

Charlotte Zolotow Award. For outstanding writing in a picture book published in the United States in the previous year. *Offered by:* Cooperative Children's Book Center, University of Wisconsin–Madison. *Winner:* Meg Medina for *Evelyn Del Rey Is Moving Away*, illustrated by Sonia Sanchez (Candlewick Press).

Part 6
Directory of Organizations

Directory of Library and Related Organizations

Networks, Consortia, and Other Cooperative Library Organizations

This list is taken from the current edition of *American Library Directory* (Information Today, Inc.), which includes additional information on member libraries and primary functions of each organization.

United States

Alabama

Alabama Health Libraries Assn., Inc. (AL-HeLa), Lister Hill Lib., Univ. of Alabama, Birmingham 35294-0013. SAN 372-8218. Tel. 205-975-8313, fax 205-934-2230. *Pres.* Monica Hodge.

Library Management Network, Inc. (LMN), 1405 Plaza St. S.E., Ste 309, Decatur 35603. SAN 322-3906. Tel. 256-822-2371. *Pres.* Derrick Griffey.

Marine Environmental Sciences Consortium, Dauphin Island Sea Laboratory, 101 Bienville Blvd., Dauphin Island 36528. SAN 322-0001. Tel. 251-861-2141, fax 251-861-4646, e-mail disl@disl.org. *Exec. Dir.* John Valentine.

Network of Alabama Academic Libraries, c/o Alabama Commission on Higher Education, 100 N. Union St., Montgomery 36104. SAN 322-4570. Tel. 334-242-2211, fax 334-242-0270. *Exec. Dir.* Sheila Snow.

Alaska

Alaska Library Network (ALN), P.O. Box 230051, Anchorage 99523-0051. SAN 371-0688. Tel. 907-205-5362, e-mail info@aklib.net. *Exec. Dir.* Steve Rollins.

California

49-99 Cooperative Library System, c/o Southern California Lib. Cooperative, 254 N. Lake Ave., Suite 874, Pasadena 91101. SAN 301-6218. Tel. 626-359-6111, fax 626-283-5949. *Exec. Dir.* Diane Bednarski.

Bay Area Library and Information Network (BayNet), 1462 Cedar St., Berkeley 94702. SAN 371-0610. Tel. 415-355-2826, e-mail infobay@baynetlibs.org. *Pres.* Dean Jones.

Califa, 330 Townsend St., Ste. 133, San Francisco 94107. Tel. 888-239-2289, fax 415-520-0434, e-mail califa@califa.org. *Exec. Dir.* Paula MacKinnon.

Gold Coast Library Network, 3437 Empresa Dr., Suite C, San Luis Obispo 93401-7355. Tel. 805-543-6082, fax 805-543-9487. *Admin. Dir.* Maureen Theobald.

National Network of Libraries of Medicine–Pacific Southwest Region (NN/LM-PSR), Louise M. Darling Biomedical Lib., 10833 Le Conte Ave., 12-077 Center for Health Science, Box 951798, Los Angeles 90095-1798. SAN 372-8234. Tel. 310-825-1200, fax 310-825-5389, e-mail psr-nnlm@library.ucla.edu. *Dir.* Judy Consales.

Northern California & Nevada Medical Library Group (NCNMLG), Barton Memorial Hospital Lib., 2170 South Ave., South Lake Tahoe 96150. SAN 370-0445. Tel. 530-543-

5844, fax 530-541-4697. *Senior Exec. Coord.* Laurie Anton.

Northern California Assn. of Law Libraries (NOCALL), 268 Bush St., #3736, San Francisco, 94104. E-mail admin@nocall.org. *Pres.* Delia Montesinos.

Northern and Central California Psychology Libraries (NCCPL), 1453 Mission St, San Francisco 94103. SAN 371-9006. Tel. 415-575-6180. *Pres.* Scott Hines.

Peninsula Libraries Automated Network (PLAN), 32 West 25th Avenue, Suite 201, San Mateo 94403. SAN 371-5035. Tel. 650-349-5538, fax 650-349-5089. *CEO* Carol Frost.

Santa Clarita Interlibrary Network (SCIL-NET), College of the Canyons, 26455 Rockwell Canyon Road, Santa Clarita 91355. SAN 371-8964. Tel. 661-362-3758, fax 661-362-2719. *Libn.* John Stone.

Serra Cooperative Library System, Serra c/o SCLC, 254 N. Lake Ave., Suite 874, Pasadena 91101. SAN 301-3510. Tel. 626-283-5949. *Dir.* Diane Bednarski.

Southern California Library Cooperative (SCLC), 254 N. Lake Ave., Suite 874, Pasadena 91101. SAN 371-3865. Tel. 626-283-5949. *Dir.* Diane Bednarski.

Colorado

Colorado Alliance of Research Libraries, 3801 E. Florida Ave., Suite 515, Denver 80210. SAN 322-3760. Tel. 303-759-3399, fax 303-759-3363. *Exec. Dir.* George Machovec.

Colorado Assn. of Law Libraries, c/o William A Wise Law Library, 2450 Kittredge Loop Dr., 402 UCB, Boulder 80309. SAN 322-4325. Tel. 303-492-7535, fax 303-492-2707. *Pres.* Catherine Dunn.

Colorado Council of Medical Librarians (CCML), P.O. Box 101058, Denver 80210. SAN 370-0755. Tel. 303-724-2124, fax 303-724-2154. *Pres.* Ben Harnke.

Colorado Library Consortium (CLiC), 7400 E. Arapahoe Rd., Suite 75, Centennial 80112. SAN 371-3970. Tel. 303-422-1150, fax 303-431-9752. *Exec. Dir.* Jim Duncan.

Connecticut

Bibliomation, 24 Wooster Ave., Waterbury 06708. Tel. 203-577-4070, fax 203-577-4077. *Exec. Dir.* Carl DeMilia.

Connecticut Library Consortium, 234 Court St., Middletown 06457-3304. SAN 322-0389. Tel. 860-344-8777, fax 860-344-9199, e-mail clc@ctlibrarians.org. *Exec. Dir.* Jennifer Keohane.

CTW Library Consortium, Olin Memorial Lib., 252 Church St., Middletown 06459-6065. SAN 329-4587. Tel. 860-685-3887, fax 860-685-2661. *Libn. for Collaborative Projects* Lorri Huddy.

Libraries Online, Inc. (LION), 100 Riverview Center, Suite 252, Middletown 06457. SAN 322-3922. Tel. 860-347-1704, fax 860-346-3707. *Exec. Dir.* Joseph Farara.

Library Connection, Inc., 599 Matianuck Ave., Windsor 06095-3567. Tel. 860-937-8261, fax 860-298-5328. *Systems Librn.* Sam Cook.

District of Columbia

Association of Research Libraries, 21 Dupont Circle N.W., Suite 800, Washington 20036. Tel. 202-296-2296, fax 202-872-0884. *Exec. Dir.* Mary Lee Kennedy.

Council for Christian Colleges and Universities, 321 8th St. N.E., Washington 20002. SAN 322-0524. Tel. 202-546-8713, fax 202-546-8913, e-mail council@cccu.org. *Pres.* Shirley V. Hoogstra.

FEDLINK/Federal Library and Information Network, c/o Federal Lib. and Info. Center Committee, 101 Independence Ave. S.E., Washington 20540-4935. SAN 322-0761. Tel. 202-707-4800, fax 202-707-4818, e-mail flicc@loc.gov. *Exec. Dir.* Laurie Neider.

Washington Theological Consortium, 487 Michigan Ave. N.E., Washington 20017-1585. SAN 322-0842. Tel. 202-832-2675, fax 202-526-0818, e-mail wtc@washtheocon.org. *Exec. Dir.* Larry Golemon.

Florida

Consortium of Southern Biomedical Libraries (CONBLS), c/o Harriet F Ginsburg Health Sciences Library, 6850 Lake Nona Blvd., Orlando 32867. SAN 370-7717. Chair Nadine Dexter.

Florida Academic Library Services Cooperative (FALSC), 1753 W Paul Dirac Dr., Tallahassee 32310. Tel. 850-922-6044, fax 850-922-4869. *Exec. Dir.* Elijah Scott.

Florida Library Information Network, R.A. Gray Bldg., State Library and Archives of Florida, Tallahassee 32399-0250. SAN 322-0869. Tel. 850-245-6600, fax 850-245-6744, e-mail library@dos.myflorida.com. *Bureau Chief* Cathy Moloney.

Library and Information Resources Network, 25400 US 19 N., Ste. 220, Clearwater 33763. Tel. 727-536-0214, fax 727-530-3126. *Pres. & CEO* Andrew Anderson.

Midwest Archives Conference (MAC), 2598 E Sunrise Blvd., Suite 2104, Fort Lauderdale 33304. E-mail membership@midwestarchives.org. *Pres.* Tamar Chute.

Northeast Florida Library Information Network (NEFLIN), 2233 Park Ave., Suite 402, Orange Park 32073. Tel. 904-278-5620, fax 904-278-5625, e-mail office@neflin.org. *Exec. Dir.* Brad Ward.

Panhandle Library Access Network (PLAN), Five Miracle Strip Loop, Suite 8, Panama City Beach 32407-3850. SAN 370-047X. Tel. 850-233-9051, fax 850-235-2286. *Exec. Dir.* Charles Mayberry.

SEFLIN/Southeast Florida Library Information Network, Inc., Wimberly Lib., Office 452, Florida Atlantic Univ., 777 Glades Rd., Boca Raton 33431. SAN 370-0666. Tel. 561-208-0984, fax 561-208-0995. *Exec. Dir.* Brock Peoples.

Southwest Florida Library Network (SWFLN), 13120 Westlinks Terrace, Unit 3, Fort Myers 33913. Tel. 239-313-6338, fax 239-313-6329. *Exec. Dir.* Luly Castro.

Tampa Bay Library Consortium, Inc., 4042 Park Oaks Blvd., Suite 430, Tampa 33619. SAN 322-371X. Tel. 813-622-8252, fax 813-628-4425. *Exec. Dir.* Jim Walther.

Tampa Bay Medical Library Network, Medical Lib., Department 7660, 501 Sixth Ave. South, Saint Petersburg 33701. SAN 322-0885. Tel. 727-767-8557. *Interim Chair* Deanna Stevens.

Three Rivers Regional Library Consortium, 176 S.W. Community Cir., Mayo 32066. Tel. 386-294-3858, e-mail hello@3riverslibrary.com. *Dir.* Dale Collum.

Georgia

Association of Southeastern Research Libraries (ASERL), c/o Robert W. Woodruff Library, 540 Asbury Circle, Suite 316, Atlanta 30322-1006. SAN 322-1555. Tel. 404-727-0137. *Exec. Dir.* John Burger.

Atlanta Health Science Libraries Consortium, Fran Golding Medical Lib. at Scottish Rite, 1001 Johnson Ferry Rd. N.E., Atlanta 30342-1600. Tel. 404-785-2157, fax 404-785-2155. *Pres.* Kate Daniels.

Atlanta Regional Council for Higher Education (ARCHE), 141 E. College Ave., Box 1084, Decatur 30030. SAN 322-0990. Tel. 404-651-2668, fax 404-880-9816, e-mail arche@atlantahighered.org. *Exec. Dir.* Tracey Brantley.

GOLD Georgia Resource Sharing for Georgia's Libraries (GOLD), c/o Georgia Public Lib. Service, 1800 Century Pl. N.E., Suite 150, Atlanta 30345-4304. SAN 322-094X. Tel. 404-235-7128, fax 404-235-7201. *Project Mgr.* Elaine Hardy.

LYRASIS, 1438 W. Peachtree St. N.W., Suite 150, Atlanta 30309. SAN 322-0974. Tel. 800-999-8558, fax 404-892-7879. *CEO* Robert Miller.

Public Information Network for Electronic Services (PINES), 2872 Woodcock Blvd., Suite 250, Atlanta 30341. Tel. 404-235-7200. *Prog. Mgr.* Terran McCanna.

Hawaii

Hawaii-Pacific Chapter, Medical Library Assn. (HPC-MLA), Health Sciences Lib., Honolulu 96813. SAN 371-3946. Tel. 808-692-0810, fax 808-692-1244. *Chair* Kris Anderson.

Idaho

Cooperative Information Network (CIN), 8385 N. Government Way, Hayden 83835-9280. SAN 323-7656. Tel. 208-772-5612, fax 208-772-2498.

Library Consortium of Eastern Idaho (LCEI), 113 S. Garfield, Pocatello 83204-3235. SAN 323-7699. Tel. 208-237-2192. *Pres.* Marilyn Kamoe.

LYNX Consortium, c/o Boise Public Lib., 715 S. Capitol Ave., Boise 83702-7195. SAN 375-0086. Tel. 208-384-4238, fax 208-384-4025. *Dir.* Kevin Booe.

Illinois

American Theological Library Assn., 200 S. Wacker Dr., Ste. 3100, Chicago, 60606-5829. Tel. 872-310-4200. *Exec. Dir.* Brenda Bailey-Hainer.

Assn. of Chicago Theological Schools (ACTS), Univ. of St. Mary of the Lake, 1000 E. Maple Ave., Mundelein 60060-1174. SAN 370-0658. Tel. 847-566-6401. *Coord.* Jennifer Ould.

Big Ten Academic Alliance (formerly Committee on Institutional Cooperation), 1819 S. Neil St., Suite D, Champaign 61820-7271. Tel. 217-333-8475, fax 217-244-7127, e-mail btaa@staff.cic.net. *Exec. Dir.* Keith A. Marshall.

Center for Research Libraries, 6050 S. Kenwood, Chicago 60637-2804. SAN 322-1032. Tel. 773-955-4545, fax 773-955-4339. *Pres.* Gregory Eow.

Consortium of Academic and Research Libraries in Illinois (CARLI), 100 Trade Center Dr., Suite 303, Champaign 61820. SAN 322-3736. Tel. 217-244-4664, fax 217-244-7596, e-mail support@carli.illinois.edu. *Chair* Taran Ley.

East Central Illinois Consortium (ECIC), c/o CARLE Foundation Hospital, 611 W. Park St., Urbana 61801. SAN 322-1040. Tel. 217-383-3311, 217-383-4513. *Coord.* Frances Drone-Silvers.

Illinois Library and Information Network (ILLINET), c/o Illinois State Lib., Gwendolyn Brooks Bldg. 300 S. Second St., Springfield 62701-1796. SAN 322-1148. Tel. 217-785-5600. *Dir.* Greg McCormick.

LIBRAS, Inc., North Park Univ., 3225 W. Foster Ave., Chicago 60625-4895. SAN 322-1172. Tel. 773-244-5584, fax 773-244-4891. *Pres.* Estevon Montano.

Network of Illinois Learning Resources in Community Colleges (NILRC), P.O. Box 120, Blanchardville, WI 53516-0120. Tel. 608-523-4094, fax 608-523-4072. *Bus. Mgr.* Lisa Sikora.

System Wide Automated Network (SWAN), 800 Quail Ridge Dr., Westmont 60559. Tel. 844-792-6542. *Exec. Dir.* Aaron Skog.

Indiana

Consortium of College and University Media Centers (CCUMC), Indiana Univ., 306 N. Union St., Bloomington 47405-3888. SAN 322-1091. Tel. 812-855-6049, fax 812-855-2103, e-mail ccumc@ccumc.org. *Exec. Dir.* Aileen Scales.

Evergreen Indiana Consortium, Indiana State Lib., 315 W. Ohio St., Indianapolis 46202.

Tel. 317-234-6624, fax 317-232-0002. *Coord.* Anna Goben.

Indiana Library Federation, 941 E. 86th St., Ste. 260, Indianapolis, 46240. Tel. 317-257-2040. *Exec. Dir.* Lucinda Nord.

Iowa

National Network of Libraries of Medicine–Greater Midwest Region (NN/LM-GMR), c/o Hardin Library for the Health Sciences, 600 Newton Road, Iowa City, 52242. SAN 322-1202. Tel. 319-353-4479. *Dir.* Linda Walton.

Polk County Biomedical Consortium, c/o Broadlawns Medical Center Lib., Des Moines 50314. SAN 322-1431. Tel. 515-282-2394, fax 515-282-5634. *Treas.* Elaine Hughes.

State of Iowa Libraries Online (SILO), State Lib. of Iowa, Des Moines 50319. SAN 322-1415. Tel. 515-281-4105, fax 515-281-6191. *State Libn.* Michael Scott.

Kansas

Greater Western Library Alliance, 5200 W. 94th Terrace, Ste. 200, Prairie Village 66027. Tel. 913-370-4422. *Exec. Dir.* Joni Blake.

State Library of Kansas/Statewide Resource Sharing Div., 300 S.W. 10 Ave., Room 312-N., Topeka 66612-1593. SAN 329-5621. Tel. 785-296-3296, fax 785-368-7291. *Dir.* Jeff Hixon.

Kentucky

Appalachian College Assn., 3816 Camelot Dr., Lexington 40517. Tel. 859-986-4584, fax 859-986-9549. *Pres.* Beth Rushing.

Assn. of Independent Kentucky Colleges and Universities (AIKCU), 484 Chenault Rd., Frankfort 40601. SAN 322-1490. Tel. 502-695-5007, fax 502-695-5057. *Pres.* Gary S. Cox.

Kentuckiana Metroversity, Inc., 200 W. Broadway, Suite 800, Louisville 40202. SAN 322-1504. Tel. 502-897-3374, fax 502-895-1647.

Kentucky Medical Library Assn., University of Louisville Bldg. D, Rm 110A, 500 S. Preston St., Louisville 40292. SAN 370-0623. Tel. 502-852-8530. *Contact* Tiffney Gipson.

Louisiana

Health Sciences Library Assn. of Louisiana (HSLAL), 433 Bolivar St., New Orleans

70112. SAN 375-0035. Tel. 504-568-5550. *Pres.* Rebecca Bealer.

Loan SHARK, State Lib. of Louisiana, 701 N. Fourth St., Baton Rouge 70802. SAN 371-6880. Tel. 225-342-4918, fax 225-219-4725, e-mail ill@state.lib.la.us. *Admin.* Kytara Christophe.

Louisiana Library Network (LOUIS), 1201 N. Third St., Suite 6-200, Baton Rouge 70802. E-mail louisresources@regents.la.gov. *Exec. Dir.* Terri Gallaway.

New Orleans Educational Telecommunications Consortium, 2045 Lakeshore Dr., Suite 541, New Orleans 70122. Tel. 504-524-0350, e-mail noetc@noetc.org. *Dir.* Michael Adler.

Maryland

Maryland Interlibrary Loan Organization (MILO), c/o Enoch Pratt Free Lib., Baltimore 21201-4484. SAN 343-8600. Tel. 410-396-5498, fax 410-396-5837, e-mail milo@prattlibrary.org. *Mgr.* Emma E. Beaven.

National Network of Libraries of Medicine (NNLM), National Lib. of Medicine, Bldg. 38, 8600 Rockville Pike, Room B1-E03, Bethesda 20894. SAN 373-0905. Tel. 301-496-4777, fax 301-480-1467. *Head, National Network Coordinating Office* Amanda J. Wilson.

National Network of Libraries of Medicine–Southeastern Atlantic Region (NN/LM-SEA), Univ. of Maryland Health Sciences and Human Services Lib., 601 W. Lombard S., Baltimore 21201-1512. SAN 322-1644. Tel. 410-706-2855, fax 410-706-0099, e-mail hshsl nlmsea@hshsl umaryland.edu. *Dir.* Mary Tooey.

Southeastern Chapter of the American Assn. of Law Libraries (SEAALL), c/o University of Baltimore School of Law, 1420 N. Charles St., Baltimore 21201. *Pres.* Charles Pipins.

U.S. National Library of Medicine (NLM), 8600 Rockville Pike, Bethesda 20894. SAN 322-1652. Tel. 301-594-5983, fax 301-402-1384, e-mail custserv@nlm.nih.gov. *Coord.* Martha Fishel.

Washington Research Library Consortium (WRLC), 901 Commerce Dr., Upper Marlboro 20774. SAN 373-0883. Tel. 301-390-2000, fax 301-390-2020. *Exec. Dir.* Mark Jacobs.

Massachusetts

Boston Library Consortium, Inc., 401 Edgewater Place, Suite 600, Wakefield 01880. SAN 322-1733. Tel. 781-876-8859, fax 781-623-8460, e-mail admin@blc.org. *Exec. Dir.* Susan Stearns.

Boston Theological Interreligious Consortium, P.O. Box 391069, Cambridge 02139. Tel. 207-370-5275, e-mail btioffice@boston theological.org. *Exec. Dir.* Stephanie Edwards.

Cape Libraries Automated Materials Sharing Network (CLAMS), 270 Communication Way, Unit 4E, Hyannis 02601. SAN 370-579X. Tel. 508-790-4399, fax 508-771-4533. *Exec. Dir.* Gayle Simundza.

Central and Western Massachusetts Automated Resource Sharing (C/W MARS), 67 Millbrook St., Suite 201, Worcester 01606. SAN 322-3973. Tel. 508-755-3323 ext. 30, fax 508-755-3721.

Fenway Libraries Online, Inc. (FLO), c/o Wentworth Institute of Technology, 550 Huntington Ave., Boston 02115. SAN 373-9112. Tel. 617-989-5032. *Exec. Dir.* Walter Stein.

Massachusetts Health Sciences Libraries Network (MAHSLIN), Lamar Soutter Lib., Univ. of Massachusetts Medical School, Worcester 01655. SAN 372-8293. http://nahsl.libguides.com/mahslin/home. *Pres.* Stephanie Friree Ford.

Merrimack Valley Library Consortium, 4 High St., North Andover 01845. SAN 322-4384. Tel. 978-557-1050, fax 978-557-8101. *Exec. Dir.* Eric C. Graham.

Minuteman Library Network, 10 Strathmore Rd., Natick 01760-2419. SAN 322-4252. Tel. 508-655-8008, fax 508-655-1507. *Exec. Dir.* Susan McAlister.

National Network of Libraries of Medicine–New England Region (NN/LM-NER), Univ. of Massachusetts Medical School, 55 Lake Ave. N., Room S4-241, Worcester 01655. SAN 372-5448. Tel. 800-338-7657, fax 508-856-5977. *Dir.* Elaine Martin.

North of Boston Library Exchange, Inc. (NOBLE), 42-A Cherry Hill Drive, Danvers 01923. SAN 322-4023. Tel. 978-777-8844, fax 978-750-8472, e-mail staff@noblenet. org. *Exec. Dir.* Ronald A. Gagnon.

SAILS Library Network, 10 Riverside Dr., Suite 102, Lakeville 02347. SAN 378-0058. Tel. 508-946-8600, fax 508-946-8605, e-mail support@sailsinc.org. *Exec. Dir.* Deborah K. Conrad.

Michigan

Detroit Area Library Network (DALNET), 5150 Anthony Wayne Dr., Detroit 48202. Tel. 313-577-6789, fax 313-577-1231, info@dalnet.org. *Exec. Dir.* John E. Sterbenz, Jr.

Lakeland Library Cooperative, 4138 Three Mile Rd. N.W., Grand Rapids 49534-1134. SAN 308-132X. Tel. 616-559-5253, fax 616-559-4329. *Dir.* Carol Dawe.

The Library Network (TLN), 41365 Vincenti Ct., Novi 48375. SAN 370-596X. Tel. 248-536-3100, fax 248-536-3099. *Dir.* Steven Bowers.

Michigan Health Sciences Libraries Assn. (MHSLA), 1407 Rensen St., Suite 4, Lansing 48910. SAN 323-987X. Tel. 517-394-2774, fax 517-394-2675. *Pres.* Jill Turner.

Mideastern Michigan Library Cooperative, 503 S. Saginaw St., Suite 839, Flint 48502. SAN 346-5187. Tel. 810-232-7119, fax 810-232-6639. *Dir.* Eric Palmer.

Mid-Michigan Library League, 201 N Mitchell, Suite 302, Cadillac 49601-1835. SAN 307-9325. Tel. 231-775-3037, fax 231-775-1749. *Dir.* Sheryl L. Mase.

Midwest Collaborative for Library Services, 1407 Rensen St., Suite 1, Lansing 48910. Tel. 800-530-9019, fax 517-492-3878. *Exec. Dir.* Scott Garrison.

Southeastern Michigan League of Libraries (SEMLOL), Lawrence Technological Univ., 21000 W. Ten Mile Rd., Southfield 48075. SAN 322-4481. Tel. 810-766-4070, fax 248-204-3005. *Treas.* Gary Cocozzoli.

Southwest Michigan Library Cooperative, 401 Wix St., Ostego 49078. SAN 308-2156. Tel. 269-657-3800, e-mail aestelle@otsegoli brary.org. *Dir.* Andrea Estelle.

Suburban Library Cooperative (SLC), 44750 Delco Blvd., Sterling Heights 48313. SAN 373-9082. Tel. 586-685-5750, fax 586-685-5750. *Dir.* Tammy Turgeon.

Upper Peninsula of Michigan Health Sciences Library Consortium, c/o Marquette Health System Hospital, 580 W. College Ave., Marquette 49855. SAN 329-4803. Tel. 906-225-3429, fax 906-225-3524. *Lib. Mgr.* Janis Lubenow.

Upper Peninsula Region of Library Cooperation, Inc., 1615 Presque Isle Ave., Marquette 49855. SAN 329-5540. Tel. 906-228-7697, fax 906-228-5627. *Treas.* Suzanne Dees.

Valley Library Consortium, 3210 Davenport Ave., Saginaw 48602-3495. Tel. 989-497-0925, fax 989-497-0918. *Exec. Dir.* Randall Martin.

White Pine Library Cooperative, 429 N State St., Ste. 207, Caro 48723. Tel. 989-793-7126. *Dir.* Kate Van Auken.

Minnesota

Capital Area Library Consortium (CALCO), c/o Minnesota Dept. of Transportation, Lib. MS155, 395 John Ireland Blvd., Saint Paul 55155. SAN 374-6127. Tel. 651-296-5272, fax 651-297-2354. *Libn.* Shirley Sherkow.

Central Minnesota Libraries Exchange (CMLE), Miller Center, Room 130-D, Saint Cloud 56301-4498. SAN 322-3779. Tel. 320-308-2950, fax 320-654-5131, e-mail cmle@stcloudstate.edu. *Exec. Dir.* Mary Wilkins-Jordan.

Cooperating Libraries in Consortium (CLIC). See MNPALS.

Metronet, 1619 Dayton Ave., Suite 314, Saint Paul 55104. SAN 322-1989. Tel. 651-646-0475, fax 651-649-3169, e-mail information@metrolibraries.net. *Exec. Dir.* Ann Walker Smalley.

Metropolitan Library Service Agency (MELSA), 1619 Dayton Ave., No. 314, Saint Paul 55104-6206. SAN 371-5124. Tel. 651-645-5731, fax 651-649-3169, e-mail melsa@melsa.org. *Exec. Dir.* Ken Behringer.

MINITEX, Univ. of Minnesota–Twin Cities, 60 Wilson Library, 309 19th Ave. S., Minneapolis 55455-0439. SAN 322-1997. Tel. 612-624-4002, fax 612-624-4508. *Dir.* Valerie Horton.

Minnesota Library Information Network (MnLINK), Univ. of Minnesota–Twin Cities, Minneapolis 55455-0439. Tel. 800-462-5348, fax 612-624-4508. *Info. Specialist* Nick Banitt.

Minnesota Theological Library Assn. (MTLA), Luther Seminary Lib., 2375 Como Ave., Saint Paul 55108. SAN 322-1962. Tel. 651-641-3447. *Exec. Dir.* Sandra Oslund.

MNPALS, Minnesota State Univ. Mankato, 3022 Memorial Library, Mankato 56001.

Tel. 507-389-2000, fax 507-389-5488. *Exec. Dir.* Johnna Horton.

Northern Lights Library Network (NLLN), 1104 7th Ave. S., Box 136, Moorhead 56563. SAN 322-2004. Tel. 218-477-2934. *Exec. Dir.* Kathy Brock Enger.

Prairielands Library Exchange, 109 S. 5th St., Marshall 56258. SAN 322-2039. Tel. 507-532-9013, fax 507-532-2039, e-mail info@sammie.org. *Exec. Dir.* Shelly Grace.

Southeastern Libraries Cooperating (SELCO), 2600 19th St. N.W., Rochester 55901-0767. SAN 308-7417. Tel. 507-288-5513, fax 507-288-8697. *Exec. Dir.* Ann Hutton.

Twin Cities Biomedical Consortium (TCBC), c/o Fairview Univ. Medical Center, 2450 Riverside Ave., Minneapolis 55455. SAN 322-2055. Tel. 612-273-6595, fax 612-273-2675. *Mgr.* Colleen Olsen.

Mississippi

Central Mississippi Library Council (CMLC), c/o Millsaps College Lib., 1701 N. State St., Jackson 39210. SAN 372-8250. Tel. 601-974-1070, fax 601-974-1082. *Chair* Justin Huckaby.

Mississippi Electronic Libraries Online (MELO), Mississippi State Board for Community and Junior Colleges, Jackson 39211. Tel. 601-432-6518, fax 601-432-6363, e-mail melo@colin.edu. *Dir.* Audra Kimball.

Missouri

Health Sciences Library Network of Kansas City (HSLNKC), Univ. of Missouri–Kansas City Health Sciences Lib., 2411 Holmes St., Kansas City 64108-2792. SAN 322-2098. Tel. 816-235-1880, fax 816-235-6570. *Pres.* Cindi Kerns.

Kansas City Library Service Program (KC-LSP), 14 W. 10 St., Kansas City 64105. Tel. 816-701-3520, fax 816-701-3401, e-mail kc-lspsupport@kclibrary.org. *Lib. Systems and Service Prog. Mgr.* Melissa Carle.

Mid-America Library Alliance/Kansas City Metropolitan Library and Information Network, 15624 E. 24 Hwy., Independence 64050. SAN 322-2101. Tel. 816-521-7257, fax 816-461-0966. *Exec. Dir.* Mickey Coalwell.

Missouri Evergreen, c/o Poplar Bluff Public Library, 318 N. Main St., Poplar Bluff 63901. Tel. 573-203-4680. *Chair* Sue Szostak.

Mobius, 111 E. Broadway, Suite 220, Columbia 65203. Tel. 877-366-2487, fax 541-264-7006. *Exec. Dir.* Donna Bacon.

Saint Louis Regional Library Network, 1190 Meramec Station Rd., Suite 207, Ballwin 63021. SAN 322-2209. Tel. 800-843-8482, fax 636-529-1396, e-mail slrln@amigos.org. *Pres.* Nina O'Daniels.

Western Council of State Libraries, 1190 Meramec Station Rd., Suite 207, Ballwin 63021-6902. Tel. 972-851-8000, fax 636-529-1396.

Montana

Treasure State Academic Information and Library Services (TRAILS), Montana State Univ., P.O. Box 173320, Bozeman 59717. Tel. 406-994-4432, fax 406-994-2851. *Coord.* Pamela Benjamin.

Nebraska

ICON Library Consortium, McGoogan Lib. of Medicine, Univ. of Nebraska, Omaha 68198-6705. Tel. 402-559-7099, fax 402-559-5498. *Exec. Secy.* Cindy Perkins.

Nevada

Information Nevada, Interlibrary Loan Dept., Nevada State Lib. and Archives, 100 N. Stewart St., Carson City 89701-4285. SAN 322-2276. Tel. 775-684-3360, fax 775-684-3330. *Asst. Admin., Lib. and Development Svcs.* Tammy Westergard.

New Hampshire

Council of State Library Agencies in the Northeast (COSLINE), c/o New Hampshire State Library, 20 Park St., Concord 03301. SAN 322-0451. Tel. 603-5271-2397, fax 603-271-6826. *Pres.* Michael York.

GMILCS, Inc., 31 Mount Saint Mary's Way, Hooksett 03106. Tel. 603-485-4286, fax 603-485-4246, e-mail helpdesk@gmilcs.org. *Systems Admin.* Marilyn Borgendale.

Librarians of the Upper Valley Coop. (LUV Coop), c/o Converse Free Library, 38 Union St., Lyme 03768. SAN 371-6856. Tel. 603-795-4622. *Coord.* Judith G. Russell.

Merri-Hill-Rock Library Cooperative, c/o Sandown Public Lib., 305 Main St., P.O. Box 580, Sandown 03873. SAN 329-5338.

E-mail director@sandownlibrary.us. *Chair* Deborah Hoadley.

New Hampshire College and University Council, 3 Barrell Court, Suite 100, Concord 03301-8543. SAN 322-2322. Tel. 603-225-4199, fax 603-225-8108. *Pres.* Thomas R. Horgan.

Nubanusit Library Cooperative, c/o Frost Free Lib., 28 Jaffrey Rd., Marlborough 03455. SAN 322-4600. *Chair* Kristin Readel.

Rochester Area Librarians, c/o Milton Free Public Lib., 13 Main St., Milton Mills 03852. E-mail mfpl@metrocast.net. *Dir.* Betsy Baker.

New Jersey

Basic Health Sciences Library Network (BHSL), Overlook Hospital Health Science Lib., 99 Beauvoir Ave., Summit 07902. SAN 371-4888. Tel. 908-522-2886, fax 908-522-2274. *Coord.* Pat Regenberg.

Bergen County Cooperative Library System (BCCLS), 21-00 Route 208 S., Ste. 130, Fair Lawn 07410. Tel. 201-498-7300, fax 201-489-4215, e-mail bccls@bccls.org. *Exec. Dir.* David Hanson.

Burlington Libraries Information Consortium (BLINC), 5 Pioneer Blvd., Westampton 08060. Tel. 609-267-9660, fax 609-267-4091, e-mail hq@bcls.lib.nj.us. *Dir.* Ranjna Das.

Libraries of Middlesex Automation Consortium (LMxAC), 27 Mayfield Ave., Edison 08837. SAN 329-448X. Tel. 732-750-2525, fax 732-750-9392. *Exec. Dir.* Eileen M. Palmer.

LibraryLinkNJ, New Jersey Library Cooperative, 44 Stelton Rd., Suite 330, Piscataway 08854. SAN 371-5116. Tel. 732-752-7720, fax 732-752-7785. *Exec. Dir.* Susanne Sacchetti.

Morris Automated Information Network (MAIN), 16 Wing Dr., Suite 212, Cedar Knolls 07927. SAN 322-4058. Tel. 973-862-4606, fax 973-512-2122. *Exec. Dir.* Phillip Berg.

Morris-Union Federation, 214 Main St., Chatham 07928. SAN 310-2629. Tel. 973-635-0603, fax 973-635-7827. *Exec. Dir.* Karen Brodsky.

New Jersey Health Sciences Library Network (NJHSN), Overlook Hospital Lib., 99 Beauvoir Ave., Summit 07902. SAN 371-4829.

Tel. 908-522-2886, fax 908-522-2274. *Lib. Mgr.* Patricia Regenberg.

New Jersey Library Network, Lib. Development Bureau, 185 W. State St., Trenton 08608. SAN 372-8161. Tel. 609-278-2640 ext. 152, fax 609-278-2650. *Admin.* Ruth Pallante.

Virtual Academic Library Environment (VALE), NJEdge/NJIT, 218 Central Ave., GITC 3902, Newark 07102-1982. Tel. 855-832-3343. *Prog. Mgr.* Melissa Lena.

New Mexico

Estacado Library Information Network (ELIN), 509 N. Shipp, Hobbs 88240. Tel. 505-397-9328, fax 505-397-1508.

New Mexico Consortium of Academic Libraries, c/o Donnelly Library, 802 National Ave., Las Vegas. SAN 371-6872. *Pres.* Poppy Johnson-Renval.

New York

Academic Libraries of Brooklyn, Long Island Univ. Lib. LLC 517, One University Plaza, Brooklyn 11201. SAN 322-2411. Tel. 718-488-1081, fax 718-780-4057. *Dir.* Ingrid Wang.

Associated Colleges of the Saint Lawrence Valley, SUNY Potsdam, 288 Van Housen Extension, Potsdam 13676-2299. SAN 322-242X. Tel. 315-267-3331, fax 315-267-2389. *Admin. Coord.* Ben Dixon.

Brooklyn–Queens–Staten Island–Manhattan–Bronx Health Sciences Libns. (BQSIMB), 150 55th St., Brooklyn 11220. Tel. 718-630-7200, fax 718-630-8918. *Pres.* Sheryl Ramer Gesoff.

Capital District Library Council (CDLC), 28 Essex St., Albany 12206. SAN 322-2446. Tel. 518-438-2500, fax 518-438-2872. *Exec. Dir.* Kathleen Gundrum.

Central New York Library Resources Council (CLRC), 5710 Commons Park Dr., East Syracuse 13057. SAN 322-2454. Tel. 315-446-5446, fax 315-446-5590. *Exec. Dir.* Marc Wildman.

CONNECTNY, Inc., 6721 U.S. Highway 11, Potsdam 13676. Tel. 716-930-7752. *Exec. Dir.* Pamela Jones.

Library Assn. of Rockland County (LARC), P.O. Box 917, New City 10956-0917. Tel. 845-359-3877, e-mail president@rocklandlibraries.com.

Library Consortium of Health Institutions in Buffalo (LCHIB), Abbott Hall, SUNY at Buffalo, 3435 Main St., Buffalo 14214. SAN 329-367X. Tel. 716-829-3900 ext. 143, fax 716-829-2211, e-mail hubnet@buffalo.edu; ulb-lchib@buffalo.edu. *Exec. Dir.* Martin E. Mutka.

Long Island Library Resources Council (LILRC), 627 N. Sunrise Service Rd., Bellport 11713. SAN 322-2489. Tel. 631-675-1570. *Dir.* Tim Spindler.

Medical and Scientific Libraries of Long Island (MEDLI), c/o Palmer School of Lib. and Info. Science, Brookville 11548. SAN 322-4309. Tel. 516-299-2866, fax 516-299-4168. *Pres.* Claire Joseph.

Metropolitan New York Library Council (METRO), 599 Eleventh Ave., 8th Fl., New York 10036. SAN 322-2500. Tel. 212-228-2320, fax 212-228-2598, e-mail info@metro.org. *Exec. Dir.* Nate Hill.

New England Law Library Consortium (NELLCO), 756 Madison Ave., Suite 102, Albany 12208. SAN 322-4244. Tel. 518-694-3025, fax 518-694-3027. *Exec. Dir.* Corie Dugas.

Northeast Foreign Law Libraries Cooperative Group, c/o Fordham University School of Law, 5th Flr., 150 W 62nd St., New York 10023. Tel. 212-636-6913. *Librn.* Janet Kearney.

Northern New York Library Network, 6721 U.S. Hwy. 11, Potsdam 13676. SAN 322-2527. Tel. 315-265-1119, fax 315-265-1881, e-mail info@nnyln.org. *Exec. Dir.* Meg Backus.

Rochester Regional Library Council, 3445 Winton Pl., Ste. 204, Rochester 14623. SAN 322-2535. Tel. 585-223-7570, fax 585-223-7712, e-mail rrlc@rrlc.org. *Exec. Dir.* Laura Ousterhout.

South Central Regional Library Council, 108 N. Cayuga St., Clinton Hall, 3rd Floor, Ithaca 14850. SAN 322-2543. Tel. 607-273-9106, fax 607-272-0740, e-mail scrlc@scrlc.org. *Exec. Dir.* Mary-Carol Lindbloom.

Southeastern New York Library Resources Council (SENYLRC), 21 S. Elting Corners Rd., Highland 12528-2805. SAN 322-2551. Tel. 845-883-9065, fax 845-883-9483. *Exec. Dir.* Tessa Killian.

SUNYConnect, Office of Lib. and Info. Services, Office of Library & Information Services, SUNY Administration Plaza, 353 Broadway, Albany 12246. Tel. 518-443-5577, fax 518-443-5358. *Asst. Provost for Lib. and Info. Svcs.* Carey Hatch.

United Nations System Electronic Information Acquisitions Consortium (UNSEIAC), c/o United Nations Lib., New York 10017. SAN 377-855X. Tel. 212-963-3000, fax 212-963-2608, e-mail unseiac@un.org. *Coord.* Amy Herridge.

Westchester Academic Library Directors Organization (WALDO), 118 N. Bedford Rd., Ste 100, Mount Kisco 10549. Fax 914-729-1966. *Pres.* Maureen Clements.

Western New York Library Resources Council, 4950 Genesee St., Buffalo 14225. SAN 322-2578. Tel. 716-633-0705, fax 716-633-1736. *Exec. Dir.* Sheryl Knab.

North Carolina

Carolina Consortium, Walter Clinton Jackson Library, 320 College Avenue, Rm. 224G, Greensboro 27412-0001. Tel. 336-256-1216, e-mail bucknall@uncg.edu. *Chief Negotiator* Tim Bucknall.

North Carolina Community College System, 200 W. Jones St., Raleigh 27603-1379. SAN 322-2594. Tel. 919-807-7100, fax 919-807-7165. *Pres.* Peter Hans.

Northwest AHEC Library at Hickory, Catawba Medical Ctr., 810 Fairgrove Church Rd., Hickory 28602. SAN 322-4708. Tel. 828-326-3662, fax 828-326-3484. *Dir.* Karen Lee Martinez.

Northwest AHEC Library Information Network, Wake Forest Univ. School of Medicine, Medical Center Blvd., Winston-Salem 27157-1060. SAN 322-4716. Tel. 336-713-7700, fax 336-713-7701.

Triangle Research Libraries Network, Wilson Lib., CB No. 3940, Chapel Hill 27514-8890. SAN 329-5362. Tel. 919-962-8022, fax 919-962-4452. *Exec. Dir.* Lisa Croucher.

Western North Carolina Library Network (WNCLN), c/o Appalachian State Univ., 218 College St., Boone 28608. SAN 376-7205. Tel. 828-262-2774, fax 828-262-3001. *Libn.* Ben Shirley.

North Dakota

Central Dakota Library Network, Morton Mandan Public Lib., Mandan 58554-3149.

SAN 373-1391. Tel. 701-667-5365, e-mail mortonmandanlibrary@cdln.info.

Ohio

Assn. of Christian Librarians (ACL), P.O. Box 4, Cedarville 45314. Tel. 937-766-2255, fax 937-766-5499, e-mail info@acl.org. *Pres.* Leslie Starasta.

Christian Library Consortium (CLC), c/o ACL, P.O. Box 4, Cedarville 45314. Tel. 937-766-2255, fax 937-766-5499, e-mail info@acl.org. *Coord.* Beth Purtee.

Consortium of Ohio Libraries, P.O. Box 38, Cardington 43315-1116. E-mail Info@info.cool-cat.org. *Chair* Lisa Murray.

Consortium of Popular Culture Collections in the Midwest (CPCCM), c/o Popular Culture Lib., Bowling Green 43403-0600. SAN 370-5811. Tel. 419-372-2450, fax 419-372-7996. *Head Libn.* Nancy Down.

Five Colleges of Ohio, 173 West Lorain Street, Room 208, Oberlin College, Oberlin 44074. Tel. 440-775-5500, e-mail info@ohio5.com. *Exec. Dir.* Sarah Stone.

Northeast Ohio Regional Library System (NEO-RLS), 1737 Georgetown Rd., Ste. B, Hudson 44236. SAN 322-2713. Tel. 330-655-0531, fax 330-655-0568. *Exec. Dir.* Betsy Lantz.

NORWELD (formerly Northwest Regional Library System), 181½ S. Main St., Bowling Green 43402. SAN 322-273X. Tel. 419-352-2903, fax 419-353-8310. *Exec. Dir.* Arline V. Radden.

OCLC Online Computer Library Center, Inc., 6565 Kilgour Place, Dublin 43017-3395. SAN 322-2748. Tel. 614-764-6000, fax 614-718-1017, e-mail oclc@oclc.org. *Pres. & CEO* Skip Pritchard.

Ohio Health Sciences Library Assn. (OHSLA), Medical Lib., South Pointe Hospital, Warrensville Heights 44122. Tel. 216-491-7454, fax 216-491-7650. *Pres.* Mary Pat Harnegie.

Ohio Library and Information Network (OhioLINK), 1224 Kinnear Rd., Columbus 43215. SAN 374-8014. Tel. 614-485-6722, fax 614-228-1807, e-mail info@ohiolink.edu. *Exec. Dir.* Amy Pawlowski.

Ohio Network of American History Research Centers, Ohio Historical Society Archives–Lib., Columbus 43211-2497. SAN 323-9624. Tel. 614-297-2510, fax 614-297-

2546, e-mail reference@ohiohistory.org. *Exec. Dir.* Jackie Barton.

Ohio Public Library Information Network (OPLIN), 2323 W. 5 Ave., Suite 130, Columbus 43204. Tel. 614-728-5252, fax 614-728-5256, e-mail support@oplin.org. *Exec. Dir.* Don Yarman.

OHIONET, 1500 W. Lane Ave., Columbus 43221-3975. SAN 322-2764. Tel. 614-486-2966, fax 614-486-1527. *Exec. Officer* Nancy S. Kirkpatrick.

Serving Every Ohioan Library Center, SEO, 40780 Marietta Rd., Caldwell 43724. SAN 356-4606. Tel. 740-783-5705, fax 800-446-4804. *Dir.* John Stewart.

Southeast Ohio and Neighboring Libraries (SWON), 10250 Alliance Rd., Suite 112, Cincinnati 45242. SAN 322-2675. Tel. 513-751-4422, fax 513-751-0463, e-mail info@swonlibraries.org. *Exec. Dir.* Cassondra Vick.

Southeast Regional Library System (SERLS), 252 W. 13 St., Wellston 45692. SAN 322-2756. Tel. 740-384-2103, fax 740-384-2106. *Dir.* Jay Burton.

Southwestern Ohio Council for Higher Education (SOCHE), Miami Valley Research Park, 3155 Research Blvd., Suite 204, Dayton 45420-4015. SAN 322-2659. Tel. 937-258-8890, fax 937-258-8899, e-mail soche@soche.org. *Exec. Dir.* Cassie Barlow.

Oklahoma

Mid-America Law Library Consortium (MALLCO), 800 N. Harvey Ave., Oklahoma City 73102. Tel. 405-208-5393, e-mail mallcoexecutivedirector@gmail.com. *Exec. Dir.* Susan Urban.

Oklahoma Health Sciences Library Assn. (OHSLA), HSC Bird Health Science Lib., Univ. of Oklahoma, Oklahoma City 73190. SAN 375-0051. Tel. 405-271-2285 ext. 48755, fax 405-271-3297. *Exec. Dir.* Joy Summers-Ables.

Oregon

Chemeketa Cooperative Regional Library Service, 4000 Lancaster Dr. N.E., Rm. 9/136, Salem 97305-1453. SAN 322-2837. Tel. 503-399-5165, fax 503-399-7316, e-mail contact@cclrs.org. *Dir.* John Goodyear.

Library Information Network of Clackamas County (LINCC), 1810 Red Soils Court, #110, Oregon City 97045. SAN 322-2845. Tel. 503-723-4888, fax 503-794-8238. *Lib. Network Mgr.* Kathryn Kohl.

Orbis Cascade Alliance, 2300 Oakmont Way, Eugene 97401. SAN 377-8096. Tel. 541-246-2470. *Exec. Dir.* Kim Armstrong.

Washington County Cooperative Library Services, 111 N.E. Lincoln St., MS No. 58, Hillsboro 97124-3036. SAN 322-287X. Tel. 503-846-3222, fax 503-846-3220.

Pennsylvania

Berks County Library Assn. (BCLA), c/o Berks County Public Libraries, 1040 Berks Rd., Leesport 19533. SAN 371-0866. Tel. 610-478-9035, 610-655-6350. *Pres.* Amy Resh.

Central Pennsylvania Consortium (CPC), c/o Franklin & Marshall College, Goethean Hall 101, Lancaster 17604. SAN 322-2896. Tel. 717-358-2896, fax 717-358-4455, e-mail cpc@dickinson.edu. *Exec. Asst.* Kathy Missildine.

Central Pennsylvania Health Sciences Library Assn. (CPHSLA), Office for Research Protections, Pennsylvania State Univ., 212 Kern Graduate Bldg., University Park 16802. SAN 375-5290. Fax 814-865-1775. *Pres.* Helen Houpt.

Eastern Mennonite Associated Libraries and Archives (EMALA), 2215 Millstream Rd., Lancaster 17602. SAN 372-8226. Tel. 717-393-9745, fax 717-393-8751. *Chair* John Weber.

Greater Philadelphia Law Library Assn. (GPLLA), P.O. Box 335, Philadelphia 19105. SAN 373-1375. *Pres.* Lori Strickler Corso.

HSLC/Access PA (Health Science Libraries Consortium), 3600 Market St., Suite 550, Philadelphia 19104-2646. SAN 323-9780. Tel. 215-222-1532, fax 215-222-0416, e-mail support@hslc.org. *Exec. Dir.* Maryam Phillips.

Interlibrary Delivery Service of Pennsylvania (IDS), c/o Bucks County IU, No. 22, 705 N Shady Retreat Rd., Doylestown 18901. SAN 322-2942. Tel. 215-348-2940 ext. 1625, fax 215-348-8315, e-mail ids@bucksiu.org. *Admin. Dir.* Pamela Dinan.

Keystone Library Network, 1871 Old Main Drive, Shippensburg 17257. Tel. 717-720-4088, fax 717-720-4211. *Interim Coord.* Ed Zimmerman.

Lehigh Valley Assn. of Independent Colleges, 1309 Main St., Bethlehem 18018. SAN 322-2969. Tel. 610-625-7888, fax 610-625-7891. *Exec. Dir.* Diane Dimitroff.

Montgomery County Library and Information Network Consortium (MCLINC), 301 Lafayette St., 2nd Fl., Conshohocken 19428. Tel. 610-238-0580, fax 610-238-0581, e-mail webmaster@mclinc.org. *Exec. Dir.* Sharon Moreland-Sender.

National Network of Libraries of Medicine–Middle Atlantic Region (NN/LM-MAR), Univ. of Pittsburgh, 3550 Terrace St., 200 Scaife Hall, Pittsburgh 15261. Tel. 412-684-2065, fax 412-648-1515, e-mail nnlmmar@pitt.edu. *Exec. Dir.* Renae Barger.

Partnership for Academic Library Collaboration and Innovation (PALCI; formerly Pennsylvania Academic Library Consortium), 1005 Pontiac Road, Suite 330, Drexel Hill, PA 19026. Tel. 215-567-1755. *Exec. Dir.* Jill Morris.

Pennsylvania Library Assn., 220 Cumberland Pkwy, Suite 10, Mechanicsburg 17055. Tel. 717-766-7663, fax 717-766-5440. *Exec. Dir.* Christi Buker.

Philadelphia Area Consortium of Special Collections Libraries (PACSCL), P.O. Box 22642, Philadelphia 19110-2642. Tel. 215-985-1445, fax 215-985-1446, e-mail lblanchard@pacscl.org. *Exec. Dir.* Laura Blanchard.

Southeastern Pennsylvania Theological Library Assn. (SEPTLA), c/o Biblical Seminary, 200 N. Main St., Hatfield 19440. SAN 371-0793. Tel. 215-368-5000 ext. 234. *Pres.* Patrick Milas.

State System of Higher Education Library Cooperative (SSHELCO), c/o Bailey Lib., Slippery Rock 16057. Tel. 724-738-2630, fax 724-738-2661. *Coord.* Mary Lou Sowden.

Tri-State College Library Cooperative (TCLC), c/o Rosemont College Lib., 1400 Montgomery Ave., Rosemont 19010-1699. SAN 322-3078. Tel. 610-525-0796, e-mail office@tclclibs.org. *Coord.* Mary Maguire.

Rhode Island

Library of Rhode Island Network, One Capitol Hill, Providence 02908. Tel. 401-574-9300, fax 401-574-9320. *Chief of Library Svc.* Karen Mellor.

Ocean State Libraries (OSL), 300 Centerville Rd., Suite 103S, Warwick 02886-0226. SAN 329-4560. Tel. 401-738-2200, e-mail support@oslri.net. *Exec. Dir.* Stephen Spohn.

RILINK, 317 Market St., Warren 02885. SAN 371-6821. Tel. 401-245-4998. *Exec. Dir.* Dorothy Frechette.

South Carolina

Partnership Among South Carolina Academic Libraries (PASCAL), 1122 Lady Street, Suite 300, Columbia 29201. Tel. 803-734-0900, fax 803-734-0901. *Exec. Dir.* Rick Moul.

South Carolina AHEC, c/o Medical University of South Carolina, 1 South Park Circle, Suite 203, Charleston 29407. SAN 329-3998. Tel. 843-792-4431, fax 843-792-4430. *Exec. Dir.* David Garr.

Tennessee

Knoxville Area Health Sciences Library Consortium (KAHSLC), Univ. of Tennessee Preston Medical Lib., 1924 Alcoa Hwy., Knoxville 37920. SAN 371-0556. Tel. 865-305-9525, fax 865-305-9527. *Pres.* Cynthia Vaughn.

Tennessee Health Science Library Assn. (THeSLA), Holston Valley Medical Center Health Sciences Lib., 130 W. Ravine Rd., Kingsport 37660. SAN 371-0726. Tel. 423-224-6870, fax 423-224-6014. *Pres.* Sandy Oelschlegel.

Tenn Share, P.O. Box 331871, Nashville 37203-7517. Tel. 615-669-8670, e-mail execdir@tenn-share.org. *Exec. Dir.* Jenifer Grady.

Texas

Abilene Library Consortium, 3305 N. 3 St., Suite 301, Abilene 79603. SAN 322-4694. Tel. 325-672-7081, fax 325-672-7082. *Exec. Dir.* Edward J. Smith.

Amigos Library Services, Inc., 4901 LBJ Freeway, Suite 150, Dallas 75244-6179. SAN 322-3191. Tel. 972-851-8000, fax 972-991-6061, e-mail amigos@amigos.org. *Chief Prog. Officer* Tracy Byerly.

Council of Research and Academic Libraries (CORAL), P.O. Box 6733, San Antonio

78212. SAN 322-3213. Tel. 210-710-4475. *Pres.* Michelea Mason.

Del Norte Biosciences Library Consortium, El Paso Community College, El Paso 79998. SAN 322-3302. Tel. 915-831-4149, fax 915-831-4639. *Coord.* Becky Perales.

Harrington Library Consortium, 413 E. 4 Ave., Amarillo 79101. SAN 329-546X. Tel. 806-378-6037, fax 806-378-6038. *Dir.* Amanda Barrera.

Health Libraries Information Network (Health LINE), 3500 Camp Bowie Blvd. LIB-222, Fort Worth 76107-2699. SAN 322-3299. E-mail dfwhealthline@gmail.com. *Pres.* Michele Whitehead.

National Network of Libraries of Medicine–South Central Region (NN LM-SCR), c/o UNT Health Science Center, Gibson D. Lewis Library, Room 310, 3500 Camp Bowie Blvd., Fort Worth 76107. SAN 322-3353. Tel. 713-799-7880, fax 713-790-7030, e-mail nnlm-scr@exch.library.tmc.edu. *Dir.* Brian Leaf.

South Central Academic Medical Libraries Consortium (SCAMeL), c/o Lewis Lib.-UNTHSC, 3500 Camp Bowie Blvd., Fort Worth 76107. SAN 372-8269. Tel. 817-735-2380, fax 817-735-5158. *Chair* Kelly Gonzalez.

Texas Council of Academic Libraries (TCAL), VC/UHV Lib., 2602 N. Ben Jordan, Victoria 77901. SAN 322-337X. Tel. 361-570-4150, fax 361-570-4155. *Chair* Cate Rudowsky.

TEXSHARE—Texas State Library and Archives Commission, 1201 Brazos St., Austin 78701. Tel. 512-463-5455, fax 512-936-2306, e-mail texshare@tsl.texas.gov. *Dir. and State Libn.* Mark Smith.

Utah

National Network of Libraries of Medicine–MidContinental Region (NN/LM-MCR), Spencer S. Eccles Health Sciences Lib., Univ. of Utah, Salt Lake City 84112-5890. SAN 322-225X. Tel. 801-587-3650, fax 801-581-3632. *Dir.* Catherine Soehner.

Utah Academic Library Consortium (UALC), Univ. of Utah, Salt Lake City 84112. SAN 322-3418. Tel. 801-581-7701, 801-581-3852, fax 801-585-7185, e-mail UALCmail@library.utah.edu. *Chair* Wendy Holliday.

Vermont

Catamount Library Network, 43 Main St., Springfield 05156. *Mailing Address:* Ten Court St., Rutland 05701-4058. *Pres.* Amy Howlett.

Collaborative Libraries of Vermont, Vermont Dept. of Libraries, 60 Washington St., Ste. 2, Barre 05641. Tel. 802-636-0040. *Ref. Libn.* April Shaw.

Virginia

American Indian Higher Education Consortium (AIHEC), 121 Oronoco St., Alexandria 22314. SAN 329-4056. Tel. 703-838-0400, fax 703-838-0388, e-mail info@aihec.org. *Pres. & CEO* Carrie Billy.

Lynchburg Information Online Network (LION), 2315 Memorial Ave., Lynchburg 24503. SAN 374-6097. Tel. 434-381-6311, fax 434-381-6173. *Systems Admin.* Lisa Broughman.

Richmond Academic Library Consortium (RALC), James Branch Cabell Lib., Virginia Commonwealth Univ., 901 Park Ave., Richmond 23284. SAN 322-3469. Tel. 804-828-1110, fax 804-828-1105. *Pres.* Christopher Richardson.

Southwestern Virginia Health Information Librarians, Sentara RMH Virginia Funkhouser Health Sciences Library, 2010 Health Campus Dr., Harrisonburg 22801. SAN 323-9527. Tel. 540-689-1772, fax 540-689-1770, e-mail mdkhamph@sentara.com. *Libn.* Megan Khamphavong.

Virginia Independent College and University Library Assn., c/o Elizabeth G. McClenney, Roanoke College—Fintel Library, 220 High St., Salem 24153. SAN 374-6089. Tel. 540-375-2508. *Chair* Elizabeth G. McClenney.

Virginia Tidewater Consortium for Higher Education (VTC), 4900 Powhatan Ave., Norfolk 23529. SAN 329-5486. Tel. 757-683-3183, fax 757-683-4515, e-mail lgdotolo@aol.com. *Pres.* Lawrence G. Dotolo.

Virginia's Academic Library Consortium (VIVA). George Mason University, 4400 University Dr., Fenwick 5100, Fairfax 22030. Tel. 703-993-4652, fax 703-993-4662. *Dir.* Anne Osterman.

Washington

Assn. for Rural and Small Libraries, P.O. Box 33731, Seattle 98133. Tel. 206-453-3579. *Exec. Dir.* Kate Laughlin.

National Network of Libraries of Medicine–Pacific Northwest Region (NN/LM-PNR), T-344 Health Sciences Bldg., Univ. of Washington, Seattle 98195. SAN 322-3485. Tel. 206-543-8262, fax 206-543-2469, e-mail nnlm@u.washington.edu. *Assoc. Dir.* Catherine Burroughs.

Washington Community & Technical College Library Consortium (WACTCLC), c/o Big Ben Community College, 7662 Chanute St. NE, Moses Lake 98837. Tel. 509-760-4474. *Mgr.* Wade Guidry.

West Virginia

Mid-Atlantic Law Library Cooperative (MALLCO), College of Law Lib., West Virginia Univ., Morgantown 26506-6135. SAN 371-0645. Tel. 304-293-7641, fax 304-293-6020. *Lib. Dir.* Lynn Maxwell.

Wisconsin

Fox River Valley Area Library Consortium (FRVALC), c/o Polk Lib., Univ. of Wisconsin–Oshkosh, 800 Algona Blvd., Oshkosh 54901. SAN 322-3531. Tel. 920-424-3348, 920-424-4333, fax 920-424-2175. *Coord.* Holly Egebo.

NorthEast Wisconsin Intertype Libraries, Inc. (NEWIL), c/o Nicolet Federated Library System, 1595 Allouez Ave. Suite 4, Green Bay 54311. SAN 322-3574. Tel. 920-448-4410, fax 920-448-4420. *Coord.* Jamie Matczak.

Southeastern Wisconsin Health Science Library Consortium, Veterans Admin. Center Medical Lib., Milwaukee 53295. SAN 322-3582. Tel. 414-384-2000 ext. 42342, fax 414-382-5334. *Coord.* Kathy Strube.

Southeastern Wisconsin Information Technology Exchange, Inc. (SWITCH), 6801 North Yates Rd., Milwaukee 53217. Tel. 414-382-6710. *Coord.* Jennifer Schmidt.

Wisconsin Library Services (WILS), 1360 Regent St., No. 121, Madison 53715-1255. Tel. 608-216-8399, e-mail information@wils.org. *Dir.* Stef Morrill.

Wisconsin Public Library Consortium (WPLC), c/o WILS, 1360 Regent St., No. 121, Madison 53715-1255. Tel. 608-216-

8399, e-mail information@wils.org. *Dir.* Stef Morrill.

Wisconsin Valley Library Service (WVLS), 300 N. 1 St., Wausau 54403. SAN 371-3911. Tel. 715-261-7250, fax 715-261-7259. *Dir.* Marla Rae Sepnafski.

WISPALS Library Consortium, c/o Gateway Technical College, 3520 30th Ave., Kenosha 53144-1690. Tel. 262-564-2602, fax 262-564-2787. *Chair* Scott Vrieze.

Wyoming

WYLD Network, c/o Wyoming State Lib., 2800 Central Ave., Cheyenne 82002-0060. SAN 371-0661. Tel. 307-777-6333, e-mail support@wyldnetwork.com. *State Libn.* Jamie Marcus.

Canada

Alberta

The Alberta Library (TAL), 623 Seven Sir Winston Churchill Sq. N.W., Edmonton T5J 2V5. Tel. 780-414-0805, fax 780-414-0806, e-mail admin@thealbertalibrary.ab.ca. *CEO* Grant Chaney.

Council of Prairie and Pacific University Libraries (COPPUL), c/o High Density Library, University of Calgary, 150 B – 11711 85th St. N.W., Calgary T3R 1J3. Tel. 403-220-2414. *Exec. Dir.* Vivian Stieda.

NEOS Library Consortium, Cameron Lib., 5th Fl., Edmonton T6G 2J8. Tel. 780-492-0075, fax 780-492-8302. *Mgr.* Anne Carr-Wiggin.

British Columbia

British Columbia Electronic Library Network (BCELN), WAC Bennett Lib., 7th Fl., Simon Fraser Univ., Burnaby V5A 1S6. Tel. 778-782-7003, fax 778-782-3023, e-mail office@eln.bc.ca. *Exec. Dir.* Anita Cocchia.

Center for Accessible Post-Secondary Education Resources, Langara College Library, 100 W. 49th Ave., Vancouver V5Y 2Z6. SAN 329-6970. Tel. 604-323-5639, fax 604-323-5544, e-mail caperbc@langara.bc.ca. *Dir.* Patricia Cia.

Electronic Health Library of British Columbia (e-HLbc), c/o Bennett Lib., 8888 University Dr., Burnaby V5A 1S6. Tel. 778-782-5440,

fax 778-782-3023, e-mail info@ehlbc.ca. *Exec. Dir.* Anita Cocchia.

Northwest Library Federation, 12495 Budds Rd., Prince George V2N 6K7. Tel. 250-988-1860, e-mail director@nwlf.ca. *Dir.* Anna Babluck.

Public Library InterLINK, 5489 Byrne Rd., No 158, Burnaby V5J 3J1. SAN 318-8272. Tel. 604-517-8441, fax 604-517-8410, e-mail info@interlinklibraries.ca. *Exec. Dir.* Michael Burris.

Manitoba

Manitoba Library Consortium, Inc. (MLCI), c/o Lib. Admin., Univ. of Winnipeg, 515 Portage Ave., Winnipeg R3B 2E9. SAN 372-820X. Tel. 204-786-9801, fax 204-783-8910. *Chair* Heather Brydon.

Nova Scotia

Maritimes Health Libraries Assn. (MHLA-AB-SM), W.K. Kellogg Health Sciences Lib., Halifax B3H 1X5. SAN 370-0836. Tel. 902-494-2483, fax 902-494-3750. *Libn.* Shelley McKibbon.

NOVANET, The Consortium of Nova Scotia Academic Libraries, 120 Western Pkwy., No. 202, Bedford B4B 0V2. SAN 372-4050. Tel. 902-453-2470, fax 902-453-2369, e-mail office@novanet.ca. *Mgr.* Bill Slauenwhite.

Ontario

Canadian Assn. of Research Libraries (Association des Bibliothèques de Recherche du Canada), 203-309 Cooper St., Ottawa K2P 0G5. SAN 323-9721. Tel. 613-482-9344, fax 613-562-5297, e-mail info@carl-abrc. ca. *Exec. Dir.* Susan Haigh.

Canadian Health Libraries Assn. (CHLA-AB-SC), 468 Queen St. E., LL-02, Toronto M5A 1T7. SAN 370-0720. Tel. 416-646-1600, fax 416-646-9460, e-mail info@chla-absc. ca. *Exec. Dir.* Perry Ruehlen.

Canadian Heritage Information Network, 1030 Innes Rd., Ottawa K1B 4S7. SAN 329-3076. Tel. 613-998-3721, fax 613-998-4721, e-mail pch.rcip-chin.pch@canada.ca. *Dir.* Charlie Costain.

Canadian Research Knowledge Network (CRKN), 11 Holland Ave., Suite 301, Ottawa K1Y 4S1. Tel. 613-907-7040, fax 866-903-9094. *Exec. Dir.* Clare Appavoo.

Health Science Information Consortium of Toronto, c/o Gerstein Science Info. Center, Univ. of Toronto, 9 King's College Circle, Toronto M5S 1A5. SAN 370-5080. Tel. 416-978-6359, fax 416-971-2637. *Exec. Dir.* Lori Anne Oja.

Ontario Council of University Libraries (OCUL), 130 Saint George St., Toronto M5S 1A5. Tel. 416-946-0578, fax 416-978-6755. *Exec. Dir.* John Barnett.

Ontario Library Consortium (OLC), c/o Brant Public Lib., 12 William St., Paris M3L 1K7. *Pres.* Kelly Bernstein.

Perth County Information Network (PCIN), c/o Stratford Public Lib., 19 St. Andrew St., Stratford N5A 1A2. Tel. 519-271-0220, fax 519-271-3843, e-mail webmaster@pcin. on.ca. *CEO* Sam Coglin.

Toronto Health Libraries Assn. (THLA), 3409 Yonge St., Toronto M4N 2L0. SAN 323-9853. Tel. 416-485-0377, fax 416-485-6877, e-mail medinfoserv@rogers.com. *Pres.* Zack Osborne.

Woodstock Hospital Regional Library Services, Woodstock General Hospital, 310 Juliana Dr., Woodstock N4V 0A4. SAN 323-9500. Tel. 519-421-4233 ext. 2735, fax 519-421-4236. *Contact* Bailey Urso.

Quebec

Assn. des Bibliothèques de la Santé Affiliées a l'Université de Montréal (ABSAUM), c/o Health Lib., Univ. of Montreal, Montreal H3C 3J7. SAN 370-5838. Tel. 514-343-6826, fax 514-343-2350. *Dir.* Monique St-Jean.

Réseau BIBLIO de l'Ouatouais, 2295 Saint-Louis St., Gatineau, Quebec J8T 5L8. SAN 319-6526. Tel. 819-561-6008. *Exec. Gen.* Sylvie Thibault.

Saskatchewan

Consortium of Academic and Special Libraries of Saskatchewan (CASLS), Courthouse, 2425 Victoria Ave., Regina S4P 3M3. *Mailing address:* P.O. Box 5032, Regina S4P 3M3. *Chair* Melanie Hodges Neufeld.

Library and Information-Industry Associations and Organizations, U.S. and Canada

AIIM—The Association for Information and Image Management

Chair, Kramer Reeves
President and CEO, Peggy Winton
8403 Colesville Rd., Suite 1100, Silver Spring, MD 20910
800-477-2446, 301-587-8202, fax 301-587-2711, e-mail hello@aiim.org
World Wide Web http://www.aiim.org
European Office: Broomhall Business Centre, Lower Broomhall Farm, Broomhall Ln., Worcester WR5 2NT, UK
Tel. 44-1905-727600, fax 44-1905-727609, e-mail info@aiim.org

Objective

AIIM is an international authority on enterprise content management, the tools and technologies that capture, manage, store, preserve, and deliver content in support of business processes. It was founded in 1943.

Officers (2022)

Chair Kramer Reeves, Work-Relay; *V.Chair* Ron Cameron, KnowledgeLake; *Treas.* Martin Birch, ibml; *Past Chair* Dave Jones, Instinctive Solutions.

Board Members

Jason Cassidy, Rikkert Engels, Karen Hobert, Shukra Kichambare, Lorelei Chernyshov, Riley McIntosh, Chris McNulty, Julia Sweeney.

Publication

The AIIM Blog.

American Association of Law Libraries

Executive Director, Vani Ungapen
230 West Monroe St., Suite 2650, Chicago, IL 60606
312-939-4764, fax 312-431-1097, e-mail vungapen@aall.org
World Wide Web http://www.aallnet.org

Our Mission

The American Association of Law Libraries advances the profession of law librarianship and supports the professional growth of its members through leadership and advocacy in the field of legal information and information policy.

Membership

4,000 members. For law librarians and other legal information professionals of any professional sector. Dues (Indiv.) $281; (Ret.) $70; (Student) $70. Year. March–February.

Officers (2021–2022)

Pres. Diane Rodriguez; *V.P.* Elizabeth Adelman; *Secy.* Mary Jenkins; *Treas.* Cornell H. Winston; *Past Pres.* Emily Florio.

Board of Directors

Susan David Demaine, Michelle Hook Dewey, Stacy Etheredge, Emily M. Janoski-Haehlen, Kristina Neidringhaus, Jason R. Sowards.

Publications

AALL EBriefing.
AALL ENewsletter (mo.).
AALL Weekly ENewsletter.

AALL Spectrum (bi-mo.; free; digital only starting 2021).
AALL State of the Profession Report (print, digital, or print-digital bundle).
Law Library Journal (q.; digital; free).
AALL Biennial Salary Survey and Organizational Characteristics (biennial; memb. only online; print e-mail orders@aall.org).
Index to Foreign Legal Periodicals (print or online).
AALL White Papers (digital).
Guide to Fair Practices for Legal Publishers.
KnowItAALL (memb. only; digital; free).
LegalTrac.
Principles and Practices for Licensing Electronic Sources.
Universal Citation Guide.

American Indian Library Association

Executive Director, Heather Devine-Hardy (Eastern Shawnee)
E-mail hhdevine@gmail.com
World Wide Web https://ailanet.org

Objective

To improve library and information services for American Indians. Founded in 1979; affiliated with the American Library Association in 1985.

Membership

Any person, library, or other organization interested in working to improve library and information services for American Indians may become a member. Dues (Inst.) $40; (Indiv.) $20; (Student) $10.

Officers (2021–2022)

Pres. Aaron LaFromboise; *Secy.* Rhiannon Sorrell (Diné); *Treas.* Liana Juliano; *Past Pres.* Cindy Hohl; *Memb.-at-Large* Carla Davis-Castro (Chippewa-Cree), Stacy Wells, Mary Kunesh-Podein.

Publication

AILA Newsletter (bi-ann.; memb. and non-memb.: electronic; print: memb. only). *Ed.* George Gottschalk.

American Library Association

Executive Director, Tracie D. Hall
225 N. Michigan Ave, Suite 1300
Chicago, IL 60601
312-944-6780, 800-545-2433, fax 312-440-9374, e-mail ala@ala.org
World Wide Web http://www.ala.org

Objective

The objective of the American Library Association (ALA) shall be to promote library service and librarianship. The mission of ALA is to provide leadership for the development, promotion, and improvement of library and information services and the profession of librarianship in order to enhance learning and ensure access to information for all. It was founded 1876.

Membership

Memb. (Indiv.) 51,842; (Inst.) 5,189; (Corporate) 146; (Total) 57,177. Any person, library, or other organization interested in library service and librarians. Dues (Indiv.) 1st year, $75; 2nd year, $114; 3rd year and later, $150; (Trustee and Assoc. Memb.) $68; (Lib. Support Staff) $54; (Student) $40; (International Indiv.) $90; (Non-Salaried/In Transition/Retired) $54; (Inst.) $175 and up, depending on population served.

Divisions

See the separate entries that follow: American Assn. of School Libns.; Assn. for Lib. Service to Children; Assn. of College and Research Libs; Core: Leadership, Infrastructure, Futures; Public Lib. Assn.; Reference and User Services Assn.; United for Libraries; Young Adult Lib. Services Assn.

Officers (2021–2022)

Pres. Patricia "Patty" M. Wong, Santa Monica Public Library, Santa Monica, CA 90401; *Pres.-Elect* Lessa Kanani'opua Pelayo-Lozada, Palos Verdes Library District, Rolling Hills Estates, CA 90274; *Treas.* Maggie Farrell, Univ.

of Nevada–Las Vegas, Las Vegas, NV 89001; *Past Pres.* Julius C. Jefferson, Jr., Private Citizen, Washington, DC.

Board Members

Latrice Booker (2020–2023); Ana Elisa de Campos Salles (2021–2024); Sam Helmick (2021–2024); Eboni M. Henry (2019–2022); Larry Neal (2020–2023); Alexandra Rivera (2020–2023); Christina Rodriques (2021–2024); Karen G. Schneider (2019–2022).

Round Table Chairs

Ethnic and Multicultural Information Exchange (EMIERT). Deborah Dolores Allman.
Film and Media (FMRT). Benjamin Aleksandr Franz.
Games and Gaming Round Table (GameRT). Thomas Vose.
Government Documents Round Table (GODORT). Robbie Sittel.
Graphic Novel and Comics (GNCRT). Matthew Noe.
Intellectual Freedom (IFRT). Rhonda Evans.
International Relations (IRRT). Jim Neal.
Learning Round Table (LearnRT). Kim Bishop.
Library History (LHRT). Danielle M. Ponton (staff liaison).
Library Instruction (LIRT). Susan Mythen.
Library Research (LRRT). Dr. Africa S. Hands.
Library Support Staff Interests (LSSIRT). Nina Manning.
Map and Geospatial Information (MAGIRT). Min Zhang.
New Members (NMRT). Dani Brecher Cook.
Rainbow Round Table (RRT) Kathleen Breitenbach.
Retired Members (RMRT). Nancy M. Bolt.
Social Responsibilities (SRRT). Sherre L. Harrington.

Staff Organization (SORT). Danielle M. Ponton.

Sustainability. Lisa Gangemi Kropp.

Committee Chairs

Accreditation. Dr. Linda C. Smith.

ALA-Children's Book Council Joint. Dr. Nicole A. Cooke.

American Libraries Advisory. Dr. Sian Dorian Brannon.

Appointments. None listed

Awards. Andrew Mangels.

Budget Analysis and Review. Rodney E. Lippard.

Chapter Relations. Jennifer A. Alvino

Code of Conduct. Thomas Lamanna, II.

Committee on Committees. Lessa Kanani'opua Pelayo-Lozada.

Conference. Robin Kear.

Constitution and Bylaws. Aaron W. Dobbs

Council Orientation. Rhonda K. Gould.

Diversity. Kiera O'Shea Vargas.

Diversity, Literacy, and Outreach Services Advisory. Jennifer Shimada

Education. Dr. LaVerne Gray.

Election. Cathy Wolford.

Human Resource Development and Recruitment Advisory. Libby Holtmann.

Information Technology Advisory. Gina Seymour.

Information Technology Policy Advisory. James K. Teliha

Intellectual Freedom. Dr. Martin L. Garnar.

International Relations. Dr. Min Chou.

Legislation. Joseph A. Thompson, Jr.

Library Advocacy. Dr. Steven D. Yates.

Literacy. Gwendolyn N. Weaver.

Membership. Miranda Henry Bennett.

Nominations. Rebekkah Smith Aldrich.

Organization. James Neal.

Policy Monitoring. Toni Negro.

Professional Ethics. Johana Emperatriz Orellana Cabrera.

Public and Cultural Programs Advisory. Mimosa Shah.

Public Awareness. Stephanie R. Freas.

Publishing. Heather M. Campbell.

Research and Statistics. Dr. Kimberley Bugg.

Resolutions. Aaron W. Dobbs.

Rural, Native, and Tribal Libraries of All Kinds. Leslie A. Warren.

Scholarships and Study Grants. Regina M. Beard.

Status of Women in Leadership. Loida A. Garcia-Febo.

Sustainability. Rebekkah Smith Aldrich.

Training, Orientation, and Leadership Development. Dora T. Ho.

Publications

American Libraries (6 a year; memb.; organizations in U.S., Canada, and Mexico $74; elsewhere $84; single copy $7.50).

Booklist (22 a year, with digital edition access to current and past issues of *Book Links* and 24/7 access to *Booklist Online*; U.S. and Canada $169.50; foreign $188).

Library Studies, Issues and Trends report.

Library Technology Reports (8 a year, online and print $340, non-U.S. $385).

Smart Libraries Newsletter (mo., online, and print $101, non-U.S. $111)

American Library Association
American Association of School Librarians

Executive Director, Sylvia Knight Norton
225 N. Michigan Ave., Ste. 1300, Chicago, IL 60601
312-280-4382, 800-545-2433 ext. 4382, fax (312) 280-5276, e-mail snorton@ala.org
World Wide Web http://www.aasl.org, e-mail aasl@ala.org

Objective

The American Association of School Librarians (AASL) empowers leaders to transform teaching and learning. Established in 1951 as a separate division of the American Library Association, AASL understands the current realities and evolving dynamics of the professional environment and is positioned to help members achieve universal recognition of school librarians as indispensable educational leaders. AASL publishes standards for the profession—National School Library Standards for Learners, School Librarians, and School Libraries (2018, its latest)—providing a comprehensive approach through integrated frameworks consisting of four domains (Think, Create, Share, Grow) and six Shared Foundations (Inquire, Include, Collaborate, Curate, Explore, Engage).

Membership

Memb. 5,900+. Open to all school librarians, librarians, libraries, interested individuals, and business firms, with requisite membership in ALA.

Board of Directors (2021–2022)

Pres. Jennisen Lucas, Park County School District #6, District Librarian, WY; *Pres.-Elect* Kathy Lester, East Middle School, School Librarian, MI; *Treas.* Erika Long, Thurgood Marshall Middle School, School Libn., TN; *Past Pres.* Kathy Carroll, Westwood HS, Lead Lib. Media Specialist, SC; *Div. Councilor* Diane R. Chen, Stratford STEM School, School Libn.,TN; *Dirs.* Becky Calzada, Lori Donovan, Sylvia Knight Norton, Jennifer Sharp Heather Thore.

Section Leadership

AAS /ESLS. Joyce Valenza, Pamela R. Moore, Jenna Spiering, Daniella Smith.
AASL/ISS. Maegen Rose, Kate Lewallen, Bianca N. Spurlock.
AASL/SPVS. Jennifer Sturge, Jenny Takeda, Cherity Pennington, Christina Shepard Norman.
(Subcommittees may be found on section websites.)

Committee Chairs

AASL/ALSC/YALSA Joint Committee on School/Public Library Cooperation. Sylvia Knight Norton (staff liaison).
Annual Conference. Allison Cline (staff liaison).
Association of American University Presses Book Selection. Catherine Kerns.
Awards. Cynthia Zervos, Allison Cline (staff liaison).
Budget and Finance. Erika Long. Sylvia Knight Norton (staff liaison).
Bylaws and Organization. Robbie Leah Nickel.
CAEP Coordinating Committee. Mary Ann Harlan.
Knowledge Quest. Sarah Searles, Meg Featheringham.
Leadership Development. Kathy Carroll.
Legacy. Cassandra Barnett. Allison Cline (staff liaison).
Member Engagement. Allison Cline (staff liaison).
National Conference. Allison Cline (staff liaison).
Practice. Laura Hicks and Amanda Kordeliski.
Professional Learning. Buffy Edwards. Jennifer Habley (staff liaison).
Publications. Stephanie Book (staff liaison).
School Library Event Promotion Committee. Lisa Brackel.

School Library Research. Audrey Church and Elizabeth Burns.
School Librarian Preparation National Recognition. Judy T. Bevins.
Standards. Sylvia Knight Norton (SL).

Editorial Board Chairs

Knowledge Quest Editorial Board. Sarah Searles (chair). Meg Featheringham (editor).
School Library Research Editorial Board. Audrey Church and Elizabeth Burns (co-editors).

Task Force Chairs

School Librarian Preparation Program National Recognition. Judy T. Bivens.

Awards Committee Chairs

ABC-CLIO Leadership Grant. Cynthia Zervos.
Best Digital Tools for Teaching and Learning. Samuel Northern.
Chapter of the Year Award. Brittany Tignor.

Collaborative School Library Award. Stacy Brown.
Distinguished School Administrator Award. Sarah Hunicke.
Frances Henne Award. Martha Pangburn.
Innovative Reading Grant. Alexa Lalejini.
Inspire Collection Development Grant. Nicolle Mazzola.
Inspire Special Event Grant. Zandra Lopez.
Intellectual Freedom Award. Christy James.
National School Library of the Year Award. Phoebe Warmack.
Research Grant. Allison Cline (staff liaison).
Roald Dahl Miss Honey Social Justice Award. Allison Cline (staff liaison)

Publications

Knowledge Quest (bi-mo.; memb.; nonmemb. $50 per year; outside U.S. $60 per year; https://knowledgequest.aasl.org/subscription). *Ed.* Meg Featheringham. E-mail mfeatheringham@ala.org.
School Library Research (electronic, free, at http://www.ala.org/aasl/slr). *Ed.* Meg Featheringham. E-mail mfeatheringham@ala.org.

American Library Association
Association for Library Service to Children

Interim Executive Director, Alena Rivers
225 N. Michigan Ave., Suite 1300

Chicago, IL 60601
800-545-2433 ext. 2163, alsc@ala.org
World Wide Web http://www.ala.org/alsc

Objective

The Association for Library Service to Children (ALSC) develops and supports the profession of children's librarianship by enabling and encouraging its practitioners to provide the best library service to our nation's children. It was founded in 1901.

ALSC is interested in the improvement and extension of library services to children in all types of libraries. It is responsible for the evaluation and selection of book and nonbook library materials and for the improvement of techniques of library service to children from preschool through the eighth grade of junior high school age, when such materials and techniques are intended for use in more than one type of library. ALSC has specific responsibility for the following:

- Continuous study and critical review of activities assigned to the division

- Conduct of activities and carrying on of projects within its area of responsibility

- Cooperation with all units of ALA whose interests and activities have a relationship to library service to children

- Interpretation of library materials for children and of methods of using such materials with children, to parents, teachers, and other adults, and representation of librarians' concern for the production and effective use of good children's books to groups outside the profession

- Stimulation of the professional growth of its members and encouragement of participation in appropriate type-of-library divisions

- Planning and development of programs of study and research in the area of selection and use of library materials for children for the total profession

- Development, evaluation, and promotion of professional materials in its area of responsibility

Membership

Memb. 3,797. Open to anyone interested in library services to children. Dues in addition to ALA membership (Regular) $50; (Student) $20; (Nonsalaried/Ret.) $35; (Associate) $25.

Address correspondence to the ALSC Office, http://www.ala.org/alsc/aboutalsc/contact.

Officers (2021–2022)

Pres. Lucia Martinez Gonzalez; *V.P./Pres.-Elect.* Amy Koester, Skokie Public Library, IL; *Past Pres.* Kirby McCurtis. E-mail kirbyalsc@gmail.com; *Div. Councilor* Kimberly Anne Patton; *Fiscal Officer* Amber Lea Creger.

Board Members

Ariana Augustine Sani Hussain (2020–2023), Maggie Jacobs (2019–2022), April Mazza (2019–2022), Sada Mozer (2021–2024), Tori Ann A. Ogawa (2021–2024), Georgina M. Rivas-Martinez (2021–2024), Soraya Anne-Machel Silverman-Montano (2020–2023), Ms. Meredith C. Steiner (2020–2023), Alena Rivers (ex officio, 2021–2022).

Committee Chairs

AASL/ALSC/YALSA Interdivisional Committee on School/Public Library Cooperation. Ms. Jodi Silverman.
BIOPC (Black, Indigenous and/or People of Color) Discussion Group. Alia R. Jones, Hanna Lee.

Budget. Robin Ellis Friedman.

Children and Libraries Editorial Advisory. Amalia Elizabeth Butler and Jennifer Knight.

Children and Technology. Manuela Victoria Aronofsky and Tina L. Bartholoma.

Children's Collections Management Discussion Group. Kay M. Weisman (consultant).

Children's Literature Lecture Award. Debra S. Gold.

Early Childhood Programs and Services. Josephine G. Caisse and Darla R. Salva Cruz.

Early and Family Literacy. Ruth Guerrierpierre and Joanna Ward.

Education. Edith Campbell and Casey O'Leary.

Excellence for Early Learning Digital Media. Heather Love Beverley.

Intellectual Freedom. Dr. Allison G. Kaplan and Andrew Medlar.

Library Service to Underserved Children and Their Caregivers. Jaime Lee Eastman and Melody T. Leung

Managing Children's Services. Michael A. Rogalla and Kristin Kelly Williamson.

Membership. Amy Seto Forrester and Allison M. Knight.

Nominating and Leadership Development–2023. Anna Taylor and Sophia Kenney.

Notable Children's Books. Madeline C. Tyner.

Notable Children's Digital Media. Melanie A. Lyttle and Brittany A. Tavernaro.

Notable Children's Recordings. Jessica Gillis.

Organizational Effectiveness. Jenna Friebel and Michelle Ng.

Preschool Services Discussion Group. Lisa Gangemi Kropp.

Program Coordinating. Ericka Brunson-Rochette and Tara Phethean.

Public Awareness and Advocacy. Cassie Chenoweth and Ana-Elba Pavon.

Quicklists Consulting. Ms. Kit Ballenger and Destinee Renee Sutton.

School-Age Programs and Services. Sierra McKenzie and Stephanie C. Prato.

Storytelling Discussion Group. Kay M. Weisman (consultant).

Task Force Chairs

Diversifying Revenue Streams Task Force. Nina Lindsay.

Equity, Diversity, and Inclusion (EDI) within ALSC Implementation. Danielle Jones and Sophia Kenney.

National Institute Planning. Crystal Faris.

Research Agenda. Kay M. Weisman (consultant).

Summer/Out-of-School-Time Learning. Lisa Gangemi Kropp (consultant).

Awards Committee Chairs

Mildred L. Batchelder Award 2023. Barbara Scotto.

Pura Belpré Award 2023. Diane Marie Olivo-Posner.

Randolph Caldecott Award 2023. Dr. Robert Bittner.

Children's Literature Legacy Award Selection Committee–2023. Maegen Janine Rose.

Theodor Seuss Geisel Award 2023. Julie Ann Corsaro.

John Newbery Award 2023. Christina Vortia.

Odyssey Award 2023. Lynda Salem Poling.

Professional Recognition and Scholarships. Rachel Fryd and Brooke E. Newberry.

Programs and Services Recognition. Erin Lovelace and Stephanie Luyt.

Robert F. Sibert Informational Book Award 2023. Elisa Gall.

Excellence for Early Learning Digital Media. Heather Love Beverley.

Award Manual Revision Working Group. Caitlin D. Jacobson and Carol K. Phillips.

Publications

ALSC Matters! (q., electronic; open access).

Children and Libraries: The Journal of the Association for Library Service to Children (q.; print and online; memb.; nonmemb. $50; intl. $60).

American Library Association
Association of College and Research Libraries

Executive Director, Robert Jay Malone
225 N. Michigan Ave, Suite 1300, Chicago, IL 60601
312-280-2523, 800-545-2433 ext. 2523, fax 312-280-2520, e-mail acrl@ala.org
World Wide Web http://www.ala.org/acrl

Objective

The Association of College and Research Libraries (ACRL) is a forum for and an advocate of academic and research librarians and library personnel. The object of ACRL is to provide leadership for the development, promotion, and improvement of academic and research library resources and services and to advance learning, research, and scholarly communication. It was founded 1940.

Membership

Memb. 9,108. For information on dues, see ALA entry.

Officers (2021–2022)

Pres. Julie Ann Garrison, Western Michigan University; *Pres.-Elect* Erin L. Ellis, Indiana University; Budget and Fin. Chair Carolyn Henderson Allen, University of Arkansas Libraries; *Div. Councilor* Jacquelyn A. Bryant, Community College of Philadelphia; *Past Pres.* Jon E. Cawthorne, Wayne State University Library System.

Board of Directors

Toni Anaya (2020–2024), Jessica Brangiel (2020–2024), Faye Chadwell (2018–2022), Kim Copenhaver (2019–2023), April D. Cunningham (2018–2022), Cinthya Ippoliti (2019–2023), Mary Mallery (2021–2025), Yasmeen L. Shorish (2021–2025), Robert (Jay) Malone (ex officio).

Committee Chairs

ACRL Coordinating. John P. Culshaw.

ACRL Contributed Papers. Dr. Erla P. Heyns and Howard C. Marks.
ACRL Experience and Inclusion. Emily Daly and Katelyn Quirin Manwiller.
ACRL Invited Presentations. Federico Martinez-Garcia, Jr. and Lisa M. Stillwell.
ACRL Keynote Speakers. Heidi Steiner Burkhardt and Alexia Hudson-Ward.
ACRL Lightning Talks. Brett Cloyd and Orlando Duffus.
ACRL Local Arrangements. Carrie Donovan and Martha Cheatham Yancey.
ACRL Panel Sessions. Bethann Zani Rea and Constance M. Wade.
ACRL Poster Sessions. Angie Cox and Alyssa Koclanes.
ACRL Roundtable Discussions Committee. Sarah Bankston and Caroline Fuchs.
ACRL Scholarships. Willie Miller and Rita Marie Suarez.
ACRL Virtual Conference. Rachel Besara and Michelle Demeter.
ACRL Workshops. Matthew P. Ciszek and Christine E. Woods.
ACRL/CORE Interdivisional Academic Library Facilities Survey. Dr. Anne Marie Casey and Eric A. Kidwell.
Appointments. Kara M. Whatley.
Budget and Finance. Carolyn Henderson Allen.
Communities of Practice Assembly. Ms. Tahirah Z. Akbar-Williams.
Equity, Diversity, and Inclusion. Maisha Duncan Carey.
External Liaisons. Christine Ruotolo.
Government Relations. Dr. Erik Nordberg.
Immersion Program. Nicole Pagowsky.
Information Literacy Frameworks and Standards. Wayne Bivens-Tatum.
Dr. E.J. Josey Spectrum Scholar Mentor. Dr. K.T.L. Vaughan.
Leadership Recruitment and Nomination. Rachel M. Minkin.
Liaisons Assembly. Kathleen H. Flynn.
Membership. Russell S. Michalak.

New Roles and Changing Landscapes. Marilyn Myers.

President's Program Planning. Erin L. Ellis (board liaison).

Professional Development. Jodie Borgerding

Professional Values. Lisa Lee Broughman.

Publications Coordinating. Jennifer A. Maddox Abbott.

Research Planning and Review. Dr. Alex McAllister.

Research and Scholarly Environment. Sandra Enimil.

Section Membership. Ilka Datig.

Standards. Elizabeth A. Burns.

Student Learning and Information Literacy. Meg Meiman.

Value of Academic Libraries. Dr. Rebecca Croxton.

Editorial Board Chairs

Academic Library Trends and Statistics Survey. Devin Savage.

ACRL/CORE Interdivisional Academic Library Facilities Survey. Anne Marie Casey, Eric A. Kidwell.

Choice. Diane G. Klare.

C&RL. Wendi Arant Kaspar.

C&RL News. Dr. Leo S. Lo.

New Publications Advisory. Courtney Greene McDonald.

Project Outcome for Academic Libraries. Jennifer Arnold.

Publications in Librarianship. Dr. Mark E. Shelton.

RBM: A Journal of Rare Books, Manuscripts, and Cultural Heritage. Dr. Richard Saunders.

Resources for College Libraries. Tammera M. Race.

Task Force Chairs

ACRL/ALA/ARL IPEDS Advisory. Adrian K. Ho and Erik Mitchell.

Awards. Kara Malenfant (staff liaison).

Diversity Alliance. Dr. José A. Aguiñaga and Annie Belanger.

Member Accommodation/Compensation Janice D. Welburn.

National Survey of Student Engagement (NSSE) Information Literacy Module Review. Merinda Kaye Hensley.

Nominations and Policies Audit. Matthew Weirick Johnson.

Discussion Group Conveners

Assessment. Nancy B. Turner.

Balancing Baby and Book. Laura Bornella.

Copyright. Sandra Enimil, April Hathcock.

First-Year Experience. Kimberly Shotick.

Heads of Public Services. William H. Weare, Jr.

Hip Hop Librarian Consortium. Craig E. Arthur.

Human Resources and Organizational Development. Agnes K. Bradshaw.

Language and Linguistics. Katie E. Gibson and Dan Mandeville.

Leadership. Russell S. Michalak.

Learning Commons. Diane M. Fulkerson.

Librarians from Very Small Academic Institutions. Linda Kern and Linda M. Kramer.

Librarianship in For-Profit Educational Institutions. Mary A. Snyder.

Philosophical, Religious, and Theological Studies. Frederick Charles Carey and Dr. Karen Keesing.

Scholarly Communication. Jennifer Chan and Ashley D.R. Sergiadis.

Student Retention. Nicole Helregel.

Undergraduate Librarians. Chris Davidson.

Interest Group Conveners

Academic Library Services to Graduate Students. Jessica Hagman, Matt Ogborn.

Academic Library Services to International Students. Mihoko Hosoi.

Access Services. Renise Johnson, Joanna Messer Kemmitt.

African-American Studies Librarians. Valerie Amele Tagoe.

Asian, African, and Middle Eastern Studies. Deepa Banerjee, Triveni S. Kuchi.

Contemplative Pedagogy. Madeleine Charney and Sarah Morris.

Digital Badges. Dr. Michael Gutierrez and Wendy G. Pothier.

Evidence Synthesis Methods. Dr. Zahra Premji and Sarah Young.

Health Sciences. Anna Ferri.

History Librarians. Jessica Sheara Epstein and Rebecca Ann Lloyd.

Image Resources. Jacqueline K. Fleming.
Library Marketing and Outreach. Jillian Christine Eslami and Tori Golden.
Research Assessment and Metrics. Laura Bowering Mullen.
Residency. Jessica Dai.
Technical Services. Laurie Palumbo and David A. Van Kleeck.
Universal Accessibility. Maya Hobscheid and Trisha Prevett.
Virtual Worlds. Carla Downer Pritchett and Breiana Theodore.

Awards Committee Chairs

Academic/Research Librarian of the Year Award. Adrian Morales.
Hugh C. Atkinson Memorial Award. Angela M. Gooden, Rebecca L. Mugridge.
Excellence in Academic Libraries Awards. Karen Munro.

Publications/Editorial Board Chairs

Academic Library Trends and Statistics Survey. Devin Savage.
ACRL/CORE Interdivisional Academic Library Facilities Survey. Dr. Anne Marie Casey and Eric A. Kidwell.
C&RL. Wendi Arant Kaspar.
C&RL News. Dr. Leo S. Lo.
Choice. Diane G. Klare.
New Publications Advisory Board. Courtney Greene McDonald.
Project Outcome for Academic Libraries. Jennifer Arnold.
Publications in Librarianship. Dr. Mark E. Shelton.
RBM. Dr. Richard Saunders.
Resources for College Libraries. Tammera M. Race.

Section Chairs

Anthropology and Sociology (ANSS). Triveni S. Kuchi.

Arts Section. Tiffany Bailey.
College Libraries Section (CLS). Kevin Butterfield.
Community and Junior College Libraries Section (CJCLS). Robin Brown.
Digital Scholarship Section. Elisandro Cabada.
Distance and Online Learning Section (DOLS). Samantha Harlow.
Education and Behavioral Sciences Section (EBSS). April Hines.
European Studies Section (ESS). Dr. Hélène Huet.
Instruction Section (IS). Veronica Arellano Douglas.
Literatures in English Section (LES). Glenda M. Insua.
Politics, Policy and International Relations Section (PPIRS). Chelsea Nesvig.
Rare Books and Manuscripts (RBMS). Heather M. Smedberg.
Science and Technology Section (STS). Hannah Gascho Rempel.
University Libraries Section (ULS). Jennifer Sharkey.
Women and Gender Studies Section (WGSS). Julie M. Adamo.

Publications

Choice (12 a year; $513; Canada and Mexico $551; other international $660). *Ed.* Diane G. Klare.
Choice Reviews-on-Cards (requires subscription to *Choice* or *Choice Reviews* $576; Canada and Mexico $618; other international $713).
C&RL (6 a year; open access online-only). *Ed.* Wendi Arant Kaspar.
C&RL News (11 a year; memb.; nonmemb. $58; Canada and other PUAS countries $63; other international $68). *Ed.* Dr. Leo S. Lo.
RBM: A Journal of Rare Books, Manuscripts, and Cultural Heritage (s. ann.; $52; Canada and other PUAS countries $58; other international $69). *Ed.* Richard Saunders. Southern Utah Univ., 351 W. University Blvd. Gerrald R. Sherratt Lib., Cedar City, UT 84720-2415. Tel. 435-865-7947, fax 435-865-8152, e-mail rsaunders@suu.edu.

American Library Association
CORE: Leadership, Infrastructure, Futures

Executive Director, Kerry Ward
225 N. Michigan Ave, Suite 1300, Chicago, IL 60601
800-535-2433, e-mail core@ala.org
World Wide Web http://www.ala.org/core

Vision

Core members play a central role in every library, shaping the future of the profession through community-building, advocacy, and learning.

Mission

To cultivate and amplify the collective expertise of library workers in core functions through building, advocacy, and learning.

Membership

Memb. 5,931. For information on dues, see ALA entry.

Officers (2021–2022)

Pres. Lindsay Anne Cronk; *Pres.-Elect* Margaret Heller; *Past Pres.* Christopher J. Cronin; *Div. Councilor* Jodie Gambill; *Chair of Advocacy Coord.* Kellie Barbato; *Chair of Budget* Miranda Henry Bennett.

Board of Directors

Galen Charlton (2020–2022), Tyler Dzuba (2021–2023), Ms. Hong Ma (2020–2022), Alexandra P. Rivera (executive board liaison, 2020–2022), Lori P. Robare (2020–2022), Evviva R. Weinraub Lajoie (2021–2023), Afiya Farrell (ex officio).

Committee Chairs

Advocacy Coordination. Kellie Barbato.
Appointments. Margaret Heller.
Awards and Scholarships Coordination. Maggie Dull and Gabrielle Somnee Wiersma.
Budget and Finance. Miranda Henry Bennett.
Bylaws and Organization. Kerry Ward (staff liaison).
Committee Recognizing Excellence in Children's and Young Adult Science Fiction. Elizabeth Nebeker.
Communications Coordination. Elyssa M. Gould.
Competencies Development. Nancy A. Cunningham.
Conference Program Coordination. Lacie Griffin and Richard R. Guajardo.
Content Coordination. Robin P. Sofge.
Continuing Education Coordination. Amanda A. Stone.
CORE Reading Club Facilitation. Michelle Elaine Colquitt.
Diversity and Inclusion. Amber Billey and Dr. Ashley Ruth Lierman.
Exchange Planning. Julie Reese (staff liaison).
Forum Planning. Wendy Tressler.
Fundraising and Sponsorships. Tabatha Farney.
Interest Group Coordination. Susan Martin.
International Relations. Aubrey Iglesias.
Leadership Development and Mentoring. Maurini R. Strub.
Member Engagement Coordination. Monica R. Harris.
Nominating Committee. Emily Drabinski.
Preservation Outreach Committee. Jessica Bitely.
Publications Coordination. Susan E. Thomas.
Standards. Matthew W. Wise.
Top Technology Trends. Thomas Lamanna II.

Awards Committees

ALA John Cotton Dana library Public Relations Award. Gregg Dodd.
Hugh C. Atkinson Memorial Award. Angela M. Gooden and Rebecca L. Mugridge.
Christian Larew Memorial Scholarship. David Ratledge.

CORE Margaret Mann Citation. Jessica L. Hayden.

CORE/OCLC Frederick G. Kilgour Award for Research in Library and Information Technology. Patricia M. Dragon.

CORE PR Xchange Awards. Dr. Naomi Gold and Markaaron Polger.

Editorial Boards

ITAL. Ken Varnum.
LL&M. Elizabeth Nelson.
LRTS. Mary Beth Weber.

Interest Group Chairs

Artificial Intelligence and Machine Learning in Libraries. Andromeda Yelton.

Authority Control. Melanie Polutta.

Bibliographic Conceptual Models. Thomas M. Dousa and Paloma Graciani Picardo.

Book and Paper. Carrie Beyer.

Cartographic Resources Cataloging (CORE/ MAGIRT). Amy Runyon.

Catalog Form and Function. Jim Hahn.

Catalog Management. Lauren Geiger and Peggy Griesinger.

Cataloging and Classification Research. Tim Keller and Junjiro Nakatomi.

Cataloging Norms. Elizabeth Barrera Rush.

Chief Collection Development Officers of Large Research Libraries. Mihoko Hosoi.

Collection Development Issues for the Practitioner. Russell S. Michalak.

Collection Evaluation and Assessment. Arthur Aguilera and Anne Koenig.

Collection Management in Public Libraries. Jessica Russell.

Competencies and Education for a Career in Cataloging. Robin Fay and Dr. Athena Salaba.

Consortium Management. Tracy Byerly.

Copy Cataloging. Ms. Keiko Suzuki and Rachel Turner.

Creative Ideas in Technical Services. Susan Martin and Laura A. Sill.

Dialogue with Directors. Shelly McCoy and Denise Shorey.

Digital Conversation. Faye Mazzia.

Ebooks. Michael L. Blackwell.

Electronic Resources. Christine Davidian and Kerry R. Walton.

Faceted Subject Access. Lana Soglasnova.

Heads of Library Technology. Bohyun Kim and David Schuster.

Imagineering. Athina Livanos-Propst.

Instructional Technologies. Breanne Ariel Kirsch.

Library Consulting. Valerie A. Edwards and Dr. Martha Kyrillidou.

Library Facilities and Interiors. Gili Meerovitch.

Library Leaders and Managers. Dr. Anne Cooper Moore and Dr. Erik Nordberg.

Library Storage. Jennifer A. Maddox Abbott.

Linked Data. Kevin M. Ford and Benjamin M. Riesenberg.

Maker Technology. Leanne Nay.

MARC Formats Transition. Brian Patrick Clark and Cindy Tian.

Metadata. Anne M. Washington.

Middle Managers. Jeffrey Scott Bullington and Carissa Ann Tomlinson.

Newspaper. Brian Geiger.

Open Access. Emma Molls.

Open-Source Systems. James Mitchell and Robert T. Wilson.

Preservation Administration. Mark Coulbourne and Miriam Nelson.

Project Management. Kristen Clark and Anastasia G. Guimaraes.

Promoting Preservation. Shelby Strommer.

Public Libraries Technical Services. Yu-Lan Margaret Chou and Michael P. Santangelo.

Publisher-Vendor-Library Relations. Ellen Amatangelo, Ajaye Bloomstone, and Carolyn Morris.

Role of the Professional Librarian in Technical Services. Mr. Sherab Chen and Sofia A. Slutskaya.

Solo Practitioners. Susan Kusel.

Technical Services Managers in Academic Libraries. Gregory Ferguson.

Technical Services Workflow Efficiency. Sai Deng and Mrs. Yan Liao.

WebServices4Lib. Ilana Kingsley.

Publications

Information Technologies and Libraries (4 a year). *Ed.* Ken Varnum.

Library Leadership and Management (4 a year). *Ed.* Elizabeth Nelson.

Library Resources and Technical Services (4 a year). *Ed.* Mary Beth Weber.

American Library Association
Public Library Association

Executive Director, Mary Davis Fournier
225 N. Michigan Ave., Suite 1300, Chicago, IL 60601
312-280-5752, 800-545-2433 ext. 5752, fax 312-280-5029, e-mail pla@ala.org
World Wide Web http://www.pla.org

The Public Library Association (PLA) has specific responsibility for the following:

- Conducting and sponsoring research about how the public library can respond to changing social needs and technical developments
- Developing and disseminating materials useful to public libraries in interpreting public library services and needs
- Conducting continuing education for public librarians by programming at national and regional conferences, by publications such as the newsletter, and by other delivery means
- Establishing, evaluating, and promoting goals, guidelines, and standards for public libraries
- Maintaining liaison with relevant national agencies and organizations engaged in public administration and human services, such as the National Association of Counties, the Municipal League, and the Commission on Postsecondary Education
- Maintaining liaison with other divisions and units of ALA and other library organizations, such as the Association for Library and Information Science Education and the Urban Libraries Council
- Defining the role of the public library in service to a wide range of user and potential user groups
- Promoting and interpreting the public library to a changing society through legislative programs and other appropriate means
- Identifying legislation to improve and to equalize support of public libraries

PLA enhances the development and effectiveness of public librarians and public library services. This mission positions PLA to:

- Focus its efforts on serving the needs of its members
- Address issues that affect public libraries
- Commit to quality public library services that benefit the general public

The goals of PLA are:

- Advocacy and Awareness: PLA is an essential partner in public library advocacy.
- Leadership and Transformation: PLA is the leading source for learning opportunities to advance transformation of public libraries.
- Literate Nation: PLA will be a leader and valued partner of public libraries' initiatives to create a literate nation.
- Organizational Excellence: PLA is positioned to sustain and grow its resources to advance the work of the association.

Membership

Memb. 8,800+. Open to all ALA members interested in the improvement and expansion of public library services to all ages in various types of communities.

Officers (2021–2022)

Pres. Melanie Huggins, Richland Library, Columbia, SC; *Pres.-Elect* Dr. Maria Taesil Hudson McCauley, Cambridge Public Library, Cambridge, MA; *Past Pres.* Michelle Jeske, City Librarian, Denver, CO; *Div. Councilor* Stephanie Chase, Libraries of Eastern Oregon and Consultant, Constructive Disruption, Portland, OR; *Fiscal Officer* Clara Nalli Bohrer, West Bloomfield Township Public Library, West Bloomfield, MI; *Exec. Dir.* Mary Davis Fournier, PLA/American Library Association, Chicago, IL. E-mail mfournier@ala.org (ex officio).

Board of Directors

Erica Freudenberger (2021–2024), Toby Greenwalt (2019–2022), Amita Lonial (2019–2022), Candice Wing-Yee Mack (2021–2024), Brandy A. McNeil (2020–2023), Dara Hanke Schmidt (2020–2023).

Committee Chairs

Advocacy and Strategic Partnerships. Susan Hempstead.
Annual Conference Program Subcommittee. Denise Rae Lyons.
Budget and Finance. Clara Nalli Bohrer.
Conference. Michelle M. Jeske and Carrie N. Willson.
Continuing Education Advisory Group. Erin J. Collier-Plummer.
Digital Literacy. Angela Kay Craig and Dr. Brandy A. McNeil.
Equity, Diversity, Inclusion and Social Justice. Tamara M. King and Amita Kaur Lonial.
Family Engagement. Amber Lea Creger and Rebecca Simone Shaknovich.

Leadership Development. Kent L. Oliver.
Measurement, Evaluation and Assessment. Linda Hofschire.
Membership Advisory Group. Kim DeNero-Ackroyd and Rachel Nowell.
Nominating. Ramiro S. Salazar.
Public Libraries Advisory. Douglas A. Crane.
Technology. Anastasia Diamond-Ortiz.
Web Content Working Group. Jay Dela Cruz.

Task Force Chairs

Social Worker. Debra Walsh Keane, Patrick Lloyd, and Tiffany Russell.

Publication

Public Libraries (6 a year; memb.; nonmemb. $65; Canada and Mexico $75; Int'l. $100). *Ed.* Kathleen Hughes, PLA, 50 E. Huron St., Chicago, IL 60611. E-mail khughes@ala.org.

American Library Association
Reference and User Services Association

Executive Director, Bill Ladewski
225 N. Michigan Ave, Suite 1300, Chicago, IL 60601
800-545-2433 ext. 4395, 312-280-4395, fax 312-280-5273, e-mail bladewski@ala.org or rusa@ala.org
World Wide Web http://www.ala.org/rusa

Objective

The Reference and User Services Association (RUSA) is responsible for stimulating and supporting excellence in the delivery of general library services and materials and the provision of reference and information services, collection development, readers' advisory, and resource sharing for all ages in every type of library.

The specific responsibilities of RUSA are the following:

- Conduct of activities and projects within the association's areas of responsibility
- Encouragement of the development of librarians engaged in these activities and stimulation of participation by members of appropriate type-of-library divisions
- Synthesis of the activities of all units within the American Library Association that have a bearing on the type of activities represented by the association
- Representation and interpretation of the association's activities in contacts outside the profession
- Planning and development of programs of study and research in these areas for the total profession
- Continuous study and review of the association's activities

Membership

Memb. 2,600+

Officers (2021–2022)

Pres. Christina Pryor; *Pres.-Elect* Cynthia A. Johnson; *Secy.* Jenny L. Presnell.; *Past Pres.* Courtney Greene McDonald; *Div. Councilor* Alesia M. McManus.

Board of Directors

Nanette Wargo Donohue (2021–2022), Sam Cordell Helmick (executive board liaison, (2021–2022), Sarah McHone-Chase (2021–2022), Dr. Chad J. Pearson (2021–2024), Fatima K. Perkins (2021–2022), Kathy Shields (2021–2022), Ilana Stonebraker (2020–2022), Bill Ladewski (ex officio).

Committee Chairs

Access to Information. Ninah Moore (staff liaison).
Accessibility Assembly. Lauren Sarah Kehoe.
AFL-CIO/ALA Labor. Jane Billinger and Shuntai Sykes.
Budget and Finance. Cynthia A. Johnson.
Conference Program Coordinating. Barry Trott.
Leadership Council. Christina Pryor.
Member Engagement. Jennifer Washburn.
Nominating. Elizabeth Marie German.
President's Program Planning. Ninah Moore (staff liaison).
Professional Development. Tatiana Pashkova-Balkenhol.
Professional Resources. Shatha Baydoun and Hilary M. Kraus.
Volunteer Development. Geoffrey W. Morse.

RUSA Sections

Business Reference and Services Section (BRASS). https://www.ala.org/rusa/business-reference-and-services-section-brass-committees.
Collection Development and Evaluation Section (CODES). https://www.ala.org/rusa/collection-development-and-evaluation-section-codes-committees.
Emerging Technologies Section (ETS). https://www.ala.org/rusa/emerging-technologies-section-ets-committees.
History Section (HS). https://www.ala.org/rusa/history-section-hs-committees.
Reference Services Section (RSS). https://www.ala.org/rusa/reference-services-section-rss-committees.
Sharing and Transforming Access to Resources Section (STARS). https://www.ala.org/rusa/sharing-and-transforming-access-resources-section-stars-committee.
(Subcommittees may be found on section websites.)

Awards Committee Chairs

Achievement Award. Chris Le Beau.
Andrew Carnegie Medal for Excellence in Fiction and Nonfiction. William Patrick Kelly, Jr.
Awards Coordinating Committee. Nanette Wargo Donohue.
Excellence in Reference and Adult Services Award. Chris Le Beau.
Isadore Gilbert Mudge Award. Chris Le Beau.
Gail Schlachter Memorial Research Grant. Chris Le Beau.
John Sessions Memorial Award. Ninah Moore (staff liaison).
Margaret E. Monroe Library Adult Services Award. Chris Le Beau.

Publications

Reference & User Services Quarterly (online only at http://journals.ala.org/index.php/rusq) (memb.).
RUSA Update (q., online newsletter, at http://www.rusaupdate.org).

American Library Association
United for Libraries: Association of Library Trustees, Advocates, Friends, and Foundations

Executive Director, Beth Nawalinski
600 Eagleview Blvd., Suite 300, Exton, PA 19341
800-545-2433, ext. 2161, fax 215-545-3821, e-mail bnawalinski@ala.org or united@ala.org
World Wide Web http://www.ala.org/united

Objective

United for Libraries was founded in 1890 as the American Library Trustee Association (ALTA). It was the only division of the American Library Association (ALA) dedicated to promoting and ensuring outstanding library service through educational programs that develop excellence in trusteeship and promote citizen involvement in the support of libraries. ALTA became an ALA division in 1961. In 2008 the members of ALTA voted to expand the division to more aggressively address the needs of friends of libraries and library foundations, and through a merger with Friends of Libraries USA (FOLUSA) became the Association of Library Trustees, Advocates, Friends and Foundations (ALTAFF). In 2012 members voted to add "United for Libraries" to its title.

Memb. 5,000. Open to all interested persons and organizations. Dues (prorated to match ALA membership expiration) $55; (student with ALA membership) $20.

Officers (2021–2022)

Pres. Charity Tyler, Cedar Rapids (Iowa) Public Library Foundation; *V.P./Pres.-Elect* Gordon Baker, Clayton State (Georgia) University Library; *Secy.* Kathleen McEvoy, EBSCO Information Services; *Past Pres.* David Paige, Libraries Unlimited; *Div. Councilor* Andrea Lapsley, Texas Library and Archives Foundation; *Fiscal Officer* Amandeep Kochar, Baker & Taylor.

Board of Directors

Trustees at Large Chris Chanyasulkit, Debbie Smart, Mary Soucie. *Friends at Large* Ari Brooks, Ben Carter, Patricia Hofmann, Camille McCutcheon. *Foundations at Large* Brenda Langstraat, Chicago (Illinois) Public Library Foundation; Kristi Pearson, Friends of the Hennepin County (Minnesota) Library; Marie Ciepiela, Friends of the San Francisco (California) Public Library; Lauren Trujillo, Santa Barbara (California) Public Library Foundation. *Corporate at Large* Steve Laird, Data Axle Reference Solutions; Skip Dye, Penguin Random House; Gary Kirk, Tech Logic. *Board Members at Large* Maura Deedy, Alan Fishel, Deborah Doyle, Kathy Kosinski, Mark Miller, Peter Pearson. *Lifetime Board Member* Pat Schuman.

Committee and Task Force Chairs

Awards & Honors Committee. Position Open.
Finance Committee. Position Open.
Governance Committee. Position Open.
Leadership Development Committee. Position Open.
Membership Committee. Position Open.
Nominating Committee. Position Open.
Partnership & Fundraising Committee. Position Open.
Programs Committee. Position Open.
Public Policy & Advocacy Committee. Position Open.

Publications

All Ages Welcome: Recruiting and Retaining Younger Generations for Library Boards, Friends Groups, and Foundations.
The Complete Library Trustee Handbook.
Even More Great Ideas for Libraries and Friends.
The Good, the Great, and the Unfriendly: A Librarian's Guide to Working with Friends Groups.

A Library Board's Practical Guide to Hiring Outside Experts by Christine Lind Hage, Mary Pergander, and Jean Tabor.
A Library Board's Practical Guide to Self-Evaluation by Nicholas Spillios and Sally G. Reed.

Getting Grants in Your Community by Sally Gardner Reed and Beth Nawalinski.
Making Our Voices Heard: Citizens Speak Out for Libraries by Sally Gardner Reed and Beth Nawalinski.
Proving Your Library's Value: Persuasive, Organized, and Memorable Messaging.

American Library Association
Young Adult Library Services Association

Interim Executive Director, LaMoya Burk
225 N. Michigan Ave, Chicago, IL 60601
312-280-4390, 800-545-2433 ext. 4390, fax 312-280-5276, e-mail yalsa@ala.org
World Wide Web http://www.ala.org/yalsa
YALSA blog http://yalsa.ala.org/blog, The Hub http://yalsa.ala.org/thehub
Wiki http://wikis.ala.org/yalsa, Twitter http://twitter.com/yalsa
Facebook http://www.facebook.com/YALSA

Objective

In every library in the nation, high-quality library service to young adults is provided by a staff that understands and respects the unique informational, educational, and recreational needs of teenagers. Equal access to information, services, and materials is recognized as a right, not a privilege. Young adults are actively involved in the library decision-making process. The library staff collaborates and co-operates with other youth-serving agencies to provide a holistic, community-wide network of activities and services that support healthy youth development.

To ensure that this vision becomes a reality, the Young Adult Library Services Association (YALSA) does the following:

- Advocates extensive and developmentally appropriate library and information services for young adults ages 12–18
- Promotes reading and supports the literacy movement
- Advocates the use of information and digital technologies to provide effective library service
- Supports equality of access to the full range of library materials and services, including existing and emerging information and digital technologies, for young adults

- Provides education and professional development to enable its members to serve as effective advocates for young people
- Fosters collaboration and partnerships among its individual members with the library community and other groups involved in providing library and information services to young adults
- Influences public policy by demonstrating the importance of providing library and information services that meet the unique needs and interests of young adults
- Encourages research and is in the vanguard of new thinking concerning the provision of library and information services for youth

Membership

Memb. 3,600+. Open to anyone interested in library services for and with young adults. For information on dues, see ALA entry.

Officers (2021–2022)

Pres. Kelly Czarnecki; *Pres.-Elect* Franklin Escobedo; *Div. Councilor* Elizabeth Nebeker; *Fiscal Officer* Kate Denier; *Secy.* Carrie Kausch; *Past Pres.* Amanda Barnhart.

Board of Directors

Kelsey Ford, Traci Glass, Susannah Goldstein, Dawn Kirkpatrick, Karen Lemmons, Abby Phillips, Valerie Tagoe, LaMoya N. Burks (ex officio), Elizabeth Molina (ex officio), Stacey Shapiro (ex officio), Joel Shoemaker (ex officio), Tess Wilson (ex officio).

Committee Chairs

AASL/ALSC/YALSA Committee on School and Public Library Cooperation. Jodi Silverman (YALSA).
Annual Conference Marketing and Local Arrangements. Carla Jamison (staff liaison).
Board Development. Amanda Barnhart.
Division and Membership Promotion. Jessica Hilbun Schwartz.
Education Advisory. Sarah Evans.
Executive Committee. Kelly Czarnecki.
Financial Advancement. Joel Shoemaker.
Hub Advisory Board. Stephanie Johnson.
Organization and Bylaws Committee. Tess Wilson.
Research Committee. Wendy Stephens.
Research Journal Advisory Board. Melanie Wachsmann.
Selection List Oversight Committee. Erin Durrett.
Social Media Marketing. Aimee Haslam and Christine Pyles.
Teen Civic Engagement. Melissa Malanuk.
Teens' Top Ten. Shira Pilarski.
YALS/YALSAblog Editorial Advisory. Yolanda Hood and Tess Wilson.

Task Force Chairs

Amazing Audiobooks Blogging Team. Jennifer Sutton.
Best Fiction Blogging Team. Caitlyn Seale.

CORE/YALSA Toolkit. Kathleen Barker.
Evaluating Volunteer Resources. Dora Ho.
Graphic Novel Selection Blogging Team. Kelley Blue.
Mid-Winter Marketing and Local Arrangements. Position Open.
President's Implementation. Kelly Czarnecki.
Quick Pick Blogging Team. Jordeana Kruse.
Teen Programming HQ. Position Open.
YA Symposium Planning and Marketing Task Force. Karen Lemmons.

Awards Committee Chairs

ALSC/Booklist/YALSA Odyssey Award Committee. Pat Toney (ALSC).
Alex Award Committee. Jane Gov
Book Awards Committees' Oversight Committee. Courtney Waters.
Margaret Edwards Committee. Joni Bodart.
Michael L. Printz Award. Valerie Davis.
Morris Award Committee. Candice Mack.
Nonfiction Award. B. Allison Gray.

Publications

Journal of Research on Libraries and Young Adults (q.) (online, open source, peer-reviewed). *Ed.* Denise Agosto. E-mail yalsaresearch@gmail.com.
Young Adult Library Services (*YALS*) (q.) (online only; member; nonmember $70; foreign $70). *Ed.* Yolanda Hood. E-mail: yalseditor@gmail.com.

ARMA International

CEO, Mona Buckley
312 SW Greenwich Dr, Suite 515

Lee's Summit, MO 64082
913-444-9174, 844-565-2120, fax 913-257-3855, e-mail headquarters@armaintl.org
World Wide Web https://www.arma.org

Objective

To be the driving force that enables organizations to harness the strategic power of information, empowering the community of information professionals to advance their careers, organizations, and the profession. ARMA International is committed to finding innovative ways to provide our personal and professional communities with guidance, learning, development, and opportunity. We value the open exchange of ideas, good governance, free flow of information, and thought leadership by seeking diversity, inclusivity, and equity in all its forms. The membership of ARMA International has reached a consensus that the association's most unique value to the information community is derived from the following: (1) professional standard-setting and best practice frameworks, (2) current news, events, and industry trends, (3) network of local chapters providing opportunities for in-person training and leadership development, (4) certification preparation and continuing education.

Membership

More than 6,000 in more than 30 countries besides its U.S. base. Annual dues (Professional) $175; (Assoc.) $95. Chapter dues vary.

Officers (2021–2022)

Pres. Michael Haley, Cohasset Associates. E-mail michael.haley@armaintl.org; *Pres.-Elect* Margaret Hermesmeyer, PNC Financial Services Group; *Treas.* Michael Landau, Veritas Technologies. E-mail michaelhaley.arma@ gmail.com; *Past Pres.* Jason C. Stearns, Arrayo. E-mail jason.stearns@armaintl.org.

Board of Directors

Tyrene Bada, Megan Butcher, Cindy Chmura, Melonie Jones, Ellie Kim.

Publications

Implementing the Generally Accepted Recordkeeping Principles (PDF).
inDEPTH newsletter (bi-mo. memb.).
INFORMATION: The Comprehensive Overview of the Information Profession (PDF).
Information Management (IM) (bi-mo., memb., e-magazine https://magazine.arma.org). *Ed.* Nick Inglis. Tel. 913-312-5567, e-mail nick. inglis@armaintl.org.
Records and Information Management: Fundamentals of Professional Practice, 3rd Edition (PDF).
RIM and IG Around the World (mo.).

Art Libraries Society of North America

Executive Director, Cambria Happ
4 Lan Drive, Suite 310, Westford, MA 01886
978-674-6211, 800-817-0621, fax 414-768-8001, e-mail n.short@arlisna.org
World Wide Web https://www.arlisna.org

Objective

The object of the Art Libraries Society of North America (ARLIS/NA) is to foster excellence in art librarianship and visual resources curatorship for the advancement of the visual arts. It was established 1972.

Membership

Memb. 1,000+. Dues (Business Affiliate) $250; (Introductory) $100 (two-year limit); (Indiv.) $150; (Student) $50 (three-year limit); (Ret.) $75; (Unemployed/Bridge) $50. Year. Jan. 1–Dec. 31. Membership is open to all those interested in visual librarianship, whether they be professional librarians, students, library assistants, art book publishers, art book dealers, art historians, archivists, architects, slide and photograph curators, or retired associates in these fields.

Officers (2021–2022)

Pres. Mark Pompelia, Rhode Island School of Design. Tel. 401-709-5935; *V.P./Pres.-Elect* Rebecca Price, University of Michigan. Tel. 734-647-5274; *Secy.* Sarah Carter, Indiana University; *Treas.* Douglas Litts, United States Military Academy West Point; *Past Pres.* Amy Trendler, Ball State Univ., Muncie. Tel. 765-285-5858, e-mail aetrendler@bsu.edu.

Board Members

Amy Furness, Stephanie H. Grimm, Roger Lawson, Heather Slania, Kai Alexis Smith.

Committee Chairs

Advocacy and Public Policy. Michael A. Wirtz.
Anti-Racism. Rebecca M. Price.
Awards. Suzanne Rackover.
Cataloging Advisory. William T Blueher.
Conference Planning Advisory. Mark Pompelia.
Development. Allison R. Benedetti.
Diversity and Inclusion. Alex Watkins.
Documentation. Rachel Resnik.
Finance. Matthew Gengler.
International Relations. Gabrielle Reed.
Membership. Beth Owens.
Nominating. Jon Evans.
Professional Development. Courtney A. Hunt.
Strategic Directions. Suzanne Rackover and Amy Trendler.

Editorial Board Chair

Roger Lawson.

Awards Committee Chairs

Awards Chair: Suzanne Rackover.
ARLIS/NA Applauds. Sylvia Roberts.
Distinguished Service. Katharine Keller.
Melva J. Dwyer Award. Amy Furness.
Samuel H. Kress Foundation Award for International Travel. Amy Trendler.
Research. Jeanne-Marie Musto.
Student Advancement. Gwen Mayhew.
Travel. Courtney L. Stine.
George Wittenborn Memorial Book Award. David Green and John Latour.

Publications

ARLIS/NA Multimedia & Technology Reviews (bi-mo.; memb.). *Eds.* Melanie Emerson, Gabriella Karl-Johnson, Alexandra Provo. E-mail arlisna.mtr@gmail.com.
ARLIS/NA Research and Reports.
ARLIS/NA Reviews (bi-mo.; memb.). *Eds.* Rebecca Price, e-mail rpw@umich.edu; Terrie Wilson, e-mail wilso398@msu.edu.
Art Documentation (2 a year; memb., subscription). *Ed.* Judy Dyki. E-mail jdyki@cranbrook.edu.
Miscellaneous others (request current list from headquarters).

Asian/Pacific American Librarians Association

Executive Director, Lessa Kanani'opua Pelayo-Lozada
P.O. Box 1598, San Pedro, CA, 90733
310-377-9584 x237, e-mail ed@apalaweb.org
World Wide Web http://www.apalaweb.org

Objective

To provide a forum for discussing problems and concerns of Asian/Pacific American librarians, to provide a forum for the exchange of ideas by Asian/Pacific American librarians and other librarians, to support and encourage library services to Asian/Pacific American communities, to recruit and support Asian/Pacific American librarians in the library/information science professions, to seek funding for scholarships in library/information science programs for Asian/Pacific Americans, and to provide a vehicle whereby Asian/Pacific American librarians can cooperate with other associations and organizations having similar or allied interests. It was founded in 1980, incorporated in 1981, and affiliated with the American Library Association in 1982.

Membership

Memb. approximately 300. Dues (Corporate) $250; (Inst.) $70; (Lib. Support Staff) $20; (Life) $400; (Personal) $35 (one-year limit); (Ret.) $20 (one-year limit); (Student) $15 (Unemployed) $20. Open to all librarians and information specialists of Asian/Pacific descent working in U.S. libraries and information centers and other related organizations and to others who support the goals and purposes of the association. Asian/Pacific Americans are defined as people residing in North America who self-identify as Asian/Pacific American.

Officers (2021–2022)

Pres. Ray Pun; *V.P./Pres.-Elect* Annie Pho; *Secy.* Rebecca Martin; *Treas.* Jaena Rae Cabrera; *Past Pres.* Candice (Wing-yee) Mack; *Memb.-at-Large* Tarida Anantachai (2021–2023), Cynthia Mari Orozco (2021–2023), Yen Tran (2020–2022), Anu Vedantham (2020–2022).

Committee Chairs

Constitution and Bylaws. Iliana Burgos and Rebecca Martin.
Family Literacy Focus. Amy Breslin Bartko and Sarah Nguyễn.
Finance and Fundraising. Kat Bell and Ding Yi.
Literature Awards. Helen Look, Zoë McLaughlin, and Candice Mack.
Media and Publicity. Silvia Lew and Amanda Cheung.
Membership. Maria (Pontillas) Shackles.
Mentorship. Alvina Lai and Elizabeth Joseph.
Nominating. Candice Wing-Yee Mack.
Program Planning. Regina Gong.
Scholarships and Awards. Jennifer Embree and Ayshea Khan.

Publication

APALA Newsletter (2–3 a year).

Association for Information Science and Technology

Executive Director, Lydia Middleton
673 Potomac Station Drive, Suite 155, Leesburg, VA
301-495-0900, e-mail asist@asist.org
World Wide Web http://www.asist.org

Objective

The Association for Information Science and Technology (ASIS&T) provides a forum for the discussion, publication, and critical analysis of work dealing with the design, management, and use of information, information systems, and information technology. The mission of the association is to advance research and practice in information science and technology.

Membership

Regular Memb. (Indiv.) 1,100; (Student) 500; (Student Developing) $15; Dues (Professional) $150; (Professional Developing) $25; (Early Career and Ret.) $75; (Student) $45.

Officers (2021–2022)

Pres. Naresh Agarwal, Simmons University, Boston, MA; *Pres.-Elect* Abebe Rorissa, University of Tennessee, Knoxville, TN; *Treas.* Ina Fourie, Univ. of Pretoria, Pretoria, South Africa; *Parliamentarian* Chris Cunningham, North Carolina Central University, Hattiesburg, MS; *Past Pres.* Brian Detlor, McMaster Univ., Hamilton, ON, Canada.

Board of Directors

Joan Bartlett (2021–2024), Maria Bonn (2021–2024), Jia Tina Du (2021–2024), Anna Maria Tammaro (2019–2022), Dan Wu (2020–2023).

Committee Chairs

Awards and Honors. Heidi Julien.
Budget and Finance. Ina Fourie.
Executive. Naresh Agarwal.
Governance. Michael Leach.
History. Tatjana Aparac-Jelusic.
Membership. Daniel Alemneh.
Nominations. Steve Hardin.
Professional Development. Louis Spinelli.
Publications. Keren Dali.
Research Engagement. Rebekah Willson.
Standards. Mark Needleman and Timothy Dickey.

Publication

Inside ASIS&T newsletter (bi-mo.).

Periodicals

Journal of the Association for Information Science and Technology. (JASIST) (mo.). Available with ASIS&T membership or from Wiley Blackwell.
Bulletin of the Association for Information Science and Technology (bi-mo.; memb.; online only).
Proceedings of the ASIS&T Annual Meeting. Available from ASIS&T.
Annual Review of Information Science & Technology (ARIST).

Association for Library and Information Science Education

Executive Director, Cambria Happ
4 Lan Dr., Suite 310, Westford, MA 01886
978-674-6190, e-mail office@alise.org
World Wide Web https://www.alise.org

Objective

The Association for Library and Information Science Education (ALISE) is an independent nonprofit professional association whose mission is to promote excellence in research, teaching, and service for library and information science education through leadership, collaboration, advocacy, and dissemination of research. Its enduring purpose is to promote research that informs the scholarship of teaching and learning for library and information science, enabling members to integrate research into teaching and learning. The association provides a forum in which to share ideas, discuss issues, address challenges, and shape the future of education for library and information science. Founded in 1915 as the Association of American Library Schools, it has had its present name since 1983.

Membership

Memb. 700+ in four categories: Personal, Institutional, International Affiliate Institutional, and Associate Institutional. Dues (Indiv. full-time) $155; (Emerging Professional/Part-Time/Ret.) $85; (Student) $40; (Inst. varies, based on school budget) $400–$2,900; (Inst. Int'l./Assoc.) $350. Personal membership is open to anyone with an interest in the association's objectives.

Officers (2021–2022)

Pres. Lisa O'Connor, University of North Carolina–Greensboro. E-mail lgoconno@uncg.edu; *Pres.-Elect* Rong Tang, Simmons University. E-mail rong.tang@simmons.edu; *Secy.-Treas.* Shimelis Assefa, University of Denver. E-mail Shimelis.Assefa@du.edu; *Past Pres.* Sandy Hirsh, San José State Univ. E-Mail sandy.hirsh@sjsu.edu.

Directors

Denice Adkins, Monica Colon-Aguirre, Mega Subramaniam.

Publications

Journal of Education for Library and Information Science (*JELIS*) (q.; online only; memb.; nonmemb. $139 individual subscription; $360 institutional subscription). *Eds.* John M. Budd and Denice Adkins. E-mail jeliseditor@alise.org.

Library and Information Science Education Statistical Report (ann.; electronic; memb.; nonmemb. $135).

ALISE Book Series. *Eds.* Jaya Raju and Dietmar Wolfram. E-mail jaya.raju@uct.ac.za.

Association for Rural and Small Libraries

Executive Director, Kate Laughlin
P.O. Box 33731, Seattle, WA, 98133. Tel. 206-453-3579 e-mail info@arsl.org
World Wide Web https://www.arsl.org
Twitter @RuralLibAssoc

Objective

The Association for Rural and Small Libraries (ARSL) was established in 1978 in the Department of Library Science at Clarion University of Pennsylvania as the Center for Study of Rural Librarianship.

ARSL is a network of people throughout the United States dedicated to the positive growth and development of libraries. ARSL believes in the value of rural and small libraries and strives to create resources and services that address national, state, and local priorities for libraries situated in rural communities.

Its objectives are the following:

* To organize a network of members concerned about the growth and development of useful library services in rural and small libraries

* To provide opportunities for the continuing education of members

* To provide mechanisms for members to exchange ideas and to meet on a regular basis

* To cultivate the practice of librarianship and to foster a spirit of cooperation among members of the profession, enabling them to act together for mutual goals

* To serve as a source of current information about trends, issues, and strategies

* To partner with other library and non-library groups and organizations serving rural and small library communities

* To collect and disseminate information and resources that are critical to this network

* To advocate for rural and small libraries at the local, state, and national levels

Membership

Dues (Indiv. varies, based on salary) $15–$49; (Inst.) $150; (Business) $200; (Affiliate) $150.

Officers (2022)

Pres. Bailee Hutchinson, Altus Public Library, Altus, OK; *V.P./Pres.-Elect* Jennie Garner, North Liberty Library, North Liberty, Iowa; *Secy.* Krist Obrist, Monmouth Public Library, Monmouth, OR; *Treas.* Beth Vendetti, Kingsville Public Library, Kingsville, Ohio; *COSLA Rep.* Wendy Knapp, State Library of Ohio, Columbus, OH; *Past Pres.* Kathy Zappitello, Conneaut Public Lib., Conneaut, OH. E-mail kathy.zappitello@conneaut.lib.oh.us.

Directors

Patrick Bodily, Kevin Bourque, Philip Carter, Erin Silva, Kate Laughlin (ex officio).

Committee Chairs

Advocacy. Elizabeth "Beth" Anderson and Tyler Hahn.
Conference. Erica Testani and Sulin Jones.
Continuing Education. Allie Stevens and Joy Worland.
Elections. Position Open.
Finance. Beth Vendetti.
Governance. Kristi Chadwick and John A. Clexton.
Marketing and Communications. Elektra Greer and Suzanne Macaulay.
Membership. Amy Golly and Molly Schock.
Partnership. Kelly Kreps-Depin and Johnna Schultz.
Scholarship. Amanda Bundy and Savannah Kitchens.

Association of Academic Health Sciences Libraries

Executive Director, Louise Miller
2150 N. 107 St., Suite 205, Seattle, WA 98133
206-209-5261, fax 206-367-8777, e-mail office@aahsl.org
World Wide Web https://www.aahsl.org

Objective

The Association of Academic Health Sciences Libraries (AAHSL) comprises the libraries serving the accredited U.S. and Canadian medical schools belonging to or affiliated with the Association of American Medical Colleges. Its goals are to promote excellence in academic health science libraries and to ensure that the next generation of health practitioners is trained in information-seeking skills that enhance the quality of healthcare delivery, education, and research. It was founded in 1977.

Membership

Memb. 150+. Full membership is available to nonprofit educational institutions operating a school of health sciences that has full or provisional accreditation by the Association of American Medical Colleges. Full members are represented by the chief administrative officer of the member institution's health sciences library. Associate membership (and nonvoting representation) is available to organizations having an interest in the purposes and activities of the association. For dues information, contact the association.

Officers (2021–2022)

Pres. Melissa De Santis, Strauss Health Sciences Library, University of Colorado. Tel. 303-724-2152; *Pres.-Elect* Nadine Dexter, Harriet F. Ginsburg Health Sciences Library, University of Central Florida College of Medicine. Tel. 407-266-1421; *Secy./Treas.* Tania Bardyn, Health Sciences Lib., Univ. of Washington. Tel. 206-543-0422, e-mail bardyn@uw.edu; *Past Pres.* Chris Shaffer, UCSF Lib., Univ. of California. Tel. 415-476-2336, e-mail chris.shaffer@ucsf.edu.

Board of Directors

Fatima Barnes, Kelly Gonzalez, Gabe Rios.

Committee Chairs

Assessment and Statistics. Matthew Wilcox.
Diversity, Equity and Inclusion. Bart Ragon.
Future Leadership. Terrie Wheeler.
Program and Education. Colleen Cuddy.
Scholarly Communication. Susan Kendall.

Task Force Chairs

Implementation. Amy Blevins.
Joint Legislative. Philip Walker.

Association of Christian Librarians

Executive Director, Janelle Mazelin
P.O. Box 4, Cedarville, OH 45314
937-766-2255, fax 937-766-5499, e-mail info@acl.org
World Wide Web http://www.acl.org
Facebook https://www.facebook.com/ACLibrarians
Twitter @ACLibrarians

Objective

The mission of the Association of Christian Librarians (ACL) is to strengthen libraries through professional development of evangelical librarians, scholarship, and spiritual encouragement for service in higher education. ACL is a growing community that integrates faith, ministry, and academic librarianship through development of members, services, and scholarship. It was founded 1957.

Membership

Memb. 600+ individual and 200+ institutional members. Membership is open to those who profess the Christian faith as outlined by the association's statement of faith and are employed at an institution of higher education. Associate memberships are available for nonlibrarians who both agree with ACL's statement of faith and are interested in libraries or librarianship. Dues (Indiv. 1st Year) $40; (Ret. Libn., Lib. School Student) $35; (Varies, based on income) $40–$120.

Officers

Pres. (2020–2022) Leslie Starasta, Lincoln Christian University; *V.P. (2017–2023)* Nate Farley, Univ. of Northwestern–St. Paul; *Secy. (2020–2023)* Denise Nelson, Point Loma Nazarene Univ.; *Treas. (2019–2021)* Rodney Birch, Northwest Nazarene Univ.; *Dirs.-at-Large* Andrea Abernathy *(2019–2023)*, Eric Bradley *(2020–2023)*, Sarah Davis *(2020–2023)*, Erinn Huebner *(2021–2024)*, Jeremy Labosier *(2019–2022)*, Jaime Pitt *(2021–2024)*.

Section Chairs

Bible Core. Jon Jones.
Liberal Arts. Garrett Trott.
Seminary. Craig Kubic.

Publications

The Christian Librarian. (2 a year; memb.; nonmemb. $30). *Ed.* Garrett Trott.
Christian Periodical Index (q.; electronic).
Librarian's Manual (English or Spanish; electronic or print; $40).
Library Guidelines for ABHE Colleges and Universities (memb.).

Association of Independent Information Professionals

President, Karen Klein
8550 United Plaza Blvd., Suite 1001, Baton Rouge, LA 70809
225-408-4400, e-mail office@aiip.org
World Wide Web https://aiip.org
Facebook https://www.facebook.com/officialaiip
Twitter @AIIP

Objective

Members of the Association of Independent Information Professionals (AIIP) are owners of firms providing such information-related services as online and manual research, document delivery, database design, library support, consulting, writing, and publishing.

The objectives of the association are the following:

- To advance the knowledge and understanding of the information profession
- To promote and maintain high professional and ethical standards among its members
- To encourage independent information professionals to assemble to discuss common issues
- To promote the interchange of information among independent information professionals and various organizations
- To keep the public informed of the profession and of the responsibilities of the information professional

Membership

Memb. 200+. Dues (Full) $200; (Assoc.) $200; (Student) $50; (Supporting) $500; (Ret.) $75; (Emeritus) $50.

Officers (2021–2022)

Pres. Karen Klein, Fulcrum Information Resources; *Pres. Elect* Denise Carter, DCision Consult; *Secy.* Troy Wason, Axxess Point, Inc.; *Treas.* Beth Plutchak, Beth Plutchak Consulting, LLC; *Past Pres.* Jennifer Pflaumer, Paroo.

Directors

Membership, Edward J. Ajaeb; Professional Development, Kelly Berry; Outreach, Janel Kinlaw.

Publications

"AIIP Connections" (blog).
Member Directory (ann.).
Professional papers series.

Association of Jewish Libraries

President, Kathleen Bloomfield
P.O. Box 1118, Teaneck, NJ 07666
201-371-3255, e-mail info@jewishlibraries.org
World Wide Web https://jewishlibraries.org
Facebook https://www.facebook.com/jewishlibraries
Twitter @JewishLibraries

Objective

The Association of Jewish Libraries (AJL) is an international professional organization that fosters access to information and research in all forms of media relating to all things Jewish. The association promotes Jewish literacy and scholarship and provides a community for peer support and professional development.

AJL membership is open to individuals and libraries, library workers, and library supporters. There are two divisions within AJL: RAS (Research Libraries, Archives, and Special Collections) and SSCPL (Synagogue, School Center and Public Libraries). The diverse membership includes libraries in synagogues, JCCs, day schools, yeshivot, universities, Holocaust museums, and the Library of Congress. Membership is drawn from North America and places beyond, including China, the Czech Republic, the Netherlands, Israel, Italy, South Africa, Switzerland, and the United Kingdom.

Goals

The association's goals are to:

- Maintain high professional standards for Judaica librarians and recruit qualified individuals into the profession
- Facilitate communication and exchange of information on a global scale

- Encourage quality publication in the field in all formats and media, print, digital, and so forth and to stimulate publication of high-quality children's literature
- Facilitate and encourage establishment of Judaica library collections
- Enhance information access for all through application of advanced technologies
- Publicize the organization and its activities in all relevant venues: stimulate awareness of Judaica library services among the public at large; promote recognition of Judaica librarianship within the wider library profession; and encourage recognition of Judaica library services by other organizations and related professions
- Ensure continuity of the association through sound management, financial security, effective governance, and a dedicated and active membership

AJL conducts an annual conference in the United States or Canada in late June.

Membership

Memb. 600. Year: Oct. 1–Sept. 30. Dues (Indiv.) $77; (First-year Lib. School Student) Free; (Second/third-year Lib. School Student) $36; (Ret./unemployed) $36; (Large Inst.) (Greater than 100 FTE/includes personal membership) $118; (Small Inst.) (100 or fewer FTE/ includes 1 personal membership) $90; (Corporate) $118.

Board of Directors

Pres. Kathleen Bloomfield, Seal Beach, CA 90740 e-mail kathybloomfield@gmail.com; *V.P./Pres.-Elect* Michelle Margolis; *V.P. Development* Jackie Ben-Efraim, Ostrow Lib., American Jewish Univ., 15600 Mulholland Dr., Los Angeles, CA 90077. Tel. 818-383-9672, e-mail ajladmanager@gmail.com; *V.P. Membership* Sharon Benamou, UCLA, Hebraica/Judaica and Music Catalog Librarian. E-mail benamou@library.ucla.edu; *Secy.* Eitan Kensky, Stanford Univ. E-mail kensky@stanford.edu; *Treas.* Holly Zimmerman, AARP,

601 E. St. N.W., Washington, DC 20049. E-mail hzimmerman@aarp.org; *RAS Pres.* Amalia Levi; *RAS V.P.* Anna Levia; *SSCPL Pres.* Sean Boyle; SSCPL V.P. Rebecca Levitan; *Past Pres.* Dina Herbert, National Archives and Records Admin., Alexandria, VA. E-mail dina.herbert@gmail.com; *Parliamentarian* Joy Kingsolver.

Council Members

Paula Breger, Joseph Galron, Haim Gottschalk, Rachel Leket-Mor, Andrew Lillien, Heidi Rabinowitz, Daniel Scheide, Laura Schutzman, Lisa Silverman, Sheryl Stahl, Sally Steigletz.

Committee Chairs

Accreditation. Shaindy Kurzmann.
Advertising. Jackie Ben-Efriam.
Cataloging. Neil Frau-Cortes.
Conference. Lisa Silverman.
Conference Stipends. Lenore Bell.
Endowment. Jackie Ben-Efraim and Holly Zimmerman.
Librarianship and Education. Haim Gottschalk.
Member Relations. Heidi Rabinowitz.
Public Relations. Paula Breger.
Publications. Laura Schutzman.
Strategic Planning. Sean Boyle.
Web. Sheryl Stahl.

Editorial Board Chairs

AJL News and Reviews. Sally Stieglitz.
Conference Proceedings Compiler. Elana Gensler.
Judaica Librarianship. Rachel Leket-Mor.

Awards Committee Chairs

Fanny Goldstein Merit Award. Rachel Kamin.
Groner-Wikler Scholarship. Sean Boyle.
Jewish Fiction Award. Laura Schutzman.
Reference and Bibliography Award. Anna Levia.
Student Scholarship. Tina Weiss.
Sydney Taylor Book Award. Martha Simpson.
Sydney Taylor Manuscript Award. Aileen Grossberg.

Publications

AJL Conference Proceedings.
AJL News and Reviews (q., digital; memb.).
Ed. Sally Stieglitz. Tel. 631-6751-570 ext.
2005, e-mail sstieglitz@lilrc.org.
Judaica Librarianship (annual, digital).
Ed. Rachel Leket-Mor, Arizona State Univ.
Libs. E-mail rachel.leket-mor@asu.edu.

Affiliate Liaisons

American Library Association (ALA). Emily
Bergman and Susan Kusel.
American Theological Library Association
(ATLA). Sheryl Stahl.
Association for Jewish Studies (AJS). Rachel
Greenblatt.
Catholic Library Association (CATHLA). Daniel Stuhlman.
International Liaison. Michael Young.

Association of Research Libraries

Executive Director, Mary Lee Kennedy
21 Dupont Circle N.W., Suite 800, Washington, DC 20036
202-296-2296, fax 202-872-0884, e-mail webmgr@arl.org
World Wide Web https://www.arl.org

Objective

The Association of Research Libraries (ARL)
is a nonprofit organization of 125 research libraries in Canada and the United States whose
mission is to advance research, learning, and
scholarly communication. The association fosters the open exchange of ideas and expertise;
advances diversity, equity, and inclusion; and
pursues advocacy and public policy efforts that
reflect the values of the library, scholarly, and
higher education communities. ARL forges
partnerships and catalyzes the collective efforts
of research libraries to enable knowledge creation and to achieve enduring and barrier-free
access to information.

Membership

Memb. 125. Membership is institutional. Dues:
$30,605 for 2022.

Officers

Pres. K. Matthew Dames, Edward H. Arnold
University Librarian, Univ. of Notre Dame; *V.P./
Pres.-Elect* Susan Parker, University Librarian,
University of British Columbia; *Treas.* Bob Fox,
Dean of University Libraries, University of Louisville; *Past Pres.* John Culshaw, Jack B. King
University Librarian, Univ. of Iowa.

Board of Directors

Jon E. Cawthorne, Wayne State University
(2021–2024); Trevor A. Dawes, University of
Delaware (2020–2023); Melissa Just, University of Saskatchewan (2021–2024); Joe Lucia, Temple University (2019–2022); Robert
McDonald, University of Colorado–Boulder
(2020–2023); Lisa O'Hara, University of Manitoba (2021–2024); Sarah Pritchard, Northwestern University (2019–2022); Lorelei Tanji,
University of California–Irvine (2021–2024).

Advisory Group, Task Force, and Working Group Chairs

Advocacy and Public Policy Committee. Claire
Stewart.
ARL Academy Advisory Committee. Barbara
Rockenbach.
ARL/CARL Joint Task Force on Marrakesh
Treaty Implementation. Victoria Owen.
Association Meeting Planning Task Force.
Rick Anderson.
Audit Committee. Sarah Pritchard.
Code of Conduct Committee. John Culshaw.
Digital Scholarship Institute Advisory Group.
Robert McDonald.
Diversity, Equity, and Inclusion Task Force.
Rhea Ballard-Thrower.
Fall Forum Task Force. Susan Parker.
Finance Committee. Bob Fox.

Governance Committee. Robert McDonald.

Kaleidoscope Program Selection Working Group. DeLa Dos.

Kaleidoscope Program Task Force. Ebony Magnus.

Leadership and Career Development Program Selection Working Group. DeLa Dos.

Leadership and Career Development Program Task Force. Andrea Malone.

Leadership Fellows Selection Working Group. John Ulmschneider.

Leadership Fellows Task Force. Hilary Seo.

Member Engagement and Outreach Committee. Evviva Weinraub.

Membership Committee. Joe Lucia.

Nominating Committee. John Culshaw.

Program Strategy Committee. Mary Lee Kennedy.

Research and Analytics Committee. Joe Salem.

Scholars and Scholarship Committee. Gwen Bird.

Task Force on Vision, Mission, and Guiding Principles. Susan Parker.

Publications

Annual Report (ann.)

ARL Academic Health Sciences Library Statistics (ann.).

ARL Academic Law Library Statistics (ann.).

ARL Annual Salary Survey (ann.).

ARL Statistics (ann.).

Research Library Issues (irregular).

ARL Membership

Nonuniversity Libraries

Boston Public Lib.; Center for Research Libs.; Lib. of Congress; National Agricultural Lib.; National Archives and Records Administration; National Lib. of Medicine; New York Public Lib.; Smithsonian Libs. and Archives.

University Libraries

Alabama; Albany (SUNY); Alberta; Arizona; Arizona State; Auburn; Boston College; Boston Univ.; Brigham Young; British Columbia; Brown; Buffalo (SUNY); Calgary; California–Berkeley; California–Davis; California–Irvine; California–Los Angeles; California–Riverside; California–San Diego; California–Santa Barbara; Case Western Reserve; Chicago; Cincinnati; Colorado–Boulder; Colorado State; Columbia; Connecticut; Cornell; Dartmouth; Delaware; Duke; Emory; Florida; Florida State; George Washington; Georgetown; Georgia; Georgia Inst. of Technology; Guelph; Harvard; Hawaii–Manoa; Houston; Howard; Illinois–Chicago; Illinois–Urbana-Champaign; Indiana–Bloomington; Iowa; Iowa State; Johns Hopkins; Kansas; Kent State; Kentucky; Laval; Louisiana State; Louisville; McGill; McMaster; Manitoba; Maryland; Massachusetts–Amherst; Massachusetts Inst. of Technology; Miami (Florida); Michigan; Michigan State; Minnesota; Missouri; Nebraska–Lincoln; New Mexico; New York; North Carolina–Chapel Hill; North Carolina State; Northwestern; Notre Dame; Ohio; Ohio State; Oklahoma; Oklahoma State; Oregon; Ottawa; Pennsylvania; Pennsylvania State; Pittsburgh; Princeton; Purdue; Queen's (Kingston, Ontario); Rice; Rochester; Rutgers; Saskatchewan; Simon Fraser; South Carolina; Southern California; Southern Illinois–Carbondale; Stony Brook (SUNY); Syracuse; Temple; Tennessee–Knoxville; Texas–Austin; Texas A&M; Texas State; Texas Tech; Toronto; Tulane; Utah; Vanderbilt; Virginia; Virginia Commonwealth; Virginia Tech; Washington; Washington, Saint Louis; Washington State; Waterloo; Wayne State; Western; Wisconsin–Madison; Yale; York.

Association of Vision Science Librarians

Co-Chairs Dede Rios, Heather Edmonds
World Wide Web http://www.avsl.org

Objective

To foster collective and individual acquisition and dissemination of vision science information, to improve services for all persons seeking such information, and to develop standards for libraries to which members are attached. Founded in 1968.

Membership

Memb. (Indiv.) approximately 150, (Inst.) 100+.

Leadership Team

Co-Chair Dede Rios, Rosenberg School of Optometry, Univ. of the Incarnate Word, San Antonio, TX. E-mail dmrios1@uiwtx. edu; *Co-Chair* Heather Edmonds, New England College of Optometry, Boston, MA. E-mail edmondsh@neco.edu; *Secy.* Karen Alcorn, MCPHS University, Worcester, MA. E-mail karen.alcorn@mcphs.edu; *Archivist* Gale Oren, Univ. of Michigan Kellogg Eye Ctr., John W. Henderson Lib., Ann Arbor, MI. E-mail goren@umich.edu.

Meetings

Spring and fall meetings are held each year. The annual fall meeting runs 3–4 days and is usually timed alongside the annual meeting of the American Academy of Optometry.

Atla

Executive Director, Brenda Bailey-Hainer
200 S. Wacker Dr., Suite 3100, Chicago, IL 60606
888-665-2852 or 312-454-5100; e-mail connect@atla.com
World Wide Web http://www.atla.com

Mission

The mission of Atla (formerly known as the American Theological Library Association) is to foster the study of theology and religion by enhancing the development of theological and religious libraries and librarianship.

Membership

Dues (Inst.) $100–$1,000; (Indiv. varies, based on income) $35–$181.50; (Student) $35; (Affiliates) $100.

Officers (2021–2022)

Pres. Christina Torbert. Univ. of Mississippi Libs., P.O. Box 1848, University, MS 38655. E-mail ctorbert@olemiss.edu; *V.P.* Armin Siedlecki, Pitts Theology Library, Emory University, 1531 Dickey Dr., Suite 560, Atlanta, GA 30322. E-mail asiedle@emory.edu; *Secy.* Leslie A. Engelson, University Libraries, Murray State University; *Treas.* Jérémie LeBlanc, Jean Leon Allie Library, Saint Paul University; *Past Pres.* Stephen Sweeney, Saint John Vianney Theological Seminary, 1300 South Steele St., Denver, CO 80210-2599. E-mail stephen. sweeney@archden.org.

Board of Directors

Yasmine Abou-El-Kheir, Kerrie Burn, Susan Ebertz, Leslie Michelle Spomer, Karl Stuzman, Matthew Thiesen, Kristine Veldheer, Brenda Bailey-Hainer (ex officio).

Committee Chairs

Conference. Vance Thomas.
Diversity, Equity, and Inclusion. Daniel Baek and David Kriegh.
Endowment. Pat Graham.
International Theological Librarianship Education Task Force. Kelly Campbell.
Professional Development. Patsy Yang.
Scholarly Communication and Digital Initiatives. Matt Davis.

Publications

Theological Librarianship (open access journal) http://serials.atla.com/theolib.
Theology Cataloging Bulletin (open access journal) http://serials.atla.com/tcb/index.
Atla Annual Yearbook (online open access ann. serial) http://serials.atla.com/yearbook.
Atla Newsletter (mo.; online).

Atla Proceedings (online open access ann. serial) http://serials.atla.com/proceedings.

books@Atla Open Press (online open access monographs) https://books.atla.com/atlapress.

Beta Phi Mu
(International Library and Information Studies Honor Society)

Administrative Assistant, Romina Rodons
P.O. Box 292992, Davie, FL 33329
e-mail headquarters@betaphimu.org
World Wide Web http://www.betaphimu.org

Objective

To recognize distinguished achievement in and scholarly contributions to librarianship, information studies, or library education and to sponsor and support appropriate professional and scholarly projects relating to these fields. Founded at the University of Illinois in 1948.

Membership

Memb. 40,000. Eligibility for membership in Beta Phi Mu is by invitation of the faculty from institutions where the American Library Association, or other recognized accrediting agency approved by the Beta Phi Mu Executive Board, has accredited or recognized a professional degree program. Candidates must be graduates of a library and information science program and fulfill the following requirements: complete the course requirements leading to a master's degree with a scholastic average of 3.75 where A equals 4 points or complete a planned program of advanced study beyond the master's degree that requires full-time study for one or more academic years with a scholastic average of 3.75 where A equals 4.0. Each chapter or approved institution is allowed to invite no more than 25 percent of the annual graduating class, and the faculty of participating library schools must attest to their initiates' professional promise.

Officers

Pres. Tom Rink, Northeastern State University, Broken Arrow Campus, 3100 East New Orleans Street, Broken Arrow, OK 74014. Tel. 918-449-6457, E-mail: rink@nsuok.edu; *V.P./ Pres.-Elect* Adrienne Teague, Rudisill Branch, Tulsa City-County Library System. E-mail adrienne.teague@gmail.com; *Treas.* Vicki Gregory, School of Information, College of Arts and Sciences, University of South Florida, 4202 E. Fowler Ave., CIS 2036, Tampa, FL 33620. Tel. 813-974-3520, E-mail gregory@usf.edu; *Past Pres.* Emily Knox, School of Information Sciences, Univ. of Illinois, 501 E. Daniel St., Champaign, IL 61820. Tel. 217-300-0212, e-mail knox@illinois.edu.

Directors

At-Large Lisa Hussey (2021–2023), Camille McCutcheon (2020–2022); *Dirs.* Mirah J. Dow (2020–2022), Jack Fisher (2020–2022), Kimberly M. Gay (2021–2023), Elizabeth Jones (2021–2023).

Publications

Beta Phi Mu Scholars Series. Available from Rowman & Littlefield, Publishers, 4501 Forbes Blvd., Suite 200, Lanham, MD 20706. *Ed.* Andrea Falcone. E-mail bpmseries@gmail.com.

Newsletter. *The Pipeline* (biennial; electronic only). *Ed.* Alison Lewis.

Chapters

Alpha. Univ. of Illinois–Urbana-Champaign, School of Info. Sciences; *Gamma.* Florida State Univ., College of Communication and Info.; *Epsilon.* Univ. of North Carolina–Chapel Hill, School of Info. and Lib. Science; *Theta.* c/o Pratt Inst., School of Info.; *Iota.* Catholic Univ. of America, Dept. of Lib. and Info. Science;

Univ. of Maryland, College of Info. Studies; *Lambda.* Univ. of Oklahoma, School of Lib. and Info. Studies; *Xi.* Univ. of Hawaii–Manoa, Lib. and Info. Science Program; *Omicron.* Rutgers Univ., Grad. School of Communication, Info. and Lib. Studies; *Pi.* Univ. of Pittsburgh, School of Info. Sciences; *Sigma.* Drexel Univ., College of Computing and Informatics; *Psi.* Univ. of Missouri–Columbia, School of Info. Science and Learning Technologies; *Omega.* San José State Univ., School of Info.; *Beta Beta.* Simmons Univ., School of Lib. and Info. Science; *Beta Delta.* State Univ. of New York–Buffalo, Dept. of Lib. and Info. Studies; *Beta Epsilon.* Emporia State Univ., School of Lib. and Info. Management; *Beta Zeta.* Louisiana State Univ., School of Lib. and Info. Science; *Beta Iota.* Univ. of Rhode Island, Grad. School of Lib. and Info. Studies; *Beta Kappa.* Univ. of Alabama, School of Lib. and Info. Studies; *Beta Lambda.* Texas Woman's Univ., School of Lib. and Info. Sciences; *Beta Mu.* Long Island Univ., Palmer School of Lib. and Info. Science; *Beta Nu.* St. John's Univ., Div. of Lib. and Info. Science *Beta Xi.* North Carolina Central Univ., School of Lib. and Info. Sciences; *Beta Pi.* Univ. of Arizona, School of Info.; *Beta Rho.* Univ. of Wisconsin–Milwaukee, School of Info. Science; *Beta Phi.* Univ. of South Florida, School of Lib. and Info. Science; *Beta Psi.* Univ. of Southern Mississippi, School of Lib. and Info. Science; *Beta Omega.* Univ. of South Carolina, College of Lib. and Info. Science; *Beta Beta Epsilon.* Univ. of Wisconsin–Madison, School of Lib. and Info. Studies; *Beta Beta Theta.* Univ. of Iowa, School of Lib. and Info. Science; *Pi Lambda Sigma.* Syracuse Univ., School of Info. Studies; *Beta Beta Mu.* Valdosta State Univ., Lib. and Info. Science Program; *Beta Beta Nu.* Univ. of North Texas, College of Info.; *Beta Beta Omicron.* East Carolina Univ., Dept. of Interdisciplinary Professions; *Beta Beta Xi.* St. Catherine Univ., Master of Lib. and Info. Science Program.

Bibliographical Society of America

Executive Director, Erin McGuirl
67 West Street Suite 401, Unit C17, Brooklyn, NY 11222
e-mail erin.mcguirl@bibsocamer.org
World Wide Web http://www.bibsocamer.org

Objective

To promote bibliographical research and to issue bibliographical publications. Organized in 1904.

Membership

Dues (Partner) $80; (Sustaining) $125; (Leadership) $250; (Advancing) $500; (Lifetime) $1,250; (Emerging bibliographers, 35 and under) $25. Year. Jan.–Dec.

Officers

Pres. Caroline Duroselle-Melish, Folger Shakespeare Library; *V.P.* Megan Peiser, Oakland University; *Secy.* John T. McQuillen, Morgan Museum and Library; *Treas.* G. Scott Clemons, Brown Brothers Harriman; *Delegate to the ACLS* David Vander Meulen, University of Virginia.

Council

(2025) Rebecca Romney, Alice Schreyer, Kenneth Soehner, Derrick Spires; (2024) María Victoria Fernández, Thomas Goldwasser, Adam G. Hooks, Nick Wilding; (2023) Mary Crawford, Andrew T. Nadell, Elizabeth Ott, Douglas Pfeiffer.

Committee Chairs

Audit. Joan Friedman.
BibSite Editorial Group. Eric Ensley.
Development. Caroline Duroselle-Melish.
Digital Strategy Working Group. Erin McGuirl.
Events. Ashley Cataldo.
Fellowship. Hope Mayo.
Investments. Mary Crawford.
Liaisons. Catherine M. Parisian.
Membership. Elizabeth Ott.
New Scholars. Barbara Heritage.
Nominating. Barbara A. Shailor.
Policy and Procedures Manual Working Group. Joan Friedman.
Publications. Nicholas Wilding.

Publication

Papers of the Bibliographical Society of America (q.; memb.). *Eds.* Sarah Werner, independent scholar, and Jesse R. Erickson, Morgan Museum and Library. E-mail editor. pbsa@bibsocamer.org.

Bibliographical Society of Canada
(La Société Bibliographique du Canada)

President, Chris Young
360 Bloor St. W., P.O. Box 19035, Walmer, Toronto, ON M5S 3C9
E-mail secretary@bsc-sbc.ca
World Wide Web http://www.bsc-sbc.ca/en

Objective

The Bibliographical Society of Canada is a bilingual (English/French) organization that has as its goal the scholarly study of the history, description, and transmission of texts in all media and formats, with a primary emphasis on Canada, and the fulfillment of this goal through the following objectives:

- To promote the study and practice of bibliography: enumerative, historical, descriptive, analytical, and textual
- To further the study, research, and publication of book history and print culture
- To publish bibliographies and studies of book history and print culture
- To encourage the publication of bibliographies, critical editions, and studies of book history and print culture
- To promote the appropriate preservation and conservation of manuscript, archival, and published materials in various formats
- To encourage the utilization and analysis of relevant manuscript and archival sources as a foundation of bibliographical scholarship and book history
- To promote the interdisciplinary nature of bibliography and to foster relationships with other relevant organizations nationally and internationally
- To conduct the society without purpose of financial gain for its members and to ensure that any profits or other accretions to the society shall be used in promoting its goal and objectives

Membership

The society welcomes as members all those who share its aims and wish to support and participate in bibliographical research and publication. Dues (Reg.) $80; (Student) $35; (Ret.) $50; (Inst.) $100; (Life) $1,000.

Executive Council (2021–2022)

Pres. Christopher Young. E-mail president@bsc-sbc.ca; *1st V.P.* Svetlana Kochkina. E-mail vice_president_1@bsc-sbc.ca; *2nd V.P.* Jocelyne Thompson. E-mail vice_president_2@bsc-sbc.ca; *Secy.* Andrew Stewart. E-mail secretary@bsc-sbc.ca; *Assoc. Secy.* Laurence Patenaude; *Treas.* Tom Vincent. E-mail treasurer@bsc-sbc.ca; *Assoc. Treas.* Meaghan Scanlon; *Past Pres.* Karen Smith. E-mail past_president@bsc-sbc.ca.

Councilors

(2019–2022) Susan Cameron, Scott Schofield, Myra Tawfik; (2020–2023) Christopher Lyons, Chelsea Shriver, Danielle Van Wagner; (2021–2024) Mathieu Bouchard, Myron Groover, Christina Ionescu.

Committee Chairs

Awards. Scott Schofield.
Communications. Chris Young.
Fellowships. Susan Cameron.
Publications. Geoffrey Little.
Special Collections Interest Group. Scott Schofield and Christopher Lyons.

Publications

Bulletin (s. ann). *Ed.* Ellen Forget.
Journal Manager. Sarah Severson.
Papers of the Bibliographical Society of Canada/Cahiers de la Société Bibliographique du Canada (s. ann.). *Ed.* Elizabeth Willson Gordon; *Review Ed.* (English) Rachel Harris; *Review Ed.* (French) Philippe Rioux.

Black Caucus of the American Library Association

President, Shauntee Burns-Simpson
P.O. Box 174, New York, NY 10159-0174
646-721-1358
World Wide Web https://www.bcala.org

Mission

The Black Caucus of the American Library Association (BCALA) serves as an advocate for the development, promotion, and improvement of library services and resources for the nation's African American community and provides leadership for the recruitment and professional development of African American librarians. It was founded in 1970.

Membership

Membership is open to any person, institution, or business interested in promoting the development of library and information services for African Americans and other people of African descent and willing to maintain good financial standing with the organization. The membership is currently composed of librarians and other information professionals, library support staff, libraries, publishers, authors, vendors, and other library-related organizations in the United States and abroad. Dues (Lifetime) $500; (Corporate) $200; (Inst.) $60; (Reg.) $45; (Library Support Staff) $20; (Student) $10; (Ret.) $25.

Officers

Pres. Shauntee Burns-Simpson; *V.P./Pres.-Elect* Nichelle M. Hayes; *Secy.* Brenda Johnson-Perkins; *Treas.* Brandy McNeil; *Past Pres.* Richard E. Ashby. Jr.

Board Members

(2020-2022) KC Boyd, Dolores Brown, Valerie Carter, Taryn Fouche, Derek Mosley, Fayrene Muhammed, Satia Orange; (2019–2021) Latrice Booker, Vivian Bordeaux, Rudolph Clay, James Allen Davis, Jr., Tashia Munson, Ana Ndumu, Regina Renee Ward, Shamika Simpson.

Committee Chairs

Affiliates. Tiffany Alston.
ALA Relations. Latrice Booker
Awards. John Page.
Budget and Finance. Stanton Biddie.
Constitution and Bylaws. Jos Holman.
Fundraising. Kelvin Watson.
History. Sybyl Moses.
International Relations. Eboni M. Henry, Vivian Bordeaux.
Marketing and Public Relations. Shaundra Walker.
Membership. Rudolph Clay, Jr.
National Conference. Tracey Hunter Hayes.
Nomination and Election. Richard E. Ashby.
President's Advisory. Shauntee Burns-Simpson.
Programs. Shauntee Burns-Simpson, Nichelle M. Hayes.
Publications. Nichelle Hayes.
Recruitment and Professional Development. Ana Ndumu.
Services to Children and Families of African Descent. Karen Lemmons.
Technology Advisory. Zakia Ringgold.

Awards Committee Chairs

Literary Awards. Gladys Smiley Bell.
Dr. E.J. Josey Scholarship. Sylvia Sprinkle-Hamlin.

Publication

BCALA News (3 a year; memb.). *Ed.* Nichelle M. Hayes.

Canadian Association for Information Science (L'Association Canadienne des Sciences de l'Information)

President, Philippe Mongeon
World Wide Web http://www.cais-acsi.ca

Objective

To promote the advancement of information science in Canada and encourage and facilitate the exchange of information relating to the use, access, retrieval, organization, management, and dissemination of information.

Membership

Institutions and individuals interested in information science and involved in the gathering, organization, and dissemination of information (such as information scientists, archivists, librarians, computer scientists, documentalists, economists, educators, journalists, and psychologists) and who support Canadian Association for Information Science (CAIS) objectives can become association members.

Officers

Pres. Philippe Mongeon, Dalhousie Univ.; *Secy.* Fei Shu, Hangzhou Dianzi Univ.; *Treas.* Michael Ridley, Western Univ.; *Past Pres.* Heather Hill, Western Univ.; *Memb.-at-Large* Danica Pawlick-Potts.

Board Members

Roger Chabot, Western Univ.; Christina Parsons, Robyn Stobbs, Univ. of Alberta; Sam A. Vander Kooy, Western Univ.

Publication

Canadian Journal of Information and Library Science. (q.; memb.; print; online). For nonmember subscription information visit https://ojs.lib.uwo.ca/index.php/cjils. *Ed.* Heather Hill, Information and Media Studies, Western Univ. E-mail cjils@cais-acsi.ca.

Canadian Association of Research Libraries (Association des Bibliothèques de Recherche du Canada)

Executive Director, Susan Haigh
309 Cooper St., Suite 203, Ottawa, ON K2P 0G5
613-482-9344 ext. 101, e-mail info@carl-abrc.ca
World Wide Web http://www.carl-abrc.ca
Twitter @carlabrc

Membership

The Canadian Association of Research Libraries (CARL), established in 1976, is the leadership organization for the Canadian research library community. The association's members are the 29 major academic research libraries across Canada together with Library and Archives Canada and the National Research Council Canada, National Science Library. Membership is institutional and is open primarily to libraries of Canadian universities that have doctoral graduates in both the arts and the sciences. CARL is an associate member of the Association of Universities and Colleges of Canada (AUCC) and is incorporated as a not-for-profit organization under the Canada Corporations Act.

Mission

The association provides leadership on behalf of Canada's research libraries and enhances their capacity to advance research and higher education. It promotes effective and sustainable scholarly communication and public policy that enables broad access to scholarly information.

Officers (2021–2023)

Pres. Vivian Lewis, McMaster University, Hamilton, ON; *V.P.* Brett Waytuck, University of Regina, Regina, SK; *Secy.* Dr. Guylaine Beaudry, Concordia University, Montréal, PQ; *Treas.* Lesley Balcom, Harriet Irving Library, University of New Brunswick, Fredericton, NB.

Board of Directors

Talia Chung, Univ. of Ottawa, ON (Ontario Region Representative); Dr. Susan Parker, Univ. of British Columbia, Vancouver, BC (Western Region Representative).

Committee Chairs

Advancing Research. Talia Chung.
Assessment. Mary-Jo Romaniuk.
Policy. Susan Parker.
Strengthening Capacity. Melissa Just.

Member Institutions

National Members

Lib. and Archives Canada, National Research Council Canada

Regional Members

Univ. of Alberta, Univ. of British Columbia, Brock Univ., Univ. of Calgary, Carleton Univ., Concordia Univ., Dalhousie Univ., Univ. of Guelph, Univ. Laval, McGill Univ., McMaster Univ., Univ. of Manitoba, Memorial Univ. of Newfoundland, Univ. de Montréal, Univ. of New Brunswick, Univ. of Ottawa, Univ. du Québec à Montréal, Queen's Univ., Univ. of Regina, Ryerson Univ., Univ. of Saskatchewan, Université de Sherbrooke, Simon Fraser Univ., Univ. of Toronto, Univ. of Victoria, Univ. of Waterloo, Western Univ., Univ. of Windsor, York Univ.

Catholic Library Association

Executive Director, Melanie Talley
8550 United Plaza Blvd., Suite 1001, Baton Rouge, LA 70809
225-408-4417, e-mail cla2@cathla.org
World Wide Web http://www.cathla.org

Objective

The promotion and encouragement of Catholic literature and library work through cooperation, publications, education, and information. Founded in 1921.

Membership

Memb. 1,000. Dues $25–$500. Year. July–June.

Officers

Pres. Kathryn Shaughnessy, e-mail shaughnk@stjohns.edu; *V.P./Treas.* Bro. Andrew J. Kosmowski, SM, e-mail kosmowskia1@udayton.edu; *Past Pres.* Jack Fritts, 5700 College Rd., Lisle, IL 60532. Tel. 630-829-6060, e-mail jfritts@ben.edu.

Board Members

Eva Gonsalves, Kathy Harty, Elyse Hayes, Jean McManus.

Section Chairs

Academic Libraries, Archives and Library Education. Bro. Andrew J. Kosmowski, SM.
High School and Young Adult Library Services. Eva Gonsalves.
Parish and Community Library Services. Phyllis Petre.

Publication

Catholic Library World (q.; memb.; nonmemb. $100 domestic, $125 international). *General Ed.* Sigrid Kelsey. E-mail sigridkelsey@gmail.com.

Chief Officers of State Library Agencies

Executive Director, Jeremy Johannesen
201 E. Main St., Suite 1405, Lexington, KY 40507
859-514-9150, fax 859-514-9166, e-mail info@cosla.org
World Wide Web https://www.cosla.org
Twitter @COSLA_US

Objective

Chief Officers of State Library Agencies (COSLA) is an independent organization of the chief officers of state and territorial agencies designated as the state library administrative agency and responsible for statewide library development. Its purpose is to identify and address issues of common concern and national interest, to further state library agency relationships with federal government and national organizations, and to initiate cooperative action for the improvement of library services to the people of the United States.

COSLA's membership consists solely of these top library officers, variously designated as state librarian, director, commissioner, or executive secretary. The organization provides a continuing mechanism for dealing with the problems and challenges faced by these officers. Its work is carried on through its members, a board of directors, and committees.

Officers (2021–2023)

Pres. Jennie Stapp, State Libn., Montana State Lib. Tel. 406-444-3116, e-mail jstapp2@mt.gov; *V.P./Pres.-Elect* Julie Walker, State Libn., Georgia Public Lib. Svcs. Tel. 404-406-4519, e-mail jwalker@georgialibraries.org; *Secy.* Jennifer Nelson, State Library Svcs. and Charter Ctr., Minnesota Dept. of Ed. Tel. 651-582-8791, e-mail jennifer.r.nelson@state.mn.us; *Treas.* Jamie Ritter, State Libn., Maine State Lib Tel. 207-287-5604, e-mail james.ritter@maine.gov; *Past Pres.* Stacey Aldrich, State Libn., Hawaii State Public Lib. System. Tel. 808-586-3704, e-mail stacey.aldrich@librarieshawaii.org.

Directors

Holly Henley, State Librarian, Arizona State Library. Tel. 602-542-6181, e-mail hhenley@azlibrary.gov; Mary Soucie, State Librarian, North Dakota State Library. Tel. 701-328-4654, e-mail msoucie@nd.gov.

Chinese American Librarians Association

Executive Director, Lian Ruan
E-mail lruan@illinois.edu
World Wide Web https://cala-web.org

Objective

To enhance communications among Chinese American librarians as well as between Chinese American librarians and other librarians, to serve as a forum for discussion of mutual problems and professional concerns among Chinese American librarians, to promote Sino-American librarianship and library services, and to provide a vehicle whereby Chinese American librarians can cooperate with other associations and organizations having similar or allied interests.

Membership

Memb. approximately 600. Membership is open to anyone interested in the association's goals and activities. Dues (Reg.) $30; (International/Student/Nonsalaried/Overseas) $15; (Inst.) $100; (Affiliated) $100; (Life) $300.

Officers (2021–2024)

Pres. Wenli Gao. E-mail wgao5@central. uh.edu; *V.P./Pres.-Elect* Ray Pun. E-mail raypun101@gmail.com; *Treas.* Suzhen Chen. E-mail suzhen@hawaii.edu; *Past Pres.* Hong Yao. E-mail Hong.Yao@queenslibrary.org; *Incoming V.P./Pres.-Elect.* Vincci Kwong. E-mail vkwong@iusb.edu.

Board of Directors

(2019–2022) Ying Liao, Jianye He, Hong Miao, Vincci Kwong, Xiaocan Wang; (2020–2023) Leping He, Yan He, Amy Jiang, Mingyan Li, Le Yang; (2021–2024) Ying Zhang, Michael Huang, Katherina Lee, Lei Jin, Xiaoyu Duan.

Chapter Presidents (2021–2022)

NCA: Yi Liang; SCA: Joy Wang; GMA: Andrew Yanqing Lee; MW: Anlin Yang; NE: Alvina Lai; SE: Xiying Mi; SW: Hui-Fen, Chang; Canada: Haiyun Cao.

Committee Chairs

Assessment and Evaluation. Xiaoyin Zhang.
Awards. Leping He and Kuei Chiu.
Conference Program. Wenli Gao.
Constitution and Bylaws. Liya Deng.
Election. Lian Ruan.
International Relations. Michael Huang.
Mentorship Programming. Zeng Yang.
Membership. Xiaoyu Duan.
Nominating. Fu Zhuo.
Public Relations/Fundraising. Katherina Lee and Ray Pun.
Publications. Guoying Liu.
Web Committee. Jingshan Xiao.

Publications

CALA Newsletter (2 a year; memb.; online). *Eds.* Xiying Mi. E-mail mixiying@gmail. com; Esther DeLeon. E-mail esther.dele on@ttu.edu.
International Journal of Librarianship (IJoL). *Ed.* Grace Liu. E-mail editors@calaijol.org.

Coalition for Networked Information

Executive Director, Clifford A. Lynch
21 Dupont Circle, Suite 800, Washington, DC 20036
202-296-5098, fax 202-872-0884, e-mail clifford@cni.org
World Wide Web https://www.cni.org
Facebook https://www.facebook.com/cni.org
Twitter @cni_org
YouTube https://www.youtube.com/user/cnivideo
Vimeo http://vimeo.com/cni

Mission

The Coalition for Networked Information (CNI) promotes the transformative promise of networked information technology for the advancement of scholarly communication and the enrichment of intellectual productivity.

Membership

Memb. 240+. Membership is institutional. Dues $8,660. Year. July–June.

Staff

Assoc. Exec. Dir. Joan K. Lippincott, 21 Dupont Cir., Suite 800, Washington, DC 20036. Tel. 202-296-5098, e-mail joan@cni.org; *Asst. Exec. Dir.* Diane Goldenberg-Hart. E-mail diane@cni.org; *Admin. Asst.* Sharon Adams. E-mail sharon@cni.org; *Systems Coord.* Maurice-Angelo F. Cruz. E-mail angelo@cni.org; *Office Mgr.* Jacqueline J. Eudell. E-mail jackie@cni.org; *Communications Coord.* Paige Pope. E-mail paige@cni.org.

Steering Committee Members (2021–2022)

Kristin Antelman, University of California–Santa Barbara; Dale Askey, University of Alberta; Daniel Cohen, Northeastern University; Gina M. Siesing, Bryn Mawr College; Jenn Stringer, University of California–Berkeley; Ann Thornton, Columbia University; Donald J. Waters; Mary Lee Kennedy, Association of Research Libraries (ex officio); Clifford A. Lynch, Coalition for Networked Information (ex officio); John O'Brien, EDUCAUSE (ex officio).

Publications

CNI-ANNOUNCE (https://www.cni.org/resources/follow-cni/cni-announce)
CNI Executive Roundtable Reports (https://www.cni.org/tag/executive-roundtable-report).

Council on Library and Information Resources

Chair, Buhle Mbambo-Thata
211 North Union Street, Suite 100-PMB 1027, Alexandria, VA 22314
E-mail contact@clir.org
World Wide Web http://www.clir.org
Twitter @CLIRnews

Objective

In 1997 the Council on Library Resources (CLR) and the Commission on Preservation and Access (CPA) merged and became the Council on Library and Information Resources (CLIR). CLIR is an independent, nonprofit organization that forges strategies to enhance research, teaching, and learning environments in collaboration with libraries, cultural institutions, and communities of higher learning.

CLIR promotes forward-looking collaborative solutions that transcend disciplinary, institutional, professional, and geographic boundaries in support of the public good. CLIR identifies and defines the key emerging issues relating to the welfare of libraries and the constituencies they serve, convenes the leaders who can influence change, and promotes collaboration among the institutions and organizations that can achieve change. The council's interests embrace the entire range of information resources and services from traditional library and archival materials to emerging digital formats. It assumes a particular interest in helping institutions cope with the accelerating pace of change associated with the transition into the digital environment.

While maintaining appropriate collaboration and liaison with other institutions and organizations, CLIR operates independently of any particular institutional or vested interests. Through the composition of its board, it brings the broadest possible perspective to bear upon defining and establishing the priority of the issues with which it is concerned.

Officers

Chair Buhle Mbambo-Thata, National Univ. of Lesotho; *V.Chair* Guy Berthiaume, Librarian and Archivist of Canada Emeritus; *Pres.* Charles Henry; *Treas.* John Price Wilkin, Univ. of Illinois–Urbana-Champaign.

Board of Directors

Edward Ayers, University of Richmond; Michele Casalini, Casalini Libri; Christopher Celenza, Johns Hopkins University; Dan Cohen, Northeastern University; Tess Davis, Antiquities Coalition; Kurt De Belder, Leiden University; Kathleen Fitzpatrick, Michigan State University; Fenella France, Library of Congress; Michael A. Keller, Stanford University; W. Joseph King, Lyon College; Carol Mandel, New York University Division of Libraries; Max Marmor, Samuel H. Kress Foundation; Asma Naeem, Baltimore Museum of Art; Richard Ovenden, University of Oxford; Sandra Phoenix, HBCU Library Alliance; Winston Tabb, Johns Hopkins University; Ben Vinson III, Case Western Reserve University; Sohair Wastawy, The Information Guild.

Address correspondence to headquarters.

Publications

Annual Report.
CLIR Issues (bi-mo.; electronic).

EveryLibrary

Executive Director, John Chrastka
P.O. Box 406, 45 E. Burlington St.,
Riverside, IL 60546
312-574-5098
E-mail info@everylibrary.org
World Wide Web https://www.everylibrary.org | https://action.everylibrary.org
Facebook https://www.facebook.com/EveryLibrary
LinkedIn https://www.linkedin.com/company/3801587
Twitter @EveryLibrary

Object

EveryLibrary is a national political action committee for libraries. Organized as a 501(c)4, the organization provides pro bono advising and consulting to libraries about their funding requests, either when it appears on a ballot or through a municipal funding partner. Its school-library-focused digital activism platform SaveSchoolLibrarians.org works to support school librarian positions and budgets for school library programs. Its national network in 2021 included more than 355,000 Americans. EveryLibrary's mission is to "build voter support for libraries" at all levels of government, and it works to fulfill that mission as a completely donor-supported organization.

Board Members

Jeannie Allen, Lori Bowen Ayer, Peter Bromberg, John Chrastka, Roberto Delgadillo, Harmony V. Faust, Erica Findley, Brian D. Hart, Gary Kirk, Kathleen McEvoy, Patrick Sweeney.

EveryLibrary Institute, NFP

Executive Director, John Chrastka
P.O. Box 406, 45 E. Burlington St.,
Riverside, IL 60546
312-574-5098
E-mail info@everylirbaryinstitute.org
World Wide Web https://www.everylibraryinstitute.org
Facebook https://facebook.com/everylibraryinstitute
Twitter @ELInstituteNFP

Object

The EveryLibrary Institute, NFP is a public policy and tax policy think tank for libraries that is focused on the future of public library and school library funding in the United States and abroad. Its nonprofit 501(c)3 mission is to develop research, programmatic opportunities, trainings, fiscal sponsorships, and scholarship that advance the image and impact of libraries and librarians to the general public and policymakers. Domestically, this includes publishing its journal, supporting public outreach and education across the EveryLibrary network, and providing crowdfunding services through its FundLibraries.org platform. Internationally, it partners with CILIP, the Chartered Institute for Library and Information Professionals, to host the LibrariesDeliver.uk outreach campaign about libraries in England.

Board Members

K.C. Boyd, John Chrastka, Kyle Courtney, Trevor A. Dawes, Erica Findley, Britten Follett, Amy Garmer, Fran Glick, Kafi Kumasi, Steve Potter, Rivkah Sass, Cal Shepard, Maureen Sullivan, Patrick Sweeney, Jill Hurst-Wahl, Lance Werner.

Publication

The Political Librarian (irreg.; open access). *Ed.* Christopher Stewart.

Federal Library and Information Network

Executive Director, Laurie Neider
Library of Congress, Washington, DC 20540-4935
202-707-4801, e-mail lneider@loc.gov
World Wide Web http://www.loc.gov/flicc
Twitter @librarycongress

Objective

The Federal Library and Information Network (FEDLINK) is an organization of federal agencies working together to achieve optimum use of the resources and facilities of federal libraries and information centers by promoting common services, coordinating and sharing available resources, and providing continuing professional education for federal library and information staff. FEDLINK serves as a forum for discussion of the policies, programs, procedures, and technologies that affect federal libraries and the information services they provide to their agencies, to Congress, to the federal courts, and to the public.

Membership

The FEDLINK voting membership is composed of representatives of the following U.S. federal departments and agencies: Each of the national libraries (the Library of Congress, National Agricultural Library, National Library of Education, National Library of Medicine, and National Transportation Library); each cabinet-level executive department, as defined in 5 U.S.C. § 101; additional departments and agencies (the Defense Technical Information Center; departments of the Air Force, Army, and Navy; Executive Office of the President; Government Accountability Office; General Services Administration; Government Printing Office; Institute of Museum and Library Services; National Aeronautics and Space Administration; National Archives and Records Administration; National Technical Information Service (Department of Commerce); Office of Management and Budget; Office of Personnel Management; Office of Scientific and Technical Information (Department of Energy); Office of the Director of National Intelligence; and the Smithsonian Institution); the U.S. Supreme Court and the Administrative Office of the U.S. Courts; the District of Columbia; and other federal independent agencies and government corporations.

Address correspondence to the executive director.

Publication

FEDLINK Bulletin (bi-wk.; electronic).

Librarians, Archivists, and Museum Professionals in the History of the Health Sciences

President, Jennifer Nieves
E-mail jks4@case.edu
World Wide Web http://iis-exhibits.library.ucla.edu/alhhs/index.html

Objective

Librarians, Archivists, and Museum Professionals in the History of the Health Sciences (LAMPHHS; formerly ALHHS/MeMA) was established exclusively for educational purposes, to serve the professional interests of librarians, archivists, and other specialists actively engaged in the librarianship of the history of the health sciences by promoting the exchange of information and by improving the standards of service.

Membership

Memb. approximately 150. Dues $15.

Officers (2020–2022)

Pres. Jennifer Nieves, Dittrick Medical History Ctr., Cleveland, OH. E-mail jks4@case.edu; *V.P.* Polina Ilieva, Archives and Special Collections, UCSF Library, San Francisco, CA. E-mail jpolinailieva@ucsf.edu; *Secy.* Jamie Rees, Clendening History of Medicine Library and Museum, University of Kansas Medical Center, Kansas City, KS. E-mail lamphhs.org@gmail.com; *Treas.* Tegan Kehoe, Paul S. Russell, MD, Museum of Medical History and Innovation, Massachusetts General Hospital, Boston, MA.

E-mail lamphhs.treasurer@gmail.com; *Past Pres.* Melissa Grafe, Medical Historical Lib., Harvey Cushing/John Hay Whitney Medical Lib., Yale Univ. New Haven, CT. E-mail melissa.grafe@yale.edu. *Memb.-at-Large* Judy M. Chelnick, Mary Hague-Yearl, Megan Keller Young, Christine Ruggere.

Committee Chairs

Annual Meeting Local Arrangements. Elise DeAndrea.
Annual Meeting Program. Dan Cavanaugh.
Archivist. Jodi Koste.
Communications. Jamie Rees.
Membership Directory. Jamie Rees.
Nominating. Lucy Waldrop.
Recruiting. Jonathan Erlen.
Travel Scholarships. Stephen Greenberg.
Website. Sara Alger and Beth DeFrancis Sun.

Awards Committee Chairs

Publications Awards. Carrie Meyer.
Recognition Awards. Megan Keller Young.
Watermark (q.; memb.). *Ed.* Stephen E. Novak. Augustus C. Long Health Sciences Library, Columbia University. E-mail sen13@cumc.columbia.org.

Medical Library Association

Executive Director, Kevin Baliozian
225 West Wacker Dr., Suite 650, Chicago, IL 60606-1210
312-419-9094, fax 312-419-8950, e-mail websupport@mail.mlahq.org
World Wide Web http://www.mlanet.org
Twitter @MedLibAssn

Objective

The Medical Library Association (MLA) is a nonprofit professional education organization with nearly 4,000 health sciences information professional members and partners worldwide. MLA provides lifelong educational opportunities, supports a knowledge base of health information research, and works with a global network of partners to promote the importance of high-quality information for improved health to the healthcare community and the public.

Membership

Memb. (Inst.) 400+; (Indiv.) 3,200+, in more than 50 countries. Dues (Indiv.) $75–$225; (Student) $50; (Int'l.) $150; (Affiliate) $140; (Inst.) $325–$880. Year. Institutional members are medical and allied scientific libraries. Individual members are people who are (or were at the time membership was established) engaged in professional library or bibliographic work in medical and allied scientific libraries or people who are interested in medical or allied scientific libraries. Members can be affiliated with one or more of MLA's more than 20 special-interest sections and its regional chapters.

Officers

Pres. Kristine M. Alpi, Oregon Health & Science Univ.; *Pres.-Elect*; Shannon D Jones, Medical Univ. of South Carolina; *Secy.* Heather N. Holmes, Medical University of South Carolina; *Treas.* J. Dale Prince, Louisiana State University Health Sciences Center - New Orleans; *Past Pres.* Lisa K. Traditi, Univ. of Colorado Anschutz Med. Campus; *Exec. Dir.* Kevin Baliozian. Med. Lib. Assn.

Board of Directors

Tara Douglas-Williams, Sally Gore, Heather N. Holmes, Janna C. Lawrence, Brenda M. Linares, Meredith I. Solomon; *Chapter Council Chairs* Donna R. Berryman, Adela V. Justice.

Committee Chairs

Awards. Rose L. Turner.
Books Panel. Jamie L. Conklin.
Bylaws. David Charles Duggar and Amy Gische Lyons.
Credentialing. Lindsay E. Blake.
Diversity, Equity, and Inclusion. Jane Morgan-Daniel.
Education: Health Information Professionalism Curriculum. Elizabeth Irish.
Education: Information Management Curriculum. Margaret Henderson.
Education: Information Services Curriculum. Amy Chatfield.
Education: Instruction and Instructional Design Curriculum. Shenita Peterson.
Education: Leadership and Management Curriculum. Tamara M. Nelson.
Education: Research and Evidence-Based Practive Curriculum. Andrea C. Kepsel.
Education: Steering. Stephanie M. Swanberg.
Finance. J. Dale Prince.
Governmental Relations. Mary M Langman (staff liaison).
Grants and Scholarships. Andrew Todd.
Joseph Leiter NLM/MLA Lectureship. Patrick McLaughlin.
Membership. Nell Aronoff.
National Program. Kate Flewelling and Ryan Harris.
Nominating. Lisa K. Traditi.
Oral History. Ansley Stuart and Gregory Laynor.
Professional Recruitment and Retention. Sheila Green.

Editorial Board Chairs

JMLA Interim *Editor-in-Chief.* Alexander J. Carroll.
MLAConnect Ed. Christine Willis.

Task Force Chairs

125-Year Retrospective Task Force. Michelle R Lieggi.
Archives Task Force. Brandon Pieczko.
Joint MLA/AAHSL Legislative Task Force. Margaret Ansell.
Vision 2048 Task Force. Charlotte Beyer.

Awards Committee Chairs

Virginia L. and William K. Beatty Volunteer Service. Basia (Barbara) Delawska-Elliott.
Estelle Brodman Award for the Academic Medical Librarian of the Year. Derek Johnson.
Chapter Project of the Year. Carolyn Ching Dennison.
Lois Ann Colaianni Award for Excellence and Achievement in Hospital Librarianship. Olivia A. Glotfelty-Scheuering.
Consumer Health Librarian of the Year Award Jury. Jessi Van Der Volgen.
Louise Darling Medal for Distinguished Achievement in Collection Development in the Health Sciences. Angela Dixon.
Janet Doe Lectureship. Chana Kraus-Friedberg.
Ida and George Eliot Prize. Bethany S. McGowan.
Fellows and Honorary Members. Debra Berlanstein.
Carla J. Funk Governmental Relations. Kathryn M. Houk.
T. Mark Hodges International Service. Linda M. Hartman.
Lucretia W. McClure Excellence in Education. Jenny Pierce.
Erich Meyerhoff Prize. Lisa Huang.
Research Advancement in Health Sciences Librarianship Awards Jury. Traci Jean Mays.
Rising Stars Award. Susan Arnold.
Rittenhouse Award. Bethany Figg.
Frank Bradway Rogers Information Advancement. Maria Lopez (staff liaison).

Grants, Scholarships, and Fellowships Juries

Ysabel Bertolucci MLA Annual Meeting Grant. Maria Lopez (staff liaison).
Naomi C. Broering Hispanic Heritage Grant. Carol Seiler.
Continuing Education Grant. Ellen Rothbaum.
Cunningham Memorial International Fellowship. Kathy Kwan.
Financial Support Jury: Annual Conference and Exhibits. Danielle N. Linden.
Financial Support Jury: CE Passports. Maria Lopez (staff liaison).
Eugene Garfield Research Fellowship. Julia Stumpff.
David A. Kronick Traveling Fellowship. Maria Lopez (staff liaison).
Librarians Without Borders Ursula Poland International Scholarship. Mirian Ramirez Rojas.
Donald A.B. Lindberg Research Fellowship. Megan De Armond.
MLA Doctoral Fellowship. Maria Lopez (staff liaison).
MLA EBSCO Annual Conference Support. Maria Lopez (staff liaison).
MLA Hospital Libraries Professional Development Grant. Emily Petersen.
MLA Librarians Without Borders/Elsevier Foundation/Research4Life Grants. Megan Fratta.
MLA Medical Informatics Career Development Grant. Gail Kouame.
MLA Research, Development, and Demonstration Project Grant. Jenessa Marie McElfresh.
MLA Scholarships (including for underrepresented students). Tova Johnson.
Research Training Institute Jury. Carrie Grinstead.

Publication

Journal of the Medical Library Association (q.; electronic version, free to all through PubMed Central). *Interim Ed.-in-Chief* Alexander J. Carroll. E-mail jmla@journals.pitt.edu.

Music Library Association

President, Liza Vick
1600 Aspen Commons, Suite 100, Middleton, WI 53562
608-836-5825, fax 608-831-8200, e-mail mla@areditions.com
World Wide Web https://www.musiclibraryassoc.org
Facebook https://www.facebook.com/Music.Library.Association
Twitter @musiclibassoc
Vimeo https://vimeo.com/musiclibraryassoc

Objective

The Music Library Association provides a professional forum for librarians, archivists, and others who support and preserve the world's musical heritage. To achieve this mission, it does the following:

- Provides leadership for the collection and preservation of music and information about music in libraries and archives
- Develops and delivers programs that promote continuing education and professional development in music librarianship
- Ensures and enhances intellectual access to music for all by contributing to the development and revision of national and international codes, formats, and other standards for the bibliographic control of music
- Ensures and enhances access to music for all by facilitating best practices for housing, preserving, and providing access to music
- Promotes legislation that strengthens music library services and universal access to music
- Fosters information literacy and lifelong learning by promoting music reference services, library instruction programs, and publications
- Collaborates with other groups in the music and technology industries, government, and librarianship to promote its mission and values

Membership

Memb. 1,200+. Dues (Inst.) $175; (Indiv.) $140; (Ret.) $105; (Paraprofessional) $75; (Student) $65. (Foreign, add $10.) Year. July 1–June 30.

Officers

Pres. Liza Vick. E-mail lizavick@upenn.edu; *V.P./Pres.-Elect*; Paula Hickner. E-mail paula.hickner@uky.edu; *Recording Secy.* Veronica Wells. E-mail vmalzalde@gmail.com; *Chief Fin. Officer* Elizabeth Hille Cribbs. E-mail elizabethhillecribbs@gmail.com; Asst. Chief Fin. Officer Serena Vaquilar. E-mail serena.vaquilar@wayne.edu; *Past Pres.* Susannah Cleveland. E-mail Susannah.Cleveland@unt.edu.

Board of Directors

(2021–2023) Parliamentarian Kristi Bergland; Fiscal Officer Marci Cohen; *Planning and Reports Officer* Scott Stone. *(2022–2024) Asst. Parliamentarian* Ray Heigemeir; *Asst. Fiscal Officer* Katie Buehner; *Asst. Planning and Reports Officer* Sonia Archer-Capuzzo. *(2022–2023) Student/Early Career Rep.* Elizabeth Uchimura.

Committee Chairs

Archives and Special Collections. Maristella J. Feustle.
Career Development and Services. Emma Dederick and Timothy Sestrick.
Career Development and Services: New Members Forum. Jessica M. Abbazio and Karen I. Berry.
Cataloging and Metadata. Hermine Vermeij.
Development. Sara White.
Diversity. Callie Holmes.
Education. Sonia Archer-Capuzzo.
Emerging Technologies and Services. Amy S. Jackson.
Finance. Casey A. Mullin.
Legislation. Kyra Folk-Farber.

Membership. Lisa Shiota.
Music Library Advocacy. Linda B. Fairtile.
Nominating. Joe C. Clark.
Oral History. Catherine Hammer and Sara Wallace.
Planning. Diane L. Steinhaus.
Preservation. Treshani Perera.
Program. Rachel Smiley.
Public Libraries. Kristine E. Nelsen.
Public Services. Andrea L. Beckendorf.
Publications. Deborah A. Campana.
Resource Sharing and Collection Development. Stephanie Bonjack.
Web. Kerry C. Masteller.

Awards Committee Chairs

Best of Chapters. Casey Burgess.
Conference Travel Grants. Chris Durman.
Lenore Coral IAML Travel Grant. Katie Buehner and Laura Stokes.
Diversity Scholarship. Sara J. Manus.

Dena Epstein Award for Archival and Library Research in American Music. Bret McCandless.
Gerboth and Bradley Award. Joe C. Clark.
Publications. Sofia Becerra-Licha.

Publications

Basic Manual Series. *Series Ed.* Kathleen A. Abromeit.
Basic Music Library. *Ed.* Daniel Boomhower.
Index and Bibliography Series (irreg.; price varies). *Ed.* Maristella Feustle.
MLA *Newsletter.* (6 a year; memb.). *Ed.* Jacey Kepich.
Music Cataloging Bulletin (mo.; online subscription only, $35). *Ed.* Kirk-Evan Billet.
Notes (q.; memb.). *Ed.* Jonathan J. Sauceda.
Technical Reports and Monographs in Music Librarianship (irreg.; price varies). *Ed.* Anna E. Kijas.

NASIG

President, Ted Westervelt
PMB 305, 1902 Ridge Road, West Seneca, NY 14224-3312
716-324-1859, e-mail: info@nasig.org
World Wide Web: https://nasig.org
Twitter: @NASIG
Facebook: https://www.facebook.com/groups/2399345882
Instagram: https://www.instagram.com/nasig_official
LinkedIn: https://www.linkedin.com/groups/149102
YouTube: https://www.youtube.com/channel/UCVvnh_CzXS8YgftuvIypTiQ

Vision and Mission

Established in 1985, NASIG is an independent organization working to advance and transform the management of information resources. NASIG's goal is to facilitate and improve the distribution, acquisition, and long-term accessibility of information resources in all formats and business models. There are three key components to the organization's mission:

1. NASIG supports a dynamic community of professionals including, but not limited to, librarians, publishers, and vendors engaging in understanding one another's perspectives and improving functionality throughout the information resources life cycle with an emphasis on scholarly communications, serials, and electronic resources.

2. NASIG provides a rich variety of conference and continuing education programming to encourage knowledge-sharing among its members and to support their professional and career development.

3. NASIG promotes the development and implementation of best practices and standards for the distribution, acquisition, and long-term accessibility of information resources in all formats and business models throughout their life cycle.

In addition to developing best practices, NASIG supports the development of standards by NISO, an affiliated organization.

Membership

Memb. 525. For any person, library, or organization interested in information resources and scholarly communication. Dues (Indiv. based on salary range) $75–$100; (Ret.) $25; (Student) Free; (Lifetime) $1,000/one time; (Inst.) $195.

Executive Board (2021–2022)

Pres. Ted Westervelt, Library of Congress; *V.P./ Pres.-Elect* Dana Sinclair, SUNY Old Westbury; *Past Pres.* Betsy Appleton, University of Texas–Austin; *Sec.* Willa Tavernier, Indiana University–Bloomington; *Treas.* Cris Ferguson, Murray State University; *Memb.-at-Large* Keondra Bailey, Duke University Press; Treasa Bane, University of Wisconsin–Madison; Katy DiVittorio, University of Colorado–Denver; Moon Kim, Ohio State University; Mary Ann Jones, Mississippi State University; Courtney McAllister, EBSCO; *Newsletter Editor-in-Chief* Angela Dresselhaus, ProQuest, LLC (ex officio).

Committee Chairs

Archivist. Peter Whiting.
Awards and Recognition. Dejah Rubel.
Bylaws. Stephen Sweeney and Maria Aghazarian.
Communications. Rebecca Tatterson and Sofia Slutskaya.
Conference Coordinator. Anna Creech.
Conference Planning. Jacque Brellenthin and Maria Aghazarian.
Conference Proceedings Editors. Caitlin Harrington and Kate Banet Moore.
Continuing Education. Amy Carlson and Kate Hill.

Digital Preservation. Heather Staines and Michelle Polchow.
Equity and Inclusion. Kristin Twardowski and Ilda Cardenas.
Evaluation and Assessment. Bonnie Thornton and Victoria Koger.
Membership Services. Suzy Kozaitis.
Mentoring and Student Outreach. Juliya Borie and Rachel Scott.
Newsletter. Angela Dresselhaus.
Nominations and Elections. Steve Kelley and Danielle Williams.
Open Initiatives. Melissa Hart Cantrell.
Proceedings. Paul Moeller.
Program Planning. Sarah Dennis and Jennifer Zuccaro.
Registrar. Stephanie J. Adams.
Standards. Beverly Geckle and Jacque Brellenthin.

Task Force Chairs

Vendor and Publisher Engagement. Kristy White.

Publications

Conference Proceedings (currently published in two issues of *Serials Librarian*).
Core Competencies for Electronic Resources Librarians.
Core Competencies for Print Serials Management.
Core Competencies for Scholarly Communication Librarians.
NASIG Newsletter.
Various NASIGuides.
NASIG Blog.
NASIG Jobs Blog.

Meetings

Annual conference held in the summer. Continuing education events and webinars throughout the year.

National Association of Government Archives and Records Administrators

Executive Director, Johnny Hadlock
444 N. Capitol Street, N.W. Suite 237, Washington, DC 20001
202-508-3800, fax 202-508-3801, e-mail info@nagara.org
World Wide Web http://www.nagara.org
Twitter @InfoNAGARA

Objective

Founded in 1984, the National Association of Government Archives and Records Administrators (NAGARA) is a nationwide association of local, state, and federal archivists and records administrators and others interested in improved care and management of government records. NAGARA promotes public awareness of government records and archives management programs, encourages interchange of information among government archives and records management agencies, develops and implements professional standards of government records and archival administration, and encourages study and research into records management problems and issues.

Membership

Most NAGARA members are federal, state, and local archival and records management agencies. Dues (Org.) $225–$750 dependent on number of contacts; (NARA Employees Indiv.) $40; (Students/Ret.) $50; (All other Indiv.) $89.

Officers (2021–2022)

Pres. Patricia C. Franks, San José State Univ. E-mail patricia.franks@sjsu.edu; *Pres.-Elect* Jennifer Green, The City of Oklahoma, jennifer.green@okc.gov; *V.P.* Jen Haney Conover, Warren County (Ohio) Records Center & Archives; *Secy.* Marissa Paron, Lib. and Archives Canada. E-mail marissa.paron@canada.ca; *Treas.* Pari J. Swift, Ohio State University; *Past Pres.* Caryn Wojcik, Michigan Records Management Svcs. E-mail wojcikc@michigan.gov.

Board of Directors

Tara Bell, Shante Ellis, Anne Frantilla, JA Pryse, Lindsey Rambow, Kristopher Stenson, Kathleen Williams.

Publication

Newsletter (q.; memb.; electronic).

National Information Standards Organization

Executive Director, Todd Carpenter
3600 Clipper Mill Rd., Suite 302, Baltimore, MD 21211-1948
301-654-2512, e-mail nisohq@niso.org
World Wide Web http://www.niso.org

Objective

The National Information Standards Organization (NISO) fosters the development and maintenance of standards that facilitate the creation, persistent management, and effective interchange of information so that it can be trusted for use in research and learning. To fulfill this mission, NISO engages libraries, publishers, information aggregators, and other organizations that support learning, research, and scholarship through the creation, organization, management, and curation of knowledge. NISO works with intersecting communities of interest and across the entire life cycle of an information standard. NISO standards apply both traditional and new technologies to the full range of information-related needs, including discovery, retrieval, repurposing, storage, metadata, business information, and preservation.

NISO also develops and publishes recommended practices, technical reports, white papers, and information publications. NISO holds regular educational programs on standards, technologies, and related topics where standards-based solutions can help solve problems. These programs include webinars, online virtual conferences, in-person forums, and teleconferences.

Experts from the information industry, libraries, systems vendors, and publishing participate in the development of NISO standards and recommended practices. The standards are approved by the consensus body of NISO's voting membership, representing libraries, publishers, vendors, government, associations, and private businesses and organizations. NISO is supported by its membership and grants.

NISO is a not-for-profit association accredited by the American National Standards Institute (ANSI) and serves as the U.S. Technical Advisory Group Administrator to ISO/TC 46 Information and Documentation as well as the secretariat for ISO/TC 46/SC 9, Identification and Description.

Membership

Voting Members: 80+. Open to any organization, association, government agency, or company willing to participate in and having substantial concern for the development of NISO standards. Library Standards Alliance Members: 60+. Open to any academic, public, special, or government-supported library interested in supporting the mission of NISO.

Officers

Chair; Mary Sauer-Games, OCLC, Inc.; *V. Chair* Maria Stanton, Atla; *Treas.* Wayne Strickland, NTIS; *Past Chair* Peter Simon, NewsBank, Inc.

Directors

Ryan Bernier, Karim Boughida, Jonathan Clark, Trevor A. Dawes, Salwa Ismail, Allan Lu, Rebecca McCloud, Wendy Queen, Rhonda Ross, Chris Shillum, Greg Suprock, Robert Wheeler.

Committee Chairs

Audit. Rhonda Ross.
Finance. Wayne Strickland.
Governance. Peter Simon.
Nominating. Ryan Bernier.

Staff

Assoc. Exec. Dir. Nettie Lagace; *Dir. of Content* Jill O'Neill; *Dir. of Strategic Initiatives* Jason Griffey.

Publications

Information Standards Quarterly (back issues available in open access from the NISO website).

NISO's published standards, recommended practices, and technical reports are available free of charge as downloadable PDF files from the NISO website (http://www.niso. org). Hard-copy documents are available for sale from the website.

For additional NISO publications, see the article "NISO Standards" in this volume.

Patent and Trademark Resource Center Association

President, Sharyl Overhiser
Reference Department, University of Delaware Library, Newark, DE 19717-5267
World Wide Web https://ptrca.org

Objective

The Patent and Trademark Resource Center Association (PTRCA) provides a support structure for the more than 80 patent and trademark resource centers (PTRCs) affiliated with the U.S. Patent and Trademark Office (USPTO). The association's mission is to discover the interests, needs, opinions, and goals of the PTRCs and to advise USPTO in these matters for the benefit of PTRCs and their users and to assist USPTO in planning and implementing appropriate services. Founded in 1983 as the Patent Depository Library Advisory Council, the name changed to Patent and Trademark Depository Library Association in 1988, and it became an American Library Association affiliate in 1996. In 2011 the association was renamed the Patent and Trademark Resource Center Association.

Membership

Open to any person employed in a patent and trademark resource center library whose responsibilities include the patent and trademark collection. Affiliate membership is also available. Dues (Reg.) $65; (Student) $10.

Officers (2021–2022)

Pres. Sharyl Overhiser, Philadelphia, PA. E-mail overhisers@freelibrary.org; *V.P./Pres.-*

Elect John Schlipp, Highland Heights, KY. E-mail schlippj1@nku.edu; *Secy.* Tallie Casucci, Salt Lake City, UT; *Treas.* Jim Miller, McKeldin Lib., Univ. of Maryland, Library Lane, College Park. Tel. 301-405-9152, e-mail jmiller2@umd.edu; *Past Pres.* Rebecca M. (Missy) Murphey, Orlando, FL. E-mail rebecca.murphey@ucf.edu.

Directors

Academic Libraries Division Reps. Ran Raider (2020–2022), Suzanne Reinman (2021–2023); *Public Libraries Division Reps.* Stella Mittelbach (2020–2022), James Bettinger (2021–2023).

Committee Chairs (2021–2022)

Bylaws. Marian Armour-Gemman.
Conferences. Sharyl Overhiser.
Database. Lisha Li.
Election. Position Open.
Membership and Mentoring. John Schlipp.
Publications. Suzanne Reinman.

Publication

PTRCA Journal. Electronic at https://ptrca.org/newsletters.

Polish American Librarians Association

President, Ewa Barczyk
984 N. Milwaukee Avenue, Chicago, IL 60642
World Wide Web http://palalib.org

Objective

Founded in 2009, the mission of the Polish American Librarians Association (PALA) is to positively affect services provided to library patrons of Polish descent and individuals interested in Polish culture.

The organization's vision is the following:

- To enhance professional knowledge by developing forums for discussion and networks of communication among library staff working with Polish collections and patrons of Polish origin
- To promote understanding and respect among all cultures by expanding the means to access reliable, current information about Polish and Polish American culture
- To promote Polish American librarianship
- To provide opportunities for cooperation with other library associations

Membership

Membership is open to librarians, students of library schools, library support staff, and others who support the vision of PALA. Dues $50 (one-time dues to support the goals of PALA).

Officers

Pres. Ewa Barczyk, Golda Meir Lib., Univ. of Wisconsin–Milwaukee, 2311 E. Hartford Ave., Milwaukee. Tel. 414-412-5456, e-mail ewa@uwm.edu; *Secy.* Paulina Poplawska, New Ulm Public Lib., New Ulm, MN. E-mail ppoplaws ka@tds.lib.mn.us; *Treas.* Bernadetta Koryciarz, Niles-Maine District Lib., 6960 Oakton St., Niles, IL 60714. Tel. 847-663-6642, e-mail bkorycia@nileslibrary.org; *Past Pres.* Leonard Kniffel (dec.). *Dirs.-at-Large* Iwona Bozek, Krystyna Matusiak, Hanna Przybylski, Marianne Ryan.

REFORMA (National Association to Promote Library and Information Services to Latinos and the Spanish-Speaking)

President, Oscar Beaza
P.O. Box 71651, Los Angeles CA 90071
E-mail admin@reforma.org
World Wide Web https://www.reforma.org

Objective

Promoting library services to the Spanish-speaking for nearly 40 years, REFORMA, an affiliate of the American Library Association, works in a number of areas to advance the development of library collections that include Spanish-language and Latino-oriented materials, the recruitment of more bilingual and bicultural professionals and support staff, the development of library services and programs that meet the needs of the Latino community, the establishment of a national network among individuals who share its goals, the education of the U.S. Latino population in regard to the availability and types of library services, and lobbying efforts to preserve existing library resource centers serving the interest of Latinos.

Membership

Memb. 800+. Membership is open to any person who is supportive of the goals and objectives of REFORMA. Dues (Indiv.) $10–$50; (Int'l.) Free; (Life) $450; (Inst.) $100–$250. Year.

Executive Committee (2021–2022)

Pres. Nicanor Diaz, Denver Public Library. E-mail president@reforma.org; *V.P./Pres.-Elect* Romelia Salinas, Mt. San Antonio College. E-mail vice-president@reforma.org; *Secy.* Alma Ramos-McDermott, Lake Trafford Elementary School. E-mail secretary@reforma.org; *Treas.* Denice Adkins, Univ. of Missouri. E-mail treasurer@reforma.org; *Past Pres.* Oscar Baeza, El Paso Community College. E-mail past-president@reforma.org; *Memb.-at-Large* Alda Allina Migoni, Library of Congress. E-mail at-large-rep@reforma.org; *Chapter Reps.* Manny Figueroa, Queens Lib. E-mail chapter-east-region@reforma.org; Balladolid (Dolly) Lopez, California State University Fresno. E-mail chapter-west-region@reforma.org; Position Open. E-mail chapter-central-region@reforma.org.

Committee Chairs

Awards. Mary Marques.
Children and Young Adult Service Committee (CAYASC). Maria Estrella.
Education. Michele A.L. Villagran.
Finance. Oscar Baeza.
Fundraising. Kenny Garcia.
International Relations. Elizabeth Garcia and Tess Tobin.
Legislative. Mario Ascencio and Madeleine Ildefonso.
Membership. Tess Tobin.
Mentoring. Antonio Apodaca.
Nominations. Kenny Garcia.
Organizational Development and New Chapters. Manny Figueroa.
Program. Romelia Salinas.
Public Relations. Celia Avila and Libbhy Romero.
REFORMA National Conferences Coordinating Committee. Abigail Morales and Roxana Benavides.
Scholarship. Position Open.
Technology. Madeline Peña (web manager) and Edwin Rodarte.
Translations. Joanna M. Arteaga La Spina.

Publication

REFORMA (e-newsletter). *Ed.* Libbhy Romero.

Meetings

General membership and board meetings take place at the American Library Association Midwinter Meeting and Annual Conference and Exhibition.

Scholarly Publishing and Academic Resources Coalition

Executive Director, Heather Joseph
1201 Connecticut Ave. N.W., P.O. 607/608, Washington, DC 20036
202-630-5090, e-mail sparc@sparcopen.org
World Wide Web https://sparcopen.org
Twitter @SPARC_NA

Objective

SPARC, the Scholarly Publishing and Academic Resources Coalition, is a global organization that promotes expanded sharing of scholarship in the networked digital environment. It is committed to faster and wider sharing of outputs of the research process to increase the impact of research, fuel the advancement of knowledge, and increase the return on research investments.

Launched as an initiative of the Association of Research Libraries, SPARC has become a catalyst for change. Its pragmatic focus is to stimulate the emergence of new scholarly communication models that expand the dissemination of scholarly research and equip libraries for the inexorable growth in research output.

Action by SPARC in collaboration with stakeholders—including authors, publishers, and libraries—builds on the unprecedented opportunities created by the networked digital environment to advance the conduct of scholarship.

SPARC's role in stimulating change focuses on the following:

- Educating stakeholders about the problems facing scholarly communication and the opportunities for them to play a role in achieving positive change
- Advocating policy changes that advance scholarly communication and explicitly recognize that dissemination of scholarship is an essential, inseparable component of the research process
- Incubating demonstrations of new publishing and sustainability models that benefit scholarship and academe

SPARC is an advocate for changes in scholarly communication that benefit more than the academic community alone. Founded in 1997 and now operating independently of ARL, SPARC has expanded to represent more than 800 academic and research libraries in North America, the United Kingdom, Europe, and Japan.

Membership

Memb. 240+ institutions. SPARC membership is open to international academic and research institutions, organizations, and consortia that share an interest in creating a more open and diverse marketplace for scholarly communication. Dues are scaled by membership type and budget. For more information, visit SPARC's website at https://sparcopen.org/become-a-member, SPARC Europe at https://sparcopen.org/people/sparc-europe, SPARC Japan at http://www.nii.ac.jp/sparc, or SPARC Africa at https://sparcopen.org/people/sparc-africa.

Steering Committee

Jennifer Beamer, Gwen Bird, Chris Bourg, Talia Chung, Vicki Coleman, Christopher Cox, Karen Estlund, Antoinette Foster, Scarlet Galven, Carrie Gits, Harriet Green, Lorraine Harricombe, April Hathcock, Heather Joseph, Mary Lee Kennedy, Beth McNeil, Carmelita Pickett, Ariana Santiago, Virginia Steel, Elaine Thornton.

Staff

Open Education Cdtr. Aisha Abdullah. E-mail aisha@sparcopen.org.; *Dir., Open Education* Nicole Allen. E-mail nicole@sparcopen.org; *Open Education Project Mgr.* Hailey Babb. E-mail hailey@sparcopen.org; *VPO for U.S. Repository Network* Tina Baich; *HELIOS Project Coord.* Caitlin Carter. E-mail caitlin@sparcopen.org; *Senior Consultant* Raym Crow. E-mail crow@sparcopen.org; *Prog. & Oper. Specialist* Lese Fandel. E-mail lese@sparcopen.org; *Chief Operating Officer* Val Hollister. E-mail val@sparcopen.org; *Exec. Dir.* Heather Joseph. E-mail heather@sparcopen.org; *Sr. Fellow* Sarah Lamdan; *Asst. Dir., Right to Research Coalition* Joseph McArthur. E-mail joe@righttoresearch.org; *Community Mgr., Open Research Funders Group*, Erin McKiernan. E-mail erin@sparc.open.org; *Open & Equitable Civic Science Fellow* Eunice Mercado-Lara. E-mail eunice@sparcopen.org; *Open Education Project Mgr.* Trudi Radtke. E-mail trudi@sparcopen.org; *Dir. of Programs and Engagement* Nick Shockey. E-mail nick@sparcopen.org; *Instructor, Open Educ. Leadership Program* Tanya Spilovoy. E-mail leadership@sparcopen.org; *Manager of Public Policy and Advocacy* Katie Steen. E-mail katie@sparcopen.org; *Consultant* Greg Tananbaum. E-mail greg@sparcopen.org.

Publications

Open Educational Resources (OER) State Policy Playbook (2020 ed.) (https://sparcopen.org/our-work/oer-state-policy-playbook).

SPARC Landscape Analysis and Roadmap for Action (2020 update) by Claudio Aspesi (lead author), Nicole Allen, Raym Crow, Shawn Daugherty, Heather Joseph, Joseph McArthur, and Nick Shockey. (https://infrastructure.sparcopen.org/2020-update).

Society for Scholarly Publishing

Executive Director, Melanie Dolechek
1120 Route 73, Suite 200, Mount Laurel, NJ 08054
856-439-1385, fax 856-439-0525, e-mail info@sspnet.org
World Wide Web https://www.sspnet.org
Twitter @ScholarlyPub

Objective

To draw together individuals involved in the process of scholarly publishing. This process requires successful interaction of the many functions performed within the scholarly community. The Society for Scholarly Publishing (SSP) provides the leadership for such interaction by creating opportunities for the exchange of information and opinions among scholars, editors, publishers, librarians, printers, booksellers, and all others engaged in scholarly publishing.

Membership

Memb. 1,000+. Open to all with an interest in the scholarly publishing process and dissemination of information. Dues (Indiv. Renewal) $200; (Libn.) $85; (Early Career New) $60; (Student) $40; (Supporting Organization) $2,195; (Sustaining Organization) $5,747; (Intl. Indiv.) $50; (Intl. Early Career) $25; (Intl. Libn.) $25; (Intl. Student); $10. Year. Jan.–Dec.

Officers

Pres. Alice Meadows, NISO; *Pres.-Elect* Miranda Walker, Wolters Kluwer; *Secy./Treas.* Emelie Delquie, Copyright Clearance Ctr.; *Past Pres.* Lauren Kane, Morressier.

Board of Directors

Meredith Adinolfi, Mike Di Natale, Gabe Harp, Lisa Hinchliffe, Sai Konda, Rebecca McLeod, Charlotte Roh, Sara Rouhi, Randy Townsend, David Crotty (ex officio), Melanie Dolechek (ex officio).

Committee Chairs

Advancement. Richard Kobel and Kim Smilay.
Annual Meeting Program. Lori Carlin, Yael Fitzpatrick, and Tim Lloyd.
Audit. Gabriel P. Harp and Cason Lynley.
Career Development. Michelle M. English, Karen G. Stanwood, and Sanjay Tangri.
Community Engagement. Megan M. McCarty, Lindsay Best Miller, and Byron A. Russell.
Diversity, Equity, and Inclusion. Chhavi Chauhan, Sabby Kaur Jivanji, and Damita Snow.
Education. Stephanie F. Decouvelaere, Jeff Lang and Will Schweitzer.
Finance. Emilie Delquie and Dr. Anna Wetterberg.
Funder Task Force. Adrian Stanley and Michelle Urberg.
Marketing & Communications. Mike Groth, Nicola Poser, and Jennifer Regala.
Membership. Caroline Breul and Patrick Franzen.
Nominating and Awards. Lauren Kane.

Publications

Learned Publishing (memb.). Published by the Association of Learned and Professional Society Publishers (ALPSP) in collaboration with SSP. *Ed.* (N.A.) Lette Y. Conrad.
The Scholarly Kitchen (moderated blog). *Ed.* David Crotty.

Meetings

An annual meeting is held in late May/early June.

Society of American Archivists

Executive Director, Jacqualine Price Osafo
17 N. State St., Suite 1425, Chicago, IL 60602
312-606-0722, toll-free 866-722-7858, fax 312-606-0728, e-mail saahq@archivists.org
World Wide Web https://www2.archivists.org
Twitter @archivists_org

Object

Founded in 1936, the Society of American Archivists (SAA) is North America's oldest and largest national archival professional association. Representing more than 6,000 individual and institutional members, SAA promotes the value and diversity of archives and archivists and is the preeminent source of professional resources and the principal communication hub for American archivists.

Membership

Memb. 6,200+. Dues (Indiv.) $80 to $325, graduated according to salary; (Assoc.) $115; (Ret.) $77; (Student/Bridge) $55; (Inst.) $340; (Sustaining Inst.) $595.

Officers

Pres. Courtney Chartier, Columbia University. E-mail president@archivists.org; *V.P./Pres.-Elect* Terry Baxter, Multnomah County Records Program; *Treas.* Shamila Bhatia, National Archives at College Park.

Leadership

Exec. Dir. Jacqualine Price Osafo; *Dir. of Publishing* Teresa Brinati; *Dir. of Finance and Admin.* Peter Carlson; *Dir. of Ed.* Rana Hutchinson Salzmann; *Web and Info. Syst. Admin.* Matthew Black; *Governance Prog. Mgr.* Felicia Owens; *Mgr./Svc. Ctr.* Carlos L. Delgado.

SAA Council

Eric Chin, Stephen R. Curley, Jasmine Jones, Dominique Luster, Derek P. Mosley, Mario Ramirez, Tonia Sutherland. Meg Tuomala, Rachel E. Winston; Jacqualine Price Osafo (ex officio).

Committee Chairs

American Archivist Editorial Board. Amy Cooper Cary.
Appointments. Selena Ortega-Chiolero.
Awards. Cara Bertram and Megan Keller Young.
Diversity. Tammi Kim.
Education. Carli Lowe.
Ethics and Professional Conduct. Cliff Hight and Mary Larson.
Finance. Sharmila Bhatia.
Host. Rakashi Chand.
Membership. Alison Clemens.
Nominating. Maria Angel Diaz.
Programming. Natalie Bauer and Sarah Quigley.
Public Awareness. Rachel Seale.
Public Policy. Bryan Whitledge.
Publications Board. Stacie Williams.
Research, Data, and Assessment. Jennifer King and Erin Passehl Stoddart.
Selection of SAA Fellows. Tanya Zanish-Belcher.
Standards. Kira Dietz.

Task Force and Working Groups Chairs

Archival Compensation Task Force. Greta Pittenger.
A*CENSUS II Working Group. Elizabeth Myers.

Publications

American Archivist (s. ann.; $289). *Ed.* Amy Cooper Cary. Tel 414-288-5901, e-mail AmericanArchivist@archivists.org; *Reviews Eds.* Rose Buchanan and Stephanie Luke. Tel. 217-333-0798, e-mail Reviews Editor@archivists.org.
Archival Outlook (bi-mo.; memb.).
In the Loop e-newsletter (bi-wk.).

Software and Information Industry Association

President, Jeff Joseph
1090 Vermont Ave. N.W. Sixth Floor, Washington, DC 20005-4905
202-289-7442, fax 202-289-7097
World Wide Web http://www.siia.net
Twitter @SIIA

The Software and Information Industry Association (SIIA) was formed January 1, 1999, through the merger of the Software Publishers Association (SPA) and the Information Industry Association (IIA).

Membership

Memb. 800+ companies. Open to companies that develop software and digital information content. For details on membership and dues, see the SIIA website, http://www.siia.net.

Leadership

Pres. Jeff Joseph. Tel. 202-789-4440. E-mail jjoseph@siia.net; *Senior V.P. and Managing Dir., FISD* Tom Davin; *Chief Financial Officer* Carl Walker; *Sr. V.P., Global Public Policy* Paul Lekas; *V.P. for Intellectual Property and Gnl. Cnsl.* Christopher Mohr; *Dir. Associations Council* Jen Smith.

Special Libraries Association

Executive Director, Amy Lestition Burke
7918 Jones Branch Drive, Suite 300, McLean, VA 22102
703-647-4900, fax 703-506-3266, e-mail aburke@sla.org
World Wide Web https://www.sla.org
Twitter @SLAhq

Mission

The Special Libraries Association (SLA) promotes and strengthens its members through learning, advocacy, and networking initiatives.

Strategic Vision

SLA is a global association of information and knowledge professionals who are employed in every sector of the economy. Its members thrive where data, information, and knowledge intersect, and its strategic partners support SLA because they believe in the association's mission and the future of its members. SLA's goal is to support information professionals as they contribute, in their varied and evolving roles, to the opportunities and achievements of organizations, communities, and society.

Membership

Memb. 9,000+ in 75 countries. Dues (Org.) $750; (Indiv.) $100–$200; (Student/Intl./Salary less than $18,000 income per year) $50; (Ret.) $100.

Officers (2022)

Pres. Catherine Lavallée-Welch, Bishop's Univ., Sherbrooke, PQ. E-mail clw@ubishops.ca; *Pres.-Elect* Seema Rampersad, British Library, London, England. E-mail seemarampersad@hotmail.com; *Treas.* Valerie Perry, University of Kentucky, Lexington, KY. E-mail vperry@uky.edu; *Past Pres.* Tara Murray Grove, Pennsylvania State Univ., University Park, PA. E-mail tem10@psu.edu.

Directors

Anne Barker (2022–2024), JonLuc Christensen (2022–2024), PK Jain (2020–2023), Debal Kar (2022), Heather Kotula (2022–2024), Elaine Lasda (2020–2023), Kendra Levine (2022–2024), Jim Miller (2020–2023), Julie Snyder (2020–2023), Ty Webb (2022).

Council and Committee Chairs

Annual Conference Advisory Council. Janel Kinlaw.
Awards and Honors. Jill Strand.
Content Advisory Council. Helen Kula and Brian McCann.
Finance. Willem Noorlander.

Governance and Strategy. Position Open.
Leadership Advisory Council. Tara Murray Grove.
Membership Advisory Council. Lateka Grays.
Nominating. Nick Collison.
Professional Development Advisory Council. Lateka Grays.
Public Policy Advisory Council. Kevin Adams.
Public Relations Advisory Council. Elizabeth Deegan.
Students and New Professionals Advisory Council. Laura Walesby.
Technology Advisory Council. Christine Geluk, Samuel Russell.
Workplace Preparedness and Response Advisory Council (PREP). Eric Tans.

Theatre Library Association

President, Francesca Marini
c/o New York Public Library for the Performing Arts
40 Lincoln Center Plaza, New York, NY 10023
E-mail theatrelibraryassociation@gmail.com
World Wide Web http://www.tla-online.org
Twitter @theatrelibassn

Objective

To further the interests of collecting, preserving, and using theater, cinema, and performing arts materials in libraries, museums, and private collections. Founded in 1937.

Membership

Memb. 300. Dues (Indiv.) $50; (Student/Nonsalaried) $25; (Inst.) $75; (Sustaining) $150. Year. Jan.–Dec.

Officers

Pres. Francesca Marini, Cushing Lib., Texas A&M Univ. E-mail fmarini@library.tamu. edu; *V.P.* Diana King, Univ. of California–Los Angeles. E-mail diking@library.ucla.edu; *Exec. Secy.* Dale Stinchcomb, Houghton Lib., Harvard University. E-mail dstinchcomb@fas. harvard.edu; *Treas.* Sophie Glidden-Lyon, La MaMa. E-mail sophie.gliddenlyon@gmail.

com; *Past Pres.* (ex officio) Colleen Reilly, Houston Community College. E-mail colleen. reilly@hccs.edu.

Board of Directors

(2020–2022) Drew Barker, William Daw, Kylie Goetz, Karin Suni; (2021–2023) Kristin Dougan Johnson, Suzanne Lipkin, David Nochimson, Gabriella Steinberg; (2012–2023) Stephanie Bonjack, Arianne Hartsell-Gundy, Mary Huelsbeck, Megan Reichelt.

Committee Chairs

Book Awards. Suzanne Lipkin and Annemarie van Roessel.
Conference Planning. Diana King.
Membership. Matt DiCintio.
Nominating. Angela Weaver.
Professional Awards. Drew Barker.
Publications. Joseph Tally.

Strategic Planning. Diana King.
Website Editorial. William Daw.

Publications

Broadside Archive (digital back issues). *Ed.* Angela Weaver *(2008–2014).*

Performing Arts Resources (occasional) see http://www.tla-online.org/publicationsper forming-arts-resources/performing-arts-resources-volumes for links to subscription and https://www.proquest.com/products-services/iipa_ft.html for database from Pro-Quest.

Urban Libraries Council

President and CEO, Susan Benton
1333 H St. N.W., Suite 1000 West, Washington, DC 20005
202-750-8650, e-mail info@urbanlibraries.org
World Wide Web http://www.urbanlibraries.org
Facebook https://www.facebook.com/UrbanLibrariesCouncil
Twitter @UrbanLibCouncil

Objective

Since 1971 the Urban Libraries Council (ULC) has worked to strengthen public libraries as an essential part of urban life. A member organization of North America's leading public library systems, ULC serves as a forum for research widely recognized and used by public- and private-sector leaders. Its members are thought leaders dedicated to leadership, innovation, and the continuous transformation of libraries to meet community needs.

ULC's work focuses on helping public libraries to identify and utilize skills and strategies that match the challenges of the 21st century.

Membership

Membership is open to public libraries and to corporate partners specializing in library-related materials and services. The organization also offers associate memberships. Annual membership dues for libraries are based on the size of a library's operating budget (local + state).

Officers (2021–2022)

Chair Mary J. Wardell-Ghirarduzzi; *V.Chair/Chair-Elect* Karl Dean; *Secy./Treas.* J. Brandon Neal; *Past Chair* Richard Reyes-Gavilan; *Memb.-at-Large* Karl Dean.

Board Members

Dr. Michele Bria, Sarah Campbell, Joey Crawford, Dr. Patrick Dowd, Pilar Martinez, Michael Meyer, Skye Patrick, Jesus Salas, Meghann Silverthorn, Rebecca Stavick, Michelle VonderHaar, Roosevelt Weeks.

State, Provincial, and Regional Library Associations

The associations in this section are organized under three headings: United States, Canada, and Regional. Both the United States and Canada are represented under Regional associations.

United States

Alabama

Memb. 1,200. Publication. *ALLA COMmunicator* (q.).

Pres. Laura Pitts, Scottsboro Public Library. Tel. 256-574-4335, e-mail, laurap@scottsboro. org; *Pres.-Elect* Amanda Melcher, University of Montevallo. Tel. 205-665-6104, e-mail melcheras@montevallo.edu; *Secy.* Paula Webb, Univ. of South Alabama. Tel. 251-461-1933, e-mail pwebb@southalabama.edu; *Treas.* Karen Preuss, Montgomery City-County Public Lib. (retired), P.O. Box 1950, Montgomery 36102-1950. Tel. 334-240-4300, e-mail kpreuss@mccpl.lib.al.us; *Memb.-at-Large* (Central Alabama) Emily Allee, Birmingham Public Library. Tel. 205.226.3720, emily.allee@cobpl. org; (North Alabama) Craig Scott, Gadsden Public Library. Tel. 256-549-4699, ext. 2120, e-mail craig@gadsdenlibrary.org; (South Alabama) Wendy Congairdo, Thomas B. Norton Public Lib., 221 W. 19th Ave., Gulf Shores 36542. Tel. 251-968-1176, e-mail wcongiardo@hotmail.com. *Past Pres.* Daniel Tackett, Vestavia Hills Library in the Forest. Tel. 205-978-3683, e-mail daniel.tackett@vestavialibrary.org; *Assn. Admin.* (ex officio) Angela Moore, Alabama Lib. Assn., 6030 Monticello Dr., Montgomery 36117. Tel. 334-414-0113, e-mail allaadmin@allanet.org.

Address correspondence to administrator. Alabama Lib. Assn., 6030 Monticello Dr., Montgomery 36117. Tel. 334-414-0113, e-mail allibraryassoc@gmail.com.

World Wide Web https://www.allanet.org.

Alaska

Memb. 450+. Publication. *Newspoke* (q.) (online at http://akla.org/newspoke).

Pres. Jonas Lamb; *Pres.-Elect* Jessica Ieremia; *Secy.* Paul Adasiak. E-mail pfadasiak@ alaska.edu; *Treas.* Samantha Blanquart; *Conference Coord.* Deborah Rinio; *ALA Rep.* Lorelei Sterling. E-mail lsterling@alaska.edu; *PNLA Rep.* MJ Grande; *Past Pres.* Deborah Rinio.

Address correspondence to the secretary. Alaska Lib. Assn., P.O. Box 81084, Fairbanks 99708. E-mail akla@akla.org.

World Wide Web https://akla.org.

Arizona

Memb. 1,000. Term of Office. Nov.–Nov. Publication. *AzLA Newsletter* (6x yearly).

Pres. Corey Christians; *Pres.-Elect* John Walsh; *Secy.* Amber Kent, Casa Grande Public Lib., 449 N. Drylake St., Casa Grande 85122. Tel. 520 421-8710, e-mail AKent@casagrandeaz.gov; *Treas.* Natalie Menger, Glendale Public Library. Tel. 623-930-3530, e-mail nmenger@ @glendaleaz.com; *Northern Regional Rep.* Martha Baden; *Central Regional Rep.* Rachel Martinez; *Southern Regional Rep.* Carrie Dawson; *ALA Councilor* Dan Stanton; *MPLA Rep.* Amadee Ricketts; *Past Pres.* Michelle Simon, Pima County Public Lib., 101 N. Stone Ave., Tucson 85701. Tel. 520-594-5654, e-mail michesimon54@gmail.com.

Address correspondence to Arizona 2532 N 4th St #271, Flagstaff 86004. Tel. 928.288.2011, e-mail admin@azla.org.

World Wide Web https://www.azla.org.

Arkansas

Memb. 600. Publication. *Arkansas Libraries* (4x yearly).

Pres. Rachel Shankles, 891 Hwy 7, Bismarck 71929. Tel. 501-276-4949, e-mail president@arlib.org; *Pres.-Elect* Carol Coffey, Central Arkansas Library System Main Library. Tel. 501-918-3008, e-mail president-elect@ arlib.org; *Secy.* Janice Weddle, Hendrix College–Bailey Library, 1600 Washington Avenue, Conway 72032; *Treas.* Kathleen Ashmore, Lonoke County Library System, 909 West Main St., Cabot 72023. Tel. 406-480-6249, e-mail info@arlib.org; *ALA Councilor* Crystal Gates, William F. Laman Public Library System, 2801 Orange St., North Little Rock 72114. Tel. 501-404-2919, e-mail crystal.gates@lamanlibrary.org; *Non-Voting: SELA State Rep.* Emily Rozario, William F. Laman Public Lib., 2801 Orange St., North Little Rock 72114. E-mail emily.rozario@lamanlibrary.org; *Past Pres.* Philip Shackelford, South Arkansas Community College, El Dorado 71730. Tel. 870-864-7116, e-mail pshackelford@southark.edu.

Address correspondence to Arkansas Lib. Assn., P.O. Box 3821, Little Rock 72203. Tel. 406-480-6249, e-mail info@arlib.org.

World Wide Web https://arlib.org.

California

Memb. 2,500.

Pres. Jené Brown, Los Angeles Public Library. E-mail jbrown@lapl.org; *V.P./Pres.-Elect* Gary Shaffer, Glendale Library Arts & Culture District. E-mail gshaffer@glendaleca.gov; *Treas.* Mark Fink, Yolo County Library. E-mail dwolfgram@redwoodcity.org; *Past Pres.* Jayanti Addleman, Hayward Public Library. E-mail JayantiAddleman@gmail.com.

Address correspondence to California Lib. Assn., 1055 E. Colorado Blvd., 5th Floor, Pasadena 91106. Tel. 626-204-4071, e-mail info@cla-net.org.

World Wide Web https://www.cla-net.org.

Colorado

Pres. Tiah Frankish, Adams 12 Five Star Schools. E-mail tfrankish@gmail.com; *Pres.-Elect* Jenn Cook, Garfield County Public Library District. E-mail jcook@gcpld.org; *Secy.* Sandy Hancock, Pikes Peak Library District. E-mail shancock@ppld.org; *Treas.* Nanette Fisher, Anythink Libs. E-mail nfisher@anythinklibraries.org; *Membs.-at-Large* Christine Dyar, Arapahoe Libraries. E-mail cdyar@ald.lib.co.us; B Spenser Snarr, Durango Public Library. spenser.snarr@durangogov.org. *Past Pres.* Ryan F. Buller, Univ. of Denver. E-mail ryan.buller@du.edu.

Address correspondence to Colorado Assn. of Libs., P.O. Box 740905, Arvada 80006-0905. Tel. 303-463-6400, e-mail cal@cal-webs.org.

World Wide Web https://cal-webs.org.

Connecticut

Memb. 1,000+. Term of Office. July–June. Publication. *CLA Today* (6x yearly; online). E-mail editor@ctlibrarians.org.

Pres. Colleen Balie. E-mail cbailie@west havenlibrary; *V.P./Pres.-Elect* Douglas C. Lord. E-mail dlord@chboothlibrary.org; *Recording Secy.* Danielle Duffy Valenzano, Milford Public Lib. E-mail dvalenzano@milfordct.gov; *Treas.* Kristina Edwards, Central Connecticut State Univ. E-mail kristina.edwards@uconn.edu; *Past Pres.* Thomas Piezzo, Brainerd Memorial Lib. E-mail tpiezzo@brainerdlibrary.org.

Address correspondence to Connecticut Lib. Assn., 55 North Main St., Unit 49, Belchertown 01007. Tel. 860-346-2444, e-mail mscheier@ctlibraryassociation.org.

World Wide Web https://ctlibraryassociation.org.

Delaware

Memb. 200+. Publication. *DLA Bulletin* (q.; online). E-mail Nicole.Ballance@lib.de.us.

Pres. Jen Wilson, New Castle Public Library. Tel. 302-328-1995, e-mail jennifer.wilson@lib.de.us; *V.P./Conference Chair* Rachel Jackson, Georgetown Public Library, 123 West Pine St., Georgetown 19947. Tel. 302-856-7958, e-mail rachel.jackson@lib.de.us; *Secy.* Katherine Goff, Delaware Technical Community College, Terry Campus. E-mail kgoff1@dtcc.edu; *Treas.* Jaclyn Hale, Delaware Division of Libraries, 121 Martin Luther King Jr. Blvd. N., Dover 19901. Tel. 302-257-3004, e-mail jaclynhaledla@gmail.com; *ALA Councilor* Tameca Beckett, Delaware State University, William C. Jason Library Reference and Access Services Librarian, 1200 N. DuPont Highway, Dover 19901. Tel. 302-857-7886, e-mail tbeckett@desu.edu; *Delaware State Libn.* Annie Norman, Delaware Div. of Libs., 121 Martin Luther King Jr. Blvd. N., Dover 19901. Tel. 302-257-3001, fax 302-739-6787, e-mail annie.norman@state.de.us; *Pres., Friends of Delaware Libs.* Kay Bowes. E-mail kaybowes@gmail.com; *Past Pres.* Catherine Wimberley, New Castle County Libs., 2020 W. 9th St., Wilmington 19805. Tel. 302-571-7425, e-mail catherine.wimberley@newcastlede.gov. Tel. 302-831-1730, e-mail alisonwessel.dla@gmail.com.

Address correspondence to Delaware Lib. Assn., c/o Delaware Division of Libs., 121 Martin Luther King Jr. Blvd. N., Dover 19901. E-mail dla@lib.de.us. World Wide Web https://dla.lib.de.us.

District of Columbia

Memb. 300+. Term of Office. July–June. *Pres.* Maria Thurder. E-mail president@ dcla.org; *Secy.* Leah Castaldi. E-mail secretary@dcla.org; *Treas.* Karen Janka. E-mail treasurer@dcla.org; *ALA Councilor* Erica Harbeson. E-mail ala_councilor@dcla.org; *Past Pres.* Meg Metcalf. E-mail past_president@ dcla.org.

Address correspondence to District of Columbia Lib. Assn., Union Station, 50 Massachusetts Ave. N.E., P.O. Box 1653 Washington, DC 20002.

World Wide Web https://dcla.org.

Florida

Memb. (Indiv.) 1,000+. Publication. *Florida Libraries* (s. ann.).

Pres. Phyllis Gorshe, Dunedin Public Library; *V.P./Pres.-Elect* Shane Roopnarine, University of Central Florida; *Secy.* Marina Morgan, Roux Library, Florida Southern College; *Treas.* Matthew David, Tampa-Hillsborough County Public Library; *State Libn.* Amy Johnson, Division of Lib. and Info. Svcs. E-mail Amy.Johnson@dos.myflorida.com; *ALA Councilor* Heather Sostrom, SJC-BOCC Branch Manager, Anastasia Island Branch.

Address correspondence to the executive director. Florida Lib. Assn., 545 E. Tennessee St., #103, Tallahassee 32308. Tel. 850-270-9205, e-mail admin@flalib.org.

World Wide Web https://www.flalib.org.

Georgia

Memb. 800+. Publication. *Georgia Library Quarterly* (q., online).

Pres. Karen Manning, Georgia Institute of Technology. E-mail km17@mail.gatech.edu, president@georgialibraryassociation.org; *1st V.P./Pres.-Elect* Michele Bennett-Copeland, Fayette County Public Library. E-mail vice-president@georgialibraryassociation.org; *2nd V.P./Membership* Rebecca Ballard, Athens Regional Library System. E-mail membership@

georgialibraryassociation.org; *V.P. Marketing and Branding* Marquita Gooch, Clayton County Public Library. E-mail mgooch@claytongal ib.org, marketing@georgialibraryassociation. org; *Secy.* Kelly Williams, Gwinnett County Public Library. E-mail secretary@georgiali braryassociation.org; *Treas.* Justin Nobles, West Georgia Regional Library System. E-mail treasurer@georgialibraryassociation.org; *Past Pres.* Wendy Cornelisen, GPLS. E-mail wcor nelisen@georgialibraries.org, pastpresident@ georgialibraryassociation.org.

Address correspondence to Georgia Lib. Assn., 1502 W Broadway, Suite 102, Madison, 53713. Tel. 912-376-9155, e-mail memberser vices@georgialibraryassociation.org.

World Wide Web https://gla.georgialibrar ies.org.

Hawaii

Memb. 250. Publication. *KoleKole* (3x yearly).

Pres. Jenny Silbiger, State Law Librarian & Access to Justice; *V.P.* Carina Chernisky, James & Abigail Campbell Library, University of Hawaii-West Oahu; *Secy.* Stephanie Robertson, Joseph F. Smith Library, Brigham Young University-Hawaii; *Treas.* Joy Oehlers, Lama Library, Kapi'olani Community College; *Past Pres.* Joyce Tokuda, Kapi'olani Community College. E-mail jtokuda@hawaii.edu.

Address correspondence to Hawai'i Lib. Assn., P.O. Box 4441, Honolulu 96812-4441. E-mail hawaii.library.association@gmail.com.

World Wide Web https://www.hawaiili braryassociation.org.

Idaho

Memb. 420. Term of Office. Oct.–Oct.

President Amy Campbell, Marshall Public Library, Pocatello. Tel. 208-232-1263, ext. 105, e-mail acampbell@marshallpl.org; *V.P.* Jessica Bowman, Community Library Network at Hayden. Tel. 208-610-3959, e-mail jessg bowman@gmail.com; *Secy.* Jennifer Redford, Idaho Commission for Libraries. Tel. 208-991-8271, e-mail jennifer.redford@idaho.libraries. gov; *Treas.* Gretchen Casserotti, Meridian Library District. Tel. 208-888-2451, ext. 1226; *Membership Committee Chair* Mary DeWalt, Ada Community Library, Boise. Tel. 208-437-2774, e-mail mdewalt@adalib.org.

Address correspondence to Idaho Lib. Assn., 4911 N. Shirley Ave., Boise 83703. World Wide Web http://idaholibraries.org.

Illinois

Memb. 3,000. Publication. *ILA Reporter* (bi-mo.; online).

Pres. Jeanne Hamilton, Bloomington Public Library; *V.P./Pres.-Elect* Heather Jagman, DePaul University Library; *Treas.* Joe Filapek, Aurora Public Library; *ALA Councilor* Paul Mills, Fountaindale Public Library District; *Past Pres.* Veronica De Fazio, Plainfield Public Lib. Dist.

Address correspondence to the executive director. Illinois Lib. Assn., 33 W. Grand Ave., Suite 401, Chicago 60654-6799. Tel. 312 644-1896, fax 312 644-1899, e-mail ila@ila.org. World Wide Web https://www.ila.org.

Indiana

Indiana Lib. Federation. Memb. 2,000+. Publication. *Focus on Indiana Libraries* (mo.; memb.).

Pres. Michael Williams, Indianapolis Public Library, 40 E. Saint Clair St., Indianapolis 46204. Tel. 317-275-4302; *V.P.* Karen Evans, Indiana State University; *Secy.* Cheryl Blevens, Indiana State University; *Treas.* Lynn Hobbs, Pendleton Community Public Library; *ALA Councilor* Jos N. Holman, Tippecanoe County Public Library, 627 South St., Lafayette 47901; *Past Pres.* Leslie Sutherlin, South Dearborn Community Schools, 5770 Highlander Place, Aurora 47001; *Exec. Dir.* Lane Valeyo. Tel. 317-257-2040 ext. 101, e-mail exec@ilfonline. org.

Address correspondence to Indiana Lib. Federation, 941 E. 86 St., Suite 260, Indianapolis 46240. Tel. 317-257-2040, fax 317-257-1389, e-mail askus@ilfonline.org. World Wide Web https://www.ilfonline.org.

Iowa

Memb. 1,600+. Publication. *Catalyst* (bi-mo., online).

Pres. Sarah Uthoff, Kirkwood Community College; *V.P.* Sam Helmick, Iowa City Public Library; *Secy.* Eric Jennings, University of Northern Iowa; *Treas.* Megan Klein-Hewett, Ames Public Library; *Parliamentarian* Tracy Clair, Ely Public Library; *ALA Councilor* Amanda Vazquez, Dubuque County Library; *Past Pres.* Stacy Goodhue. E-mail sgoodhue@carlisle.lib.ia.us.

Address correspondence to Iowa Lib. Assn., 6919 Vista Dr., West Des Moines 50266. Tel. 515-282-8192. World Wide Web https://www.iowalibrary association.org.

Kansas

Kansas Lib. Assn. Memb. 1,500. Term of Office. July–June. Publication. *Kansas Libraries!* (6x yearly; online). E-mail kilbmag@gmail. com.

Pres. Holly Mercer, Southwest Kansas Lib. System; *1st V.P.* Shanna Smith-Ritterhouse; *2nd V.P.* Sean Bird; *Secy.* Sean Stacey; *Treas.* Terri Wojtalewicz, Lancing Community Library; *Exec. Secy.* George Seamon; *Parliamentarian* Dan Ireton; *ALA Councilor* Heather Van Dyne, Allen Community College; *Past Pres.* Meagan Zampieri-Lillipopp, Hays Public Lib.

Address correspondence to the president. Kansas Lib. Assn., Northwest Kansas Lib. System, 2 Washington Sq., Norton 67654. Tel. 785-877-5148. World Wide Web https://kslibassoc.org.

Kentucky

Memb. 1,600. Publication. *Kentucky Libraries Journal* (q.).

Pres. Mark Adler; *Pres.-Elect* Adele Koch; *Secy.* Andrew Adler; *Past Pres.* Kandace Rodgers.

Address correspondence to the president Andrew Adler. 1588 Leestown Rd., Ste. 130-310, Lexington 40511. Tel. 502-863-8405. info@kla.memberclicks.net. World Wide Web https://www.klaonline.org.

Louisiana

Memb. 1,000+. Term of Office. July–June. Publication. *Louisiana Libraries* (q.).

Pres. Jeremy Bolom. E-mail llabolom@gmail.com; *1st V.P.* Lora Amsberryaugier. E-mail lamsberr@uno.edu; *2nd V.P.* Jenny Mayer. E-mail mayerj@stpl.us; *Secy.* Jessica Styons. E-mail jstyons@slol.lib.la.us; *Treas.* Giovanni Tairov. E-mail director@mylpl.info; *ALA Councilor* Vivian McCain.

Tel. 318-513-5508, e-mail straitviv@gmail.com; *Parliamentarian* Chris Achee. E-mail cachee@myapl.org; *Past Pres.* Sonnet Ireland. Tel. 504-390-6834, e-mail sonnet@sonnetireland.com.

Address correspondence to Louisiana Lib. Assn., 1190 Meramec Station Rd., Suite 207, Ballwin, MO 63021. Tel 800-969-6562 ext. 3, fax 972-991-6061, e-mail lla@amigos.org.

World Wide Web https://llaonline.org.

Maine

Maine Lib. Assn. Memb. 950. Publication. *MLA to Z* (q., online).

Pres. Wynter Giddings, Curtis Memorial Lib., 23 Pleasant St., Brunswick 04011. Tel. 207-725-3542, e-mail giddingswynter@gmail.com; *V.P.* Sonya Durney. E-mail vicepresident@mainelibraries.org; *Secy.* Matt DeLaney, Millinocket Memorial Lib., 5 Maine Avenue, Millinocket, 04462. E-mail matt@millinocketmemoriallibrary.org; *Treas.* Amy Wisehart, Ellsworth Public Lib., 20 State Street, Ellsworth, 04605. E-mail awisehart@ellsworthlibrary.net; *Past Pres.* Jennifer Alvino, Windham Public Lib., 217 Windham Center Rd., Windham 04062. Tel. 207-892-1908, e-mail jaalvino@windhammaine.us; *Membs.-at-Large* Meg Gray, Bangor Public Library. Tel. 207-947-8336, ext. 129; Kate Wing, George J. Mitchell Department of Special Collections & Archives, Bowdoin College and Curtis Memorial Library, Brunswick. E-mail katemwing@gmail.com; *ALA Councilor* Kara Reiman, Maine State Lib., 64 State House Station, Augusta, 04333. Tel. 207-287-5660, e-mail kara.reiman@maine.gov; *NELA Rep.* Michelle Sampson, York Public Lib., 15 Long Sands Rd., York 03909. Tel. 207-363-2818, e-mail msampson@york.lib.me.us.

Address correspondence to Maine Lib. Assn., 55 Main St., Unit 49, Belchertown 01007. Tel. 207-744-7919. E-mail mainelibrary@gmail.com.

World Wide Web https://www.mainelibraries.org.

Maryland

Maryland Lib. Assn. Memb. 1,000+. Term of Office. July–July. Publication. *The Crab* (q., memb., online).

Pres. Mary Anne Bowman, St. Mary's County Public Lib., 23250 Hollywood Rd., Leonardtown 20650. Tel. 301-475-2846 ext. 1015, fax 410-884-4415, e-mail mabowman@stmalib.org; *Treas.* Carl Olson, Towson Univ., Cook Lib., 8000 York Rd., Towson 21252. Tel. 410-704-3267, e-mail colson@towson.edu; *ALA Councilor* David Dahl, Univ. of Maryland. Tel. 301-314-0395, e-mail ddahl1@umd.edu; *Conference Dir.* Naomi Keppler, Baltimore County Public Lib., 6105 Kenwood Ave., Rosedale 21237. Tel. 410-887-0521, e-mail nkeppler@bcpl.net; *Past Pres.* Morgan Miller, Cecil County Public Lib. 301 Newark Ave., Elkton 21921. Tel. 410-996-1055, e-mail mmiller@ccplnet.org; *Exec. Dir.* Joshua Stone, Maryland Lib. Assn., 1401 Hollins St., Baltimore 21223. Tel. 410-947-5090, e-mail jstone@mdlib.org.

Address correspondence to Maryland Lib. Assn., 1401 Hollins St., Baltimore 21223. Tel. 410-947-5090, fax 410-947-5089, e-mail mla@mdlib.org.

World Wide Web https://www.mdlib.org.

Massachusetts

Massachusetts Lib. Assn. Memb. (Indiv.) 1,000; (Inst.) 100.

Pres. Joanne Lamothe, Sandwich Public Lib. E-mail president@masslib.org; *V.P.* Kim Hewitt, Waltham Public Library. E-mail vicepresident@masslib.org; *Secy.* Noelle Boc, Tewksbury Lib., 300 Chandler St., Tewksbury 01876. Tel. 978-640-4490, e-mail secretary@masslib.org; *Treas.* Bernadette Rivard, Bellingham Public Lib., Bellingham. E-mail treasurer@masslib.org; *Past Pres.* Nora Blake, Emily Williston Memorial Lib., Easthampton. E-mail pastpresident@masslib.org.

Address correspondence to Massachusetts Lib. Assn., P.O. Box 404, Malden 02148. Tel. 781-698-7764, e-mail manager@masslib.org.

World Wide Web https://mla.wildapricot.org.

Michigan

Memb. 1,200+.

Pres. Ryan Wieber, Kalamazoo Public Library; *Secy./Treas.* Scott Duimstra, Capital Area District Libraries; *State Librarian* Randy Riley, Library of Michigan; *Past Pres./ALA Councilor* Jennifer L. Dean, University of Detroit Mercy Libraries; *Exec. Dir.* Deborah E. Mikula, Michigan Lib. Association. Tel. 517-394-2774 ext. 224, e-mail dmikula@milibraries.org.

Address correspondence to the executive director. Michigan Lib. Assn., 3410 Belle Chase Way, Suite 100, Lansing 48911. Tel. 517-394-2774, e-mail MLA@milibraries.org. World Wide Web https://www.milibraries.org.

Minnesota

Memb. 1,100. Term of Office. (*Pres., Pres.-Elect*) Jan.–Dec. Publication. *Roundup* (mo., online).
Pres. Stacey Hendren, Anoka County Lib.; *Pres.-Elect* Steve Harsin, Southeastern Libraries Cooperating; *Secy.* Sara Fillbrandt, Rasmussen College; *Treas.* Sarah Ethier, Scott County Lib.; *Memb.-at-Large* Katie Sundstrom, Two Harbors Public Lib.; *ALA Chapter Councilor* Hannah Buckland, Minnesota Dept. of Education; *Past Pres.* Kirsten Clark, Enterprise Systems, University of Minnesota Libraries; *Exec. Dir.* Joy DesMarais-Lanz. E-mail office@mnlibraryassociation.org.
Address correspondence to the executive director. 1611 County Road B West, Ste 315, Saint Paul 55113. Tel. 612-294-6549, e-mail office@mnlibraryassociation.org.
World Wide Web https://www.mnlibraryassociation.org.

Mississippi

Memb. 625. Term of Office. Jan.–Dec. Publication. *Mississippi Libraries* (q.).
Pres. Stephen Parks, State Law Lib. of Mississippi. Tel. 601-359-3612; *V.P.* Philip Carter, Starkville-Oktibbeha Public Library System. Tel. 662-323-2766, ext.7; *Secy.* Ryda Worthy, South Mississippi Regional Library. Tel. 601-736-5516; *Treas.* Audrey Beach, Mississippi Delta Community College. Tel. 662-246-6353; *Parliamentarian* Patsy C. Brewer, Waynesboro-Wayne County Library. Tel. 601-735-2268; *ALA Councilor* Amanda Clay Powers, Fant Memorial Library. Tel. 662-329-7332; *Past Pres.* Mara Polk, Central Mississippi Regional Lib. System. Tel. 601-825-0100; *Admin.* Paula Bass, P.O. Box 13687, Jackson 39236-3687. Tel. 601-981-4586, e-mail info@misslib.org.
Address correspondence to the administrator. Mississippi Lib. Assn., P.O. Box 13687, Jackson 39236-3687. Tel. 601-981-4586, e-mail info@misslib.org.
World Wide Web http://www.misslib.org.

Missouri

Memb. 800+. Term of Office. Jan.–Dec. Publication. *MO INFO* (bi-mo.).
Pres. Claudia Cook, Missouri River Regional Lib. E-mail mlapresident@molib.org; *Pres.-Elect* Otter Bowman, Daniel Boone Regional Library; *Secy./Memb.-at-Large* Rachelle Brandel, Missouri Baptist University; *Treas./Memb.-at-Large* Brent Sweany, University of Missouri-Kansas City; *Asst. Treas./Memb.-at-Large* Jason Phinney, Windsor Branch, Jefferson County Library; *Memb. Committee Chair/Memb.-at-Large* Kimberly Moeller, University of Missouri–Columbia; *Membs.-at-Large* Amy Held, Jefferson County Lib. Arnold Branch; Diana Platt, Kansas City Public Lib.; *ALA Councilor* Margaret Conroy, Daniel Boone Regional Lib.; *Past Pres.* Cindy Thompson, UMKC Univ. Libs. E-mail cindy@molib.org.
Address correspondence to the president. Missouri Lib. Assn., 1190 Meramec Station Rd., Suite 207, Ballwin, 63021-6902. E-mail mlapresident@molib.org.
World Wide Web http://molib.org.

Montana

Memb. 600. Term of Office. July–June. Publication. *Focus* (bi-mo.).
Pres. Kit Stephenson, Bozeman Public Lib.; *V.P./Pres.-Elect* Angela Archuleta, KW-Vina Elementary School; *Secy./Treas.* Kelly Reisig, Sidney-Richland County Public Library; *ALA Rep.* Matt Beckstrom, Lewis & Clark Lib., 120 S. Last Chance Gulch, Helena 59601; *Past Pres.* Gavin Woltjer, Billings Public Lib., 510 North Broadway, Billings 59101; *Exec. Dir.* Kirk Vriesman, Montana Lib. Assn., P.O. Box 823, Arlee 59821. Tel. 406-579-3121. E-mail kirkv@mtlib.org.
Address correspondence to the executive director. Montana Lib. Assn, P.O. Box 823, Arlee 59821. Tel. 406-579-3121. E-mail kirkv@mtlib.org.
World Wide Web https://mlai.wildapricot.org.

Nebraska

Term of Office. Jan.–Dec.
Pres. Emily Nimsakont. E-mail nlapresident@nebraskalibraries.org; *Pres.-Elect* Holli Duggan. E-mail nlapresidentelect@nebraskalibraries.org; *Secy.* Allison Sillik.

E-mail nlasecretary@nebraskalibraries.org; *Treas.* Anneka Ramirez. E-mail nlatreasurer@ nebraskalibraries.org; *ALA Councilor* Brenda Ealey. E-mail nla-ala@nebraskalibraries. org; *Past Pres.* Laura England-Biggs. E-mail nlapastpresident@nebraskalibraries.org; *Exec. Dir.* Ginger Jelinek. E-mail nlaexecutivedirec tor@nebraskalibraries.org.

Address correspondence to the executive director. Nebraska Lib. Assn., P.O. Box 21756, Lincoln 68542-1756.

World Wide Web https://nebraskalibraries. org.

Nevada

Memb. 450. Term of Office. Jan.–Dec. Publication. *Nevada Libraries* (q.).

Pres. Tod Colegrove, Carson City Lib., E-mail tcolegrove@carson.org; *Pres.-Elect* Marcie Smedley, Henderson Libraries. E-mail mlsmedley@hendersonlibraries.com. *Exec. Secy.* Carla Land, Las Vegas–Clark County Lib. District. E-mail bookdiva@gmail.com; *Treas.* Joy Gunn, Henderson Libs. E-mail jgunn@ hendersonlibraries.com; *Finance* Morgan Tiar, Washoe County Lib. System. E-mail matiar@ washoecounty.us; *State Libn.* Mike Strom, Nevada State Lib. Administrator. E-mail mstrom@admin.nv.gov; *ALA Delegate* Amy Geddes, Lyon County Lib. District. E-mail ageddes@lyon-county.org; *Past Pres.* Forrest Lewis, North Las Vegas Lib. District. E-mail lewisf@cityofnorthlasvegas.com.

Address correspondence to the executive secretary.

World Wide Web https://nevadalibraries.org.

New Hampshire

Memb. 600+.

Pres. Yvette Couser, Merrimack Public Lib., 470 Daniel Webster Hwy., Merrimack 03784. Tel. 603-424-5021 ext. 108, e-mail ycouser@ merrimacklibrary.org; *V.P./Pres.-Elect* Denise M. van Zanten, Manchester City Lib., 405 Pine Street, Manchester 03104. Tel. 603-624-6550 ext. 3329, e-mail dvanzant@manchesternh. gov; *Secy.* Mindy Atwood, Abbott Library, 11 Soonipi Circle P.O. Box 314, Sunapee 03782. Tel. 603-763-5513; e-mail director@abbottli brary.org; *Treas.* Kim Gabert, Wadleigh Memorial Lib., 49 Nashua St., Milford 03055. Tel. 603-249-0645, e-mail treasurer@nhlibrarians.

org; *ALA Councilor* Lori Fisher, New Hampshire State Lib., 20 Park St., Concord 03301. Tel. 603-271-2393, e-mail lori.fisher@dncr. nh.gov; *Past Pres.* Amy Lappin, Lebanon Public Libs., 80 Main St., West Lebanon 03784. Tel. 603-298-8544, e-mail president@nhlibrar ians.org.

Address correspondence to New Hampshire Lib. Assn., c/o New Hampshire State Lib., 20 Park St., Concord 03301-6314. E-mail nhlaex ecutive@googlegroups.com.

World Wide Web http://nhlibrarians.org.

New Jersey

Memb. 1,800. Term of Office. July–June. Publication. *New Jersey Libraries NEWSletter* (q.). E-mail newsletter_editor@njlamembers.org.

Pres. Kate Jaggers, Highland Park Public Lib. E-mail librariankatej@gmail.com; *1st V.P./Pres.-Elect* Jessica Trujillo, Montclair Public Library. E-mail jbmtrujillo@gmail. com; *2nd V.P.* Allen McGinley, Westfield Memorial Library. E-mail allen.mcginley@gmail. com; *Secy.* Selwa Shamy, Montclair Public Library. E-mail selwashamy@gmail.com; *Treas.* Samantha McCoy, West Caldwell Public Lib. E-mail mccoy@westcaldwell.bccls.org; *ALA Councilor* Eileen Palmer, LMxAC. E-mail em palmer@lmxac.org; *Past Pres.* Jen Schureman, Gloucester County Lib. System. E-mail jmsch ureman@gmail.com; *Exec. Dir.* Juliet Machie. E-mail jmachie@njla.org.

Address correspondence to the executive director. E-mail jmachie@njla.org.

World Wide Web https://www.njla.org.

New Mexico

Memb. 550. Term of Office. Apr.–Apr. Publication. *NMLA Newsletter* (bi-mo., online). E-mail newsletter@nmla.org.

Pres. Dean Smith. E-mail president@nmla. org; *V.P./Pres.-Elect* Kate Alderete. E-mail vicepresident@nmla.org; *Secy.* Sarah Obenauf. E-mail secretary@nmla.org; *Treas.* Kelli Murphy. E-mail treasurer@nmla.org; *Membs.-at-Large* Julia Kelso. E-mail librarydirector@ vglibrary.org; Cassandra Osterloh. E-mail cas sandra.osterloh@state.nm.us; Ellen Bosman. E-mail ebosman@nmsu.edu; Anne Lefkosfsky. E-mail alefkofsky@cabq.gov; *ALA-APA Councilor* Aubrey Iglesias. E-mail aiglesia@nmsu. edu.

Address correspondence to New Mexico Lib. Assn., P.O. Box 26074, Albuquerque 87125. Tel. 505-400-7309, e-mail contact@nmla.org.

World Wide Web https://nmla.org.

New York

Memb. 4,000. Term of Office. Nov.–Nov. Publication. *The eBulletin* (6x yearly, online).

Pres. Beth Merkle, The Strong Museum of Play; *Pres.-Elect* Arlene LaVerde, Townsend Harris High School; *Treas.* Kelly Harris, John Jermain Memorial Library; *Treas.-Elect* Frank McKenna, Seaford Public Library; *ALA Chapter Councilor* Cassie Guthrie, Greece Public Lib.; *Past Pres.* Barbara Stripling, iSchool, Syracuse University; *Exec. Dir.* AnnaLee Dragon, New York Lib. Assn., 6021 State Farm Rd., Guilderland 12084. Tel. 518-432-6952, fax 518-427-1697, e-mail director@nyla.org.

Address correspondence to New York Lib. Assn., 6021 State Farm Rd., Guilderland 12084. Tel. 518-432-6952, fax 518-427-1697, e-mail info@nyla.org.

World Wide Web https://www.nyla.org.

North Carolina

Memb. 1,100. Term of Office. Oct.–Oct. Publication. *North Carolina Libraries* (1–2x yearly, online).

Pres. Libby Stone. E-mail president@nclaonline.org; *V.P./Pres.-Elect* Dawn Behrend. E-mail vicepresident@nclaonline.org; *Secy.* Jenneffer Sixkiller. E-mail secretary@nclaonline.org; *Treas.* Lara Luck. E-mail treasurer@nclaonline.org; *Treas.-Elect* Kate Engelbrecht. E-mail treasurer.elect@nclaonline.org; *ALA Councilor* Siobhan Loendorf. E-mail sloendorf@catawbacountync.gov; *Interim State Libn.* Susan Forbes (ex officio). E-mail susan.forbes@ncdcr.gov; *Past Pres.* Lorrie Russell. E-mail pastpresident@nclaonline.org.

Address correspondence to North Carolina Lib. Assn., 265 Eastchester Dr., Suite 133, #364, High Point 27262. E-mail nclaonline@gmail.com.

World Wide Web https://nclaonline.org.

North Dakota

Memb. (Indiv.) 300+. Term of Office. Sept.–Sept. Publication. *The Good Stuff* (q.). *Ed.* Shannon Yarbrough. E-mail shannon.yarbrough@und.edu.

Pres. Will Martin, Chester Fritz Library, University of North Dakota. E-mail william.d.martin@und.edu; *Pres.-Elect* Kerrianne Boetcher, Ward County Public Library. E-mail kerrianne.boetcher@co.ward.nd.us. *Secy.* Abby Ebach, North Dakota State Library. E-mail aebach@nd.gov; *Treas.* Aaron Stefanich, Grand Forks Public Library. E-mail aaron.stefanich@gflibrary.com; *ALA Councilor* Sara Westall, School of Medicine and Health Sciences, University of North Dakota. E-mail sara.westall@und.edu; *State Libn.* Mary J. Soucie, North Dakota State Lib. E-mail msoucie@nd.gov.

Address correspondence to the president. North Dakota Lib. Assn., 604 E. Boulevard Ave., Bismarck 58505.

World Wide Web https://ndla.info.

Ohio

Memb. 2,700+. Term of Office. Jan.–Dec. Publication. *OLC News* (online).

Chair Tom Dillie, Minerva Public Lib. Tel. 330-868-4101; *V.Chair/Chair-Elect* Laura Lee Wilson, Huron County Community Library. Tel. 419-933-2544; *Secy./Treas.* Carol Herrick, Washington-Centerville Public Library. Tel. 937-609-4267; *Immediate Past Chair* Cheryl Kuonen, Mentor Public Lib. Tel. 440-255-8811 ext. 2323; *ALA Councilor*, Nick Tepe, Athens County Public Libraries. Tel. 740-737-6003; *Exec. Dir.* Michelle Francis. Tel. 614-410-8092 ext. 105, e-mail mfrancis@olc.org.

Address correspondence to the executive director. Ohio Lib. Council, 495 Metro Place South, Suite 350, Dublin 43017. Tel. 614-410-8092.

World Wide Web https://olc.org.

Oklahoma

Memb. 500–600. Term of Office. July–June.

Pres. Cherity Pennington. E-mail president@oklibs.org; *V.P./Pres.-Elect* Tim Miller. E-mail president-elect@oklibs.org; *Secy.* Jenny Bodenhamer. E-mail secretary@oklibs.org; *Treas.* Michael Hull. E-mail treasurer@oklibs.org; *ALA Councilor* Kelly Sitzman. E-mail ala_councilor@oklibs.org; *Past Pres.* Cathy Blackman. E-mail finance@oklibs.org.

Address correspondence to Oklahoma Lib. Assn., 1190 Meramec Station Rd., Suite 207,

Ballwin, MO 63021-6902. Tel. 800-969-6562 ext. 5, fax 636-529-1396, e-mail ola@amigos. org.

World Wide Web https://www.oklibs.org.

Oregon

Memb. (Indiv.) 1,000+. Publications. *OLA Hotline.* (bi-w.). E-mail olahotline@olaweb.org; *OLA Quarterly* (q.).

Pres. Arlene Weible, State Lib. of Oregon. E-mail olapresident@olaweb.org; *V.P./Pres.- Elect* Marci Ramiro-Jenkins, McMinnville Public Library. E-mail olavp@olaweb.org; *Secy.* Star Khan, Driftwood Public Library. E-mail olasecretary@olaweb.org. *Treas.* Stuart Levy, Parkrose High School. E-mail olatreasurer@olaweb.org; *Memb.-at-Large* Sami Kerzel, Deschutes Public Library. E-mail samik@dpls. lib.or.us; *ALA Rep.* Kirsten Brodbeck-Kenney, Driftwood Public Lib. E-mail olachaptercouncilor@olaweb.org; *Past Pres.* Kate Lasky, Josephine Community Lib. District. E-mail olapastpresident@olaweb.org.

Address correspondence to Oregon Lib. Assn., P.O. Box 3067, La Grande 97850. Tel. 541-962-5824, e-mail ola@olaweb.org.

World Wide Web https://www.olaweb.org.

Pennsylvania

Memb. 1,900+. Term of Office. Jan.–Dec. Publication. *PaLA Bulletin* (q.).

Pres. Jen Knisely; *1st V.P.* Melissa Rowse; *2nd V.P. (Harrisburg Conference)* Brianna Crum; *2nd V.P. (Kalahari Conference)* Rose Chiocchi; *3rd V.P.* Dana Barber; *Treas.* Kate Cummings; *ALA Councilor* Barbara McGary; *Past Pres.* Tom Reinsfelder; *Exec. Dir.* Christi Buker. Pennsylvania Lib. Assn., 220 Cumberland Pkwy., Suite 10, Mechanicsburg 17055. Tel. 717-766-7663, e-mail christi@palibraries.org.

Address correspondence to the executive director. Pennsylvania Lib. Assn., 220 Cumberland Parkway, Suite 10, Mechanicsburg 17055. Tel. 717-766-7663, fax 717-766-5440.

World Wide Web https://www.palibraries. org.

Rhode Island

Memb. (Indiv.) 350+; (Inst.) 50+. Term of Office. June–June. Publication. *RILA Bulletin* (6x yearly).

Pres. Rachael Juskuv, Bryant Univ. Tel. 401-232-6299, e-mail president@rilibraries. org; *V.P.* Beatrice Pulliam, Providence Public Library. Tel. 401-455-8101, e-mail vice-president@rilibraries.org; *Secy.* Celeste Dyer, Cumberland Public Lib. Tel. 401-333-2552, e-mail secretary@rilibraries.org; *Treas.* Sam Simas, Providence Public Library. Tel. 401-455-8101. E-mail treasurer@rilibraries.org; *Memb.-at-Large* Megan Hamlin-Black, Rhode Island State Libn. Tel. 401-330-3184, e-mail mblack@sos.ri.gov; *ALA Councilor* Jack Martin, Providence Public Lib. Tel. 401-455-8100, e-mail jmartin@provlib.org; *Past Pres.* Julie Holden, Cranston Public Lib. Tel. 401-943-9080 ext. 101.

Address correspondence to Rhode Island Lib. Assn., P.O. Box 6765, Providence 02940.

World Wide Web https://www.rilibraries.org.

South Carolina

Memb. 350+. Term of Office. Jan.–Dec. Publication. *South Carolina Libraries Journal* (s.-ann., online).

Pres. Sara DeSantis, Univ. of South Carolina–Upstate. Tel. 864-503-5006, e-mail sarabd@uscupstate.edu; *1st V.P.* Sunny Peterson, Richland Library, Sandhills. Tel. 803-699-9230, e-mail speterson@richlandlibrary.com; *2nd V.P.* Jimmie Epling, Darlington County Library System. Tel. 843-398-4940, e-mail jimmie.epling@darlington-lib.org; *Secy.* Position Open; *Treas.* Danielle Robinson. Tel. 864-430-8796, e-mail sclatreasurersc@gmail.com; *ALA Councilor* Danielle Thornton, Greenville County Library System. Tel. 864-963-9031, e-mail dthornton@greenvillelibrary.org; *Past Pres.* Megan Palmer, Clemson Univ. Tel. 864-656-5179, e-mail mpalme4@clemson.edu. *Exec. Sec.* Donald Wood, South Carolina Lib. Association, P.O. Box 1763, Columbia, 29202. Tel. 803-252-1087, fax 803-252-0589, e-mail scla@capconsc.com.

Address correspondence to the executive secretary. South Carolina Lib. Assn., P.O. Box 1763, Columbia 29202. Tel. 803-252-1087, e-mail scla@capconsc.com.

World Wide Web https://www.scla.org.

South Dakota

Memb. (Indiv.) 450+; (Inst.) 60+. Publication. *Book Marks* (q.).

Pres. Shari Theroux, HM Briggs Lib, South Dakota State University, Brookings. E-mail Shari.Theroux@sdstate.edu; *V.P./Pres.-Elect* Jamie Formanek, Watertown Regional Library. E-mail jformanek@watertownsd.us; *Recording Secy.* Sean Minkel, Rapid City Public Lib, Rapid City. sminkel@rcplib.org; *Exec. Secy./ Treas.* Krista Ohrtman, Mikkelsen Lib., Augustana University, Sioux Falls. E-mail SDLibraryAssociation@gmail.com; *ALA Councilor* Danielle De Jager-Loftus, University of South Dakota, Vermillion. E-mail Danielle.Loftus@usd.edu; *Past Pres.* Julie Erickson, TIE, Rapid City. E-mail jerickson@tie.net.

Address correspondence to the executive secretary. South Dakota Lib. Assn., Mikkelsen Lib., 2001 S. Summit Ave., Sioux Falls 57197. Tel. 605-743-0889.

World Wide Web https://www.sdlibraryassociation.org.

Tennessee

Memb. 600+. Term of Office. July–June. Publications. *Tennessee Libraries* (q.; online); *TLA Newsletter* (q.; online).

Pres. Sharon Edwards. E-mail sharonedwards405@gmail.com; *V.P./Pres.-Elect* Dwight Hunter. E-mail dwight.hunter@chattanoogastate.edu; *Recording Secy.* Holly Hebert. E-mail holly.hebert@mtsu.edu; *Past Pres.* Erika Long. E-mail erika.long.lib@gmail.com; *Exec. Dir.* Cathy Farley. E-mail exdirtla@gmail.com.

Address correspondence to the executive director. Tennessee Lib. Assn., P.O. Box 6297, Sparta 38583. Tel. 931-607-1182, e-mail exdirtla@gmail.com.

World Wide Web https://www.tnla.org.

Texas

Memb. 6,000. Term of Office. Apr.–Apr. Publication. *Texas Library Journal* (q).

Pres. Daniel Burgard, University of North Texas Health Science Center; *Pres.-Elect* Mary Woodard, Mesquite ISD; *Treas.* Dianna Morganti, Texas A&M University; *ALA Councilor* Dorcas Hand, Students Need Libraries in HISD; *Past Pres.* Christina Gola, Univ. of Houston; *Exec. Dir.* Shirley Robinson, Texas Lib. Assn., 3420 Executive Center Dr., Ste. 301, Austin 78731. Tel. 512-328-1518 ext. 151, e-mail shirleyr@txla.org.

Address correspondence to the executive director. Texas Lib. Assn., 3420 Executive Center Dr., Ste. 301, Austin 78731. Tel. 512-328-1518, e-mail tla@txla.org.

World Wide Web https://txla.org.

Utah

Memb. 650. Publication. *Utah Libraries News* (q.; online).

Pres. Rita Christensen, Orem Public Library. E-mail rchristensen@orem.org; *Pres.-Elect* Marissa Bischoff, Harold B. Lee Library, Brigham Young University. E-mail marissa_bischoff@byu.edu; *Treas.* Allen Arnoldsen. E-mail allen_arnoldsen@byu.edu; *ALA Chapter Councilor* Trish Hull, Kearns Branch, Salt Lake County Library. E-mail thull@slcolibrary.org; *Past Pres.* Daniel Mauchley, Duchesne County Library. E-mail dmauchley@duchesne.utah.gov; *Exec. Dir.* Mindy Hale. E-mail mhale@ula.org.

Address correspondence to the executive director.

World Wide Web https://ula.org.

Vermont

Memb. 300+. Publication. *VLA News* (q.).

Pres. Michael D. Roy, Middlebury College, Middlebury 05753. Tel. 802-443-5490, e-mail president@vermontlibraries.org; *V.P./ Pres.-Elect* Kelly McCagg, Burnham Memorial Library, 898 Main St., Colchester 05446. Tel. 802-264-5660, e-mail vicepresident@vermontlibraries.org; *Secy.* Barbara Ball, Windsor Public Library, 43 State St., Windsor 05089. Tel. 802-674-2556, e-mail secretary@vermontlibraries.org; *Treas.* Lisa Milchman, Norwich Public Library, P.O. Box 290, Norwich 05055. Tel. 802-649-1184, e-mail treasurer@vermontlibraries.org; *Past Pres.* Kevin Unrath, Pierson Lib., 5376 Shelburne Road, Shelburne 05482. Tel. 802-264-5017, e-mail kunrath@shelburnevt.org.

Address correspondence to Vermont Lib. Assn., P.O. Box 803, Burlington 05402.

World Wide Web https://www.vermontlibraries.org.

Virginia

Memb. 950+. Term of Office. Oct.–Oct. Publication. *Virginia Libraries* (ann.).

Pres. K.T. Vaughan, Washington & Lee University. E-mail kvaughan@wlu.edu; *Pres.-Elect* Kimberly Knight, Alexandria Library. E-mail kknight@alexlibraryva.org; *2nd V.P.* Zach Elder, Chesapeake Public Library. E-mail zwelder@infopeake.org; *Secy.* Lisa Broughman, Randolph College. E-mail llee@randolphcollege.edu; *Treas.* Kyle Binaxas, Suffolk Public Library. E-mail k.binaxas@gmail.com; *ALA Councilor* Lucy Rush Wittkower, Old Dominion Univ. E-mail lrush@odu.edu; *Past Pres.* Jennifer Resor-Whicker, Radford University, McConnell Lib., P.O. Box 6881, Radford 24142. Tel. 540-831-5691, e-mail jrwhicker@radford.edu; *Exec. Dir.* Lisa Varga, Virginia Lib. Assn., P.O. Box 56312, Virginia Beach 23456. Tel. 757-689-0594, e-mail vla.lisav@cox.net.

Address correspondence to the executive director. Virginia Lib. Assn., P.O. Box 56312, Virginia Beach 23456. Tel. 757-689-0594, fax 757-447-3478, e-mail vla.lisav@cox.net.

World Wide Web https://www.vla.org.

Washington

Memb. (Indiv.) 742, (Inst.) 47. Publication. *Alki: The Washington Library Association Journal* (3x yearly, online).

Pres. Ahniwa Ferrari, The Evergreen State College. E-mail ferraria@evergreen.edu; *V.P./ Pres.-Elect* Johanna Jacobsen Kiciman, University of Washington. E-mail jmjk@uw.edu; *Treas.* Muriel Wheatley, Timberland Regional Lib. E-mail mwheatley@trl.org; *ALA Councilor* Steven Bailey, King County Lib. System. E-mail sbailey@kcls.org; *Past Pres.* Danielle Miller, Washington Talking Book & Braille Lib. E-mail dan-ielle.miller@sos.wa.gov; *Exec. Dir.* Brianna Hoffman, Washington Lib. Association. E-mail brianna@wla.org.

Address correspondence to the executive director. Washington Lib. Assn., P.O. Box 33808, Seattle 98133. Tel. 206-823-1138, e-mail info@wla.org.

World Wide Web https://www.wla.org.

West Virginia

Memb. 700+.

Pres. Breana Roach Bowen, Cabell County Public Library. Tel. 304-528-5700, fax 304-528-5701, e-mail breana.bowen@cabell.lib.wv.us; *1st V.P.* Angela Strait, Marshall

University Library; *2nd V.P.* Angela Arthur, Cox Landing Library; Secy. Larissa Cason, Marion County Public Library; *Treas.* Erika Connelly, Kanawha County Public Library; *ALA Councilor* Majed Khader, Marshall University. Tel. 304-696-3121, fax 304-696-5219, e-mail khader@marshall.edu; *Exec. Dir.* Kerry Trahan, Marion County Public Library.

Address correspondence to the president.

World Wide Web https://wvla.org.

Wisconsin

Memb. 1,900. Term of Office. Jan.–Dec. Publication. *WLA eNewsletter* (3–4x yearly; online).

Pres. Nyama Reed. E-mail n.reed@wfblibrary.org; *V.P.* Kris Turner. E-mail kris.turner@wisc.edu; *Secy.* Desiree Bongers, Ripon Public Lib., Ripon. E-mail dbongers@riponlibrary.org; *Treas.* Rachel Arndt. E-mail rachel.arndt27@gmail.com; *ALA Councilor* Kristina Gómez. E-mail kgomez@madisonpubliclibrary.org; *Past Pres.* Sherry Machones. E-mail sherrymachones@gmail.com; *Exec. Dir.* Laura Sauser. E-mail sauser@wisconsinlibraries.org.

Address correspondence to Wisconsin Lib. Assn., P.O. Box 6437, 112 Owen Rd., #6437, Monona 53716. Tel. 608-245-3640, e-mail wla@wisconsinlibraries.org.

World Wide Web https://www.wisconsinlibraries.org.

Wyoming

Memb. 450+. Term of Office. Oct.–Oct. Publication. Newsletter (ann.; August).

Pres. Conrrado Saldivar, Wyoming State Library. Tel. 307-777-6330, e-mail conrrado.saldivar@wyo.gov; *V.P.* Position Open; *ALA Councilor* Lisa Scroggins, Natrona County Library. Tel. 307-237-4935, ext. 115, e-mail lscroggins@natronacountylibrary.org; *State Libn. (ex officio)* Jamie Markus, Wyoming State Lib. Tel. 307-777-5914, e-mail jamie.markus@wyo.gov; *Past Pres.* Katrina Brown, Casper College Goodstein Foundation Library. Tel. 307-268-2036, e-mail katrina.brown@caspercollege.edu; *Communications Advisor (ex officio)* Elizabeth Thorson, Laramie County Lib. System. Tel. 307-773-7230, e-mail ethorson@lclsonline.org.

Address correspondence to Wyoming Lib. Assn., 1190 Meramac Station Rd., Suite 207,

Ballwin, MO 63201. Tel. 800-969-6562 ext. 6, e-mail wla@amigos.org.
World Wide Web https://wyla.org.

Canada

Alberta

Memb. 800+. Term of Office. May–April.
Pres. Kirk MacLeod, Alberta Law Libraries. E-mail president@laa.ca; *1st V.P.* Jessica Knoch, Yellowhead Regional Library. E-mail 1stvicepresident@laa.ca; *2nd V.P.* Jocie Wilson, Yellowhead Regional Library. E-mail 2ndvicepresident@laa.ca; *Treas.* Charla Majeran, Tofield School. E-mail treasurer@laa.ca; *Dirs.* Kait McClary, Shortgrass Library System. E-mail director1@laa.ca; Carla Lewis, University of Calgary Library. E-mail director2@laa.ca; Robert Tiessen, University of Calgary Library. E-mail director3@laa.ca; *Comm. Officer* Lorisia MacLeod, The Alberta Library. E-mail info@laa.ca.
Address correspondence to Lib. Assn. of Alberta, c/o The Alberta Library, #623, 7 Sir Winston Churchill Sq. NW, Edmonton T5J 2V.
World Wide Web https://www.laa.ca.

British Columbia

Memb. 750+. Term of Office. April–April. Publication. *BCLA Perspectives* (q.; online).
Pres. Todd Mundle, Kwantlen Polytechnic University Library; *Incoming Pres.* Tracey Therrien, Nelson Public Library; *Recording Secy.* Rina Hadziev, BCLA Executive Director; *Treas.* Anne O'Shea, Vancouver Island Regional Library; *Incoming Treas.* Donald Taylor, SFU Library; *Past Pres.* Chris Middlemass, Vancouver Public Lib.; *Exec. Dir.* Rina Hadziev. E-mail execdir@bcla.bc.ca.
Address correspondence to the executive director. British Columbia Lib. Assn., P.O. Box 19008 Rocky Point PO, Port Moody V3H 0J1. E-mail bclaoffice@bcla.bc.ca.
World Wide Web https://bclaconnect.ca.

Manitoba

Memb. 500+. Term of Office. May–May.
Pres. Melanie Sucha; *V.P.* Position Open; *Secy.* Caralie Heinrichs. E-mail secretary@mla.mb.ca; *Treas.* Kelly Murray; *Past Pres.* Kerry Macdonald.

Address correspondence to Manitoba Lib. Assn., 606-100 Arthur St., Winnipeg R3B 1H3. E-mail secretary@mla.mb.ca.
World Wide Web https://mla.mb.ca.

Ontario

Memb. 5,000+. Publication. *Open Shelf* (mo., multimedia).
Pres. Sabrina Saunders, The Blue Mountains Public Lib. E-mail ssaunders@thebluemountains.ca; *V.P./Pres.-Elect* Melanie Mills, Huron University College, Western University. E-mail melanie.mills@uwo.ca; *Treas.* Lori Hallahan, Seneca College. E-mail lori-ann.hallahan@senecacollege.ca; *Past Pres.* Andrea Cecchetto, Markham Public Lib. E-mail acecch@markham.library.on.ca; *Exec. Dir.* Shelagh Paterson, Ontario Lib. Assn. E-mail spaterson@accessola.com.
Address correspondence to Ontario Lib. Assn., 2080 Danforth Ave., Toronto M4C 1J9. Tel. 877-340-1730, e-mail info@accessola.com.
World Wide Web https://accessola.com.

Quebec

Memb. (Indiv.) 100+. Term of Office. May–April. Publication. *ABQLA Bulletin* (3x yearly).
Pres. Position Open; *V.P.s* Barbara Whiston and Maria Ressina; *Treas.* Taylor Gammon; *Past Pres.* Sandy Hervieux.
Address correspondence to the president. Assn. des Bibliothecaires du Quebec/Quebec Lib. Assn., C.P. 26717, CPS Beaconsfield H9W 6G7.
World Wide Web https://abqla.qc.ca/en.

Saskatchewan

Memb. 200+.
Pres. Amy Rankin, CMP Resource Centre, P.O. Box 6500, Regina. Tel. 639-625-3537, e-mail amy.rankin@rcmp-grc.gc.ca; *V.P. Engagements and Communications* Elaina St. Onge, Campion College Lib, 3737 Wascana Parkway, Regina, S4S 0A2. Tel. 306-359-1233. E-mail: elaina.st.onge@uregina.ca; *V.P. Advocacy and Development* Vacant; *Treas.* Darrel Yates. E-mail darrel.yates@dal.ca; *Past Pres.* Alison Jantz, RCMP Resource Centre; *Exec. Dir.* Dorothea Warren Saskatchewan Lib.

Assn., #15–2010 7th Ave, Regina S4R 1C3. Tel. 306-780-9413, fax 306-780-9447, e-mail slaexdir@sasktel.net.

Address correspondence to the executive director. Saskatchewan Lib. Assn., 10-2010 7th Ave., Regina S4R 1C3. Tel. 306-780-9413, fax 306-780-3633, e-mail slaexdir@sasktel.net. World Wide Web https://saskla.ca.

Regional

Atlantic Provinces: N.B., N.L., N.S., P.E.I.

Memb. (Indiv.) 320+.

Pres. Marc Harper, Bibliothèque Champlain, 18 avenue Antonine-Maillet (local 164), Moncton, NB E1A 3E9. Tel. 506-858-4154, e-mail president@apla.ca; *V.P./Pres.-Elect* Cate Carlyle, Mount Saint Vincent University, Halifax, NS. E-mail president-elect@apla.ca; *V.P. Nova Scotia* Margaret Vail, St. Francis Xavier University, Antigonish, NS. E-mail ns@apla. ca; *V.P. New Brunswick* Chantale Saulnier, New Brunswick Public Library Service, Fredericton, NB. E-mail nb@apla.ca; *V.P. Newfoundland and Labrador* Su Cleyle, Memorial University of Newfoundland, St. John's, NL. E-mail nl@apla.ca; *V.P. Prince Edward Island* Krystal Dionne, Montague Rotary Library, Public Library Service, Montague, PEI. E-mail pe@apla.ca; *Secy.* Victoria Volkanova, Université de Moncton, Moncton, NB. E-mail secretary@apla.ca; *Past President* Ann Smith, Acadia University, Wolfville, NS. E-mail past-president@apla.ca.

Address correspondence to Atlantic Provinces Lib. Assn., Dalhousie Univ., Kenneth C. Rowe Mgt. Bldg., 6100 University Ave., Suite 4010, P.O. Box 15000, Halifax, NS B3H 4R2. E-mail president@apla.ca or secretary@apla.ca.

World Wide Web https://www.apla.ca.

Mountain Plains: Ariz., Colo., Kan., Mont., Neb., Nev., N.Dak., N.Mex., Okla., S.Dak., Utah, Wyo.

Memb. 700. Term of Office. Oct.–Oct. Publication. *MPLA Newsletter* (6x yearly, online).

Pres. Robin Newell, Emporia Public Lib., 110 E. Sixth Ave., Emporia, KS 66801. Tel. 620-340-6464, e-mail president@mpla.us; *V.P./Pres.-Elect* Brenda Hemmelman, South Dakota State Library, 800 Governors Drive, Pierre, SD 57501. Tel. 605-773-5075, fax 605-773-6962, e-mail vicepresident@mpla.us; *Recording Secy.* Whitney Hilley, Oklahoma State Univ., Edmon Low Lib., Stillwater, OK 74078. Tel. 405-744-7142, e-mail secretary@mpla. us; *Past Pres.* Stephen Sweeney, St. John Vianney Seminary, Cardinal Stafford Lib., 1300 South Steele St., Denver, CO 80210. Tel. 303-715-3192, fax 303-715-2037, e-mail pastpresident@mpla.us; *Exec. Secy.* Judy Kulp, 14293 West Center Dr., Lakewood, CO 80228. Tel. 303-985-7795, e-mail execsecretary@mpla.us.

Address correspondence to the executive secretary. Mountain Plains Lib. Assn., 14293 West Center Drive, Lakewood, CO 80228. Tel. 303-985-7795, e-mail execsecretary@mpla.us.

World Wide Web https://mpla.us.

New England: Conn., Maine, Mass., N.H., R.I., Vt.

Memb. (Indiv.) 650+. Term of Office. Nov.–Oct. Publication. "NELA News" (blog).

Pres. Kimberly Usselman, Cumberland Public Lib., Cumberland, RI. Tel. 413-323-5925 ext. 102; *V.P.* Bethany Klem, Bedford Free Public Library, Bedford, MA. Tel. 413-323-5925, ext. 103, e-mail vice-president@nelib. org; *Secy.* Lucinda Walker, Norwich Public Lib., Norwich, VT. Tel. 413-323-5925 ext. 106; *Treas.* Bernie Prochnik, Bath Public Lib., Bath, NH. Tel. 413-323-5925 ext. 105; *Past Pres.* Mike Zeller, Shrewsbury Public Lib, Shrewsbury, MA. Tel. 413-323-5925 ext. 102; *Admin.* Robert Scheier, NELA Office, 55 N. Main St., Unit 49, Belchertown, MA 01007. Tel. 413-323-5925 ext. 100, rscheier@nelib.org.

Address correspondence to the administrator. New England Lib. Assn., 55 N. Main St., Unit 49, Belchertown, MA 01007. Tel. 413-323-5925, e-mail rscheier@nelib.org.

World Wide Web https://www.nelib.org.

Pacific Northwest: Alaska, Idaho, Mont., Ore., Wash., Alberta, B.C.

Memb. 170+. Term of Office. Aug.–Aug. Publication. *PNLA Quarterly.*

Pres. Nicole Thode, Tumwater Timberland Lib., Thurston County, WA; *Vice-Pres./Pres.-Elect* Gavin Woltjer, Billings Public Library, Billings, MT; *2nd V.P./Membership Chair* Ilana Kingsley, Univ. of Alaska–Fairbanks,

Rasmuson Lib., Fairbanks, AK. Tel. 907-474-7518; *Secy.* Christina Brischetto, Kids Read Books, Randle, WA; *Treas.* Position Open; *Past Pres.* Pam Henley, Montana State Lib., Helena (and Bozeman), MT. Tel. 406-461-9049.

Address correspondence to Pacific Northwest Lib. Assn., 1430 Willamette Street, #764, Eugene, OR 97401.

World Wide Web https://pnla.org.

Southeastern: Ala., Ark., Fla., Ga., Ky., La., Miss., N.C., S.C., Tenn., Va., W.Va.

Memb. 500. Publication. *The Southeastern Librarian* (*SELn*) (q.; online, open access).

Pres. SELA President: Melissa Dennis, University of Mississippi, University, MS. E-mail president@selaonline.org; *Pres.-Elect* Crystal Gates, William F. Laman Public Lib, North Little Rock, AR. E-mail president.elect@selaonline.org; *Secy.* Kristin Rogers, University of Mississippi University, MS. E-mail secretary@selaonline.org; *Treas.* Vicki Gregory, University of South Florida (Professor Emeritus), Tampa, FL. E-mail treasurer@selaonline.org; *Archivist* Camille McCutcheon, Univ. of South Carolina Upstate, Spartanburg, SC. E-mail archivist@selaonline.org; *Past Pres.* Tim Dodge, Auburn University Libraries, Auburn, AL.

Address correspondence to Southeastern Lib. Assn., Admin. Services, P.O. Box 30703, Savannah, GA 31410. Tel. 912-999-7979, e-mail selaadminservices@selaonline.org.

World Wide Web http://selaonline.org.

State and Provincial Library Agencies

The state library administrative agency in each of the U.S. states will have the latest information on its state plan for the use of federal funds under the Library Services and Technology Act (LSTA). The directors and addresses of these state agencies are listed below.

United States

Alabama

Nancy Pack, Dir., Alabama Public Lib. Svc., 6030 Monticello Dr., Montgomery 36117. Tel. 334-213-3900, fax 334-213-3993, e-mail npack@apls.state.al.us. World Wide Web https://aplsws1.apls.state.al.us/aplsnew/web/content/contactapls.

Alaska

Patience Frederiksen, State Libn., Alaska State Lib., P.O. Box 110571, Juneau 99811-0571. Tel. 907-465-2920, fax 907-465-2151, e-mail patience.frederiksen@alaska.gov. World Wide Web https://library.alaska.gov.

Arizona

Holly Henley, State Libn. and Dir. of Lib. Svcs., Arizona State Lib., Archives and Public Records, 1901 W. Madison St., Phoenix 85009. Tel. 602-542-6200. World Wide Web https://azlibrary.gov.

Arkansas

Jennifer Chilcoat, State Libn., Arkansas State Lib., 900 W. Capitol, Suite 100, Little Rock 72201. Tel. 501-682-2053, e-mail jennifer. chilcoat@ade.arkansas.gov. World Wide Web https://www.library.arkansas.gov.

California

Greg Lucas, State Libn., California State Lib., 900 N Street, Sacramento 95814-4869. Tel. 916-323-9759, fax 916-323-9768, e-mail csl-adm@library.ca.gov. World Wide Web https://www.library.ca.gov.

Colorado

Katy Anthes, Commissioner, Colorado State Lib., 201 E. Colfax Ave., Denver 80203-1799. Tel. 303-866-6600, fax 303-830-0793, e-mail commissioner@cde.state.co.us. World Wide Web http://www.cde.state.co.us/cdelib.

Connecticut

Deborah Schander, State Libn., Connecticut State Lib., 231 Capitol Ave., Hartford 06106. Tel. 860-757-6510, fax 860-757-6503, e-mail deborah.schander@ct.gov. World Wide Web https://ctstatelibrary.org.

Delaware

Annie Norman, Dir., Delaware Division of Libs., 121 Martin Luther King Jr. Blvd. N., Dover 19901. Tel. 302-257-3001, fax 302-739-6787, e-mail annie.norman@delaware.gov. World Wide Web https://libraries.delaware. gov.

District of Columbia

Richard Reyes-Gavilan, Exec. Dir., District of Columbia Public Lib., 901 G Street, NW, Suite 301, Washington, DC 20001. Tel. 202-727-1101, fax 202-727-1129, e-mail rrg@dc.gov. World Wide Web https://www.dclibrary.org.

Florida

Amy L. Johnson, State Libn. and Div. Dir., Division of Lib. and Info. Svcs., R.A. Gray Bldg., 500 S. Bronough St., Tallahassee 32399-0250. Tel. 850-245-6600, fax 850-245-6622, e-mail info@dos.myflorida.com. World Wide Web https://dos.myflorida.com/library-archives.

Georgia

Julie Walker, State Libn., Georgia Public Lib. Svc., 2872 Woodcock Boulevard, Suite 250, Atlanta 30341. Tel. 404-235-7200, e-mail jwalker@georgialibraries.org. World Wide Web https://georgialibraries.org.

Hawaii

Stacy A. Aldrich, State Libn., Hawaii State Public Lib. System, Office of the State Libn., 44 Merchant St., Honolulu 96813. Tel. 808-586-3704, fax 808-586-3715, e-mail stlib@librarieshawaii.org. World Wide Web https://www.librarieshawaii.org.

Idaho

Stephanie Bailey-White, State Libn., Idaho Commission for Libs., 325 W. State St., Boise 83702. Tel. 208-639-4145, fax 208-334-4016, e-mail stephanie.bailey-white@libraries.idaho.gov. World Wide Web https://libraries.idaho.gov.

Illinois

Greg McCormick, Dir., Illinois State Lib., Gwendolyn Brooks Bldg., 300 S. Second St., Springfield 62701-1796. Tel. 217-785-5600, fax 217-785-4326, e-mail islinfo@ilsos.net. World Wide Web https://www.ilsos.gov/departments/library/home.html.

Indiana

Jacob Speer, State Libn., Indiana State Lib., 315 W. Ohio St., Indianapolis 46202. Tel. 317-232-3675, e-mail jspeer@library.in.gov. World Wide Web https://www.in.gov/library.

Iowa

Michael Scott, State Libn., State Lib. of Iowa, 1112 E. Grand Ave., Des Moines 50319-0233. Tel. 800-248-4483, fax 515-281-6191, e-mail Michael.Scott@iowa.gov. World Wide Web https://www.statelibraryofiowa.gov.

Kansas

Cindy Roupe, Acting State Libn., Kansas State Lib., Capitol Bldg., 300 S.W. 10th Ave., Rm. 312-N, Topeka 66612. Tel. 785-296-5437, e-mail cindy.roupe@ks.gov. World Wide Web https://kslib.info.

Kentucky

Terry Manuel, Commissioner, Kentucky Dept. for Libs. and Archives, 300 Coffee Tree Rd., P.O. Box 537, Frankfort 40602-0537. Tel. 502-564-8303, e-mail terry.manuel@ky.gov. World Wide Web http://www.kdla.ky.gov.

Louisiana

Rebecca Hamilton, State Libn., State Lib. of Louisiana, 701 N. 4th St., P.O. Box 131, Baton Rouge 70821-0131. Tel. 225-342-4923, fax 225-219-4804, e-mail rhamilton@crt.la.gov. World Wide Web http://www.state.lib.la.us.

Maine

James Ritter, State Libn., Maine State Lib., 64 State House Sta., Augusta 04333-0064. Tel. 207-287-5600, fax 207-287-5615, e-mail james.ritter@maine.gov. World Wide Web https://www.maine.gov/msl.

Maryland

Irene M. Padilla, State Libn., Maryland State Lib., 22 S. Calhoun St., Baltimore 21223. Tel. 667-219-4800, fax 667-219-4798, e-mail elizabeth.fletcher@maryland.gov. World Wide Web https://www.marylandlibraries.org.

Massachusetts

James Lonergan, Dir., Massachusetts Board of Lib. Commissioners, 90 Canal St., Suite 500, Boston, 02114. Tel. 617-725-1860, ext. 222, fax 617-725-0140, e-mail james.lonergan@state.ma.us. World Wide Web https://mblc.state.ma.us.

Michigan

Randy Riley, State Libn., Lib. of Michigan, 702 W. Kalamazoo St., P.O. Box 30007, Lansing 48909-7507. Tel. 517-335-1517, e-mail rileyr1@michigan.gov. World Wide Web https://www.michigan.gov/libraryofmichigan.

Minnesota

State Libn. and Dir. of State Lib. Svcs., Minnesota State Lib. Agency, Div. of State Lib. Svcs., MN Dept. of Educ., 1500 Hwy. 36 West, Roseville 55113. Tel. 651-582-8791, fax 651-582-8752, e-mail mde.lst@state.mn.us. World Wide Web https://education.mn.gov/MDE/dse/Lib/sls/index.htm.

Mississippi

Hulen Bivins, Exec. Dir., Mississippi Lib. Commission, 3881 Eastwood Dr., Jackson 39211. Tel. 601-432-4038, e-mail hbivins@mlc.lib.ms.us. World Wide Web http://www.mlc.lib.ms.us.

Missouri

Robin Westphal, State Libn., Missouri State Lib., 600 W. Main St., P.O. Box 387, Jefferson City 65101. Tel. 573-526-4783, e-mail robin.westphal@sos.mo.gov. World Wide Web http://www.sos.mo.gov/library.

Montana

Jennie Stapp, State Libn., Montana State Lib., 1515 E. 6th Ave., P.O. Box 201800, Helena, 59620-1800. Tel. 406-444-3116, fax 406-444-0266, e-mail jstapp2@mt.gov. World Wide Web https://msl.mt.gov.

Nebraska

Rodney G. Wagner, Dir., Nebraska Lib. Commission, 1200 N St., Suite 120, Lincoln 68508-2023. Tel. 402-471-4001, fax 402-471-2083, e-mail rod.wagner@nebraska.gov. World Wide Web http://www.nlc.nebraska.gov.

Nevada

Mike Strom, Admin., Nevada State Lib. and Archives, 100 N. Stewart St., Carson City 89701. Tel. 775-684-3410, fax 775-684-3311, e-mail mstrom@admin.nv.gov. World Wide Web https://nsla.nv.gov/home.

New Hampshire

Michael York, State Libn., New Hampshire State Lib., 20 Park St., Concord 03301. Tel. 603-271-2397, e-mail michael.york@dncr.nh.gov. World Wide Web http://www.state.nh.us/nhsl.

New Jersey

Jennifer R. Nelson, State Libn., New Jersey State Lib., an affiliate of Thomas Edison State Univ., P.O. Box 520, Trenton 08625-0520. Tel. 609-278-2640 ext. 101, fax 609-278-2652, e-mail jnelson@njstatelib.org. World Wide Web https://www.njstatelib.org.

New Mexico

Eli Guinnee, State Libn., New Mexico State Lib., 1209 Camino Carlos Rey, Santa Fe 87507-5166. Tel. 505-476-9762, e-mail Eli.Guinnee@state.nm.us. World Wide Web https://www.nmstatelibrary.org.

New York

Lauren Moore, State Libn., New York State Lib., Cultural Educ. Ctr., 222 Madison Ave., Albany 12230. Tel. 518-474-5930, fax 518-474-5786, e-mail statelibrarian@nysed.gov. World Wide Web https://www.nysl.nysed.gov.

North Carolina

Timothy G. Owens, State Libn., State Lib. of North Carolina, Administrative Section, 4640 Mail Svc. Ctr., Raleigh 27699-4600; 109 E. Jones St., Raleigh 27601. Tel. 919-814-6784, fax 919-733-8748, e-mail timothy.owens@ncdcr.gov. World Wide Web https://statelibrary.ncdcr.gov.

North Dakota

Mary J. Soucie, State Libn., North Dakota State Lib., 604 E. Boulevard Ave., Dept. 250, Bismarck 58505-0800. Tel. 701-328-4654, fax 701-328-2040, e-mail msoucie@nd.gov. World Wide Web http://www.library.nd.gov.

Ohio

Wendy Knapp, State Libn., 274 E. First Ave., Suite 100, Columbus 43201. Tel. 616-644-6843, e-mail jward@library.ohio.gov.. World Wide Web https://library.ohio.gov.

Oklahoma

Melody Kellogg, Dir., Oklahoma Dept. of Libs., 200 N.E. 18th St., Oklahoma City 73105-3298. Tel. 405-521-2502, fax 405-525-7804, World Wide Web http://www.odl.state.ok.us.

Oregon

Wendy Cornelisen, State Libn., State Lib. of Oregon, 250 Winter St., N.E., Salem 97301. Tel. 503-378-4367, fax 503-585-8059, e-mail wendy.cornelisen@slo.oregon.gov. World Wide Web https://www.oregon.gov/Library.

Pennsylvania

Susan Banks, Acting Deputy Secy. of Educ., Commissioner of Libs., and State Libn., State Lib. of Pennsylvania, Commonwealth Keystone Bldg., Plaza Lib. (Museum Plaza Wing), 400 North St., Harrisburg 17120-0211. Tel. 717-787-2646, fax 717-772-3265, e-mail ra-edo cldeptysecty@pa.gov. World Wide Web https://www.statelibrary.pa.gov/Pages/default.aspx.

Rhode Island

Karen Mellor, Chief of Lib. Services, Rhode Island Office of Lib. and Info. Svcs., One Capitol Hill, Providence 02908. Tel. 401-574-9304, fax 401-574-9320, e-mail karen.Mellor@olis.ri.gov. World Wide Web https://olis.ri.gov.

South Carolina

Leesa M. Aiken, Dir., South Carolina State Lib., 1500 Senate St., Columbia 29201. Tel. 803-734-8668, fax 803-734-8676, e-mail laiken@statelibrary.sc.gov. World Wide Web https://www.statelibrary.sc.gov.

South Dakota

Brenda Hemmelman, Interim State Libn., South Dakota State Lib., MacKay Bldg., 800 Governors Dr., Pierre 57501. Tel. 605-773-3131, option 6, fax 605-773-6962, e-mail brenda.hemmelman@state.sd.us. World Wide Web https://library.sd.gov.

Tennessee

Charles A. Sherrill, State Libn. and Archivist, Tennessee State Lib. and Archives, 403 7th Ave. N., Nashville 37243. Tel. 615-741-7996, fax 615-532-9293, e-mail chuck.sherrill@tn.gov. World Wide Web https://sos.tn.gov/tsla.

Texas

Gloria Meraz, Dir. and Libn., Texas State Lib. and Archives Commission, 1201 Brazos St., Austin 78701; P.O. Box 12927, Austin 78711-2927. Tel. 512-463-5460, fax 512-463-5436, e-mail director.librarian@tsl.texas.gov. World Wide Web https://www.tsl.texas.gov.

Utah

Chaundra Johnson, State Libn., Utah State Lib. Div., 250 N. 1950 W., Suite A, Salt Lake City 84116-7901. Tel. 801-715-6770, fax 801-715-6767, e-mail crjohns@utah.gov. World Wide Web https://library.utah.gov.

Vermont

Catherine Delneo, State Libn., Vermont State Lib., 60 Washington St., Suite 2, Barre, VT 05641. Tel. 802-636-0040, e-mail catherine.delneo@vermont.gov. World Wide Web https://libraries.vermont.gov/state_library.

Virginia

Sandra Treadway, Libn. of Virginia, Lib. of Virginia, 800 E. Broad St., Richmond 23219-8000. Tel. 804-692-3535, fax 804-692-3556, e-mail sandra.treadway@lva.virginia.gov. World Wide Web https://www.lva.virginia.gov.

Washington

Sara Jones, State Libn., Washington State Lib., Office of the Secretary of State, Point Plaza E., 6880 Capitol Blvd., Tumwater 98501; P.O. Box 42460, Olympia 98504-2460. Tel. 360-704-5276, e-mail sara.jones@sos.wa.gov. World Wide Web https://www.sos.wa.gov/library.

West Virginia

Karen Goff, Dir./State Libn., West Virginia Lib. Commission Cultural Ctr., Bldg. 9, 1900 Kanawha Blvd. E., Charleston 25305. Tel. 304-558-2041 ext. 2084, fax 304-558-2044, e-mail karen.e.goff@wv.gov. World Wide Web https://librarycommission.wv.gov/Pages/default.aspx.

Wisconsin

Kurt Kiefer, Asst. State Superintendent, Div. for Libs. and Tech., Wisconsin Dept. of Public Instruction, 125 S. Webster St., Madison 53703; P.O. Box 7841, Madison 53707-7841. Tel. 608-266-2205, fax 608-267-9207, e-mail Kurt.Kiefer@dpi.wi.gov. World Wide Web https://dpi.wi.gov/libraries.

Wyoming

Jamie Markus, State Libn., Wyoming State Lib., 2800 Central Ave., Cheyenne 82002. Tel. 307-777-5914, e-mail jamie.markus@wyo.gov. World Wide Web http://library.wyo.gov.

American Samoa

Justin H. Maga, Territorial Libn., Feleti Barstow Public Lib., Box 997687, Pago Pago 96799. Tel. 684-633-5816, fax 684-633-5823, e-mail justinmaga@gmail.com. World Wide Web https://www.feletibarstow.org.

Federated States of Micronesia

Augustine Kohler, Ntl. Historic Preservation Officer, Office of National Archives, Culture, and Historic Preservations, PS175, Palikir, Pohnpei State 96941. Tel. 691-320-2343, fax 691-320-5632, e-mail hpo@mail.fm. World Wide Web https://www.fsmgov.org.

Guam

Sandra Stanley, Admin. Officer, Guam Public Lib. System, 254 Martyr St., Hagatna 96910-5141. Tel. 671-475-4765, fax 671-477-9777, e-mail sandra.stanley@guampls.guam.gov. World Wide Web https://gpls.guam.gov.

Northern Mariana Islands

Erlinda Naputi, Lib. Dir., CNMI Joeten-Kiyu Public Lib., P.O. Box 501092, Saipan 96950. Tel. 670-235-7322, fax 670-235-7550, e-mail ecnaputi@gmail.com. World Wide Web https://cnmilib.org.

Palau

Sinton Soalablai, Chief, Div. of School Mgt., Palau Ministry of Educ., Madalaii Box 189, Koror, Palau 96940. Tel. 680-488-2570, fax 680-488-2380, e-mail ssoalablai@palaumoe.net. World Wide Web https://www.palaugov.pw/executive-branch/ministries/education.

Puerto Rico

Mary Jean Haver, Acting Dir., Lib. and Info. Svcs. Program, Puerto Rico Dept. of Educ., P.O. Box 190759, San Juan 00919-0759. Tel. 787-773-3570, fax 787-753-6945, e-mail haverbmj@de.pr.gov. Website not available.

Republic of the Marshall Islands

Wisse Amram, Exec. Dir., Alele Museum, Lib. and National Archives, P.O. Box 629, Majuro 96960. Tel. 011-692-625-3372, fax 011-692-625-3226, World Wide Web https://www.alele.org.

U.S. Virgin Islands

Arlene Pinney-Benjamin, Acting Dir., The Division of Libraries, Archives and Museums, c/o Florence Augusta Williams Public Lib., 1122 King St. Christiansted, St. Croix 00820. Tel. 340-773-5715, fax 340-773-5327, e-mail arlene.benjamin@dpnr.vi.gov. World Wide Web https://www.usvipubliclibraries.com.

Canada

Alberta

Diana Davidson, Dir., Alberta Public Lib. Svcs., Municipal Affairs, 8th fl., 10405 Jasper Ave., Edmonton T5J 4R7. Tel. 780-415-0284, fax 780-415-8594, e-mail diana.davidson@gov.ab.ca or libraries@gov.ab.ca. World Wide Web http://www.municipalaffairs.alberta.ca/alberta_libraries.cfm.

British Columbia

Mari Martin, Dir., Libs. Branch, Ministry of Educ., P.O. Box 9831, Stn. Prov. Govt., Victoria V8W 9T1. Tel. 250-886-2584, fax 250-953-4985, e-mail Mari.Martin@gov.bc.ca. World Wide Web https://www2.gov.bc.ca/gov/content/sports-culture/arts-culture/public-libraries/tool-resources-library-administrators/about-the-libraries-branch.

Manitoba

Trevor Surgenor, Dir., Public Lib. Services Branch, Manitoba Culture, Sport and Heritage Dept., B10 - 340 9th St., Brandon R7A 6C2. Tel. 204-726-6590, fax 204-726-6868, e-mail trevor.surgenor@gov.mb.ca. World Wide Web https://www.gov.mb.ca/chc/pls/index.html.

New Brunswick

Ella Nason, Acting Exec. Dir., New Brunswick Public Libs., Provincial Office, 570 Two Nations Crossing, Suite 2, Fredericton E3A 0X9. Tel. 506-453-2354, fax 506-444-4064, e-mail ella.nason@gnb.ca. World Wide Web https://www2.gnb.ca/content/gnb/en/departments/nbpl.html.

Newfoundland and Labrador

Andrew Hunt, Exec. Dir., Provincial Info. and Lib. Resources Board, 48 St. George's Ave., Stephenville A2N 1K9. Tel. 709-643-0900, fax 709-643-0925, e-mail ahunt@nlpl.ca. World Wide Web https://nlpl.ca.

Northwest Territories

Brian Dawson, Territorial Libn., Northwest Territories Public Lib. Services, 75 Woodland Dr., Hay River X0E 1G1. Tel. 867-874-6531, fax 867-874-3321, e-mail brian_dawson@gov.nt.ca. World Wide Web https://www.ece.gov.nt.ca/en/services/nwt-public-libraries.

Nova Scotia

Lynn Somers, Dir., Provincial Lib., Nova Scotia Provincial Lib., 6016 University Ave., 5th Fl., Halifax B3H 1W4. Tel. 902-424-2457, fax 902-424-0633, e-mail nspl@novascotia.ca. World Wide Web https://library.novascotia.ca.

Nunavut

Ron Knowling, Mgr., Nunavut Public Lib. Svcs., P.O. Box 270, Baker Lake X0C 0A0. Tel. 867-793-3353, fax 867-793-3360, e-mail rknowling@gov.nu.ca. World Wide Web https://publiclibraries.nu.ca.

Ontario

Rob Lavery, Ontario Heritage, Tourism, and Culture Division, Programs and Services Branch, 401 Bay St., Suite 1700, Toronto M7A 0A7. Tel. 416-314-7154, fax 416-212-1802, e-mail rob.lavery@ontario.ca. World Wide Web http://www.mtc.gov.on.ca/en/libraries/contact.shtml.

Prince Edward Island

Kathleen Simmonds, Dir., Libs. and Archives, Education and Lifelong Learning, Sullivan Bldg., 16 Fitzroy St., 1st Fl., Charlottetown, PE CIA 7N8. Tel. 902-314-5523, fax 902-894-0342, e-mail kesimmonds@gov.pe.ca. World Wide Web https://www.princeedwardisland.ca/en/topic/libraries-and-archives.

Quebec

Marie Grégoire, Chairman and CEO, Bibliothèque et Archives Nationales du Québec (BAnQ), 475, Boulevard de Maisonneuve Est, Montreal, H2L 5C4. Tel. 800-363-9028 or 514-873-1100, e-mail pdg@banq.qc.ca. World Wide Web https://www.banq.qc.ca/accueil/index.html.

Saskatchewan

Alison Hopkins, Provincial Libn./Exec. Dir., Provincial Lib. and Exec. Dir., Ministry of Educ., 409A Park Street, Regina, SK, S4N 5B2. Tel. 306-787-2972, fax 306-787-2029, e-mail alison.hopkins@gov.sk.ca. World Wide Web https://www.saskatchewan.ca/residents/education-and-learning/library-system-in-saskatchewan.

Yukon Territory

Melissa Yu Schott, Dir. of Public Libs., Community Development Div., Dept. of Community Svcs., Government of Yukon, 1171 Front St., Whitehorse, Y1A 0G9. Tel. 867-335-8600, e-mail Melissa.YuSchott@gov.yk.ca. World Wide Web https://yukon.ca/en/arts-and-culture/yukon-public-libraries.

State School Library Associations

Alabama

Youth Services and School Libns. Div., Alabama Lib. Assn. (ALLA). Memb. 600+.

Chair Caitlin Rogers, The Altamont School. E-mail crogers@altamontschool.org; *Chair-Elect* Cristina Castor, Homewood Public Lib. E-mail cristina.castor@homewoodpubliclibrary.org.

Address correspondence to the Youth Services and School Libns. Div., ALLA, 6030 Monticello Dr., Montgomery 36117. Tel. 334-414-0113, e-mail allaadmin@allanet.org.

World Wide Web https://www.allanet.org/youth-services-and-school-library-division-yssld-.

Alaska

Alaska Assn. of School Libns. (AkASL). Memb. 100+. Publication. *The Puffin* continuing basis online at http://akasl.org/puffin-news. Submissions e-mail akasl.puffin@gmail.com.

Pres. Katie Conover Clark. E-mail akasl.presidentelect@gmail.com; *Secy.* Jessica Tonnies. E-mail akasl.secretary@gmail.com; *Treas.* Janet Madsen. E-mail janet.madsen@alaska.gov; *Past Pres.* Pam Verfaillie (Valdez).

Address correspondence to AkASL, P.O. Box 101085, Anchorage 99510-1085, e-mail akasl.webmaster@gmail.com.

World Wide Web http://www.akasl.org.

Arizona

Teacher-Libn. Div., Arizona Lib. Assn. (AZLA). Memb. 1,000. Term of Office. Jan.–Dec.

Co-Chair Jean Kilker, Maryvale High School, 3415 N. 59th Ave., Phoenix 85033. Tel. 602-764-2134, e-mail jkilker@phoenixunion.org; *Co-Chair* Judi Moreillon, Tel. 520-603-4868, e-mail info@storytrail.com.

Address correspondence to the chairpersons, AZLA, c/o Arizona Lib. Assn., 2532 N 4th St., #271, Flagstaff 86004. Tel. 928.288.2011, e-mail admin@azla.org.

World Wide Web https://www.azla.org/azla-groups/teacher-librarian-division.

Arkansas

Arkansas Assn. of School Libns. (ARASL), div. of Arkansas Lib. Assn.

Chair Rachel Shankles, 891 Hwy. 7, Bismarck 71929. Tel. 501-276-4949, e-mail arasl.chair@gmail.com; *Past Chair* Daniel Fouts II, Osceola High School, 2800 W. Semmes Ave., Osceola 72370. Tel. 870-563-1863, e-mail dfouts@glaucus.org.

Address correspondence to the chairperson via e-mail.

World Wide Web https://arasl.weebly.com.

California

California School Lib. Assn. (CSLA). Memb. 1,200+. Publications. *CSLA Journal* (2x yearly). *Ed.* Mary Ann Harlan, San José State Univ. E-mail maryann.harlan@sjsu.edu; *CSLA Newsletter* (10x yearly, memb., via e-mail).

(State Board)

Pres. Nina Jackson, Franklin Classical Middle School, 540 Cerritos Ave., Long Beach 90802. E-mail njcatsandbooks@gmail.com; *Pres.-Elect* Rosan Cable, Pacifica High School, Garden Grove. E-mail cablesclasses@outlook.com; *Secy.* Lori Broger-Mackey, Columbus Middle School, Canoga Park. E-mail lorib.csla@gmail.com; *Treas.* Lori Stevens, Rialto Unified School Dist. E-mail lstevens2@rialtousd.org; *Past Pres.* Lisa Bishop, Aptos Middle School, 105 Aptos Ave., San Francisco 94127.

Address correspondence to CSLA, 6444 E. Spring St., No. 237, Long Beach 90815-1553. Tel./fax 888-655-8480, e-mail info@csla.net.

World Wide Web http://csla.net.

Colorado

Colorado Assn. of Libs. School Library Interest Group. Memb. 18+.

Chair Terri Brungardt, Widefield School Dist. 3. E-mail brungardtt@wsd3.org.

Address correspondence to Colorado Assn. of Libs., P.O. Box 740905, Arvada 80006-0905. Tel. 303-463-6400.

World Wide Web https://cal-webs.org/School_Libraries_Interest_Group.

Connecticut

Connecticut Assn. of School Libns. (CASL).
Memb. 500+. Term of Office. July–June.
Pres. Melissa Thom. E-mail President@ct
casl.org; *V.P.* Jenny Lussier. E-mail Vicepresi
dent@ctcasl.org; *V.P. Intern* Valerie DiLorenzo.
E-mail VPIntern@ctcasl.org; *Recording Secy.*
Margo Nabors. E-mail Secretary@ctcasl.org;
Treas. Laura Hedenberg. E-mail treasurer@
ctcasl.org; *Past Pres.* Barbara Johnson. E-mail
bjohnson@ctcasl.org.
Address correspondence to the president.
CASL, 4 Wotton Lane, Burlington 06013.
World Wide Web https://casl.wildapricot.org.

Delaware

Delaware Assn. of School Libns. (DASL), div.
of Delaware Lib. Assn. Memb. 100+. Publications. *DASL Newsletter* (online; irreg.); column
in *DLA Bulletin* (2x yearly).
Pres. Katelynn Scott, Alfred G. Waters Mid-
dle School, 1235 Cedar Lane Rd., Middletown
19709. Tel. 302-449-3490 ext. 2134, e-mail
katelynn.scott@appo.k12.de.us; *V.P./Pres.-
Elect* Patty Brown, Everett Meredith Middle
School, 504 S. Broad St., Middletown 19709.
Tel. 302-378-5001, e-mail patricia.brown@
appo.k12.de.us; *Secy.* Patty Crilley, Old State
Elementary School, 580 Tony Marchio Dr.,
Townsend 19734. Tel. 302-378-6720, e-mail
Patricia.Crilley@appo.k12.de.us; *Treas.* Jaclyn
Hale, Dover Public Lib., 35 Loockerman Plz.,
Dover 19901. Tel. 302-736-7185, e-mail jaclyn-
haledla@gmail.com; *Past Pres.* Kim Read, St.
George's Technical High School, 555 Hyatt's
Corner Rd., Middletown 19709, Tel. 302-449-
3360, e-mail kim.read@nccvt.k12.de.us.
Address correspondence to the president,
DASL, c/o Delaware Lib. Assn., Delaware
Division of Libs., 121 Martin Luther King, Jr.
Blvd. N., Dover 19901.
World Wide Web https://dla.lib.de.us/divisions/
dasl.

District of Columbia

District of Columbia Assn. of School Libns.
(DCASL). Memb. 8. Publication. Newsletter
(4x yearly).
Dir. Angela Falkenberg; *Assistant Dir.*
Christopher Stewart.
Address correspondence to DCASL, Union
Station, 50 Massachusetts Ave. NE, P.O. Box
1653 Washington, DC 20002. Tel. 301-502-
4203, e-mail contactdcasl@gmail.com.
World Wide Web https://dcla.org/School-
Library-Section.

Florida

Florida Assn. for Media in Educ. (FAME).
Memb. 1,400+. Term of Office. Nov.–Oct. Pub-
lication. *Florida Media Quarterly* (q.; memb.).
Ed. Okle Miller. E-mail okle.miller@gmail.com.
Pres. Ashlee Cornett. E-mail noblebeach@
gmail.com; *Pres.-Elect* Michelle Jarrett; *Secy.*
Kathleen Daniels; *Treas.* Angela Michael. *Parliamentarian* Vic Burke; *Past Pres.* Lorraine
Stinson. E-mail Lorraine.Stinson@stjohns.
k12.fl.us.
Address correspondence to FAME, P.O. Box
941169, Maitland 32794-1169. Tel. 863-585-
6802, e-mail FAME@floridamediaed.org.
World Wide Web https://www.floridamedi
aed.org.

Georgia

Georgia Lib. Media Assn. (GLMA). Memb.
700+.
Pres. Martha Bongiorno. E-mail president@
glma-inc.org; *Pres.-Elect* Amanda Lee; *Secy.*
Sarah Sansbury; *Treas.* Lora Taft. E-mail treas-
urer@glma-inc.org; *Past Pres.* Holly Frilot.
Address correspondence to GLMA, P.O.
Box 148, Waverly Hall 31831. E-mail info@
glma-inc.org.
World Wide Web https://www.glma-inc.org.

Hawaii

Hawaii Assn. of School Libns. Memb. (HASL).
145. Term of Office. June–May.
Co-Pres. Maricar Kawasaki *Co-Pres.* Dani-
elle Fujii; *V.P. Programming* Caitlin Ramirez,
Mokapu Elementary; *V.P. Membership* Elodie
Arellano, Ahuimanu Elementary; *Secy.* Susan
Clark, Punahou Schools; *Treas.* Donna Takara,
Kailua High.
Address correspondence to HASL, P.O. Box
29691 Honolulu 96820. E-mail hasl.contactus@
gmail.com.
World Wide Web https://haslhawaii.weebly.
com.

Idaho

School Libs. Services and Consulting, Idaho
Commission for Libs. (ICfL).

School Library Action Planning Committee: School Lib. Consultant Jeannie Standal. Tel. 208-639-4139, e-mail jeannie.standal@libraries.idaho.gov; Kit Anderson, Teton High School, Teton School Dist.; Sherrilynn Bair, Snake River School Community Lib.; Dennis Hahs, Rocky Mountain High School, Joint School Dist #2; Lynn Johnson, Mountain View School Dist.; Kiersten Kerr, Coeur d'Alene School Dist.; Susan Tabor-Boesch, Wood River Middle School.

Address correspondence to Jeannie Standal, Idaho Commission for Libs., 325 W. State St., Boise 83702. Tel. 208-334-2150, fax 208-334-4016, e-mail jeannie.standal@libraries.idaho.gov.

World Wide Web https://libraries.idaho.gov/school-libraries.

Illinois

Assn. of Illinois School Lib. Educators (AISLE). Memb. 1,000. Term of Office. July–June. Publications. Newsletter (4x yearly). *Ed.* David P. Little. E-mail newsletter@aisled.org.

Pres. Christy Semande, Canton USD #66, Canton. E-mail president@aisled.org; *Pres.-Elect* Mary Jo Matousek. E-mail preselect@aisled.org; *Secy.* Joanna Marek, La Grange School Dist. 105. E-mail secretary@aisled.org; *Treas.* Michelle Glatt. E-mail; treasurer@aisled.org; *Past Pres.* Anna Kim, Chappell Elementary, Chicago. E-mail pastpres@aisled.org; *Exec. Secy.* Carolyn Kinsella. E-mail ecsecretary@aisled.org.

Address correspondence to Assn. of Illinois School Lib. Educators. P.O. Box 110, Seneca 61360. Tel./fax 815-357-6023, e-mail execsecretary@aisled.org.

World Wide Web https://www.aisled.org.

Indiana

Assn. of Indiana School Lib. Educators (AISLE), affiliation of the Indiana Lib. Federation.

Chair Emily Wilt, Chesterton High School. E-mail ewilt@duneland.k12.in.us; *Chair Elect* Position Open; *Past Chair* Diane Rogers, Ben Davis 9th Grade Ctr. Tel. 317-988-7577; *Secy.* Ben Moore, Summit Middle School.

Address correspondence to AISLE, c/o Indiana Lib. Federation, 941 E. 86 St., Suite 260, Indianapolis 46240. Tel. 317-257-2040, e-mail askus@ilfonline.org.

World Wide Web https://www.ilfonline.org/page/AISLE.

Iowa

Iowa Assn. of School Libns. (IASL), div. of the Iowa Lib. Assn. Memb. 180+. Term of Office. Jan.–Jan.

Pres. Michelle Kruse, Cedar Rapids Middle School. E-mail michelle.kruse.2011@gmail.com; *V.P./Pres.-Elect* Ron Frascht, Lewis Central Community School District, Council Bluffs; *Secy/Treas.* Lisa Newgard, Orchard Hill Elementary, Cedar Falls; *Past Pres.* Jenahlee Chamberlain, Iowa City. E-mail iaslwebpage@gmail.com; *Membs.-at-Large* Diana Geers, Carrie Teske.

Address correspondence to the president, IASL, c/o the Iowa Lib. Assn., 6919 Vista Dr., W. Des Moines 50266. Tel. 515-282-8192.

World Wide Web https://www.iasl-ia.org.

Kansas

Kansas Assn. of School Libns. (KASL). Memb. 600.

Pres. Gail Becker E-mail gbecker@usd259.net; *1st V.P.* Rachel Yoder. E-mail rachel.yoder@usd460.org; *2nd V.P.* Tonya Foster. E-mail tonya_foster@cox.net; *Secy.* Rachel Hodges. E-mail hodgesrac@gmail.com; *Treas.* Amanda Harrison. E-mail amanda.harrison@mcpherson.com; *Past Pres.* Tonya Foster. E-mail tonya_foster@cox.net.

Address correspondence to the president, KASL, c/o Kansas Lib. Assn., 2 Washington Sq., Norton 67654.

World Wide Web http://www.ksschoollibrarians.org.

Kentucky

Kentucky Assn. of School Libns. (KASL), section of Kentucky Lib. Assn. Memb. 600+. Publication. *KASL Blog.* (blog) http://www.kaslblog.com.

Pres. Deidra Bowling-Meade. E-mail deidra.bowlingmeade@ashland.kyschools.us; *Pres.-Elect* Jen Gilbert. E-mail jennifer.gilbert@eminence.kyschools.us; *Secy.* Carrie Wilkerson. E-mail carrie.wilkerson@daviess.kyschools.us; *Treas.* Fred Tilsley. E-mail tilsley.kasl@

gmail.com; *Past Pres.* Sam Northern. E-mail samuel.northern@simpson.kyschools.us.
Address correspondence to the president. World Wide Web http://www.kasl.us.

Louisiana

Louisiana Assn. of School Libns. (LASL), section of the Louisiana Lib. Assn. Memb. 230. Term of Office. July–June.
Pres. Kim "Lovie" Howell, Benton Middle School. E-mail kim.howell@bossierschools.org; *1st V.P.* Amanda Jones, Live Oak Middle School. E-mail amanda.jones@lpsb.org; *2nd V.P.* Tammy Chaffin, French Settlement High School. E-mail tammy.chaffin@lpsb.org; *Secy.* Kelsye Baudoin, Belle Place Elementary School. E-mail kebaudoin@iberiaschools.org; *Parliamentarian* Tiffany Whitehead, Episcopal School Library. E-mail librariantiff@gmail.com; *Past-Pres.* Amanda Blanco, Lafayette High School.
Address correspondence to LASL, c/o Louisiana Lib. Assn., 1190 Meramec Station Rd., Suite 207, Ballwin, 63021. Tel. 1-800-969-6562 ext. 3, e-mail lla@amigos.org.
World Wide Web http://laslonline.weebly.com.

Maine

Maine Assn. of School Libs. (MASL). Memb. 200+.
Pres. Jennifer Stanbro, Skillin Elementary, South Portland; *Pres.-Elect* Heather Perkinson, Greely High School; *Secy.* Cathy Potter, Falmouth Middle School, Falmouth; *Treas.* Amy Denecker–Windham High School; *Past Pres.* Amanda Kozaka, Cape Elizabeth Middle School. E-mail akozaka@capeelizabethschools.org.
Address correspondence to the president, MASL, c/o Maine State Lib. Assn., 64 State House Station, Augusta 04333-0064. E-mail maslibraries@gmail.com.
World Wide Web http://www.maslibraries.org.

Maryland

Maryland Assn. of School Libns (MASL). Publication. Newsletter (mo.; online).
Pres. Lindsey Weaver, Middletown Middle School, Frederick County Public Schools. E-mail president@maslmd.org; *Pres.-Elect*

Tatanisha Love, Loch Raven Technical Academy, Baltimore County Public Schools. E-mail presidentelect@maslmd.org; *Secy.* Mary Jo Richmond, Media Services, Frederick County Public Schools. E-mail secretary@maslmd.org; *Treas.* Brittany Tignor, Snow Hill High School, Worcester County Public Schools. E-mail treasurer@maslmd.org; *Past Pres.* Jen Sturge, Calvert County Public Schools. E-mail president@maslmd.org; *Membs.-at-Large*, Simone Harris-Woodard, Prince George's County Public Schools. E-mail memberatlarge1@maslmd.org; Amanda O'Neil, Chopticon High School, St. Mary's County Public Schools. E-mail memberatlarge2@maslmd.org; *Delegate* Marianne Fitzgerald, Severna Park High School, Anne Arundel County Public Schools. E-mail delegate@maslmd.org; *MSDE Rep.* Laura Hicks. E-mail msde@maslmd.org.
Address correspondence to the secretary via e-mail to secretary@maslmd.org.
World Wide Web https://www.maslmd.org.

Massachusetts

Massachusetts School Lib. Assn. (MSLA). Memb. 800. Publication. *MSLA Forum* (irreg.; online). *Eds.* Katherine Steiger, Reba Tierney.
Pres. Jennifer Varney, MLKing, Jr. School, Cambridge. E-mail jvarney@maschoolibraries.org; *Secy.* Emma Kwon, Weston Elementary Schools. E-mail ekwon@maschoolibraries.org; *Treas.* Michelle Fontaine. E-mail mfontaine@maschoolibraries.org; *Past Pres.* Laura Luker, Pioneer Valley Chinese Immersion Charter, Hadley. E-mail lluker@maschoolibraries.org.
Address correspondence to Emily Kristofek, office manager, P.O. Box 336. Wayland 01778. Tel. 508-276-1697, e-mail ekristofek@maschoolibraries.org.
World Wide Web https://www.maschoolibraries.org.

Michigan

Michigan Assn. for Media in Educ. (MAME). Memb. 1,200. Publication. *Media Matters!* newsletter (mo.). *Eds.* Beverly Banks. E-mail beverlybanks@wlcsd.org and Jonathan Richards. E-mail jrichards@vanburenschools.net.
Pres. Erica Trowbridge, Oakridge Public Schools, Muskegon. E-mail etrow-bridge@

mimame.org; *Pres.-Elect* Carma Roesch, Oakridge Public Schools, Muskegon. E-mail croesch@mimame.org; *V.P. Continuing Ed.* Carrie Betts. E-mail cbetts@mimame.org; *Secy.* Kelly Hinks. E-mail khincks@mimame.org; *Treas.* Lisa Kelley, Rochester Community Schools, University Hills, 600 Croydon, Rochester Hills 48309. Tel. 248-726-4404, e-mail lkelley@mimame.org; *Past Pres.* Shannon Torres, Northville Public Schools, 45700 W. Six Mile Rd., Northville 48167. E-mail torressh@mimame.org; *Exec. Secy.* Teri Belcher. E-mail tbelcher@mimame.org.

Address correspondence to MAME, 1407 Rensen, Suite 3, Lansing 48910. Tel. 517-394-2808, fax 517-492-3878, e-mail mame@mimame.org.

World Wide Web http://www.mimame.org.

Minnesota

Info. and Technology Educators of Minnesota (ITEM) (formerly Minnesota Educ. Media Organization). Memb. 400+. Term of Office. July–June.

Co-Pres. Ashley Krohn, Minneapolis Public Schools; *Co-Pres.* Marie Hydukovich, South Saint Paul Public Schools; *Secy.* Sarah Rose, Minneapolis Public Schools; *Treas.* Jenifer Shier, Saint Paul Public Schools; *Past Co-Pres.* Dana Woods, Bemidji Public Schools; *Past Co-Pres.* Sara Florin, Centennial Public Schools; *Past Co-Pres.* Kim Haugo, Osseo Public Schools.

Address correspondence to ITEM, P.O. Box 130555, Roseville 55113. Tel. 651-771-8672, e-mail admin@mnitem.org.

World Wide Web https://mnitem.org.

Mississippi

School Lib. Section, Mississippi Lib. Assn. (MLA). Memb. 1,300.
School Lib. Section Chair Angela Mullins, Simpson Central School/Simpson County School Dist. Tel. 601-847-2630, e-mail angelamullins39073@gmail.com.

Address correspondence to School Lib. Section, MLA, P.O. Box 13687, Jackson 39236-3687. Tel. 601-981-4586, e-mail info@misslib.org.

World Wide Web http://www.misslib.org/page-1860236.

Missouri

Missouri Assn. of School Libns. (MASL). Memb. 1,000. Term of Office. July–June.
Pres. Kris Baughman, Eastwood Hills Elementary School, Raytown C-2 School Dist. E-mail kris.baughman@raytownschools.org; *1st V.P.* Melissa Corey, Robidoux Middle School, St. Joseph School Dist. E-mail melissa.corey@sjsd.k12.mo.us; *2nd V.P.* Tom Bober, Ralph M. Captain Elementary, School District of Clayton. E-mail tombober@claytonschools.net; *Secy.* Jenn Baldwin, Jasper R-5 School District. E-mail jbaldwin@jasper.k12.mo.us; *Treas.* Becky Haynes, Cassville Middle School, Cassville R-IV School Dist. E-mail beckbeckhaynes@gmail.com; *AASL Delegate* Matt King, Discovery Elementary, Orchard Farm School Dist. E-mail mking@ofr5.com; *Past Pres.* Kirsten Shaw, Martin Warren Elementary School, Warrensburg School Dist. E-mail kshaw@warrensburgr6.org.

Address correspondence to MASL, P.O. Box 2107, Jefferson City 65102. Tel. 573-893-4155, fax 573-635-2858, e-mail info@maslonline.org.

World Wide Web https://maslonline.org.

Montana

School Lib. Div., Montana Lib. Assn. (MLA). Memb. 200+.
Co-Chair Chani Craig, Whitefish Middle School Library; *Co-Chair* Vic Mortimer, Corvallis Middle School Lib.; *MLA Exec. Dir.* Kirk Vriesman, Montana Library Association, P.O. Box 823, Arlee 59821. E-mail kirkv@mtlib.org.

Address correspondence to the MLA executive director.

World Wide Web https://mlai.wildapricot.org/SLD.

Nebraska

Nebraska School Libns. Assn. (NSLA). Memb. 300+. Term of Office. July–June. Publication. *NSLA News* (blog; mo.).
Pres. Angela Blankenship. E-mail NSLApres@gmail.com; *Pres.-Elect* Crys Bauermeister. E-mail cbauermeister@gmail.com; *Secy.* Kelly Kenny. E-mail kenny.kelly@westside66.net; *Treas.* Beth Eilers. E-mail beth.eilers@ops.org; *Past Pres.* Cynthia Stogdill.

E-mail cynstogdill@gmail.com; *Exec. Secy.* Mandy Peterson. E-mail contactnsla@gmail.com.

Address correspondence to the executive secretary via e-mail.

World Wide Web https://www.neschoollibrarians.org.

Nevada

Nevada School and Children Libns. Section (NSCLS) of the Nevada Lib. Assn. (NLA). Memb. 120.

Chair Susan Thurnbeck, Las Vegas–Clark County Lib. Dist. E-mail susantnvlibrary.@gmail.com; *Past Chair* Larry Johnson, Las Vegas–Clark County Lib. Dist.; *Exec. Secy. NLA* Carla Land, Las Vegas–Clark County Lib. District. E-mail bookdiva@gmail.com.

Address correspondence to the chair, NLA School and Children Libns. Section, via e-mail.

World Wide Web http://nevadalibraries.org/Handbook-NSCLS.

New Hampshire

New Hampshire School Lib. Media Assn. (NSHLMA). Memb. 250+. Term of Office. July–June. Publication. *NHSLMA Newsletter* (irreg.; online).

Pres. Justine Thain, Hooksett School Dist., Hooksett. E-mail president@nhslma.org; *V.P.* Mary Lou O'Connor, Stratham Memorial School, Stratham School District. E-mail vice-president@nhslma.org; *Secy.* Kristin Whitworth, Dover High School. E-mail secretary@nhslma.org; *Treas.* Audra Lewis, Horne Street School, Dover. E-mail treasurer@nhslma.org; *Past Pres.* Karen Abraham, Laconia High School. E-mail past-president@nhslma.org.

Address correspondence to the president, NHSLMA, P.O. Box 418, Concord 03302-0418. E-mail nhslma@gmail.com.

World Wide Web https://nhslma.wildapricot.org.

New Jersey

New Jersey Assn. of School Libns. (NJASL). Memb. 1,000+. Term of Office. Aug. 1–July 31. Publication. *Bookmark Newsletter* (mo.; memb.). *Ed.* Casey Schaffer. E-mail bookmark@njasl.org.

Pres. Lisa Straubinger, T. Baldwin Demarest School, Old Tappan. E-mail president@njasl.org; *Pres.-Elect.* Ewa Dziedzic-Elliott, Lawrence Township High School, Lawrence. E-mail presidentelect@njasl.org; *V.P.* Beth Raff, Mt. Tabor Elementary School, Parsippany-Troy Hills School District. E-mail vp@njasl.org; *Recording Secy.* Casey Jane Schaffer DeMasi Schools. E-mail secretary@njasl.org; *Treas.* Elizabeth (Beth) Willoughby, Dunellen Public Schools. E-mail treasurer@njasl.org; *Membs.-at-Large* Karen Grant, Steve Tetreault. E-mail membersatlarge@njasl.org; *Past Pres.* Beth Thomas, Lawton C. Johnson Middle School, Summit. E-mail pastpresident@njasl.org.

Address correspondence to the recording secretary, NASL, P.O. Box 1460, Springfield 07081.

World Wide Web https://njasl.org.

New York

Section of School Libns., New York Lib. Assn. (NYLA). Memb. 800+. Term of Office. Nov.–Oct. Publication. *School Library Update* (3x yearly; memb.; online).

Pres. Lisa Perkowski. E-mail lehnski16@gmail.com; *Pres.-Elect* Madelyn Haussner, E-mail nfogoddess@gmail.com; *Secy.* Jessica Regitano. E-mail jlregitano@gmail.com; *Treas.* Anne Paulson. E-mail anneppaulson@gmail.com; *V.P. of Conferences* Annarose Foley. E-mail annarose.foley@icsd.k12.ny.us; *V.P. of Communications* Heather Turner. E-mail hturner@ocmboces.org; *Past Pres.* Dawn Pressimone. E-mail dpressimone@waynecsd.org.

Address correspondence to the Section of School Libns., NYLA, 6021 State Farm Rd., Guilderland 12084. Tel. 518-432-6952, fax 518-427-1697, e-mail info@nyla.org.

World Wide Web https://www.nyla.org/4DCGI/cms/review.html?Action=CMS_Document&DocID=136&MenuKey=ssl.

North Carolina

North Carolina School Lib. Media Assn. (NCSLMA). Memb. 1,000+. Term of Office. Nov.–Oct.

Pres. Jenny Umbarger. E-mail jennyumbarger@ncslma.org; *Pres.-Elect* Jennifer Abel.

E-mail jenniferabel@ncslma.org; *Secy.* Jen Baker. E-mail jenbaker@ncslma.org; *Treas.* Bitsy Griffin. E-mail bitsygriffin@ncslma.org; *Past Pres.* Cindy Sturdivant. E-mail cindysturdivant@ncslma.org.

Address correspondence to the president, NCSLMA, 151 NC Hwy. 9, Suite B-188, Black Mountain 28711.

World Wide Web https://ncslma.wildapricot.org.

North Dakota

School Lib. and Youth Svcs. section of the North Dakota Lib. Assn. (NDLA). Memb. 100.

Chair Sharri Mosser, North Dakota State Lib. E-mail ssandwick@nd.gov; *Chair-Elect* Jennifer Hess, Eagles Elementary School, Fargo Public Schools. E-mail hessj@fargo.k12.nd.us; *Secy.* Carmen Redding, North Dakota State Lib. E-mail Carmen.Redding@k12.nd.us; *Past Chair* Leslie Allan, Williston Public Schools. E-mail lesley.allan@willistonschools.org.

Address correspondence to the School Lib. and Youth Svcs. Section, NDLA, 604 E. Boulevard Ave., Bismarck 58505.

World Wide Web https://ndla.info/School-Library-and-Youth-Services.

Ohio

Ohio Educ. Lib. Media Assn. (OELMA). Memb. 1,000.

Pres. Karen Gedeon, Cuyahoga Falls City Schools. E-mail president@oelma.org; *V.P.* Lisa Barnes Prince, Manchester Local Schools. E-mail vicepresident@oelma.org; *Secy.* Amy Keister, Louisville City Schools. E-mail secretary@oelma.org; *Treas.* Jennifer Schwelik. E-mail treasurer@oelma.org; *Past Pres.* Brandi Young, South-Western City School Dist., Westland High School. E-mail pastpresident@oelma.org.

Address correspondence to OELMA, 675 Alpha Drive, Suite E and K, Highland Heights 44143. Tel. 614-647-3487.

World Wide Web https://www.oelma.org.

Oklahoma

Oklahoma School Libns. Div., Oklahoma Lib. Assn. (OLA). Memb. 200+.

Chair Ashleigh Dautermann. E-mail oksl@oklibs.org; *Chair-Elect* Dr. Alesha Baker.

E-mail bakera@nsuok.edu; *Secy.* Molly Dettmann. E-mail mdettmann@norman.k12.ok.us; *Treas.* Lisa Battige. E-mail Lisabattige@gmail.com; *Past Chair* Amanda Kordeliski. E-mail akordelis2@norman.k12.ok.us.

Address correspondence to the chairperson, School Libns. Div., OLA, 1190 Meramec Station Rd., Suite 207, Ballwin MO 63021-6902. Tel. 800-969-6562 ext. 5, fax 636-529-1396.

World Wide Web https://www.oklibs.org/page/OKSL.

Oregon

Oregon Assn. of School Libs. (OASL). Memb. 600. Publication. *Interchange* (3x yearly). Co-ord. Ed. Dana Berglund. E-mail interchange@oasl.olaweb.org.

Pres. Arlene Weible, State Library of Oregon. E-mail olapresident@olaweb.org; *V.P./Pres.-Elect* Marci Ramiro-Jenkins, McMinnville Public Library. E-mail olavp@olaweb.org; *Secy.* Star Khan, Driftwood Public Library. E-mail olasecretary@olaweb.org; *Treas.* Stuart Levy, Parkrose High School. E-mail olatreasurer@olaweb.org; *Past Pres.* Kate Lasky, Josephine Community Library District. E-mail olapastpresident@olaweb.org; *Memb.-at-Large* Sami Kerzel, Deschutes Public Library. E-mail samik@dpls.lib.or.us.

Address correspondence to the president, OASL, c/o Oregon Lib. Assn., P.O. Box 3067, La Grande 97850. Tel. 541-962-5824, e-mail president@oasl.olaweb.org.

World Wide Web https://www.olaweb.org/oasl-home.

Pennsylvania

Pennsylvania School Libns. Assn. (PSLA). Memb. 800+. Publication. *PSLA Pulse* (blog).

Pres. Laura Ward, Fox Chapel Area School Dist. E-mail lward@psla.org; *Pres.-Elect.* Aimee Emerson, Floyd C. Fretz Middle School, Bradford Area School District. E-mail aemerson@psla.org; *V.P.* Mary Schwander, New Hope-Solebury High School. E-mail mschwander@psla.org; *Secy.* Elizabeth Henry, Lampeter-Strasburg School District. E-mail secretary@psla.org; *Treas.* Jeffrey Weiss, Bradford Area High School, Bradford Area School Dist. E-mail pslatreasurer@gmail.com; *Past Pres.* Robin Burns, Salisbury Township School Dist. E-mail rburns@psla.org.

Address correspondence to the president, PSLA, Hershey Square #125, 1152 Mae St., Hummelstown 17036.

World Wide Web https://www.psla.org.

Rhode Island

School Libns. of Rhode Island, section of the Rhode Island Lib. Assn. (RILA). Memb. 350+. Publication. *SLRI Update* (irreg.; online).

Pres. Joan Mouradjian. E-mail slri@rili braries.org.

Address correspondence to the president, School Libns. of Rhode Island, RILA, P.O. Box 6765, Providence 02940.

World Wide Web https://rilibraries.org/slri.

South Carolina

South Carolina Assn. of School Libns. (SCASL). Memb. 900. Term of Office. July–June. Publication *SCASL Messenger* (q., online, memb.). *Ed.* Anya Bonnette. E-mail anya.bonnette@ocsd5.net.

Pres. Katherine Malmquist. E-mail president@scasl.net; *Pres.-Elect* Tamara Cox. E-mail president.elect@scasl.net; *Secy.* Gloria Coleman. E-mail secretary@scasl.net; *Treas.* Camellia Harris; *Past Pres.* Heather Loy.

Address correspondence to SCASL, P.O. Box 2442, Columbia 29202. Tel./fax 803-492-3025.

World Wide Web https://www.scasl.net.

South Dakota

South Dakota School Lib. Media Section, South Dakota Lib. Assn. (SDLA). Memb. 140+. Term of Office. Oct.–Sept.

Chair Korey Erickson, Sioux Falls Public Schools, Sioux Falls. E-mail korey.erickson@k12.sd.us; *Past Chair* Kimberly Darata, Douglas School Dist. E-mail kimberly.darata@k12.sd.us.

Address correspondence to the chairperson. South Dakota School Lib. Media Section, SDLA, Mikkelsen Lib., 2001 S. Summit Ave., Sioux Falls 57197. Tel. 605-743-0889.

World Wide Web https://www.sdlibraryas sociation.org/page/Sections.

Tennessee

Tennessee Assn. of School Libns. (TASL). Memb. 450. Term of Office. Jan.–Dec. Publication. *TASL Talks* (wk.; blog).

Pres. Katie Capshaw; *Pres.-Elect* Katelyn Jernigan; *Secy.* Becca Chen; *Treas.* Ginny Britt, Robertson County Schools. E-mail ginny.britt@rcstn.net; *Past Pres.* Lindsey Kimery, Woodland Middle School, 1500 Volunteer Pkwy., Brentwood 37027. E-mail lindskander son@gmail.com.

Address correspondence to the president, TASL, P.O. Box 2013, Goodlettsville 37072.

World Wide Web https://www.tasltn.org.

Texas

Texas Assn. of School Libns. (TASL), div. of Texas Lib. Assn. Memb. 4,500+. Term of Office. Apr.–Mar.

Chair Jill Bellomy. E-mail jillbellomy@gmail.com; *Chair-Elect* Lucy Podmore. E-mail lucy.podmore@nisd.net; *Secy.* Linda Kay. E-mail linda_kay@roundrockisd.org; *Councilor* Nicole Cruz. E-mail ncruz@sharylandisd.org; *Alternate Councilor* Jen Hampton. E-mail hamptoj@hpisd.org; *Private Schools* Abby Harrison. E-mail harrisona@greenhill.org; *Past Chair* Kristi Starr. E-mail kristi.starr@lubbockisd.org; *TLA Exec. Dir.* Shirley Robinson. E-mail shirleyr@txla.org.

Address correspondence to the chairperson, TASL, c/o Texas Lib. Assn., 3420 Executive Center Dr., Suite 301, Austin 78731. Tel. 512-328-1518, fax 512-328-8852.

World Wide Web https://www.txla.org/groups/tasl.

Utah

Utah Educ. Lib. Media Assn. (UELMA). Memb. 500+. Publication. *UELMA Works* (q.).

Pres. Tricia Fenton, Cyprus High School, Granite School Dist. E-mail pmfenton@grani teschools.org; *Pres.-Elect* Michele Edgley; *Secy.* Stephanie Jones, Alpine School Dist. E-mail sjones@alpinedistrict.org; *Past Pres.* Emily DeJong, Beacon Heights Elementary, Salt Lake. E-mail board@uelma.org; *Exec. Dir.* Davina Sauthoff, Granite Dist. E-mail execu tivedirector@uelma.org.

Address correspondence to the executive director.

World Wide Web https://uelma.org.

Vermont

Vermont School Lib. Assn. (VSLA). Memb. 220+. Term of Office. May–May.

Pres. Peter Langella; *Pres.-Elect* Meg Allison; *Secy.* Martine Gulick. E-mail vslasecretary@gmail.com; *Treas.* Megan Sutton. E-mail msutton@acsdvt.org; *Past Pres.* Deborah Ehler-Hansen. E-mail vermonthan1@gmail.com.

Address correspondence to VSLAmembership@gmail.com.

World Wide Web https://vsla.wildapricot.org.

Virginia

Virginia Assn. of School Libns. (VAASL). Memb. 1,200. Term of Office. Nov.–Nov. Publication. *VAASL Voice* (q.; memb.).

Pres. Judy Deichman. E-mail president@vaasl.org; *Pres.-Elect* Nathan Sekinger. E-mail presidentelect@vaasl.org; *Secy.* Megan Moore. E-mail secretary@vaasl.org; *Treas.* Tonia Erickson. E-mail Treasurer@vaasl.org; *Past Pres.* Jennifer Cooper. E-mail pastpresident@vaasl.org; *Exec. Dir.* Margaret Baker. E-mail executive@vaasl.org.

Address correspondence to the executive director, VAASL, P.O. Box 2015, Staunton 24402-2015. Tel. 540-416-6109, e-mail exec utive@vaasl.org.

World Wide Web https://www.vaasl.org.

Washington

School Lib. Div., Washington Lib. Assn. (WLA). Memb. 700+. Term of Office. Apr.–Apr.

Chair Ryan Grant, Medical Lake School District. E-mail rgrant@mlsd.org; *V. Chair/Chair-Elect* Elizabeth Roberts, Bellevue School District. E-mail elizabeth.k.roberts@gmail.com.

Address correspondence to WLA School Lib. Div., P.O. Box 33808, Seattle 98133. Tel. 206-823-1138, e-mail info@wla.org.

World Wide Web https://www.wla.org/school-libraries.

West Virginia

School Lib. Div., West Virginia Lib. Assn. (WVLA). Memb. 50. Term of Office. Nov.–Nov.

Chair Leigh Ann Hood, East Park Elementary, 805 Pittsburgh Ave., Fairmont 26554. Tel. 304-534-0927, e-mail lahood@k12.wv.us; *Past Chair* Lynda Suzie Martin, Brookhaven Elementary, 147 Estate Dr., Morgantown 26508. Tel. 304-282-0147, e-mail librarynbct@gmail.com.

Address correspondence to the chairperson, WVLA School Lib. Div., P.O. Box 1432, Morgantown 26507.

World Wide Web https://wvla.org.

Wisconsin

Wisconsin Educ. Media and Technology Assn. (WEMTA). Memb. 800+.

Pres. Raquel Rand; *Pres.-Elect* Kay Koepsel-Benning; *V.P.* Tina Birkett; *Secy.* Dawn Totzke; *Treas.* Pamela Hansen; *Past Pres.* Micki Uppena.

Address correspondence to WEMTA, 1502 W. Broadway, Suite 102, Madison 53713. Tel. 608-588-6006, e-mail wemta@wemta.org.

World Wide Web https://www.wemta.org.

Wyoming

School Lib. Interest Group, Wyoming Lib. Assn. (WLA). Memb. 100+.

Co-Chair Melissa Brumsted Snider, Teton County School Dist. Tel. 307-733-3020; *Co-Chair* Megan Bietz, Campbell County School Dist. Tel. 307-682-7289; *Secy.* Maggie Unterseher, Weston County School Dist. #1. Tel. 307-629-0190.

Address correspondence to the chairperson, SLIG, c/o WLA, 1190 Meramac Station Rd., Suite 207, Ballwin MO 63201.

World Wide Web https://wyla.org/School-Library-Interest-Group.

International Library Associations

International Association of Law Libraries

Kurt Carroll, President
P.O. Box 5709, Washington, DC 20016
E-mail president@iall.org
World Wide Web https://iall.org

Objective

The International Association of Law Libraries (IALL) is a worldwide organization of librarians, libraries, and other persons or institutions concerned with the acquisition and use of legal information emanating from sources other than their jurisdictions and from multinational and international organizations.

IALL's purpose is to facilitate the work of librarians who acquire, process, organize, and provide access to foreign legal materials. IALL has no local chapters but maintains liaison with national law library associations in many countries and regions of the world.

Membership

More than 400 members in more than 50 countries on five continents.

Officers

Pres. Kurt Carroll, Library of Congress, Washington, DC 20550. Tel. 202-707-1494, e-mail president@iall.org; *V.P.* Kerem Kahvecioglu, Haciahment Mahellesi, Pir Hüsamettin Sokak 20, 34440 Beyoğlu, Istanbul. Tel: 90 212 311 5157, e-mail vicepresident@iall.org; *Secy.* David Gee, Institute of Advanced Legal Studies, Univ. of London, 17 Russell Sq., London. Tel. 44 (0)20 7862 5822, fax 44 (0)20 7862 5770, e-mail David.Gee@sas.ac.uk; *Treas.* Barbara Garavaglia, Univ. of Michigan Law Lib., Ann Arbor 48109-1210. Tel. 734-764-9338, fax 734-764-5863, e-mail bvaccaro@umich.edu; *Past Pres.* Jeroen Vervliet, The Hague. Tel. 31-70-302-4242, e-mail j.vervliet@ppl.nl.

Board of Directors

Kristina J. Alayan, Howard Univ. School of Law, Washington, DC. Tel. 202-806-8047, e-mail kristina.alayan@law.howard.edu; Rebecca J. Five Bergstrøm, Univ. of Oslo Law Lib. Tel. 4722859306, e-mail r.j.f.bergstrom@ub.uio.no; Heather Casey, Georgetown Univ. Law Lib., Washington, DC. Tel. 202-661-6573, e-mail hec29@georgetown.edu; François Desseilles, Univ. of Liège Lib., Liège (Sart-Tilman). E-mail fdesseills@uliege.be; Mark D. Engsberg, MacMillan Law Lib., Emory School of Law, Atlanta, GA. Tel. 404-727-6983, e-mail mengsbe@emory.edu; Michel Fraysse, Université Toulouse, France. Tel. 00 33 (5) 34 61 34, e-mail michel.fraysse@ut-capitole.fr; Trung Quach, Melbourne Law School, Univ. of Melbourne, Victoria. Tel. 61 3 9035 3061, e-mail trung.quach@unimelb.edu.au; Jean M. Wenger, Chicago-Kent College of Law, Chicago, IL 60661. Tel. 312-906-5610, e-mail jwenger@kentlaw.iit.edu.

Publications

International Journal of Legal Information (*IJLI*) (3x yearly; memb.).

International Association of Music Libraries, Archives, and Documentation Centres

Anders Cato, Secretary-General
Slots- og Kulturstyrelsen, Danish Agency for Culture and Palaces, H.C. Andersens Boulevard 2,
DK-1553 Copenhagen V Denmark
Tel: +45 5376 6337, e-mail secretary@iaml.info
World Wide Web https://www.iaml.info

Objective

The objective of the International Association of Music Libraries, Archives, and Documentation Centres (IAML) is to promote the activities of music libraries, archives, and documentation centers and to strengthen the cooperation among them; to promote the availability of all publications and documents relating to music and further their bibliographical control; to encourage the development of standards in all areas that concern the association; and to support the protection and preservation of musical documents of the past and the present.

Membership

Memb. approximately 1,700 in about 40 countries worldwide.

Officers

Pres. Pia Shekhter, Gothenburg Univ. Lib., Sweden. E-mail president@iaml.info; *V.P.s* Jürgen Diet, Bayerische Staatsbibliothek, Munich; Jane Gottlieb, The Juilliard School, New York; Anna Pensaert, Cambridge Univ. Lib. and the Pendlebury Lib. of Music; and Rupert Ridgewell, British Lib., London; *Secy.-Gen.* P. Anders Cato, Danish Agency for Culture and Palaces, Copenhagen, Denmark. E-mail secretary@iaml.info; *Treasurer* Thomas Kalk, Stadtbüchereien Düsseldorf, Germany. E-mail treasurer@iaml.info; *Past Pres.* Stanislaw Hrabia, Uniwersytet Jagiellonski, Kraków, Poland.

Publication

Fontes Artis Musicae (q.; memb.). *Ed.* James P. Cassaro, Univ. of Pittsburgh, B-30 Music Bldg., Pittsburgh, PA 15260. Tel. 412-624-4131, e-mail fontes@iaml.info.

Institutional Sections

Archives and Music Documentation Centres. *Chair* Joseph Hafner, McGill Library, Montréal. E-mail archives@iaml.info.

Broadcasting and Orchestra Libraries. *Chair* Sabina Benelli, Teatro alla Scala, Milan. E-mail broadcasting-orchestra@iaml.info.

Libraries in Music Teaching Institutions. *Chair* Charles Peters, William & Gayle Cook Music Lib., Indiana Univ., Bloomington. E-mail teaching@iaml.info.

Public Libraries. *Chair* Blanka Ellederová, Municipal Lib. of Prague. E-mail public-libraries@iaml.info.

Research Libraries. *Chair* Ruprecht Langer, Deutsche Nationalbibliothek, Leipzig. E-mail research-libraries@iaml.info.

Subject Sections

Audio-Visual Materials. *Chair* Zane Grosa, National Library of Latvia, Riga. E-mail ajustice@usc.edu.

Bibliography. *Chair* Stefan Engl, Österreichische Nationalbibliothek, Vienna. E-mail bibliography@iaml.info.

Cataloguing. *Chair* Kimmy Szeto, Baruch College, New York. E-mail cataloguing@iaml.info.

Service and Training. *Chair* Katherine Penner, University of Manitoba. E-mail service@iaml.info.

International Association of School Librarianship

Jill Hancock, Executive Director
P.O. Box 684, Jefferson City, MO 65102
Tel. 573-635-2173, e-mail iasl@c2pro.solutions
World Wide Web https://iasl-online.org

Mission and Objectives

The mission of the International Association of School Librarianship (IASL) is to provide an international forum for those interested in promoting effective school library programs as viable instruments in the education process. IASL also provides guidance and advice for the development of school library programs and the school library profession. IASL works in cooperation with other professional associations and agencies.

Membership is worldwide and includes school librarians, teachers, librarians, library advisers, consultants, education administrators, and others who are responsible for library and information services in schools. The membership also includes professors and instructors in universities and colleges where there are programs for school librarians and students who are undertaking such programs.

The objectives of IASL are to advocate the development of school libraries throughout all countries; to encourage the integration of school library programs into the instruction and curriculum of the school; to promote the professional preparation and continuing education of school library personnel; to foster a sense of community among school librarians in all parts of the world; to foster and extend relationships between school librarians and other professionals in connection with children and youth; to foster research in the field of school librarianship and the integration of its findings with pertinent knowledge from related fields; to promote the publication and dissemination of information about successful advocacy and program initiatives in school librarianship; to share information about programs and materials for children and youth throughout the international community; and to initiate and coordinate activities, conferences, and other projects in the field of school librarianship and information services.

IASL was founded in 1971.

Membership

Approximately 825.

Officers

Pres. Katy Manck, Independent Book Reviewer, Gilmer, Tex. E-mail katyroo@gmail.com or Katy.Manck@gmail.com; *V.P. Assn. Operations* Fredrik Ernerot, School Library West, Gothenburg, Sweden. E-mail fredrik.ernerot@grundskola.goteborg.se; *V.P. Assn. Relations* Albert Boekhorst, Brasil, Netherlands. E-mail albertkb@gmail.com; *V.P. Advocacy and Promotion* Annie Tam, the Independent Schools Foundation Academy, Hong Kong, China. E-mail atam@isf.edu.hk; *Treas.* Jennifer Branch-Mueller, Univ. of Alberta, Canada. E-mail jbranch@ualberta.ca.

Regional Board of Directors

Jerry Mathema, Africa; Dr. Chavvi Jain, Asia; Eleanor Duggan, East Asia; Meghan Harper, North America; Mark-Jeffery O'Niel Deans, Latin America/Caribbean; Vanja Jurilj, Europe; Sevgi Arioglu, North Africa/Middle East; Susan La Marca, Oceania; Zakir Hossain, International Schools.

Publications

School Libraries Worldwide (http://www.iasl-online.org/publications/slw/index.html), the association's refereed research and professional journal (online only; 2x yearly; memb.).

IASL Newsletter (http://www.iasl-online.org/publications/newsletter.html) (print; 4x yearly; memb.).

International Association of University Libraries (IATUL)

Charles Eckman, President
World Wide Web https://www.iatul.org

Objective

The main objective of the International Association of Scientific and Technological University Libraries (IATUL) is to provide a forum where library directors and senior managers can meet to exchange views on matters of current significance and to provide an opportunity for them to develop a collaborative approach to solving problems. IATUL also welcomes into membership organizations that supply services to university libraries, if they wish to be identified with the association's activities.

Membership

260 in 60 countries.

Officers

Pres. Dr. Anna Walek, GUT Library, Gdańsk University of Technology, Poland. E-mail anna.walek@pg.edu.pl; *V.P.* Dr. Charles Eckman, Otto G. Richter Library, University of Miami, U.S. E-mail ceckman@miami.edu; *Secy.* Donna Bourne-Tyson, Killam Library, Dalhousie University, Canada. E-mail donna.bourne-tyson@dal.ca; *Treas.* Mag. Gerda Winkler, Universitiy Library, Free University of Bozen-Bolzano, Italy. E-mail library@unibz.it.

Board Members

Jill Benn, Univ. of Western Australia, Perth. E-mail jill.benn@uwa.edu.au; Lars Egeland, Oslo Metropolitan Univ., Norway. E-mail larse@oslomet.no; Kate Robinson, University of Bath, England. E-mail liskmr@bath.ac.uk; Ujala Satgoor, University of Cape Town, South Africa. E-mail ujala.satgoor@uct.ac.za.

Publication

IATUL Conference Proceedings (https://www.iatul.org/publications/proceedings).

International Council on Archives

David Fricker, President
60 rue des Francs-Bourgeois, 75003 Paris, France
Tel. 33-1-40-27-63-06, fax 33-1-42-72-20-65, e-mail ica@ica.org
World Wide Web https://www.ica.org/en

Objective

The mission of the International Council on Archives (ICA) is to establish, maintain, and strengthen relations among archivists of all lands and among all professional and other agencies or institutions concerned with the custody, organization, or administration of archives, public or private, wherever located. ICA was established in 1948.

Membership

Approximately 1,900 in nearly 200 countries and territories.

Officers

Pres. David Fricker, Australia; *V.P.s* Meg Phillips, U.S.; Henri Zuber, France.

Board Members

Hamad bin Mohammed al-Dhawyani, Oman; Françoise Banat-Berger, France; Avril Belfon, Trinidad and Tobago; Alexander Lukas Bieri, Switzerland; Caroline Brown, United Kingdom; Yolanda Cagigas Ocejo, Spain; Montserrat Canela Garayoa, Switzerland; Søren Bitsch Christensen, Denmark; Emma de Ramon Acevedo, Chile; Charles Farrugia, Malta; Emilie Gagnet Leumas, United States; Becky Haglund Tousey, United States; Jeff James, United Kingdom; James Lowry, United States; Guoqiang Lu, China; Victorino M. Manalo, Philippines; Vitor Manoel Marques da Fonseca, Brazil; Paolo Massa, Italy; Mathias Massode, Benin; Noa Petueli Tapumanaia, Tuvalu; Fina Solà i Gasset, Spain; Atakilty Assefa Asgedom, Ethiopia (ex officio).

Publications

Comma (print and online; 2x yearly, memb.).
Flash (online only; 2x yearly; memb.).
ICA e-newsletter (online only; mo.).
Conference papers and proceedings.

International Federation of Film Archives
(Fédération Internationale des Archives du Film)

Michael Loebenstein, Secretary-General
Secretariat, 42 rue Blanche, B-1060 Brussels, Belgium
Tel. 32-2-538-30-65, fax 32-2-534-47-74, e-mail info@fiafnet.org
World Wide Web http://www.fiafnet.org

Objective

Founded in 1938, the International Federation of Film Archives (FIAF) brings together not-for-profit institutions dedicated to rescuing films and any other moving-image elements considered both as cultural heritage and as historical documents.

FIAF is a collaborative association of the world's leading film archives whose purpose has always been to ensure the proper preservation and showing of motion pictures. Almost 90 member archives in more than 50 countries collect, restore, and exhibit films and cinema documentation spanning the entire history of film.

FIAF seeks to promote film culture and facilitate historical research, to help create new archives around the world, to foster training and expertise in film preservation, to encourage the collection and preservation of documents and other cinema-related materials, to develop cooperation between archives, and to ensure the international availability of films and cinema documents.

Officers

Pres. Frédéric Maire; *V.P.* Chalida Uabumrungjit; *Secy.-Gen.* Michael Loebensten; *Treas.* Jon Wengström.

Address correspondence to Christophe Dupin, Senior Administrator, FIAF Secretariat. E-mail c.dupin@fiafnet.org.

Publications and Databases

FIAF Bulletin Online.
FIAF Directory (print).
International Index to Film Periodicals database. (OVID, ProQuest).
Journal of Film Preservation. Ed. Elaine Burrows. E-mail jfp.editor@fiafnet.org.
Treasures from the Film Archives database.
Extensive selection of books through the FIAF Bookshop.

International Federation of Library Associations and Institutions

Halo Locher, Interim Secretary General
Prins Willem-Alexanderhof 5, 2595 BE The Hague, Netherlands
Tel. 31-70-314-0884, fax 31-70-383-4827, e-mail ifla@ifla.org
World Wide Web https://www.ifla.org

Objective

The objective of the International Federation of Library Associations and Institutions (IFLA) is to promote international understanding, cooperation, discussion, research, and development in all fields of library activity, including bibliography, information services, and the education of library personnel, and to provide a body through which librarianship can be represented in matters of international interest. IFLA is the leading international body representing the interests of library and information services and their users. It is the global voice of the library and information profession. IFLA was founded in 1927.

Officers

Pres. Barbara Lison, Stadtbibliothek, Bremen, Germany. E-mail barbara.lison@stadtbiblio thek.bremen.de; *Pres.-Elect* Antonia Arahova, General Council for Libraries, Ministry of Education and Religious Affairs, Greece; *Treas.* Perry Moree, ZB - Library of Zeeland, Netherlands; *Past Pres.* G Christine Mackenzie, Australia.

Governing Board

At-Large Kirsten Boelt, Denmark; Jonathan Hernández Pérez, Mexico; Yasuyo Inoue, Japan; Ayub Khan, United Kingdom; Mandla Ntombela, South Africa; *Chair, Professional Council* Adjoa Boateng, Germany; *Chair, Regional Council* Nthabiseng Kotsokoane,

South Africa; *Chair, Management of Library Assns. Section* Halo Locher, Switzerland.

Publications

IFLA Annual Report.
IFLA Journal (4x yearly).
IFLA Trend Reports.
IFLA Professional Reports.
IFLA Publications Series.
IFLA Series on Bibliographic Control.
Global Studies in Libraries and Information (irreg. series).
Access and Opportunity for All: How Libraries Contribute to the United Nations 2030 Agenda.

American Membership

Associations

American Lib. Assn., Assn. for Lib. and Info. Science Educ., Assn. of Research Libs., Chief Officers of State Lib. Agencies, Medical Lib. Assn., Special Libs. Assn., Urban Libs. Council, Chinese American Libns. Assn., Polish American Lib. Assn.

Institutional Members

More than 100 libraries and related institutions are institutional members or consultative bodies and sponsors of IFLA in the United States (out of a total of more than 1,000 globally), and more than 100 are individual affiliates (out of a total of more than 300 affiliates globally).

International Organization for Standardization

Sergio Mujica, Secretary-General
ISO Central Secretariat, Chemin de Blandonnet 8, CP 401 1214 Vernier, Geneva, Switzerland
Tel. 41-22-749-01-11, fax 41-22-733-34-30, e-mail central@iso.org
World Wide Web https://www.iso.org/home.html

Objective

Founded in 1947, the International Organization for Standardization (ISO) is a worldwide federation of national standards bodies that currently comprises members from 164 countries and 785 technical committees and subcommittees working on various aspects of standards development. The objective of ISO is to promote the development of standardization and related activities in the world with a view to facilitating international exchange of goods and services and to developing cooperation in the spheres of intellectual, scientific, technological, and economic activity. The scope of ISO covers international standardization in all fields except electrical and electronic engineering standardization, which is the responsibility of the International Electrotechnical Commission (IEC). The results of ISO's technical work are published as international standards.

Officers

Pres. Ulrika Francke, Sweden; *Pres.-Elect* Ulrika Francke, Sweden; *V.P.s* Christoph Winterhalter, Germany *(Policy)*, Sauw Kook Choy, Singapore *(Technical Management)*, Mitsuo Matsumoto, Japan *(Finance)*; *Treas.* Jacqueline Curzon, Switzerland; *Past Pres.* Eddy Njoroge, Kenya; *Secy.-Gen.* Sergio Mujica, Chile.

Technical Work

The technical work of ISO is carried out by groups of experts collaborating worldwide, representing every imaginable sector, from soaps to spacecraft, from MP3 to coffee. Among its technical committees are:

ISO/TC 46—Information and documentation (Secretariat, Association Française de Normalization, 11 rue Francis de Pressensé, 93571 La Plaine Saint-Denis, Cedex, France). Scope: Standardization of practices relating to libraries, documentation and information centers, indexing and abstracting services, archives, information science, and publishing.

ISO/TC 37—Language and terminology (Secretariat, Standardization Administration of China, No. 9 Madian Donglu, Haidian District, Beijing 100088, China). Scope: Standardization of descriptions, resources, technologies, and services related to terminology, translation, interpreting, and other language-based activities in the multilingual information society.

ISO/IEC JTC 1—Information technology (Secretariat, American National Standards Institute, 1899 L St. NW, 11th Fl., Washington, DC 20036). Scope: Standardization in the field of information technology.

Publications

ISO Annual Report.
ISOfocus (6x yearly).
Extensive selection of titles on the ISO website (https://www.iso.org/publication-list.html).

Foreign Library Associations

The following is a list of regional and national library associations around the world. A more complete list can be found in *International Literary Market Place* (Information Today, Inc.).

Regional

Africa

Standing Conference of Eastern, Central, and Southern African Lib. and Info. Assns. (SCECSAL), c/o General-Secretary, Uganda Library and Information Association, P.O. Box 5894, Kampala, Uganda. Tel. +256-772-488937, +256-782-617623, +256-782-42204, e-mail info@ulia.or.ug, World Wide Web https://www.scecsal.org.

The Americas

Assn. of Caribbean Univ., Research, and Institutional Libs. (ACURIL), P.O. Box 23317, San Juan, Puerto Rico 00931-3317. Tel. 787-612-9343, e-mail executivesecretariat@acuril.org, World Wide Web https://acuril.org. *Pres.* Jeannette Lebrón Ramos; *Exec. Secy.* Elizabeth Pierre-Louis.

Seminar on the Acquisition of Latin American Lib. Materials (SALALM), c/o SALALM Secretariat, Latin American Lib., 422 Howard Tilton Memorial Lib., Tulane Univ., 7001 Freret St., New Orleans, LA 70118-5549. Tel. 504-247-1366, fax 504-247-1367, e-mail salalm@tulane.edu, World Wide Web https://salalm.org. *Exec. Dir.* Hortensia Calvo. E-mail hcalvo@tulane.edu.

Asia

Congress of Southeast Asian Libns. (CONSAL), Razathingaha Road, Uottra Thiri TSP, Naypyitaw, Myanmar. Tel. 95 67 418427, fax 95 67 418426, e-mail info@consalxvii.org.

The Commonwealth

Commonwealth Lib. Assn. (COMLA), P.O. Box 144, Mona, Kingston 7, Jamaica. Tel. +1-876-978-2274, fax +1-876-927-1926, e-mail comla72@yahoo.com, World Wide Web https://www.commonwealthofnations.org/commonwealth-directory/organisations-by-sector/libraries. *Interim Pres.* Elizabeth Watson, University of the West Indies, Cave Hill Campus, Barbados; *Hon. Exec. Secy.* Norma Y Amenu-Kpodo (Jamaica).

U.K. Library and Archives Group on Africa (SCOLMA), c/o Sarah Rhodes, Bodleian Social Science Lib., Univ. of Oxford, Manor Rd. Bldg., Manor Rd., Oxford OX1 3UQ, England. Tel. 01865-277162, World Wide Web http://scolma.org. *Chair* Lucy McCann, Weston Library, Bodleian Libraries, Broad Street, Oxford, OX1 3BG, England; *Secy.* Sarah Rhodes.

Europe

European Bureau of Library, Information and Documentation Associations (EBLIDA), c/o EBLIDA Secretariat, Koninklijke Bibliotheek (National Library of the Netherlands), Prins Willem-Alexanderhof 5, 2595 BE, The Hague. Tel. 31 (0) 70 3140137, e-mail eblida@eblida.org, World Wide Web http://www.eblida.org. *Dir.* Giuseppe Vitiello.

Ligue des Bibliothèques Européennes de Recherche (LIBER) (Assn. of European Research Libs.), P.O. Box 90407, 2509 LK The Hague, Netherlands. Tel. 31-70-314-07-67, fax 070-314-01-97, e-mail liber@kb.nl, World Wide Web http://www.libereurope.eu. *Pres.* Jeannette Frey; *V.P.* Julien Roche; *Secy.-Gen.* Anja Smit; *Exec. Dir.* Astrid Verheusen.

National

Argentina

ABGRA (Asociación de Bibliotecarios Graduados de la República Argentina) (Assn. of Graduate Libns. of Argentina), Paraná 918, 2do Piso, C1017AAT Buenos Aires. Tel. 54-11-4811-0043, fax 54-11-4816-3422, e-mail info@abgra.org.ar, World Wide Web https://abgra.org.ar. *Pres.* Maria Silvia LaCorazza; *Secy. Gen.* Jessica Soledad Castaño.

Australia

Australian Lib. and Info. Assn., Box 6335, Kingston, ACT 2604. Tel. 61-2-6215-8222, fax 61-2-6282-2249, e-mail enquiry@alia. org.au, World Wide Web https://www.alia. org.au. *Pres.* Vicki Edmunds. E-mail ALI-ABoard@alia.org.au.

Australian Society of Archivists, P.O. Box 576, Crows Nest, NSW 1585. Tel. 61-2-6190-7983, e-mail office@archivists.org. au, World Wide Web https://www.archivists. org.au. *Pres.* Nicola Laurent; *V.P.* Hannah Hibbert; *Gen. Mgr.* James Polley.

National and State Libs. Australia (NSLA), State Lib. Victoria, 328 Swanston St., Melbourne VIC 3000. Tel. 03 8664 7512, e-mail nsla@slv.vic.gov.au, World Wide Web https://www.nsla.org.au. *Chair* Vicki McDonald; *Exec. Officer* Barbara Lemon.

Austria

Österreichische Gesellschaft für Dokumentation und Information (Austrian Society for Documentation and Info.), c/o Österreichische Computer Gesellschaft OCG, Wollzeile 1, 1010 Vienna. E-mail office@oegdi. at, World Wide Web http://oegdi.at. *Chair* Gerhard Frohlich.

Vereinigung Österreichischer Bibliothekarinnen und Bibliothekare (VOEB) (Assn. of Austrian Libns.), Universitätsbibliothek Graz, Universitätsplatz 3, 8010 Graz. E-mail voeb@ub.tuwein.ac.at, World Wide Web https://www.univie.ac.at/voeb/php. *Interim Presidents* Pamela Stückler and Eva Ramminger; *Secy.* Markus Lackner.

Bangladesh

Bangladesh Assn. of Libns., Info. Scientists and Documentalists (BALID), House # 67/B (3rd floor), Road # 9/A, Dhanmondi, Dhaka-1209, Bangladesh. E-mail balidbd@ gmail.com, info@balidbd.org, World Wide Web https://www.balid.org. *Chair* Muhammad Hossam Haider Chowdhury.

Belgium

Archief-en Bibliotheekwezen in België (Belgian Assn. of Archivists and Libns.), Royal Library of Belgium, Boulevard de l'Empereur 2, 1000 Brussels. Tel. 2-519-53-93, fax 2-519-56-10, e-mail abb@kbr.be, World Wide Web http:// www.archibib.be. *Pres.* Marc Libert; *Admin. Secy.* Anja Marginet

Assn. Belge de Documentation/Belgische Vereniging voor Documentatie (Belgian Assn. for Documentation), 4 Boulevard de l'Empereur, 1000 Bruxelles. Tel. 2-675-58-62, fax 2-672-74-46, e-mail abdbvd@ abd-bvd.be, World Wide Web https://www. abd-bvd.be/fr. *Pres.* Sara Decoster, e-mail sara.decoster.pro@gmail.com; *Secy. Gen.* Guy Delsaut, e-mail delsautg@gmail.com.

Association des Professionales des Bibliothèques Francophones de Belgique (APBFB), Rue Nanon 98, 5002 Namur. Tel. 32-492-31-09-41, e-mail info@apbfb.be, World Wide Web http://www.apbfb.be. *Pres.* Françoise Dury.

Vlaamse Vereniging voor Bibliotheek-, Archief-, en Documentatiewezen (Flemish Assn. of Libns., Archivists, and Documentalists), Statiestraat 179, B-2600 Berchem, Antwerp. Tel. 3-281-44-57, e-mail vvbad@ vvbad.be, World Wide Web https://www. vvbad.be. *Coord.* Jessica Jacobs. E-mail jessica.jacobs@vvbad.be.

Bolivia

Centro Nacional de Documentación Científica y Tecnológica (National Scientific and Technological Documentation Center), Av. Mariscal Santa Cruz 1175, Esquina c Ayacucho, La Paz. Tel. 02-359-583, fax 02-359-586, e-mail iiicndct@huayna.umsa.edu.bo, World Wide Web http://www.bolivian.com/ industrial/cndct.

Bosnia and Herzegovina

Drustvo Bibliotekara Bosne i Hercegovine (Libns. Society of Bosnia and Herzegovina), Zmaja od Bosne 8B, 71000 Sarajevo. Tel. 33-275-301, e-mail nubbih@nub.ba, World Wide Web https://www.nub.ba. *Pres.* Ismet Ovcina. E-mail ured.direktora@nub.ba.

Botswana

Botswana Lib. Assn., Box 1310, Gaborone. Tel. 267-732-31047, e-mail secretary@bla. org.bw, *Pres.* Lynn Jabril. E-mail president@bla.org.bw, World Wide Web https:// www.facebook.com/BotsLibAssociation.

Brunei Darussalam

Persatuan Perpustakaan Negara Brunei Darussalam (National Lib. Assn. of Brunei), c/o Class 64 Lib., SOASC, Jalan Tengah, Bandar Seri Begawan BS8411. Fax 2-222-330, e-mail po box.bla@gmail.com, World Wide Web http:// bruneilibraryassociation.wordpress.com.

Cameroon

Assn. des Bibliothécaires, Archivistes, Documentalistes et Muséographes du Cameroun (Assn. of Libns., Archivists, Documentalists, and Museum Curators of Cameroon), BP 12092, Yaoundé. Tel. 237-2-22-22-28-98, e-mail abadcameroun@gmail.com, World Wide Web http://www.abadcam.sitew.com. *Pres.* Alim Garga. E-mail a_garga@yahoo.fr.

Chile

Colegio de Bibliotecarios de Chile (Chilean Lib. Assn.), Avda. Diagonal Paraguay 383, Torre 11, Oficina 122, 6510017 Santiago. Tel. 2-222-5652, e-mail cbc@bibliotecarios. cl, World Wide Web http://www.bibliote carios.cl. *Pres.* María Angélica Fuentes Martínez.

China

Library Society of China, c/o National Library of China, 33 Zhongguancun Nandajie, Hai Dian District, Beijing 100081. Tel: 4006006988, (+86 10) 88545426. E-mail webmaster@nlc.cn, World Wide Web http:// www.nlc.cn/newen. *Secy. Gen.* Wang Yanhang.

Colombia

Asociación Colombiana de Bibliotecólogos y Documentalistas (Colombian Assn. of Libns. and Documentalists), Calle 21, No. 6-58, Oficina 404, Bogotá D.C. Tel. 1-282-3620, fax 1-282-5487, e-mail secretaria@ ascolbi.org, World Wide Web http://www. ascolbi.org. *Dir.* Monica Sandoval.

Croatia

Hrvatsko Knjiznicarsko Drustvo (Croatian Lib. Assn.), c/o National and Univ. Lib., Hrvatske bratske zajednice 4, 10 000 Zagreb. Tel./fax 1-615-93-20, e-mail hkd@nsk.hr, World Wide Web http://www.hkdrustvo.hr. *Pres.* Dijana Machala; *Secy.* Andreja Tominac.

Cuba

Asociación Cubana de Bibliotecarios (AS-CUBI) (Lib. Assn. of Cuba), P.O. Box 6670, Havana. Tel. 7-555-442, fax 7-816-224, e-mail ascubi@bnjm.cu, World Wide Web http://ascubi.blogspot.com. *Chair* Margarita Bellas Vilariño. E-mail ascubi@bnjm.cu.

Cyprus

Cyprus Association of Librarians - Information Scientists (KEVEP), T.Th. 21100, 1501 Nicosia, Cyprus. Tel.: 99-277-758, e-mail ke bepcy@gmail.com, World Wide Web http:// kebep.blogspot.com.

Czech Republic

Svaz Knihovniku a Informacnich Pracovniku Ceske Republiky (SKIP) (Assn. of Lib. and Info. Professionals of the Czech Republic), National Library of the Czech Republic, Mariánské náměstí 190/5, 110 00 Prague 1. Tel. 420-221-663-379, fax 420-221-663-175, e-mail skip@nkp.cz, World Wide Web https://www.skipcr.cz. *Chair Mgr.* Roman Giebisch.

Denmark

Arkivforeningen (Archives Society), Ingrid Nostberg, Vestfoldmuseene IKS, Department Vestfoldarkivet, 3205 Sandefjord. Tel. 958 21 501, e-mail post@arkivarforeningen. no, World Wide Web http://www.arkivar foreningen.no. *Chair* Ingrid Nostberg.

Danmarks Biblioteksforening (Danish Lib. Assn.), Vartov, Farvergade 27D, 1463 Copenhagen K. Tel. 3325-0935, fax 3325-7900, e-mail db@db.dk, World Wide Web http://www.db.dk. *Chair* Steen Bording Andersen. e-mail steen.a@aarhus.dk; *Dir.* Michel Steen-Hansen, e-mail msh@db.dk.

Danmarks Forskningsbiblioteksforening (Danish Research Lib. Assn.), c/o University of Southern Denmark, Studiestræde 6, 1455 Copenhagen K. Tel. 45-4220-2177, e-mail secretariat@dfdf.dk, World Wide Web http://www.dfdf.dk. *Chair* Karin Englev. e-mail kabe@kb.dk.

Dansk Musikbiblioteks Forening (Assn. of Danish Music Libs.), c/o Helene Olsen,

Sundby Library, Jemtelandsgade 2300, Copenhagen S. E-mail sekretariat@dmbf.nu, World Wide Web https://www.dmbf.nu.

Ecuador

Asociación Ecuatoriana de Bibliotecarios (Ecuadoran Lib. Assn.), c/o Casa de la Cultura Ecuatoriana, Casillas 87, Quito. E-mail asoecubiblio@gmail.com, World Wide Web http://aeb-nacional.blogspot.com.

El Salvador

Asociación de Bibliotecarios de El Salvador (ABES) (Assn. of Salvadorian Libns.), Residencial La Cima, Avenida 7, Calle 5 house # 15G, San Salvador. Tel. 503-2212-7600, e-mail abeselsalvador@gmail.com, World Wide Web https://bibliotecarios-de-el-salvador.webnode.es. *Pres.* Claudia Oviedo.

Finland

Suomen Kirjastoseura (Finnish Lib. Assn.), Runeberginkatu 15 A 6, 00100 Helsinki. Tel. 44-522-2941, e-mail info@fla.fi, World Wide Web http://www.fla.fi. *Exec. V.P.* Rauha Maarno. E-mail rauha.maarno@fla.fi.

France

Association des Archivistes Français (Assn. of French Archivists), 8 rue Jean-Marie Jego, 75013 Paris. Tel. 1-46-06-39-44, fax 1-46-06-39-52, e-mail secretariat@archivistes.org, World Wide Web http://www.archivistes.org.

Association des Bibliothécaires de France (Assn. of French Libns.), 31 rue de Chabrol, F-75010 Paris. Tel. 1-55-33-10-30, fax 1-55-30-10-31, e-mail info@abf.asso.fr, World Wide Web http://www.abf.asso.fr. *Pres.* Hélène Brochard; *Gen. Secy.* Mélanie Roson.

Association des Professionnels de l'Information et de la Documentation (Assn. of Info. and Documentation Professionals), 25 rue Claude Tillier, 75012 Paris. Tel. 06-81-39-82-14, e-mail adbs@adbs.fr, World Wide Web http://www.adbs.fr. *Secy. Gen.* Valérie Rostowski.

Germany

Arbeitsgemeinschaft der Spezialbibliotheken (Assn. of Special Libs.), c/o German-French Institute (dfi) – France Library, Asperger Str. 30, 71634 Ludwigsburg. Tel. +49-7141-930338, e-mail geschaeftsstelle@aspb.de, World Wide Web http://aspb.de. *Chair* Monika Sommerer.

Berufsverband Information Bibliothek (Assn. of Info. and Lib. Professionals), P.O. Box 13 24, 72703 Reutlingen. Tel. 7121-3491-0, fax 7121-3491-34, e-mail mail@bib-info.de, World Wide Web http://www.bib-info.de. *Chair* Ute Engelkenmeier.

Deutsche Gesellschaft für Informationswissenschaft und Informationspraxis eV (German Society for Information Science and Practice eV), Windmühlstr. 3, 60329 Frankfurt-am-Main. Tel. 69-43-03-13, fax 69-490-90-96, e-mail mail@dgi-info.de, World Wide Web http://www.dgi-info.de. *Pres.* Margarita Reibel-Felten.

Deutscher Bibliotheksverband eV (German Lib. Assn.), Fritschestr. 27–28, 10585 Berlin. Tel. 30-644-98-99-10, fax 30-644-98-99-29, e-mail dbv@bibliotheksverband.de, World Wide Web http://www.bibliotheksverband.de. *Dir.* Barbara Schleihagen.

VdA—Verband Deutscher Archivarinnen und Archivare (Assn. of German Archivists), Woerthstr. 3, 36037 Fulda. Tel. 661-29-109-72, fax 661-29-109-74, e-mail info@vda.archiv.net, World Wide Web http://www.vda.archiv.net. *Chair* Ralf Jacob; *Managing Dir.* Thilo Bauer.

Verein Deutscher Bibliothekare eV (Society of German Libns.), University and State Library, 06108 Hall, August-Bebel-Str. 13, Saxony-Anhalt. Tel. 09131-85-22150, e-mail geschaeftsstelle@vdb-online.org, World Wide Web http://www.vdb-online.org. *Chair* Konstanze Söllner. e-mail chairman@vdb-online.org.

Ghana

Ghana Lib. Assn., Box GP 4105, Accra. Tel. 244-17-4930, e-mail info@gla-net.org, World Wide Web http://gla-net.org. *Pres.* Comfort Asare.

Greece

Enosis Hellinon Bibliothekarion (Association of Greek Librarians), Akadimias 84, PC 106 78, Athens. Tel./fax 210-330-2128, e-mail info-eebep@eebep.gr, World Wide Web http://www.eebep.gr. *Pres.* Dr. Anthi Katsirikou; *Gen. Secy.* Eleni Molfesi.

Guyana

Guyana Lib. Assn., c/o Department of Public Information, Area 'B' Homestretch Ave., D'Urban Park, Georgetown. Tel. 592-226-6715, fax 592-227-4052, e-mail info@dpi. gov.gy, World Wide Web https://dpi.gov.gy/ tag/guyana-library-association.

Hong Kong

Hong Kong Lib. Assn., GPO Box 10095, Hong Kong, China. E-mail hkla@hkla.org, World Wide Web http://www.hkla.org. *Pres.* Wilson Chu. E-mail president@hkla.org. *Membership Secy.* Bernice Chan. E-mail membership@hkla.org.

Hungary

Magyar Könyvtárosok Egyesülete (Assn. of Hungarian Libns.), 1827 Budapest, Budavári Palota Building F. Tel./fax 1-311-8634, e-mail mke@oszk.hu, World Wide Web http://www.mke.info.hu. *Chair* Dr. Ágnes Hajdu; *Secy. Gen.* Judit Gerencsér.

Iceland

Upplysing—Felag bokasafns-og upplysingafraeoa (Information—The Icelandic Lib. and Info. Science Assn.), Mailbox 8865, 128 Reykjavík. Tel. 354-864-6220, e-mail upplysing@upplysing.is, World Wide Web http://www.upplysing.is. *Chair* Þórný Hlynsdóttir. E-mail chairman@upplysing.is.

India

Indian Assn. of Special Libs. and Info. Centres, P-291, CIT Scheme 6M, Kankurgachi, Kolkata 700-054. Tel. 33-2362-9651, e-mail iaslic@vsnl.net, World Wide Web http://www.iaslic1955.org.in. *President* Narendra Lahkar; *Gen. Secy.* Abhijit Kumar.

Indian Lib. Assn., A/40-41, Flat 201, Ansal Bldg., Mukerjee Nagar, New Delhi 110009. Tel./fax 11-2765-1743, e-mail dvs-srcc@re diffmail.com, World Wide Web http://www. ilaindia.net. *Pres.* B.D. Kumbar; *Gen. Secy.* O.N. Chaubey.

Indonesia

Ikatan Pustakawan Indonesia (Indonesian Lib. Assn.), Jl. Salemba Raya, RT.8/RW.8, Kramat Senen, Kota Jakarta Pusat, DKI Jakarta 10430. Tel. (021) 3900944, World Wide Web http://ipi.web.id. *Chair* T. Syamsul Bahri.

Ireland

Cumann Leabharlann na hEireann (Lib. Assn. of Ireland), c/o 138–144 Pearse St., Dublin 2. E-mail honsecretary@libraryassociation. ie, World Wide Web http://www.libraryas sociation.ie. *Pres.* Cathal McCauley. E-mail president@libraryassociation.ie; *Hon. Secy.* Niall O'Brien. E-mail honsecretary@li braryassociation.ie.

Israel

Israeli Center for Libs., 22 Baruch Hirsch St., P.O. Box 801, 51108 Bnei Brak. Tel. 03-6180151, fax 03-5798048, e-mail meida@ gmail.com or icl@icl.org.il, World Wide Web http://www.icl.org.il. *Chair* Moshe Perl.

Italy

Associazione Italiana Biblioteche (Italian Lib. Assn.), Biblioteca Nazionale Centrale, Viale Castro Pretorio 105, 00185 Rome RM. Tel. 6-446-3532, fax 6-444-1139, e-mail segre teria@aib.it, World Wide Web http://www. aib.it.

Jamaica

Lib. and Info. Assn. of Jamaica, P.O. Box 125, Kingston 5. Tel./fax 876-927-1614, e-mail liajapresident@yahoo.com, World Wide Web https://www.facebook.com/ groups/147277112846.

Japan

Info. Science and Technology Assn., 1-11-14, Shinkawa, Chuo-ku, Tokyo 104-0033. Tel. 81-3-6222-8506, fax 81-3-6222-8107, e-mail infosta@infosta.or.jp, World Wide Web http://www.infosta.or.jp.

Nihon Toshokan Kyokai (Japan Lib. Assn.), 1-11-14 Shinkawa, Chuo-ku, Tokyo 104 0033. Tel. 3-3523-0811, fax 3-3523-0841, e-mail info@jla.or.jp, World Wide Web http://www.jla.or.jp. *Chair* Mitsuhiro Oda. Senmon Toshokan Kyogikai (Japan Special Libs. Assn.), c/o Japan Lib. Assn., Bldg. F6, 1-11-14 Shinkawa Chuo-ku, Tokyo 104-0033. Tel. 3-3537-8335, fax 3-3537-8336, e-mail jsla@jsla.or.jp, World Wide Web http://www.jsla.or.jp. *Co-Chairs* Akio Mimura and Toru Ishida.

Jordan

Jordan Lib. and Info. Assn., P.O. Box 6289, Amman 11118. Tel./fax 00962-64629412, World Wide Web http://jlia.org/component/content/en. *Pres.* Dr. Naguib Al-Sharbaji.

Kenya

Kenya Assn. of Lib. and Info. Professionals (formerly Kenya Lib. Assn.), Buruburu, P.O. Box 49468-00100 Nairobi. Tel. 20-733-732-799, e-mail info@kenyalibraryassociation. or.ke, World Wide Web http://www.kenyali braryassociation.or.ke.

Korea (Republic of)

Korean Lib. Assn., 201 Banpo-daero (Banpo-dong), Seocho-gu, Seoul. Tel. 2-535-4868, fax 2-535-5616, e-mail license@kla.kr, World Wide Web http://www.kla.kr. *Pres.* Nam Young-joon.

Laos

Association des Bibliothécaires Laotiens (Lao Lib. Assn.), c/o Direction de la Bibliothèque Nationale, Ministry of Educ., BP 704, Vientiane. Tel. 21-21-2452, fax 21-21-2408, e-mail bailane@laotel.com.

Latvia

Latvian Libns. Assn., c/o Latvian National Lib., Mukusalas iela 3, Riga, LV-1423. Tel. 67806100, fax 67280851, e-mail lnb@lnb. lv, World Wide Web http://www.lnb.lv. *Dir.* Andris Vilks, e-mail andris.vilks@lnb.lv.

Lebanon

Lebanese Lib. Assn., P.O. Box 113/5367, Beirut. Tel. 1-786-456, e-mail leblibassocia tion@gmail.com, World Wide Web https://www.facebook.com/LebaneseLibrary

Association. *Pres.* Fawz Abdallah. E-mail fabdallas@gmail.com.

Lithuania

Lietuvos Bibliotekininkų Draugija (Lithuanian Libns. Assn.), Gedimino pr. 51, Vilnius, LT-01504. Tel. 370-5-231-8585, e-mail lbd.sekretore@gmail.com, World Wide Web http://www.lbd.lt. *Chair* Jolita Stephonaitiene. E-mail jolita.stephonaitiene@lnb.lt.

Luxembourg

Association Luxembourgeoise des Bibliothécaires, Archivistes, et Documentalistes (ALBAD) (Luxembourg Assn. of Libns., Archivists, and Documentalists), c/o National Lib. of Luxembourg, BP 295, L-2012 Luxembourg. Tel. 352-621-46-14-15, World Wide Web http://www.albad.lu. *Pres.* Estelle Beck. E-mail presidence@albad.lu. *Secy. Gen.* Bernard Linster. E-mail secreta rie@albad.lu.

Malaysia

Persatuan Pustakawan Malaysia (Libns. Assn. of Malaysia), P.O. Box 12545, 50782 Kuala Lumpur. Tel./fax 3-2694-7390, e-mail pustakawan55@gmail.com, World Wide Web http://ppm55.org. *Pres.* Dr. Rashidah binti Bolhassan, E-mail rashidahb@sar awak.gov.my.

Mali

Association Malienne des Bibliothécaires, Archivistes et Documentalistes (Mali Assn. of Libns., Archivists, and Documentalists) (AMBAD), BP E4473, Bamako. Tel. 20-29-94-23, fax 20-29-93-76, e-mail dnambko@afribone.net.ml.

Malta

Malta Lib. and Info. Assn. (MaLIA), c/o Univ. of Malta Lib., Msida MSD 2080. E-mail info@malia-malta.org, World Wide Web https://www.facebook.com/malia.malta.

Mauritania

Association Mauritanienne des Bibliothécaires, Archivistes, et Documentalistes (Mauritanian Assn. of Libns., Archivists, and Documentalists), c/o Bibliothèque Nationale, BP 20, Nouakchott. Tel. 525-18-62, fax 525-18-68, e-mail bibliothequenationale@yahoo.fr.

Mauritius

Mauritius Lib. Assn., Quatre Bornes, Mauritius 230. Tel. 230 5769 7392, fax 454-9553, e-mail mauritiuslibassociation@gmail.com, World Wide Web https://www.facebook.com/Mauritius-Library-Association-MLA-142991592578201.

Mexico

Asociación Mexicana de Bibliotecarios (Mexican Assn. of Libns.), Angel Urraza 817-A, Colonia Del Valle, Benito Juárez, Mexico DF, CP 03100. Tel. 55-55-75-33-96, e-mail correo@ambac.org.mx, World Wide Web http://www.ambac.org.mx. *Chair* Brenda Cabral Vargas; *V.P.* María Guadalupe Vega Díaz.

Myanmar

Myanmar Lib. Assn., Room 003, Diamond Jubilee Hall, Yangon University, Yangon, Myanmar. Tel. 95-9-420728446, e-mail libraryassociation@mlamyanmar.org, World Wide Web http://myanmarlibraryassociation.org. *Pres.* Daw Ah Win.

Namibia

Namibia Information Workers Assn., P.O. Box 308, Windhoek. Tel. 264-8148-10713, e-mail niwaassociation@gmail.com. *Contact* Ms. Namutenya Hamwaalwa, e-mail hnamutenya@gmail.com.

Nepal

Nepal Lib. Assn., KVPL, Bhrikuti Mandap, Kathmandu. Tel. 01-4221163, e-mail nepal-libraryassociation@gmail.com, World Wide Web https://nla.org.np. *Pres.* Indra Prasad Adhikari; *Gen. Secy.* Reshma Dangol.

The Netherlands

KNVI—Koninklijke Nederlandse Vereniging van Informatieprofessionals (Royal Dutch Association of Information Professionals), Ambachtsstraat 15, 3861 RH Nijkerk. Tel. 033-2473427, e-mail info@knvi.nl, World Wide Web http://knvi.nl.

New Zealand

New Zealand Lib. Assn. (LIANZA), 70 Molesworth St., Wellington 6140. Tel. 027-347-5326, e-mail officeadmin@lianza.org.nz, World Wide Web http://www.lianza.org.nz. *Pres.* Erica Rankin.

Nicaragua

Asociación Nicaraguense de Bibliotecarios y Profesionales Afines (ANIBIPA) (Nicaraguan Assn. of Libns.), Bello Horizonte, Tope Sur de la Rotonda 1/2 cuadra abajo, J-11-57, Managua. Tel. 277-4159, e-mail anibipa@hotmail.com. World Wide Web https://www.facebook.com/ANIBIPA.

Nigeria

National Lib. of Nigeria, Plot 274 Sanusi House, Central Business District, Abuja. Tel. 09-234-6773, e-mail info@nln.gov.ng, World Wide Web https://www.nln.gov.ng. *Chair* Prof. Zaynab Alkali.

Norway

Arkivar Foreningen (Assn. of Archivists), Vestfoldmuseene IKS. department Vestfoldarkivet, 3205 Sandefjord. Tel. 936 56 026, e-mail post@arkivarforeningen.no, World Wide Web http://www.arkivarforeningen.no/. *Chair* Ingrid Nøstberg.

Norsk Bibliotekforening (Norwegian Lib. Assn.), Universitetsgata 14, 0164 Oslo. Tel. 23 24 34 30, e-mail nbf@norskbiblioteksforening.no, World Wide Web https://norskbibliotekforening.no. *Dir.* Vidar Lund; *Gen. Secy.* Ann Berit Hulthin. E-mail abh@norskbibliotekforening.no.

Panama

Asociación Panameña de Bibliotecarios (Lib. Assn. of Panama), c/o Biblioteca Interamericana Simón Bolivar, Estafeta Universitaria, Panama City. E-mail biblis2@arcon.up.ac.pa, Tel. 507-6527-1904, e-mail ocastillos@hotmail.com, World Wide Web https://www.facebook.com/asociacionpanamenabibliotecarios/info.

Paraguay

Asociación de Bibliotecarios Graduados del Paraguay (Assn. of Paraguayan Graduate Libns.), Facultad Politécnica, Universidad Nacional de Asunción, 2160 San Lorenzo. Tel. 21-585-588, e-mail abigrap@pol.una.py, World Wide Web https://www.facebook.com/AGCIPy.

Peru

Asociación Peruana de Archiveros y Gestores de la Información (Peruvian Assn. of Archivists and Info. Managers), Av. Manco Capac No. 1180, Dpto 201, La Victoria, Lima. Tel. 51-934-182079, e-mail contacto@archiverosdelperu.org, World Wide Web http://archiverosdelperu.org. Pres. Ricardo Arturo Moreau Heredia.

Philippines

Assn. of Special Libs. of the Philippines, c/o Goethe-Institut Philippinen, G/4-5/F Adamson Centre, 121 Leviste St., Salcedo Village, 1227 Makati City. Tel. 2-840-5723, e-mail aslplibrarians@gmail.com, World Wide Web https://aslplibrarians.org/home. Pres. Eugene Jose T. Espinoza.

Philippine Libns. Assn., Room 301, National Lib. Bldg., T. M. Kalaw St., 1000 Ermita, Manila. Tel. 525-9401. World Wide Web http://plai.org.ph. Pres. Emma Rey.

Poland

Stowarzyszenie Bibliotekarzy Polskich (Polish Libns. Assn.), al Niepodleglosci 213, 02-086 Warsaw. Tel. 22-608-28-24, e-mail biuro@sbp.pl, World Wide Web http://www.sbp.pl. Dir. Aldona Zawałkiewicz. E-mail a.zawalkiewicz@sbp.pl; Secy. Małgorzata Dargiel-Kowalska. E-mail m.dargielkowalska@sbp.pl.

Portugal

Associação Portuguesa de Bibliotecários, Arquivistas e Documentalistas (Portuguese Assn. of Libns., Archivists, and Documentalists), Praça Dr. Nuno Pinheiro Torres 10-A, 15500 246 Lisbon. Tel. +351-218-161-980, e-mail bad@bad.pt, World Wide Web http://www.apbad.pt. Pres. Ana Paula Gordo.

Puerto Rico

Sociedad de Bibliotecarios de Puerto Rico (Society of Libns. of Puerto Rico), Apdo 22898, San Juan 00931-2898. Tel./fax 787-764-0000, World Wide Web https://sociedad bibliotecariospr.wordpress.com. Pres. Juan Ramón Soto Rosa.

Russia

Rossiiskaya Bibliotechnaya Assotsiatsiya (Russian Lib. Assn.), 18 Sadovaya St., St. Petersburg 191069. Tel./fax 812-110-5861, e-mail rba@nlr.ru, World Wide Web http://www.rba.ru. Exec. Secy. Trushina Irina Aleksandrovna.

Senegal

Association Sénégalaise des Bibliothécaires, Archivistes et Documentalistes (Senegalese Assn. of Libns., Archivists, and Documentalists), BP 2006, Dakar RP, Université Cheikh Anta Diop, Dakar. Tel. 77-651-00-33, fax 33-824-23-79, e-mail asbadsn@gmail.com.

Serbia

Jugoslovenski Bibliografski Informacijski Institut, Terazije 26, 11000 Belgrade. Tel. 11-2687-836, fax 11-2687-760.

Sierra Leone

Sierra Leone Assn. of Archivists, Libns., and Info. Scientists, 7 Percival Street, Freetown. Tel. 022-220-758.

Singapore

Lib. Assn. of Singapore, National Lib. Board, 100 Victoria St., No. 14-01, Singapore 188064. Tel. 6332-3255, fax 6332-3248, e-mail lassec@las.org.sg, World Wide Web http://www.las.org.sg. Pres. Dr. Sadie-Jane Nunis. E-mail president@las.org.sg.

Slovenia

Zveza Bibliotekarskih Društev Slovenije (Union of Assns. of Slovene Libns.), Turjaöka 1, 1000 Ljubljana. Tel. 1-2001-176, fax 1-4257-293, e-mail info@zbds-zveza.si, World Wide Web http://www.zbds-zveza.si. Pres. Damjana Vovk. E-mail damjana.vovk@nuk.uni-lj.si.

South Africa

Lib. and Info. Assn. of South Africa, P.O. Box 1598, Pretoria 0001. Tel. 27 (0) 12-328-2010, 27 (0) 12-323-4912, fax 27 (0) 12-323-1033, e-mail liasa@liasa.org.za, World Wide Web http://www.liasa.org.za. *Pres.* Naziem Hardy. E-mail naziem.hardy@capetown.gov.za.

Spain

Federación Española de Archiveros, Bibliotecarios, Arqueólogos, Museólogos y Documentalistas (ANABAD) (Spanish Federation of Assns. of Archivists, Libns., Archaeologists, Museum Curators, and Documentalists), de las Huertas, 37, 28014 Madrid. Tel. 91-575-1727, fax 91-578-1615, e-mail anabad@anabad.org, World Wide Web http://www.anabad.org. *Pres.* José María Nogales Herrera.

Sri Lanka

Sri Lanka Lib. Assn., Sri Lanka Professional Centre 275/75, Stanley Wijesundara Mawatha, Colombo 7. Tel./fax 11-258-9103, e-mail slla@slltnet.lk, World Wide Web https://www.slla.lk. *Pres.* Dr. Ananda Tissa, e-mail president@slla.lk; *Gen. Secy.* M P P Dilhani, e-mail gs@slla.lk.

Sweden

Foreningen for Archiv & Informationsforvaltening (Society of Archives and Records Management in Sweden—FAI), c/o Foreningshuset Sedab AB, Virkesvägen 26, 120 30 Stockholm. Tel. 08-121 513 21, e-mail info@fai.nu, World Wide Web https://fai.nu. *Pres.* Katarina Ekelof.

Svensk Biblioteksförening (Swedish Lib. Assn.), Oxtorgsgrand 2, 111 57 Stockholm. Tel. 08-545-132-30, fax 8-545-132-31, e-mail info@svbib.se, World Wide Web http://www.biblioteksforeningen.se. *Pres.* Johanna Hansson; *Secy. Gen.* Karin Linder.

Svensk Förening för Informationsspecialister (Swedish Assn. for Info. Specialists), c/o Föreningshuset Sedab, Virkesvägen 26, 120 30 Stockholm. E-mail info@sfis.nu, World Wide Web http://www.sfis.nu. *Chair* Elisabeth Hammam Lie.

Switzerland

Verein Schweizer Archivarinnen und Archivare (Assn. of Swiss Archivists), Schweizerisches Bundesarchiv, Büro Pontri GmbH, Solohurnstr. 13, Postfach CH-3322, Urtenen Schönbühl. Tel. 41-31-312-26-66, fax 41-31-312-26-68, e-mail info@vsa-aas.ch, World Wide Web http://www.vsa-aas.org.

Taiwan

Lib. Assn. of the Republic of China (LAROC), 20 Zhongshan South Rd., Taipei 10001. Tel. 2-2361-9132, fax 2-2370-0899, e-mail lac@msg.ncl.edu.tw, World Wide Web http://www.lac.org.tw.

Tanzania

Tanzania Lib. Assn., P.O. Box 33433, Dar es Salaam. Tel./fax 255-744-296-134, e-mail info@tla.or.tz, World Wide Web http://www.tla.or.tz.

Thailand

Thai Lib. Assn., 1346 Songkhon 5 Road (between Sri Burapha Road 8-9), Klong Chan, Bang Kapi, Bangkok 10240. Tel. 02-734-9022, fax 02-734-9021, e-mail tla2497@gmail.com, World Wide Web http://tla.or.th.

Trinidad and Tobago

Lib. Assn. of Trinidad and Tobago, P.O. Box 1275, Port of Spain. Tel. 868-687-0194, e-mail latt46@gmail.com, World Wide Web http://www.latt.org.tt. *Pres.* Beverly Ann Williams.

Turkey

Türk Kütüphaneciler Dernegi (Turkish Libns. Assn.), Necatibey Cad Elgun Sok 8/8, 06440 Kizilay, Ankara. Tel. 312-230-13-25, fax 312-232-04-53, e-mail tkd.dernek@gmail.com, World Wide Web https://kutuphaneci.org.tr. *Pres.* Ali Fuat Kartal.

Uganda

Uganda Lib. and Info. Assn., P.O. Box 25412, Kampala. Tel. 256-704-885-246, e-mail secretariat@ulia.org.ug. World Wide Web https://www.facebook.com/

Uganda-Library-and-Information-Associa tion-179998355458703.

Ukraine

Ukrainian Lib. Assn., a/c 62, Kiev, 03057. Tel. 380-44-383-14-32, e-mail info@ula.org.ua, World Wide Web https://ula.org.ua/en. *Pres.* Oksana Brui; *Exec. Dir.* Yaroslava Soshynska.

United Kingdom

Archives and Records Assn., U.K. and Ireland (formerly the Society of Archivists), Prioryfield House, 20 Canon St., Taunton TA1 1SW, England. Tel. 1823-327-077, fax 1823-271-719, e-mail societyofarchivists@ archives.org.uk, World Wide Web https:// www.archives.org.uk. *Chief Exec.* John Chambers; *Chair* Lisa Snook.

Bibliographical Society, Institute of English Studies, Senate House, Malet St., London WC1E 7HU, England. E-mail admin@bib soc.org.uk, World Wide Web http://www. bibsoc.org.uk. *Pres.* James Raven. E-mail president@bibsoc.org.uk.

Chartered Institute of Lib. and Info. Professionals (CILIP), 7 Ridgmount St., London WC1E 7AE, England. Tel. 20-7255-0500, fax 20-7255-0501, e-mail info@cilip.org. uk, World Wide Web http://www.cilip.org. uk.

School Lib. Assn., 1 Pine Court, Kembrey Park, Swindon SN2 8AD, England. Tel. 1793-530-166, fax 1793-481-182, e-mail info@sla.org.uk, World Wide Web http:// www.sla.org.uk. *Chair* Sue Bastone; *Chief Exec.* Allison Tarrant.

Scottish Lib. and Info. Council, 175 W. George St., Glasgow G2 2LB, Scotland. Tel. 141-202-2999, e-mail info@scottishlibraries. org, World Wide Web http://www. scottishlibraries.org. *Chair* Ian Ruthven.

Society of College, National, and Univ. Libs. (SCONUL) (formerly Standing Conference of National and Univ. Libs.), 94 Euston St., London NW1 2HA, England. Tel. 20-7387-0317, fax 20-7383-3197, e-mail info@sconul.ac.uk, World Wide Web http://www.sconul.ac.uk. *Exec. Dir.* Ann Rossiter.

Uruguay

Agrupación Bibliotecológica del Uruguay (Uruguayan Lib. and Archive Science Assn.) and Asociación de Bibliotecólogos del Uruguay (Uruguayan Libns. Assn.), Eduardo V. Haedo 2255, CP 11200, Montevideo. Tel. 2409-9989, e-mail abu@adinet.com.uy, World Wide Web https://www.abu.net.uy. *Pres.* Alicia Ocaso Ferreira.

Vietnam

Hôi Thu-Vien Viet Nam (Vietnam Lib. Assn.), National Lib. of Vietnam, 31 Trang Thi, Hoan Kiem, 10000 Hanoi. Tel. 43-9366596, e-mail info@nlv.org.vn, World Wide Web http://www.vla.org.vn. *Chair* Nguyen Huu Gioi.

Zambia

Lib. and Info. Assn. of Zambia, P.O. Box 50183 Ridgeway, Lusaka. Tel. 260-965-024914, e-mail liaz@zambia.co.zm, World Wide Web https://zambia.co.zm.

Zimbabwe

Zimbabwe Lib. Assn., ZimLA Midlands Branch, P.O. Box 1521, Gweru. Tel. 263-773-568-837, e-mail information@ zimla.org.zw, World Wide Web https://zim babwereads.org/zimla.

Directory of Book Trade and Related Organizations

Book Trade Associations, United States and Canada

For more extensive information on the associations listed in this section, see the annual edition of *Literary Market Place* (Information Today, Inc.).

AIGA—The Professional Assn. for Design, 222 Broadway, New York, NY 10038. Tel. 212-807-1990, fax 212-807-1799, e-mail general@aiga.org, World Wide Web https://www.aiga.org. *Exec. Dir.* Bennie F. Johnson; *Senior Dir. of Admin.* Amy Chapman.

American Book Producers Assn. (ABPA), 31 West 8th Street, #2, New York, NY 10011. Tel. 212-944-6600, e-mail office@ABPA online.org, World Wide Web https://abpa online.org. *Pres.* Richard Rothschild; *V.P./ Treas.* Nancy Hall; *Admin.* Michael Centore.

American Booksellers Assn., 333 Westchester Ave. Suite S202, White Plains, NY 10604. Tel. 800-637-0037, fax 914-417-4013, e-mail info@bookweb.org, World Wide Web https://www.bookweb.org. *Pres.* Christine Onorati, WORD Bookstores, Brooklyn, NY and Jersey City, NJ; *Co-V.P.* Kelly Estep, Carmichael's Bookstore & Carmichael's Kids, Louisville, KY; *Co-V.P.* Angela María Spring, Duende District, Albuquerque, NM and Washington, DC; *CEO* Allison Hill. E-mail allisonhill@bookweb.org.

American Literary Translators Assn. (ALTA), University of Arizona, Esquire Building #205, 1230 N. Park Ave., Tucson, AZ 85721. World Wide Web https://literarytranslators. org. *Exec. Dir.* Elisabeth Jaquette. E-mail elisabeth@literarytranslators.org.

American Printing History Assn., Box 4519, Grand Central Sta., New York, NY 10163-4519. World Wide Web https://printinghisto ry.org. *Pres.* J. Fernando Peña; *Treas.* David Goodrich; *Board Secy.* Meghan Constanti-

nou; *Exec. Secy.* Lyndsi Barnes. E-mail sec retary@printinghistory.org.

American Society for Indexing, 1628 E. Southern Ave., No. 9-223, Tempe, AZ 85282. Tel. 480-245-6750, e-mail info@asindexing.org, World Wide Web https://www.asindexing. org. *Pres.* Michele Combs. E-mail presi dent@asindexing.org; *V.P./Pres.-Elect.* Gina Guilinger. E-mail presidentelect@asindex ing.org; *Exec. Dir.* Gwen Henson. E-mail gwen@asindexing.org.

American Society of Journalists and Authors, 355 Lexington Ave., 15th Fl., New York, NY 10017-6603. Tel. 212-997-0947, fax 212-937-2315, e-mail asjaoffice@ asja.org, World Wide Web https://www. asja.org. *Pres.* Laura Laing. E-mail presi dent@asja.org; *V.P.* Emily Paulsen. E-mail vicepresident@asja.org; *Exec. Dir.* James Brannigan.

American Society of Media Photographers, Four Embarcadero Center, Suite 1400, San Francisco, CA 94111. Tel. 877-771-2767, fax 231-946-6180, e-mail asmp@vpconnec tions.com, World Wide Web https://www. asmp.org. *Chair* Michael Shay. E-mail chair@asmp.org; *V. Chair* Gabriella Marks; *CEO* James Edmund Datri. E-mail jdatri@ asmp.org.

American Translators Assn., 225 Reinekers Lane, Suite 590, Alexandria, VA 22314. Tel. 703-683-6100, fax 703-683-6122, e-mail ata@atanet.org, World Wide Web https://www.atanet.org. *Pres.* Madalena Sánchez Zampaulo; *Pres.-Elect* Veronika

Demichelis; *Secy.* Alaina M. Brandt; *Treas.* John M. Milan; *Exec. Dir.* Walter W. Bacak, Jr. E-mail walter@atanet.org.

Antiquarian Booksellers Assn. of America, 20 W. 44 St., No. 507, New York, NY 10036-6604. Tel. 212-944-8291, fax 212-944-8293, World Wide Web https://www.abaa.org. *Pres.* Sheryl Jaeger; *V.P.* Alexander Akin; *Secy.* Elizabeth Young; *Treas.* Peter Blackman; *Exec. Dir.* Susan Benne. E-mail sbenne@abaa.org.

Assn. Media and Publishing Network, P.O. Box 34340, Washington, DC 20043. Tel. 202-289-7442, World Wide Web https://www.siia.net/amp-network. *Exec. Dir.* Matthew Kinsman.

Assn. of American Publishers, 455 Massachusetts Ave. N.W., Suite 700, Washington, DC 20001. Tel. 202-347-3375, fax 202-347-3690, World Wide Web https://publishers.org. *Pres./CEO* Maria A. Pallante. E-mail ceo@publishers.org. *Chair* Michael Pietsch; *V. Chair* Julia Reidhead; *Treas.* Jeremy North.

Assn. of University Presses, 1412 Broadway, Suite 2135, New York, NY 10018. Tel. 212-989-1010, fax 212-989-0275, e-mail info@aupresses.org, World Wide Web https://aupresses.org. *Pres.* Lisa Bayer, Univ. of Georgia Press; *Pres.-Elect* Charles Watkinson, Univ. of Michigan Press; *Chief Financial Officer* Alice Ennis, Univ. of Illinois Press; *Exec. Dir.* Peter Berkery. Tel. 917-288-5594, e-mail pberkery@aupresses.org.

Assn. of Canadian Publishers, 174 Spadina Ave., Suite 306, Toronto, ON M5T 2C2. Tel. 416-487-6116, fax 416-487-8815, e-mail admin@canbook.org, World Wide Web https://publishers.ca. *Pres.* Ruth Linka, Orca Book Publishers, Victoria, BC; *V.P.* Karen Boersma, Owlkids Books, Toronto, ON; *Treas.* Brian Lam, Arsenal Pulp Press, Victoria, BC; *Exec. Dir.* Kate Edwards. Tel. 416-487-6116 ext. 2340, e-mail kate_edwards@canbook.org.

Audio Publishers Assn., 333 Hudson Street Suite 503, New York, NY 10013. Tel. 646-688-3044, e-mail info@audiopub.org, World Wide Web https://www.audiopub.org. *Pres.* Ana Maria Allessi; *V.P.* Amy Metsch; *Secy.* Natalie Fedewa; *Treas.* Lee Jarit; *Exec. Dir.* Michele Cobb. E-mail mcobb@audiopub.org.

Authors Guild, 31 E. 32 Street, 7th Floor, New York, NY 10016. Tel. 212-563-5904, e-mail staff@authorsguild.org, World Wide Web https://www.authorsguild.org. *Pres.* Douglas Preston; *V.P.s* Monique Truong and W. Ralph Eubanks; *Secy.* Rachel Vail; *Treas.* Peter Petre; *Exec. Dir.* Mary Rasenberger.

Book Industry Study Group, 232 Madison Ave., Suite 1400, New York, NY 10016. Tel. 646-336-7141, e-mail info@bisg.org, World Wide Web https://bisg.org. *Chair* Kathleen Reid, Elsevier; *V.Chair* Joshua Tallent, Firebrand Technologies; *Secy.* Kelvin Watson, Las Vegas-Clark County Library District; *Treas.* Joe Matthews, Independent Publishers Group; *Exec. Dir.* Brian O'Leary. Tel. 646-336-7141, e-mail brian@bisg.org.

Book Manufacturers' Institute (BMI), 7282 55th Avenue East, #147, Bradenton, FL 34203. Tel. 386-986-4552, fax 386-986-4553, World Wide Web https://www.bmibook.com. *Pres.* David McCree, Lakeside Book Company; *V.P.* Mark Levin, HP, Inc.; *Treas.* Suzanne Wiersma, Wallaceburg Bookbinding; *Exec. Dir./Secy.* Matthew J. Baehr.

Bookbuilders of Boston, 115 Webster Woods Lane, North Andover, MA 01845. Tel. 781-378-1361, fax 419-821-2171, e-mail office@bbboston.org, World Wide Web https://www.bbboston.org. *Pres.* James Taylor. E-mail james.taylor@bbboston.org; *1st V.P.* Margaret Rosewitz. E-mail margaret.rosewitz@bbboston.org; *2nd V.P.* Michele DeVenuto. E-mail michelle.devenuto@bbboston.org; *Treasurer* Isabel Tran. E-mail isabel.tran@bbboston.org; *Clerk* Laura Rodriguez. E-mail laura.rodriguez@bbboston.org.

Bookbuilders West. See Publishing Professionals Network.

Canadian International Standard Numbers (ISNs) Agency, c/o Lib. and Archives Canada, 395 Wellington St., Ottawa, ON K1A 0N4. Tel. 866-578-7777 (toll-free) or 613-996-5115, World Wide Web https://www.bac-lac.gc.ca/eng/services/isbn-canada/Pages/isbn-canada.aspx.

Canadian Printing Industries Assn., 4000 Blvd Industriel, Laval, QC H7L 4R9. World Wide Web https://cpia-aci.ca. *Pres.* Richard Kouwenhoven, Tel. 604-438-2456, e-mail richard@hemlock.com; *Assoc. Mgr.* Gerry

Lacombe, e-mail admin@cpia-aci.ca; *Dir.* Tracey Preston, Tel. 905-602-4441, e-mail tpreston.opia@on.aibn.com.

Children's Book Council, 54 W. 39 St., 14th Fl., New York, NY 10018. Tel. 917-890-7416, e-mail cbc.info@cbcbooks.org, World Wide Web https://www.cbcbooks.org. *Chair* Yolanda Scott; *Vice Chair* Shimul Tolia; *Treas.* Terry Borzumato-Greenberg; *Secy.* Karen Walsh; *Exec. Dir.* Carl Lennertz.

Community of Literary Magazines and Presses, 154 Christopher St., Suite 3C, New York, NY 10014. Tel. 212-741-9110, e-mail info@clmp.org, World Wide Web https://www.clmp.org. *Chair* Nicole Dewey; *Exec. Dir.* Mary Gannon. E-mail mgannon@clmp.org.

Copyright Society of the USA, 1 E. 53 St., 8th Fl., New York, NY 10022. Tel. 212-354-6401, World Wide Web https://www.csusa.org. *Pres.* Naomi Jane Gray; *V.P./Pres.-Elect* Casey Chisick; *Secy.* Chad Rutkowski; Treas. Theodore Cheng; *Exec. Dir.* Kaitland E. Kubat.

Educational Book and Media Assn., P.O. Box 3363, Warrenton, VA 20188. Tel. 540-318-7770, e-mail info@edupaperback.org, World Wide Web https://www.edupaperback.org. *Pres.* Lisa Maisonneuve; *V.P.* Ben Conn; *Treas.* Bryan Thompson; *Secy.* Marin Foster; *Exec. Dir.* Brain Gorg.

Evangelical Christian Publishers Assn., 9633 S. 48 St., Suite 140, Phoenix, AZ 85044. Tel. 480-966-3998, fax 480-966-1944, e-mail info@ecpa.org, World Wide Web https://www.ecpa.org. *Pres./CEO* Stan Jantz; *Chair* Jeff Crosby; *V. Chair* Dan Kok; *Secy.* Barb Sherrill; *Treas.* Dan Baker.

Graphic Artists Guild, 31 West 34th St., 8th Fl., New York, NY 10001. Tel. 212-791-3400, e-mail admin@graphicartistsguild.org, World Wide Web https://www.graphicartistsguild.org. *Pres.* Liz DiFiore. E-mail president@graphicartistsguild.org; *Treas.* Yanique DaCosta; *Admin. Dir.* Paula Hinkle. E-mail membership@graphicartistsguild.org.

Great Lakes Independent Booksellers Assn., 3123 Andrea Court, Woodridge, IL 60517. Tel. 630-841-8129, e-mail larry@gliba.org, World Wide Web https://www.gliba.org. *Pres.* Lynn Mooney, Women & Children First, 5233 N. Clark St., Chicago, IL 60640. Tel. 773-769-9299. *Exec. Dir.* Larry Law.

Guild of Book Workers, 521 Fifth Ave., New York, NY 10175. Tel. 212-292-4444, e-mail communications@guildofbookworkers.org, World Wide Web https://guildofbookworkers.org. *Pres.* Bexx Caswell. E-mail president@guildofbookworkers.org; *V. Pres.* Henry Hebert. E-mail vicepresident@guildofbookworkers.org; *Secy.* Lindsey Jackson. E-mail secretary@guildofbookworkers.org; *Treas.* Lawrence Houston. E-mail treasurer@guildofbookworkers.org.

Horror Writers Assn., P.O. Box 56687, Sherman Oaks, CA 91413. E-mail hwa@horror.org, World Wide Web https://horror.org. *Pres.* John Palisano. E-mail president@horror.org; *V.P.* Meghan Arcuri. E-mail vp@horror.org; *Secy.* Becky Spratford. E-mail secretary@horror.org; *Treas.* Leslie Klinger. E-mail treasurer@horror.org; *Admin.* Brad Hodson. E-mail admin@horror.org.

Independent Book Publishers Assn., 1020 Manhattan Beach Blvd., Suite 204, Manhattan Beach, CA 90266. Tel. 310-546-1818, fax 310-546-3939, e-mail info@ibpa-online.org, World Wide Web https://www.ibpa-online.org. *Chair* Karla Olson, Patagonia Books; *Treas.* Peter Trimarco, Notable Kids Publishing; *Secy.* Maggie Langrick, Wonderwell; *CEO* Angela Bole. E-mail angela@ibpa-online.org.

International Standard Book Numbering U.S. Agency, 531 Route 22 East, PMB 344, Whitehouse Station, NJ 08889. Tel. 877-310-7333, e-mail isbn-san@bowker.com, World Wide Web http://www.isbn.org. *Dir., Identifier Svcs.* Beat Barblan.

Jewish Book Council, 520 Eighth Ave., 4th Fl., New York, NY 10018. Tel. 212-201-2920, fax 212-532-4952, e-mail info@jewishbooks.org, World Wide Web https://www.jewishbookcouncil.org. *Pres.* Jane Weitzman; *V.P.s* Joy Greenberg, Carol Levin, Lenore J. Weitzman; *Secy.* Elisa Spungen Bildner; *Treasurer* Alan Kadish; *Exec. Dir.* Naomi Firestone-Teeter.

Midwest Independent Publishers Assn. (MIPA), P.O. Box 580475, Minneapolis, MN 55458-0475. Tel. 651-917-0021, World Wide Web https://mipa.org. *Pres.* Nayt Rundquist, New Rivers Press, Tel. 218-477-5870, e-mail president@mipa.org; *V.P.* Paul Nylander, Illustrada Design. Tel. 612-325-1228, e-mail vicepresident@mipa.

org; *Secy.* Ron Peterson, PTB Books, e-mail secretary@mipa.org; *Treas.* Joshua Weber, Calumet Editions, e-mail treasurer@mipa. org; *Exec. Dir.* Jennifer Baum, e-mail boo kawards@mipa.org.

Miniature Book Society. Tel. 619-226-4441, e-mail member@mbs.org, World Wide Web https://www.mbs.org. *Pres.* Tony Firman; *V.P.* Ron Wood; *Secy.* Cynthia Cosgrove; *Treas.* Kim Herrick.

Minnesota Book Publishers' Roundtable. E-mail information@publishersround table.org, World Wide Web https://pub lishersroundtable.org. *Pres.* Ashley Kuehl, Ashley Kuehl Editorial, e-mail president@ publishersroundtable.org; *V.P.* Allison Juda, Bearport Publishing, e-mail vice.presi dent@publishersroundtable.org; *Secy.* Ar nold Ringstad, Red Line Editorial, e-mail a.ringstad@redlineeditorial.com; *Treas.* Paul Nylander, illustrada design, e-mail treasurer@publishersroundtable.org.

Mountains and Plains Independent Booksell ers Assn., PO Box 746, Denver, CO 80201. Tel. 800-752-0249, e-mail info@moun tainsplains.org, World Wide Web https:// www.mountainsplains.org. *Pres.* Stephanie Schindhelm; *Vice Pres.* Cristina Rodriguez; *Secy.* Allison Senecal; *Treas.* Brian Contine; *Exec. Dir.* Heather Duncan. E-mail heath er@mountainsplains.org.

MPA—The Assn. of Magazine Media, 1211 Connecticut Avenue NW, #610, Washing ton, DC 20036. Tel. 202-296-7277, e-mail mpa@magazine.org, World Wide Web https://www.magazine.org. *Chair* Bonnie Kintzer; *Vice Chair* Debi Chirichella; *Treas.* Andrew W. Clurman; *Pres. & CEO* Brigitte Schmidt Gwyn, e-mail bsgwyn@magazine. org.

National Assn. of College Stores, 500 E. Lo rain St., Oberlin, OH 44074-1294. Tel. 800-622-7498, 440-775-7777, fax 440-775- 4769, e-mail info@nacs.org, World Wide Web https://www.nacs.org. *Pres. and Treas.* Steve Westenbroek; *Pres.-Elect* Andy Dunn; *CEO* Eric Schlechenmayer. E-mail eschli chenmayer@nacs.org.

National Book Foundation, 90 Broad St., Suite 604, New York, NY 10004. Tel. 212-685- 0261, fax 212-213-6570, e-mail national book@nationalbook.org, World Wide Web https://www.nationalbook.org. *Chair* David Steinberger, Arcadia Publishing; *V. Chair* Fiona McCrea, Graywolf Publishing; *Secy.* Calvin Sims, CNN; *Treas.* Elpidio Villar real; *Exec. Director* Ruth Dickey. E-mail rdickey@nationalbook.org.

National Coalition Against Censorship (NCAC), 19 Fulton St., Suite 407, New York, NY 10038. Tel. 212-807-6222, fax 212-807- 6245, e-mail ncac@ncac.org, World Wide Web https://ncac.org. *Dirs.* Jon Anderson, Michael Bamberger, Chris Finan, Eric M. Freedman, Robie Harris, Michael Jacobs, Randall Kennedy, Emily Knox, Gina Maria Leonetti, Chris Peterson, Larry Siems, Oren J. Teicher, Emily Whitfield; *Exec. Dir.* Chris Finan. E-mail chris@ncac.org.

New Atlantic Independent Booksellers Assn. (NAIBA), 2667 Hyacinth St., Westbury, NY 11590. Tel. 516-333-0681, fax 516-333- 0689, e-mail naibabooksellers@gmail.com, World Wide Web https://www.naiba.com. *Pres.* Hannah Oliver Depp, Loyalty Book stores; *V.P.* Erin Matthews, The Last Word; *Secy.* Amanda Zirn Hudson, Bethany Beach Books; *Treas.* Michael Triebwasser, Politics & Prose; *Exec. Dir.* Eileen Dengler. E-mail eileen@naiba.com.

New England Independent Booksellers Assn. (NEIBA), One Beacon Street, 15th Floor, Boston, MA 02108. Tel. 617-547-3642, fax 617-830-8768, e-mail beth@neba.org, World Wide Web https://newenglandbooks. org. *Pres.* Beth Wagner, Phoenix Books, Es sex Junction, VT; *V.P.* Emily Russo, Print: A Bookstore, Portland, ME; *Treas.* Emily Crow, An Unlikely Story, Plainville, MA; *Exec. Dir.* Beth Ineson. E-mail beth@neba. org.

Northern California Independent Booksellers Assn., 148 Redding Road, Campbell, CA 95008. Tel. 415-561-7686, e-mail info@ nciba.com, World Wide Web https://calibal liance.org/default.aspx. *Pres.* Melinda Pow ers; *Treas.* Bridget Schinnerer; *Secy.* Carolyn Hutton; *Co-Exec. Dirs.* Ann Seaton, e-mail ann@caliballiance.org, and Kristin Rasmus sen, e-mail kristin@caliballiance.org.

PEN American Center, Div. of International PEN, 588 Broadway, Suite 303, New York, NY 10012. Tel. 212-334-1660, fax 212-334- 2181, e-mail pen@pen.org, World Wide Web https://pen.org. *Pres.* Ayad Akhtar; *Exec. V.P.* Markus Dohle; *V.P.s* Masha

Gessen and Tracy Higgins; *Treas.* Yvonne Marsh; *CEO* Susanne Nossel. E-mail snossel@pen.org.

Publishing Professionals Network (formerly Bookbuilders West), c/o Postal Annex, 274 Redwood Shores Parkway, Box 129, Redwood City, CA 94065-1173. E-mail operations@pubpronetwork.org, World Wide Web https://pubpronetwork.org. *Pres.* Dave Peattie. E-mail dave@bookmatters.com; *V.P.* David Zielonka. E-mail zielonka@stanford.edu; *Secy.* Mimi Heft. E-mail mimi.heft.design@gmail.com; *Treas.* Kelly Lee. E-mail klee@bkpub.com.

Romance Writers of America, 5315-B Cypress Creek Parkway, #111, Houston, TX 77069. Tel. 832-717-5200, e-mail info@rwa.org, World Wide Web https://www.rwa.org. *Pres.* Clair Brett. E-mail president@rwa.org; *Secy.* Siera London. E-mail secretary@rwa.org; *Treasurer* Brooke Wills. E-mail treasurer@rwa.org; *Exec. Dir.* Leslie Scantlebury. E-mail leslie.scantlebury@rwa.org.

Science Fiction and Fantasy Writers of America, P.O. Box 215, San Lorenzo, CA 94580. World Wide Web https://www.sfwa.org. *Pres.* Jeffe Kennedy. E-mail president@sfwa.org; *V.P.* Tobias S. Buckell. E-mail tobias.buckell@sfwa.org; *Secy.* Adam Rakunas. E-mail secretary@sfwa.org; *CFO* Nathan Lowell. E-mail cfo@sfwa.org. *Exec. Dir.* Kate Baker, E-mail office@sfwa.org

SIBA (formerly Southern Independent Booksellers Alliance), 51 Pleasant Ridge, Asheville, NC 28805. Tel. 803-994-9530, e-mail siba@sibaweb.com, World Wide Web https://sibaweb.com. *Exec. Dir.* Linda-Marie Barrett, E-mail lindamarie@sibaweb.com.

Society of Children's Book Writers and Illustrators (SCBWI), 4727 Wilshire Blvd., Suite 301, Los Angeles, CA 90010. Tel. 323-782-1010, e-mail scbwi@scbwi.org, World Wide Web https://www.scbwi.org. *Exec. Dir.* Sarah Baker, E-mail sarahbaker@scbwi.org.

Society of Illustrators (SI), 128 E. 63 St., New York, NY 10065. Tel. 212-838-2560, fax 212-838-2561, e-mail info@societyillustrators.org, World Wide Web https://societyillustrators.org. *Pres.* Tim O'Brien; *Exec. Secy.* Leslie Cober; *Treas.* David Reuss; *Exec. Dir.* Anelle Miller. E-mail anelle@societyillustrators.org.

Southern Independent Booksellers Alliance. See SIBA.

Western Writers of America, c/o Candy Moulton, 271 CR 219, Encampment, WY 82325 Tel. 307-329-8942, e-mail wwa.moulton@gmail.com, World Wide Web https://westernwriters.org. *Pres.* Chris Enss; *V.P.* Phil Mills, Jr.; *Exec. Dir., Secy./Treas.* Candy Moulton.

Women's National Book Assn., P.O. Box 237, FDR Sta., New York, NY 10150. Tel. 866-610-WNBA (9622), e-mail info@wnba-books.org, World Wide Web https://wnba-books.org. *Pres.* Natalie Obando-Desai; e-mail nationalpresidentWNBA@gmail.com; *Co-V.P.s* Andrea Panzeca and NC Weil; *Secy.* Prithi Rajan; *Treasurer* Karen Holly.

International and Foreign Book Trade Associations

For Canadian book trade associations, see the preceding section, "Book Trade Associations, United States and Canada." For a more extensive list of book trade organizations outside the United States and Canada, with more detailed information, consult *International Literary Market Place* (Information Today, Inc.), which also provides extensive lists of major bookstores and publishers in each country.

International

African Publishers' Network, c/o Ghana Book Publishers Assn., Bureau of Ghana Languages Building, Kawukudi Culture, P.O. Box Lt 471, Laterbiokorshie, Accra, Ghana. Tel. 233-302-912764, 233-209-115191, e-mail info.africanpublishers@gmail.com, World Wide Web https://african-publishers. net. *Acting Exec. Dir.* Ernest Oppong.

Afro-Asian Book Council, 4259/3, Ansari Road, Darya Ganj, New Delhi 110 002, India. Tel. 91-11-45355555, fax 91-11-23275542, e-mail aabookcouncil@gmail.com, World Wide Web http://www.aabookcouncil.org. *Secretary-General* Ramesh Mittal. E-mail rkmittal@dkagencies.com; *Dir.* Pranav Gupta. E-mail pgprintsindia@gmail.com.

Centro Regional para el Fomento del Libro en América Latina y el Caribe (CERLALC) (Regional Center for Book Promotion in Latin America and the Caribbean), Calle 70, No. 9-52, Bogotá, Colombia. Tel. 571-518-70-70, e-mail cerlalc@cerlalc.com, World Wide Web https://cerlalc.org. *Dir.* Andrés Ossa.

Federation of European Publishers, Chaussee d'Ixelles 29/35, Box 4, 1050 Brussels, Belgium. Tel. 32-2-770-11-10, fax 32-2-771-20-71, e-mail info@fep-fee.eu, World Wide Web https://fep-fee.eu. *Pres.* Peter Kraus vom Cleff; *Dir.* Anne Bergman-Tahon.

International Board on Books for Young People (IBBY), Nonnenweg 12, Postfach CH-4009, Basel, Switzerland. Tel. 41-61-272-29-17, fax 41-61-272-27-57, e-mail ibby@ibby.org, World Wide Web https://www.ibby.org. *Pres.* Mingzhou Zhang; *Exec. Dir.* Elizabeth Page.

International League of Antiquarian Booksellers (ILAB), c/o Rue Toepffer 5, Case postale 499, 1211 Geneva 12, Switzerland. E-mail secretariat@ilab.org, World Wide Web https://ilab.org. *Pres.* Sally Burdon; *Exec. Secy.* Angelika Elstner.

International Publishers Assn. (Union Internationale des Editeurs), 23 ave. de France, CH-1202 Geneva, Switzerland. Tel. 41-22-704-1820, fax 41-22-704-1821, e-mail info@internationalpublishers.org, World Wide Web https://www.internationalpublishers.org. *Pres.* Bodour Al Qasimi; *Secy.-Gen.* José Borghino.

STM: The International Assn. of Scientific, Technical, and Medical Publishers, Prins Willem-Alexanderhof 5, 2595 BE The Hague, The Netherlands. Tel. 31-70-314-09-30, fax 31-70-314-09-40, e-mail info@stm-assoc.org, World Wide Web http://www.stm-assoc.org. *CEO* Caroline Sutton.

National

Argentina

Cámara Argentina del Libro (Argentine Book Assn.), Av. Belgrano 1580, 4 piso, C1093AAQ Buenos Aires. Tel. 54-11-4381-8383, fax 54-11-4381-9253, e-mail cal@editores.org.ar, World Wide Web http://www.editores.org.ar. *Pres.* Martín Gremmelspacher.

Fundación El Libro (Book Foundation), Yrigoyen 1628, 5 piso, C1089AAF Buenos Aires. Tel. 54-11-4370-0600, fax 54-11-4370-0607, e-mail fundacion@el-libro.com.ar, World Wide Web https://www.el-libro.org.ar. *Pres.* Gabriel Waldhuter; *Admin. Dir.* José Gutiérrez Brianza.

Australia

Australian and New Zealand Assn. of Antiquarian Booksellers (ANZAAB), 40 Charlotte St. (Ground Floor), Brisbane, Q 4000. E-mail admin@anzaab.com, World Wide Web http://www.anzaab.com. *Pres.* Douglas Stewart.

Australian Booksellers Assn., 828 High St., Unit 9, Kew East, Vic. 3102. Tel. 3-9859-7322, fax 3-9859-7344, e-mail mail@aba.org.au, World Wide Web https://www.book sellers.org.au. *CEO* Robbie Egan.

Australian Publishers Assn., 60/89 Jones St., Ultimo, NSW 2007. Tel. 2-9281-9788, e-mail apa@publishers.asn.au, World Wide Web https://www.publishers.asn.au. *Pres.* James Kellow.

Austria

Hauptverband des Österreichischen Buchhandels (Austrian Publishers and Booksellers Assn.), Grünangergasse 4, A-1010 Vienna. Tel. 43-1-512-15-35, fax 43-1-512-84-82, e-mail office@hvb.at, World Wide Web https://www.buecher.at. *Pres.* Benedikt Föger.

Verband der Antiquare Österreichs (Austrian Antiquarian Booksellers Assn.), Grünangergasse 4, A-1010 Vienna. Tel. 1-512-1535-14, e-mail sekretariat@hvb.at, World Wide Web https://www.buecher.at/antiquar.

Belgium

Boek.be (formerly Vlaamse Boekverkopersbond, Flemish Booksellers Assn.), Te Buelaerlei 37, 2140 Borgerhout. Tel. 03-230-89-23, fax 3-281-22-40, World Wide Web http://www.boek.bc/over-buckbe.

Brazil

Câmara Brasileira do Livro (Brazilian Book Assn.), Rua Cristiano Viana 91, Pinheiros-São Paulo-SP, CEP: 05411-000. Tel./fax 11-3069-1300, e-mail cbl@cbl.org.br, World Wide Web http://www.cbl.org.br. *Pres.* Vitor Tavares.

Sindicato Nacional dos Editores de Livros (Brazilian Publishers Assn.), Rue da Ajuda 35 / 18th Fl., 20040-000 Rio de Janeiro-RJ. Tel. 21-99472-6066, 21-2533-0399, fax 21-2533-0422, e-mail snel@snel.org.br, World Wide Web http://www.snel.org.br. *Pres.* Dante Jose Alexandre Cid.

Chile

Câmara Chilena del Libro AG (Chilean Assn. of Publishers, Distributors, and Booksellers), Av. Libertador Bernardo O'Higgins 1370, Oficina 501, Santiago. Tel. 2-672-0348, fax 2-687-4271, e-mail prolibro@tie.cl, World Wide Web https://camaradellibro.cl. *Pres.* Eduardo Castillo.

Colombia

Câmara Colombiana del Libro (Colombian Book Assn.), Calle 35, No. 5A 05, Bogotá. Tel. 57-1-323-01-11, fax 57-1-285-10-82, e-mail camlibro@camlibro.com.co, World Wide Web http://www.camlibro.com.co. *Exec. Pres.* Emiro Aristizábal; *Secy.-Gen.* Manuel José Sarmiento Ramírez.

Czech Republic

Svaz ceských knihkupcu a nakladatelu (Czech Publishers and Booksellers Assn.), Fugnerovo nameisti 1808/3, Prague 2, 120 00. Tel. 420-227-660-644, e-mail sckn@sckn.cz, World Wide Web https://www.sckn.cz. *Dir.* Marcela Turečková. E-mail tureckova@sckn.cz.

Denmark

Danske Boghandlerforening (Danish Booksellers Assn.), Slotsholmsgade 1 B, 1216 Copenhagen K. Tel. 45-32-54-2255, fax 45-32-54-0041, e-mail info@boghandlerne.dk, World Wide Web https://boghandlerforenin gen.dk. *Chair* Lone Haagerup; *Vice Chair* Trine Thougaard

Danske Forlæggerforening (Danish Publishers Assn.), Stock Exchange, Slotsholmsgade 1, 1217 Copenhagen K. Tel. 45-33-15-66-88, e-mail info@danskeforlag.dk, World Wide Web https://www.danskeforlag.dk. *Chair* Morten Hesseldahl; *Dir.* Christine Bødtcher-Hansen.

Ecuador

Câmara Ecuatoriana del Libro, N29-61 Eloy Alfaro and England, 9th Floor, Quito. Tel. 593-2-2553311, fax 593-2-2553314, e-mail info@celibro.org.ec, World Wide Web https://www.celibro.org.ec/pagina. *Pres.* Oswaldo Almeida Mora.

Egypt

General Egyptian Book Organization (GEBO), 1194 Corniche El Nil, Ramlet Boulaq, Book

Authority Building, Cairo 1194. Tel. 2-577-5367, e-mail info@gebo.gov.eg, World Wide Web http://www.gebo.gov.eg.

Estonia

Estonian Publishers Assn., Roosikrantsi 6-207, 10119 Tallinn. Telephone 372-644-9866, fax 372-617-7550, e-mail kirjastusteliit@eki.ee, World Wide Web http://www.est book.com. *Managing Dir.* Kaidi Urmet. E-mail kirjastusteliit@eki.ee.

Finland

Kirjakauppaliitto Ry (Booksellers Association of Finland), Eteläranta 10, 00130 Helsinki. Tel. 040-689-9112, e-mail toimisto@kir jakauppaliitto.fi, World Wide Web https://kirjakauppaliitto.fi. *Managing Director* Laura Karlsson. E-mail laura.karlsson@kir jakauppaliitto.fi.

Suomen Kirjasaatio (Finnish Book Foundation). Eteläranta 10, FI-00130 Helsinki. Tel. 358 9 228 77 255, World Wide Web https://kustantajat.fi. *Chair* Timo Julkunen; *Mgr.* Sakari Laiho.

France

Bureau International de l'Edition Française (BIEF) (International Bureau of French Publishing), 115 blvd. Saint-Germain, F-75006 Paris. Tel. 01-44-41-13-13, fax 01-46-34-63-83, e-mail info@bief.org, World Wide Web http://www.bief.org. *Pres.* Antoine Gallimard. *New York Branch* French Publishers Agency, 30 Vandam Street, Suite 5A, New York, NY 10013. Tel./fax 212-254-4540, World Wide Web https://www.french rights.com.

Cercle de la Librairie (Circle of Professionals of the Book Trade), 35 rue Grégoire-de-Tours, F-75006 Paris. Tel. 01-44-41-28-00, fax 01-44-41-28-65, e-mail support@elec tre.com, World Wide Web https://accueil.electre.com.

Syndicat de la Librairie Française, Hotel Massa, 38 rue du Faubourg Saint-Jacques, F-75014 Paris. Tel. 01-53-62-23-10, fax 01-53-62-10-45, e-mail contact@syndicat -librairie.fr, World Wide Web https://www.syndicat-librairie.fr/accueil. *Admin. Secy.* Gaëlle Sacase. E-mail g.sacase@syndicat -librairie.fr.

Syndicat National de la Librairie Ancienne et Moderne (SLAM) (National Assn. of Antiquarian and Modern Booksellers), 4 rue Gît-le-Coeur, F-75006 Paris. Tel. 01-43-29-46-38, fax 01-43-25-41-63, World Wide Web https://slamlivrerare.org. *Pres.* Jean-Marc Dechaud; *Secy.-Gen.* Charles-Henri de Boissieu.

Syndicat National de l'Edition (SNE) (National Union of Publishers), 115 blvd. Saint-Germain, F-75006 Paris. Tel. 01-44-41-40-50, fax 01-44-41-40-77, World Wide Web https://www.sne.fr. *Pres.* Vincent Montagne.

Germany

Börsenverein des Deutschen Buchhandels e.V. (Stock Exchange of German Booksellers), Braubachstr. 16, 60311 Frankfurt-am-Main. Tel. 49-69-1306-0, fax 49-69-1306-201, e-mail info@boev.de, World Wide Web https://www.boersenverein.de. *Chair* Karin Schmidt-Friderichs.

Verband Deutscher Antiquare e.V. (German Antiquarian Booksellers Assn.), Geschäftsstelle, Seeblick 1, 56459 Elbingen. Tel. 49-0-6435-90-91-47, fax 49-0-6435-90-91-48, e-mail buch@antiquare.de, World Wide Web https://www.antiquare.de/aktuelles. *Chair* Sibylle Wieduwilt. E-mail s.wieduwilt@antiquare.de.

Hungary

Magyar Könyvkiadók és Könyvterjesztök Egyesülése (Assn. of Hungarian Publishers and Booksellers), Kertész u. 41. I / 4, 1073 Budapest. Tel. 06-1-343-2538, e-mail mkke@mkke.hu, World Wide Web http://www.mkke.hu. *Pres.* Katalin Gál.

Iceland

Félag Islenskra Bókaútgefenda (Icelandic Publishers Assn.), Brautarholti 8, 105 Reykjavik. Tel. 517-7200, e-mail fibut@fibut.is, World Wide Web http://www.fibut.is. *Chair* Heidar Ingi Svannsson; *Man. Dir.* Benedikt Kristjánsson.

India

Federation of Indian Publishers, Federation House, 18/1C Institutional Area, Aruna Asaf Ali Marg, New Delhi 110067. Tel. 11-2696-

4847, fax 11-2686-4054, e-mail fippresi
dent@gmail.com, World Wide Web https://
www.fiponline.org. *Exec. Dir.* Shri. Ramesh
K. Mittal.

Indonesia

Ikapi (Indonesian Publisher Association), Ikapi
Building, Jalan Kalipasir, No. 32, Cikini,
Central Jakarta, 10340. Tel. 62 21 314 1907,
e-mail sekretariat@ikapi.org, World Wide
Web https://www.ikapi.org/. *Chair* Arys
Hilman Nugraha; *Secy.* Novi Arsianti.

Ireland

Publishing Ireland/Foilsiu Eireann (formerly
CLÉ: The Irish Book Publishers' Assn.), 63
Patrick St., Dun Laoghaire, Co Dublin. Tel.
353-1-639-4868, e-mail info@publishin
gireland.com, World Wide Web https://
www.publishingireland.com. *Pres.* Ruth
Hallinan; *Gen. Mgr.* Orla McLoughlin.

Israel

Israeli Association of Book Publishers, 29 Car-
lebach St., 67132 Tel Aviv. Tel. 3-561-4121,
fax 3-561-1996, e-mail info@tbpai.co.il,
World Wide Web https://www.tbpai.co.il.
Chair Benjamin Trivaks.

Italy

Associazione Italiana Editori (Italian Publishers Assn.), Corso di Porta Romana 108,
20122 Milan. Tel. 2-89-28-0800, fax 2-89-
28-0860, e-mail info@aie.it, World Wide
Web https://www.aie.it. *Pres.* Ricardo Fran-
co Levy.
Associazione Librai Antiquari d'Italia (Antiquarian Booksellers Assn. of Italy), Via
Luigi Cadorna 22, 22100 Como. Tel. 39-
349-0748229; e-mail alai@alai.it, World
Wide Web https://www.alai.it. *Pres.* Gabri-
ele Maspero.

Japan

Antiquarian Booksellers Assn. of Japan, Koku-
sai Hamamatsucho Bldg., 9th Floor, 1-9-
18 Kaigan, Minato-ku, Tokyo, 105-0022.
Tel. 81-3-6367-6070, fax 81-3-6367-6196,
e-mail abaj@abaj.gr.jp, World Wide Web
http://www.abaj.gr.jp. *Chair* Shoichi Takagi.

Japan Assn. of International Publications,
1-1-13-4F Kanda, Jimbocho, Chiyodak-
ku, Tokyo 101-0051. Tel. 3-5479-7269, fax
3-5479-7307, e-mail office@jaip.jp, World
Wide Web http://www.jaip.jp/jp/index.html.
Exec. Dir. Mark Gresham.
Japan Book Publishers Assn., 5th Fl., Shup-
pan-Club Building 1-32, Kanda-Jimbocho,
Chiyoda-ku, Tokyo, 101-0051. Tel. 81-0-3-
6273-7065, fax 81-0-3-6811-0959, e-mail
research@jbpa.or.jp, World Wide Web
http://www.jbpa.or.jp. *Pres.* Masaru On-
odera.

Kenya

Kenya Publishers Assn., P.O. Box 42767,
Nairobi 00100. Tel. 254-724-255848, e-
mail info@kenyapublishers.org, World
Wide Web https://www.facebook.com/
kenyapublishersassociation. *Chair* Lawrence Njagi.

Korea (Republic of)

Korean Publishers Assn., Publishing Culture
Center, 6 Samcheong-ro (Sagan-dong),
Jongno-gu, Seoul. Tel. 2-733-8402, fax
2-738-5414, e-mail webmaster@kpa21.
or.kr, World Wide Web http://kpa21.
or.kr/?ckattempt=1. *Chair* Yoon Cheol-ho.

Latvia

Latvian Publishers' Assn., Baznicas iela 37-3,
LV-1010 Riga. Tel./fax 67-217-730, e-mail
lga@gramatizdeveji.lv, World Wide Web
https://www.gramatizdeveji.lv. *Pres.* Renāte
Punka; *Exec. Dir.* Marika Celma.

Lithuania

Lithuanian Publishers Assn., Vokiečių st. 18A,
LT 01130, Vilnius. Tel. 370-675-75692, fax
370-670-32287, e-mail info@lla.lt, World
Wide Web https://lla.lt/lt. *Pres.* Lolita
Varanavičienė; *Exec. Dir.* Rūta Elijošaitytė-
Kaikarė.

Malaysia

Malaysian Book Publishers' Assn., No. 7-6,
Block E2, Jl PJU 1/42A, Dataran Prima,
47301 Petaling Jaya, Selangor. Tel. 3-7880-
5840, fax 3-7880-5841, e-mail info@

mabopa.com.my, World Wide Web http://www.mabopa.com.my. *Pres.* Arief Hakim Sani Rahmat.

Mexico

Cámara Nacional de la Industria Editorial Mexicana (Mexican Publishers' Assn.), Holanda No. 13, Col. San Diego Churubusco, Deleg. Coyoacán, 04120 Mexico DF. Tel. 155-56-88-20-11, fax 155-56-04-31-47, e-mail contacto@caniem.com, World Wide Web https://caniem.online. *Pres.* Juan Luis Arzoz Arbide. E-mail presidencia@caniem.com.

The Netherlands

KVB—Koninklijke Vereeniging van het Boekenvak (Royal Society for the Book Trade), P.O. Box 12040, AA Amsterdam-Zuidoost. Tel. 020-430-9115, e-mail info@kvb.nl, World Wide Web https://kvb.nl. *Dirs.* M.K.J. David and A. Schroën.

Nederlands Uitgeversverbond (Royal Dutch Publishers Assn.), Postbus 12040, 1100 AA Amsterdam. Tel. 20-430-9150, fax 20-430-9199, e-mail info@mediafederatie.nl, World Wide Web https://mediafederatie.nl. *Chair* Derk Haank; *Dir.* Peter Stadhouders. E-mail pstadhouders@mediafederatie.nl.

Nederlandsche Vereeniging van Antiquaren (Netherlands Assn. of Antiquarian Booksellers), P.O. Box 503, 4200 AM Gorinchem. Tel. 31-0-114-3142-09, fax 31-0-114-e-mail rashi@xs4all.nl, World Wide Web https://nvva.nl. *Gen. Secy.* Ingrid Oey.

Nederlandse Boekverkopersbond (Dutch Booksellers Assn.), Hamburgerstraat 28a, 512 NS, Utrecht. Tel. 088-600-9500, e-mail info@boekbond.nl, World Wide Web https://www.boekbond.nl. *Chair* Jan Peter Prenger.

New Zealand

Booksellers New Zealand, Ground Floor, Red Shield House, 79 Boulcott St., Wellington 6011. Tel. 4-472-1908, fax 4-472-1912, e-mail info@booksellers.co.nz, World Wide Web https://www.booksellers.co.nz. *Chair* Juliet Blyth. E-mail juliet.blyth@booksellers.co.nz. *CEO* Dan Slevin. E-mail dan.slevin@booksellers.co.nz.

Nigeria

Nigerian Publishers Assn., 1st Floor Premium House, Opp. Evans Brothers (Nig. Publishers) Ltd., Jericho, GPO Box 2541, Dugbe, Ibadan, Oyo States. Tel. 234-816-248-9037, e-mail nigerianpublishers@ymail.com, World Wide Web https://www.facebook.com/nigerianpublishers. *Pres.* Adedapo Gbadega.

Norway

Norske Bokhandlerforening (Norwegian Booksellers Association), Sehesteds gate 6, 0164 Oslo. Tel. 47-22-39-68-00, e-mail firmapost@bokhandlerforeningen.no, World Wide Web https://bokhandlerforeningen.no. Chair Hans Antonsen; *Dir.* Anne Schiøtz. E-mail direktor@bokhandlerforeningen.no.

Norske Forleggerforening (Norwegian Publishers Assn.), Sehesteds gate 6, 0164 Oslo. Tel. 22-00-75-80, fax 22-33-38-30, e-mail dnf@forleggerforeningen.no, World Wide Web https://forleggerforeningen.no. *Chair* Edmund Austigard; *Admin. Dir.* Heidi Austlid.

Peru

Cámara Peruana del Libro (Peruvian Publishers Assn.), Av. Cuba 427, Jesús María, Apdo. 10253, Lima 11. Tel. (511) 265-0735, fax (511) 265-0735, e-mail cp-libro@cpl.org.pe, World Wide Web http://www.cpl.org.pe. *Pres.* José Wilfredo Del Pozo Alarcón.

Philippines

Philippine Educational Publishers Assn., Phoenix Building, 927 Quezon Ave., Quezon City. Tel. (632) 376-4041 local 334, fax (632) 376-4031, e-mail pepasecretariat@gmail.com, World Wide Web http://www.pepa.org.ph. *Pres.* Jose Paolo M. Sibal.

Poland

Władze Stowarzyszenie Księgarzy Polskich (Assn. of Polish Booksellers), ul. Złota 65/25, 00-819 Warsaw. Tel./fax 0-22-827-93-81, e-mail skp@ksiegarze.org.pl, World Wide Web http://ksiegarze.org.pl. *Chair* Zofia Szpojankowska; *Gen. Secy.* Katarzyna Balicka-Więckowska.

Portugal

Associação Portuguesa de Editores e Livreiros (Portuguese Assn. of Publishers and Booksellers), Av. dos Estados Unidas da America 97, 6 Esq., 1700-167 Lisbon. Tel. 21-843-51-80, e-mail geral@apel.pt, World Wide Web http://www.apel.pt. *Exec. Dir.* Pedro Sobral; *Gen. Secy.* Bruno Pires Pacheco.

Russia

Assn. of Book Publishers of Russia, 101000, Lubyanka, Luchnikov per., D.4, p. 1, Moscow. Tel. 7-926-900-85-27, e-mail askibook@gmail.com, World Wide Web http://www.aski.ru. *Pres.* Chechenev Konstantin Vasilievich.

Rossiiskaya Knizhnaya Palata (Russian Book Chamber), Zvezdny boulevard 17, building 1, 129085, Moscow. Tel. 495-688-96-89, fax 495-688-99-91, e-mail info@bookchamber.ru, World Wide Web http://www.bookchamber.ru.

Singapore

Singapore Book Publishers Assn., 9 Jurong Town Hall Road, 02-02 Trade Association Hub, Jurong Town Hall, Singapore 609431. Tel. 65-6957-7093, e-mail info@singaporebookpublishers.sg, World Wide Web https://www.singaporebookpublishers.sg. *President* Max Phua. E-mail schoppert@nus.edu.sg. *Exec. Dir.* Cecilia Woo.

Slovenia

Zdruzenie Zaloznikov in Knjigotrzcev Slovenije Gospodarska Zbornica Slovenije (Assn. of Publishers and Booksellers of Slovenia), Dimičeva 13, SI-1504 Ljubljana. Tel. 386-1-5898-000, fax 386-1-5898-100, e-mail info@gzs.si, World Wide Web https://www.gzs.si/zbornica_knjiznih_zaloznikov_in_knjigotrzcev. *Pres.* Tibor Šimonka; *Gen. Mgr.* Aleš Cantarutti.

South Africa

Publishers Assn. of South Africa (PASA), House Vincent, Wynberg Mews, 10 Brodie Rd., Wynberg, Cape Town 7800. Tel. 21-762-9083, fax 21-762-2763, e-mail pasa@publishsa.co.za, World Wide Web http://www.publishsa.co.za. *Chair* Brian Wafawarowa; *Exec. Dir.* Mpuka Radinku.

South African Booksellers Assn. (formerly Associated Booksellers of Southern Africa), Regus Business Centre, 2 Fir Street, Observatory, 7925, Cape Town. Tel. 27 21 003 8098, e-mail saba@sabooksellers.com, World Wide Web https://www.sabooksellers.com. *Pres.* Melvin Kaabwe. E-mail melvin.kaabwe@vanschaik.com.

Spain

Federación de Gremios de Editores de España (Federation of Spanish Publishers Assns.), Calle de Cea Bermúdez 44, 28003 Madrid. Tel. 91-534-51-95, fax 91-535-26-25, e-mail fgee@fge.es, World Wide Web http://www.federacioneditores.org. *Acting Pres.* D. Daniel Fernandez; *Secy.* Antonio María Ávila.

Sweden

Svenska Förläggareföreningen (Swedish Publishers Assn.), c/o Svenska Publisher AB, Kungstensgatan 38, 2 tr, 113 59 Stockholm. Tel. 8-736-19-40, e-mail info@forlaggare.se, World Wide Web https://forlaggare.se. *Chair* Jesper Monthán.

Switzerland

Swiss Booksellers and Publishers Association (SBVV), Limmatstrasse 111, Postfach 8031, Zürich. Tel. 44-421-36-00, fax 44-421-36-18, e-mail info@sbvv.ch, World Wide Web https://www.sbvv.ch. *Pres.* Thomas Kramer. E-mail t.kramer@scheidegger-spiess.ch; *Gen. Mgr.* Tanja Messerli. E-mail tanja.messerli@sbvv.ch.

Thailand

Publishers and Booksellers Assn. of Thailand, 83/159 Soi Ngam Wong Wan 47 (Chinnaket 2), Thung Song Hong, Lak Si, Bangkok 10210. Tel. 2-954-9560-4, fax 02-954-9565-6, e-mail info@pubat.or.th, World Wide Web https://pubat.or.th.

Uganda

Uganda Publishers Assn., P.O. Box 7732, Kampala. Tel. 256-752-707327. World Wide

Web https://www.facebook.com/Uganda-Publishers.

United Kingdom

Antiquarian Booksellers Assn., 21 John Street, London WC1N 2BF, England. Tel. 44-0-20-8004-9512, e-mail admin@aba.org.uk, World Wide Web https://aba.org.uk. *Pres.* Pom Harrington.

Assn. of Learned and Professional Society Publishers, Egale 1, 80 St Albans Road, Watford, Hertfordshire WD17 1DL England. Tel. 44 (0)1245 260571, e-mail ad min@alpsp.org, World Wide Web https://www.alpsp.org. *Chair* Niamh O'Connor; *Chief Exec.* Wayne Sime.

Booktrust, G8 Battersea Studios, 80 Silverthorne Rd., Battersea, London SW8 3HE, England. Tel. 020 7801 8800, e-mail que ry@booktrust.org.uk, World Wide Web http://www.booktrust.org.uk. *Pres.* Michael Morpurgo; *Chief Exec.* Diana Gerald.

Publishers Assn., 50 Southwark Street, London SE1 1UN, England. Tel. 44 0 20 7378 0504, e-mail mail@publishers.org.uk, World Wide Web http://www.publishers.org.uk. *Pres.* Stephen Lotinga.

Scottish Book Trust, Sandeman House, Trunk's Close, 55 High St., Edinburgh EH1 1SR, Scotland. Tel. 131-524-0160, e-mail info@scottishbooktrust.com, World Wide Web https://www.scottishbooktrust.com.

Welsh Books Council (Cyngor Llyfrau Cymru), Castell Brychan, Aberystwyth, Ceredigion SY23 2JB, Wales. Tel. 1970-624-151, fax 1970-625-385, e-mail info@wbc.org.uk, World Wide Web https://llyfrau.cymru/en. *Hon. Counsel* Gwydion Hughes.

Uruguay

Cámara Uruguaya del Libro (Uruguayan Publishers Assn.), Colón 1476, Apdo. 102, 11000 Montevideo. Tel. 2-916-93-74, fax 2-916-76-28, e-mail gerencia@camaradel libro.com.uy, World Wide Web https://www.camaradellibro.com.uy. *Chair* Alicia Guglielmo.

Venezuela

Cámara Venezolana del Libro (Venezuelan Publishers Assn.), Av. Andrés Bello, Centro Andrés Bello, Torre Oeste 11, piso 11, of. 112-0, Caracas 1050. Tel. 212-793-1347, fax 212-793-1368, e-mail cavelibro@gmail.com, World Wide Web https://www.facebook.com/CamaradelLibro.

Zimbabwe

Zimbabwe Book Publishers Assn., P.O. Box 3041, Harare. Tel. 263-77-706-4272, e-mail danielle.zbpa@gmail.com. World Wide Web https://www.facebook.com/zimbabwebookpublishers.

National Information Standards Organization (NISO)

NISO, the National Information Standards Organization, a nonprofit association accredited by the American National Standards Institute (ANSI), identifies, develops, maintains, and publishes technical standards to manage information in today's continually changing digital environment. NISO standards apply to both traditional and new technologies and to information across its whole lifecycle, from creation through documentation, use, repurposing, storage, metadata, and preservation. The following listing includes NISO standards of interest to readers of *Library and Book Trade Almanac*.

Content and Collection Management

ANSI/NISO Z39.2-1994 (R2016)	Information Interchange Format ISBN 978-1-937522-70-4
ANSI/NISO Z39.4-2021	Criteria for Indexes ISBN 978-1-950980-14-7
ANSI/NISO Z39.14-1997 (R2015)	Guidelines for Abstracts ISBN 978-1-937522-44-5
ANSI/NISO Z39.18-2005 (R2010)	Scientific and Technical Reports— Preparation, Presentation, and Preservation ISBN 978-1-937522-21-6
ANSI/NISO Z39.19-2005 (R2010)	Guidelines for the Construction, Format, and Management of Monolingual Controlled Vocabularies ISBN 978-1-937522-22-3
ANSI/NISO Z39.23-1997 (S2015)	Standard Technical Report Number Format and Creation ISBN 978-1-937522-45-2
ANSI/NISO Z39.29-2005 (R2010)	Bibliographic References ISBN 978-1-937522-26-1
ANSI/NISO Z39.32-1996 (R2012)	Information on Microfiche Headers ISBN 978-1-937522-29-2
ANSI/NISO Z39.41-1997 (S2015)	Placement Guidelines for Information on Spines ISBN 978-1-937522-46-9

ANSI/NISO Z39.43-1993 (R2017) Standard Address Number (SAN) for the
Publishing Industry
ISBN 978-1-937522-75-9

ANSI/NISO Z39.48-1992 (R2009) Permanence of Paper for Publications and
Documents in Libraries and Archives
ISBN 978-1-937522-30-8

ANSI/NISO Z39.71-2006 (R2011) Holdings Statements for Bibliographic
Items
ISBN 978-1-937522-31-5

ANSI/NISO Z39.73-1994 (R2012) Single-Tier Steel Bracket Library Shelving
ISBN 978-1-937522-32-2

ANSI/NISO Z39.74-1996 (R2012) Guides to Accompany Microform Sets
ISBN 978-1-937522-40-7

ANSI/NISO Z39.78-2000 (R2018) Library Binding
ISBN 978-1-937522-86-5

ANSI/NISO Z39.84-2005 (R2010) Syntax for the Digital Object Identifier
ISBN 978-1-937522-34-6

ANSI/NISO Z39.85-2012 The Dublin Core Metadata Element Set
ISBN 978-1-937522-14-8

ANSI/NISO Z39.86-2005 (R2012) Specifications for the Digital Talking Book
ISBN 978-1-937522-35-3

ANSI/NISO Z39.96-2021 JATS: Journal Article Tag Suite, version 1.3
ISBN 978-1-950980-13-0

ANSI/NISO Z39.98-2012 Authoring and Interchange Framework for
Adaptive XML Publishing Specification
ISBN 978-1-937522-07-0

ANSI/NISO Z39.102-2017 STS: Standards Tag Suite
ISBN 978-1-937522-78-0

ANSI/NISO Z39.104-2022 CRediT, Contributor Roles Taxonomy
ISBN 978-1-950980-18-5

ANSI/NISO/ISO 12083-1995 Electronic Manuscript Preparation and
(R2009) Markup
ISBN 978-1-880124-20-8

Standards for Discovery to Delivery

ANSI/NISO Z39.19-2005 (R2010) Guidelines for the Construction, Format,
and Management of Monolingual
Controlled Vocabularies
ISBN 978-1-937522-22-3

ANSI/NISO Z39.50-2003 (S2014) Information Retrieval (Z39.50) Application
Service Definition and Protocol
Specification
ISBN 978-1-937522-42-1

ANSI/NISO Z39.83-1-2012	NISO Circulation Interchange Part 1: Protocol (NCIP), version 2.02 ISBN 978-1-937522-03-2
ANSI/NISO Z39.83-2-2012	NISO Circulation Interchange Protocol (NCIP) Part 2: Implementation Profile 1, version 2.02 ISBN 978-1-937522-04-9
ANSI/NISO Z39.85-2012	The Dublin Core Metadata Element Set ISBN 978-1-937522-14-8
ANSI/NISO Z39.87-2006 (R2017)	Data Dictionary—Technical Metadata for Digital Still Images ISBN 978-1-937522-76-6
ANSI/NISO Z39.88-2004 (R2010)	The OpenURL Framework for Context-Sensitive Services ISBN 978-1-937522-38-4
ANSI/NISO Z39.89-2003 (S2014)	The U.S. National Z39.50 Profile for Library Applications ISBN 978-1-937522-43-8
ANSI/NISO Z39.99-2017	ResourceSync Framework Specification ISBN 978-1-937522-73-5

Business Information

| ANSI/NISO Z39.7-2013 | Information Services and Use: Metrics and Statistics for Libraries and Information Providers—Data Dictionary ISBN 978-1-937522-15-5 |
| ANSI/NISO Z39.93-2014 | The Standardized Usage Statistics Harvesting Initiative (SUSHI) Protocol ISBN 978-1-937522-47-6 |

Preservation and Storage

ANSI/NISO Z39.32-1996 (R2012)	Information on Microfiche Headers ISBN 978-1-937522-29-2
ANSI/NISO Z39.48-1992 (R2009)	Permanence of Paper for Publications and Documents in Libraries and Archives ISBN 978-1-937522-30-8
ANSI/NISO Z39.73-1994 (R2012)	Single-Tier Steel Bracket Library Shelving ISBN 978-1-937522-32-2
ANSI/NISO Z39.78-2000 (R2018)	Library Binding ISBN 978-1-937522-86-5

In Development/NISO Initiatives

NISO develops new standards, reports, and best practices on a continuing basis to support its ongoing standards development program. NISO working groups are currently developing or exploring the following:

- Collection Description Specification (NISO Z39.91-200x)
- Criteria for Indexes (NISO Z39.4-201x)
- Digital Bookmarking and Annotation (NISO Z39.97-201x)
- Information Retrieval Service—Description Specification (NISO Z39.92-200x)
- Information Services and Use Metrics & Statistics for Libraries and Information Providers—Data Dictionary (NISO Z39.7-201x)
- Permanence of Paper for Publications and Documents in Libraries and Archives (ANSI/NISO Z39.48-201x)
- Scientific and Technical Reports—Preparation, Presentation, and Preservation (ANSI/NISO Z39.18-2005 [R201x])
- Standard Interchange Protocol (SIP) (NISO Z39.100-201x)
- Standards-Specific Ontology (SSOS) (NISO Z39.103-201x)

NISO Recommended Practices

A Framework of Guidance for Building Good Digital Collections, 3rd ed., 2007
ISBN 978-1-880124-74-1

NISO RP-2005-01	Ranking of Authentication and Access Methods Available to the Metasearch Environment ISBN 978-1-880124-89-5
NISO RP-2005-02	Search and Retrieval Results Set Metadata ISBN 978-1-880124-88-8
NISO RP-2005-03	Search and Retrieval Citation Level Data Elements ISBN 978-1-880124-87-1
NISO RP-2006-01	Best Practices for Designing Web Services in the Library Context ISBN 978-1-880124-86-4
NISO RP-2006-02	NISO Metasearch XML Gateway Implementers Guide ISBN 978-1-880124-85-7
NISO RP-6-2012	RFID in U.S. Libraries ISBN 978-1-937522-02-5
NISO RP-7-2012	SERU: A Shared Electronic Resource Understanding ISBN 978-1-937522-08-7
NISO RP-8-2008	Journal Article Versions (JAV) ISBN 978-1-880124-79-6
NISO RP-9-2014	KBART: Knowledge Bases and Related Tools ISBN 978-1-937522-41-4

NISO RP-10-2010   Cost of Resource Exchange (CORE) Protocol
                   ISBN 978-1-880124-84-0
NISO RP-11-2011   ESPReSSO: Establishing Suggested Practices Regarding
                   Single Sign-On
                   ISBN 978-1-880124-98-7
NISO RP-12-2012   Physical Delivery of Library Resources
                   ISBN 978-1-937522-01-8
NISO RP-14-2014   NISO SUSHI Protocol: COUNTER-SUSHI
                   Implementation Profile
                   ISBN 978-1-937522-45-2
NISO RP-15-2013   Recommended Practices for Online Supplemental Journal
                   Article Materials
                   ISBN 978-1-937522-12-4
NISO RP-16-2013   PIE-J: The Presentation and Identification of E-Journals
                   ISBN 978-1-937522-05-6
NISO RP-17-2013   Institutional Identification: Identifying Organizations in the
                   Information Supply Chain
                   ISBN 978-1-937522-11-7
NISO RP-19-2020   Open Discovery Initiative: Promoting Transparency in
                   Discovery
                   ISBN 978-1-950980-08-6
NISO RP-20-2014   Demand Driven Acquisition of Monographs
                   ISBN 978-1-937522-44-5
NISO RP-21-2013   Improving OpenURLs Through Analytics (IOTA):
                   Recommendations for Link Resolver Providers
                   ISBN 978-1-937522-18-6
NISO RP-22-2015   Access License and Indicators
                   ISBN 978-1-937522-49-0
NISO RP-22-2021   Access & License Indicators (2021 Revision)
                   ISBN 978-1-950980-17-8
NISO RP-23-2015   Protocol for Exchanging Serial Content (PESC)
                   ISBN 978-1-937522-66-7
NISO RP-24-2019   Transfer Code of Practice, version 4.0
                   ISBN 978-1-937522-90-2
NISO RP-25-2016   Outputs of the NISO Alternative Assessment Project
                   ISBN 978-1-937522-71-1
NISO RP-26-2019   KBART Automation: Automated Retrieval of Customer
                   Electronic Holdings
                   ISBN 978-1-937522-91-9
NISO RP-27-2019   Resource Access in the 21st Century
                   ISBN 978-1-937522-99-5
NISO RP-29-2022   E-Book Bibliographic Metadata Requirements in the Sale,
                   Publication, Discovery, Delivery, and Preservation Supply
                   Chain
                   ISBN 978-1-950980-01-7

NISO RP-30-2020	Manuscript Exchange Common Approach (MECA) ISBN 978-1-950980-02-4
NISO RP-31-2021	Reproducibility Badging and Definitions ISBN 978-1-950980-03-1
NISO RP-32-2019	JATS4R Subject & Keyword Guidelines ISBN 978-1-950980-04-8
NISO RP-33-2020	NISO JATS4R Ethics Statements ISBN 978-1-950980-05-5
NISO RP-35-2020	JATS4R Preprint Citations ISBN 978-1-950980-07-9
NISO RP-36-2020	JATS4R Data Citations ISBN 978-1-950980-09-3
NISO RP-37-2021	JATS4R Funding, Version 1.3 ISBN 978-1-950980-15-4
NISO RP-38-2021	Content Platform Migrations ISBN 978-1-950980-11-6
NISO RP-39-2021	JATS4R Peer Review Materials ISBN: 978-1-950980-12-3
NISO RP-40-2021	JATS4R Software Citations, Version 1.0 ISBN 978-1-950980-16-1

NISO Technical Reports

NISO TR-01-1995	Environmental Guidelines for the Storage of Paper Records by William K. Wilson ISBN 978-1-800124-21-5
NISO TR-02-1997	Guidelines for Indexes and Related Information Retrieval Devices by James D. Anderson ISBN 978-1-880124-36-X
NISO TR-03-1999	Guidelines for Alphabetical Arrangement of Letters and Sorting of Numerals and Other Symbols by Hans H. Wellisch ISBN 978-1-880124-41-6
NISO TR-04-2006	Networked Reference Services: Question/Answer Transaction Protocol ISBN 978-1-880124-71-0
NISO TR-05-2013	IOTA Working Group Summary of Activities and Outcomes ISBN 978-1-937522-17-9
NISO TR-06-2017	Issues in Vocabulary Management ISBN 978-1-937522-79-7

Other NISO Publications

The Case for New Economic Models to Support Standardization
by Clifford Lynch
ISBN 978-1-880124-90-1

The Exchange of Serials Subscription Information
by Ed Jones
ISBN 978-1-880124-91-8

The Future of Library Resource Discovery
by Marshall Breeding
ISBN 978-1-937522-41-4

Information Standards Quarterly (ISQ) [NISO quarterly open access magazine]
ISSN 1041-0031

Internet, Interoperability and Standards—Filling the Gaps
by Janifer Gatenby
ISBN 978-1-880124-92-5

Issues in Crosswalking Content Metadata Standards
by Margaret St. Pierre and William P. LaPlant
ISBN 978-1-880124-93-2

Making Good on the Promise of ERM: A Standards and Best Practices Discussion Paper
by the ERM Data Standards and Best Practices Review Steering Committee
ISBN 978-1-9357522-00-1

Metadata Demystified: A Guide for Publishers
by Amy Brand, Frank Daly, and Barbara Meyers
ISBN 978-1-880124-59-8

The Myth of Free Standards: Giving Away the Farm
by Andrew N. Bank
ISBN 978-1-880124-94-9

NISO Newsline [free monthly e-newsletter]
ISSN 1559-2774

NISO Working Group Connection (free quarterly supplement to *Newsline*)
Patents and Open Standards
by Priscilla Caplan
ISBN 978-1-880124-95-6

The RFP Writer's Guide to Standards for Library Systems
by Cynthia Hodgson
ISBN 978-1-880124-57-4

Streamlining Book Metadata Workflow
by Judy Luther
ISBN 978-1-880124-82-6

Understanding Metadata: What Is Metadata, and What Is It For?: A Primer
by Jenn Riley
ISBN 978-1-937522-72-8

*Up and Running: Implementing Z39.50: Proceedings of a Symposium
   Sponsored by the State Library of Iowa*
   edited by Sara L. Randall
   ISBN 978-1-880124-33-8

Z39.50: A Primer on the Protocol
   ISBN 978-1-880124-35-2

Z39.50 Implementation Experiences
   ISBN 978-1-880124-51-2

NISO standards are available at http://www.niso.org/publications/standards.

Recommended Practices, technical reports, white papers, and other publications are available on the NISO website at http://www.niso.org/publications.

For more information, contact NISO, 3600 Clipper Mill Rd., Suite 302, Baltimore, MD 21211. Tel. 301-654-2512, e-mail nisohq@niso.org, World Wide Web http://www.niso.org.

Calendar, 2022–2028

This listing contains information on association meetings and promotional events that are, for the most part, national or international in scope. U.S. state and regional library association meetings are also included.

Due to changing guidelines regarding public gatherings, many conferences scheduled for 2022 and into 2023 have been canceled, rescheduled, or moved to a virtual or hybrid format. The calendar indicates where meetings are scheduled to be held as virtual only. Events with cities listed are expected to include an in-person component; hybrid meetings that offer both an in-person gathering and a virtual component are indicated by (H) next to the meeting location.

A web URL is included for each event. For meetings scheduled in 2022 and early 2023, the URL will often deliver a dedicated event webpage; for meetings further in the future, the URL may point to event basics, including date, venue, and contact information. To confirm the status of a particular conference as well as its start and end dates, please refer to the sponsoring organization's website or contact the association directly.

For information on additional book trade and promotional events, see *Literary Market Place* and *International Literary Market Place*, published by Information Today, Inc., and other library and book trade publications such as *Library Journal*, *School Library Journal*, and *Publishers Weekly*. The American Library Association (ALA) keeps an online calendar at http://www.ala.org/conferencesevents/planning-calendar. An Information Today, Inc. events calendar can be found at http://www.infotoday.com/calendar.shtml.

2022

June

7–9	Assn. of Canadian Publishers Annual Meeting https://publishers.ca/save-the-date-acp-2022-mid-winter-meeting	Calgary, AB (H)
13–15	Assn. of Christian Librarians http://www.acl.org/index.cfm/conference	Wichita, KS (H)
18–20	Assn. of American University Presses https://aupresses.org/programs-events/annual-meeting aupresses-2022	Washington, DC
23–28	American Library Assn. Annual Conference https://2022.alaannual.org	Washington, DC (H)
26–July 1	IEEE International Symposium on Information Theory https://www.isit2022.org	Espoo, Finland (H)

27–29	Assn. of Jewish Libraries https://jewishlibraries.org/2022-conference	Philadelphia, PA

July

6–8	Assn. of European Research Libraries https://liberconference.eu	Odense, Denmark
11–15	International Assn. of School Librarianship https://www.iasl2022.com	Columbia, SC (H)
14–15	Computing Conference https://saiconference.com/Computing	Virtual
16–19	American Assn. of Law Libraries (AALL) https://www.aallnet.org/conference	Denver, CO
20–26	Hong Kong Book Fair https://hkbookfair.hktdc.com/en/ About-Book-Fair/Fair-Details.html	Hong Kong
21–24	Comic-Con International https://comic-con.org/cci	San Diego, CA
26–29	International Federation of Library Assns. (IFLA) General Conf. and Assembly https://2022.ifla.org	Dublin, Ireland
31–Aug. 2	Special Libraries Assn. https://www.sla.org/attend/sla-2022-annual- conference-source-forward	Charlotte, NC

August

13–19	Edinburgh International Book Festival https://www.edbookfest.co.uk	Edinburgh, U.K. (H)
20–27	Society of American Archivists https://www2.archivists.org/am2022	Boston, MA (H)
24–27	Beijing International Book Fair https://www.bibf.net/en	Beijing, China

September

8–10	Colorado Library Assn. https://cal-webs.wixsite.com/ calcon2022	Westminster, CO
22–25	Gothenburg Book Fair https://goteborg-bookfair.com	Gothenburg, Sweden
28–30	Ohio Library Council http://conventionexpo.olc.org	Toledo, OH

| 28–30 | South Dakota Library Assn.
 https://www.sdlibraryassociation.org/page/
 Conference2022 | Brookings, SD |

October

5–7	Nebraska Library Assn. https://nebraskalibraries.org meetinginfo.php?id=11&ts=1552601863	Kearney, NE
12–14	Iowa Library Assn. https://www.iowalibraryassociation.org/index. php/conference	Coralville, IA
14–16	Arkansas Library Assn. https://www.arlib.org/conference	Fort Smith, AR
16–19	Pennsylvania Library Assn. https://www.palibraries.org/page/ 2022ConferencePrelim	Harrisburg, PA
17–22	International Conference on Information and Knowledge Management (CIKM) https://www.cikm2022.org	Atlanta, GA (H)
18–20	Illinois Library Assn. https://www.ila.org/events/future-ila-annual- conferences	Rosemont, IL
18–20	Internet Librarian https://internet-librarian.infotoday.com/ 2022/default.aspx	Monterey, CA
19–21	Virginia Library Assn. https://www.vla.org/vla-annual-conference	Norfolk, VA
19–23	Frankfurt Book Fair https://www.buchmesse.de/en	Frankfurt, Germany
23–25	New England Library Assn. . https://nela2022.godaddysites.com	Manchester, NH
25–27	International Conference of Indigenous Archives, Libraries, and Museums https://www.atalm.org/node/533	Temecula, CA
26–28	Arizona Library Assn. https://www.azla.org/event/2022-azla- annual-conference	Prescott, AZ
26–28	New Mexico Library Assn. https://nmla.wildapricot.org/Conferences	Albuquerque, NM
27–30	Helsinki Book Fair https://kirjamessut.messukeskus.com/?lang=en	Helsinki, Finland

27–30	Krakow International Book Fair https://www.ksiazka.krakow.pl/gb	Krakow, Poland
29–Nov. 1	Assn. for Information Science and Technology (ASIS&T) https://www.asist.org/am22	Pittsburgh, PA

November

2–5	New York Library Assn. https://www.nyla.org/4DCGI/cms/ review.html?Action= CMS_Document&DocID=281&Menu Key=conf_info	Saratoga Springs, NY
7–10	KM World https://www.kmworld.com/Conference/2022	Washington, DC
23–27	Buch Wein International Book Fair https://www.buchwien.at	Vienna, Austria
26–Dec. 4	Guadalajara International Book Fair https://www.fil.com.mx	Guadalajara, Mexico

December

9–14	International Conference on Information Systems (ICIS) https://icis2022.aisconferences.org	Copenhagen, Denmark

2023

January

3–6	Hawaii International Conference on System Sciences https://hicss.hawaii.edu/#!future- conferences/ctld	Maui, HI
27–31	American Library Assn. LibLearnX: The Library Learning Experience (LLX) https://alaliblearnx.org	New Orleans, LA

March

28–30	Computers in Libraries https://computersinlibraries.infotoday.com/ 2022/PastEvents.aspx	Arlington, VA

April

19–22   Texas Library Assn.   Austin, TX
              https://txla.org/annual-conference/general-
              information/future-dates

June

16–18   Assn. of American University Presses   Virtual
              https://aupresses.org/programs-events/.
              annual-meeting/save-the-dates

22–27   American Library Assn. Annual Conference   Chicago, IL
              http://www.ala.org/conferencesevents/node/7

July

15–18   American Assn. of Law Libraries   Boston, MA
              https://www.aallnet.org/conference/about/
              future-meetings

October

1–4   Pennsylvania Library Assn.   Pocono Manor, PA
              https://www.palibraries.org/page/More_
              Conf

4–6   Nebraska Library Assn.   Kearney, NE
              https://nebraskalibraries.org
              meetinginfo.php?id=12&ts=1552601936

18–23   Frankfurt Book Fair   Frankfurt,
              https://www.buchmesse.de/en   Germany

19–21   American Assn. of School Librarians
              (AASL) National Conference   Tampa, FL
              http://www.ala.org/aasl/conferences/events

24–26   Illinois Library Assn.   Springfield, IL
              https://www.ila.org/events/future-ila-annual-
              conferences

November

1–4   New York Library Assn.   Saratoga Springs,
              https://www.nyla.org/4DCGI/cms/review.   NY
              html?Action=
              CMS_Document&DocID=281&Menu
              Key=conf_info

December

10–13   International Conference on Information   Hyderabad, India
https://aisnet.org/page/ICISPage   Systems (ICIS)

2024

April

3–6   Public Library Assn.   Columbus, OH
http://www.ala.org/pla/education/
conferences

16–19   Texas Library Assn.   San Antonio, TX
https://txla.org/annual-conference/general-
information/future-dates

June

11–13   Assn. of American University Presses   Montreal, QC
https://aupresses.org/programs-events/
annual-meeting/save-the-dates

27–July 2   American Library Assn. Annual Conference   San Diego, CA
https://www.ala.org/conferencesevents/
ala-upcoming-annual-and-liblearnx
-conferences

July

20–23   American Assn. of Law Libraries (AALL)   Chicago, IL
https://www.aallnet.org/conference/about/
future-meetings

October

6–9   Pennsylvania Library Assn.   Harrisburg, PA
https://www.palibraries.org/page/More_Conf

8–10   Illinois Library Assn.   Peoria, IL
https://www.ila.org/events/future-ila-annual-
conferences

16–20   Frankfurt Book Fair   Frankfurt,
https://www.buchmesse.de/en   Germany

16–20   North Carolina Library Assn.   Winston-Salem, NC
https://nclaonline.wildapricot.org/
conference

December

10–13	International Conference on Information Systems (ICIS) https://aisnet.org/page/ICISPage	Bangkok, Thailand

2025

April

1–4	Texas Library Assn. https://txla.org/annual-conference/general-information/future-dates	Dallas, TX
2–5	Assn. of College and Research Libraries http://www.ala.org/acrl/conferences	Minneapolis, MN

June

25–30	Assn. of American University Presses https://aupresses.org/programs-events/annual-meeting/save-the-dates	Virtual
26–July 1	American Library Assn. Annual Conference http://www.ala.org/conferencesevents/node/7	Philadelphia, PA

July

19–22	American Assn. of Law Libraries (AALL) https://www.aallnet.org/conference/about/future-meetings	Portland, OR

October

16–18	American Assn. of School Librarians (AASL) National Conference http://www.ala.org/aasl/conferences/events	St. Louis, MO

December

14–17	International Conference on Information Systems (ICIS) https://aisnet.org/page/ICISPage	Nashville, TN

2026

March

30–Apr. 2	Texas Library Assn. https://txla.org/annual-conference/general-information/future-dates	Houston, TX

June

13–15   Assn. of American University Presses   Seattle, WA
https://aupresses.org/programs-events/
annual-meeting/save-the-dates

25–30   American Library Assn. Annual Conference   Chicago, IL
http://www.ala.org/conferencesevents/node/7

2027

March

30–Apr. 2   Texas Library Assn.   Dallas, TX
https://txla.org/annual-conference/general-
information/future-dates

April

7–10   Assn. of College and Research Libraries   Portland, OR
http://www.ala.org/acrl/conferences

June

24–29   American Library Assn. Annual Conference   New Orleans, LA
http://www.ala.org/conferencesevents/node/7

2028

24–27   Texas Library Assn.   San Antonio, TX
https://txla.org/annual-conference/
general-information/future-dates

Acronyms

A

AACR2. Anglo-American Cataloging Rules

AAHSL. Association of Academic Health Sciences Libraries

AALL. American Association of Law Libraries

AAP. Association of American Publishers

AAPB. American Archive of Public Broadcasting

AASHE. Association for the Advancement of Sustainability in Higher Education

AASL. American Association of School Librarians

AAU. Association of American Universities

ABA. Acquisitions and Bibliographic Access Directorate

ABA. American Booksellers Association

ABAA. Antiquarian Booksellers' Association of America

ABOS. Association of Bookmobile and Outreach Services

ABPA. American Book Producers Association

ACL. Association of Christian Librarians

ACOS. Advisory Committee on Standards (IFLA)

ACP. Association of Canadian Publishers

ACRL. Association of College and Research Libraries

ACURIL. Association of Caribbean University, Research, and Institutional Libraries

AFSIC. Alternative Farming Systems Information Center

AgLaw. Agricultural Law Information Partnership

AGLINET. Agricultural Libraries Network

AgNIC. Agriculture Network Information Collaborative

AGRICOLA. AGRICultural On-Line Access

AIGA. Professional Association for Design

AIIM. Association for Information and Image Management

AIIP. Association of Independent Information Professionals

AILA. American Indian Library Association

AJL. Association of Jewish Libraries

ALA. American Library Association

ALCTS. Association for Library Collections and Technical Services

ALD. *American Library Directory*

ALIA. Australian Library and Information Association

ALIC. Archives Library Information Center

ALISE. Association for Library and Information Science Education

ALS. Academic Libraries Survey

ALSC. Association for Library Service to Children

ALTA. American Literary Translators Association

AM&P. Association Media and Publishing

ANSI. American National Standards Institute

AOMR. ALA Offices and Member Relations

APA. Audio Publishers Association

APALA. Asian/Pacific American Librarians Association

APLU. Association of Public and Land-grant Universities

APPC. Advocacy and Public Policy Committee's (ARL)

AR. Augmented reality

ARL. Association of Research Libraries

ARLIS/NA. Art Libraries Society of North America

ARMA International (formerly the Association of Records Managers and Administrators)

ARP. American Rescue Plan

ARSL. Association for Rural and Small
Libraries
ASDAL. Association of Seventh-Day
Adventist Librarians
ASGCLA. Association of Specialized
Government and Cooperative
Library Agencies
ASI. American Society for Indexing
ASIS&T. Association for Information
Science and Technology
ASJA. American Society of Journalists and
Authors
ATA. American Translators Association
ATALM. Association of Tribal Archives,
Libraries, and Museums
ATLA. American Theological Library
Association
AUPresses. Association of University
Presses
AVSL. Association of Vision Science
Librarians
AWIC. Animal Welfare Information Center

B

BARD. Braille and Audio Reading
Download
BCALA. Black Caucus of the American
Library Association
BIBCO. Bibliographic Record Cooperative
BIPOC. Black, Indigenous, and People of
Color
BISAC. Book Industry Systems Advisory
Committee
BISG (formerly Book Industry Study Group)
BLC. Boston Library Consortium
BMI. Book Manufacturers' Institute
BSA. Bibliographical Society of America
BSC-SCB. Bibliographical Society of
Canada
BtP. By the People

C

CAFS. Center for Agriculture and Food
Systems
CAIS. Canadian Association for Information
Science
CALA. Chinese American Librarians
Association
CALL. Canadian Association of Law
Libraries

CARES Act. Coronavirus Aid, Relief, and
Economic Security Act
CARL. Canadian Association of Research
Libraries
CASE. Copyright Alternative in Small-
Claims Enforcement Act
CAUL. Council of Australia University
Librarians
CBC. Children's Book Council
CCB. Copyright Claims Board
CCC. Copyright Clearance Center
CCD. Common Core of Data
CDL. Controlled Digital Lending
CDO. Collection Development Office
CFUW. Canadian Federation of University
Women
CGP. Catalog of U.S. Government
Publications
C&I. Cataloging and indexing
CIKM. International Conference on
Information and Knowledge
Management
CIP. Cataloging in Publication
CLA. Catholic Library Association
CLIR. Council on Library and Information
Resources
CLLE. Center for Learning, Literacy, and
Engagement
CLM. Committee on Copyright and Other
Legal Matters (IFLA)
CMD. Collection Management Division
CMO. Communications and Marketing
Office (ALA)
CNI. Coalition for Networked Information
COAR. SPARC/Confederation of Open
Access Repositories
COMLA. Commonwealth Library
Association
CONSAL. Congress of Southeast Asian
Libraries
CONSER. Cooperative Online Serials
COSLA. Chief Officers of State Library
Associations
CPC. Cost per Circ
CPI. Consumer Price Index
C&RL. *College & Research Libraries*
CRN. Civics Renewal Network
CRO. Chapter Relations Office (ALA)
CRRSAA. Coronavirus Response and Relief
Supplemental Appropriations Act
CRS. Congressional Research Service
CSH. Canadian Subject Headings
CUI. Controlled unclassified information

D

DAMS. Digital Asset Management System
DCMA. Digital Millennium Copyright Act
DC-PAL. Dynamic Coalition on Public
  Access in Libraries
DDC. Dewey Decimal Classification
DEI. Diversity, Equity, and Inclusion
DEL. Documenting Endangered Languages
DLF. Digital Library Federation
DLME. Digital Library of the Middle East
DMCA. Digital Millennium Copyright Act
DoD. Duplication on Demand
DoD IACs. Department of Defense
  Information Analysis Centers
DPLA. Digital Public Library of America
DSD. Digitization Services Directorate
DTIC. Defense Technical Information
  Center

E

EBLIDA. European Bureau of Library,
  Information and Documentation
  Associations
ECIP. Electronic Cataloging in Publication
  Program
ECLS. Early Childhood Longitudinal Study
EDI. Equity, Diversity, and Inclusion
ELS. Education Longitudinal Study
ELSIA. European Libraries and Sustainable
  Development Implementation and
  Assessment
EMIERT. Ethnic and Multicultural
  Information and Exchange Round
  Table
ENSUBLIB. Environment, Sustainability
  and Libraries (IFLA)
ERA. Electronic Records Archives
ERIC. Education Resources Information
  Center
ERT. Exhibits Round Table

F

FAB. FEDLINK Advisory Board
FAFLIG. Federal and Armed Forces
  Libraries Interest Group
FAIFE. Freedom of Access to Information
  and Freedom of Expression (IFLA)
FDLD. Federal Depository Library
  Directory

FDLP. Federal Depository Library Program
FEDLINK. Federal Library and Information
  Network
FIAF. International Federation of Film
  Archives
FMRT. Film and Media Round Table
FNIC. Food and Nutrition Information
  Center
FOIA. Freedom of Information Act
FRCs. Federal Records Centers
FSRIO. Food Safety Research Information
  Office

G

GameRT. Games and Gaming Round Table
GBA. Green Book Alliance
GDPR. General Data Protection Regulation
GLBTRT. Gay, Lesbian, Bisexual, and
  Transgendered Round Table
GNCRT. Graphic Novel and Comics Round
  Table
GODORT. Government Documents Round
  Table
GPO. U.S. Government Publishing Office

H

HBCU. Historically Black Colleges and
  Universities
HEERF. Higher Education Emergency
  Relief Fund
HESI. Higher Education Sustainability
  Initiative
HRDR. Office for Human Resource
  Development and Recruitment
  (ALA)

I

IACs. Information Analysis Centers
IAL. Innovative Approaches to Literacy
IALL. International Association of Law
  Libraries
IAML. International Association of
  Music Libraries, Archives and
  Documentation Centres
IASL. International Association of School
  Librarianship
IATUL. International Association of
  Scientific and Technological
  University Libraries

IAU. International Association of
Universities

IBBY. International Board on Books for
Young People

IBPA. Independent Book Publishers
Association

ICA. International Council on Archives

ICIS. International Conference on
Information Systems

ICP. International Cataloging Principles

ICSD. International Conference on
Sustainable Development

IFLA. International Federation of Library
Associations and Institutions

IFRT. Intellectual Freedom Round Table

ILA. International Literacy Association

ILAB. International League of Antiquarian
Booksellers

IMLS. Institute of Museum and Library
Services

IPA. International Publishers Association

IPEDS. Integrated Postsecondary Education
Data System

IRO. International Relations Office (ALA)

IRRT. International Relations Round Table

ISBD. International Standard
Bibliographical Description

ISBN. International Standard Book Number

ISLD. International Sustainable Library
Development interest group

ISNs. Canadian International Standard
Numbers

ISO. International Organization for
Standardization

ISOO. Information Security Oversight
Office

ISSN. International Standard Serial Number

J

JCLC. National Joint Conference of
Librarians of Color

JDR&E. *Journal of DoD Research and
Engineering*

JELIS. *Journal of Education for Library and
Information Science*

L

LAC. Library and Archives Canada

LAMPHHS. Librarians, Archivists, and
Museum Professionals in the History

of the Health Sciences (formerly
ALHHS)

LARC. Library and Research Center
(ALA)

LC. Library of Congress

LCA. Library Copyright Alliance

LCDP. Leadership and Career Development
Program

LCI. Leading Change Institute

LearnRT. Learning Round Table (formerly
CLENERT)

LHRT. Library History Round Table

LIBER. Association of European Research
Libraries (Ligue des Bibliotheques
Européennes de Recherche)

LIRT. Library Instruction Round Table

LIS. Library and information science

LITA. Library and Information Technology
Association

LJ. *Library Journal*

LLAMA. Library Leadership and
Management Association

LLX. Library Learning Experience

LMPI. Library Materials Price Index

LOC. Library of Congress

LRM. Library Reference Model

LRRT. Library Research Round Table

LSCM. Library Services and Content
Management

LSSIRT. Library Support Staff Interests
Round Table

LSTA. Library Services and Technology
Act

LTC. Libraries Transforming Communities

M

MAGIRT. Map and Geospatial Information
Round Table

MARC. Machine Readable Cataloging

MARS. Material Acquisition Request
Service

MeSH. Medical Subject Headings

METRO. Metropolitan New York Library
Council

MFA. Museums for America

MIPA. Midwest Independent Publishers
Association

MLA. Maryland Library Association

MLA. Medical Library Association

MLA. Music Library Association

MLIS. Master of Library and Information
Science

MLSA. Museum and Library Services Act

MMLIS. Master of Management in Library and Information Science

MPA. Association of Magazine Media

MPLA. Mountain Plains Library Association

N

NAC. National Archives Catalog

NACO. Name Authority Cooperative

NACS. National Association of College Stores

NAGARA. National Association of Government Archives and Records Administrators

NAIBA. New Atlantic Independent Booksellers Association

NAL. National Agricultural Library

NALC. National Agricultural Law Center

NALDC. National Agricultural Library Digital Collection

NALT. National Agricultural Library Thesaurus

NARA. National Archives and Records Administration

NASIG (formerly North American Serials Interest Group)

NCAC. National Coalition Against Censorship

NCES. National Center for Education Statistics

NCTE. National Council of Teachers of English

NDC. National Declassification Center

NDNP. National Digital Newspaper Program

NDSA. National Digital Stewardship Alliance

NEH. National Endowment for the Humanities

NEIBA. New England Independent Booksellers Association

NHES. National Household Education Survey

NHPRC. National Historical Publications and Records Commission

NIH. National Institutes of Health

NILPPA. National Impact of Library Public Programs Assessment

NISIC. National Invasive Species Information Center

NISO. National Information Standards Organization

NIST. National Institute of Standards and Technology publications

NLE. National Library of Education

NLM. National Library of Medicine

NLS. National Library Service for the Blind and Print Disabled

NLW. National Library Week

NLWD. National Library Workers Day

NMRT. New Members Round Table

NNLM. Network of the National Library of Medicine

NPA. Norwegian Publishers Association

NTIS. National Technical Information Service

NTPS. National Teacher and Principal Survey

NTRL. National Technical Reports Library

NYPL. New York Public Library

O

OCIO. Office of the Chief Information Officer (LC)

OCLC. Online Computer Library Center

ODL. Office of Digital Humanities

ODLOS. Office for Diversity, Literacy and Outreach Services (ALA)

OECD. Organisation for Economic Co-operation and Development

OGIS. Office of Government Information Services

OIB. USSBY Outstanding International Books

OIF. Office for Intellectual Freedom (ALA)

OLOS. Office for Literacy and Outreach Services

OLS. Office of Library Services

ORFG. Open Research Funders Group

P

PALA. Polish American Librarians Association

PCC. Program for Cooperative Cataloging

PCPAC. Public and Cultural Programs Advisory Committee (ALA)

PENS. Public Law Electronic Notification Service

PLA. Public Library Association

PLS. Public Library Survey

PMC. PubMed Central

PPAO. Public Policy and Advocacy Office (ALA)
PPO. Public Programs Office (ALA)
PRH. Penguin Random House
PSLF. Public Service Loan Forgiveness
PTRCA. Patent and Trademark Resource Center Association

R

RBMS. Rare Books and Manuscripts Section (ACRL)
RDA. Resource Description and Access
RDaF. NIST Research Data Framework
REALM. REopening Archives, Libraries, and Museums
REFORMA. National Association to Promote Library and Information Services to Latinos and the Spanish-Speaking
RIC. Rural Information Center
RMS. Research Management and Support
RNTLOAK. Rural, Native and Tribal Libraries of All Kinds (ALA)
RRS. Researcher and Reference Services Division (LC)
RRT. Rainbow Round Table
RUSA. Reference and User Services Association
RWA. Romance Writers of America

S

SAA. Society of American Archivists
SACO. Subject Authority Cooperative
SALALM. Seminar on the Acquisition of Latin American Library Materials
SAN. Standard Address Number
SASS. Schools and Staffing Survey
SCBWI. Society of Children's Book Writers and Illustrators
SCCR. Standing Committee on Copyright and Related Rights (IFLA)
SCECSAL. Standing Conference of Eastern, Central, and Southern African Libraries and Information Associations
SCOLMA. U.K. Library and Archives Group on Africa
SDGs. Sustainable Development Goals

SDSN. Sustainable Development Solutions Network
SI. Society of Illustrators
SIBA (formerly Southern Independent Booksellers Alliance)
SIGL. Stitching IFLA Global Libraries
SIIA. Software and Information Industry Association
SLA. Special Libraries Association
SLAA. State Library Administrative Agency
SLIDE. School Librarian Investigation—Decline or Evolution?
SORT. Staff Organization Round Table
SPARC. Scholarly Publishing & Academic Resources Coalition
SRA. Sequence Read Archive
SRRT. Social Responsibilities Round Table
SSP. Society for Scholarly Publishing
ST&B. Science, Technology and Business Division (LC)
STEAM. Science, Technology, Engineering, Arts, and Mathematics
STEM. Science, Technology, Engineering, and Mathematics
STM. International Association of Scientific, Technical, and Medical Publishers
SU. Simultaneous use

T

TDR. Trustworthy Digital Repository
TLA. Theatre Library Association
TOME. Toward an Open Monograph Ecosystem
TPS. Teaching with Primary Sources
TRAIL. Technical Report Archive & Image Library

U

ULC. Urban Libraries Council
UMLS. Unified Medical Language System
USAIN. United States Agricultural Information Network
USBBY. United States Board on Books for Young People
USPPI. U.S. Periodical Price Index

V

VHP. Veterans History Project

W

WAIC. Water and Agriculture Information
  Center
WIPO. World Intellectual Property
  Organization
WLIC. World Library and Information
  Congress

WNBA. Women's National Book
  Association

Y

YALSA. Young Adult Library Services
  Association

Index

Note: Page numbers followed by "f" and "t" represent figures and tables respectively. The Directory of Organizations (Part 6) is not included in the index.

F

G